Sadly, porn

Edward Teach, M.D.

Paperback ISBN 978-1-7344608-2-7

Ebook - Kindle ISBN 978-1-7344608-3-4

Table of Contents

See the woman?

The bloom on the woman?

You can see her again and again.

Anytime you want.

Disclaimer

I went down yesterday to Piraeus-- no, wait, that wasn't me.

What is pornography? "I can't define it, but I know it when I see it." So you're the one who decides? "No, it's subjective, porn could be different things to different people." So everyone gets to decide? "No, there's no objective criteria." So no one gets to decide? "No--" Thank God.

Many people find it hard to have a rational discussion about pornography with other people, because other people don't exist. You may as well try to discuss porn with an ox, if you can find one, if you will listen. Other generations exist, because you hate them, but such dialogues are tricky because the old can't help but see sexuality as part of a continuum towards death because they are closer to death than they are to lust, so much so that rather than an old guy thinking the young are sex obsessed, he forgets they are sex obsessed, forgets how sex and love frame all their decisions, forgets that the kid looking idly around a train car isn't thinking about bladder capacities or his boss's incompetence, he's daydreaming about gazing at his beloved or ejaculating on a chick as he explains to her that she knows she likes it.[1] Worse, they forget how hyperspecific love and lust is, a recently middle

---

1 [7.14] Of course, in real life he wouldn't be daydreaming about sex, he'd be looking at it on his Pornotron. That's not a joke, it is the central problem of our time. Men regularly whisper what women wonder out loud: why do the most desirable women have the least devoted boyfriends? The usual explanation of arrogance and misogyny assume what's impossible if you spend a moment on it, that these desirable women somehow can't attract devoted men. And because these men all seem to have the same kind of tattoos, the assumption presumes they attract men who are reliably unreliable. But it's evident that these men aren't invested, everyone easily leaving his woman to the mercy of greater numbers. Intercourse happens only with fear, so every man husbands his girlfriend just enough to make due, making no plans and planting no seeds, because you don't know when some other bull will inevitably invade and carry her away. God knows you can't keep her walled in, and if you landed her, she's got to be easy to plough. "Why commit? She'll just end up cheating anyway." You expected a desirable woman to be devoted enough for the both of you? Such men simply settle to be the boyfriend of any such woman, plowing just enough to satisfy themselves day to day, and make no bones about being with someone else next year. But because of this they never show any ability, either for wealth or achievement or anything else. The most desirable of the women are always the most susceptible to these turnovers of boyfriends. The desirability of these

aged guy looks around and thinks college girls today are hotter than they've ever been, meanwhile a sophomore can look at identical twin cheerleaders and still need a few beers before he can get it up for the ugly one. You can play the game backwards, too, the creepy old perv, age 35-55, is creepy to a sophomore because it's unimaginable anyone that old still experiences lust in 3D; the simple fact that he noticed the consequences of an 18-24 year old's computer engineered bra is evidence of sociopathy unless those women have been branded as for-profit media combustibles in which case it's un-American if you don't look. The NFL put a lot of money into designing what's left of those cheerleading uniforms, so unless you want to end up registered on a database

---

women increases the power of their men, but makes these men susceptible to betrayal, and to the plottings of others. Thus the woman least fought over invites the most devotion, the combination of the two being able to build an empire.

Porn becomes the solution to a problem you didn't know you had, which isn't genetic, but arithmetic. Rather than evolution magically matching fecund brunettes to instinct driven reproduction machines that want to impregnate as many uteros as possible (using the Darwinian strategy of facials) the men do a quick calculation: how much energy should I give to what will surely be taken from me, especially if beforehand I make it radiate even more brightly?

"Why am I attracted to those I can't have?" "Why do I date people I shouldn't?" "Why don't I understand myself better?" Like the Delphic Oracle commands, KNOW THYSELF? You know the Oracle isn't really all knowing, right? Did you stop and wonder why professional manipulators carved this into their temple? "Didn't Socrates also believe it?" The liars certainly told you so.

The answers to your questions are irrelevant, those aren't your questions, those are your defenses that safely protect you from asking other questions. "What am I getting out of porn?" Try: What is porn getting you out of? The media scienticians tell us that it destroys self-esteem, relationships and careers, but the media can't show porn so talking about it is their way of capitalizing on it while taking credit for being above it. Don't listen to them, they are using you. If they made up the woman to deliver the news, you can be sure they made up the news for it to be delivered.

"Porn is just unreal images, it doesn't mean anything, it isn't bad or good." So-- nothing in excess?

One interesting discovery I made-- and you're going think this was obvious-- is that most people masturbate while they are watching porn... to completion. Easy, baby steps: they don't watch it, then retreat to a safe room and masturbate the rest of the way to a porn-inspired fantasy, re-shot, re-casted and re-directed in their head. *There is no fantasy.* They are lead mechanically to the orgasm. But what makes it diabolical is that it feels like you are fantasizing, it feels like they got it, like it's your fantasy presciently or coincidentally acted on screen. "I know porn isn't real, but how did they know this is what I liked?" Change "liked" from past tense back to future conditional and then contrast the Pornotron to how Judge Reinhold masturbated to a red bikinied Phoebe Cates coming out of the pool in *Fast Times At Ridgemont High*: he's not actually seeing it, he is imagining it. Note that this famous scene which we have mostly forgotten didn't happen also inspired a generation of real life masturbation fantasies, which is why it is a great contrast for the way we fantasize now: Reinhold took what he saw and then masturbated to a fantasy. We want the reality to obliterate the fantasy.

Edging is the porn addict's response to getting too much of what he wants. With all the truth and none of the fantasy, it's your brain trying to take some autonomy back from the automation, and in the future that will be built into the software so you don't miss the lack. Anybody who has ever been deep in even the best video porn for too long has experienced the paradoxical relief that comes when you stumble on static photos-- suddenly there's room to breathe, suddenly you're free to fantasize.

you better not be caught not pretending not to notice.

Lust wanes with age; and if the old have good characters, they may feel some relief at having escaped such a frenzied and savage master. And if they lament it, and feel like they are being deprived of something very important, then I suspect that youth was hard for them as well. But what blocks all such dialogues isn't the age or the hormone levels, it's the demographic. The hardest thing to swallow is that your lust is not your own, while it feels primal there's little innate or instinctive about it. This is not a happy thought, with so-co individualism being all the rage in the age of Know Thyself you're not going to want to hear about how little of you is you rather than the work

---

Now what? Now you need a video. Fast.

Generating your own sexual fantasy has no payoff and thus no reinforcement because after the orgasm there's nothing left, all that work you put in refining what you want becomes afterwards merely a memory of what you'll never have, you're way better off spending hours a day watching videos of your deceased child. "Whoah, why'd you bring that up?" Because the mechanism is the same, the lack of payoff is the same. "Drowning out reality with unreal images?" No, drowning in video reality to drown out unreality, anything so your mind is not ruminating, *fantasizing*, the painful video memories seem masochistic but they are 100% defensive because to a person stuck in mourning-- sorry, complicated bereavement-- sorry, Major Depressive Disorder------ do you see how they want to castrate you and leave you only   porn? the only way to know yourself is with their jargon------ the videos are absolutely more tolerable than closing your eyes and seeing him in your obsessive imagination, over, and over, and over, and over.... the pathology isn't in the fact of the images, it is in the replacement of the images: it is a disorder of thinking, it is a disorder of math. You can say the digital images are painful, but they are far less threatening than imagination. You are sad, you are so so sad, but you are not changed, you are still you. Because the sadness feels like it's all on you,   everyone else seems to have moved on. So you condemn yourself to the entire mourning, those videos and your grief are the only thing keeping him alive. One might suggest that the way to lessen the pain of perpetual mourning is to take your pathology literally: since you are obsessed by the thoughts, then you must commit yourself to the full OCD: give yourself a ritual that has a fixed set of rules you must be compelled to follow: I must eat peas in his honor every Tuesday; I must carry a red Lego in my pocket, I must spend ten seconds every day reciting his favorite quote that then seemed so banal yet now proves his soul was timeless: 'Life is made up of meetings and partings. Such is the way of it.' "Job 2:13?" Kermit The Frog.

You keep the fetish, and then slowly it will let you go. When General Pericles lay dying and the surrounding idiots were taking credit for recalling his achievements, he borrowed three seconds from the afterlife to reanimate and declare his most praiseworthy achievement: "No one can say that because of me the Athenians were clad in the black clothes of complicated bereavement." That is something a man can be proud of, though it's an odd thing to assert when a quarter of the population has just died, not because he sent them far from home to fight a war but because he kept them home to avoid fighting it, and I know this isn't what he meant but in one way he was literally correct: the Athenians didn't mourn *him*. Well, they should have.

With porn there's no work in fantasizing and no guilt in the fantasy, after all, it's not yours.   So too with actual sex, as long as the cheating was pornographic, there can be no guilt-- this has always been true. "Always true? You do know that in the Victorian Era if a woman was caught in adultery she could be burned as a witch?"   I think you're confusing two eras, two books and three punishments. In the Salem Witch Trials of 1692, the standard high school teaching is that though they may have believed in witches, the trials were "really" about the established patriarchal order punishing women who represented ideological threats to their power. But as the accusers were primarily teenage girls, you could also say the Trials reveal how easy it is for hysterical nobodies to

product of whatever media agency targets the demo they've decided you're in. You're not taught what to want, but how to want, the modern innovation is to let you think you came up with you on your own. "I love a shaved pussy," says the man who just doesn't get it, as if this his genetic preference. "Ugh!" says some equally oblivious antithesis, "it's like you're with a child." Now he has to imagine she's an adult. "She is actually an adult." Yes, but he has to imagine it. If you practice seeing pieces of images, images of pieces are hard to unsee. When a guy looks at porn back from his own sexual prime, the enthusiastic reaction he has to the now hysterical hair and makeup or decade/exercise/diet specific body type is just as reflexive as if it came from ten gazillion years of

---

manipulate the existing power structure via their dad with nothing more than spectral evidence to turn on those who may once have had some power but society was now mostly done with so were an easy comparator to peacock self-righteousness and thus cause mass hysteria, all for no reason, except possibly the desire to brand themselves as relevant to the debate, and spite. NB it's not a perspective that you'll be allowed to bring up in class. If the logic is that the Trials were a form of ideological persecution, then the one victim who refused to confess technically died a martyr against the patriarchy. Unfortunately for this logic, it was a man. My guess is you don't know his name or that he was a powerlifter.

"America has always seen sex as something shameful." Yes, shame, I figured you'd bring that up. Which is more shameful: getting caught masturbating to porn or getting caught masturbating with your eyes closed? Because one of those makes you a sociopath. Your inner thoughts are always more depraved to everyone else. Porn is less shameful because, well, it's not yours. Before you finish nodding please observe that it's kind of the opposite for women.

You are living through the product recall of Freud's steam driven invention: the obliteration of all unconscious fantasy, thus locking us down into the existing reality: someone else's unconscious. At first the fantasies were encouraged because advertisers could use them to draw us in. Well, we're all inside the walls, and we're not going anywhere. So now the fantasies are at best superfluous and at worst a threat.

"So porn suppresses the imagination?" HA! Liar. I have to write sentences with multiple dependent clauses in order to repair the damage of your 5 word rhetorical cluster grenade. Of course it could-- if there was anything left of it. The suppression of the imagination came first and porn was the inevitable and much welcome defense against its loss, even as it could help suppress it further. I know this seems backwards, I know this seems like madness, I wish it was.

A demonstration with pornography's own logic, take Rule 34: *if you can imagine something, there's a porn of it.* If this is a valid logical proposition we should be able to make the contrapositive to our horror: if there's no porn of it, you can't imagine it.

Even attempts at fixing Rule 34 solidify the logic. *Rule 35: if there is no porn of it, then it will be made.* Which means even when the porn is made to exist, it still does not follow that you will be able to imagine it. Sorry, you're the one who wanted porn to have rules, I'm only showing you why.

If your desire and wanting were intact, then all the porn in the universe could only be a tool-- wait, I mean: all the reality of the universe would only be a tool, not to replace fantasy but to facilitate it, the way Judge Reinhold watched through a window at Phoebe Cates sitting by the pool, and then turned off the window to stop looking at her, so he could be free to *fantasize* about her coming out of the pool. NB: the movie was directed by a woman. It was not, as you might think you remember, a real life, real time embellishment of eyes wide open reality (sexier walk, sultrier look, add some mascara and let water be your proxy for touching her all over); by the time his pants are down, she hadn't even yet jumped into the pool. If you want to get psychoanalytic: the fantasy of her coming

natural selection, but it didn't. "Large hips are a cue for fecundity." That at least explains why have always avoided them. "I just love a big ass." Yes, it's the part of her furthest from her face. "You mean you can imagine her the way you want?" No, you don't have to imagine her at all. She's real. It's possible that the 1985 mustachio in the dark blazer over office-gut happened to be born at precisely the time that his unique major histocompatibility preferences coincided with the sudden popularity of white pumps and Legg's pantyhose, or that these are proxy cultural markers for biological fitness or ovulation, but the alternative explanation is that Bandolino needed market share so it targeted him as well as women, it told him not just what kinds of women a man

---

out caused her to jump in. "Come on, that's impossible." Not if it's the audience's fantasy.

The criticism I *should* be making is, "why did he pursue a fantasy and not the real girl-- why didn't he just go outside and show her his phallus or even act like a dick and see what happens? Why not some act of will?" But I was born a little too early and way too late, our desires have changed, the best I can do now is to convince you to shut the window-- to work through what you want and how you want. "So I can have more satisfying relationships?" No. So you don't destroy everyone else. No one would do that kind of detailed fantasizing today; you'll argue that no one ever did this, yet there it is on film and at that time his actions made sense to everyone, not a single person said, "why would he close his eyes? Why wouldn't he just jack it while watching her?" At this point you should wonder why, if it made sense then, do you now remember the scene wrong now?

Which is why the climax of that scene is Delphic Fate=psychic determinism: while he is fantasizing about her coming up to him as she takes her top off, she accidentally walks in on him coming with his bottoms off. "Doesn't anyone knock anymore?" he says as Cates averts her gaze, that's supposed to be the punch line. Is it funny? No, it's terrifying. Here's a knock knock joke for you, ready, go:

REPRESSED:

YOU: … aren't you supposed to say knock knock?

REPRESSED:

It's repression, not suppression, what's repressed never knocks, it just-- returns. Why would you be surprised? They were in the bathroom, after all, the only place private enough to allow the extremes of way too real and far too imaginary to coexist. A funnier and more accurate line for Reinhold would have been: "Now look what you made me do!" But the question for you in your hornet's nest heart is whether Reinhold was running the opposite game: had he unconsciously *planned* to get caught, did he know without knowing that she'd "accidentally" walk in on him sitting on that toilet, not peeing like a girl but fully erect like a man-- was he "acting out", his engorged penis a *message to her* about his sexuality, its intensity? A way of making himself less real, more like his own fantasy? Oh, that does sound complicatedly bananas, but how many times do people take only the most superficial of precautions with their porn and thus get caught by their partner, is that "on purpose"? "Look, I still have personal and unique sexual thoughts, see how big I can get when I get what I want?" Message received, though the fact that you found it on one of no more than five internationally known websites makes your uniqueness highly suspect, so you'll forgive me if I mark this message and your genitals as junk.

You can ask it the other way, the way that matters in your life: when she walked in on him, did you think that he thought that she thought he was masturbating *to her*? Or to someone else? Which would she have thought was worse? Which is more embarrassing to him: that she discovers that he likes her, or that she discovers that he lusts after her? Which discovery about him requires a response from her? You'll say love, of course, because you know that his lust has nothing to do

like him should want but what kinds of men those women would want, which is also why he thought the mustache was a good idea. "Ok, but what does it mean that I get turned on by--" Save your breath: I don't know what it means. I only know what it's for. And that it's bad for everyone else.

Here is a book about porn. If you are looking for a Table Of Contents for your own analysis, don't bother, the one you see here is fake and I don't think in chapters, only acts. As consolation I'll tell you there is a hardcore sex story right at the beginning and it's about 30 pages long so you're on notice or you're welcome. I have deliberately not written it "well", I am imitating the flow and style of that kind of porn story. I didn't try to make it unique or sensual,

---

with "her", just her body/walk/scent/moves/gaze/status-- she gets to choose when to disavow her always-on sexuality, "that isn't me." Yet his love, which is based on nothing about her anyone can point to-- is something she'd feel obligated to deal with either approvingly or through a protection order. But she'd be *literally* right: his lust has nothing to do with *her,* which is why he turned off the window. But if the lust carries the lesser risk, why are you so nervous to approach some defenseless girl in a bar, yet you have no shame sending a woman walled up in her fortress a ten page autobiopic? "I've only written Act I and I don't have financing, but the dialogue is a masterpiece and I want you to help me shoot it." You sleep now. Only dream theory can explain your behavior: things may symbolize other things, but affect is always 100% correct, so your anxiety is telling you something important: your desire to tap her drunk ass is your confused attempt at love, not lust, and your mind protected you from the mix up by failing to try, on purpose; while the spectacular love you feel writing your fictional backstory is way more about you and your character doing a dp on your DP, which is why you spent so much time writing it.

Now that you've read this here's a question that should be easy to answer: does secretly masturbating to Cates mean he would be satisfied if he got her, or not? I guess it's not that easy.

So if this hot bikini girl is the return of the repressed, then what was repressed? The "real", ordinary, skin and bones girl behind his fantasy? Not to make a normalizing judgment, but for a "real" girl she's fantastically hot. The "reality" of her hardly needs repression, if you're really fickle soft lighting and a few beers will do. But it's 1981 and he loves her as well as lusts after her, and in 1981 and today it is well nigh impossible to masturbate to a woman you love unless you're imagining her with someone else. Which is what Reinhold was doing: he's in the bathroom in the top half of his job's pirate costume while the fantasy stud making out with the topless her is in a business suit. *He has repressed himself.* He has repressed the thoughts which conflict with his ideal self, and this is hardly a surgical excision: the uniform, the lack of confidence, *and* his non-sexual desire for her-- *his love for her*-- it all goes out the window, which he then closes so he can get down to business. And then in fantasy it returned as its gender and power opposite: he approaches with the hesitation, clothes and deference of a Victorian gentleman, and she's horned up succubus, naked, powerful, and aggressively wet. Now it looks like she knows what she wants, which means he can act on it. Back to the question: under these psychic conditions, would he be satisfied by her, or not?

There is a story, maybe apocryphal but I'm going anyway, that Judge Reinhold the actor, in order to generate the scene's shock in Phoebe Cates the actress, was actually masturbating a giant dildo; so her startle/chuckle/grimace is an on-screen real life WTF. You can dismiss this as on-set shenanigans, but he wouldn't have dreamed of using a dildo if he had to perform a sex scene, bringing a dildo towards a naked woman is real-life proof of what he wants and what he's missing. But masturbating without one is an enormous risk, it must be hard for a man to be watched pretending to be masturbating to the fantasy of being desired; everyone will wonder how close that is to the truth, the best way is to negate the fantasies and offer reality: a) look, no hands! or b) look, no penis! If you want to fake masturbating, you pretend to touch your penis. If you want to fake fantasizing, you actually touch a pretend penis. *He went from desiring her to wanting to be desired,*

12

literary or even erotic; while it is explicit pornography it is vanilla by most standards, penis vs vagina, *obvious* in its language, plot, and tropes. My purpose wasn't to elevate the genre but to capture it, by which I mean photograph it. I made it easy to assure yourself that there is nothing interesting there, formulaic escapism devoid of deeper meaning, its only purpose to facilitate orgasm. And then-- well, I guess we'll see what happens next.

NB it is a specific type of porn story: a "cheating wife" story. Let me stop you right here and say I am utterly indifferent to your idiotic complaints. I am not trying to turn you on, I am not trying to explain why it does or does not

---

by her, which was exactly the point of the scene, and the inflection point of po-mo no homo sexual relations. It is the absence of the penis that makes one the object of desire. Evoke this absence in a more precise way by having him wear a cute fake one under a pirate costume, and you, or rather he, will have plenty to tell us about: the effect is 100 percent guaranteed, for men who don't beat around the bush, that is.

This kind of masturbation yields a climax that never seems to move the story forward, it goes back to the beginning and repeats, to prove this look for a commonality elsewhere that shows the story as a circle and not a mountain: e.g. it's not the first time or the last time he'll take off the pirate costume. Earlier Reinhold was working at Captain Hook Fish and Chips in the pirate uniform, and was told to go make a delivery, so he changes out of the uniform into street clothes but his boss stops him. "During deliveries you're still a representative of CHFnC-- have some pride." You can well imagine the reaction of all the recently awoken Holden Caulfields watching this scene, enraged at the boss for making him wear the humiliating costume and having to address the customers in Piratese, and consoling himself with tiny subversions like, "Arrrgh, here's a basket of hardtack and a joke for the table: a wench walks into a pirate bar and asks for seamen and a towel." HA! Funny as ever. So every 14 year old knows exactly what he's thinking: "*have some pride?* In what? In his stupid minimum wage job? Why should he have any pride? He doesn't own the means of production, he's an exploited wage slave, and we all know that pride is the lie capitalism uses to make us work harder for them." The thing is, even if this were a fact, that knowledge doesn't get anyone to do more pushups or more math or become an actual pirate let alone a captain; it doesn't move the story forward, it only gets you out of work, yours and your job's; and instead of one exploited but concrete step forward you solidify your status quo; you satisfy yourself with wearing street clothes at work and pillaging the occasional burger, to you these are a kind of compensation, you deserve to steal a little back for yourself since you have no power. The idea that he could be proud of the business itself, of what the owner had built, the form of this creative act-- whether or not he benefits-- that this respect costs him nothing and it might change him-- such an idea is so revolting to his me vs. them psychology that he pretends it's really an us vs. them philosophy, and us has more important things in store for me, yet when he ditches the job and the burger out another window and goes back home to masturbate to the girl who is literally 15 feet but two psychologies away from him, he tells everyone to keep it down because *he has work to do.* At least he had the decency of shame; today that kind of work needs to be accepted, because it is frantic, energetic, and utterly non-productive-- a defense against change.

You need to rethink how you use porn, stop listening to people who hate you, stop listening to people who want to parlay about its meaning, or lack of meaning, damn to the depths whatever man what thought of meaning. So much of the satisfaction-- not interest, not pleasure, but satisfaction-- of watching porn is not just from seeing the sex act, nor a laziness to pursue sex, but from not having to generate the fantasy. Not as "an escape from reality"-- if anything, reality sex is becoming much more like a staging of porn-- but an escape from fantasy *in to* reality. If fantasizing is daydreaming-- a semi-conscious elaboration of the unconscious-- then avoiding fantasy is a way to avoid the terrible truth that we will never get our wish fulfillment-- it is a way of not ever

turn you on, I don't care, only you care, which is equivalent to no one cares. Whether cheating wife porn arouses you or nauseates you isn't important because those feelings have the same force vector, what you think about those who do like it is also unimportant-- though it would be better than five years of undergraduate critical theory to have a ten minute discussion about why it is so important for you to hate the people who like the things you hate because other people like them, what is it about you that wants to blot out the sun whenever anyone says they want summer to come? Want to have that discussion? No? College it is then. If it makes you any feel better those people you hate will likely be responsible to pay for it. "I took out loans." My assertion is valid in all eventualities. I assure you the cheating wife genre was a random choice, any porn would have worked here, romantic, BDSM, incest, alien, snuff, the result would have been the same because the manifest content of the story is fairly irrelevant except to your genitals which are definitely irrelevant. Forget about what porn you like. It's not about you. You know how I know? You didn't make it.

Undoubtedly someone is going to toss the words heteronormative and individualizing the structural at me, and that person should stop reading immediately, not just this book but all books, your mind is broken and it is better suited for TV. I don't mean you are stupid, only that you are even more a product of the system you hate than the porn you think you reject. You think your sexual proclivities define you, they are unique to you, distinguish you; that the man who likes forced interracial porn is fundamentally different

---

wondering what our wish fulfillment might look like, and the sad reason for this is that our wish fulfillment doesn't actually contain us-- it's impossible. "I don't really want to interpret my dreams." Then your unconscious probably doesn't bother to obfuscate them, so you can take them literally. "Well, I don't remember my dreams-- I'm not even sure I do dream." Could be the alcohol or they reveal too much, are the results the same? Then it worked. You never want to know about your unconscious so you're *obsessed* with learning about your conscious-- information, studying every detail, to guard against what you are doing. So rather than fantasies that risk failure but at least clarify our real desires, we find it easier to want things that we are told to want-- that we don't want, but that there can be no guilt in wanting because they were commanded to be wanted. Since it's too painful to fantasize what will never come to pass-- or shouldn't come to pass-- we drown ourselves in other people's visions and are lead mechanically to the end, see also politics, economics, love.

It is this logic that explains why women don't watch porn, not like men do; and why the pop-feminist attempt to normalize porn for women, to progressively embrace women's "need" for porn, should be resisted as a trap: it doesn't care what you want, it's teaching you how to want: like men. "But female porn is different than male porn, you can't interpret it the same way, it has a totally different meaning." Sometimes a cigar is just a cigar, sometimes it's more than a cigar; but it's never not also a cigar.

Today we masturbate to porn-- out of obligation. "That's stupid." Are you agreeing or disagreeing? Take a guy in a 5 year cohabiting relationship and watch what happens when his woman tells him she's going to go visit her mom for the weekend. He looks forward to-- be specific-- *porn and masturbating.* But it's not like he can't do it in the garage when she's home, too, right? So? But left in the house alone for a few hours he starts to think.... well, I guess I have no choice. He feels pressured to enjoy because he has the opportunity to enjoy, and the worst sin is wasting an opportunity. "Yes, yes! What's is it called when an oppressive superego makes you feel guilty if you don't take every opportunity to enjoy?" I think it's called "capitalism" but I'm no economist.

than the woman who likes soft core lesbian porn, this is wrong: the fact that you both like a porn makes you far more similar than different, please observe that your oh-so-personal and disparate kinks are all served by the same handful of websites, we are all brothers and sisters after all. We enjoy it, surrender ourselves, we praise anyone who affects us most in this way[2]. As much as everyone believes their sexuality is fundamental to their identity, no one would say their actual sexual past is indicative of their identity. "It's different with you, those other people didn't count." I know. Neither is there anything to be gained by "analyzing" the kinds of porn you like as a window into your soul, it is meaningless and anyway chosen for you to like. Have you ever fallen asleep looking at porn? Yet that fact is far more telling than the image you fell asleep to, it doesn't matter what you want, or why you want-- it only matters how you want. You can count the drinks and pretend it's informative but too many times I've grabbed the bottle to pour myself the nth drink only to discover I hadn't finished the (n-1)th drink, the glass was still half full, or empty. So? You think the truth can be found by solving for n?

---

2 [1.17] Demography doesn't care about ratings; it serves form over content. A demographic is demarcated to serve a media company that appears to serve it; of course that company looks no further than its own enrichment, but it will spare no expense to protect itself, it must operate under maximum safety; they count their accomplishments not by their creations, but by destroying the competition. "That sounds like late stage capitalism." Yes, your demographic was told to believe that.

They also told you demographic was about who you are similar to, and not who you will become similar to. Demography is an oversimplified description suitable for journalism; an old arithmetic approach to describing a world that now requires multivariable calculus. Two completely different people of different A/G/R may like completely different TV shows, but if those shows have the same narrative form, then both of those shows will be for the same demographic, which is why they're on the same network; for example, stylized sexuality with high thread count BDSM or stylized violence with gleaming Glock gunplay: for all their advertised hard R transgressiveness, both are firmly within a conventional ethics. In other words, they're dating. And if there's a girl in it, she will finally come: up, around, back, or to her senses. And if it's on a network, it will be episodic; not merely there will be episodes, but that it will be a series of situations to which characters react rather than a story of desires on which characters act. You may think you're unique in liking completely different things from other people in your demographic, but even you suspect that is a demographic. Gay porn and hetero porn found on the same porn site predict similar reactive=consumer psychology, brand loyalty, comfort in the group: the desire to be lead. That the images are gay or straight is only relevant to you, and will become less so as the early childhood polymorphous perversity becomes a normalized social requirement of a system that gives you what everybody else wants. "Hey, it's all good." You're the boss, who am I to disagree? Unable to find satisfaction in your finite choices what you want now is for the choices to look infinite, which is why your demographic's most reliable porn preference is content aggregators. "That's not a kind of porn." Who decides? "It's just easier to find what I want if it's all in one place." You do know that that's not really a place and the search occurs in a different place anyway? Yet knowing this won't stop you from doing this. You think you want the content but your history shows it's only the form, you keep coming back for the system, and it obliges, it lets you be autonomous and individuated and pursue your unique interests, it let's you think you came up with them on your own-- it only asks that you use your unique individual autonomy here, not there. "Yes, yes, what's it called when a benevolent consumerist superego absolves you from guilt by offering only what is possible to want?" I think it's called a tyranny, but I'm no historian.

So consider this your final warning. I have written a book, and the only thing I use in this book is words. *Everything else that happens is your fault.*

How far my efforts agree with those of other writers I will not decide. What I've here written makes no claim to novelty in points of detail, and therefore I give no sources, I do not care whether what I've thought was already thought before me by someone else. So shut it.

I have not ornamented or stuffed this work with bombastic foot-and-a-half long words, superfluous ornamentation or any other stylistic graces that might make the rhetoric more pleasing. And unless you're a gynecologist don't tell me I need more regular periods, I've read both of the primary sources and it doesn't say that anywhere. I have avoided the use of jargon, at most you will find id, ego, and superego, which I don't even use correctly, on purpose. And I use bemused as a synonym for nonplussed. Good luck. I've tried to make this book as simple as possible, so if there's a part that you can't understand-- not agree with, *understand*-- then you should ask whether the problem is your own resistance. If at the end you conclude I'm wrong, then either you will be right or you will be a liar. That's a big difference and there are no other possibilities, you should take your time and double check your math. In this book you will find one sentence that will engage you and one sentence that will enrage you, and if you tell both those sentences to anyone else they will have all the information necessary to determine whether to sleep with you or abandon you at a rest stop.

"Will this book help me learn more about myself?" Ugh. The whole earth is sick of your search for knowledge. In here you will not find explanations, I am not offering you information, this is an attempt to destroy the wisdom of the wise and frustrate the intelligence of the intelligent. "But is this book accurate?" Your question is meaningless, in America we divide our books between fiction and non-fiction, not fact and non-fact, the standard is the fiction, the standard is the green. This is not a "deconstruction of the text", it is the interpretation of a dream, I am not looking to explain the meaning of pornography in general, only how it's used, by you. Let's face it, you're the only one you really care about anyway.

Final warning: this is not a good book, and no, you will not like it. If I had more time to write-- to read, to think-- maybe I could have done a better job, or at least caught the typos. Who knows? I'm not a good writer. Or person. I think in life I did fulfill my primary duty, but I didn't keep a ledger and anyway it's not really for me to say. But I had to write it in a car during stolen time in the middle of the woods or night, and eventually it took a global pandemeconium for me to Philip K. Dick the book during a manic week off just to get what you see here. But the more time passes, the greater the risk of apathy, personal tragedies, alcoholic hallucinosis, or the measured judgment of advancing age, all of which would result in no book at all. Publish and perish, stabs the spur, time's running out.

Well, there's my whole introduction. I fully agree that it is completely useless, but since it's been written, let it stand. And now to business.

It is customary in these introductions to thank the people who assisted in the work, but this is not the kind of project that permits outside help. You have to be alone.

The best of what you can know, cannot be said to boys.

--Mark 1:34

A journalist is interviewing a physicist about multi-dimensional mathematics. The journalist says, "I can sort of see how you might visualize five dimensions, but how can anyone possibly visualize 13 dimensions?" "It's really quite easy," says the physicist. "First, you visualize it in n dimensions. Then let n=13."

My Husband And His Rival Bet Who Was The Better Man-- And I Won

(… in media's res....[3])

It was too late to stop now-- there was nothing I could do! Here I was, climaxing on this guy's dick as he smugly thrust into me-- and my husband was right outside the door! I had been tricked into cheating-- and I was loving it!

This isn't something I wanted, let alone tried to make happen. How did I end up in this here? Let's start from the beginning-- all the way back, when bikinis had two pieces!

In college my sorority sisters and I went to a beach themed fraternity party. We all wore matching white string bikinis with our letters stitched in red on the left cup, strappy heels, and mesh sarongs (which didn't hide very much.) The guys came shirtless in lettered trunks and flip flops, and most had whistles (so the girls could blow them, what cornballs!) Late into the party I spotted a cute guy, but he wasn't in a frat. While he was well built and rugged looking, he spent most of his time cloistered in the library, so at this beach he was a fish out of water.   I said hi (I may be in a sorority, but I'm not stuck up!) We hit it off, we were both econ majors and had a lot in common.   As a freshman he didn't have a whole lot of experience with these kind of parties, so he was respectful and didn't try anything with me, which was really nice-- and weird!

3

Act I: Inciting event (Denial)

Act II: 1. Conflict (Rage) 2. Reversal (Despair) 3. Trial (Sacrifice)

Act III: Climax (Acceptance)

Rule of repetition compulsion: Perform only Acts I, II, and III. Act IV is repressed. It returns as Act I.

But I did have experience with these parties... All around us drunk people were hooking up with willing partners, and by that point I was pretty drunk and pretty willing. While we were standing around chatting the bartender in red trunks (very cute, and we had been flirting a little earlier!) comes over to us holding two pitchers of beer.

"Could you hold this real quick?" He handed me the full pitchers.

"Ok ..." I said surprised, my coordination triply impaired by the beers I drank and the beers I was holding.

As soon as I had them, he leans in, cups my ass and kisses me! I was so surprised I just went along with it! I just stood there, high in my heels, a pitcher in each hand, making out with a guy whose name I didn't even know while people around cheered. "Woah, okay then!" I said, breaking the kiss.

My poor fish out of water stood there with his mouth hanging open, not sure what he was allowed to feel, but certainly envious. The bartender slapped him on the back jovially. "Sorry buddy, house rules, she's too hot to keep to yourself!"

He was at a loss for words. "Um, no problem."

The bartender didn't hesitate. "Well, if you're ok with it..." And in a flash we were making out again, this time his hands sliding to my ribs! I have to admit, he was a good kisser.

"What do you say we get out of here?" he says, boldly snapping my top from the front.

Cocky bastard, right in front of a guy he probably assumed was my boyfriend! I handed back the pitchers, "I'm sure there are a lot of other girls who would be happy to have your beer spilled on them."

He laughed and turned to leave. "You better keep your girlfriend on a short leash, she's a wild one!"

My new "boyfriend" tried to be a good sport, but he was a little disoriented. "It was just a kiss," I assured him, "it doesn't really count." I made a little sexy pose and winked at him. "You can't blame him for trying."

We spent the rest of the night talking about everything, it was like we were totally in synch with each other. He even tried to impress me with a card trick, which was dorky, but still totally fooled me! He was so handsome, and so sweet-- was I meeting the perfect guy at a party, of all places? He seemed to be everything I could ever have asked for in man. I had to remind myself to take it slow, I didn't want him to think this was some impulsive fling, like kissing the bartender, that I'd forget tomorrow. I wanted him to feel what I felt. I was actually thinking that that night could be the start of a beautiful relationship with a wonderful man. And I was right.

I had only one regret from that night, and even though it doesn't have anything to do with him I still feel kinda bad about it. I was young, tipsy, and-- you only live once, okay? So we're trying to have a conversation, which was difficult with all the loud music, alcohol and half naked debauchery going on around us. At one point we heard the sounds of sex coming over the music speakers and I figured someone was playing a porno as a joke, but I realized it was actually two real people somewhere at the party having sex! The sounds were being played for the amused partiers. After a minute I could tell the girl knew everyone could hear them, because she was hamming it up, squealing and cooing, talking dirty, telling him how big he was, how hard he was-- she was definitely playing the part of the drunk slut for the benefit of her unseen audience.

It was hard for both of us-- well, him-- to concentrate on our conversation, especially after I told him she was one of my sorority sisters-- which she wasn't, I just said it to blow his mind. So with that I excused myself to go to the bathroom, leaving him to enjoy the "bikini beach soundtrack". I made my way past drunk and giggly girls and drunk and handsy boys, and past the guy at the top of the stairs who told me that the top floor was now a Caribbean resort and I had to give him my top. I dodged him and went down the hall, opened the door to the bathroom and-- oops!

There was the same bartender guy, naked, balls deep in some gorgeous brunette who was perched on the bathroom sink. She had one long leg over his shoulder and the other wrapped around his pumping ass.

"Oh--!" I said.

"Doesn't anybody knock?" she said in mock annoyance, then giggling, her big eyes never averting from his ripped and thrusting body. Her pink bikini bottoms (the other Alpha sorority, of course!) untied at both ends, were laying beneath his trunks on the floor. I assume Caribbean Resort guy had her top because I didn't see it anywhere.

"I'm so sorry--" I repeated, backing out.

"It's ok, sweetie," she said breathlessly, "you can come in,"

"Yes, sweetie," mimicked the guy, blatantly looking me over. Typical guy! "Don't mind us, I'll just be over here railing this chick."

So what could I do? I peed, trying not to look at them. Then-- what? Was I supposed to wash my hands at the sink full of a sorority girl's ass?

I'm going to say I was drunk, that's what I'll say. I'm not sure if that makes it better or worse. But I just looked at her, glowing, moaning, lost in what the guy was doing to her. That could have been me, I thought to myself. If I had just let myself go with the flow... would that have been so bad?

She was so open about it, unashamed. Even proud to be watched, like she was performing. It was some performance! I stared openly at them as they showed off for me, each in their own way. She turned her head upwards towards him and hooked her manicured fingers around his neck, gently pulling him towards her. She snaked her tongue lustily into his mouth, pulling his ass into her with her supple calf. She was showing me how she had sex, what it was like to be with her. It was so feminine, so hot! He... he spread her thigh open to show me his big dick, and winked. Such a guy! I rolled my eyes but smiled.

"Come here," she casually offered.

"Oh no," I laughed, "this is your show." But I slid up to them anyway. I slapped Bartender Guy's butt playfully. "Come on, stud, fuck her, fuck her so she remembers it."

"Oh god, yes," she agreed.

I watched as she moaned, breathed, climaxed. I don't know if it was the alcohol, or the effect of watching a man I had just kissed have sex with a woman I felt like I should kiss, but the whole thing just looked so-- right. Two amazingly gorgeous people, stealing away together just to fuck, no pretense, no strings, no games. What could be wrong about that?

I had a naughty thought. "Honey?" I said to her as I slinked my hand beneath her ass to cup his heavy balls. "What's this guy's name?"

For an instant she stopped squealing, and then rolled her head back in mock embarrassment. "Oh my God, I have no idea!"

I smiled at him, sharing his amusement, and felt his dick and balls swell. "You little slut!" I teased her. "Spreading your legs for some guy whose name you don't even know!"

"I thought he was cute," she said dreamily looking into his eyes.

"I think your boyfriend is rushing my frat," he said.

"Oops," she giggled and sighed at the same time. "He better not, I know how you guys are around women."

I stood there, watching him pound her, drive his fat dick upwards into a pussy that didn't look like it could take it, but boy oh boy could it take it. I wondered how many other women he had fucked like this, and how many other men she had fucked like this.

Wickedly, I leaned in and whispered in her ear while slyly looking into his eyes. She bit her bottom lip and repeated it.

"Wow, your dick is thick," she said. "I don't think my boyfriend would approve."

"Fuck," he agreed.

"I can't believe you got your dick in me," she recited. "I'm a very bad girlfriend."

It didn't take much. "I'm going to cum," he grunted. Was it to me? "I'm going to cum in this slut's tight cunt."

"Oh fuck," we both said.

"I want to see it," I said excitedly. "Cum on her, cum all over her!"

"I'm--"

"I want to do it!" I said, I don't know what came over me but I grabbed his dick as he unsheathed it. I jacked it in front of her, aiming it, all three of us staring down at the swollen head as it blasted forceful jets of cum over her spectacular body.

"Take that, you sexy bitch!" I shouted, hosing the horny coed with his semen. He started growling as he stiffened, gripping my ass for balance.

Some cum shot high and hit her face, tracing down over her lips, and she squealed in surprise and delight. I continued to stroke him as she made a show of licking it. Either he hadn't had sex in a while, which I found impossible to believe, or he was really turned on by all this. I loved feeling how hard he was in my hand. I aimed further blasts at her beautiful tits, and she turned her head to look at me doing this to her. Our eyes met, we were sharing a slo-mo totally ho-mo moment. Then she rolled her eyes back into her head and came, just from our look. I felt like it was me cumming on her, and I made more cum land on her ecstatic face.

Finally he was totally spent. "Fuck yeah," he said, admiring his conquest.

"Fuck yeah," I agreed, also spent. He casually grabbed his camera off the counter and I reflexively went into sorority pose mode. She and I leaned close and air kissed each other. He'd be quite the stud showing the photo to everyone, a blonde in a string bikini kissing a smiling brunette with cum on her face and tits. No big deal-- just another Friday night!

"Take a cropped one and send it to her boyfriend," I playfully suggested, popping off my top.

He smirked and took a few lips-down shots: my hand holding his big dick, my tits mashed into her arm, her cum covered body. "Tease him it's his girlfriend! He won't believe it!"

"You're so bad!" she said to me, our lips smiling for the camera.

"I know," I said, "I can't help it!"

I was still holding his now rapidly deflating cock. He looked utterly drained, poor guy would need a week to recover from this. "I'll leave you two to awkward silences!" I said. I felt too charged to put the top on immediately. Clutching it in my hand and covering my tits with my arm, I ran to the door and stepped out, but then turned to face them. I looked at them and wickedly sucked a finger clean. Then I shut the door.

I did finally tell my husband about that night. Well, that's kind of a lie. About a year later we were discussing our sexual pasts and I told him this story. But I pretended like it happened before I met him. I didn't really consider it cheating because while they both had orgasms, I didn't. That may not sound like a hard line but you got to make one somewhere! I only lied because I didn't think he'd handle it well if he knew it happened the same night we met. No doubt he would have compared it to the chaste but hopeful peck on the cheek I gave him before he left, obsessing on the chaste part and ignoring how much hope was invested in it. But even thinking the story happened before him made him irrationally jealous, like I was willing to be more sexual with other men than with him. That wasn't true. From a certain perspective I guess it appeared that way, but it was only because those other guys didn't matter in the same way, and I didn't matter to them. It's hard to explain.

Anyway, a few years later we were on our honeymoon in the islands, and we were out on a deck, taking in the sun and the sea air. Of course it was topless and I was a little nervous, but when in Rome...

My new husband (it felt amazing to say that!) was getting us drinks. So it was in this relaxed and exposed condition that I felt a strong, masculine hand gently touch my shoulder. "Hey, Christey. Love the shades. Is your agent around?"

I knew who it was the moment I felt the hand: a topless girl will attract a lot of attention, but I didn't know anyone else who had the balls to just walk up to one and touch her. So it had to be Jack. Out here? What were the odds one of his coworkers would show up on the island? At this secluded deck near our cabana?

I had met Jack at the various office parties. I was not at all attracted to Jack, but I couldn't deny Jack was a complete stud. I probably shouldn't say that out loud, but that's what he was. Standing in front of me bare chested, abs chiseled, muscles defined from MMA training. And it was impossible not to notice the freely flopping beer can filling his otherwise baggy shorts, right at my eye level, while I lounged before him wearing nothing but a pink thong and a wedding ring.

Jack had a complicated reputation. Like my husband, he was a young superstar who climbed quickly to partner; but unlike him, on the way up he had left behind him a trail of sexual devastation. Receptionists, coworkers, the wives of coworkers-- if he wanted he unfailingly bed them. He was an arrogant bully who treated men like shit and women like sluts, but no man would stand up to him and no woman seemed to want to. Worse, he was a hugely important part of the company. Even though many of the men were resentful of him, there was a collective sense that he deserved his success, not to mention "all that pussy" (of course, they didn't know that included their own wives.) I guess many of the women quietly thought the same.

His ego finally got him into trouble. He kept pushing the board to do a takeover of another firm, both out of a desire to cross the others, with whom he was at odds in other work issues, and also because of the veiled criticisms he made in his speech, but mostly because he wanted a promotion, hoping the takeover would make him a lot of money and earn for himself all the glory. His ego was already overinflated by being a quasi-celebrity to the lower employees who had only heard about him anecdotally, and this led him to overindulge his tastes beyond what his income would bear, in cars and in the rest of his expenses; and later on this had more than a little to do with the bankruptcy of the company. Most of the senior managers were alarmed at his ambitiousness, and how much license he took with the job, his life and habits, and… the female employees, and the bulk of them saw him as wanting to make himself CEO and so became his enemies. And although in his public life his handling of the job was as good as anyone could have ever wanted, in his private life his behavior enraged everyone, and caused them to give promotions to others less able, to the ruin of the company. Eventually he went to work for their main competitor. I'm sure he did very well for himself.

Jack was not the kind of guy my husband would have been friends with, but he tacitly respected Jack's act-on-what-you-want attitude. I don't know about the boardroom, but as for the bedroom I had often tried to argue that Jack's success wasn't something to admire, it required him to be callous and unempathic, oblivious to any resistance or hesitation from the woman. "You're not going to understand this," I said, "but sometimes a woman feels like she has to go along with it. If it gets to a certain point, she feels obligated to submit." I was right, he didn't understand this. He thought women could always do what they wanted, which in this case was what Jack wanted.

But respect wasn't the only thing that drove my husband to maintain friendly relations. He got a perverse enjoyment from being around Jack because of me. My husband knew that Jack saw me as just another of the many trophy wives that would fall into his bed-- except that, try as he might, I didn't. Sorry, bub, the only man I want I marrying. That rejection pleased my then fiance so much that he tolerated Jack's increasingly bold flirtations. If we were at a party and he saw me talking to Jack he wouldn't interfere at all, he wouldn't even glance in our direction; meanwhile Jack took full advantage of our time to ply me with flattery or provoke me with manipulative complements, all of which I parried by reminding him I had a fiance, and right over there, and that there were plenty of other women who would adore his attentions. Of course, Jack assumed he just needed to get me away from the "giant cock blocker over there...." (yes, I got it!)

God knows I never would have gone out with him even if I single, his cockiness and smug superiority totally turned me off. But if you knew how to handle him he could actually be quite fun to be around. He was undeniably attractive, and I admit I was flattered that the man who was known for bedding beautiful women wanted me. He was charming and funny, and despite his cockiness was never pushy with me or made me feel uncomfortable. I found I could let my guard down, even flirt a little (it's fun!) and he wouldn't overestimate it. So I played the part of the curious but honorable fiancee and just as playfully shut him down when it got too hot. Jack's ego never suffered, I'm sure. He was man enough not to take the rejection personally, even if I sometimes meant it personally. Meanwhile, each time Jack flirted with me, my husband saw it as another championship match for the trophy wife which he kept winning again and again. Undefeated-- against his single rival.

Perhaps because my husband never directly confronted him, Jack even began to tease my husband a little, letting him know that it was only a matter of time before he got me out of my clothes.

I rolled my eyes when I heard his fantastic predictions of my complicit nudity. And yet now he was standing above me, grinning broadly, while I was topless in a pink thong that served no other purpose than to prove I was naked. For years he had been eyeing my breasts, and now they were fully displayed for his enjoyment. What was I supposed to do? Wouldn't it have been weirder to cover up? Thank

God I was wearing sunglasses, it made me look way more self-assured than I felt.

Beyond nervous, I stood up and did that thing where you overcompensate pretending to be excited to see a person in a new context. "Oh my God, Jack, how are you! When did you get here?" By reflex I greeted him with an awkward bent-over hug, careful to make sure our hips didn't touch, but the result was my naked tits swayed against his bare chest. Oops. His one hand slid to the small of my back, and then lingered at the edge of my thong. I quickly lay back in the chaise, but of course not putting on a shirt only made it look like an invitation, which he took. He perched himself on the edge.

"I had no idea you were here until the desk told me you were on your honeymoon. Congratulations, I'm sure you've made him a very happy man. Here, let me help you with that." He took a nearby bottle of sunscreen and began to rub it into my already glistening, well lotioned calves-- exactly as my husband came out to the deck. I froze. What should I do? I saw his eyes momentarily widen as he tried to process what he was seeing, but he otherwise didn't react and maintained a poker face as he continued walking casually towards us. So I nervously did nothing, and passively let Jack continue rubbing my legs.

"Hey, man, congratulations on your wedding," Jack said as he caressed under my knees. "Why don't you leave the drinks here and meet us for dinner later?"

I was so tense I couldn't help it-- a loud laugh escaped me, which he took as assent to sliding his hand further up my inner thighs. I sat upright and crossed my legs, ending his recklessness.

Nevertheless, Jack stayed put on my chaise. We all began chatting, awkwardly at first, my husband tried to seem cool but I knew he was tense, he had a pack of cards that he was fiddling with in his hands, hoping to seem nonchalant but also to break the tension. But it was Jack who made it all very light and smooth, and soon we fell into easy conversation, talking and drinking. He even asked to see a card trick! Truth is, Jack hadn't really done anything wrong, rubbing my calves was typical Jack, and its very brazenness proved it was meaningless. He was just fun to be around, easy going and friendly. Periodically of course he dropped flirty innuendos, commented on my spectacular "boob job" (as if he was fooled-- ha), and even managed to get me (after my eyes rolled) to let him rub lotion on my back as if it was the most normal thing in the world. And my husband seemed ok with everything, too, no secret signals, no signs of discomfort beyond the card twirling. They were both having a good time, and it was fun for me to be the center of attention. So I relaxed. Topless. On a chaise lounge between my hunky husband and his studly rival.

Whew. He did give nice back rubs, though.

At some point Jack left to get us more drinks, and all at once my husband's cool demeanor completely imploded. It was so forceful and abrupt that I reflexively threw on a tank top and raised my sunglasses to my head.

"He'd kill to fuck you," he told me urgently.

"He's not going to," I said, sobering up quickly. "I have no desire to be with any other man, let alone him."

"I don't think he thinks that."

"Would you like me to tell him?"

He thought about this for a moment. "No, because he wouldn't believe you. He thinks he just needs to get you away from me."

I laughed. "You want me to seduce him into the hot tub and turn him down there?"

"No..." he said in a way that made me think he was considering it. "The key is to lead him on into a situation where there is no way I could catch you, and then shut him down. Let him know I beat you."

"How you think," I rolled my eyes. "Do you run a business this way?"

"Do something really sexy, I don't know, flirt, show him your tits."

"He's already seen my tits," I reminded him, tugging my tank top down. Where the hell did I ever get it? It was my old sorority crop top, cut obscenely high so that it barely covered my breasts, and right below the logo was written in squintingly tiny letters, "take a picture, you'll last longer." My dorky husband thought it was hilarious. Did wearing it make me look more covered or less?

"Show him your ass then, I don't know."

"Oh my god, what am I to you, shark bait?"

"Just drive him crazy, do something."

"So you want me to be a cock please," I said.

"Tease," he smirked.

"Oops," I said. "Sorry-- tease."

"Can you do it?"

I smirked back and gestured to my body. "Umm, yeah, I'm pretty sure I can do

30

it. I just don't think I should do it."

My husband was nuts. Work parties are one thing, but I couldn't believe he was letting this cocky alpha male anywhere near his intoxicated and basically naked wife, let alone asking me to inflame him. What did he think would happen?

Jack returned with the drinks, and there was no way I couldn't glance at the beer can in his shorts swinging as he walked. The big dick had a big dick. Urf. I lowered my sunglasses and lay back on the chaise, and was about to take off my top again when I realized that it would look like I had covered up when alone with my husband, and was now going to re-present myself to Jack. Oh God, they were making me as nuts as they were, these two horny mountain goats were getting high on their own pheromones and I was getting it from both ends, so I resolved to just be myself, act naturally, keep my own limits and have a little fun, and let them lock horns and misinterpret my behavior any way they needed to. If my husband wanted me to stop or do something different, all he had to do was just say so.

Jack studied the shirt for a moment, then looked into my glasses. "Pig," I mouthed.

Alcohol and innuendo continued, and I have to admit that all the attention I was getting was making me giddy. I know this won't make sense to a man, but that jump from being single to being married made me feel more free, not less. Marriage made it possible for me to enjoy desires without the pressure to pursue them or the guilt that I didn't. It made it safer to flirt because there was a line around you, and anything outside was inconsequential when before I'd have to figure out what I wanted, my feelings about it, weighing the consequences of acting on it against the risks of a missed opportunity. If I had been topless in front of Jack back when I was dating, I would have been just as mortified and just as turned on as I was now, but too mixed up inside to enjoy it. And while I never would have pursued him I admit I would have been way easier to seduce. But married, on my honeymoon? I was a queen guarded by a king, playing with... jacks.

And so with my new husband right there beside me, I even felt safe enough to enjoy being provocative. I had placed my drink on the table slightly behind me so that I had to twist my body to reach it, causing the shirt to stretch and expose the bottom of my breasts. Of course I was aware. Both boys noticed, and both guys knew the other noticed. Oh boy. I was drunk, I was tingling. Everyone's attention was on me, it felt electric, it made me feel so sexy, so desired, so charged.

And that's when my seemingly laid back, likely drunk, and evidently dumb husband suggested we... play poker. Uh oh, I know I've seen this movie before.

Good thing I put the shirt on.

I'm sure in his head he thought it was a good way taunt Jack, to show me off and show him up, frustrating and humiliating him, but Dummy hadn't thought through how that scene would play out. So when he proudly won the first hand, he suddenly went silent, realizing he had to command me to take my top off in front of his coworker and--

"I know you want me to undress in front of your wife," gloated Jack, "but you'll have to say please. Or do you want us to undress each other?"

Yeah. He's a dummy. Thinking fast, he instead "demanded" I give him a lap dance while Jack had to sit and watch. "Oh my God," I laughed "You're such a dork! Are we in college?" But I wanted to dance, I had to get the erotic energy out of me and dancing was a safe way to discharge it. I got up, moving my hips and shoulders to a beat I hummed out loud. I had a lot of practice dancing; minimal movements was all I needed for maximum effect and plausible deniability. At one point I sat in my husband's lap facing Jack and blew him an innocent kiss. He responded by discreetly but deliberately adjusting his giant penis inside his trunks. "Bad boy," I mouthed to him.

Dummy's improvised reward brought about the obvious. The next hand went to Jack, and of course he wanted a dance with the newlywed. I got up and moved towards him with completely fake confidence. "You guys better hope I don't win any hands."

Overcompensating for my anxiety, I danced around him, stroked his hair and then his chest (sexy!) Fortunately, even this arrogant prick had the sense not to try anything too crazy in front of my husband, and I was still wearing the tank, which gave me a little more freedom to tease him.

I tried to safely straddle his lap facing him, but as I grinded on him his dick was impossible to avoid. I tried to avoid it... honest! But it was so prominent that even with his shorts on, playful writhing on his lap became subtly rubbing my pussy along his pole. My hands were on the back of his chair, my tank covered chest (thank god!) pushed forward into his face, my nipples confessing my arousal through the white material.

"Take off your top," he whispered in my ear. "I want to feel you."

"I'm maaaaarrrried," I teased, exaggeratedly slurring my words. "My husband would not like that."

"If he loved you, he'd want you to enjoy yourself."

"Yes," I said leaning into his ear, "but I'm pretty sure he wouldn't want you to enjoy yourself."

"What does he want?" Dummy said proudly.

"He wants," I said, looking at Jack stare into my mirrored sunglasses, "to see my tits." I giggled.

"He's seen them." Ok, true, but he wasn't supposed to say it out loud! I felt myself flush. "Show him your ass."

I caught a flash of my new wedding ring, with all its magic powers. I spun around and sat facing away from Jack, pushing my ass against his crotch. He slapped it playfully. "Any tan lines?" he asked. Without waiting for an answer, he tugged on the side of my strap to reveal the light arc that traced over my hips and... down.

"Hey, now," I cautioned, in what probably sounded like assent.

"Are you a natural blonde?" he asked, covertly speaking into the back of my neck. My husband sat across us smiling, gloating over the frustration Jack must have felt.

"No," I admitted.

"I should check," he said.

I turned my head and bit my bottom lip. "There's nothing to check," I slurred.

Of course he checked anyway, pulling up the straps like a puppeteer. "You're bad," I whispered.

Of course Jack had been around enough women to know my dance was intended as fun, meaningless teasing-- of both of men-- and he played along. He put his hands on my sides and daringly slid them slowly upwards. His hands felt so good, no man since my husband had touched me there, like that. I was nervous and excited, pretending like I was enjoying it while hiding how much I was really enjoying it. And Jack knew just how to playfully push the envelope. He began to slide his hands higher... and forwards... deliberately provoking the expected response: I slapped his hands away, giggling. "Hey, no touching," I pretended to whisper, "you know my husband is right there, right?"

"That guy?" he said loudly. "You think he's going to do anything?"

And then he started to go for it. He let me know that he was going for it, making me self-conscious of the fact that neither I nor my husband was stopping him. He slid his hands slowly up under my shirt. I had been topless before, but this was different-- he was touching me, touching my bare flesh while I was covered to my husband, the significance of the action impossible to ignore. Our touch had become private. He was taking possession of me. I waited to see how my husband would react: would he jump up? Stop this? Give me a signal, anything? But he did nothing! He just watched Jack's hands under the shirt. I tried to hide how turned on I was, but it was hard. Hard for me… I had even forgotten what I was sitting on… My breathing became ragged and my heart was pounding right through my breasts, I know Jack could feel it. I was so mixed up with anxiety and arousal I was trembling. Jack's hands slid all the way forward, cupping and massaging my breasts, and then his fingers finally reached my nipples.

I came.

"Oh!" I didn't mean to, it surprised me, and I really tried not to show it. My back stiffened as I tried to resist its arching. My hands gripped his through the shirt. My hips drove downwards even as my weight shifted to my toes. My mouth fell open but I stifled the moan with a long breath, oh god please don't let him notice; yet through my sunglasses my taunting eyes screamed at my husband: look what he's doing to me! But he was so focused on what Jack's hands were doing to my breasts that he didn't appreciate what Jack was doing to the rest of me, how easy it was for him to do it to me. Jack, of course, knew exactly what he was doing to me.

"Nice," he whispered, very pleased with himself, politely letting me ride out my orgasm. His hands remained on my swollen tits.

"Oh my," I said finally, preposterously playing it off like I didn't just have a massive orgasm in his lap. I looked at my still oblivious husband, feigning an amused shock while trying to reset my hormones. "Are you just going to sit there and let this very naughty man maul your wife's tits?"

He eyed me suspiciously but said nothing.

I heard Jack chuckle. "Told you." He pulled my shirt completely off, tossing it at my husband, hitting him in the face. I couldn't help it-- I giggled.

His eyes widened, but he forced a smile and took up the shirt. Jack kept up his gentle assault of my now full displayed breasts. Oh God. I was both terrified and-- turned on. Was he too drunk or not drunk enough to stop this?

"Your wife's tits are real," Jack informed him. He weighed them from behind, gently pulling my body back to lay on his chest. His hands looked so masculine and powerful on my swollen boobs that I moaned out loud just from the visual. My husband no doubt thought I was just acting the part of strip club dancer, but I was so aroused that I felt like I would come again from the craziness of what was happening. Under the sunglasses I closed my eyes to block it out, and lay my head back on Jack's shoulder, pretending to be faking enjoying it. He kissed my neck.

I know a lot of people would be horrified that I let another man touch me like that, right in front of my husband, but you have to believe me that I never would have done it except that my husband was right in front of me. Of course he was shocked, maybe a little jealous, maybe turned on, who knows? But he had all the power, he could stop it any time he wanted. I felt safe and protected because I had placed myself totally in his hands (well, Jack's hands, too!)

"No one at the office is going to believe they're real," Jack taunted.

The mention of the others hearing about any of this craziness should have made me ashamed, but instead it aroused my naughty side. What's it to me, my drunk brain asked? They'll just be jealous of my husband, and isn't that what he wanted all along? I moaned into Jack's ear (maybe I gave it a little kiss!) as he pulled my nipples towards the hot sun. Arf. My husband started this. I snaked my one hand in front of Jack's neck and up through his hair, and shot my husband a sneaky wink to let him know I was still just pretending and totally in control. I guess I forgot that he couldn't see my eyes through the sunglasses.

In retrospect, I get now that the thought of his coworkers drooling over the story-- or being jealous of the wrong man-- or my expression, my sounds, the way I sat-- lay-- writhed-- on Jack as his hands traveled my body, it may have finally been too much for my poor hubby. "All right, you two," he said laughingly, "break it up before I have to remarry."

"No, baby," I said, thinking it was all part of the teasing, "I love you, being your wife is so much fun."

"I'm sure security would agree."

Of course I wasn't going to go any further, but I couldn't resist the banter. "Ooh, are we on camera?" I said in my best dumb blonde voice, biting my lip. "Does this look cute?" I leaned into Jack's face, our lips grazing each other's.

"Come on, I've been a good sport, but fun time with the bride is over."

"No, not yet," I said smiling into Jack's face. "He still has to remove my garter."

"Just a gentle tug..." Jack playfully snapped my thong.

"All right, let go of my wife," he said, "this is bordering on disrespectful."

"Oh, relax," said Jack, "it's not all about you. You don't have to prove your dick is bigger by being all bossy."

"Yeah," I teased vampishly as my lips brushed Jack's, "I can figure out whose dick is bigger on my own." I stuck my tongue out and licked his lips.

Jack's hands slid under the straps and took hold of my hip bones, directing my pelvis. I hooked one arm behind Jack's head while I nibbled the fingernail of the other hand, turning to look deep into my husband's eyes. I was going to call his bluff. "Baby?" I said sweetly, his frozen stare trying to see into my thoughts-- thank god for my sunglasses-- "would you come over here and slip off my thong? I'm afraid this very bad man might rip it."

He stopped breathing. "I said that's enough!" His voice cracked like a teenager's. I thought it had all been teasing fun, but clearly I had better control of Jack than my husband did of himself. I raised my body up and slinked off Jack's lap, trying to make it look natural. Well, that was something! I stood up, fluffed my hair and adjusted my thong, playing like I was totally in control. I took the shirt back, but rather than putting it on, I used it to dab the sweat off my breasts, then tossed it playfully at Jack. Oh, well, now he had a little trophy.

Knowing he must have come off looking insecure, my husband tried to laugh it off and overcompensated by dealing the cards. "Come on, a few more hands and then I guess we better jet." Jet? Since when did he talk like that? And a few more hands? It only took two hands to get me to orgasm. "Next hand, if I win, I get two of your accounts, my choice."

Jack laughed. "That's some bet, what's the other side?"

"If you win, you get two of mine."

"I'm going to get them anyway, I don't need win them in poker." He looked like he had a sudden inspiration. "How about a blowjob? Relax, I mean from Christey." He winked at me.

Even my husband laughed. "In your wildest dreams."

"She's going to give me one anyway," Jack said, "this way you can pretend she had no choice."

My husband didn't even pause. "Deal."

What?! I started to blurt out a protest, but something told me not to break character, and so my involuntary "no!" turned into an "oh!" I can't imagine how that sounded to the boys. My husband had me set up as some kind of party chick who was down for anything, and so far I had what he wanted, and more. A sexy lap dance, second base, ok-- and never mind I would never do it, but he wasn't actually

36

risking me blowing his rival, was he?

"I know Christey is down for it," Jack said smiling at me, "but how do I know you won't turn into a homicidal maniac?"

My husband spread out his arms. "Come on, I'm a man, I know the rules: bros before hoes!"

I couldn't help myself-- I laughed out loud. I was no ho, but I was way more of a ho than he was a bro!

"You're on, bro!" said Jack, seeing no protest from me. I twirled my hair and smiled like a dumb blonde, trying to appear relaxed, compliant and willing to play. WTF? A blowjob?

Jack shuffled the deck, but I took it from him. "I'll deal," I said, laughing, "I don't trust either of you two." I wasn't sure why I said that. But what poor old Jack didn't know was that this wasn't my first game of strip poker with horny guys, I had learned a thing or two about trick dealing in college. Sorry, mister, you can have a lap dance, even paw my tits, but I no way am I going to blow you! So with nimble fingers I let Jack come out with three Queens but my husband was about to win with a flush.

Imagine my surprise when instead of the flush he turned over... three Jacks! How had that happened? It was impossible! I know I didn't mess up! Did I mess up?

"On your knees, baby," Jack said laughing, "let's see if practice made perfect!"

I froze, my dumb smile locked on my face. My husband stared blankly at the cards. As if he couldn't believe it either...

"Come on," Jack said. He was milking it, but obviously joking with no intention of collecting. "Let's put my money where your mouth is!"

"Wait a second," my dumbfounded husband said, still looking at the cards. "Hold on. You cheated..."

"How could I cheat, I wasn't even dealing!"

"You must have hidden a card..."

"Where, under my dick?" he said laughing. I had a sudden image of me on my knees finding his heavy slab of cock easily securing a winning hand against his balls. He winked at me, having so much fun torturing my poor husband.

"Wait a second..."

"Come on, dude," Jack said. "You proposed the bet, not me. Didn't hear her complain, either. I won her fair and square. If you want to go back on your debt, well, that's your choice, but you did say you would be a man." He sat there, grinning like a big dicked frat boy. I sat there, smiling like a blonde sorority girl.

What I didn't know then was that my husband had also cheated-- he had 3 Jacks pulled out of the deck already. But it made no sense, he knew I was good at trick dealing. Unless… was he actually afraid I might make Jack win?

"No way, wait," he insisted, maybe a little too aggressively. "She's not going through with it."

"I'm not going to force her," sending me another quick wink, "she isn't going to do anything she doesn't choose to do, right, Christey?" I smiled nonchalantly, terrified-- electrified. "But she seems into it."

On the inside I was a vortex of conflicted feelings, but I was also very self-conscious of how I looked on the outside. How obscenely I was un-dressed. Perched felinely at the edge of the chair, sunglasses turning my apprehension into coy passivity, stomach muscles taut from anxiety resulting in centerfold perfect posture; topless, swollen breasts proudly displayed and on offer. I felt like my entire body looked horny. And-- whether it was the atmosphere, or the alcohol, or the heightened energy of two men fighting over me, instead of getting frightened I was getting really, really turned on. It was insane, but at that moment I wanted them to physically fight over me like gorillas, naked gorillas, the winner tossing me down on the chaise, tearing off my little thong and fucking his prize, either my husband with his jealousy enraged dick or Jack with has arrogantly triumphant cock--- oh God, think about baseball!

But this was no fantasy, it was real, but real like I was watching a movie. To my amazement, my husband stood up and squared off against Jack, who rolled his eyes. "Seriously, you want to fight me?"

It was now evident just how drunk he was and how drunk Jack wasn't. My husband lunged forward, took a swing, stumbled, and grabbed an umbrella pole for balance. Oh my God! The pole fell and struck Jack square in the face, but he didn't even flinch-- he laughed!

"That all you got?" straightening himself up. "Here's what's going to happen. After I lay you out, I'm going to take that gorgeous wife of yours and watch her try and suck my dick. And then I'm going cum all over her fat tits, and she's going to love it. Then she'll pose for a few pictures, which I'll send you. Eventually."

He lunged at Jack again, drunkenly and clumsily. Jack gave him a single jab to the face and he fell onto a chair, knocked out cold!

"Man," said Jack out loud to no one, almost surprised. "That was too easy. And I have to admit, a little wrong."

He shrugged, offered me his hand, and gently pulled me up from the chaise. I was in shock. He guided me into his arms, took my sunglasses off and tossed them next to my husband. He put his hands on my waist and traced upwards, his fingers sliding into the grooves between my ribs. Wait, had he been joking about being serious, or--? Frozen, I just stood there, mouth hanging open. He leaned in slowly and kissed it. I closed my eyes and reflexively kissed him back. I wasn't even thinking. I didn't know what was happening. "Umm..." I said, breaking the kiss and looking over at my husband lying on the chaise, "is he going to be all right?"

"He'll be fine," he said, "I barely touched him, it was more the alcohol than the anything else."

"Shouldn't we do something for him?"

"We should settle his debt." He leaned in for a kiss.

Ha! Topless, in a thong, as if the proper etiquette after beating up my husband was to give myself to his rival!

I swear it was out of habit, it wasn't about Jack, it was context, my hands just did what they... naturally... did in those situations. Reflex, muscle memory, as we kissed my eyes closed and my hands went gently to his abs, hips, and then down that crease towards his... I felt a movement, and opened my eyes to see he was undoing his shorts. Oh my God! They fell away. He was naked, big dick now fully erect before me. He pulled me closer to him.

"What are you doing!" I asked, half jokingly, half honestly, still in shock, eyes drawn down to a dick that came almost up to my tits. "My husband that you knocked out is right there!"

"So? A deal's a deal, this is America. Kind of." He touched my arm and I just stood there, compliant. The way he was caressing my arm made me not think about pulling away from him. The way his dick grazed my belly made me think about pulling closer to him. "Your body is spectacular," he said admiringly. "One guy couldn't possibly be enough for you." Taking my lack of resistance as an invitation, he hooked a finger into the front of my thong and pulled me up against him.

"Fuck you, get off me," I told him, partially coming to my senses. But not pushing him away.

"What's wrong?" he said, gently holding me in his powerful arms.

"I don't like you," I managed.

"That's fine with me." He had started caressing my back, lightly, my breasts smashed up against his chest and his lips hovered over my ears. I weakly tried to push him off, but he grabbed my wrists and with one hand pinned them over my head against the wall. His other hand slid behind my neck, and we kissed again. He tasted like lust.

"Fuck you!" I whispered, pushing his tongue out of my mouth with my tongue.

Then he kissed my neck. I let him. I don't know why. I hated this guy, I hated how he had treated my husband, how he treated women, his arrogance-- and how much it was turning me on.

He kissed my neck, then slowly turned me sideways to kiss my hips. One hand on my breast, the other on my ass, his lips making their way to my shoulders. "Your curves are so sexy," he said, dragging his lips back up towards the back of my neck, inhaling deeply as he kissed. "I love your smell, everything about you is making me crazy for you."

He turned me facing the wall and slid down towards my ass, kissing and gnawing on it. I arched my back involuntarily, facilitating his control of my ass. "I don't think any guy could handle you the way you need to be handled."

As he devoured my body, my mind drifted to all the women he had seduced. Right now he wanted me, he was hungry for me. I had some power. I spun around. I took Jack's head and gave him a deep and passionate kiss. Then I would push him off me and get the hell out of there.

"I love how receptive your body is," he said.

"You just like my big tits," I said mischievously.

"It's so sexy, it needs to be touched more."

Smug bastard, did he think that would work on me? I tried-- I wanted to try-- to stop kissing him. Boy did he know how to kiss me. Meanwhile, his hands kept moving, roaming, touching… why was I still here? Ok, I told myself, this was still harmless. I hadn't wanted it. I ended up in this situation, but it wasn't out of hand. I hadn't cheated yet, and I could stop it at any time… why not… just… kiss… a few moments more?

Jack's hand went to my thong. Uh uh, I laughingly moved it back up to my nipple. He could do whatever he wanted with my tits, but the thong stayed on, that would be the limit.

Even though I didn't like him as a person, our slow exploration of each other was making me want him. And it felt so hot to kiss this jerk, to give my body to a man I didn't like but still wanted.

I had a pang of guilt when I caught a glimpse of my husband laying there. Here I was, practically naked, in the arms of another man. Bad enough I was doing this, but I was doing it with my husband's rival, a guy he hated, a guy he felt insecure about, and a guy who outplayed him and outmuscled him. The thought that this man could take another man's woman made me flush. Urf. I knew I wasn't a prize to be passed around... but it was so hot imagining myself as one. Oh God, I was revving myself up!

Jack must have been reading my mind, or my body, because instead of trying to take my thong off, he tugged it slightly outwards, and I actually watched as he purposefully slipped his long, thick cock up through it, so it poked obscenely out the top while the shaft found a welcoming groove against my unprotected pussy.

"I can't believe how sexy you are," he said. "Naked is definitely your best look."

"Fuck," was all I could say. He kissed me like this, his strong arms pinning my shoulder blades back and forcing my tits outwards into him. Fuck. I'm in trouble.

I should have stopped it. I should have told him to back off. Somehow I convinced myself that my thong being on-- even if he was using it to secure his dick against my pussy-- made up for how slutty I was acting. His head went to a breast and I pulled him closer to it. Oh god, I hate this guy, and I'm letting him suck my tits. What kind of a woman am I? I tried to drag my pussy lips along his shaft without letting him notice. How could he not notice? I was the one who was trying not to notice. This was so wrong, so hot. I have to stop this, soon.

He pulled back a little, his unyielding cock tugging the thong outwards. Wow. Not only was this wrong, it looked really wrong. Giving in to a reckless passionate moment was one thing, but now he was just posing us, forcing me to observe how perfect our bodies looked together.

I looked down at the erection that had plowed through so many other beautiful women, under the noses or over the objections of their boyfriends or husbands. "You think I'm that easy?" I said in response to a question he hadn't even asked.

He laughed almost humbly. "Would you mind pretending you are?"

Umf.

"You know what I want?" he said, tracing a nipple. Yeah. I'm pretty sure I did. My left hand drifted to his cock jutting up past my thong, my fingers holding the bulbous head like a delicate egg I should not squeeze. I am not going to cheat on my husband, I thought, as I looked at my engagement ring flush against... Wow. I needed distance, I needed to get this arrogant prick away from my body.

"Someone should photograph us," he said, leaning back, admiring how our bodies fit together. "Where would you put your thighs while I worked my dick into you?"

I tried not to think of an answer, but I couldn't not think of lots of answers.

I looked in his face. He leered at me. To him I was just another blonde bimbo whose promiscuous pussy would soon be climaxing on his careless cock, smirking at my shameless and sinful squeals. I hated this jerk. I wanted to taste his cum. Oh god, what was the matter with me? I started making crazy deals with myself: ok, I had to suck him off, that had been the deal, but then I'd be free. And he wouldn't be touching me anymore, I'd be in control. A blowjob wasn't so bad, far less intimate than sex. My poor husband. This was like a porno fantasy, some imaginary hotwife overwhelmed by lust for the alpha male, and here I was about to give this fantasy to someone else. I was supercharged, but I didn't want Jack to know that, I didn't want him to have that satisfaction. I wanted to punish this guy, give him just a taste of the kind of sex my husband got that I would deprive Jack of. It was worth giving Jack a few cheap feels so it would hurt more when I showed him I had been in control and I wouldn't let him have me.

His eyes devoured me, his cock pressed up against my pussy, his hands weighed my swollen tits as his thumbs and fingers rubbed my nipples. His tongue and lips worshiped my body everywhere, mixing our scents, mixing our tastes. Meanwhile I leaned back against the door frame and in between kisses casually stroked my hand up and down his big cock.

I was looking for reasons to give a blowjob to my husband's rival.

Fuck.

I stepped back. I took the straps of my thong and daintily pulled the ties. Arrogant prick. Pay attention, it's never going to be this good for you again. I let the thong fall away, fluffed my hair and then ran my hands along his chest with a little sway of my hips. I stepped my now naked body up to him with all the confidence of a professional seductress, my pussy's heat directly warming his balls. I gave him the lustiest kiss I could manage, spreading my legs apart, dangerously daring his cock head to penetrate me. And even then I wasn't sure… I know it sounds crazy, but even at that point I didn't know what I was going to do. I really believed I could stop at any moment, yet I also felt this guy had me completely in his power.   Sucking him off was no longer his reward, it was my only escape. I know my husband wouldn't understand how I could give a blowjob to a man I didn't like… in order to deprive him. How I could want it and not want it at the same time. How I could hate a man and still want to make him cum all over me. How I could want to make him cum because I hated him. "It takes two to tango," he'd insist. But sometimes the best dances are with partners you don't like, right?

Jack gently but assertively pushed me down to my knees, as if he was entitled to use me for his lust. But I was tipsy, naked, and horny-- I was headed down there anyway.   At that moment I knew I had no choice but to give him the most spectacular blowjob I could perform.   I looked over at my defeated husband. Making sure Jack was watching me, I pulled his shaft to the outside of my cheek and simultaneously blew my sleeping husband a kiss. "Sorry honey, but it's no big deal. Jack's been blown by a lot of other wives. I know you'd want him to think your wife was the best at it." I sucked the head. "Besides," I said sweetly. "He did win the bet. You wouldn't want him to tell people you don't pay your debts, would you?"

Jack looked down at me tonguing his shaft. "Either your husband is the luckiest guy in the world, or I am."

I sat back on my thighs and spread my legs open so Jack could see every inch of the sexy body he was never going to have.

"Well, he did say we should always pay our debts."

"Fuck, you are amazingly hot," he said.

"I know," I responded. I squeezed my own tits, partly for show but also because they were tingling. Oh, god, I was so turned on by this. My body and my mind were completely at odds.

He gloated, at ease, casually placing his hands up in the door frame and spreading his legs slightly, the light from behind him framing his spectacular body. His erection was rock hard, and I felt so proud, I felt so-- fucking hot. It was like watching a movie of us, and I suddenly had the crazy thought that since I was so hot it was my obligation to pleasure him. I had no doubt this arrogant stud thought the same.

I had never sucked a cock that big, there was no way I could take it all, but I didn't want him to know that. I placed my lips around the shaft, like a harmonica, and dragged my mouth up and down its length, snaking my tongue over and under it.

"Where'd you learn to do that?" he said, nudging me towards the response.

"With tits like mine?" I said smiling up at him. "I've had lots of practice"

He smirked. "I figured, a body like yours gets a lot of attention."

I ran my lips over the bulbous head of his dick, popping on it.

"Don't I deserve it?" I said trying to match his cockiness. He didn't just have me blowing him, he had me performing for him.

"You sexy bitch, you know that every time I'm around your husband I'm going to think of his slutty wife on her knees with her lips around my dick?"

Who the fuck did this guy think he was that he could call me names? Yet here I was, on my knees, one hand on his huge dick and the other on my tits, my own thighs spread open in lewd display-- and also to prevent myself from squeezing them towards an orgasm. No way was I going to give him the satisfaction of knowing he made me orgasm just from sucking his dick! I had come this far, so I'd give him a blowjob that he'd remember forever, and then leave him wanting more. He would never get to watch me riding him. He'd have to imagine my clit grinding onto his pelvis as he thrust upwards into me. He'd never know what it sounded like to have his balls slap against my ass as he plowed roughly into me from behind. He would only get to fantasize about what it looked like when I climaxed helplessly over and over as he pinned me on my back and repeatedly slammed his magnificent dick in and out of me. Oh god, what was I doing? I was fantasizing about fucking him while I was blowing him to prevent him from fucking me!

"You're such a sexy whore, sucking my big dick," he said.

"Awww," I giggled, "anyone who sucks your dick is a whore, or only whores ever suck your dick?"

His dick flexed. "Fuck," he said.

"Fuck," I agreed. His body was so masculine, his cock thick and hard, and right now he wanted me-- and while I was pretending to be aroused by sucking him, I was very much aroused by sucking him. The worst part was that even though I knew I'd stop after the blowjob, part of me wanted him to win, to see through my little game and just dominate me, throw me on the bed and fuck the ambivalence out of me. But I couldn't allow that to happen. For my poor husband's sake, I had to make this stud cum hard.

I lovingly tongued the leaking tip of his perfect dick. I looked up at him with innocent eyes. "You know I hate you, right?"

"I can tell," he said, watching me make love to his shaft.

"But I have to admit you have a beautiful cock." It looked even bigger, pulsing, oozing with his precum. He was so close. "How does it look between my lips?"

"Spectacular," he groaned. Really close.

"But I'm only doing this," I said, in between french kissing his cock head, "to show you how you couldn't even fuck me." Cum for me, you thick dicked bastard, cum.

He laughed and groaned at the same time. "What makes you think I'm not going to fuck you?" his dick swelling suddenly, balls rising, as he tried in vain to hold back.

"Because," I said, looking up at him, licking his shaft from balls to tip and finally bringing him off, "I'm going to make you cum all over my face."

Our eyes locked-- mine sparkling and innocent, his glazing over, and then he came. Wow! He slipped one hand to the back of my head to keep me from moving, but I wasn't going anywhere, I was committed. I took most of the whole shaft in my mouth, swallowing eagerly. With each burst I dragged slowly back and forth, tickling the shaft with my tongue as I pulled slowly back to the tip. He was cumming hard, and I felt pulses of pride at how easily I had made him lose control.

"Swallow it, you cheating slut," he growled.

I giggled out loud and to myself. He could call me any kind of names, but I had all the power. I gazed up at him as he moaned, gloating over his vulnerability. His ass clenched repeatedly as I drained him into my victorious mouth. I let out a gleeful squeal   to let him know that I was having fun with my toy cock, I was in control of it.   I pulled back to the head and lightly traced my fingers on the underside of his still spurting cock and heavy balls, swallowing lustily. "Mmmmmm," I cooed, as my other hand snaked between his legs and held his ass. I'd give this jerk something to remember.

My poor husband, he would die if he saw me on my knees like this, eagerly taking this jerk's cum, draining him, gloating through my squeals-- even if it was all for show.

"Fuck yeah, you slut," Jack groaned through his orgasm, "Your husband would be so proud." His enraged dick blasted cum into me to reinforce his point. I part chuckled, part moaned. He was right, on some level he would have been proud. Here I was, acting like a big titted bimbo, doing exactly what guys always fantasized about-- but I was doing it with another man he didn't like. And I was loving it.

I swallowed every drop. When he finished I let him watch me trace the drooling cock-tip on my mouth like lip gloss. I puckered my lips and kissed it. Then I stood up, my hands raised daintily, shoulders back and tits thrust forward.

"You are an amazing, beautiful, and very naughty, girl," he said admiringly.

I slowly, pointlessly, dabbed my juicy lips with the back of my hand, and said innocently, "did I do something bad?"

"Look at your sexy body." He put his hand in the small of my back and pulled my curves into him, and we gazed into the mirror. It did look... hot. His hard masculine body towering behind me, and my hand-- my engagement ring-- resting on his muscular chest. He saw me looking at it and smiled, relishing in the fact that yet again he had taken another man's wife.

"Fuck," he said. "Someone should photograph this."

Before I could stop him, he stretched out his hand and snap-- he had a picture of himself holding a trophy of his conquest, a picture of another tipsy blonde he had seduced away from her husband and corrupted at the end of his dick. I was simultaneously horrified-- and aroused--

"Don't you dare--!"

And then I realized he was holding my camera!

"You could always delete it," he said with enraging confidence. He knew I couldn't, how could I? No matter how dangerous it was to keep it I could never bring myself to delete it. "Show it to your girlfriends, they'll be jealous of you," he suggested. I looked at the picture as he ran his hands along my ribs. I tried to see it objectively. It was porno hot. Fuck, why did it have to look so perfect with this jerk?

He pointed the camera again. "Let's take a cropped one to send to your husband... you can tease him that it's you and me."

"You are so bad!" I said, obligingly posing.

"You could say no," he said, and took the picture.

"He'd never believe it's me," I said. "But it'll blow his mind if we pretend it is." Oh! What had come over me!

"It's not enough that you'll be thinking of me when you have sex, now you want him to think of me?"

So full of himself! I turned to look at his his now spent dick, and lightly rubbed my big tits. It was time to go on the offensive. "I must have really turned you on." I snaked my hand down to his cock. "I knew you wouldn't be able to handle me."

"Looks to me like I handled you just fine" he said, slapping my ass.

I took his now deflated dick in my hand. It was still thick and heavy, but now flaccid it seemed to me so defeated, chastised. I had beaten him, poor guy would need a week to recover and I'd be long gone. "Do you know how stupid you are?" I said, standing as confidently like a vixen as I could. "I never liked you, and it was only an accident you got me topless in the first place. But what kind of a guy has a gorgeous blonde naked in his arms, and doesn't try to get his dick in her? A blowjob? What are we, in high school?" I took a long drink from his nearby beer, at the end deliberately letting the foam surprise me by swelling up and overflowing out of my mouth and onto my chest. Oops. I dabbed my lips with my hand.

"I thought you didn't like me," he said, surprised.

I laid it back on thick again, letting him realize that I had been in control the whole time. My erect nipples pressed against his chest, reminding him that he had left me unsatisfied; I stood on my toes on one leg while I raised the other one to rub his muscular thigh, teasing his spent and defeated dick with my moist and exposed pussy, tracing his weary and saliva slicked cock riskily along the outside of my very wet and hungry cunt lips, and I kissed him lustily. "A real man would have satisfied me anyway."

"Sounds like a challenge," he said. And he picked me up, flung me over his shoulder, and carried me into the cabana.

I squealed in surprise, instantly knowing I had made a terrible mistake. I had underestimated how much he wanted to fuck me, and definitely underestimated his ability to fuck. He laid me down on the bed, one hand cupping my ass and the other tracing a line from my neck to my pussy. I let him. Ok, let's see if you're bluffing. I spread my legs lewdly, defiantly. I didn't know what my plan was. I was daring him to try to fuck me, betting that he wouldn't be able to, then turn up the pressure by teasing him that his flaccid dick was unable to match his bravado. Boy was I wrong. He put one hand on my hip bone, pinning me to the bed, the other hand held one of my tits as he slid his pelvis-- and his impossibly re-hardening cock-- in between my thighs. "I've wanted to do this since I met you," he said, "I knew it was only a matter of time before I got between your legs." He tugged on a nipple, causing me to arch my back in involuntary arousal. This bastard was rocking my body.

I looked down at our hips, my spread thighs, his muscular ass above me. I had that crazy thought again, that since we both had such sexy bodies it was expected that I should fuck him. Well.

He undulated his hips a little, causing his solid column of cock to slicken along my wetness. His big dick was sliding frictionlessly all around the outside of my pussy, making it swell even more. We kissed intensely. He would split my pussy lips like a hot dog in a bun, rubbing the whole length of his long shaft along it, dragging it endlessly across my clit. He was masturbating himself on my pussy lips, he was masturbating me with his cock, and it was driving me wild. I watched, helplessly, trying not to moan as his engorged cock stimulated my clit, while the rest of his body loomed over me proudly watching a blonde amateur involuntarily cream his manhood. It was so easy for him to do this to me. In between kissing him and trying to suppress dozens of orgasms I was angry at myself for getting so aroused, for letting him see how aroused I was. But I still couldn't bring myself to stop what his cock was doing to me. I didn't know what I wanted anymore.

"Oh god," I moaned, helplessly near climax. "Do you have a condom?"

He laughed at me. "Of course not."

"Uhhhh…." I moaned deliriously, closing my eyes. How much could I get away with enjoying without letting him know I was enjoying it…?

"You're so wet, so open," he said. "I bet I could make you come just doing this."

Oh my God he had no idea. My hands went to his chest-- holding him up for me, holding him off of me, as if that would stop him from doing what he was built to do. I refused to let him have the satisfaction of seeing me come. Blowing him was nothing, I told myself, meaningless, I had been in total control. This was different. I had to defy his cock's reckless assault on my cheating pussy.

It was a race to see who could cum last. Oh fuck. I was going to lose.

"Even I never guessed how spectacular you'd be in bed." Was I? "If I had known, I would have fucked you a lot sooner."

Ahhhh-- he popped the head of his now fully erect cock inside me and I clamped down on the head. I had to stop this, this thing that felt so necessary but was so wrong, but my body's arousal betrayed me by lubricating his bullying cock head. What kind of a woman was I? My poor husband, I had to stop this for his sake.   But Jack pumped the head in and out of the opening, battering it open, forcing it to surrender.   This guy was a sexual machine, as much as I knew I should stop, just the selfish and dominating way he wanted my body was making my lust overwhelm me. I squeezed my pussy as tight as I could, pointlessly trying to prevent him from penetrating me.

"Oh, god," I groaned guiltily, "it's so fucking thick."

I wanted this jerk off me, and deep inside me.   So the result of my ambivalence was that I was simultaneously spreading my legs wide to invite him in yet clamping my drooling pussy tight to keep him out.

In other words, I was giving him the perfect fuck.

"Unnggghhh," I moaned.

"You are so sexy," he responded.

"Ohhh,… God, no, I'm married... please don't make me cheat on my husband..." I was half saying it to remain faithful, half to dare him to take me.

He smirked. "Don't worry, baby, it isn't cheating until it's more than half in."

"Ahhhh," I moaned.

He forced his thick cock deeper into my pussy despite my squeezing.

"Fuck, you're perfect," he said. "I can't take it. You're a goddess."

"Ahhhhhhhhhhh," I moaned. His hands were supporting his weight so he could watch my body squirm freely beneath him.   He leaned in and lecherously sucked on my tits. Why were my legs so spread open for him? I couldn't squeeze my pussy forever, and every time I tired he managed to slide another inch into me before I locked tight again. The result was that not only was I getting more and more stretched by his giant cock, but I was basically kegeling myself towards orgasm on his rock hard pole.   The idea of coming hard on this arrogant dick bullying into my tight but frictionless pussy...

"Oh fuck, oh fuck," I said as it slid in further. Was this guy going to have all of me? Was nothing going to be reserved for my poor husband? He was resizing my pussy, it would never fit my husband again. Oh God. I had to keep him out, I could not let myself come, but then he shifted his hips and drove his cock upwards. My legs spread wider, my back arched, and my head tilted backwards, my breasts presented themselves to his greedy mouth.

"Fuck you're so sexy, look at your spectacular body, look at how it moves. I wish your husband could see you right now."

What would he see? A wife submitting to an arrogant stud? A big titted blonde getting devastated by her husband's chauvinistic rival?

He leaned in and sucked my upturned chin, "let me in, you gorgeous slut, I want in..."

"Ahhh" I cried again, trying to squeeze him out. So thick-- I couldn't let myself cum!

"Please, oh God, no more, I can't take it." I could take it, I could take all of it--

"So fucking tight," he insisted, purposely swelling his massive cock to make the point. "I can't believe how easy it was to get between your legs."

I cooed involuntarily, "easy? Oh, god, I'm married..." and then I sucked his tongue into my mouth. I arched my back and caressed him with my thighs. "I shouldn't be doing this... it's so big.... This is so wrong." He had me laid out like a starfish and the only resistance I offered was my squeezed pussy muscles. "Oh, baby," I sighed into his mouth, "don't make me cheat on my husband by making me come with you."

But of course that was what he wanted. He laughed nastily, the big jerk, gloating over his conquest. "You're a very bad wife, I'm going to have to punish your pussy for him," he said. Here I was, flat on my back with my pussy totally full of barely half his shaft, and all I could do was narrate, "ohhhh.... you're so thick....." He leaned down and licked my conquered lips.

I reluctantly, passionately, moaned into his mouth as we kissed.

"Does it feel good?" he said.

"Ahhh."

"I can't understand why your husband doesn't like me," he teased. "It's just sex. I'm not going to hurt you."

"Fuck," I said.

"Just stretch you a little. So you can enjoy it more."

"Fuck!"

"Maybe next time we should let him watch so he can see how much you enjoy it."

"Fuck," I said again.

"He'd probably jack off, watching how sexy you look taking my dick, no way he'd be able to help himself."

Oh god, what a thought! He kept inching his cock further into me while I pointlessly tried to squeeze him out, but I was so wet that it was no use. Finally that arrogant bastard got his dick all the way inside my unfaithful pussy, and just to prove he'd conquered me, he thrust upwards and bottomed out. "Tight fit," he said. "There isn't going to be any room for my cum."

"Ooooooohh!" I squealed at this, and almost came immediately. No! I had resigned myself to getting fucked by this stud, and by the way he knew how to handle my body, I guess I never stood a chance. But even if he was going to use me as a fuck toy for his selfish pleasure, no way was I going to cum, no way was I going to give him the satisfaction of knowing he could make me climax-- no way would I let him talk to my clueless husband as he recalled the look, the feel, the sounds of my adulterous orgasm. I tried to concentrate on how much I hated him to distract my mind, but the fact that I didn't like him made it even hotter, it intensified the feeling of his shaft which I was never supposed to feel plowing my pussy with deep, deliberate strokes.

He must have sensed that I was holding back. He took it as a challenge. "I want to watch you cum," he said.

"Not going to happen," I said breathlessly kissing him, holding his magnificent shoulders.

Without slowing his strokes at all, he smirked and gently slapped my tits. "Yes it is, many times."

So fucking arrogant, so sure of himself. Ahhhhh. I was so close, please, no, no. He leaned down again and kissed me, his forceful tongue fucking my mouth like his cock was fucking my cunt. Oh, God. I arched my back, I threw my hands behind my head in partial submission. "Oh, oh, oh, you fucking bastard, oh, God, please, no, don't make me cum…" I couldn't take it anymore, just the thought of this jerk bringing me to orgasm so soon, so easily, feeding his ego, watching yet another pliable blonde climax over his perfect cock-- the thought itself was making me orgasm against my will. Helplessly, I begged him in the lustiest voice, "oh, please, baby, no more, I don't want to cheat on my husband…"

With a laugh, he fucked me with more power, more lust, more--- cock--- and I was lost.

"Oh---- fuck--- ooooohhhhhhh!" The orgasm ripped through my body. "Oh, God, you fucker, you're making me cum! You're making me cum!" He didn't change his stroke at all, he powered through my climax, watching me cum beneath him. He knew how to move, how to ride my spasming cunt through my orgasm, his dick rigid, hard and forceful, letting me max out around him as he enjoyed the spectacle. Oh! I know it's crazy, but I thought I owed it to my husband to at least think about him-- at least a little!

"Oh, god, you bastard, I'm coming on you, I can't stop coming on you!" I looked right into his eyes with devilish delight. "Ahhh, my husband will not be happy when he hears about this!"

He started laughing, laughing at me climaxing! He had taken me and made sure I knew it. "That's it, squeeze it, baby, squeeze my cock as you come."

Oh, how did this happen? He wasn't even supposed to see me naked, let alone this get his dick in me, let alone... I twitched my hips wildly, deep contractions traveling across my hips and abdomen, he was so hard I could feel the cap of his cock pushing in and then dragging back out. "Oh, oh!"

Just as I started to come down he leaned completely over me, his face aligned with mine. I was beaten. I opened my mouth and slid my tongue into his, completely submitting. He was going to fuck me any way he wanted, and I was going to love it.

He pumped into me like a machine, in total control of my writhing, unfaithful body. When he spun me around and to slide into me from behind, I deliberately arched my back like a kitten so he could grab my ass. I couldn't tell if I was acting like a slut or I was a slut. I looked back over my shoulder with lust and viciousness, I hated this stud; and when I saw the arrogant expression on his smug face for so easily seducing another man's wife, I came again, loudly.

And then the door opened.

A stunning brunette in a bikini top and sarong stood in the doorway, very amused. "Hi," she said. "Sorry to bother you."

"Hey," Jack said nonchalantly, not changing his rhythm or his grip on my ass. I was mortified, aroused-- but I couldn't stop either. I looked up at her through glazed eyes.

She stifled back a giggle, putting her finger to her lips. This was evidently not a new scenario for her. "There's a man outside," she said with obvious delight, "he says he's looking for a blonde in a pink bikini... and I'm like, 'aren't we all?'" She giggled. "Actually, he's only looking for the blonde, we already found the bikini... well, half of it..."

"It's their honeymoon," said the cocky cocksman filling me with cock. "We're celebrating." Oh god! My husband would die!

Then I heard someone approaching the cabana. It had to be--

The brunette smiled wickedly at us. "These walls are really thin, they were kinda not designed for privacy. He probably heard… someone… having sex." Her eyes lit up excitedly. "Would it be super awkward or super hot if he found me in here with you guys? 'Surprise!'" Pausing to consider, she blew us a kiss and then slipped out the door, closing it quickly behind her. She wouldn't--!

A man in the distance said something we couldn't hear, because she responded, "Have you checked these cabanas?" That bitch!

Jack kept fucking me. "You should be a little more quiet," he said helpfully.

"This one, too?" said the brunette, right outside our door. I should have run, hid, but I couldn't. And I couldn't be quiet, either. My body was in total control of me, it didn't care if my husband caught us. If he walked in I'd tell him I was sorry, that I loved him, that surely he could understand, I'd make it up to him… then he'd have to wait for me to finish getting fucked. If he loved me, he'd just have to get over it. I moaned loudly.

They heard it. "Oops!" the brunette giggled, as if this was all an accident. "Yeah, that's probably someone else's wife."

"Ughhhh," I moaned again. You slut, either save me or burn me, I can't take it anymore!

"I think I saw them earlier," the brunette whispered to him but loud enough for us to hear. "She was kinda tipsy."

"Ohhhhhhh," I moaned into the pillow, my ass in the air, Jack's balls slapping against my clit as he thrust into me.

"Should we peek?" she whispered loudly. "They probably wouldn't even notice us--" and I heard the doorknob turn. That devious bitch! My husband was actually going catch us, to see me. My pussy clamped down over the thick dick.

The door clicked. "Oh, it's locked. Oh well." Then a pause. "Maybe I can… help you search some of the other cabanas?"

I got upright on my knees as Jack fucked me from behind, turning my chest around and kissing him wildly on the mouth to keep myself quiet. Was she saving me, taunting me, or was she seriously going to fuck my husband?

"Well, ok," her voice receding as they walked away, "I'm sure she'll turn up soon, there's only so many places a newlywed can go without her bikini."

Jack smiled into my moaning mouth as kissed me. "Your poor husband. Two gorgeous sluts and he can't get his dick into either one."

I giggled. I was a slut he couldn't get his dick into. It was funny.

He rolled me onto my back again. I lay underneath as he rode me. "I guess you're going to fuck that little hottie next," I teased.

"Why not? Know her number?"

"It's the same as her size, you big dicked dummy, she works at the front desk." I rolled my eyes at him as I stroked his hair. "Women helping women." The whole situation was so intense. "Oh, god, I can't stop coming with you. You handle my body so well."

"It needs to be handled, you are amazingly gorgeous. You're like a sexual fantasy."

I kissed him breathlessly, delirious from the sensations. "You don't have flatter me anymore, fucker, you already got your dick in me."

He liked that. I imagined how perfect we must have looked having sex with each other. The only way it was bad was that I had kinda promised not to. I kissed him again, rewarding myself for being so naughty.

He sat back on the bed and lifted me onto his lap, and because I had to bend my long legs to be able to sit on him his cock went even deeper and more upwards into my pussy. I rested my arms loosely around his neck and resignedly made out with him as he cupped my breast with one hand and cupped my ass cheek with the other, slowly and deeply pushing into me.

"I can't wait to tell everyone how easy it was to fuck you, the fantasy chick everyone wanted a piece of," he said.

"Oh, no," I said teasingly, knowing it would probably make this jerk more likely to do it, "it wasn't easy."

"Seems like I've been fucking you longer than it took to fuck you."

"Ahhhh," I moaned.

"I'm guessing it was the other way around for your husband," he said.

"Ohhhhh, god." I moaned. Did he have to bring him into it-- and did it have to turn me on so much? For his sake, I had to take a little bit of power back from this bragging jerk, and show him I could control him.

"Just please don't cum in me," I said, blatantly lying. "Baby, please pull out." I slid my tongue into his mouth and kissed him hotly.

The aggressiveness surprised him. "Fuck," he said.

"Come on baby, you're a strong man, you can hold it," I said naughtily. "You don't want to cum in another man's wife, do you?"

"Fuck," he said.

"Ohhhhh, ahhhhh," I cooed, getting more aroused at the game I was playing with him.

I fell to my back and pulled him over me. "Oh baby, you can't cum in your coworker's wife… that would be so wrong… what if I liked it…?"

"Ugh," he groaned, trying to hold back.

"He wouldn't be happy if you came inside me." I pouted. "I'd try to tell him it wasn't a big deal, but he'd still be jealous. How would I ever make it up to him?"

To his own surprise he erupted, pulling his head away from me to groan, but with wicked pride I pulled his head back to mine and tongued him deeply, forcing his orgasm into both ends of me at the same time, and when I had his tongue in my mouth, I let myself enjoy the feel of his spasming cock.

I arched my back, his tongue delicately bit between my teeth, and I slid one hand down his back to his pumping ass while dragging my other foot up his leg.

"Oh, god, please pull out, please don't come in me…." I said as I pinned his clenching ass into me. I was going to make this bastard unable to forget me, I was going to make him want me again and again and never have me. He groaned and thrust, his giant cock swelling even more pornographically within my selfish, insatiable pussy. "Oh, fuck! Oohhhhh!" I giggled and moaned at the same time, "ohhh, fuck, I can feel you cumming inside me! Oh god, you fucker what are you doing to me? Ahhh!" I let him blast away, hosing my cervix with his cum, my pussy squeezing and contracting against his pulsing shaft, a look of both macho ecstasy and vanquished surprise on his face. I giggled in his face, and came hard. That'll teach him!

If you are caught in the dream of another, you are fucked.

--Deleuze

Freud was wrong: "I am accustoming myself to the idea of regarding every sexual act as a process in which four persons are involved." Off by three. Should have checked the math.

[2.47] Can we assume you're a liar? I think that's fair. Let's start with the Oedipus Complex. "Totally unscientific bunk." Let's start with the single empirically verifiable part of it: *you* think it's bunk.

From which follows an observation: you don't just think the Oedipus Complex is bunk, you think the entire story of *Oedipus Rex* is stupid.

It's possible that Freud only called it the Oedipus Complex because that was the play he had just seen, had he come out of *Hamlet* he would have called it that, but you have to take a man's unconscious at its word: the purpose of art isn't to reveal the truth, but to repress the truth so that it can return as art. The psychological problem of the Oedipus story that isn't that he killed his father and had sex with his mother, but that he did not *know* he killed his father and had sex with his mother. He may have been satisfied for twenty years, but it's not like he wanted it. In other words, the tragedy of Oedipus isn't that he got what he didn't know he wanted, but that he didn't know he got what for sure he didn't want. Do you see? Well, it's too late.

Regardless of whether he wanted it or not... it was inevitable. "Fate!" Slow down, you're better off blaming the parents, after all-- it was an inherited curse. One could say that Laius and Jocasta trying to prevent a prophecy is what realized it. Had they not tried to stop it, then it wouldn't have happened, it was their fault. If you're trying to attribute powerful unconscious desires to Oedipus's 18 year, 100 mile round trip journey-- half of which he did in an infant carrier-- you're going to have to do the same with the parents. The question isn't what did Oedipus want, but what did they want?

"They wanted to avoid the prophecy." This is their first experience with prophecies, they don't know the gimmick? How may times before you realize that when a charlatan tells you the future, he chose you to tell because you are a fool? But you want to be tricked, that's why you were picked, you want to be compelled to act so you are not responsible for the decision. You want a master. "Pretty sure I don't." Then go ask out a girl you actually like. No? At least go fantasize about that girl. No? You'd prefer someone else to create a fantasy about a different girl and passively watch the results? You're free to choose that, I guess.

Do you really think that, on the one hand, King Laius was such a gullible simpleton that he blindly believed some highly dubious prophecy, yet on the other hand was such a diabolical genius that he thought he could beat Fate-- by orchestrating the utterly fool-proof plan of taking an oh my God easy to defuse time bomb, pinning its feet, and then *handing him to other people to finish the job?* More likely... the Oracle told him exactly what he needed to hear.[4]

---

4 *Oedipus Rex* is lauded as a masterpiece of plotting, irony and etc, but if one takes it literally and examines the logic, you could only marvel and despair: Jocasta claims Laius handed the baby over to some men to kill, while the slave claims Jocasta herself gave the baby to him; when the fight happens Laius is with five people, or three; many robbers killed him, or one man did; at a deserted crossroads in the middle of nowhere Oedipus kills them all or somehow *fails to even notice* one escapes; the shepherd was there during the melee, or he wasn't; and anyway fled-- fled-- in terror back to Thebes yet didn't get there until after-- after Oedipus had killed the Sphinx... and had strolled to Thebes... and had been crowned king... and had married Jocasta... But of all the WTFs, the most implicating is the very inciting event of the play: a plague has just come upon Thebes, revealed to be a punishment for Laius's murder-- a crime that occurred *sixteen years earlier*. Here

Freud called it the Oedipus Complex because he believed the play is the manifestation of Oedipus's repressed wish, the Oracle's prophecy the verbal expression of his latent wish. But then what about Laius's prophecy? If Freud's going to play by Freud's rules, then Oedipus didn't have a repressed wish to have sex with his mother; actually... Oedipus was repressed, by mom and dad, and sure enough he returned, which means that this isn't a story about Oedipus's desire to get his mother, it's a story about Laius's desire for someone to take his wife. I present to you Act IV of Western Civilization, read it one more time and look at your windows, you will see the truth of it everywhere. Turns out these plays are about transgenerational guilt after all, the men scurry to escape the past and the women scramble to ensure the present, both at the expense of the future about which they only pretend to care. "Have I not suffered?" the mother/wife hisses. "God hate you as I am hated, and him, too,

---

you have the first literary example of the statute of limitations running in reverse, the sure sign not that justice must be done but that the accused is just not worth protecting; and if there was ever a case of trumped up charges, this is it. The entire story not only couldn't win you civil damages, it would for sure trigger a countersuit, thus the fact that Oedipus is criminally convicted anyway isn't evidence of his unconscious guilt but a giant signal that the system suddenly needed someone to be convicted. Guilty? Freud will cross an ocean to tell you you can still be unconsciously guilty of something you didn't actually do; but Sophocles knew you can't be *unconsciously* guilty when someone *tells* you you are. Oedipus wasn't guilty, he was set up. "But he was *in fact* guilty!" Of what? Incest? It isn't even the crime in question. The problem of the play isn't Oedipus's penis, the problem is the *plague*-- an event of such colossal material significance that no one ever mentions it again, they entirely disavow it. Since there is no such thing as Fate without human will's involvement, the plague had to be labeled as Oedipus's fault because otherwise... it would have been no one's.

"Are we but puppets of the gods?" We're far too full of ourselves for that question, nowadays and those days we wonder: are the gods puppets of us? If this logic is confusing it is because you are making a very specific interpretive error that Freud tried to warn you against: in *Oedipus Rex*, the gods *do not exist*. There is no Fate. The gods don't *cause* anything to happen; things are *attributed* to them, thoughts are *projected* onto them. Gods shouldn't resemble mortals in their anger. When they do, it's you.

The correct way to understand the plague on Thebes is to ask yourself why, if the gods sent the plague as a punishment for Oedipus's crime of killing Laius, couldn't the gods just have targeted only him? Why did they wait a decade and a half? Presumably, three uncharacteristically unambiguous prophecies into the game, they were aware of his existence and location, and I know this because Tiresias knew it. The answer, *obvious* to us modern sophisticates but we're to believe not to the actual audience of the play, is that there aren't any gods-- the plague was a total coincidence.

But there was a plague, a plague of such Biblical violence that it infected the state and even the idea of the State. The bodies of dead men lay on top of the bodies of dying men, and half-dead zombies reeled about the streets looking for water, or brains. The temples of their gods were full of the corpses of people that just died right on the spot; and as the disaster spread beyond anyone's imagination, men, not knowing what would become of them, became utterly carefree about everything. Men now coolly did what they had previously only done behind corners. Seeing rich people suddenly die, and the poor easily taking over their property, they simply decided to spend quickly and-- enjoy themselves. The abstract notion of honor was pointless, so that more than just abandoning it, it became a settled matter that immediate enjoyment *was* honorable-- useful. Neither fear of gods nor of the laws restrained them. As for the gods, they figured it was all the same whether they worshipped them or not; and as for the laws, no one expected to live to be brought to trial, and anyway a far severer sentence had been already passed upon them all and hung ever over their heads. They did the math: it was only reasonable to enjoy life a little. This is the fictional

that begat you, and this house and all!" —But what do the children have to do with their father's sin? Why hate them? Why *call* a curse on them? All of this is to say: if there is an Oedipus Complex, it isn't your repressed desire, it's a defense against being trapped in someone else's dream.

I'm not at all saying the Oedipus Complex is of no use, or that it doesn't relate to what we are doing. It's of no use to psychoanalysts, that's true, but as psychoanalysts aren't clearly psychoanalysts, this doesn't prove anything.

The question on the 9th grade essay test was: what are the major themes of *Oedipus Rex* which resonated with audiences for two thousand years? "We're not doing Oedipus, in our

---

plague of *Oedipus Rex*, a plague so real that it made people *stop* praying.

Yes, I know how to read, the play says clearly the plague was sent by the gods. Well hold on a second, which god? Apollo gave the prophecies, but the plague was sent by Ares. Since when does Ares use plagues, did he become a girl? Why would he send a plague? He's the god of WAR. It's one thing not to impose gender roles but another not to notice them when they are imposed, like when Macbeth decides the best way to get what he wants is to tiptoe into an old man's bedroom and stab him with a letter opener while he's dead asleep. "My wife told me to act like a man." You know she's a woman, right? Reading an ancient play forces you to examine your prejudices but watching a modern play is all about deluding your mind with them, in theatre productions Macbeth is always played by a chain smoking British anorexic who totally looks like sneaky midnight backstabbing would be his standard MO, so you forget that offstage in Act I Macbeth was chopping Vikings in half, sagittally, by himself; cast him correctly as the Scottish equivalent of Thor and suddenly no way are you buying that he both needs, uses and then is terrified by his cloak and dagger, but cast him like Loki, and the results are guaranteed, at least for those who don't beat around the bush. Anyway, there's no war in *Oedipus Rex*. But there is a war in real life Athens; and their war brought their plague.

Modern readers want the play to ask whether the gods are just, whether Oedipus deserved it, but unless you believe in gods, who cares? That was Sophocles's problem. That the plague was caused by the gods doesn't require a suspension of disbelief, it's the whole *purpose* of the play-- to prove they exist, to make you believe in them; **to make you believe that they have power.**

We understand Oedipus is being punished for what the Oracle prophesied he'd do. The Oracle is omniscient, its words are true; the gods are omnipotent, their judgment is certain. Through his tragic flaw and by his own free will Oedipus will pursue the truth, will discover that the Oracle is always right. Is that what you understood? Well, that's not what happens. The Oracle isn't always right, sometimes it's wrong. Twice.

The Oracle *isn't* omniscient: for 16 years and as far as anyone knows Laius *wasn't* punished for his crime by being killed by his son—and if Laius wasn't punished by the gods for what he did, the gods are *powerless*. Even if people still believe that the gods exist, they do not think the gods have any power over them-- *the gods cannot enforce the Oracles*. This isn't a pointless deconstructive interpretation made anachronistically by a po-mo atheist from the Church of AI looking down on the superstitious simpletons of the 5th century BC or AD, it's literally the words of the play:

> For ancient oracles that dealt with Laius are withering--
> men now set them aside. Nowhere is Apollo honored publicly,
> and our religious faith is dying.

Forget about the people in the play; this is a description for what was going on in the people *watching* the play. The gods are irrelevant. If they were relevant but not revered the gods would have sent the plague as punishment for the people's hubris. They didn't. "They" "sent" it "for"

60

school we read contemporary novels." Waste of time, take the F and do more math, Literature today is defined as whatever shows that the teachers' parents' generation were jerks. Aliens will some day marvel that we made kids pretend to read 100 pages of *Heart of Darkness* for no other reason than to test them on 150 pages of *Things Fall Apart*. Why does the test ask that question, what does it hide, why ask it then, how does it train you not to see? The insightful question isn't why it resonated with audiences for so long, but why it so suddenly stopped resonating with us. Now it's boring. What happened?

The short answer is Freud interpreted the story, which was good luck for everyone. One way to give men the illusion that modernity is a clean break with the ancient world is to have someone write the primary secondary source about primary sources so we're done with the

---

Oedipus. Or, said in the correct order: if Oedipus can be shown to have been a parricide, then the Oracle was omniscient, and this plague that's here, that's the gods, the gods are omnipotent. That-- that previous sentence-- is the wish fulfillment of the *audience*. But even a cursory reading of the play shows that this is false, Apollo didn't send the plague-- or, for that matter, the Sphinx. Sophocles wants people to revere the gods, but still accept all the responsibility. And the power.

You need divine action to run a city on a hill when normal state power reveals its impotence, but unless the divine becomes manifest someone, preferably 15 year olds, have to judge the manifest action as divine in order for it to be politically useful, because just like the Anno Domini heaven/hell before it went full Roman no one else on earth will know of your punishment or indeed even of your guilt, what good is that?-- similarly a *secret* punishment by "the gods" would not serve the purpose of *displaying* power-- what was needed was the public declaration of guilt as an explanation for the punishment which preceded it to show that gods exist and have power. And get your generational conflicts right: the belief in the gods was not an old-timers' fundamentalist holdover from a bygone unscientific era; these gods are being resurrected de novo by the new crop of post-modernists, the previous generation had abandoned them. In order to *cause* the gods to exist, Oedipus had to be guilty of *causing* the plague on Thebes that therefore *they sent* for what *the Oracle predicted* he had done. If he said, and Thebans heard, "the plague has nothing to do with me, it's all bacteria and chaos theory," Thebes would have still had a plague AND the Athenians would have surrendered to whoever asked first.

It's odd that you have an ancient Greek myth turned play about divine forces *yet not a single god makes an appearance*. The Oracle does, and boy does it have a lot to say. The charlatans running the Oracle knew that the Thebans' prayers to non-existent Apollo would probably go unanswered; and eventually, whoever by temporal coincidence "saved" them from the plague by "revealing" their guilt would become their new Master, I think there's a Dostoyevsky story about it. So they got ahead of it. The best way to convince the people to stop looking for the cause of the plague-- e.g. nothing-- is to let them think they've found it. If you doubt this argument observe who appears right on cue: the demonic Tiresias, and either you believe this is one of the most contrived passages in all of Hellenism or you realize he's a goddam liar right to the genitals: "Who killed Laius? Oh, Oedipus, you don't want to know, don't ask me about it, it's better you don't know, just go on being happy, why bring this up, don't ask me any more questions..." If this is how your wife denies having an affair with your boss, get an alibi, she's setting you up for his murder. Poor Cassandra, because she gave and then withdrew consent she was cursed to know the future but could do nothing about it, and this sophist was blessed with the power to make everyone do whatever he made up. 10:1 he wasn't even blind. But he was good at his job, I can't say he wasn't, not only does he set Oedipus up, he also reverse-psychologizes the swollen footed imbecile into thinking that it was Fated. This is how it has always been, the Oracle isn't where the power is, the Power is always with the priests, even if they had to invent the oracles. "Nietzsche?" *Minority Report*.

I am aware of your secondary sources, so I know you will here assert that the Greeks did believe in the gods, but I was there, they didn't. Their gods had an entirely different psychological mandate

primary sources. Take Freud literally, I certainly do: "A legend has come down to us from classical antiquity: a legend whose profound and universal power to move can *only* be understood *if* the hypothesis I have put forward in regard to the psychology of children has an equally universal validity."[5] Freud said he was a scientist so we can use his logic to skip 9th grade:

p only if q => if p then q.

Not q.

Therefore not p.

---

than our gods, who serve as proxies for eternal life. For the Greeks, there was no eternal life; the gods were placeholders for real forces on earth. That's why only stupid people today say, "why doesn't God intervene to stop human suffering?" whereas only stupid people back then said, "why does God intervene to cause human suffering?" And anyway I do not care whether the average Athenian garlic muncher believed in the magical Oracle of Delphi, it's a democracy, they will believe what you tell them to believe, what I want to know is: did the Oracle at Delphi believe in the Oracle of Delphi? KNOW THYSELF. So that's a no?

You'll no doubt say this is like asking if a Christian priest believes in God but it isn't at all like that, because the priest has no physical contact with God, it's supposed to be all by faith; while the priests at Delphi were in gaseous communication with a supposedly materially present and physically meddlesome god who, for example, had 20 kids by 13 women at least 3 of which he raped. Do they believe in that guy? Because he sounds like a jerk. Let me tell you that Apollo or Helios or however he self-identifies is on the wrong side of every story, everything he does is malicious, petty, or spiteful. God of Medicine: he brings sickness. God of Music: couldn't out play a goat. God of Prophecy? "Well, he was a complicated god." No, he only wishes he was. The most accurate depiction of him was on *Star Trek*, look it up, when biceps and baritone don't work he cries to his daddy and mommy, feeble mortals, you will bow down to the God Of Temper Tantrums. Let me be the first person in 3000 years to say what needs to be said out loud: fuck that guy. Fuck him and his aristocratic micropenis. This has nothing to do with religious propensities and I know this is petty of me but I feel a sort of… satisfaction… in Acts 16:16: Paul is walking around former Macedon and the Delphic Oracle, on its own initiative, prophesies Paul's new religion as the true one; but instead of thanking the priestess for her support he gets annoyed and performs an exorcism: "What are you to me? The power of Christ compels you to get bent, lost, and out of her." Impressed? No? You have to read the actual lines in order to be able to read between the lines: either her knowledge legitimately came from channelling a space alien named Apollo, or she was actually possessed by a demon, or for 1000 years she was only pretending. Yet in all three cases *but especially the last*, it came out of her.

The only thing the Greeks of then and the Christians of today and the atheists of always do share in common is a wish for the omnipotence of their gods. I assure you this is not a good thing, it is a defense, and it is the sad but reliable predictor of the demise of the Polis. An entity can be omnipotent or it can be omniscient but the problem of sociology and theology is that psychologically it can not be both. The Oracle was a center of power that pretended to be a center of knowledge, it pretended to have knowledge to hide its power, and the early Greeks were happy to see it that way and just ask it questions because it meant that they could believe they retained the power. But eventually people feel like they lack power, and worse, there is no chance for more power; but there is a chance for more knowledge, which means they have to reconsider the nature of their gods and who gets what.

Trying to read Oedipus as Freud did, as we do, as a pornographic depiction of what the Greeks believed-- not wanted, believed-- and then hoping to extrapolate from that even deeper meaning is

And that's game over for Sophocles, we used Freud to modus tollens our way out of trying to understand something we want to unknow. Supposedly many people reject Freud's interpretations, maybe there was even resistance to them, but what difference does it make to you? The point is you can't read *Oedipus* without involving Freud. And since you don't agree with Freud-- you are now done with the play. And if you do agree with Freud... you are now done with the play. Are the outcomes the same? Then it was inevitable. By focusing on the incest Freud so sanitized the play it could even be performed in English, with the even more sanitized title *Oedipus Rex*. "More like *Oedipus Sex*!" Giggle. Oedipus had the good sense to gouge out his own eyes, Freud gouged out everyone else's. His method quickly became the favored procedure for knowing thyself, which means it was the defense against doing-- well, anything. This may not have been the outcome Freud wanted consciously, but the Oedipal

---

going to get you the wrong answer, and killed. You laugh? *Oedipus* was not supposed to be a possession for all time, it was written to win the applause of the moment, that moment, those people; it wasn't philosophy but *tragedy*, which means it was written for goats to train their feelings, it wasn't about what they believed but how to believe. *Sophocles could only have written about the power of the gods if it wasn't true anymore.* Sophocles was describing to the Greeks in the audience a belief that the Greeks in Thucydides so desperately wanted. If we burn this quadruped or ostracize this biped, will the god let us live? The eclipse says wait a month to find out.

Yes, I know, the Athenian geophysicists were too primitive and stupid to understand the plague as contingent materiality, and gave it metaphysical meaning by projecting it to the gods as a punishment for some perhaps collective guilt. But it's useful to review Act I to see what Sophocles was offering a theological alternative to. It wasn't atheism. It was madness. In the first year of the Athenian War the Spartans marched their army 170 miles East to the enemy's territory, only to stand pointlessly outside Athens's impenetrable walls and be confronted by nobody. "Hello?" So they chopped down some trees, tried to set fire to fresh crops, called the Athenians gay-- the bad kind, not the good kind-- and then with their you know whats in each others you know whats they just sort of looked at each other, "umm, are they coming out or what? How long can the Athenians stay cooped up in there?" With access to grain from the Ukraine? I think the answer is 1932. "Wait, you're serious?" [2.20] The typical Spartan plan for sieges was to rely on the reliably impulsive pride of the enemy's young men to come out swinging. But this-- this wasn't the kind of war the Spartans had ever seen before, let alone had a strategy for. "So... what the hell do we do now?" After two weeks, they gave up and went home.

And yet the Spartans came back the next spring. Think about this. The Spartans had a whole year to plan for this new kind of asymmetrical battle where the enemy doesn't battle. So you have to figure they came prepared with new tech, some new weapon, maybe trebuchets, dynamite, Cyclopses. Right? Nope. Again they stood outside the walls, chopped down some more trees, yelled up some more insults. And again, three weeks later, the Spartans went home. They waited a year to do the same thing they had done before? Were they insane, expecting different results? What was accomplished? Let me be clear: what did the Athenians think they had accomplished?

Meanwhile, with 200000 Athenians in a walled city, a plague broke out. Now we get to test your prejudices. Where did the Athenians think the plague came from? Do you think the Athenians thought they were being punished by Apollo? Maybe for wanting to sleep with their mothers? Do you maybe think they thought the plague was random? A coincidence? The answer was obvious. *The Spartans had caused the plague.* They poisoned the water. And if there were any doubts, the next spring when the Spartans didn't return neither did the plague, but when they came back the year after that, so did the plague. The plague lingered the entire war-- it never completely left-- yet no Spartan ever contracted it, including the ones who were held prisoner inside the Athenian walls. *Of course* it was a Spartan plot. Don't laugh; we proudly modern materialists think we're smart because we deduced that everything bad is a conspiracy of *Capitalism*. Like it's a person. "It functions like a person." Then why can't you? Zing. The war is in early stages, but the plague is

Triangle is Freud's dream, so we should probably read it as a wish fulfillment. Freud wasn't dumb, but he needed a different analyst: the method he invented is the only one that could uncover... why it was invented.

Psychoanalysis got us out from under the 2500 year oppressive weight of Greek tragedy[6], the next step was to get out from under psychoanalysis, in the same way-- not by running from it but by embracing its harsher truths. That move took only a hundred years, we are well practiced. Once psychoanalysis became widely understood, then there was no need for psychoanalysts, what secret could they help you discover that you didn't already know? The Oedipus Complex? It's been commercially packaged and marketed as a Secret® truth and you may not buy it but it's the only truth that's available in stores, and coffeehouses, and

on everyone's mind; this is why Sophocles has not Apollo but Ares send the plague, he is taking the paranoia that is projected onto the Spartans and displacing it to the Spartan god, so the Athenians have the potential for atonement, by which I mean action. They just have to figure out what they have to do, and then do it. Knowledge for the sake of action.

Unfortunately, it was destined to fail; the cracks between knowing and acting had become chasms. From then on, it was one, or the other, but not both. Fast forward past the end, to the beginning of Act IV, and observe that when the Oracle directly and unambiguously proclaimed that though Sophocles was clever there was no man wiser than Socrates, Socrates thought it was *wrong*. He went on bender trying to disprove it, proving instead that he was guilty of impiety: this is not the behavior of someone who believes that the Oracle is omniscient.

But by that point the system *required* the pretense of those gods, not because anyone believed it, they did not believe it anymore, but everyone wanted the gods to have the power, the system was organized around those placeholders. They might not believe in the theology, but they weren't going to test their luck with impiety. Not quite gods, nor demons-- call them daemons. It wasn't so much a religion as an ideology, and not so much an ideology as a fetish. Man is the measure of all things, but for precision let's measure with a machine that has a god in it. Let me highlight that the Athenian democracy everyone marvels at by the end was so invested in this system that they killed Socrates for questioning it. So when the Delphic Oracle declared Socrates the "wisest of all men", that was code for "this guy's a wiseguy, he asks too many questions." NOTHING IN EXCESS. "Your joke probably doesn't translate well to the original Greek." You're going to have to trust me: the joke works even better in the original Greek. "Are you seriously suggesting the Oracle of Delphi set up Socrates?" The alternative is that the pious Greeks executed for impiety a man the divine Oracle had identified as a national treasure. "He made the politicians angry--" What the hell is a politician? I thought it was a direct democracy? "He made them look stupid--" *He made* them? "His teachings undermined the people's belief in democracy--" Yet these democratic politicians had no problem with Socrates's former student returning from sabbatical in India or Logopolis or wherever he went and teaching the exact same Socratic lessons-- because he did it in a **school**. Do you see the difference? "None of this is possibly true." It doesn't have to be true, it just has to be necessary.

The plague and the war in Athens are felt to be on autopilot, there is nothing they can do, so they do what all impotent people do: they devote all their energy to discussing it. "Is this a coincidence, bad luck-- or inevitable?" As the Athenians obsessed over the possible links between the war and the plague, a key piece of evidence was a real life prophecy from the real life Oracle, which had long ago said, "a Doric war shall come, and with it a plague". Doric=Spartan, and plague=plague. That might not sound like great evidence, but it was still a kind of evidence; and Sophocles helpfully manifests this evidence into his play by having the Ares bring the plague. But in fact, this wasn't what the Oracle had said, it was an *interpretation* of what it had said, not written but said *out loud:* "plague" in Greek is a homophone of "famine", spelled with one letter difference. Well, which is it, famine or plague? Sophocles condenses all the possible meanings of the prophecy by having the

public agoras of all kinds, such is the tyranny of knowledge. So now it's the defense. Even your unconscious is on notice to manifest a little Oedipality in your dreams so you think you've learned about yourself-- and don't dig any deeper. "Have you ever tried lucid dreaming?" You mean porn? How badly do you want to control it, for it not to be unconscious? You are so sophisticated in your understanding of what can happen that nothing new can happen, you are even ready to criticize yourself, to expose yourself, to fully accept your guilt-- to fend off any real change.[7] Knowledge in the service of stasis. "But I don't want stasis, I want change, revolutionary change, I mean that literally!" You're an idiot. I mean that literally.

"I date these kinds of men because I'm re-enacting the childhood relationship with my

---

war god and patron god of Sparta bring a *plague* and a *famine*. Sophocles gave them the authority the Athenians wanted to appeal to.

The play we believe is called *Oedipus Tyrannos* is not about what they believed, it is about how to believe. The plague wasn't caused by the gods, it was a psychological argument for their necessity. But I don't mean this was needed by just the Oracle or the government because it materially benefitted them: everyone wanted this logic. This is why it is not simply "reality" that the humans down at the Oracle were manipulating everyone, as if political power was the only thing at stake; as if the only one who wants something are the landowners and the rest of us are manipulated thetes. "Systems of power and domination, used to control us." HA! As if it required an entire system to control you, I could do it with a TV or the hypnotic trigger of "tell me more about yourself". *You* are the system, the system is how *you* want. That's why you don't want it to change. "But I want different things than it does." Not what: how.

This explains the curious off-hand remark of Jocasta to Oedipus when she's describing to him the Oracle's first prophecy, to her and Laius, and for proper orientation and impact let me explain that this is the prophecy that convinced her it was immediately necessary to murder her little baby boy. Are you properly oriented? Ok, here's what she says:

> An oracle once came to Laius (I won't even say it was the god's, but his servants') that said--

Take a moment and re-read that, these are the words of a person who is 100% guilty of atheism but not of impiety, and 100% wants how her husband wants even if it's different than what he wants, you should write this down, you will come back to it again and again and again and again. She agreed to murder her first born on the admittedly dubious recommendation of *some guys*. Just as Freud asks us to infer Oedipus's "true" unconscious wishes voiced by the external Oracle's prophecy-- just as that Oracle is a projection-- a mis*perception* of his unconscious wishes as coming from somewhere else-- this is what Jocasta is doing when she dismisses the accuracy of the prophecy by projecting it NOT to the god, but to his servants. You could say she's simply trying to assure Oedipus the Oracle is sometimes wrong, but she's not saying the Oracle is wrong, she's saying his servants are sometimes wrong; *yet she still obeyed*. You are no doubt confused about the psychology of an insane woman who has a lot of explaining to do, so to see the arithmetic of her dementia you can begin with a single question: if god is not the one who said it, if it was "his servants"-- then does her guilt increase or decrease? Go back/forth and think it through: surprise, the answer is decrease. If you are 100% certain God commands you to murder your child, well, sorry kid, he's the boss. But you show your true faith when you act without real "proof"-- in the face of NO proof, contradictory proof-- when you believe that this is what God wants so this is what you have to do. The act isn't compelled or for some other reason; that action becomes 100% a true *act,* an act of faith, 100% your free will AND 100% your fault, you can't blame it on God no matter if He wanted it. "But then doesn't that increase your guilt??"

Yes, except *she is lying*. She has an advantage Abraham didn't that you wish you did: she didn't kill

father." And yet knowing it hasn't stopped you from doing it, that's weird. "I figured out that I'm attracted to women who look a lot like my mom did when I was a kid." That's a clever discovery-- why did you need to make it? "You're going to tell me it means I want to have sex with my mother?" As if it was your pleasure that was at stake? As if in your fantasies it's you who's satisfied? More likely you wanted to be the only one who could satisfy her. "I want to satisfy my mother?" Nice try, that's not what I said. "I know this is going to sound arrogant, but I'm just being brutally honest so I can understand myself better: every girlfriend I have ends up falling in love with me." HA! You want me to detect that your problem is an overestimation of the self? You can't fool me by pretending self-criticism is insight, I know you know the gimmick. I'm just going to take you at your word. Let's instead talk about why it's so satisfying to break up with those who love you. "It's not satisfying!" Of course it is, it's

---

her baby because the gods *or* the servants told her to, she did it because *Laius* told her to. The commandment-- and judgment-- comes from her superego, which for Jocasta is whoever is her master, and that is Laius. Gods, oracles, priests-- they impact Laius, but they don't matter to her. The Oracle isn't her excuse, it's *his*. For him it is omniscient-- so he must choose, he must ACT. For her, Laius is omnipotent. For her there are no acts possible, all she can do is want how the other wants, and the one she must want like is Laius. Consequently, she is incapable of experiencing guilt. This may seem circuitous if not downright bananastown logic, and it is, but observe the final result in its miraculous utility: she (believed she) killed her baby and had no problem living happily ever after........ wait for it...... *even after Laius was killed anyway*. Think about this, this is a woman whose soul is made of goat cheese and butyric acid, not a moment of guilt, not a moment of regret, not a moment of "Oh my God, I killed my baby-- and Laius *still* died, what was it all for?" Nothing. I'm no historian but if I have the timeline correct the very first thing she did after learning Laius was killed was shave her vagina. That's supposed to be a joke except that it's not. All the guilt died with Laius.

"At least she didn't think it was her son who killed him." Yes, I had a suspicion you would think this thought, you have too much pornography and not enough imagination. *Do you think that matters? Should* that matter? She didn't kill her baby to prevent him from being a murderer, she killed him to prevent her husband from being murdered. Laius still died-- he still got *murdered. And her son is dead*. She's telling Oedipus she's unimpressed with prophecies in the first place; you don't think at Laius's funeral she should have thought, gee, maybe we should have kept the kid alive and taken our chances, after all, Laius did live 16 more years...? She didn't. She didn't think anything, the man did all the thinking for her and then he was murdered. "Well, prepare the field for the next superego to plough, I guess."

"But that's the power of patriarchy." Sure, whatever, call it what you want, as long as the power is safely elsewhere so it's not yours. Let's be psychologically accurate: what she did was not out of love for her husband; love of this kind is a cover for rage. The rage is there, all you have to do is see the infanticide as a message to him. You shouldn't underestimate historical context, I'm told, so here you go: since Greek immortality wasn't in an afterlife but through the children, killing a husband's children becomes a powerful way of avenging yourself on your husband for... giving you children and then taking them away from you. An obsessed woman will stab you in the bathtub but a hysterical woman's vengeance doesn't employ punishment but negative reinforcement. Everyone must be deprived. "You put me through all this, and then you want to deprive me? You think that's fair??"

Now Oedipus is her superego, and fortunately for her he's utterly retarded, so she got 16 more years of guilt free matrimony with no questions asked. Why would he ask anything? He had all the answers. "Your analysis is anachronistic, back then infanticide was far more acceptable than incest. And can you not call people retarded?" I'll stop calling people retarded if you stop calling your condiment bucket a salad. You're telling me the incest taboo was inviolable, but mother-infant bonding is an easily overruled culturally dependent construct? So Jocasta's multiple orgasms riding

66

the consistent climax of all of your relationships, you're going to tell me that isn't the point of having them? "They leave me!" Come on, everything you did for the prior 6 months was a set up to compel them to do what you wanted to do but couldn't do directly. Giving oh so much of yourself in the beginning, in order to deprive them of all of yourself at the end. "That's a very wrong, and very vicious way of formulating my life." Even if wrong, it's a vicious way of living it, which is worse? Suddenly giving a guy a blowjob instead of having sex takes on a whole different backstory. "No, you don't understand, that's because intercourse is such a risk for women." Don't worry, it's the same risk for men, too, the risk is that the other person might derive too much satisfaction from you and the ledger would be unbalanced. "What ledger? What are you talking about?"

---

her thick dicked son carried more guilt than murdering him as a baby, totally the opposite of today? "Jesus, why'd you have to describe it like that?" I only did what the system does to elicit any feeling out of a person whose only honestly felt emotion is rage: I pornographized it. Asking which causes *more* guilt forces us to accept the form of the debate, I'm not falling for it. Neither made her feel guilty, she is incapable of guilt. "No guilt? She hanged herself!" Yes, but do you know why? God knows it wasn't because she tried to murder her baby or failed to protect her husband. You think it was because she found out she had committed incest with her own son? No, read the play. She hanged herself when *he* found out.

Anyone care to notice that hanging was then the preferred suicide method of women but today it's a man's game; while poison was then a woman's murder weapon and is now their go-to method for suicide? Maybe it isn't about gender after all, but about the structure of their relationships-- what's at stake aren't the consequences of success, but of failure. Because man or woman, you know too well that the one thing that stands in your way is if you are caught, your enemies will laugh at you. Best to take the shortest route, the one in which you are most skilled.

This is why Oedipus goes along with the charade that he caused the plague that is never again referenced in the play-- because the real charade is that he is king. Certainly he's not happy (anymore) that he boned Jocasta-- but what does that have to do with the plague? His defense at Colonus was, "I didn't know she was my mom." Why didn't he use the correct legal defense, "look, whoever she was, it has nothing to do with this plague"? "Speaks to character." Overruled. The guilt over incest is his misdirection-- *towards* himself, away from the causes of the plague. He feels guilty about incest and murder because he did them, but Sophocles makes him agree to connect this to the plague *so that gods exist and have power*. That's the guilt that's at stake. You can try to argue which is worse, but I already know which is worse for him: by the end of the trilogy, the gods Oedipus has caused to exist-- literally, they physically appear-- absolve him while he is still alive, this is the power of omnipotent gods. The men have little other responsibility than to know things; meanwhile Oedipus's daughter has to clean up the mess. That's another thing that changes at the height=downhill of the Athenian democracy: the State, and the men who run it, can no longer be relied on to do the right thing, so it falls to the women. Restated for literal accuracy, after all the audiences were all men: men feel the other men can no longer be relied on to do the right thing, so all men have to be disempowered. One might predict that women thus get greater power in the democracy, and sometimes that happens, but in this case what happened was the democracy collapsed.

Oedipus In Criticism holds that Oedipus represents man's pursuit of knowledge, but for a man famous for seeking the answers he didn't ask a whole lot of questions, unless they were about himself, then he was all in. Pretty clear he wasn't interested in math, his favorite knowledge was self-knowledge. Sound familiar? Superficially curious about the world around him, he only gets revved up to solve the murder when he suspects he might be a main character in that play, too. Then-- THEN-- he wants to know, this was the only kind of knowledge he wanted-- knowledge that comes from fear, knowledge to alleviate his fear. "I need to know more about my past!" Why,

"My unconscious identification with my mother unconsciously causes me to unconsciously re-enact relationships with men like the one she had with my Dad, but unconsciously." Of course! Because the alternative is that you're a nut. Why else would you lack sexual interest in your husband but be jealous of any attention he gets from other women? Sounds like the main thing is to deprive him of enjoyment.

Or maybe it's that these sluts stirred up in him some desires you had eradicated. Now you're obsessed with the thought: what is it about the other women that he wants?

"My unconscious identification with my father causes me to unconsciously re-enact relationships with women like the one he had with my Mom, but unconsciously." Sigh. If it

stupid? Because self-psychology is easier than microbiology and choosing to act?

Someone is going to tell me he did it because he was tragically driven to pursue the truth at all costs; and someone else is going to say he was selflessly driven out of a sense of duty to save his city. Those two people should probably read the play at least once:

> Who would have dared to do this [kill Laius] unless he had
> help from someone inside Thebes?... I will remove this
> pollution, not for some distant friends, but for myself.
> For whoever killed this man may soon enough kill me as well.
> Thus, in avenging Laius, I serve myself.

This isn't a dramatic exposition of his secret selfish inner thoughts. He says this out loud. To everyone.

Note well that while everyone knows incest is a pollution, the thing he labels as a pollution is the killing of Laius, it's a pollution because he might be next. Yet Sophocles makes him use the word pollution in order to symbolically link it to the incest-- so that the Oracle can be right, and the plague his fault, even though both aren't. Ain't? What kind of a nut wants to take on guilt that isn't his, when he has plenty of his own to deal with? To be precise: he wants his private guilt that is his fault to become public, and use it to take responsibility for something that has nothing to do with him. The answer is the type of person who wants to be *appointed* king and the type of person who wants to be the only thing that could satisfy his mom-- they're the same. NB: Creon is different-- he says it up front, he's not a tyrant, and too many times he's let compassion override what he knows needs to be done. He loves the country-- but he loves his children more. He has no natural craving to wear kingly robes, he would rather do kingly deeds. I admit that they are not particularly laudable deeds, but they are *deeds*; he even commands that Polynices never be buried, and in case the only thing your 9th grade mind finds worth discussing in *Antigone* is that Creon's a misogynist let me emphasize that Polynices wasn't just "bad" but extremely dangerous, had he won he would have killed the lot of them, Eteocles and Haemon and for damn sure Creon. I'm not saying we shouldn't bury our enemies but you got to figure that by this point in the trilogy Creon's just about had it with the Rexes, I don't know about inherited curse but Holy Christ have they been nothing but disaster for three generations. One of them drove Creon's sister to suicide, and Creon *forgave* him. Refuse to bury them? Creon should be given credit for not burying them alive. Creon wants power, not the shadow of power. Oedipus is 100% the opposite. Oedipus wants to be king-- not hero or lord or statesman or conqueror-- king. It's not his foot that's swollen, it's his brain, tick off the symptoms, wet, wacky, and wild, normal pressure Oedicephalos is not a man who wants battle, or glory, or honor, or something different for his subjects; he doesn't seek to expand his empire, to advance his kingdom, to remake the world, or remake himself. He does not want to change. *He does not want to act.* The Chorus tells us that up to then his reign was peaceful and prosperous. Gee that's swell, name five things Oedipus did during his 16 year reign of prosperity. No? How about two? One? Anything? Oedipus doesn't even punish Tiresias for his insolence-- not out of mercy or respect or suspiciousness or even fear, but for no reason, he does nothing. This is all he can ever do

could only be about gender so it has nothing to do with sex.

Maybe we should take the jealousy literally-- you're jealous *of* the other women-- how easy it is for them to be satisfied, they can even take a man who has nothing to offer and so effortlessly find something about him to enjoy. Or maybe you are jealous of his power-- how does he get women to want him? Hell, *even you* could satisfy those shoe models way better than he ever could. For those who think gender trumps psychology or biology trumps TV, observe that the previous three sentences require no alteration to come 100% as fluidly from a man or a woman. "I know jealousy is a big problem--" Then I can be sure it isn't yours.

No matter how you say it: you want the other person to want you, but you don't want

---

on his own. And yet the moment Creon becomes king Creon makes decisions that have consequences for which he bears all of the responsibility. Oedipus doesn't want *power.* I don't mean he is lazy or vain or weak-- or benevolent. I mean he simply does not act, he just wants to be the King. Why not live with his incestuous shame but atone by selflessly serving his kingdom? No thanks, I'll take out my eyes as long as everyone else's are on me. In the Egyptian Thebes the gimmick was the King so transforms reality that he becomes a god, he declares himself to be one; the Greek Thebes goes the other way, Oedipus uses his reign to make gods exist; then he knows his place, he gives up his power, his consolation for impotence is knowledge and a powerful backstory. If that means he has to imagine Fate controls him-- or in the more modern/aspirational "his zeal for knowledge resulted in his downfall"-- well, it's better than having to act on his own. He wants to cause the gods to exist and to be dominated by them. THAT IS US TODAY, don't let the our fashionable atheism fool you, the gods we don't believe in are only the ones we know about. Oedipus's reign achieved its purpose at the moment he took out his eyes. His life proved that the gods exist-- his life caused the gods to exist. We should review how much changed in a few hours: Oedipus was given information and accepted guilt. The people were told his secrets, and celebrated the sacrifice. Everyone knows everything, yet no one knows anything, and everyone gave up their power. And nothing changed. "Yes, ok, but all this had to happen in order to break the curse of the plague." Have you not been listening? None of this has anything to do with the plague.

The unconscious fantasy was never to sleep with his mother-- *as if it was his own satisfaction that he was pursuing.* What he wanted was to be the only person she-- the real Queen-- could be satisfied by. The fantasy isn't in the passive voice, it *is* the passive voice: to be crowned the king, to be desired, and the only way to make that fantasy happen is to do it in reverse: be given all the trappings of kingness and desirability and then never act. Be given the crown, be given the throne, be given the queen-- not a crown, a throne, a queen-- the *exact same throne, the exact same queen,* this is the limit of his imagination, the imagination of a 5 year old, an imagination which was never forced=allowed to want something different. Always: *who am I?* And never: *what do I do?* "I want to be King." You want to rule? "Easy does it, let's not get ahead of ourselves." It can't be birthright because birthright isn't you; and anyway it means you are no longer an individual but have inherited all of the responsibility of action. "I'm not so shallow to want to be the main character in my own story, what I'm really looking for is to be the main character in a play written and directed by someone else." Well, I got this short one, there's not much action in it, it's more of a character piece. "That sounds perfect." It ends tragically. "Even better, at least then people will be talking about me for years."

5 SE 4:261; contrast with Fleiss letter 10/15/97 in which the logic was initially the other way: "I now consider it a universal event in early childhood... If this is so, we can understand the gripping power of Oedipus Rex."

6 The primordial Furies, whose singular purpose is to drive the sinner insane-- these terrifying creatures who could hound even the gods-- Athena wraps them up and shuts them down in seconds, not by spear, owl attack or the Gorgon's head, she does this by bribing them with *stuff.* Even Paris

the other person to be satisfied by you. "No!!! I--" Well, at least you accept which pronoun is culpable. It's a start.

Speaking of I, you have to wonder why the title of Freud's biography of the Superego is entitled *Das Ich und Das Es... The Ego And The Id*. No one finds that weird? "It's not about the superego, stupid." Really? Then why does what it's not about appear in the book more times than what it's about? The unconscious is supposed to have the structure of a language, but Freud uses *three* languages, in German he uses Ich and Es and invents the German word "uber-Ich", but for the English he uses Latin-- ego and id-- and then invents a hybrid word "superego". Talk about not following your own logic. Let's double undo the English translation that uses Latin leaving a blank for the original German and see if the repressed

---

held out for love. Some land and honorifics, and they happily gave away their power to the new democratic State.

And it was great while it lasted, a respectfully pious populace willingly agreeing to share all the power built some durable buildings and a lot of disposable boats, but by the time of *Oedipus* something had gone wrong with the whole experiment, even as it seemed to be at its height. That was the problem-- the polis was self-aware, it knew it was at the height. The citizens still had power, even growing power; but it was enough that the velocity of its accumulation was decreasing-- and it made them bananas. They felt themselves becoming less increasingly powerful, and so became frantic, impulsive. For Aeschylus, tribal retribution and heroic vigilante justice had to be abolished, no more omnipotent gods, so Aeschylus had Athena make a parting promise that fear of the State would be sufficient to keep people from murdering their parents. Turns out she was wrong, the State is only as strong as the plague it can protect you from. Aeschylus took power from the gods and gave it to the people; Sophocles took the power they were abandoning and put it safely back in the hands of the gods, thinking he could train the people to want to take it back. They never wanted it back.

7 They say the greatest trick the devil ever did was to convince people he didn't exist, but to his surprise a lot of people were still able to find him anyway. What's his strategy nowadays? We should look online.

There's a famous internet test/meme:

> *Are you a psychopath? Answer this question!*
>
> *A woman, while at the funeral of her own mother, met a guy whom she did not know. She thought this guy was amazing, the man of her dreams, and she fell in love with him immediately. However, she never asked for his name or number and afterward could not find anyone who knew who he was.*
>
> *A few days later the girl killed her own sister.*
>
> *Question: Why did she kill her sister?*

Do you have a guess? The thing you may not have noticed is that this psychopathy test seems to be written by an autist, because there are no metaphors, nothing abstract, everything is stated objectively, literally-- except the phrase "the man of her dreams". We'll come back to this.

> *Answer: She reasoned that if the guy appeared at her mother's funeral, then he might appear at another family funeral.*
>
> *If you answered this correctly, you think like a psychopath. This was a test by a famous American psychologist...*

70

doesn't return:

Latin	German	English
ego	Ich	I
?	?	?
id	Es	it

It's a question, that much is true, but it's not a test and it's not about psychopathy and that's not the correct answer. The devil is in the details. Edgar Allen Poe told us that the best hiding spot is out in plain sight, but he was wrong, even in his story if the reward is big enough people will not stop looking until they find it. The best way to hide something is... to convince everyone they've found it.

Here you have a woman who seems to act so concretely, so ruthlessly logically in the pursuit of what she wants, but if you asked her to explain what that is, concretely, she'd be unable to. *She doesn't even know his name.* "He's the man of my dreams." Nice try. They're not your dreams.

If the riddle involves dreams we could try to do an old-school Freudian interpretation of it. This will actually be very easy to do because this riddle sounds awfully like a dream Freud had actually interpreted:

> ... another dream of a more gloomy character was offered me by a female patient in contradiction of my theory of the wish-dream. This patient, a young girl, began as follows:
>
> "You remember that my sister has now only one boy, Charles. She lost the elder one, Otto, while I was still living with her. Otto was my favorite; it was I who really brought him up. I like the other little fellow, too, but, of course, not nearly as much as his dead brother. Now I dreamt last night that I saw Charles lying dead before me. He was lying in his little coffin, his hands folded; there were candles all about; and, in short, it was just as it was at the time of little Otto's death, which gave me such a shock. Now tell me, what does this mean? You know me — am I really so bad as to wish that my sister should lose the only child she has left? Or does the dream mean that I wish that Charles had died rather than Otto, whom I liked so much better?" I assured her that this interpretation was impossible.

The riddle is nearly identical to the dream minus the autism, so is the riddle parallel thinking or plagiarism? The relevant backstory of the dreamer is that she was in love with a certain man:

> Whenever the man she loved, who was a member of the literary profession, announced a lecture anywhere, she was certain to be found among the audience; and she seized every other opportunity of seeing him unobserved... she had told me that the Professor was going to a certain concert, and that she too was going, in order to enjoy the sight of him. This was on the day before the dream; and the concert was to be given on the day on which she told me the dream. I could now easily see the correct interpretation, and I asked her whether she could think of any particular event which had occurred

I'm pretty sure the missing term should be "you", but I'm no linguist.   Not just "you," but the European formal you, aka you-plural: "Sie": *Ich, Sie, Es*. Right?   Perhaps Sie was too polyvalent, so he needed the fake word "uber-Ich"?   Admittedly, personal pronouns and adjectives are a fruitful nuisance in this language, and should have been left out. For instance, the same sound, *sie*, means *you*, and it means *she*, and it means *her*, and it means *it*, and it means *they*, and it means *them*. Think of the ragged poverty of a language which has to make one word do the work of six. But mainly, think of the exasperation of never knowing which

---

after Otto's death. She replied immediately: "Of course; the Professor returned then, after a long absence, and I saw him once more beside little Otto's coffin."

It was just as I had expected.

Wait a second, I assume he had never read the riddle, so why did Freud expect-- anything? It wasn't his dream, was it?

I interpreted the dream as follows: "If now the other boy were to die, the same thing would happen again. You would spend the day with your sister; the Professor would certainly come to offer his condolences, and you would see him once more under the same circumstances as before. The dream signifies nothing more than this wish of yours to see him again — a wish against which you are fighting inwardly."

This is the kind of Freudian interpretation that leaves you dazzled, dazed, some kind of fourth wall of reality has been breached; like the answer to the psychopathy riddle its impossible logic makes uncanny sense; you might not completely buy it but you are still left feeling... like you now *know* something about yourself. Did you get this feeling? There's a reason: like the answer to the riddle, Freud's interpretation of the dream is wrong.

First of all, that she would wish to see the man again, and thus dreams a funeral he might attend isn't an interpretation, it is *literally* the manifest content of the dream (and the riddle)-- there is no interpretation there at all, he is merely telling her what would have happened next had she stayed asleep five minutes longer.   A dream isn't what it takes to fulfill a wish, it is the fulfillment of a wish. And "seeing the Professor" is hardly a disguised latent wish she is "fighting inwardly"— she's on record as wanting him, she had seen him numerous times before and she was going to see him that very day: nothing, including her unconscious, prevents her.   Wanting him is not a repressed wish. Yet Freud says it is. *Why?*

Freud is wrong, nothing prevents her from seeing or desiring the Professor. The problem is he doesn't want her, *and now she is incapable of falling in love with anyone else*:

It looked for a time as though these barely explicit relations would end in marriage, but this happy culmination was frustrated by the sister, whose motives were never completely explained. After the rupture the man whom my patient loved avoided the house; she herself attained her independence some time after the death of little Otto, to whom, meanwhile, her affections had turned. But she did not succeed in freeing herself from the dependence due to her affection for her sister's friend. Her pride bade her avoid him, but she found it

72

of these meanings the speaker is trying to convey. This explains why, whenever a person says *sie* to me, I generally try to kill him, if a stranger. Nevertheless, "superego" *is* Sie-- yet instead of structure and grammar he uses a pop-culture reference and calls it the "uber-Ich." Don't be fooled, Nietzsche may seem sophisticated today because he lived a tenth of a millennium ago in a land you're not sure exists, but to Freud he was edgy contemporary, a reference to Nietzsche was obvious, all too obvious, he was burying the truth in the obvious references of his day.

That kind of mistake is done by a man who is trying to unknow. "The superego is the voice of the Father." Whose father? Freud doesn't think it is the Father-- he *wants* it to be the Father. He has the structure of the Mad Lib right, I'll give him that, but he filled in the

---

impossible to transfer her love to the other suitors who successively presented themselves.

The reason she can't be with any other men is her persistent unfulfilled love for this man. The reason she can't fulfill her love with this man is her sister prevented it. The dream doesn't kill the boy in order to fulfill the repressed wish of seeing the man. *The dream's repressed wish is for her sister to die.*

I see you rolling your eyes, you can't imagine any adult having that much "repressed rage" at a sibling. But there aren't any adults, here there be children. It's a *child's* wish fulfillment dream. No doubt a wish fulfillment must bring pleasure; but the question then arises, "to whom?" To the person who has the wish, of course. But a dreamer's relation to her wishes is a strange one. She repudiates them and censors them. So that their fulfillment will give her no pleasure, but just the opposite: *shock*, a fact which has still to be explained. Thus a dreamer in her relation to her dream-wishes can only be compared to an amalgamation of two separate people who are linked by some important common element. Who are the two people? The dreamer as she was as a child and the dreamer now; or, if you prefer: the unconscious, and the imagined projection of herself.

But leave her aside for a second: why did *you* roll your eyes? NOT because you can't imagine *wanting* your sister to die but because you can't imagine *repressing* it. Your heart is made of crusted glue and sawdust, so you have no problem murdering your sister in a dream because you know it's just REM and vodka metabolites-- picturing people or yourself dead is even the basis of most of your idioms. But this dream occurred to a "lady" in the era of tasteful décolletage and covered ankles, aka superego guilt; the wish for her sister to die-- let alone the wish to murder her-- has to be repressed. The reason she can dream-- does dream-- "the wish that Charles had died"-- is exactly because she has no such wish, not even as a means to an end. He's not the one she wants to die: the correct identity of that person she wants to kill is hidden-- *it has to be, or it cannot be dreamed.*

Hence the funeral: the purpose of the funeral is to cloud everything in the *appearance* of sadness that would be required if she got her wish-- it is a ruse for the adult-her-- because there is no actual sadness, Charles isn't really dead and child-- she wouldn't feel bad if the sister was. The only affect is *shock*: "I got my wish?!"

That seeing the Professor is not the repressed wish of the dream, but is made to appear to be by Freud's interpretation; and that all of this was unbelievably but verily orchestrated by her unconscious in order to stop Freud from going deeper-- that kind of trick is also in the riddle: the answer is she killed the sister in order to get the man, to hide the truth that she fell for the man in order to kill her sister.

What's so interesting about Freud's interpretation isn't merely that it's wrong but how Freud totally rationalizes it-- like an amateur, like a novice-- like a *patient*. He mistakes conscious for unconscious, manifest for latent, suppression for repression— and completely falls for the young

blanks with lies-- with hope. And using this *Insert Pronoun Here* the rest of us don't have to wonder who our Sie is, today it's "patriarchal authority". But is it? You walk down the street and think, "I'm nothing, I can't even get a girl." Is that the criticism your Dad would make of you? "I'm 30-- I'm not going to take that cubicle job that implies that I am only good enough for a cubicle-- wouldn't it be better to be unemployed and wait for the world to discover me?" Never mind the impossible logistics-- who are you talking to? But when you want to masturbate over the face of the passed out girl at a party and then take a picture, that's what you decide to label id? Because it's a weirdly complicated behavior to attribute to the instincts. Sounds like you've been taught how to want.

If we accept that Sie is the authority, the one that judges you for doing and for not doing,

---

woman's defensive batting of the eyelashes: "but Freudy poo, am I really so bad as to wish that my sister should lose the only child she has left?" With those décolletages? Not a chance! "I assured her that was impossible." Why assure her that anything is impossible? Isn't his whole gimmick, "report whatever comes to mind?" *She brought it up-- and he told her it was impossible.* Then he *published* it in a book.

"So it was countertransference?" The answer is no but the answer isn't important. This isn't about him, it's about you. So I have some questions for you first.

Literally: why did she tell him this dream?

"She wanted him to interpret it?"

No. Literally: she told it to him as a counterexample to his theory of wish fulfillment. On the most surface level: to prove him wrong. Now you can ask: to what purpose? In the 1/1000 chance it works, she wins, he loses. This is the hedge. But she more than likely figures he will detect *a* wish fulfillment in it. *She gave him what he wanted. She gave him a gift of herself.*

Why, after telling him the dream, did she herself then immediately offer up an interpretation (that she wants Charles dead, too) which even she believes is wrong?

"Obviously, she worried Freud might be thinking she wants Charles dead, too."

But Freud would *not* have thought that. What she suggested as the repressed wish (that Charles dies) was the literal, manifest content of the dream (Charles died).   An amateur might mistakenly think that's how dream wish fulfillments worked. But not Freud. The guy who invented the method wouldn't have been fooled by that... unless he could be fooled. By *her.* Dead Charles isn't Charles, dead Charles is the sister. The word she says with her conscious mouth is "Charles" but Freud's response to her unconscious wish is heard by her unconscious as about the sister. She fooled Freud into absolving her. "Am I really so bad as to wish [insert proper noun] dead?" Let me assure you and your swollen décolletage: it is impossible!

Pretend she was raised in China until she was 5 and then afterwards in Germany, so that she now no longer remembers any Chinese. One day she dreams something in Chinese, she's surprised, "why did I dream that?" Here you'd have no problem understanding that the unconscious "childhood" wishes were expressed in Chinese because that was the language those ideas were originally formed in. Except that's 50% wrong, or maybe 33% wrong, depending on the math: she dreamt in Chinese because her unconscious speaks Chinese; *and* because *she* no longer knows Chinese; AND because she assumes the analyst *does* speak Chinese, or at least can figure it out.   If he couldn't, she wouldn't have dreamt it *at all.*

Since she projects on to him her unconscious, not only will she assume Freud understands the meaning of her dream-- not only is her dream dreamt *for* him (to interpret), it was dreamt *as if she was him,* like two junior high school soulmates. You may have scientific proof that Freud was

you need only take a minute and figure out who your Sie is, and you'll have learned a lot about yourself you probably don't want to know.

"The fact that [the superego] is less firmly connected with consciousness is what calls for explanation." Here's the explanation: it's connected to someone else's consciousness. Freud thought it was the Father because Freud didn't own a TV. If he had, Sie would have been TV. "[The superego's] relation to the ego is not exhausted by the precept: 'You ought to be like this (like your father).' It also comprises the prohibition: 'You may not be like this (like your father)-- that is, you may not do all that he does; some things are his prerogative.'" Like what? Having sex with mom? He's the cock blocker? As if killing him would *automatically*

100% wrong about dreams as wish fulfillments, *but it was 100% true for her*. She dreamt according to (what she believed) were his rules, his language-- his wishes. She gave him a gift. What he wanted was for dreams to be wish fulfillments, so she dreamt for him a dream whose *manifest* content was *obviously* a wish fulfillment-- so that he would be satisfied and stop looking for the latent wish. Which is what happened. He gets a gift from her, and she gets to keep her wishes unconscious. More than that, she gets to be told she categorically doesn't have such wishes. She has been absolved by an omnipotent god, whom she fooled.

Her dream carried with it a defense *against him* in the form of an obvious interpretation that Freud can easily interpret. This keeps Freud at the manifest level of the dream. He does not want to go any further because he already got what *he* wants. Of course this interpretation is of no benefit to his patient, you could even say he was negligent in his treatment of her by using her as a way of getting what he wants; though it's hard to say that because she wanted him to fail.

Whatever Freud thought was the meaning he should have kept to himself, and instead used the meaning that she doesn't know to change her. If the wish is to see the man again, why did she use her nephew's funeral to accomplish this, instead of the concert she is actually going to in real life? What else is the funeral *used* for? Which might have lead him to ask the most insightful question: what is the dream itself used for? We know what Freud used it for (a case study); we know what she said it was for (to contradict his theory)-- well, what *else* do those things do? To hide her wish, to give Freud what he wants-- *and what else?*

In multiple ways-- this is called condensation-- the dream's structure reveals the form these latent wishes all have in common: giving the other what they want, in order to deprive them of their satisfaction.

Why was Freud fooled?

"Décolletage?"

HA! But, yeah. That's pretty much it.

An analyst has no power, he represents omniscience. At the very beginning, however, some patients may assume he is also omnipotent. What kind of patients? How about a young Victorian woman flat on her back with a man she doesn't know but heard lots about and who has lots of coke? Whatever Freud wanted, she'd feel obligated to submit.

Freud cannot see this. I don't mean he misses it; I mean it is impossible for him to see it. To him, those boobs-- her desirability-- means she has all the power. The best he can do is show her the thing that makes him desirable, which he thinks is his knowledge. To be specific: he uses his knowledge like a phallus, to impress her, and not like a penis, to satisfy her. So now the whole thing is about him. This is why, instead of useful interpretations or referral to a more objective colleague he dazzles her with ta da, with information, with his knowledge-- he gives her a gift of himself. But he already knows he's smart so for him it doesn't count; for him, fame and a woman's interest are

75

entitle you to her vagina-- as if she has no say in it? Maybe that's the important basis-- or consequence-- of the fantasy. Which story sounds more like your porn: Jocasta knew all along that she was having sex with a man she knew she shouldn't; or she had had sex with a guy she didn't know that she just met?

If we accept Freud's word that the Oedipus *story* represents the fundamental fantasy, then we better be literally precise about which part is the fantasy: either the fantasy is that we sleep with our mothers *unknowingly* or the fantasy is that the other person *has no say in it*. Oedipus "wanted" it-- so what? I want a pet chupacabra. Abracadabra? Jocasta didn't sleep with him because she wanted to or because he killed the father, she slept with him because he killed the Sphinx, was appointed King, and *so she was told she had to*. The question for later is:

---

the only two real metrics of his value, money a distant third then family a little ways down the river but there is no fifth or sixth.

"Come on, she's just a---." Were you going to say patient, or girl? I once was in a Spirituality In Medicine course for first year medical students run by the Department of Biological Psychiatry, all of those words have been typed correctly, and a-- well, let's just call him a future Clinical Assistant Professor-- had just interviewed a jaw droppingly gorgeous female patient on the bright side of a two-way mirror. Back on the dark side, during the discussion of the case, the attending psychiatrist asked the med student if he wanted to have sex with the woman. He paused, carefully admitted she was "physically attractive, perhaps even somewhat provocatively so", but of course he had no desire to have sex with her. That seemed honest, no one faulted him, which was why the attending then said this: "So millions of years of evolution have failed on you?" In other words, why is your *choice* not to sleep with her expressed not as won't or shouldn't but as a *lack of desire* to do so? What kind of a man deliberately limits his reach to his grasp? "A man who doesn't want a heaven?" "A man who prefers masturbation?" "Both?"

Of course he shouldn't, of course he won't, but why can't he say he wants to from the safety of the omnipotent side of a camera obscura? Because if he admits he wants to, he'd worry that we'd worry he might. So he says he wouldn't want to, which he thinks assures us that he wouldn't. "So he's lying?" He's not *lying*. But it is a trick: he is talking to his peers-- an audience he believes can act on their desires, but he isn't able to, *because* he wants to. Things that he thinks don't count he can get easily, but he is impotent to pursue the things that do count. You'll flip this around and say he wants the things he can't have, but he can't have a bigger penis and he doesn't really want one either. He does want her, but not because he can't have her: he can't have her *because* he wants her. That's the only reason. And so the only way to get her, right under all of our noses, is not to want her.

It's highly probable that many of the other med students in the audience, and the patient, were thinking about themselves *the exact same thing*: that they themselves can't act on whatever they want, but "everyone else", including that med student, can. *Everyone has power but you.* But he doesn't know this, and wouldn't believe it anyway.

He's defended against his impotence with some damn intricate sophistry, but it wait until you see its malevolent power: by disavowing-- not lying about, but disavowing-- his desire for her, he is freeing himself just enough to do innocuously *passive* things that set up getting her-- e.g. and especially: making *her* want *him*-- and the moment he *thinks* she does want him, nothing in the universe will be able to stop him, including her.

I've often thought about what my response to wanting to have sex with her would have been had I not been the one asking the question, and because I've been on the both sides of all kinds of two-way mirrors I think now it would be: yes. "Could you elaborate?" Nope, asked and answered, and from now on I'm taking the 5th. When I was 21 I might have said proudly, "of course I *want* to sleep with her, but I wouldn't do it," but rather than that being honest I would have been *using* the truth about my desire *in order to pretend* I had Herculean self-control. But who would have been

who told her she had to? Ok, maybe when presented with the backhaired meathead she nibbled a fingernail and cocked a unibrow, who knows, but the only reason she got on all fours was because she was the prize, she was obligated to submit. Did that make it harder or easier for her to enjoy it? I'll admit it's a fantasy for some.

Before you lament the structural misogyny of Ancient Greece, you should consider just why your low-fat cerebral cortex detected that imbalance and not the other one: Oedipus didn't sleep with her because he wanted to or because he killed his father, he slept with her because he killed the Sphinx, was appointed King, and so *he was told he had to*. The question for later is: who told him he had to? Ok, maybe when presented with her meaty backside he nailed etc etc, but the only reason he mounted her from behind was because she was the prize,

---

there to catch the form of my lie? I wouldn't have wanted to sleep with her *only*. If not for the ethical prohibition, I would probably have pursued a *relationship* with her, for all kinds of reasons, all of them projected, all of them bananas-- and I hope it is evident that that is WAY worse, and if that's not evident let me say it this way: this patient could have ended up having sex with her psychiatrist, or she could have ended up *married to me*. Yeah. Winters are cold.

No one ever doubts that some other psychiatrist's female patient might be attracted to him; the assumption is she very well might, but always only because of the "power differential." If she met him in a park the assumption is she'd call for back up, what is an adult man doing in a park other than drugs, masturbation or plotting an Amber Alert? You're saying in his office she can overlook his MWF loose fitting khakis because what's brainwashingly attractive to her is how much power he has? Then she needs to go to a psychiatrist. "That's not funny." You're right, if power is what she wanted, she wouldn't want to go to a psychiatrist, she'd want to be a psychiatrist. "But psychiatrists don't really have power, it's an illusion." So she's stupid as well? And so we've come to it: she doesn't want power, she doesn't want someone with power, she wants the illusion of power while the real power is safely monitoring them from the other side of the glass. "That's sexist." I wish that's what it was.

Freud has all these problems with this patient, but observe he has none of these problems with the Rat Man even when he goes postal in his office. This is because for all his yelling the Rat Man has no power over Freud, and so Freud does not feel pressured to give him something of himself.

He was presented with a dream which had an all too easy wish fulfillment, which he went with because it was what he wanted, the low hanging apple of being desired, instead of asking himself, "wow, this dream is way too easy to see as a wish fulfillment and as unbelievable as this sounds this woman most likely idealizes me-- therefore this is a gift to me hoping to satisfy me *temporarily*-- as a step towards depriving me-- so I don't ask anything more of her; meanwhile her strange denial likely holds the clue to the actual repressed meaning."

"You know me — am I really so bad as to wish that my sister should lose the only child she has left?" It doesn't matter what I think; what do you think your sister would think?

Instead, Freud tells her her own interpretation is impossible, shuts down the opening that would benefit her, and then puts the more *self*-serving one into a book. This is most therapy today, it goes from being useful to the patient to useful to the therapist-- self-serving-- e.g. whenever the therapist luckily detects a repressed idea, and they proudly show it to the patient to show how astute they are: "Aha! See what you just did, that negation! That's the form of a repressed idea!" *As if they were surprised themselves repression occurs,* so much for omniscience. And maybe the patient is receptive and they believe you, "wow, that's so cool, I never realized how interesting I am in bed!" What next? A different psychology book has the answer: stasis.

But maybe she ALSO wants the man? What makes you so sure she doesn't want him back at all?

he was obligated to commit. Did that make it harder or easier for him to enjoy it? I'll admit it's a fantasy for some.[8][9]

"Any son you sire will one day murder you," Laius was told. Well, isn't that supposed to be how it works? Maybe this is how a modern reading of Oedipus would go: a child born to self-absorbed parents who sabotaged his future for their status quo,   they gave him neither education nor inheritance but you can argue they did foster independence, that's something, I guess. And he's living the American dream-- no attachments, no backstory, he can be anyone he wants to be. He is free to reinvent himself.   So what did he do with all that freedom, i.e. how did he hastily guard himself against it?   He imagined himself as having a destiny, found some con men willing to confirm it, then accepted a job he was completely unqualified for

---

It's complicated. No, that's literally the answer.

The premise of the riddle is she met a man she fell in love with, but didn't ask his name. Well wait a second, how could she love someone she met once whose name she didn't know and never sees again? It's *impossible*. To be clear: if she met the man again and got to know him, he would be a different man. Imagine a woman has sex with a man whose name she doesn't know: that's a man she doesn't want to know later. *Why didn't the dreamer ask his name?* So she could want "him" and not have him.

You'll counter that this is just a riddle, her not knowing his name is a contrivance to move the riddle along. Exactly right, literally right, but towards the end of *killing her sister*. She doesn't want the man, she isn't even trying to get the man, no one pursues things they want to get this way; they pursue things they want not to get this way. The contrivance isn't in order to get him-- the contrivance is to convey the appearance that that is what she wants.

She falls in love with a man whose name she doesn't know: this is an *impossible* love. You know who fantasizes about impossible loves? Men. A hundred years after the dream, the riddle woman is wanting like a man: the prize seemingly desirable but really a symbol of your worth-- and a pretext for destroying your rivals.   Having an impossible love discharges your obligation to love, while saving you from ever having to be dependent in love.

Contrast this with the dream: she's stuck on a perfectly possible but unfulfilled love. That means the dreamer doesn't want the man either. Sure, she says she wants him, but all the energy spent stalking him is exactly equal to the energy spent not going in for an audition. If you hover around a perfectly attainable goal without action to get it, then you don't want it, you want it to want you. "I'm waiting for them to call me back." Don't you have to call them first?

Why does she want him to want her if she doesn't really want him? Because a hysterical woman's revenge fantasies don't employ punishment but negative reinforcement. He abandoned her, so she wants him to want her and never be able to have her. And the only way she knows to make that happen *without direct action* is by thinking of her life as a novel: a) she sets up contrived scenarios which are choreographed to rekindle his passion for her, like, say, oh, I don't know, a chance meeting at a concert; b) these scenarios are to convince the audience how much love she is capable of; c) they never actually hook up, or, depending on how undesirable she thinks she actually is, *never even speak,* she can't even fantasize a scenario where he doesn't immediately remember why he didn't want her in the first place. All she wants is to be wanted by him, nothing more, or, translated into jargon, there's no impediment to gazing upon him, the problem is in getting him to return the gaze, for the audience's gaze. And if by deus ex machina they end up together, she'll do to him what she did to Freud: idealize him as a god, realize he's a just guy wearing khakis, and then deprive him of his satisfaction.   Oh no, she's not going to leave him (not unless she finds someone else) because there's every chance he wouldn't feel that as deprivation, he might enjoy being without her. No: she'll stay with him to make sure he's never satisfied.

because he was right place/right time and interviewed well. I know this isn't the standard interpretation, but the Sphinx wasn't sent by Apollo to punish Laius for being a sex offender, the Sphinx was sent by Hera to punish Thebes for harboring a sex offender.

<pre>
                    SPHINX:
    Ok, T, thank you for coming out for an interview on such
    short notice, we know you must have a lot of other offers
    and I wanted to make sure we had a chance to parley before
    I catch my flight. Right now Thebes is undergoing a
    rightsizing, and as part of our talent management initiative
    we're onboarding the relevant skills sets for a balanced
</pre>

If the wish of the dream, that the sister die, is repressed, what allows the riddle to make this explicit?

The dream's repressed wish is for her sister to die. If you think that the idea of a *repressed* wish for your sister to die belongs to a bygone time of horse carriages and double entendres, you're right-- nowadays we don't have to repress those kinds of thoughts, all we have to do is explain them. So the *riddle* does not need to repress this. In fact, it makes it the explicit solution. Meanwhile, it represses something else, and covers it *by "revealing" that you are a psychopath.*

The riddle's answer makes two assumptions:

First, that only a psychopath would come up with such a deviously complicated scheme to get a man. This is totally false: psychopaths are the most direct of actors, they wouldn't go through all this unless they derived some pleasure out of the scheme itself, in which case they are more accurately perverts who get off on anything but the point. For everyone else, when you have an overly elaborate strategy to bring about what anyone else would have pursued more directly, you aren't planning like a psychopath, you are daydreaming like a child. This obsessive, crazy, fantastical logic has no problem consciously imagining all kinds of scenarios and outcomes except one: the will to act. For a child, direct action is impossible. So you fantasize situations that compel you to act-- you have no choice but to do what you wanted to do in the first place.

The second assumption of the riddle: that if you think about killing the sister just to see the man, i.e. in an instrumental way with no emotional connection to the murder itself, then you are a psychopath. That may be true-- but it is also the whole trick of the riddle: *the defense is that you are a psychopath.*

That may not sound like a defense until you should say it out loud in court. "I killed her because I was hoping he'd show up at the funeral.... I know, I always suspected there was something wrong with me." Yeah, but it's not psychopathy. In this case the defense isn't even for court, it is for your personal use: you wanted to kill her, but the only way you could do it is if it was for some other reason.

No doubt you're perplexed, isn't killing her coldly/instrumentally for some other reason, e.g. to get a guy, more pathological than doing it because you wanted to? Yes, more *pathological.* "I killed her because I am a psychopath." The direct connection between desire to kill her and action to kill her is safely severed. Now try this: "I killed her because I wanted to." That last one's all you.

This is the magical duplicity of the riddle, the meaning of "why would anyone go through all that just to see a man again?" They wouldn't, no one would. The riddle doesn't elaborately imagine a way of getting the man back; it elaborately imagines a compelling reason to have to do what you already want to do. *You cannot act* because *you want to.* It has to be compelled or for some other reason. The madness of the manifest content of the *dream--* killing Charles so that she can see the man again-- is a cover story, a defense, against having an unacceptable desire to kill the sister. And the manifest content of the *riddle--* killing the sister in order to get the man back-- is the defense

79

scorecard. I'm sure you've heard that the previous CEO
inappropriately exhibited behavior, and we need to ensure
we're sensitive to changing consumer upvotes. We want our
associates to be prophet guided, not profit seeking. This
is a buy in, lean in, work in environment. Are you in?

REX:
Wow, you guys are awfully welcoming. I heard you usually
picked apart applicants' resumes and barraged them with
complicated math questions.

SPHINX:

---

against needing to fall in love with a man in order to have cause to kill your sister-- being unable to act on desire.

NB that no one is actually dying-- everything described here is fantasy and wishes, so the core issue for the dream is, "what am I allowed to want?" but for the riddle it is, "when am I allowed to act?" It is not simply preferable to her-- to us-- to think she killed her sister instrumentally or for some reason other than that she wanted it; it is logically impossible for her to have done it because she wanted it. "I killed him because I needed the money." Aren't there richer guys to kill? "I killed her so she wouldn't suffer." Wouldn't she suffer less by killing yourself? "I killed her because--" None of these are excuses, they are causes. I know it seems like she shouldn't act; as if she was looking for an excuse to do something bad, but the obvious wrongness of murder is part of the defense, the psychological logic applies to the inability to act directly on any desire-- murder, sex, visiting a friend, borrowing a cup of olive oil. Any reason to act-- except that you wanted to act.

Just as the dream is an example of what ideas got repressed in 1900, the riddle represents the repression of our time: "I will act on my desire." *NO.*

8The true riddle of the Sphinx is-- why have a Sphinx at all? *It is the only thing in the play that doesn't exist.* You could say Apollo doesn't exist either, but he isn't in the play: things are attributed to him. The Sphinx as a fantasy creature is incongruous, even Hamlet's ghost is consistent with the logic of that play and at least someone else sees it, BTW you should observe that Horatio calls the ghost "It" but for Hamlet it's a Sie. And why doesn't the audience perceive the Sphinx as out of place? Because the whole point of tragedies was not to understand their meaning, but to be taught how to feel. This is the kind of guidance that fantasies once offered-- before we made them real and an end in themselves. The Sphinx is a crazy, dream-like amalgam of pieces of things: it is straight up definitionally the return of the repressed-- the repressed of *Laius*. When the Oracle told Laius, in spectacularly unoracular clarity, that his son would murder him-- and you'll see this every time the Oracle speaks too clearly-- *it wasn't a prophecy*, it was a *sentence*-- half a sentence-- for a crime that strangely no one seems to think relevant: Laius raped Chrysippus, son of King Pelops. Open wide, I'll spoon feed you: PELOPS. For that crime he was cursed to be murdered by his son; and when he wasn't, a second curse fell on his kingdom for not punishing Laius: to be tormented by the Sphinx. But once Laius was killed the Sphinx had no function; which is why, according to Chapter 6 Section C of the technical manual, logical consequence manifests as spatial or temporal succession: Oedipus kills Laius and then the next thing that happens in the story is the Sphinx vanishes. The solving of the riddle was merely a formality. "It doesn't vanish, it commits suicide." Um, sure. By jumping off a cliff. Here's a riddle: what has the tail of a serpent, the body of a lion, the head of a woman, and the... have you already heard this one?

But never mind the Sphinx: the King of Thebes has been murdered, who do the people of Thebes think did it? Sixteen years is a long time to forget to investigate a regicide. The real life assassin of the King of Camelot was caught red handed and on film and to this day they haven't stopped investigating it, likely because the official story actually relied on magic. You're telling me King Laius gets murdered and no one even asks *the Oracle* who did it?

```
That was the former toxicult.  We find doing that privileges
performing over conforming and IQ over EQ, so here at HQ we
obey social cues.  We want this engagement to be completely
comfortable and consensual.  Care for a Soma?

               REX:
I'm sorry?

               SPHINX:
Just kidding, only Phase II.  Ready player one?

               REX:
I'm a little nervous.
```

It's interesting that the explanation Creon gives for not investigating the murder of Laius is that he was too busy "looking into the problem we faced": the *arrival* of Sphinx. Uh oh, either Sophocles is a bad writer or someone's a bad liar. Would you like to know what question Oedipus asked that elicited this explanation from Creon?

> Oedipus: Isn't it likely Laius's murder was a conspiracy from within Thebes?

> Creon: Yes, that's what we guessed, but we were too busy looking into...

So the King is murdered, there is the possibility of political espionage, treason, assassination; then they were distracted by the Sphinx who had just arrived a decade *before* that and who suddenly/coincidentally disappeared after he was murdered; and for the next 16 years: meh? You think it's because they wanted to leave well enough alone? They valued peace? Here's the real world context of the Athenians: when the Spartan King ended the War and brokered the First Peace Of Pleistoanax, sparing countless lives on both sides, the Spartans accused *him* of treason and exiled him. Suspiciousness was the default position of the Greeks, paranoia was almost a virtue, you could here safeties clicking off if some guy started speaking too plainly. Do you think they would have been indifferent to an assassination?   "I guess it's fate." What are the chances Oedipus would find the condemned King outside the gates "guarded" by the exact same non-warrior involved in *all* of the other prophecies? Almost like they planned it. One could look at all this with sideways skepticism, but it's not like these facts were unknown, and they were certainly known to an Athenian audience at war with the *Pelopsios* and *Thebans*; what makes the facts interesting today is how ready everyone is to un-know them. The desire not to know is too consistent to be anything other than on purpose. Today it takes a just a few punch/head lines to concuss us into "knowing how things really work"; yet we assume the Greeks were too busy oppressing women to notice the enemies in their real life were the protagonists in their plays. "Hold on, Luke Skywalker and the Rebel Alliance are from Mos Kba?"

In his *Fundamentals Of Psychoanalytic Technique,* Fink discusses the difference between manifest and latent content in dreams. Then he gives an example from his own practice in which he, an analyst and academic, is analyzing his patient who is an academic and also training to be an analyst. Also, I'm pretty sure this took place in Paris. Everybody comfortable with the level of sophistication and knowledge gathered around a 60W lamp dimmed to 10? Here's the example:

> [the patient related a long dream] the only details of which he could remember were the name Chrysippus and the vague sense that in the dream he was looking for his works. Although he was initially reluctant to ponder such a "skimpy dream," he provided the following associations...

There are two general ways free association goes. One is for the patient to say, "I have no idea, I

SPHINX:
Don't be. We invested in the architecture to make this
communication full duplex, so no need to push to talk.
There are no wrong answers, only questions. You get the
extra time, right? We're about the dialectic not the
binary. Feeling safe? We can get HR support in here, or a
kimochi? No? Ok, let's ease in: What walks on four legs in
the morning, two legs in the afternoon, and three legs in
the evening?

          REX:
Man! And Woman! But a woman doesn't need to lean on anyone--

---

guess the first thing that jumps to my mind about Chrysippus is X, but that's got nothing to do with me." The second way is for the patient to reluctantly associate what he already knows about Chrysippus to himself. The first way is a true unconscious association, followed by the defensive denial "but that has nothing to do with me." The latter is *all* defense, because those associations are being consciously selected.

This is what the patient "reluctantly" comes up with.

> [Chrysippus] was a Stoic philosopher, and the analysand had been "boning up" on Stoic logic recently. It occurred to him next that he had read somewhere that "Chrysippus was as great as Aristotle," though because his works were lost it was hard to substantiate that claim. After a pause he added that, as he had not yet published his own work, I [Fink] must be like Aristotle to him whereas he is like Chrysippus, suggesting a certain wish to be as "well published" as I am. "If not better!" he added... it brought up a whole nexus of thoughts and wishes about the analysand's ambitions and his rivalry with me...

Oh boy. I am in no position to second guess Bruce Fink, but here goes. The importance of supervision is that sometimes the supervisor is thus able to hear much more of the discourse, owing not necessarily to his years of experience or "extraordinary powers of insight" but to his distance; the reason for this is that the [treating analyst] serves as a filter, or refractor, of the patient's discourse, and in this way a ready made stereograph is presented, bringing out from the start-- &c.

What they don't tell you in pop culture psychodynamics is that the patient isn't just reporting a dream for Fink to interpret. He *dreamt* the dream for Fink. In analysis, every dream is subject to report, and so it's dreamt with the knowledge that it is going to be analyzed, not just by some guy but by an analyst, and by a particular analyst. So any distortions in the dream aren't just defenses against the patient's own conscious-ness, but also Fink's.

The bluff, the double bluff, the triple bluff-- all are anticipated by a paranoid('s) unconscious. And so he reluctantly offers: maybe Chrysippus implies you're Aristotle?

"What is important, Freud tells us, is the telling of the dream — that is, in its *rhetoric*." Well, what's the first step of classical rhetoric? Ingratiate yourself to your audience-- in this case the analyst: make them think you see them the way they want to be seen.

It appears that there is very little to go on: the patient doesn't remember the dream. But see above, what is important is the *telling* of the dream, not just plot but the phrases: e.g. "skimpy dream", his "vague sense" that he was looking for Chrysippus's "works". And, most of all, the patient's own interpretation that since (=if) he is Chrysippus and Fink is Aristotle, then (=then) the wish is he wants to be well published. These aren't descriptions, these are arguments of logic. The

82

```
Man!

          SPHINX:
Nice process.  Too easy?

          REX:
Oh, no, I would never say a question is too easy, I would
only say my... privileged upbringing... afforded me the...
opportunity-- unearned opportunity... to take risks with
creativity.

          SPHINX:
```

---

associations are used *in order to* suggest that the wish is to be "well published." *He is lying.*

Chrysippus was not a student of Aristotle. In fact, there's almost no reason to think Chrysippus had even read Aristotle, or even read much about him, Chrysippus's works might be lost to us but Aristotle's were lost to him. You'll say this is impossible, a logician must have studied the only relevant logician of his past 100 years, but I don't know a single psychiatrist who has read *The Interpretation Of Dreams* and even fewer who've read an entire psychiatric journal, though I'll admit one of those is utterly useless. So the parallel to Fink and himself fails here, and it fails because it is a lousy defense-- except against Fink, he uses their *special* knowledge against Fink. From where did the patient *and* Fink *know* that Chrysippus was as great as Aristotle? They learned it from Lacan:

> I am going to try to summarize here, in a fashion which has nothing
> original about it, these two great functions that Aristotle admirably
> distinguishes, posits, affirms in their simplicity... this theory of the
> signifier which the Stoics, and specifically, for example somebody like
> Chrysippus, had pushed to an extreme point of perfection.

The connection Fink and the patient both make is to the Stoic philosopher Chrysippus; and the reason they make this *obvious* (to them) connection is Lacan and Deleuze had written about it, a fact that they both *obviously* know. You might think Laius is the more obvious association because I've been rambling about it, *but not to them*; in their microcosm the obvious reference was to the Stoic. Their knowledge protects him from the truth. Look at it like this: if the only possible association of "Chrysippus" was to Laius, *then the patient could not have had the dream at all*. The only way he could have a dream about Laius's Chrysippus is if it more easily refers to something else that a master-- *Fink*-- would think obvious and bless as correct-- AND (he hopes) Fink can be fooled into blessing it. Why such a gamble? Why not simply NOT tell him the dream? *Because it's not enough to hide the truth, because then it still remains true for him.* The master has to be used to make it mean something else. Whatever unholy thing the patient is wishing for is either something he is not *allowed* to want, or, unable to act on. So to be able to see it fulfilled, without wanting it, or acting on it, he needs someone else to make it true that it means something else: obliterate his desire, and replace it with something else.

In the Old Testament book of Daniel is the famous symbolic interpretation of King Nebuchadnezzar's dream, which is here irrelevant. At issue is what the King does with the interpretation-- the use to which it is put.

The usual telling of the story is that the King had a dream and wanted to know what the dream meant, but this misses that what the King actually wanted to know was what the dream *was*. The King had forgotten it. He asks his wise men, sorcerers and enchanters to tell him what he dreamt. Obviously they couldn't, but if you think the reason is obvious you're not going to enjoy reading the Old Testament, because that's not the reason. The King then orders the execution of all the wise men because they're ignorant, which they weren't. So to save them, Daniel approaches him with both the

Grok your dopamine the full 100. Everyone but Athena was
born from a rape, so nurturing environments become critical
when 95% of the variance is explained by genetics and all
the rest of us are equal. That's why we strive to midwife a
slice that values workplace culture over fiat rewards.

    REX:
So totally me.

    SPHINX:
That comes through in your social. Say you're in an illegal
imperialist military action and the combatants engage you in

dream and its interpretation, and because it is about the end of the world everyone is satisfied. Don't worry, this will make sense in a moment and you won't like it.

There are six things you should take note of. First, later on Nebuchadnezzar becomes mad with power, which is bad, but the alternative is mad without power, which is way worse. Second, this story happens in the second year of his reign, i.e. the beginning, shortly after a 400 year period during which 80% of human beings had mysteriously vanished. That part's not in the Bible, but it is true nevertheless. "Was it a flood?" "Plague?" "Aliens?" If there are no follow-up questions, then yes. Third, although the story feels like it was millions of years ago when superstition and magic were the customary explanations for everything, for context understand that at the same time this story was happening, Athens was reorganizing into a constitutional democracy. This is not about magic. Nebuchadnezzar's four feet were very firmly planted on the ground.

Fourth, the Book of Daniel was "written" in Aramaic, not Hebrew, and is one of only 4 places in which the odd Aramaic expression "son of god" appears, while the other three instances are in Job, which was written by a native Aramaic speaker. So this story may require a slightly different approach to interpretation than would be used elsewhere in the Old Testament.

Which brings us to fifth: when Daniel tells the King his forgotten dream, the King still can't remember it but *feels* like Daniel is right, which suggests that he hadn't merely forgotten the dream; it had been repressed. I know Nebuchadnezzar gives Daniel the credit for the making it reappear, but the real work was making it disappear.

Sixth, the whole problem of Act II of The Book of Daniel was that the King felt troubled by the dream, even though he couldn't remember it. Dreams don't cause anxiety, but they can be caused by anxiety. What made him anxious that resulted in a dream? What *wish* caused the anxiety that required its repression, that manifested as a dream that he immediately repressed *again*? Maybe that's too hard. Work backwards: what wish could a King who could have whatever he wanted need to repress, such that when it returned, it returned as *something that went forgotten*?

Forgetting is a last ditch attempt at hiding the dream from the possibility of conscious understanding when the distortions within the dream were not adequate. The dream was still too easy to interpret, so it was buried. But why not completely buried? Why not have no recollection at all of having dreamt? If what he wanted was so bad that he couldn't even bear to see it fulfilled in a dream, *why did he still ask someone to tell him what that was?*

Logically he turns to wise men. And now he's in trouble. If his assumption was that they *could* tell him what it meant, then it has to be true that he dreamt it knowing they could interpret it-- that they *could* know what it meant. *As a defense against that*, he forgot the dream. Now there was no way the wise men could interpret it correctly, and just in case he demanded that they do the impossible and tell him what it was; and double just in case, he ordered all of them executed. Immediately. Enter Daniel.

Daniel produces the dream and the interpretation. I mean that literally. Like a movie. He says it

```
a naval battle, but at exactly noon they abruptly sail back
to their shore, beach their boats, and camp until the next
day. This pattern repeats for the next few days. What's
your strategy?

        OEDIPUS:
Diplomatic signals. Clearly they don't want a full military
confrontation but likely have internal political pressures
from their more… masculoxic?-- constituents requiring
pointless shows of might, so as a sign of understanding I'd
equivalently beach our boats and camp in a place clearly
```

wasn't through any wisdom he possessed, but got the knowledge directly from God. The thing is... even if God did not *in fact* give Daniel the knowledge, it's possible Daniel could have figured out the interpretation, what it might have meant, from the telling of the dream, i.e., the kind of thing the King would need to forget. He could get at the latent wish by having the King free associate *about* not remembering the dream. But how could Daniel know the manifest content of the dream, the movie itself? The answer is that he didn't-- it wasn't the King's dream, it was Daniel's movie. Whatever dream the King actually had was disappeared forever, but Daniel constructed a formally parallel dream that the King confirmed, not because Daniel was right but because he was wrong. It was close enough and wrong enough that Nebuchadnezzar could disavow *the repression* of his own dream. In other words, Daniel's dream and the interpretation-- both-- were a new dream, the manifest content of the King's repressed, altered wish-- a distortion in the form of an interpretation-- that the King could use to defend against the latent content of his original wish-dream. To put it in Biblical terms: Daniel's "interpretation" ensured the King's wish went uninterpreted, which is what the King was really after. How do I know this? *Because the King was satisfied, and nothing changed.*

This is the interpretation Daniel gave Nebuchadnezzar, and for context Nebuchadnezzar's customary greeting was, "O King, live forever", here it is: Nebuchadnezzar's kingdom would fall. It would be replaced by another... and another... and another... and finally all earthly kingdoms would fall, replaced by God's everlasting kingdom. The King is so overjoyed by Daniel's insight that he falls to his knees and *worships him like a god.*

First of all, this dream sounds like a king's nightmare, and second of all, why would the interpretation of a dream so troubling that it needed to be repressed now make him-- happy? Because it was wrong.

The usual answer is that Daniel told Nebuchadnezzar that though his kingdom would eventually fall, his would be the greatest of all of them, until the coming of the Kingdom of God. But being the greatest isn't what the King cares about. What he cares about, what brought him such relief, was that his kingdom would fall, *period.* I know this is what he heard, what he wanted to hear, because of what he does next: he thanks/rewards/honors/*kneels before* Daniel for this interpretation, and then erects a gold idol *like the one in the dream* that he demands everyone worships. Well, what is that idol? Is it God? No. It is *literally* the end of his empire.

In year two of his reign what he is obligated to want is a kingdom that lasts forever; but he won't last forever, hence the anxiety. Not anxiety over his mortality, he is young after all, but that his kingdom might go on without him, might even be great without him; that one of his lazy sons or slutty wives will get all his money, forget where she got it, and live happily ever with all sorts of other phalluses. *He wants the kingdom to collapse after he dies.* It's certainly ok for us moderns not to give a damn about what happens to our world after we die, mostly in revenge for making us mad without power, but it was not at all ok for him not to care-- let alone to desire it. He is not allowed to want this, this wish is repressed. Daniel dreams him the way out: you're not sitting around wishing your kingdom would fall, you're paving the way for the Kingdom Of God. Of course that's what I want,

```
unsuitable for rapid redeployment.  It's about sending a
message.  Logically, as supplies on both sides dwindle no
one could be blamed for being obligated to negotiate, saving
face for both parties.

        SPHINX:
I love that your moral compass is locked on GPS.  The best
action is always no action.  Ok, why are the Athenians'
spears 8 feet long?

        OEDIPUS:
Wait, honestly, since you're asking the question, I'm sure
```

Nebuchadnezzar accepts, I'm a lion of the Lord, not an ox of the yoke. He never confronts his real wish; never has to adjust to it, because a bona fide prophet gave him the "correct" interpretation.

The dream was the manifestation of the fulfillment of the wish that his kingdom would fall, an entirely unacceptable desire, but so satisfying in its universal deprivation. Even if they dared not tell him, the wise men would have known this is what it meant, which was bad enough, but then he would have known they knew it, which was worse. So he forgot the dream. But it's not enough that he keep the dream a secret so that no one knows, because the wish still exists, it makes him anxious. It's so strong that even distortion as a dream is failing as a defense. So he has to be told by a master that the dream means something else. As much as it appears Daniel told him a lot of information about himself and his future, the knowledge didn't prompt any change; in fact, what he used it for was to guard against change. His repressed wish continues to drive him because it is protected by the interpretation. God's coming kingdom is a wonderfully useful wish to think you have, because you can postpone it indefinitely: just erect a different god, that everyone must worship. Count the successes: 1. His Kingdom will fall. 2. The Kingdom of God will replace it, but that hardly counts. 3. God is the one who promises his kingdom will fall, so if he then worships a different god, no one can say he wanted it.

Why was he so confident Daniel *wouldn't* know the meaning of the dream, that he let him try? Because Daniel was a nobody? 100% the opposite-- if he was a nobody, what he said wouldn't count. Daniel is described as already recognized to be wise and gifted, and when Nebuchadnezzar met him earlier he found him to be ten times better than any of the wise men. Yet the King didn't think to go to Daniel first-- or at all-- because then he might receive the correct interpretation. He only lets Daniel try to interpret it after Daniel approaches him, but now you have to take the story literally: Daniel approaches him not because Daniel wants to interpret the dream but explicitly because Daniel wants to save the lives of the wise men about to be executed. *Daniel's dream will have a different motive wish, and the dream will be the manifestation of the fulfillment of that wish. He will tell me exactly what I need to hear.*

The King spares the supposedly omniscient wise men because of this deal with Daniel. But why doesn't he still fire them? If he was executing them because they were useless, wouldn't they be even more useless now that he has Daniel? The wise men are omniscient, but Daniel is a prophet-- an oracle. Daniel has no knowledge of his own, it comes direct from God-- God *tells* him what's true. In fact, Daniel tells the King that God put the dream in the King's head. Be extremely careful here: does Nebuchadnezzar think this God *predicts* what will happen, or tells what He is going to *cause* to happen? This God is omnipotent. Those wise men have to stay alive because they still represent omniscience. Daniel tells the King what the dream *is*, and the wise men will tell him if the interpretation of *that* dream is correct. No, there's zero chance they are going to contradict Daniel. After all, they *know* better.

This binary of Daniel vs. the wise men isn't just a trivial juxtaposition; omniscience and omnipotence only work separately from, and in inverse relationship to, each other. Here's an example. The popular refrain that humanities grades are obviously inflated while math grades are

86

```
it's not as simple as balance or the material strength of
wood.   Let me think...  Since in a hoplite battle spears
are thrust, not thrown, the real answer is probably… small
penises?

          SPHINX:
Well done, I'm impressed by how you dig deep to deploy
empathy.  Radical prosocialism is about ennobling the answer
that is right for society and not tyrannizing society with
the right's answer.

          REX:
I very much want to... break down existing barriers?
```

---

more objective misses what the obviousness defends against: inflated or not, humanities grades are still *true*. The student has to believe they are true, even while simultaneously knowing the teacher can be fooled, manipulated; not fooled into saying something that is not true, but fooled into making something be true. Teachers have the power to grade you as an A, which means you are an A, to declare that you know, whereas a math teacher does not have this *power*-- even if he inflates the grade, he cannot change the truth about your math knowledge, he cannot make you have solved the equation correctly.   The point here is who has the power to tell you something is true; in the humanities it is the teacher, in math it is the math. But these two things are not separate, this only works because both subjects exist, this imbalance between subjective humanities grades AND objective math grades serves a *psychological* purpose; any *public* maneuvers to fix this imbalance actually serve the psychology.   E.g. attempts at standardizing the measurement of learning-- say, multiple choice tests-- have the exact opposite psychological effect than their stated purpose, on purpose: verbal scores do indeed fall because the "inflation" is reduced, but math scores *rise* because gaming standardized tests is easier than math.   The result of the *combination* of school grades and standardized tests is that it becomes true that a student is better at humanities than evidenced by the standardized test; but the standardized test indicates one's math knowledge is higher than their grades seem to show.   "I admit I'm a little lazy, but my math teacher sucks at teaching."   You mean grading.

Here's another example.   Coincidentally-- does that word mean what I think it means?-- while one god was saving Daniel from being burned alive by the King, another god was saving another King from being burned alive, though in the latter case it was the god who had sent him to be burned in the first place. Meanwhile, across the sea and after a job well done, old man Solon becomes the first Athenian to be ostracized but the only Athenian to have ostracized himself. Yes, I know what ostracism means, but I also know what it is for. It might seem like an unfair and primitive custom, but the usual alternative to casting pieces of clay against a person who we agree doesn't deserve it is throwing pieces of clay at a guy who therefore does. Solon is passing through the land of Lydia, and King Croesus invites him to the palace, and with wrinkled lip and sneer of cold command asks him who the happiest man on earth is. The adjective is important. Not the greatest, not the richest, not the one with the hottest wife-- the happiest. You can ask why Croesus thought Solon would know, but rather than the answer being that Solon was renown for being wise, the correct answer is that Croesus thought he could fool him into saying something everyone else would have to believe. The pattern will become clear later. Croesus nominally may want money, he may say he wants power, but it is clear down to his DNA that the only thing that can satisfy him is making sure others are deprived, or at least envious. Solon is not fooled by any of this. If you are almost single handedly responsible for the force vector of the next three millennia of western civilization you do not need to suffer fools gladly, lightly, or at all; so Solon tells him the names of three happiest guys no one has ever heard of and explains they all had lives well lived, and died honorable deaths. Croesus concludes he's a lunatic. Solon, unaware of what was happening back in Athens but sagely aware that in Athens anything can happen, tried to explain it using statistics and actuarial tables but failing that, finally summarizes:

```
                SPHINX:
We think you're a good person to get the best people the
concrete they need to erect better ones.  Assuming you get
this position, do you think you can be the King and
impregnate the Queen?  We'll need at least two sons for a
sibling rivalry.

                OEDIPUS:
Well, what's she... like?

                SPHINX:
```
_____

Our human life I think, and have thought, a mere shadow. Of the
mortals there is no one who is happy. If wealth comes to one he may
be perhaps luckier than another. But not happy.

Or, if you want a pithy quote to use as a caption, take it from *Oedipus*: count no man happy until his death, for no one can know what the gods have in store for him.

So Croesus does what any good tyrant would do, which is go to the Delphic Oracle and ask if it knows what the gods have in store for him. What he thinks is omniscient replies: "If you go to war, you will destroy a great kingdom." Armed with this information, soldiers, and the best   horses in the world he invades Persia, but, surprise, the Persian cavalry uses camels, proving that no one ever goes bankrupt in an arms race, except the losers. I'm sure someone in 547 BC told the Persian king that a camel cavalry was an unnecessary expense because they were already the dominant superpower, and I hope that person had the dignity to punch himself in the face a year later. I'm sure he didn't. Anyway. Anyway the Persians capture Croesus and set up his execution, and as he was tied to his funeral pyre he must have been wondering why the hell did he ever listen to the Delphic Oracle, because his last words were: Solon, Solon, why the hell didn't I listen to you?

In one version of the story Apollo comes down and stops the execution, but as this likely didn't happen because Apollo is a jerk I favor the other version: the Persian King stops the execution and asks, "wait, who's Solon, and is he a guy I should listen to?"

So Croesus tells the tale, and when he explains what convinced him that invading Persia was a good idea, he says that the Oracle mislead him. Think about that. Not that the Oracle was wrong, not that it couldn't possibly know the future, not that it gave a deliberately ambivalent prophecy that could appear correct no matter what happened-- it *mislead him on purpose*. Does that sound like he now thinks the Oracle is omniscient or omnipotent? But when out of curiosity the Persian king releases Croesus to go back and confront the Oracle, first she tries the usual dodge about not asking the right question, then finally says he was fated to lose the war because he's paying for the guilt of one of his ancestors. And when Croesus heard it... he accepted it. Do you think it's because he felt guilty? As if he thinks the Oracle *knows* something?   No. Observe that our knowledge of this episode, not the myth but the history itself, includes the Oracle: being the fulfillment of a prophecy is a lot better than being the one who stupidly starts a war for the stupidest of reasons, and then loses it because even his horses are stupid.

"What had his ancestor done?" It's a long story and you wouldn't believe it.

A dreamer in analysis assumes the analyst knows what the dream will mean. Of course, the analyst might not know. But by allowing-- encouraging-- the belief that he, the analyst, is the person who absolutely would know *but doesn't tell it*, the dreamer can act on it. The dreamer might never know what it meant, but something changes. You may find yourself tonight having a dream and thinking, I wonder what the author of this odd book on pornography would think of my dream? *He would know what it means*. And by knowing that I know what it means, you could begin to suspect some

```
Does that matter?

          OEDIPUS:
No, no, of course not, I'm not brainwashed by traditional
beauty hierarchies, women should have the privilege of
conforming to them as if it was a choice.  I'm committed to
impregnating anyone on my team equally.

          SPHINX:
You're just the kind of old school plug and play device we
need.  Welcome to Thebes.
```

It's not canon but it is pretty accurate. 16 years on the job without a single test led him

---

of what it means because its meaning is knowable-- and you will act.   And the reason you think I would know what it meant is that you dreamt it with me in mind. But if I *told* you what it meant, even on the outside chance I was dead on, you would hear it whatever perverted way you needed to but attribute that meaning to me, you would use my authority to defend against the true interpretation. You would be much more satisfied, consider me a genius, and everyone else would be miserable. The analysis failed, but the therapy was a big success. That'll be $500, please.

Unfortunately, Fink here doesn't act as the guy who knows the secret-- he becomes the guy who tells the secret. He moves from omniscience to omnipotence. He tells the patient his interpretation was correct. He gives him knowledge. He agrees with him. He accepts the analysand's interpretation at face value instead of making him wonder if this isn't precisely what he-- well, both of them-- wanted to hear. This is a dream: where is the repressed wish? The wish to be published is hardly an unconscious wish, the wish to be as good as the analyst couldn't be more conscious, and anyway dreams aren't wishes, they are the manifestation of the *fulfillment* of the wish, which is often found in the form, not just the contents: "...the vague sense that in the dream he was looking for his works." The works aren't the wish fulfillment; *looking* for his works is the wish fulfillment. Well, what are the works of Chrysippus? He got raped by Laius, that's something, I guess. Fink is Laius, safely dreamed as Aristotle; the patient is a victim of=seeking castration, used for someone else's satisfaction, safely dreamed as a great Stoic who went tragically under-celebrated-- except by people in the know. Not coincidentally, and this is something the analysand would have known, the works of the Stoic Chrysippus have evaporated, but they were so full of quotes and excerpts from other writers that if you took those out, Chrysippus's works would have evaporated.

Through this dream, the patient is accusing Fink of something that is demonstrably true for him: Fink isn't getting the analysand to change, to act; he's giving him knowledge, concrete, useless, awe-inspiring knowledge-- and then using him for his own satisfaction, e.g. not i.e. as a case history in a book. Fink decrees that the patient "secretly" and understandably wants to be like Fink. What if he's wrong? Consider that if, in the dream, the patient is Chrysippus the boy and not Chrysippus the student of Aristotle, then the person telling the patient that it's perfectly natural to be envious of him is *Laius*. Guess what happens next.

Fink allows this to become a rivalry between two people, and not a structural conflict within the analysand's unconscious against a set of forms or principles-- the system-- that he projects onto the analyst that are the basis of his struggle-- and I know this is what happened because Fink, the analyst, *calls* it a rivalry. Fink accepts it as *natural* that the analysand would have some competitive feelings, instead of having the analysand question *why* that would be natural, *why* he feels he needs to compete-- *who* wants him to compete? Whose interests does that serve? And the analysand couldn't be happier with Fink's=his interpretation (i.e. it is not a threat)-- he supplicates, "if not better!" and then right there in the paragraph rewards Fink with a thank you gift-- the gift of babbling more about his interesting thoughts and wishes-- i.e. what he believes that analyst wants from him. Nor does Fink bring the analysand to wonder why the analysand's gratitude is expressed not in certain ways (money, referrals, Christmas rum) but in gifts of *himself*.   Yes, this is an anal

to believe he deserved his success, he got it on his merits. "I have knowledge!" You're retarded. I mean that literally. I mean a lot of things literally. What his kindergarten brain didn't ask was: why me? Seriously, why would they pick me? Nor did it occur to this *wise King* to research the history of his city, the outcomes of his predecessors; not an instant of neurotic self-doubt, imposter syndrome, a moment wondering if it wasn't all too easy. Too bad, it would have helped. If true power went by birthright it would have stayed with Creon, but hmm, let's give the kingdom to this drifter like nowhere never before in history, and he took the lack of dissent as a confirming his ascent. "But why should there be dissent? Look at all I've done!" I am looking: what have you done? Which means the They who gave him that power are the ones with the actual power and they wanted a person who was too stupid to

---

joke.

The patient *wants* this to be a rivalry. Fink lets it be. It isn't. Look at the structure: what is the analysand acting like in Fink's two last sentences? An evenly, or even unevenly, matched man in competition with a rival? Or a woman who wants to be desired?

You might counter that the analyst is merely agreeing that the analysand's perception is that there is a rivalry-- not that there is a rivalry in reality. *But that's exactly what a rivalry is.* Change "being published" to "fighting over a girl" and the nature of rivalry is revealed: in any rivalry, only one of them thinks of it as a rivalry; the other thinks of it as a fait accompli.

Instead of thinking as a rivalry as a competition over a valuable trophy, look at it from the perspective of the trophy: it has value only because of the rivalry. This is why you rarely have a sexual fantasy about two equally matched dominant males fighting over a woman unless it is a female's fantasy: now the trophy must logically be valuable. There is no such thing as a love triangle, the two suitors each love a different person. The allure of those stories is that the woman is loved in two different ways-- she gets to decide not which man she likes but what kind of a person she wants to be. The men in these stories do not get this choice, they can't need it: they have to already be a kind of person. You still with me? Hang on: the reason she fantasizes about these kinds of men is because she can't find any such men in real life. Only in fantasy.

It's a modern innovation that the winner gets to keep (a replica of) the trophy, as if it was now his, as if it was valuable. And there was a time/movie when trophy wives... were replicas. Though to be correct I should say: unless she was a replica, she wasn't useful as a trophy. That kind of changes things. Long before that a single trophy would be passed around to that season's winner, up for grabs the next season. The man with a trophy wife wasn't showing he won, she is always up for grabs, having her by his side means he continues to defeat everyone. Did she know it?

[1.105] But in the original trophy days, trophies weren't prizes but merely markers of a battle: it was enough that the men were still alive and the women and children not sold into slavery. Trophies were valuable as markers when the battle was close-- when it could easily have gone the other way. Sometimes the trophy is misleading-- it leads you wrong. In 457 the Spartans defeat 14000 Athenians, hooray, and while they were setting up the trophy and heading back home otherwise empty handed, the losers were off conquering everything else.

No matter how hot the trophy, the rivalry fantasy isn't about the trophy, but what it looks like when one person deprives another. The trophy isn't merely an excuse to deprive the other, the trophy is a tool used for that purpose. The trophy's sex appeal is a necessary defensive addition after the fact, to make it appear that the motivating force is love or lust. But it isn't. It's resentment, rage. In case you can't work out the consequences, I will give you an important one that is always understood backwards, especially in porn: only the person who doesn't see it as a rivalry-- i.e. the rival-- actually values the thing/person that is the trophy because he isn't motivated by the rivalry, he actually wants the thing. The former wants to destroy the rival and can only act on that desire if it is

know his only job was to be living proof of that fact. "I was chosen by *the gods*!" Keep telling yourself that, and also everybody else, it's what we're paying you for.

"I think your explanation is anachronistic." You know what's anachronistic? The title *Oedipus Rex*. In the original Greek he's *tyrannos* which is also anachronistic since the word tyrannos wasn't invented until 1000 years after Oedipus lived. It doesn't mean king, there were plenty of other words Sophocles could have used that meant king, including, for example, the actual word king. So? One way to avoid having to think about this is to quickly translate it to the innocuous Latin, and then make Rex his last name. "That's not what it means." Really? Caesar made the same mistake, good company I guess, you can understand why we both made it: Rex was a pejorative, being a Rex was a bad thing, kind of like being

---

for something else, like a trophy. Hence the trophy won't satisfy him, should he get the trophy, he will soon not want it.

Just as the prize appears to be valuable but merely stands as pretext for battle, neither is the "better" rival to be taken as a secret aspirational self-image or "repressed homosexuality." It's not his big dick or his muscles that make the rival enviable or powerful. Nor is it his power over women. It is that he can enjoy, he can act on what he wants. Nothing compels him. He wants e.g. women, but women do not compel him to want them. He can say no to them, he doesn't appear to care what they want. The rival appears to be able to pursue a woman (=the world) for his own satisfaction-- but worse, she (=the world) appears to be satisfied by that. Therefore, the rival has to be shown winning, if not at the end then at minimum at first; the rival is hope: free me from my dependency, free me from having to be depended on. You will not believe this but it is true: win a thousand trophies and you will not be satisfied, they will not count. Let a rival beat you, take what's yours, so completely that even former friends rejoice at your humiliation-- and you may hate him but you will worship him like a god.

The fantasy that the sexist bully beats up the loving husband and takes his wife seems like the husband values the wife more than the bully who merely wants to use her for sex, but this is wrong: the fantasy is that the rival wants her, which makes her valuable to him. "You mean he wishes he had a wife so hot a rival would want her?" No. How she looks doesn't matter. In order for her to be valuable, the rival has to want her. And because he-- the husband-- does not love her the only thing he can imagine a rival would want of her is that she is hot. "But in these fantasies he loses to the rival." But in real life he's still with her. The fantasy is to lose. *Now he's free from dependency.*

So here's another consequence that may change the divorce settlement: the bully wants the wife and values her more than the husband does, even if in the fantasy he calls her a slut or uses her just for sex. In other words, if at the end of the *fantasy* she leaves the husband for the bully, it's not because he thinks she likes the bully more, it's because... he thinks the bully likes her more.

You will counter that many women are idiots and leave their husbands for all sorts of bananastown reasons; but that's on them. If it's your fantasy-- if you understand the world in terms of rivalries-- it's on you.

It's not easy to think of sexual fantasies in this way, because you have been taught to search for their "meaning." Why were you taught to do that? In this pursuit of knowledge you are safely misdirected from how they are used. In many versions of these slutwife stories, the cheating wife and loser husband end the story in a form of stalemate: she stays with him, maybe they even still have sex, but she isn't satisfied by him (e.g. "your dick is too small")-- so from then on she goes and gets her satisfaction elsewhere. This sounds like he's a humiliated wimp, but never underestimate the ingenuity of envy masking itself so it can be indulged. You may want to read this carefully, in the age of double/triple interpretations and hidden meanings, you have to read this in the language of fantasy, i.e. literally: she can *only* get her satisfaction elsewhere-- her husband can't (=won't) satisfy her. Having a smaller dick doesn't sound like much of a fantasy, but it's a

91

a... tyrant, and so here we have a situation where the original word "tyrannos" looks like tyrant but doesn't mean that, so to avoid that implication they changed it to the Latin word Rex, which no one remembers does imply tyrant, and there you go: the repressed always returns. Later they printed a new edition with an English title, *Oedipus The King*, which is flat out denial. But what does tyrannos mean? Mind made of cheese? Does it mean that he's greedy? Cruel? A dictator? That he took away everyone's power? Does it mean he will try to establish a dynasty-- and fail? Does it mean he will pretend to favor the common people because they are no threat? These things may be true, but the only thing that is axiomatic is that the tyrant's reign exists to keep himself tyrant-- at any expense, even at his own expense. But Oedipus doesn't want to be a tyrant, he wants to be anointed king. Yet his reign could

---

magnificent one if she must depend on it. Why should she get the house and your income and also *satisfaction* from you? Is she satisfying you? Doesn't seem fair, the ledger is unbalanced. If some random woman wants to have sex with you, of course you'll try and satisfy her-- that's a fair trade, tit for fat. But the women in your life-- "you know what I mean"-- scheme to get the ledger unbalanced in their favor. So the rage gets masked as a sexual fantasy and you imagine that she can only get full satisfaction with other people-- which means, in real life she isn't satisfied. Ledger balanced. Her fantasy orgasms show you just how very much she is deprived of by staying with you in real life, and it makes you cum so hard.

"I just can't imagine that I get off on the fantasy of depriving my wife." You have it backwards, it's not meaning, it's utility. The *reality* is you deprive your wife of love *already*, the fantasy lets you get away with it because now she *appears* satisfied and desired. It's such a vicious logic that you prefer to think it means you're a wimp. "No, you're wrong-- wanting to deprive my wife? It doesn't feel right to me." Huh? Of course it doesn't feel right-- did you expect to feel a weird sense of a ha? Self-realization? The uncanny shift of the unconscious becoming conscious? Of learning something about yourself, of becoming wiser? Better? You will never feel that except when you are lying, you are too well guarded by the pretense of introspection, knowledge, acknowledgement of your faults, openness to the criticism. But ask your wife, ask everyone else around you, if they think it is true that you derive not happiness or pleasure but satisfaction from the deprivation of others that you envy. "I guess it's true that, on some level, I do envy my rivals." HA! Even now you lie.

Fink's analysand wants to see things in terms of rivalries, he sees the number of publications as an important metric. *But the reason he is in analysis-- the reason he is flat on his back with a man he doesn't know-- is because he feels disconnected from these measures of value.* And the reason the analysis takes so long is that he thinks what he needs is *knowledge.* "If only I knew more about myself!" Then what? What good would that do-- your spouse? Your kids? Publishing more is an appropriate thing he (thinks he) wants, but it isn't what satisfies him because it isn't valuable to him. It isn't valuable to anyone. But he thinks it is supposed to be. What (he thinks) Fink confirms is a rivalry is actually something else; or: the reason he can't make any forward progress is that he changes his battles (with Fink's blessing) to be at the level of imaginary rivalries over things that are likely worthless. You might ask what this is if it is not a rivalry, as if seeing it as a rivalry was simply a mistake or error in judgment, as if what he needs is to be told which is the real dragon he needs to slay. This is false. There is no dragon. Even if there was, he couldn't fight it. He can't do anything. Seeing it as a rivalry is his defense against impotence.

Here's a real world example: some salarymen were having an argument with one guy who had accumulated far too many vacation days than he could actually use. Is he going to take two months off a year? Every Monday and Tuesday off for half a year? This is still America, productivity matters. The problem was that everyone covered for each other on vacations, i.e. his days off meant more work for them.

What *didn't* happen was that the employees took it to management. He didn't request to get cash for the vacation days; neither did management relieve the burden on the other staff by hiring a temp. It

have been legitimate, he could have been a King-- he actually was the heir to the throne. And the hubris that is supposed to exist in tragedy that is otherwise missing from the play-- misidentified as "arrogance about his knowledge" or "he loses his temper" (it's a sign of the times how merely being angry is today elevated to the status of crime)-- is that Oedipus wanted to believe he *earned* the job, that he deserved it, so didn't need to do anything to deserve it. And you say, why on earth would his people go along with this, why would they want a tyrant? Because they weren't going to do anything anyway, now everything that happens could only be his fault.

I wasted so much time trying to understand what psychoanalysis meant, when I should have taken it all literally and observed how it was used.

---

played out entirely as a perceived rivalry among semi-equals, not a structural conflict between labor and management. Like all rivalries, it got heated, and it got personal.

You should take special note of three things: first, the one with the fewest resources who can least afford to make the sacrifice is set up by design to be the one to make the sacrifice because his loss is least disruptive to the status quo. Second: the company not only lost nothing in the argument, it was protected from being involved in the argument *by the people suffering*; amongst the rivals, taking the vacation days became about the guy's "work ethic" and "being part of a team." Third: the vacation days problem was *already* going to be a problem in advance, even before he had accumulated them. It was a structural problem, it was built into how vacation days were handled. It may as well have said on his contract: "You can accrue up to eight weeks of vacation days, but you're going to have to give them up. Proudly."

You can say this is "systemic exploitation of labor by the capitalist", slyly exploiting the word exploitation, but that phrase is conventional wisdom, they all knew all of these words, yet the only exploitation anyone perceived was that the one guy was going to exploit the other guys if he took his earned vacation days, or that the other guys were going to exploit him into giving them up for free. Why did they see it this way? The answer is that they had already been taught to think in terms of high school, i.e. rivalries between powerless semi-equals, and not in terms of structural conflicts. How? By teaching them that the system cannot be changed. Your father/the system is so crazy, so incomprehensible, so inaccessible that it's not worth involving him; but your brother? That guy's a jerk. Your indignation, it seems, is more excited by a legal wrong than a violent wrong, because the former looks like you were cheated by an equal and the second like you were compelled by a superior.

Why can't the system be changed? The wrong answer is that rivalries between semi-equals are easier fights than structural "Oedipal" conflicts because attacking the system is too dangerous for a lowly individual. No. This fear is not the explanation for inaction, it is the defense against action. The real reason you don't attack Dad isn't that he could kill you, but that you might kill him. He is the only Dad you have, he is the only one keeping order-- he is the order-- you need him for status quo, however bad status quo is.

"What does it mean that he is 'the order'?" He is the only one with the power to say yes to himself and say no to others. "My mom was very strict, she told us no all the time." Did you listen? "She'd beat us with meat tenderizers when we didn't." So you didn't. "Are you saying only men have the power of no?" I'm saying everyone can be omniscient, but only one entity at a time can be omnipotent. A dog cannot serve two masters-- at the same time.

That corporate power is the real power in America is a cliché, but this is not here the point: the point is that it is your desired form of power. The person embroiled in rivalries does not believe in the power of self-control, of individual control; not that it isn't effective but that it does not exist. How could it? If "personal morality" isn't keeping themselves in check, it for sure won't keep "the average person" in check (they closely follow the media, they keep an eye on what people= "they"

The key to change today is not to know consciously, it never works, we are all too clever and the defense exploits our self-aggrandizing self-criticism; "consciously" is the realm of universities and news networks all who want us to give up on belief and follow the leader out of rational choice-- as if such a thing was possible in a world with universities and news networks. Rational? We'll take just enough responsibility to become a voter or a cutter but no one is popping out their eyeballs, not today, not when everything comes in through the eyeballs. You cannot make the unconscious conscious anymore, it's impossible, all you can do is identify the return of the repressed. "I don't know why I'm afraid of spiders, but they freak me out. What does it mean?" Got me; problem solved. "But wait a second, stupid, I'm still afraid of spiders." No, stupid, that's not the problem, it's the defense.[10] "So it's an evolutionary mechanism to keep us away from poisonous spiders?" It's possible we are still at

---

are doing, and it's always bad). Self-control is the main element of self-respect, and self-respect is the main element in courage, and so we live with perpetual anxiety, and a bunker mentality. Real life Dad is totally unreliable/out of touch/impotent; and the legal system is easily manipulated (by everyone but you); the "democracy" seems dangerously in the hands of the 50% of people who are not you. The only formal constraints on behavior that everyone ALWAYS abides by are corporate, you can't go against HR, and unless you are famous nothing else will recognize you as an important, the corporation has to be protected. Of course you'll complain about it, vocal posturing as a freethinker (using their jargon) is adequate compensation, but something has to have all the power in order for no one else to have any and for you to derive satisfaction from stealing little bits back from it. Corporate power doesn't want to encroach on every day life: corporate power *has* to be extended, by you-- not it, but you-- into every day life because no other power is reliable. How many fathers threaten their kids, "that kind of behavior won't fly in the corporate world!" Fathers! So much for the tyranny of the patriarchy. These are personalities of people who don't want the power themselves, they prefer to be child-like in their interests, and also don't want anyone else to have it; they want one entity to be omnipotent, as long as it's nobody they know personally.

One might think that this is all a clever trick of capitalism, keeping conflicts at the level of rivalries, but the very fact that you figured it out means it isn't. Never mind what capitalism wants; what do you want? The fall of the USSR may have revealed the fundamental contradictions inherent in socialism, but when the ideological mushroom cloud imploded all the spores floated to the nutrient rich environment of capitalism. Now everyone is a socialist, including capitalists. "We are in LATE STAGE CAPITALISM." The capitals are theirs, because the capital is not. And they couldn't be more wrong. It's easy money to say that capitalism has so fundamentally structured our thinking that we can only imagine some form of it continuing, we lack the ability to imagine an alternative to capitalism, but I'm going to take the other side: *no one* imagines capitalism continuing; and the only alternative people have the ability to imagine is socialism. It's all anybody sees in media. It's not even abstract ideology anymore, it's pornography.

And we should really be clear about what kind of socialism we're able to imagine. The interesting thing about pop-mo socialists is how sure they are that Marx was right yet have never read Marx. You would think someone who considers himself even left of right would have at least read The Communist Manifesto. Yet look how much time they put into reading the secondary sources about or derived from Marx. That's not intellectual laziness, it's also the history of Christianity, and science; it is disavowal in order to be told what to believe. Now that you've already agreed with the glossy, seductive, poorly reasoned sophistry of whatever secondary text or article you're proud to say you read, the primary sources are a threat-- what if it's not so simple? What if they're boring? What if they tell you something else? What if it says you don't actually stand to benefit the way you were promised, e.g. and i.e., what if the other doesn't stand to lose the way you were promised? The study of Marx interferes with the use of Marx.

The superficiality of their understanding is not because they are too lazy to learn about the "problem of class struggle" but because for them class struggle isn't the problem, it is the defense. This next

94

the mercy of redundant manifestations of evolutionary processes, but the other possibility is that when we inherit a powerful and reliable way of avoiding spiders, we would use it to locate spiders everywhere and just in time, e.g. on your math homework or right before bed, now you have to watch TV or at least have another drink. "I'm self medicating an anxiety disorder." You have said it.

"My problem is I can't sleep." Turn off the TV. "I've tried that, doesn't work." So you went back to TV? "I've even tried reading." Captions don't count as reading. "My brain won't slow down, I think too much." Ok, now you're just making things up. "Ha ha, but it's true, my mind gets all tangled up in obsessive knots, ruminating about things I have no control

---

sentence will make no sense at all unless you imagine an open ledger or a midterm exam: reading Marx is not knowledge, reading about Marx is knowledge. Marx can't be an authority, but an authority can tell you about Marx. The first is theory; the second is knowledge. "Knowledge is power." Not according to Marx. You can use knowledge as a defense against impotence, but it doesn't work against omnipotence. Not when it has spears.

It's the same with Darwin, Darwinism is certainly packaged as this great war between science and religion, but the fanatical rage evident in both sides, each of which got a curved C in biochem if they took it at all pretty much guarantees Darwinism isn't science, it's hate. "Are you one of those crazies who thinks evolution isn't true?" Of course it's true. It just doesn't matter to you whether it is.

You study Marxism-- the secondary sources-- because there's safety in numbers, you may not know all the details but the fact that someone else must means your life experience is the result of a structural conflict, even if you can't really explain it. We did this with Freud, all you have to do is incorporate the jargon into the vernacular and you won't be able to see it any other way but just as importantly you won't have to see it his way either. It becomes-- obvious. And your envy, the satisfaction you derive from depriving others, is hidden from you, you go from being an oppressor to being oppressed, and if you doubt this ask yourself what Marx himself would make of your Marxism. Not just whether he thinks you got it wrong: would he feel-- used? Like you reduced him to the part that satisfied you, while obliterating the rest of him?

Here is a basic rivalry among semi-equals that pretends to be a structural conflict. That the "capitalist" they hate is more like them than unlike them, that their rage comes not from being less powerful than others but from a perceived illogical mismatch between their own knowledge and power-- how much they think they know vs. how little power they have; that it comes from an envy of their neighbor's power to act out of proportion to how much that jerk appears to know-- requires a structural understanding of the problem, because otherwise it's a psychological problem. That's why what looks to be hypocritical (touting the corporate line while calling for the beheading of the suits) is sweetly hypercritical: the goal isn't to end capitalism (and god knows not consumerism, especially since it's been rebranded experientialism), or to gain power, the whole point is to deprive someone of power. Persecutors always believe in the excellence of their cause, but in reality they hate without a cause. The cause is secondary, which ideology you adhere to is incidental, only ideological purity matters. In one case it imagines the rival (a capitalist) is unfairly hyperdominant and advantaged relative to his knowledge-- it shrouds a basic, one-sided, envy and rage driven rivalry among semi-equals into a structural conflict-- the wrong structural conflict, the one that doesn't actually have any meaning over them. "The reason he gets paid more than me is because he's a man." Maybe the reason he gets paid more than you is that he wouldn't settle for less. "I'm just explaining why, in this society, a man gets paid more than a woman." Why would you think this society wants to pay anyone more?

So it is with the proletariat, they are the idealized prize, so they have no value to you; they are only valuable because of the rivalry with the capitalists. Ironically, only one of you even perceives this as a rivalry; the rival sees it as fait accompli. In fact, if you take this to the end, the only person who

over." The wish fulfillment of an ox is to be tied to a plough, because it's better than being slaughtered for someone else's enjoyment.

What does reading *Oedipus* "through" Freud defend against? You have to wonder why so many people went all in on the Oedipus Complex despite it sounding more bananas than black bile or demonic possession. "King Oedipus, who slew his father Laius and married his mother Jocasta, merely shows us the fulfillment of our own childhood fantasies." --Yes! the people cried, which is to be translated: Phew! We fantasize about our mothers!

Look at the 20th century's materialists, they were *relieved*: someone had saved them from Sophocles.

---

actually values the prize is... "The reason she's not with me is that that guy buys her whatever she wants." Maybe the reason she's not with you is that you don't think she's worth the money. "I'm just explaining why, in this society, women want that kind of man." Why would you think she should settle for less?

That you are in a rivalry dressed up as a structural conflict can be revealed by simply asking: what do you want? For the secondary sources ideologist with all the knowledge necessary to answer-- he can't. I don't mean provide a well thought out, internally consistent philosophy, I mean he cannot say an answer to the basic question in any story: what does the main character want? "To make the world better. To promote equality." But those aren't answers, those are other people's captions.

With the reliability of a cuckoo clock in hell, he only knows that he wants to take power away from "capitalists"; then, he will try to "do what's necessary." But since this is an envy/rage rivalry that pretends it is structural as a defense, the true problem for the socialist-- not socialism, but the socialist-- is specifically that they don't want power. Neither can they directly act to get it (inability to act is the very problem) and any indirect passive attempts always deflect on approach. It's simply not what he wants. He'll only be satisfied by the deprivation of the other. I know, the mild mannered sociology professor will deny he masturbates to pictures of the guillotine, but that's only because on his screen they appear as MILFs. When they describe the utopia of their fantasies in which the capitalists lose their power, but critical questioning fails to elicit any further concrete details, you should take them at their word: their utopia is only that the other is deprived. Do they fantasize they will take the power? No. If by accident they get it they will not want it, they will push it up the party until something else-- some other omnipotent entity-- takes it. When their answer to what they want is an ideology, they will only be satisfied by a tyranny, even at their own expense. A benevolent one, whatever, but as long as it makes sure the rival is losing his power. Not has no power, not lost his power-- zero isn't satisfying, not past tense but present participle-- a continuously decreasing function. Whatever the cost to you, it will have been worth it.

And you'll pay good money to learn to see things in a way that placates your impotence with knowledge, e.g. college, e.g. science journalism, e.g. therapy. Fink's patient paid for the chance to turn an analysis into a therapy. Rather than prompting the patient to question the authority of the system to tell him how to want ("why do I think publishing is valuable when... it isn't valuable to me, only to them?") Fink takes the external authority as a valuable given and fosters a rivalry. Let me be as clear as possible: I don't think Fink wanted to do that, would do that, or perhaps even did do that. But capitalism is hyperefficient, it doesn't give you what you want or need, only what you're willing to pay for.

It looks like an analysis because the patient is on a couch free associating. But what year is it? Nowadays you can't stop at the level of the free association-- after all, the analysand already knows that gimmick, he is prepared for it, he is armor plated-- he can even weaponize it as a defense. The only way through is to provoke him: "I'm flattered that Chrysippus/Aristotle is the kind of association you would expect I was sophisticated enough to expect."

96

If you were to film the movie *Oedipus Rex*, would you make Jocasta hot, or not? Think about it, because the way it actually happened was that she was not hot: late 40s, five kids, Greek. Boy am I going to get in a lot of trouble for that one. But no one in America is going to see a movie where Jocasta looks like their mom, she has to look like someone else's mom, get it? She has to be a MILF. Not blatantly MILFy, you'd lose the white wine and wellness demographic; you want an actress whose sex is well known from earlier movies, and then class her up a bit and repress the rest. Don't worry men, that erotic desire will return in a different form, as its power and gender opposite: a steroid chiseled Oedipus, hairless and thickly flaccid, he's not there to act, he's there to be looked at; as the go-to signifier for masculinity, he causes her to be the signifier for femininity. Or did you think they wanted to film him with an erect penis but-- weren't allowed to?

The effect would be immediate: "hold, on, I know what you're thinking, but I am most emphatically not talking about that *other* Chrysippus...." Yes, that's the problem. Want to talk about it?

Another example from the same book not two pages later, another patient relates this dream:

> He was in a store after closing and had the sense that two other men were there, both from *2001: A Space Odyssey*. He turned and saw Darth Vader, who had killed the other two men. (It must, he said while recounting the dream, be *Star Wars*, not *2001*.) Darth Vader said he was going to kill the analysand, who stalled for time, saying he had to go to the bathroom. Darth Vader followed him into the bathroom; as he went to the urinal, he heard Darth Vader draw a gun, and then felt it on the back of his neck. Suddenly he had the sense that he had been shot in the back of his head, and he wondered why he did not hear it. "If I had, I'd be dead," he reasoned...

> ...The whole key to *Star Wars*, he said, is that Darth Vader is Luke Skywalker's father; the dream, he continued, was about how you survive in the world after you have been killed by your father.

Come up with that all by yourself, did you?

Let's agree that this patient has some trouble wielding his penis, by which I mean phallus, by which I mean the willingness to be what the other person wants, maybe that's power, and etc and etc and etc. The contents/images might have no symbolic meaning, sometimes they are used as logical connections: penis ↔ bathroom urinal ↔ stall for time. He certainly wasn't using his penis for his pleasure, let alone for hers.

Here you have a dream in all of its defensive splendor, it is so magnificent I wish Fink had simply made it up (because, if you care about such things, this dream and the Chrysippus dream, though ostensibly dreamt by different people, are both used by Fink for the same purpose; and the juxtaposition of these two dreams is very similar to Lacan's explanation of Kris vs. the "fresh brains" patient. Anyhoo.) The *feeling* of the dream is delay, resistance, it is the creation of an obvious crisis to avoid the truly dangerous conflict, it is stasis. The analysand delays confrontation with Darth Vader, who wants to kill him. How to delay? If you're 5, or impotent, now would be the time to pee. (That's almost not a joke, later on in the dream he is invisible and he pees in a toilet, which Conan O'Brien's (yeah) wife notices, and he is "jubilant" because "I'm having an effect on the world after all!" Then he invisibly grabs her boobs and she giggles and he wakes up, I should point out thus avoiding having to figure out she might want from him next. Yes, the Phallus is strong with this one. This is not in any way an insult but Conan's wife has very small boobs, which hardly matters as at the time of the dream Conan didn't have a wife. Guess he's not having much of an effect after all.

So you should watch your *Oedipenis* movie carefully, because it depicts Oedipus getting something... the audience wants. And now no *Oedipus* after Freud can be honest: they all exist in reaction to Freud's explanation; they are fully conscious of its "repressed" meaning. They know the audience knows the "real" story, they give them what they want. *Oedipus* thus can no longer stage a hidden psychological truth but instead the pornographization of pity into lust and fear into anxiety; the lust is a screen, but the anxiety never lies. Two logical consequences: 1) *Oedipus Rex* no longer functions as art, see above; 2) no one is interested in it. "Guy wants to sleep with his mom, what's the big deal anymore if she's super hot?" Fair enough, but if you want to reperfuse your dried sea sponge heart take an hour and ponder why you think her being hot logically explains why she'd want to sleep with him. Don't look at

---

The dream is *on purpose* interesting, linear, amenable to substitutive symbolic interpretation. It begs you to figure out what it means. Don't fall for it. Why should you? We are all well practiced liars.

He-- and you-- probably want to know what the dream means, but finding out what it means won't change you because your problem *is* that you want to know what it means-- so you don't have to change. That desire to know is why he wants to be on the couch-- but his impotence is why he *needs* to be on the couch. True change in this conventional wisdom Oedipality is only going to happen by frustrating his desire, in this case to know; and making him wonder if the most laudable and splendid of his desires-- to learn more about himself, or the world-- is *bad*, 100% a defense against change.

And where do you begin this dream analysis? Are you tempted to start with Darth Vader? As if it was-- obvious?

The way into any interpretation is the *form* of the dream. The money is in the *mistake*, the parentheses are the clue-- it is the tell, the mind's hastily appended revision when you've said too much and it's too late to say you forgot. The correction of *2001* to *Star Wars* isn't, "oh, since Darth Vader is here, I got the movie title wrong". Everything starting with "Star Wars" is the revision. If you asked about Star Wars, you wouldn't be analyzing the manifest content of the dream, but the manifest description of the disavowed manifest content of a dream. Not talking about *Star Wars* and asking him to talk about *2001* would have been very frustrating and very useful. "I told you, it wasn't *2001!*" You have said it.

So the analysand is confronted by something in *2001*, something he'd rather not know, so presto chango he turns 2001 into Darth Vader-- now they are in a safely standard Oedipal rivalry, the one he's been taught to look for, the one that now serves as a defense. So when Vader comes and shoots a hole into his head, he lives, but what he wonders about is why he didn't hear it. You might think the answer is, "who cares?" but then you're not Chrysippus and you're doing his logic wrong. The key word in that sentence is *reasoned*. "'If I had, I'd be dead,' he reasoned." Rationalization is a defense; but logic is sound. He wants the contrapositive, so asserts that he is not dead as explaining why he didn't hear it; but he concludes his dream by saying the words, "...when your father has killed you." Well, is he dead or not? The only thing we know from the telling of the dream is that he did not hear it, but we can't deduce he's alive or dead from this: if HEARD then DEAD; if NOT HEARD, then NOT DEAD: fallacy of denying the antecedent. His unconscious is snaking him. The "whole key" to *Star Wars* is indeed that Vader is Luke's "father;"-- this is called lying with the truth, because that semicolon isn't a therefore, at most it's an and-- *Star Wars* has nothing to do with the dream except obfuscate it. The dream is NOT about how to survive in the world after your father has killed you.

After hearing this long dream, the move would have been to not give the patient the *satisfaction* of talking about Darth Vader and being (not) killed by the Oedipal father, since this is obviously what the patient wants to talk about and thinks all analysts would want, too-- it is the defense.

me like that, idiot, this is your movie. Answer the question.

Since for the Greeks it was never about desire but about action, they employed a simple solution to the problem of its pornographization that is the opposite of anything that would ever be utilized today: the actors wore masks, so the audience had no guidance about how to want, it was forced to project, to... fantasize. You cannot do that now, it defeats the purpose: the Oedipus Complex isn't what's repressed, it is the defense against what is repressed.

"You mean free will vs. fate?" What's the difference? The penis is going in and the eyes are coming out, call it whatever you want but to God it's all the same, what matters is that it *happened and it is still your fault-- no one else can be blamed.* The tragedy isn't the certainty of what

---

You could ask why it was changed to Darth Vader as opposed to anyone else. There's nothing in *2001* that resembles Darth Vader; except the thing that is exactly like Darth Vader, which is Poole's breathing in a space suit, heard over (=behind) the shot of the pod menacingly turning to come kill him; and then next shot is him spinning off into space in silence.

I can't do much more with the dream without having the guy in front of me. But the bold prediction from a person thousands of days away is that if he understood *my* desire for him to be his unconscious change and not improving his conscious knowledge, and I asked him to free associate, he would be struck dumb. Now it's me he's depriving. Silence is the gambit of every overanalyzed teen asked about his day by someone who knows all his tricks. Not knowing which defense to use-- defenseless-- against an omniscient interrogator, he would try to preserve the status quo by dead silence or; if forced: irony, cynicism, criticism-- and finally rage. To be clear, all I might do is sit there and say, "well, I doubt if there's any benefit at all in discussing what it means. But why don't you tell me why you think we should keep talking about it?" Try that with sexual abuse if ten years of talking about it hasn't gotten anybody anywhere. "Do you expect me to just live with it?" But you *are* living with it.

The frustration induced is important because the correction of titles is really about how he sees his relationship to the analyst; not to press the metaphor, but he wants it to be a war, not an odyssey. Of course 1) he is trying to hide the meaning of the dream from himself; but 2) he also wants to *deprive* the analyst of the satisfaction of interpreting it correctly (he believes this to be an analyst's greatest satisfaction); but 3) deprive him not by silence or by not dreaming anything, but by pretending to give him what he wants (a dream and interpretation) with an *illusion*. In the language of porn, the wife may want to cheat; but what makes her cum-- satisfies her-- is cheating while on the phone with her oblivious husband, telling him she loves him.

You don't tell the patient any of this explicitly; it is enough only to frustrate him and get him to talk about *2001*. *He will not learn more about himself, but something will change.* In the language of porn, what ruins the wife's satisfaction-- what changes it into a whole other kind of story-- isn't the husband saying, "you cheating slut, you don't fool me, I know you're having sex with someone right now!" That doesn't change anything, that story can still continue to her orgasmic and your masturbatory satisfaction. The move is answering the phone and then *putting her on hold.*

In short, the patient here doesn't believe in the analyst's omniscience-- he believes he can fool him, likely because he just did. But he needs him to be omnipotent-- to *certify* that his lie is right. He will continue to learn a lot about himself, and nothing will change.

For example: over the course of days and interpretations, this happens:

Interestingly enough, during the night between these two sessions, he had his first ever dream about having sex with his own wife (he usually dreamt about everyone else's but his own.) This was perhaps not unrelated to his burgeoning acceptance of the validity and quality

happened but the uncertainty of what to do next, therein lies your freedom that you are desperate to avoid. Anyway it's a false dichotomy, you're not talking about free will, a more precise distinction would be determinism vs. fate: was every single atomic step from the Big Bang to the banging of Jocasta   inevitable, or are there an infinite number of paths that still inevitably converge on the same n outcomes? We pray for the former but live like the latter. The idiot's criticism of biological determinism is that if people aren't responsible for their actions they'll do whatever they want, but if we're going to be honest, you were *never* going to do what you want, what you object to is that now everyone else can. If only you had a brain tumor or a chemical imbalance or TATAAAA that caused you to act, not an excuse but a *cause*-- you could finally act. In other words, you want determinism to be true so something

---

of his own work and his own accomplishments.

Again, the obvious explanation is insecurity/inferiority vs others-- a rivalry. As if by accepting his accomplishments, he is good enough to have sex with his own wife. As if she had always been desirable to him, but only now could get her. As if she was a prize. His wife. But then who was he "good enough" compared to? His "usual" dreams were to have sex with other people's wives, but how is that a *repressed* wish? It isn't. Neither is having sex with his own wife-- he's in real life already having sex with his own wife. *He fantasizes about sex with women who are desired by others*. What must have changed is that his wife has *become* desirable to *others, in fantasy*; not necessarily to people in real life-- though this may indeed have happened, but it wouldn't count-- but something happened in his brain that he's able to perceive *in fantasy* how desirable she is *or was* to others. Now that she's desired he can desire her; but the original purpose of sex in fantasy remains unchanged. What is that purpose? I think you think there's some code to interpretation, no, everyone already knows the codes so you must take it literally: as hot as the other wives may be the fantasy is to have sex with "everyone else's *but* his own"-- the desire to deprive her of her satisfaction, a wish Fink helpfully misinterprets as insecurity instead of malice. Now having sex with his own wife *in a dream* is blessed as meaning he's more secure, but it's still for the purpose of depriving her *in real life*. Whoever wants how others want can only be satisfied by their deprivation, the deprivation of those they envy. He gets away with it, Fink rewards the patient for all his hard work on his personal growth, when what Fink should have said was, "sex with your wife-- does your wife enjoy it?"

9 Simone de Beauvoir called *The Eumenides* the founding myth of western civilization's "patriarchate", because Apollo says killing your husband is a far worse crime than killing your daughter or your mother; and Athena, who looks female but as the patron Saint of the Wisdom is therefore male, says, plainly, "I vouch myself the champion of the man, not of the woman, yea, with all my soul... in my heart, as birth, a father's child alone."

Well, ok, but it is weird de Beauvoir detected patriarchy in part 3 of a trilogy in which the only people who act by will and choice are women; all the men feel compelled. It's also telling she misses the satisfaction impossible for men that Aeschylus implies women get when they do things, including wicked things, to men, e.g. the way Clytemnestra takes her husband's blood splatter to the face is cumshot porno metaphrasis of a male's perception of the uncanny desires of woman. "It's like rain on the corn fields," says a translator who totally missed the metaphor. Meanwhile, Agamemnon and Orestes killed because they were told they had to. God knows they didn't enjoy it.

The problem wasn't that men could do whatever they wanted; the problem was that they were compelled to do things, by ritual, tyrants, tradition-- the gods. But for the primitives in The Oresteia as compared to the sophisticates watching The Oresteia, individual action was even more impossible unless you were a king or a god. If Agamemnon deserved a punishment for killing his daughter-- a big if-- then it would have been the *people's* responsibility to collectively punish him-- cause him to be punished; or, like Oedipus, cause him to punish himself. None of the sophisticates would have been up for that, no one dares stain their own hands because then everyone else who supported the

will compel you to act on what you want. If Freud reads the Oracle's prophecy as Oedipus's unconscious wish-- an incest fantasy-- then we could take all three of the Oracle's prophecies as Laius's secret wish: a cuckold fantasy. *God, compel me not to be the cause of the other's satisfaction, let this pass to someone else. I would rather die.*

---

avenger will suddenly and conveniently forget they did. "Hey, what gives you the right?" Clytemnestra's crime was way worse than Agamemnon's, not because he didn't deserve it but because she personalized it, she enjoyed it; and so Orestes was now obligated to act alone to balance the ledger, and you get a cycle of divinely required retribution that never ends as long as there's an identifiable actor. Athena takes a deep breath, the patience of a woman who has the wisdom to open carry a big stick, and tells the monkeys they could be free from all this. As long as they willingly constrained their actions, they would no longer be compelled to act. No more vengeance on behalf of the god; no more a slave to your appetites, no more mob mentality. You are free to act as long as it is just.

But who decides what's just? Men? SdB sees the gender as the deepest layer to the story, but it's really about who guarantees the freedom to act. It's not men. Orestes didn't get acquitted because Apollo said males were more valuable than females; he's an imbecile, and anyway he voted the other way. Orestes got off because Athena said so. The divided vote should not be understood as, "all else being equal, the man prevails," but rather, "all else being equal, I decide. And from now on I decide that you should form an Athens, and decide for yourselves." The temptation is to understand this new democracy as distinct from hereditary monarchies, but Athena's offer here is a continuous democracy instead of the fitful spurts of "collective action" that serve to unify a tribe while avoiding the any individual responsibility. It's the difference between sticks and stones. You can say Athena's State lets men dominate women, but Athena didn't give men that power, they brought that with them from the trees. What she gave them is the freedom from being controlled. She freed men from tyranny. She gave them power over themselves. What I would like to write is this: 2500 years later, women are finally getting it. What I have to write is this: within 100 years, no one would want it.

10 Here's a joke that made the internet rounds: guy comes home to his wife watching yet another cooking show and says, "how can you spend so much time watching cooking shows and still not know how to cook?" And she says, "how can you spend so much time watching porn...?"

An obvious comment on how media isolates the demographic. Maybe she wants better sex and maybe he wants better meals, but just take it literally and imagine what would happen if they both agreed to a fair trade: instead of retreating to isolating medias they find a space to connect, a quid pro quo, he gives her fifteen orgasms and she makes him salmon mayonnaise, and they both take pleasure in the pleasure of the other. Picture perfect? Keep the camera running and observe the horror in Act III: after cooking these elaborate meals, she starts to enjoy cooking, loves how much he enjoys her cooking, what do you think will happen next? The husband will open his ledger and his pornotron and masturbate to the new accounting: no matter how much he enjoys her cooking, since she enjoys cooking, it doesn't count. The audit shows he doesn't owe her anything, she paid herself, in fact, he's entitled to an enjoyment of his own. Which means we are back to the exact same place they started, and shows that the isolating medias weren't the cause of their insanity, they were the defense.

When did the war begin? 431? 446? Was it when Themistocles got word his walls were finished, then turned to his Spartan hosts and told them to eat it? How can you say when the war began, when the war was-- inevitable?

Incest is the symbol the play uses for guilt. But psychoanalysis took care of guilt for us, it flipped it around and made guilt a symbol for incest, and we were saved. Because today, if you woke from an alcohol blackout to discover the horny chick you ejaculated on was your mother, you'd feel a lot of shame, but you would feel no guilt. "How could I? I didn't know!" But the alcohol wasn't the excuse to do what you want-- it was the defense, the defense against realizing that even if you weren't drunk, you still wouldn't feel any guilt. One could say that the very reason you became an alcoholic in the first place is so that you would never have to wonder if you wanted what you did. "That's completely insane." Yes. Do you have a different reason why you became an alcoholic that coincidentally lead to this day? Sounds like Fate. "There's no such thing as Fate." It's hard to believe you got drunk and slept with your mother by accident. I guess the only other possibility is the Oedipus Complex: letting the other person get their enjoyment from you without compensation would make you feel guilty, yes, I wrote that correctly, so you got drunk first to obliterate your self, which means no matter how many times she came, it wasn't you. Now there's no guilt. "But why should I feel guilty over something I didn't know I did?" But you would feel ashamed? You ejaculated on your mother and the thing that bothers you is-- what other people might think?

"I'm sensitive to shame because... I'm just not self-confident. I secretly crave the approval of others." HA! You think you can convince me you want the audience's approval? You're sensitive to shame because you want the audience's gaze-- not their approval, it's enough to see them noticing you, whether they approve or not. You like their world and want to join it, even as supporting cast, even as the antagonist. *Only cowards want that.* When the white collar criminal robs millions from the masses and you say, "oh my God, did he feel no shame?" you reveal yourself to be sheep: of course he felt no shame, why would he? He doesn't want to be part of the world of sheep. Even by your own logic the correct standard should have been, "oh my genetics, did he feel no guilt?" But you would never have said this because the question makes no sense, it shows the two logics are incompatible. So he's golden and you're fleeced. All you can empathize with is........ the feeling of shame. And this is why he robbed you and why you were robbable and you will be robbed again. "We need stricter laws!" What do you need them for? "Deterrence!" I didn't ask what *we* need them for, your devotion to the society's welfare is the most hypocritical of your self-delusions, I asked what do *you* need them for? Maybe he gets 30 years in prison and you feel ten seconds of arrogant self-righteous indignant superiority; what have you gained-- other than that? The feeling that your rage helped deprive him. That was all it took to satisfy you-- and you will *set up* the world to be robbed *just* to get that feeling.

"But guilt is oppressive and painful!" What are the conditions which permit guilt to exist? Guilt can only exist in a person who can act. We don't want guilt to exist anymore because we don't want to act anymore, we don't want the responsibility, we want to be lead, we are begging for it. Give us a shame based society! Except in regard to sex, of course, in that you demand absolute shamelessness to define yourself-- because there's no risk your sex life could define you. Look back on your actual sex life: is it defining you? Hold on, I take it back-- it is perfectly defining you.

"There's no guilt in X," say the media scienticians, and you proudly accept their progressive judgment, when what you should do is turn and say: get thee behind me, Satan, who are you to tell me there's no guilt?

Wait-- were you told that *guilt* is pathological, that it is an artificial holdout from a bygone unscientific morality that pretends to be ethical but is really used as social control? And you believed-- *them*? The sheep?

Guilt is freedom: you bond yourself to yourself and free yourself from everyone else. "What if I think everything I do is right?" Then I'd say you're a person without guilt. Let's see how good you are at math... what follows? Oh, you're not good at math.

"But guilt is restrictive--" You have it backwards, self-control precedes autonomy, there's a Venn diagram about it. The movement away from guilt towards shame is a longing to get away from freedom, it wants tyranny, even if it manifests as social control by the mass of idiots, distributive justice channeled by a media just savvy enough to own the distribution channels.

"You're really stupid. Do you know how many people suffer because of excessive self-reproach, punishing themselves cruelly because of some anachronistic sense of abstract moral guilt?" Yes I do, I spent a decade with a flashlight counting them all, it is ZERO.

You're confused about what a superego does and what your superego does. Your conscience isn't cruel, *you* are cruel, you enjoy the deprivation of others, and if you can't stab them you'll cut your own wrists just deep enough to satisfy a feeling-- the feeling of what it's like to hurt someone. "I don't enjoy it, I do it to punish myself, to feel pain." Why not try some math homework? "That's not funny." I'm not joking. Punish yourself? Look around: how many other people have you caused to suffer because of your self-punishment? "Well, I can't be responsible for their feelings." You have said it.

"You shouldn't use math as a metaphor for intelligence or discipline." Now even math is a metaphor? "Most people never need more than arithmetic, and forcing them to learn it in school can be demeaning and may be at the expense of nurturing their natural talents." Come on, I'm familiar with the argument, and I know I'm supposed to counter there's benefit in training your mind to think logically and blah blah blah, but I've been through enough elections to know your trick of locking me into the form of the debate. I won't attempt to convince you that math is important, I can only convince you that you aren't important, which I hope will make you desperate to learn math. Because *someone* still has to. The debate about math isn't about math at all, but about whether you are entitled to a collection of people that reward your natural talent instead of trying to be rewarded by your natural talent. But the only way you'll get this is if some other omnipotent entity rules us all. In other words, it's a kind communism, though in practice the communists usually force everyone to learn math. "From each, according to our need." So now we have a debate about whether all natural talents have equivalent value, and it's insoluble, who should decide? We wish someone would decide. But I'm not fooled, because the trick of the argument is the axiom that math is a natural talent. It isn't. Having certain talents can help with pencil grip and parts of algebraic geometry, but nothing up through calculus requires anything more than effort. Is effort a natural talent? In college I met lots of talented people. But the only subject I ever saw being studied on a Friday night was math.

I see you barking, your egalitarianism still wants to debate that math and X are value equivalent. Still want to have that argument? I forfeit, you can win. But instead of convincing those who learned math they should share with those who didn't, you use your rhetoric to convince those who didn't that they are being deprived by those who did. You should look closely at the direction of the force vector, it starts not from ethics or equality but envy. You think I can't prove this? It's only satisfying if you feel like you got something from them: the more they feel good about giving it the less it will count. And heaven forbid they do it selflessly, plainly, for you, as if it was out of love-- you would never believe it, you'd know immediately they must have some ulterior motive. Still doubt I am talking about you, gift from god? Then replace "them" with "women".

The stereotype is the self-punishing Catholic mother who is overwhelmed with the guilt of her not-real sins and forces herself to abstain from sex and enjoyment, pray all day, say 50 Hail Marys. Well, that woman doesn't exist. "My mom was just like that!" You didn't watch her penance closely: she also forced everyone else to say 50 Hail Marys. I know your therapist told you you were the collateral damage of her neurotic guilt, but let me assure you that that is backwards. She used her guilt as a reason to hurt you, do you know why? Because she enjoys that, it is the only thing she enjoys. It doesn't make her happy, sure, but it satisfies. Where she learned how to enjoy is another matter, but if she felt truly guilty she'd ask for your forgiveness, or at the very least buy you an ice cream cone and take you to the movies and let you enjoy the story while she intones her OCD prayers silently to herself. Did she do that? No? She told you you were bad? She resents you. She doesn't know she resents you, she thinks she loves you, but she's not capable of love, the only authentically experienced emotion is rage. And so it goes. But then a question would be unavoidable: are you any better? If you were, you'd forgive her, or at least buy her an ice cream cone, take her to church and let her enjoy the story while you intone your quantized revenge fantasies to yourself. Did you do that? No? You told her she was bad? And so it goes.

I know, the Oedipus Complex is bunk because you can't imagine you wanted to kill your father to get your mother. But the part that seems unlikely isn't wanting to kill your father, on a fantasy level that part is 100% believable and hardly requires repression; the unbelievable part is loving your mother. It is so unbelievable that it took the Oracle 16 years to reveal it. Love your mother? In fact, she was often quite... enraging. Get her? You couldn't wait to get away from her.

Perhaps the problem of your life isn't that you loved your mother and hated your father, but that you didn't love your mother *as much as you were supposed to*. You were allowed to have her-- so you didn't want her.

Your father could have been a little more castrating about it, but he was busy in the home office with images of someone else's fantasy about mothers. "Look, kid, unless your mother gets implants, her tits are all yours." Dad didn't have to do much-- just love her-- then he could have been the *excuse* for why you don't have her. You do want her, of course you do! And you'd visit her more, if it wasn't for You Know Who. He could have made it ok to not want her-- to want other things. Instead you're stuck worrying that you've-- abandoned her.

And you will run this game for the rest of your life, ad infinitum=ad nauseam: X is desirable because someone else desires it-- you are told to desire it; but if you got it you'd suddenly have to deal with the realization that you don't want it; and how could you not want what the audience told you to want? So you look in desperation for a new Father to compel you not to do what you never even got a chance to decide you didn't really want. "Those blonde sluts don't want me, women are biologically hardwired to pursue high status men." The system is sound.

You don't want Mom dead, sure, but you have this uncanny, distanced fantasy in which (of course, not wanting her dead) she is dead and you don't have the obligation anymore.

106

The result is that while she is still alive, you treat her as if she was dead.

"But when I was a kid I *know* I didn't fantasize about being with my mom." Are you not listening? The unconscious is armed to the eyeballs with dependent clauses. You *can't* fantasize. It's not about your childhood but about your adulthood. The "successful resolution" of the Oedipus Complex is not "moving on to a suitable object choice." You have no problem getting naked for plenty of suitable object choices, however unsuitable they might be. The resolution is *identification with the Father*. So? How's that going? Cynical ironic detachment and mistrust of power, strongest orgasms when you're by yourself, and a serious interest in TV. I'm going to suggest not well.

Believing something is true OR believing something is not true may seem opposite, but they have the same form. The question is, can you dispense with the Oedipus Complex altogether and not require it as a premise either for belief or unbelief? In other words, can you want on your own? Can you want without it being a reaction to being told what to want? When you do want, can you act on it? Or do you first have to know why you want it, so your desire can be about something else? And the answer is Oedipal: if you're the Father, you can do whatever you want; and since you already imagine yourself as NOT the Father, you have no power. But you never wanted to be the Father, you simply don't want the responsibility. You want to be lead. "No I don't!" Yes, you do, keep reading. *I said keep reading.*

Farewell, then, Aeschylus, ascend and save our country by your art; give good advice, and educate the fools whose name is Legion.

Question: What does the translator want to be true?

In *The Devil Wears Prada*, Old Lady Couture (played by Meryl Streep) notices Pixie Millennial Prothinker (played by Anne Hathaway) giggling derisively at professional fashionistas fussing over which of two identical belts to put on a mannequin. So Streep bitch slaps her. She runs off sobbing to a middle aged man in a crisp thousand dollar suit and no briefcase (played by Stanley Tucci), who comforts her antisexually. "Listen," he says, "fashion isn't the frivolous vanity you think it is. It's a kind of art, and an aspirational safe place for kids like me who were forced to have too many brothers." Then he gives her some free expensive clothes from the Narnia wardrobe and she transitions from "I won't be objectified" to "it makes me feel good about myself."

Finding reasons to choose what you secretly wanted in the first place is a well established psychological maneuver, which is why it won't work anymore, and didn't work here. Hit rewind and listen to what Streep said that turned giggling at a mannequin into crying to a mannequin, if the devil is a liar it must mean she knows the truth, she who has ears to hear let her hear, for here is wisdom:

> Oh, okay, I see. You think this has nothing to do with you. You go to your closet and you select that lumpy blue sweater, because you're trying to tell the world that you take yourself too seriously to care about what you put on your back.

> But what you don't know is that that sweater is not just blue, it's not turquoise, it's not lapis. It's actually cerulean. And you're also blithely unaware of the fact that in 2002, Oscar de la Renta did a collection of cerulean gowns. And then Yves Saint Laurent showed cerulean military jackets. And then cerulean quickly showed up in the collections of eight different designers. And it filtered down through the department stores and then trickled on down into some tragic Casual Corner where you, no doubt, fished it out of some clearance bin. However, that blue represents millions of dollars and countless jobs and it's sort of comical how you think that you've made a choice that exempts you from the fashion industry when, in fact, you're wearing the sweater that was selected for you by the people in this room from a pile of stuff.

In this scene, Hathaway is just an intern=girl, cynically knowledgeable about how things "really" work, which, in return for a massive non-deductible charitable gift to a college, she has been assured is either incompetently, frivolously, or exploitatively. There are no other possibilities. She got accepted to law school, but opts out of the system, choosing instead to critique it from the outside. She calls this journalism. We can laugh about this later.

She takes a job as an embedded reporter=intern at a fashion magazine because she wants to critique the manipulation/exploitation of women by the fashion industry, yet she doesn't think to critique the manipulation/exploitation of women by the fashion media. This is because the fashion media isn't controlled by men, so therefore it can not be exploitative, and it must be subordinate to the male fashion industry, which every experience she has at the magazine should tell her is backwards. You might ask if, as a reporter making this assumption, she shouldn't at least wonder if her investigative reporting isn't also subordinate to some greater industry, but she doesn't wonder this, because she's not actually a reporter. She's just a girl, looking to report on her assumptions, which might get her noticed as an intern in a world controlled by industrious men. It's confusing, but 100% accurate. I'll accept the premise that she's a good writer because she puts on glasses, but her primary qualifications are being post-graduate and salary-free, thus totally unbiased and objective. She sees through the ideology. She sees reality. And it makes her giggle.

So Streep bitch-slaps her: hey womannequin, that smug detached superiority you feel working for free in a billion dollar industry you dismiss as trivial? They were able to sell you a color. So shut it.

Fashion has set a bare minimum that one must abide by to stay in, some of which, to ensure everyone stays in, is marketed as opting out. And, of course, while no man in the movie ever makes her feel bad about how she looks, every woman in the movie does nothing else. So the pressure is not to look good but to conform=confirm that fashion is invaluable. The only person unconcerned with her clothes and worried sick about her future is the patriarchy, played by her father, who is dressed like her Dad. Sweater vest under blazer because male privilege can justify anything. He buys her dinner, but I noticed she didn't eat anything. Independence.

I get that these movies aren't supposed to be high art, the whole genre is basically anime for women who liked high school, and if the only critique this scene offered was that industry or media manipulate people it wouldn't be worth the discussion, and there are better examples than *The Devil Wears Prada*. What's worthwhile here is Raggedy Ann's reaction. When Streep tells her she's been unknowingly a pawn of this omnipotent fashion industry, that she's always been inside their reality, does finding this out make her enraged? Panicked? Does she deny it? Does it crush her spirit? Does she spend the rest of the film refusing to wear colors in a suicidal martyrdom against the forces of Oscar de la Renta? No. She goes all in. She chooses the cerulean pill.

You can look all you want, you will not find any: the only other story in which a woman is happy to learn she's been manipulated for someone else's satisfaction is porn, and you should consider this seriously. We would say she secretly wanted it but would feel guilty for choosing it, after all, she's supposed to be a loyal and proper woman or a prothinking college graduate. Sure, she stole little bits of satisfaction, a drunken affair or a cerulean sweater, but she consoled herself by pretending it was a way of opting out of going totally all in. What she needs, says a therapist, is someone to tell her that it's ok to choose this, there's no guilt in wanting this.

That's the way you're supposed to think about it anyway, and god knows it makes sense, except that no one nowadays ever feels guilty for their desires.

The choice in *The Matrix* between the red and blue pills is a false choice, because it's only offered to people who already know they are slaves. The red pill is a choice for a grey reality, fine, but the blue pill is a trick so clever it could only have been invented by the robots, by which I mean humans: you already are a slave, the blue pill lets you think you can choose it.

Saying that her guilt is about what she wants-- "I shouldn't want *this*"; that-- that thought-- is absolutely a defense. She is obviously confused about what she wants and what she's allowed to want, ok, but that isn't her problem. Her problem is that no matter what she wants, she cannot act directly to get it. I don't mean things prevent her-- I mean she can *not* act.   She-- we-- explain this impotence as fear, insecurity, or guilt over what we want; but those are all retroactive defenses, the *primary* problem is the inability to act on a desire.   It doesn't matter what her desire is.   For her, acts have to be impulsive, compelled, or for some other reason, other than desire.   If the pre-modern problem was guilt, and the modern problem was the inability to feel guilt, then she exhibits the post-modern problem: the inability to act.   "Because I would feel guilty."   Keep telling yourself that.

You might criticize not her but the movie's script, the writing, it doesn't allow its lead character to make her own choices but instead has her pulled along by the plot.   That is a common critique of female lead movies, but it is absolutely also a defense. The aspirational quality of the story and her character is precisely *that* she does not act towards goals.   She reacts to situations.

Say a married woman stays loyal to her husband despite temptations.   Certainly she's had the occasional desire to cheat, but-- doesn't.   Then one day she meets a man + alcohol= they impulsively drive somewhere to have sex: "oh my god, I can't believe I'm doing this." On the way they get a flat tire, and since neither of these diplomates can change it they wait for an automotive technician to do what the chick who invented jeans shorts could do in <30 seconds.   "I'm sure I could but--"   That's the same as can't.   You might think that the delay gives her time to sober up and think things through, which means if they still have sex she is even more guilty because her choice is no longer impulsive.   This is certainly true legally, but not psychologically, because during that delay she isn't deciding whether she should GO have sex.   What she has to decide now is whether to STOP the sex that is on autopilot.   To put it as bluntly as possible: if she does nothing, she will eventually orgasm.   This hypothetical story illustrates the key psychological problem that is hoped to be a problem of guilt but has nothing to do with guilt: she does not have the ability to ACT.   The nature of the desire is irrelevant to the inability.   The only way she can act is if it's impulsive, compelled, or for some other reason.   The initial decision to have sex was sufficiently impulsive that it's likely to be met more with incredulity than guilt ("I did a bad thing, but that's not the kind of person I am"); but during the delay in Act II there is far less *will* required to go to have sex-- it's on autopilot-- then will required to stop the sex.   *The latter requires an act.*   And the problem is then identical: it is impossible to act-- in this case to stop the sex that will passively and inevitably result if she does nothing.   So while the "choices" made during the delay look like ones that would result in more responsibility and guilt, she will actually feel less guilt because she made no actual choices.   NB: regardless of whether you blame her more.   She'll invent reasons why she didn't stop it, maybe she'll figure she'd gone that far, too late to stop now.   That's an especially good rationalization for (in)action because it means she's acting on his desire, more than hers.   She could even decide she really wants to do it after all, but that "choice" is only possible because she doesn't have to choose that-- it only appears that's what she is choosing, but the only physical choice on the table is whether to stop it.   And that makes it almost impossible to stop it.   As an aside, "affirmative consent" anticipates this exact problem: publicly pretending to be a negotiation at the beginning of intimacy (where it can be safely critiqued or laughed at), it's actually only relevant in medias res, where the hard decision *for her* is not whether to continue (autopilot) but whether to stop-- so the structure requires him to stop.   It's strangely reverse-sexist, and I know you're imagining an offensive lineman bullying a semi-comatose bulimic, but in general it puts an awful lot of faith in a man's ability to act when evidently he needed to be drunk just to ask her out in the first place.

Hathaway giggles over the silliness of identical belts on a mannequin, but there's an even greater one right there: the preposterousness of a plump pensioner in pancake makeup packed into a pencil skirt and pitched on pumps people only wear to pool parties. That doesn't seem preposterous to you, just sexist? You need to pause the film and study this scene like a photograph, because while Hathaway giggles at all the fuss over dressing the mannequin, she would never dare giggle if Streep was dressing herself. That kind of fuss-- that kind of ambivalence-- is not only understandable, it is sacrosanct. But seeing it done to a mannequin lacks the illusion that the clothing reflects a unique part of your individuality-- not only are the belts the same, but whichever they choose will be worn by all of the unique individuals-- and Hathaway can't stop the giggles.

The imbeciles in the audience will hear from Tucci's monologue that fashion is a noble pursuit, there's no guilt in wanting it; and the misogynists sitting with the imbeciles would smugly observe that Hathaway ran to the person who was going to tell her what she wanted to hear so she could absolve herself of the guilt of wanting it. And then they'd debate until one of them called the other an imbecile and the other rebutted with misogynist. Have at it, it's meaningless and you're both idiots. Because at the moment she runs to Tucci, she isn't deciding whether to choose to be in fashion. Streep told her she already is in fashion, it's on autopilot-- Casual Corner and not Prada, but what's the difference to it? The guilt isn't in what's wanted, there is no guilt over that at all. The problem is inertia, the problem is physics. Fashion already extracted its benefit from her, so in order for her to derive any benefit back, i.e. to enjoy fashion, Hathaway needs what the cheating wife above needs, not an excuse to choose it but a way out of the choice. That's what Streep already gave her. All Tucci does is let her pretend she chose it.

Streep is the devil, not because she's evil and certainly not because she's powerful but because she knows. She tells the truth. Streep is part of the fashion media, but she doesn't bother to recite the standard lines of the fashion media. Streep doesn't tell her that it's a woman's right to look amazing. She doesn't say there should be no guilt in spending money on expensive clothes. She doesn't tell her that fashion empowers women. She doesn't need to lie. She's not trying to convince her it's ok to want fashion; the truth is, it doesn't matter what you want. Do you think the devil wears Prada because it *wants* to wear Prada, do you think that matters? Like it or not-- you never had a choice. *You may as well enjoy it.*

The scene features two women and a half naked dummy, so it's structured like threesome in a porn. You have a brainless mannepulator and his devilish wife tricking some naive investigative journalist into a threesome. Streep bypasses the ordinary lies of "come on baby, you know you want this" and tells her outright that fashion is manipulating her-- *that's how badly they desire her.* Of course fashion manipulates all women to get them into their clothes, but it usually doesn't tell them. The proles all think they chose fashion, but there is no power in this choice because it isn't a choice, every woman in the movie empowered by fashion is stereotypically neurotic. Hathaway gets the knowledge that she didn't choose it, it always had her in its power. But getting this knowledge means she is desirable, manifested in the movie by her seamless transformation into a supermodel. And there's your MFF: omnipotence uses both women for its satisfaction; omniscience tells her she's being manipulated; having the knowledge of her impotence makes her the most desirable of all. What gives her the most satisfaction isn't the clothes-- despite all her wardrobe changes, she never once says, "oh my god, I love this dress"-- but the *knowledge* of her manipulation. And then she's all in. She may perform the double fellatio with a little ironic distance, "this dummy thinks he's so great because he has two women worshipping him," but while she'll admit the

113

whole thing was set up for his enjoyment, "the real star of this show is me-- I'm the one everyone is looking at."

But in any situation where a person is being used for another's satisfaction, in order for the ledger to balance, someone else must be deprived of their satisfaction, of her. Take a look around. Hathaway does dump her boyfriend because he's impressed by sandwiches, but it's not the same as being married to a husband she can cuckold. So she performs an exorcism.

What is pornography? We should probably finally define our terms. "I don't know what it is, but I know it when I see it." So you're the one who decides? "No, it's subjective, porn could be different things to different people." So everyone gets to decide? "No, there's no objective criteria." So no one gets to decide? Thank God.

> *Pornography*: n. An imitation of a sex act that is serious, complete, and of a certain magnitude; in language embellished with each kind of artistic ornament, the several kinds being found in separate parts of the performance; in the form of action, not of narrative; with incidents arousing lust and anxiety, in order to accomplish a catharsis...

"Why don't you cite your sources?" Why, so you can pretend that counts as reading them?

Pornography is an imitation of the sex act: even if there is actual sex. A video of two people having sex is voyeurism. What would make it pornography is the imitation, even including the use of the orgasm to imitate an orgasm. "But I prefer a real couple to fake porn, the whole reason I like it is that it's real." Yet you found it on a porn site. Watching a real couple imitate porn.

Complete: The story unfolds logically-- despite the utter lack of necessity, the end can be traced back to the beginning and all you can say is, "because of those actions-- it was inevitable."

Incidents arousing lust... "That one's obvious." Why do they arouse lust? "Well, they are naked--" No, not why=how; *for what purpose?*

...and anxiety: this is the world that you live in, this is how it works, this could be you. Are you willing to live here, where these things happen? To you-- or not to you? But are out of your power?

In order to accomplish a catharsis: "Yes, relieving the pressure, now I can focus on work." That's not a catharsis, that's-- venting the steam. Catharsis isn't mechanical, it's not even chemical, it's alchemical, it is a rebalancing; porn is the catalyst that drives the equilibrium reaction back the other way, against entropy, in your case, *increasing* the appropriate amount of lust and anxiety, to organize it, to train you how to feel. "That's certainly not what I learned about catharsis." You learned to pronounce it a certain way, that's true. Because when you put the accent on the second syllable, you make it plural. Again and again, you go to it to be told how to want.

"This doesn't sound at all like the meaning of porn." Maybe, but what did you think it was for? "But I thought pornography literally meant, 'the writing of prostitutes'." As if what interested prostitutes enough to write about was the meaning of sex.

Say a wife complains her husband is addicted to porn, not as an instructional video or to get the prostaglandins flowing, but like every other media they're irradiating each other with it's changed how he sees reality. So now if he hears the local news not mention the suspect's race he assumes they're looking for a black guy, and if he hears a married couple mention they like to meet new people he assumes they are, too.

The wife suspects and he admits and we know that even real life sex is imitating porn, which makes it a copy of a copy, something you wouldn't tolerate in anything else, except

115

yourself. If a 25 year old guy in a fedora offered you a jellybaby you'd strangle him with the scarf he is inevitably wearing, but if a girl wants to be choked during sex we're not supposed to assume it's because the guy likes showing off his forearm tattoos? "It's not what it looks like." Then why does it look like that? The usual interpretation is that the problem is the porn, that it causes a problem in real life relationships, it affects his desire for real women. Other interpretations are that there is something wrong with the man that he's addicted to unreal images, he can't connect with reality. Did you think any these? These are the interpretations of a coward.

The coward's perspective is that the wife is the real part, the meaningful part, that the pathology has to do with the unreal images of porn. But if we're going to be honest, which we have been trained not to be, the reason no one finds the wife unreal is that she doesn't look particularly porny. Ergo, she's real, and maybe he's using unreal images to fantasize her as more porn-like. But if he's only satisfied by the images *and* he married a wife, then either the images are real or she's unreal.

It's both. The images are real, and she's not. Yes, I know you can see her. But you can see porn, too.

You want to know what's *wrong* with him. Why do you want to know this? Because you want *knowledge*.

What about the wife? What's wrong with her that she fell for him? You should probably answer that question first. He wasn't normal, got married, and then madness set in. In the beginning the euphoria and the skin hunger just made it all look like love. The pornography is not the cause, it is the response to a problem that was there long before I Do Not Have a Choice, It's On Autopilot. "Well, she didn't know!" Didn't know what? That he could only see the world through the lens of a camera? How could she not have known this, was it an arranged marriage? Or did she think how he saw the world applied to everything except their love-- the one thing that *requires* fantasy?

Why not just go cheat? Because even though he's no longer attracted to her, he's still in love with her? Love is easier than lust? As if whatever psychotic dementia you hope he has affects only his *sexual* desire-- leaving abstract reasoning intact? He's not capable of unpornographized lust, but his capacity for love is boundless?

You want porn to be the problem, you want to interpret the porn, ok: what's he looking at? What's getting him off? No, wait---------- what does he wish he could show his wife? "We need to teach couples to be able to share their fantasies safely in a non-judgmental way, but still be respectful of each other's boundaries." Hearing that sentence spoken out loud would drive any man to porn. Well, what twisted images manifest his fantasy?

Oh, it's MILF porn. The thing he's already living and the most mainstream of porn genres. The thing that used to be literally for women under the heading Romance, talk about "desire is the desire of the other." Why was he "unconsciously" drawn to that? "The age matches the demographic's?" The age of the MILF-- or the pool boy? Neither of them even look the stated age, what good is that to "visual creatures"? It's useful because it makes sense of the wife's desire, even if it is undoubtedly wrong. What makes it hysterical and confusing isn't the cheating MILFs testosteronized body but her testosteronized libido-- she wants sex all the time. What the hell happened to this woman that she is so horny? "Her husband doesn't give it to her anymore." Hold on, she's not just horny, *she's hornier than she's ever been.* She wasn't slutting her way through pizza delivery men when she was twenty, right? "Women are biologically different, they reach their sexual prime at 35." Because biology favors extra chromosomes, just in case?

It's not what she wants, it's how she wants. The porn MILF has cleanly uncoupled sex from love. Not simply she doesn't have love-- she doesn't WANT it. She doesn't believe in "love" as any kind of mystical, transcendental, "connecting" experience. Having finally freed herself from all that unsatisfying emotional complexity what's consequently magnified is a ravenous sex drive. MILFs may want sex with men but more importantly they want sex like men want-- no strings, no drama, no shame, and if she gets caught, "oh well, too late to stop now." "But many married women want lesbian porn." Forgive me, sometimes I'm not clear: *like men want*. This unrestrained drive isn't trying to get satisfied, it is the pursuit of sex only, as sex, it is infinite: she's never done, she stops only because men can't keep up. "Moneyshot... and cut."

You think she's left unsatisfied? Don't worry-- it's a male fantasy! A male fantasy about love. She's not just satisfied by him, she's satisfied through him. Maybe she came too, but it's his orgasm that makes her glow. Too bad real life sex, let alone love, doesn't guarantee such an empathy, such a closeness. He doesn't blast his cum in her eye like the alpha male she lets him think he is (wink wink), it's extracted from him by her-- the cum is the physical manifestation of his satisfaction, which she takes away from him. She takes it from him and she enjoys it, which is why he's spent and she's satisfied.

How great it would be to be the recipient-- giver?-- both?-- of that kind of satisfaction! Maybe it's the MILF's husband's fault, low T/too much TV-- he just needs to appreciate and act on his wife the way everyone else only gets to imagine. But look closely: the porn MILF will have sex with anyone, anytime-- *except* her husband. In real life we're taught to believe this is gradually "losing the spark," or "biologically programmed polyamory", because there's no greater drive for copulation than being done with ovulation, but if she was this blindingly horny or in love, then she'd *even* settle for her husband in the same way that drunk college guys settle for anyone. But she's not cheating because he's not giving her sex, she's cheating because she specifically doesn't want sex with the distraction of having to pretend to also be in love, pretending to feel something more than just horniness. That's what she wants, and her husband by definition cannot provide this: he "loves" her. Of course she knows he doesn't, but the pretense of it is inescapable. Hence role play, believing that it's hot because of the novelty of the scenario when it is really about pretending that you are only pretending that there is no love. Does anyone even know how to have sex with someone *as* an expression of love? What would that even look like? "Yes! We need to teach people about healthy sexuality, and intimacy! And boundaries!" The 4s have spoken.

"But sometimes it's hotter to have sex without love." How would you know? Did you see it in a video?

"I have fantasies that I want to incorporate into our sex, but I'm afraid my partner will think they're weird." Incorporate your fantasies? Who taught you how to speak? "I just mean--" I know what the words mean, it's how you use them that's bananas. 'Fantasies you want to incorporate'-- like a business? Are you a capitalist, do you control the means of production-- the business of porn fantasies, on the backs of the proles you're creating innovative new fantasies every day? Or have you been ruminating over the same one? "Repetition compulsion." *But it's isn't your fantasy*-- you've taken someone else's fantasy and

117

spent years making minor updates. The irony is that you are incorrectly correct: incorporate your fantasies-- "to make real as a body". Because the only thing that's real is what you can see: porn, and her body. I guess you can say you've incorporated her into your porn, and thus made the rest incorporeal. "No, you're not understanding what I'm saying--" I don't want to understand what you're saying, I am seeing how your words are used: you're using them to trick me, hoping I'll see your meaning instead of what you're doing, which is exactly how you use porn. You're using the porn to obliterate the *unreal* part of her, and you feel good about yourself because a residue of what's *real* is all that remains, which you pretend is your fantasy: "she's may not be physically perfect, but my wife is my favorite porn star." And have you really done this feat?! You've made yourself horny for your wife! Rejoice, I say! Callooh! Callay! That's how you win at life.

Porn is the *normal* way he is satisfied. Now he has to try to fit not her baggy body but her *being* into his fantasies-- except he doesn't know her being and doesn't know how to fantasize-- all he knows is porn. "Let's pretend that I'm not pretending already that this is sex without love."

Do you want to see something unsettling-- uncanny? Porn addicted men-- let's stop pretending this has anything to do with gender, or porn: media addicted hominids-- men who have adopted someone else's superego proudly settle for a real life girlfriend/wife who may not look like their porn "ideal"-- protecting them from the self-accusation of shallowness-- but can be *described* as such. "She's big titted blonde." "Long dark hair and a big ass." As long as the phrase is literally correct, it can be used metaphorically. "That sounds like a very healthy thing." If it was healthy, you wouldn't need the phrase at all.

"Are you saying a man can't love-- an ugly woman?" Ha! No, liar, I'm saying *you* can't love an ugly woman. Or a beautiful woman. Or anyone. The living, breathing woman that he loves exists only as pieces: words, images, associations. He was taught to want in pictures, translate it into words which associate to someone else's unconscious, so that then he's allowed to pursue it. "I want X." What a coincidence. We want different things.

"I do share my fantasies with her, I've tried hundreds of times to get her into them, but she always says no." Those aren't your fantasies. What you're trying to get her into is porn. Which either suggests your fantasy is only porn, or that she says no. You should probably consider that first.

So you're left with porn-- someone else's fantasy. That works, that does turn you on, because pornography is real. It is utterly meaning-less; it has no latent content at all-- none that you could know and anyway it's not your fantasy. Certainly you could load the porn with meaning, but you could load anything with meaning-- a foot, a hair color, a Glock-- make those into fetishes. But fetishes are not pornographic; they're the opposite. That's kind of their point.

Ironically, this kind of purely physical sex that porn MILFs seem to want is the kind of sex (women said) men (used to) say they want, so why wouldn't a po-mo porno couple be able to come to an agreement about the disappearance of their "love" and a future of mutual masturbation? Sometimes they can, but then it's a game of vegan chicken: if either blinks, then the absence of love becomes a beam in the other's eye and a gigantic mote in yours. "I don't really love you anymore but I'm still happy to oralate you," sounds great in theory and drunk but it's hard to hear "anymore" and remain together. No matter how freely given-- correction: especially when it's free-- that blowjob incurs a debt, on both sides. All debts must

118

be paid.

What's the solution? "How about we pretend the *sex* got stale, and the ledgers stay balanced?" With the same intensity they will do anything to maintain their identities as groupthinking individuals, they will avoid sex with each other in order to stay "in love."[11]

There was a woman's glamour magazine with an impossibly glamorous woman on the cover, but inside there were no further pictures of her because even the magazine couldn't make the impossible happen twice. Instead there was an article that explained that porn objectified women and forced women to live up to impossible porn star expectations. The irony is that looking like a porn star couldn't be easier, and I know this because of how many

---

11

> This is what I had done. I had built up false pictures in my mind and
> sat before them. I never had the courage to demand the truth.

We all come to books in our own time, they say, but always at the right time; sometimes many times and sometimes never, sometimes you come to them too late and there's nothing worse than too late. True about a lot of things, I guess. Daphne du Maurier's *Rebecca* is classic, character driven, literary romance that most young women come to by 18 and most young men come to by young women, its psychological insights are as relatable as its class insights are debatable, but I had a unique advantage in that no one had told me any of this, I came to it as #7 of the Top Mystery Books Of All Time, #1 was *And Then There Were None*, so I assumed it was a whodunit in which every word had both a meaning and a purpose, and at least one of those was a lie. Turns out the only mystery is how anyone could think *Rebecca* was a mystery, let alone #7, by this logic *A Christmas Carol* is a medallist in Top Time Travel Books Of All Time. But because I was reading with intention-- the intention of catching the bad guy-- I found some things that maybe other people overlooked.

Speaking of stories on the wrong lists, the 1931 *Frankenstein* (#14 of Top Horror Movies Of All Time) had me laughing out loud in less than two minutes because after the cold open in which a tuxedoed Edward Van Sloan comes out from behind a stage curtain to personally warn us that the what we see may be disturbing, the opening credits then horrifyingly unironically contain the following sentence which I will here transcribe with absolute precision: "From the novel by Mrs. Percy B. Shelley". Oh sweet baby Jesus, I laughed for hours. I'm even laughing now. Quentin Tarantino loved *Abbott and Costello Meet Frankenstein* because it was one of the first movies to blend horror and comedy, but I'm sorry, that line in the original is the funniest joke ever delivered in all of cinema. Her mom would be so proud.

Mrs. Browning complained that she didn't mean *Rebecca* to be a read as a romantic story but as a "study in jealousy", but it's hard to see it as either. Certainly it's about love, though a 23 year old telling a 42 year old, "why would you love me, I'm just a child, I'm not even interesting" doesn't strike me as romantic; and jealousy would require that someone want what someone else has, and in this novel no one has what someone else wants.

In Edwardian England the kind of fox hunting Eton graduate who crosses his legs at the testicles and forces brandy on women not to make them pass out but to keep them from passing out marries a commoner half his age after a week of showing her his car; she's supposed to be innocent, timid and powerless, and it will not be a spoiler to reveal here that she is indeed all of these things. "Did you notice her name is never given in the book?!" Yes, everyone notices that. Did you notice what names are given in the book? No? Next time take notes or Benzedrine.

But it's a gothic mystery, which means "the spectre of Maxim's dead first wife haunts the house," which would have been awesome if that was literally true, but it's not. "Dead first wife" means

people have tried it. Being glamorous isn't just more impossible than porn, it's also a hell of a lot more expensive, the heels, makeup and half a bikini you're going to lose in porn are way cheaper than any of the 6 essential must-haves for summer. An old joke, applicable to lots of things: how much money does it take to look your best? Answer: all of it. Never mind the psychological damages, the financial drain should be sufficient for women to go thermonuclear on pornography, let alone magazine covers, yet with women more empowered/educated/wealthier than they've ever been there's more porn and magazine covers than ever before. And the result, according to magazines?[12]

But the effect is not making men into raving beasts. On the contrary: The onslaught of porn is responsible for deadening male libido in

---

"Rebecca", "house" is "Manderley", but "spectre" is "her old belongings" and "haunts" means "are still in the drawers." Boo. "It's a psychological haunting." Your psychology needs to grow up and stop sleeping with the TV on.

For the first 2/3 of the book, we are shown something ordinary: the timid second wife trying to find her place in someone else's house. She feels inferior and overshadowed by the former wife, the beautiful socialite Rebecca, who died in a tragic boating accident. Maxim can barely speak of Rebecca without gazing into the sea/past/horizon and dramatically stoicizing his pain. The servants are reverential and I think retarded, they still call things "Rebecca's chair" and "Rebecca's envelopes"; and the head maid, Mrs. Danvers-- referred to as Danny-- had a 'psychosexual' obsession with her and has made a shrine of her old bedroom. Everything is as it should be, which is exactly where it was.

There are two ways to look at this. To someone like Danvers, the new second wife is a blotch, a stain, an intrusion of the real in the forcibly preserved Matrix world of Rebecca's Manderley. Impossible to assimilate, Danvers tries to get rid of her, by talking her into suicide-- of course by jumping out of Rebecca's bedroom window.

The other way to look at it is that for the second wife, Rebecca is the stain, an intrusion of the real in the Matrix world she is trying to create. There is no way she can "find meaning" in her own world unless the iconic Rebecca is symbolized as something else which can safely fit in the second wife's worldview.

If you try but fail to symbolize-- to compartmentalize, reduce, explain into knowledge-- the stain, as the second wife fails to do with Rebecca, your reality becomes more and more tenuous, every failed attempt at making it fit in your reality rather than you being a part of its reality leaves you increasingly hysterical; but the real mental catastrophe occurs when you realize/accept you can *never* succeed. That's when the second wife attempts suicide. The moment of her dramatic act is the moment when she realizes she has so far failed in creating her own reality and will never succeed. If you follow this, then you have an important clue in a mystery: the moment of *anyone's* dramatic act against the stain is the moment they realize they have failed and will never succeed. All set? Here we go.

There are two twists in the story. The first-- get ready-- is that the Maxim didn't love Rebecca, at all, he hated her. In fact he killed her. Don't get too excited, this part isn't the mystery, nobody figures it out, Maxim just blurts it all out to his new wife, in great detail: Rebecca had cuckolded him hundreds of times, sometimes 6 at a time, not for love or money but for no reason, because she *could*, and laughed in his face about it. Not only was she evil, "she was not even normal," which I think means she was bisexual. The horror, the horror. "You're ignoring the time and context." In what time, context or gender is bisexuality ± 2 SD more abnormal than being in an MMMMMMF? As a point of fact, Rebecca's cuckoldry wasn't a mystery to Maxim, either; right at the honeymoon Rebecca wickedly revealed what she had in store for their marriage. Oh, the hypocrisy: the perfect wife-- brains, beauty and breeding-- publicly adored by all, privately penetrated by many.

relation to real women and leading men to see fewer and fewer women as "porn-worthy." Far from having to fend off porn-crazed young men, young women are worrying that as mere flesh and blood, they can scarcely get, let alone hold, their attention.

Maybe this is the rum talking but isn't that what they wanted in the first place? What's the problem, the disappearance of one night stands? Is this what worries her for her daughters? The patriarchy is said to be powerful but it seems very inconsistent, on the one hand some women are hyper-objectified, on the other hand other women aren't objectified enough. So now she's worried that men will become disinterested in their partners because porn women are more appealing? Get rid of porn and a size 12 could be sexually attractive

I have to pause here and explain that though the second wife is the protagonist, the reason this book is beloved among educated women is Rebecca. Yes, she's "a bad wife"-- a totalizing judgment of a last gasp patriarchy dying of pneumothorax-- but they way she lived her life was a penetrating blow to the patriarchy and traditional roles. She did what she wanted, sexually, and of course the patriarchy killed her for it. I will add that breaking out of the confines of her traditional role did not include working, let alone math, which I suspect is also part of her appeal. But I digress.

So why did this privileged patriarch stay with this strumpet? "Because of the shame that would result from a divorce." Hmm. Isn't that why women stay in bad marriages? "But male infidelity was accepted and normalized, but female infidelity was a huge shame." Then why did he stay faithful to her? Why didn't he just go have sex with other abnormal women? This is a weird book. Then one night she taunted him that she was looking for a new thrill: maybe she would make him raise another man's baby, "you would enjoy it, wouldn't you Maxie Millie Waxie Weenie, to see my son growing bigger every day, to know that when you died, all this would be his?" That cuts him to the quick, which I think is a uterus. So he pulls out a gun and symbolizes her (in the heart, get it?), locks her body in the cabin of a boat, opens up the portholes, and punches holes in the deck to sink it. A few months later, by some deus ex contrivance a totally unrelated female body washes up to shore, and Maxim conveniently identifies it as Rebecca. So he got away with it. Of course the second wife is shocked when she hears this story, but the point here is that this represents the big turn in the story: the "spectre of the revered and perfect Rebecca" has been exorcised. Now the second wife is free to think of herself as Maxim's true love second wife, and to love Maxim, because Rebecca has been symbolized as the *hated* first wife, who didn't love Maxim.

There's an Oedipal interpretation here, I guess, the father kills the mother so the daughter wins the rivalry, as if killing the mom automatically entitled you to his weenie; but the reality of the complexity is that after killing the mom, the daughter has no choice, she is now stuck with the weenie, she is not allowed to want anything else. This will make sense in a moment.

Let me just pause here to report how many secondary sources about *Rebecca* claim Maxim shot Rebecca in the uterus. This isn't really up for interpretation, it literally says "heart", but the symbolic meaning of a powerful woman being shot in the uterus is too obvious to not to make up. In order for the secondary sources to get their wish, however, in order to extract this little bit of symbolic meaning, everything else Maxim says has to become true. Again, this will all make sense in a moment.

But the reason Maxim blurts this all out to his second wife now is that a diver has just found the wreckage of the real boat, with Rebecca's real body in it, and it looks very much like someone locked her in the cabin of a boat, opened up the portholes, and punched holes in the deck to sink it. Fortunately Maxim is high up in the patriarchy, and during the investigation they decide that that "someone" is Rebecca herself, i.e. it wasn't an accident, but suicide by boat. But Rebecca's lover/cousin Jack Favell doesn't buy it: he thinks Maxim killed her, because *she was in love* with Favell, and as evidence he produces a note from her he received on the day of her death: *Meet me, I have something important to tell you.* "Does that sound like someone about to suicide?" Favell

again? I assume she means to rich guys. Did you think I was going to say whites? Back in the Bush Administration I would have.

Every generation has a Princess De Leon who discovers some new spin on the "impossible expectations" critique that only applies to her grandparents generation. There was once a time women couldn't get hired as spice traders or alchemists because everyone believed they were mentally incapable of the exertion, but even though there are plenty of men who still believe a woman's place is from behind no one with credit card debt thinks women can't do the work of ten men, and they better get to it. The critique that men watch porn and then get turned off to real women is so old it was printed in pamphlets and the porn

---

asks. No, I have to agree it does not. Favell knows Maxim knew about their affair, so Favell thinks that Maxim killed her over whatever she was going to tell Favell, *for example* that she was leaving Maxim. To be very specific: Favell thinks Maxim murdered her by boat-- he has no knowledge about a gunshot. Hang in there.

Which brings us to the second twist: on the day of Rebecca's death, she had had a notation in her appointment book to see "Baker". In a series of reveals, we learn that Dr. Baker is a big city gynecologist that Rebecca went to see before she died. Can you guess who the father isn't? Now Favell thinks he has the motive for the murder. The police inspector is called, etc, and they all go see Dr. Baker. He confirms that Rebecca (under an assumed name) did indeed come to see him, but-- plot twist-- she wasn't pregnant: she had terminal cancer (of the uterus, get it?) We'd been told before she feared nothing in life but a long slow death, so now everything falls into place, the authorities have confirmed a reason for suicide. To be very clear: now the authorities and Favell think it is suicide by boat over a terminal diagnosis; and the second wife thinks Maxim got away with shooting a slutty cancer patient.

Later on, alone with his second wife, Maxim does an expository monologue in which he ties together the loose ends of the mystery: Rebecca must have been dying of cancer, and as her "last practical joke" on Maxim, she taunted him by saying she was *thinking* about getting pregnant by another man, *so that* he would kill her, so she could die quickly and he would also be jailed for her murder, and then she cackled like Maleficent. In other words, he didn't do what *he* wanted, she compelled him to act on her desire. Ta da-- a feminist hero. But her plan, in a sense, backfired: her husband did kill her, but now that everyone knows she had cancer, a motive for suicide by boat is established, and the police drop the investigation completely, Maxim is free, and Maxim's ends up with less guilt because it wasn't all his fault. The only thing left for readers to discuss is to what extent Rebecca "destabilized the patriarchy" by sleeping with other members of the patriarchy. "She laughed at all of you..." hisses Danny Danvers, "she was finally defeated not by a man, or a woman, but by the sea, the sea finally defeated her!" No, actually, it was a man. Not much of a man, a dandy man, who needed a gun to scare off a man with a penis, but penis man had already left and so things got-- out of hand. I know that must be disappointing. Don't choose your heroes based on who they hate.

So that's the ending, but at this point I am still waiting for a blow-your-mind mystery post credits scene. No? This can't be all there is to it, can it? The evidence is very weak. Rebecca may be a psychopathic cuckoldress whom Maxim hated, but the only person who says this is Maxim. Why should he be believed? I don't mean about the murder-- *how do we know Maxim didn't love Rebecca?* Maxim says there was never any love from the beginning, since the honeymoon this slut spoke plainly about the unspeakable things she was going to do, and poor Maxim, humiliated at being tricked so easily, agrees to a sham marriage. Yet this happens:

> "Mr. de Winter used to brush her hair in the mornings," Mrs. Danvers said. "I've come up to this room time and time again and seen him, in his shirt sleeves, with the two brushes. 'Harder, Max, harder,' she

was in paint, the modern innovation is to support it with every self-serving defense in academic neuroscience-- satiety, novelty seeking, conditioning, addiction.   It sounds informative, but tellingly you can't connect with these concepts except through jargon.   You copied your way to a B- in high school biology but now you've weaponized science to defend your resentment.

While there may be plenty of negative effects of porn on men, turning them off to real women simply isn't one of them, it isn't how lust works-- and women, of all people, should know this instinctively, after all, they've been lusting after cave trolls for millennia. "But men are visual creatures."   Quotes the generation glued to their teleprompters, you may want to consider you were taught that for a reason.

> would say, laughing up at him. 'Here, I shall be late,' he would say
> throwing the brushes to me, and laughing back at her. He was
> always laughing and gay then."

So what am I supposed to do with this? It's a sham marriage, yet every morning Maxim and Rebecca perform this newlywed sitcom for the benefit of Mrs. Danvers, who already knows it's a sham marriage? NB: in this loveless sham marriage, when separate beds were common anyway, he's sleeping in the same bed as his cheating whore wife. The retort to this is that Mrs. Danvers is lying, telling this story to torment the new wife. But-- and this is my point-- the only reason you would think that is because you believe *Maxim*.

If this is *supposed to be* a psychological book, then we have to accept the psychology. Danvers almost talks the second wife into suicide. How does she do that, what power does she have over her? Danvers tells the *truth*. She solidifies the reality the second wife is trapped in, closes all the available doors, so the only way out is the bedroom window. For this kind of power to work, Danvers can't be a liar, the moment any lie is even suspected, she'd be revealed as weak, her power collapses. If her manipulative power was based on lies, even if merely suspected ones, the second wife would *hate* her. No-- the anecdote above is *literally* true.

Rebecca did have affairs, but evidently conducted them with English discretion, carefully and off site. We're told of two instances where she pursues men close to Maxim: we're not 100% sure what happens with one but the second one *rejects* her and tells Maxim about it. So much for irresistible. "I think we're supposed to believe he actually succumbed but felt guilty afterwards." Because you want to believe she's powerful even if evil rather than less evil but less powerful? No, don't look away, answer that question. Husbands, I have an honest question: which is worse, that your wife seduces your friends; or tries to seduce them and fails and then they have to come tell you she's a nut?

And what if she did have affairs-- wasn't that the established protocol among the landed aristocracy? You can say that cheating was only a privilege of the men, but when a man cheated it was usually with a woman, right? If your house has a name your responsibility isn't to fidelity but... to the house. And she was loyal to the house-- to the point that she never had an affair inside it. In fact, the only anti-patriarchal sex acts she may have committed is taunting her husband and maybe having sex with Mrs. Danvers-- and there's really no textual evidence that that happened-- but to be fair you should erase from your mind the image of Mrs. Danvers as the pitchfork triggered woman in *American Gothic*, low on estrogen and high on Jesus. As far as physicality goes she was only a decade older than Rebecca, built thin and tall like Rebecca, with similar dark hair and fair skin. She might not *look* like Rebecca, but she could be *described* as Rebecca, with evocative phrases. One wonders if Danny's obsession with Rebecca wasn't so much based on projection as identification.

Which brings us back to that second twist. I've already told you what the secondary sources say the cancer reveal at Dr. Baker's office means, but maybe you should go ahead and read the primary source for yourself to see if it's not for something else.

But in order to show what the argument is actually for I'm going to flat out accept its premises: porn is everywhere; and women can't find loving mates. Assuming these are both true, what is the relationship? There are three ways to approach this question.

First, journalistic science: what are the effects of too much porn? Does it turn men off to real women? Use no math except statistics, which you are free to make up. Discuss using appeals to authority.

Second, a post-modern approach, treating porn not as the problem but as a symptom of a larger social pathology. What are the social circumstances, the "disease of society" that caused the symptoms of ubiquitous porn and stock quotes? Use no words except jargon,

> "My name is [court magistrate Colonel] Julyan. This is Mr. [Maxim] de Winter... you may have seen Mr. de Winter's name in the papers recently."
>
> "Oh," said Dr. Baker, "yes, yes, I suppose I have. Some inquest or other, wasn't it? My wife was reading all about it."
>
> [Julyan explains to the doctor about the appointment with "Baker" discovered in Rebecca's appointment book.]
>
> [Dr. Baker goes through his records]. "There must be some mistake, I never attended a Mrs. de Winter in my life... I saw a Mrs. Danvers on the twelfth at two o'clock."
>
> "Danny? What on earth..." began Favell, but Maxim cut him short.
>
> "She gave a wrong name, of course," he said. "That was obvious from the first. Do you remember the visit now, Dr. Baker?"
>
> "Yes," he said slowly. "Mrs. Danvers. I remember now."
>
> "Tall, slim, dark, very handsome?" said Colonel Julyan.
>
> "Yes," said Dr. Baker. "Yes.... Well, she asked for the truth, and I let her have it.... This Mrs. Danvers, or Mrs. de Winter rather, was not the type to accept a lie. You must have known that."

They say the greatest trick the devil ever pulled is to convince everyone that he didn't exist. They were wrong, people found him anyway. Then Poe recommended hiding the secret in plain sight, but there will always be people hell bent on finding it. If you really want to stop looking, you have to make them think they've found it.

What if in fact it the patient *was* Mrs. Danvers-- not Rebecca at all?

> "She stood it well. She did not even flinch. She said she had suspected it for some time. Outwardly she was a perfectly healthy woman," he said, "rather too thin, I remember, rather pale, but then that's the fashion nowadays, pity though it is.... the X-rays showed a certain malformation of the uterus, I remember, which meant she could never have had a child..."

Without changing anything in the text, the episode's use completely changes. Maxim goes in there *knowing* Rebecca was pregnant, because Rebecca *told* him she was pregnant, not that she was *threatening* to get pregnant. He knows the jig is up. But what fortuitous circumstance is this? The patient is Mrs. Danvers! Maxim seizes an opportunity, pretending it was Rebecca at the doctor so

which you are free to make up. Discuss using appeals to other authorities.

In theory as theory both of these approaches can be fun, but you are going to get nowhere doing it, it will be masturbation, which is why most of you will do it.

It is an imaginary worldview of structural forces that even if absolutely correct cannot change anything, indeed, it solidifies everything. If it is 100% true that porn does turn you off to real people, are you going to stop using porn-- or real people?

Do you want to be free-- do you want to have power? Then you have to give up on knowledge. Like poker, you play the opponent, not the game, stop with the statistics, stop

---

that they can ask him if "she" was pregnant, and the answer could only be no. But it gets better: "Rebecca" also has uterine cancer, now Maxim can pretend to everyone else Rebecca committed suicide by boat, and pretend to the new wife (and reader) Rebecca womanipulated him into killing her. And why wouldn't the doctor reasonably assume Mrs. Danvers is actually Maxim's wife? The description is preposterously vague yet wonderfully evocative, and unlike the new wife Danvers is the right age for Maxim, she acts the part, and any class difference is erased when moist and grubby Favell tells him "they" are cousins and anyway Danvers is the same class as the second wife standing there before him. Colonel Julyan, defender of the patriarchy, (consciously?) goes along with it. Can you imagine that "tall, dark, and handsome"-- handsome! the super slut Rebecca!-- is all the verification they need to close the case of the murder vs. suicide of Milady de Winter? "Why do you call her Milady?" Wait, seriously? I thought the reference was obvious-- i.e. a defense. Not only do they not ask for Dr. Baker's records:

> "Shall I send the report to you or to Mr. de Winter?" said Doctor Baker.

> "We may not need it at all," said Colonel Julyan. "I rather think it won't be necessary."

They tell him *not to send them at all.*

If you think this is a stretch, consider that the cancer/suicide explanation skips over the very evidence that suggested it wasn't a suicide in the first place: Rebecca's note to Favell doesn't sound like she's suicidal. Because she's not. Of course Maxim has a reason for turning a key piece of evidence into a MacGuffin, but why does Favell forget it? Surely this requires an explanation, after all he's the one who had the strongest suspicions and supposedly *loved* Rebecca. Turns out the answer is he's stupid. That's it. I'm not kidding, this is the answer that is offered in the book: he accepts she had cancer, because now he's worried he might have cancer. Because he thinks cancer is contagious. Cancer of the uterus.

"The cancer is really just a code word for venereal disease." I see. So Rebecca doesn't really have cancer?

Modern readers can be partially forgiven for accepting Rebecca has cancer, they've been trained by media to assume it, because when a woman's power is her sexuality, losing her sexuality is worse than getting cancer, which is why in media they're always given cancer, or just murdered in their prime. Time.

If the idea of murdering your wife because she's a libertine sounds like the height of misogyny in a world that sees things as black and white, even though 900% of the time those stories are for women, wait till you see it in actual black and white. You might think I'm inventing an ambiguity at the doctor's office that no sober person would have thought of, but the Academy Award winning 1940 Hitchcock film *Rebecca* reveals it is aware of the ambiguity by deliberately fixing it: the doctor describes "Mrs. Danvers" as "a very beautiful woman, tall, dark, exquisitely dressed" whom

counting cards, don't even look at your cards, they don't matter. Your bet isn't that your cards are better than his, your bet is a message to him that whatever the cards you are still taking his money, so that he folds. In the future the game will be played between two hyper-sharks where no cards need be dealt, they will imagine themselves a hand and bet their reading of the other's unconscious, even as they try to lie. You think you're ready for that game? "Sure, I've got a system." It's actually a tell. Ok, all or nothing on one hand, ready? Go: imagine for yourself a four of a kind. Got it? Ok, what are your cards? Did you remember to imagine the fifth card as a King? Did you remember to imagine a fifth card at all?

Forget about knowledge. Forget about what it all means. Instead, treat porn not as a

---

Baker "had known for a long time", and unlike in the book came to him with the specific chief complaint of feeling pregnant. He told her it was cancer: "And then she said something peculiar. When I told her it was a matter of months, she replied, 'oh no, Doctor, not that long.'" You would have thought this crack diagnostician would have picked up on that, but it would have ruined the mystery. What the movie does make ambiguous, what it completely invents as an ambiguity-- and Holy God, you should sit down for this-- is whether Maxim *murdered* her. In the movie, he describes a struggle and her falling *accidentally* and hitting her head. So what's to cover up? He didn't shoot her and she's not pregnant. At this point there's no point in portholes or inquests or gynecologists, the movie could end there, and the entire psychological drama of the second wife loving a man who murdered a succubus evaporates because he didn't actually murder her. Like all Oscar winners, this movie is completely idiotic. Hitchcock is not a great director, you're just a stupid audience.

Hitchcock's version also switches main characters, the second wife isn't the protagonist of the movie, only Maxim is. And talk about bros before hoes: Maxim makes the final scenes' premonition-driven midnight drive back to the house ("something's wrong, I can feel it") not with his wife but with-- the friend who may have slept with Rebecca! You'll say Hitchcock had to do all this because the Hayes Code wouldn't allow any murderer to get away with a crime, Maxim would have had to be visibly punished, but instead of completely inventing a scene explicitly showing that Maxim didn't murder her, the code could have been satisfied by adding a scene at the end where Maxim dies accidentally in the house fire. Nope. Rebecca's a slut, she dies, Maxim lives and he was never guilty.

And this logic also implies that if you repeal the puritanical Hayes Code we would go back to the original text. That doesn't happen, I've checked. A me-generation later the 1979 adaptation has the doctor explain that "the woman calling herself Mrs. Danvers" came with a pain, and X-rays revealed a uterine malformation so "she could never have had any children." Great news! "But there was something else." Oh? You mean, something incidental to the important question of pregnancy?

And a meh-generation later the 1997 Masterpiece Theatre version tells you directly what to believe by skipping over any preliminaries and cutting right to the doctor saying, "the woman who came to see me gave her name as Rebecca Danvers, clearly she gave me a false name, but from your description, this was your wife." We'll take your word for it, you're an authority, after all. "There is one other thing I think you ought to know. The X-ray showed a certain malformation of the uterus, which meant she would never have been able to have a child." Everybody hear that? She wasn't pregnant and there'd be no point in trying. I don't know if this typecasting or a filmography spoiler, but if Tywin Lannister is in a movie, he's the bad guy. He was once in a movie in a wig, leather skirt and leopard print blouse: still the bad guy.

My literal re-interpretation isn't superfluous but necessary to the plot. If you accept that Maxim *tricked* everyone into thinking it was Rebecca at that doctor's office, the ending of the book makes sense *where before it did not*. Maxim gets a feeling something is wrong back home; they drive all night, sure enough, Manderley is on fire. The implication is Danvers did it.

pathology, nor even as a symptom, but as the defense. What if ubiquitous porn had to be created to fill in for a lack of something else that had disappeared? That would mean porn doesn't depict fetishes, it is the fetish.

"Is it sex?" Obvious answer, so no. "Of course it's sex." I know you were told unfounded beliefs arise because of insufficient knowledge, but run that the other way: concrete knowledge is invented to fill in for insufficient belief. What don't we have anymore, that porn could fill in for? Oh, it's love.

"How silly and antiquated." Are you confirming we don't?

Well, why did she do it? Why did she do it *then*? Because Maxim had gotten away with murder? She hadn't suspected Maxim of murder before, and anyway why would the diagnosis of Rebecca's cancer make her suspect murder? Was she upset it was erroneously labeled a suicide? She hadn't set fire to anything when the inquest declared it to be a suicide, even though she didn't believe it then. More inexplicably unexplained, Mrs. Danvers was seen packing up her belongings to leave while Maxim et al are on their way to see Dr. Baker-- *before* they actually meet him. Why? Is she a medium, is that why this is a gothic tale? No-- *she knew what the doctor would say.* What she didn't know, what she was surprised to learn, was how Maxim would spin it.

And then she didn't *just* leave, she set fire to the place, and the only thing that changed is that after the doctor's meeting, Favell called her up. The exact timeline here is actually spelled out in detail preposterously superfluous-- unless it isn't. According to the official story, he must have told her that Rebecca had cancer. Was Danvers enraged Rebecca had cancer? The tenuous answer has always been that it is because Maxim got away with murder, but again, Danvers had never suspected him of murder. *Why would learning Rebecca had cancer make her suddenly think Maxim had gotten away with murder?* You can imagine Danvers beating her forehead with the phone: "No, no, no! Rebecca didn't have cancer, I had cancer; she would never have abandoned me for suicide... you're telling me Maxim convinced you all she was me, he's using my terminal illness to prove she committed suicide? He would only have done that if he killed her! Maxim got away with it-- because of me!?" The story never describes what happened to Danvers, she is never heard from again. You know who else disappears? Favell.

The second wife offers us some poetic nonsense to explain why they can never go back home, "oh, boo hoo, last night I dreamt I was in Manderley again," too many painful memories to live there; evidently not painful enough to have prevented them from living there after first having *covered up* a murder. So why not after being *exonerated*? The likely answer is more concrete: now Danvers and Favell know he did it. If Maxim and wife show their faces again, they will be exposed. In fact, based on the text, we aren't actually sure they haven't already been exposed, because Maxim and wife are literally *in hiding*.

> "It never would have occurred to me that this Mrs. Danvers and
> Rebecca were really the same person," said Dr. Baker.

Never mind the doctor-- that it never occurred to you doesn't seem odd to you? Let me say it another way: that's a quote from the book. After reading that quote from the book in the book itself--

A step into the minefield of the author's other bioweapons supports this. Du Maurier's bisexuality is said to be reflected in Rebecca, and she's celebrated for her stories' "use of the double", a thing or person becomes the manifestation of the return of the repressed, but a less literate but more literal description isn't double but "mistaken identity." Her doubles don't stand for something else; the double is actually something else, it doesn't even know it's representing anything, it is not at all what the protagonist projects on it. *Don't Look Now* (#5 on Top 20 Horror Movies Of All Time, who the

"I know you're in love with me, why can't you express it?!" says a woman to a man portrayed as too busy wielding power to know he's in love. "I don't care how much money you make or what you look like, I love you." Remember how we used to roll our eyes at women when they said that? Great news: they got the message.

The worst kind of woman wasn't a whore or slut, who trades her sex for money or pleasure-- that has a ledger's logic to it-- but a woman who compromises in love. Holly Golightly and *Pretty Woman* were presented as aspirational images to women in their times, because both were "hookers" (=wise and worldly) whose sexuality was a kind of power. But the relevance to the collateral damaged men is the real life compromise they were promised: from now on your woman is going to have a pretty extensive sexual backstory, but at least she's

---

hell writes these lists?) is a concrete example, but *The Apple Tree*, seen literally for what it is, is a story about a man who is *not* tormented by his dead wife that has returned as a tree; that tree is not his wife. I understand she "represents" his wife, but the projection is at the level of the protagonist, not the story. The suspension of disbelief isn't that in the story that *is* his wife, let's see what happens; the suspension of disbelief is that it's a tree and he's a nut, the tree has apples and the nut has an axe.

This digression is not intended to highlight the multiplicity of textual interpretations, nor do I care about the usual discussion about how the wife is willing to accept Maxim is a murderer because it proves he loves her, that discussion just lets us put a distance between her logic and our own, "I don't condone it, but I understand." What happens here is different: the readers-- all of whom I am sure would proudly prefix *feministe* to their patronymic (and yes, I know what a patronymic is)-- allow themselves to be lead, by Maxim, into *blaming the victim*. In what other story does the reader accept without reservation the account of the prime suspect, and then let him lead us in how we should understand the evolving evidence? Usually the only way to pull this off in a story is to have that prime suspect also be the unreliable narrator; but here we have a gullible narrator-- a secondary source-- brokering our acceptance of what an unreliable prime suspect wants us to believe.

For what purpose, and at what cost? What does it get us to "blame the victim"? The usual answer is it's for the benefit of the aggressor, because even though he's hardly worth the legal fees you want there to be precedent in case real-deal patriarchs want to rape a few victims, but for everyone else not involved in raping or being raped this story suggests an entirely different purpose: we blame the victim to transfer power away from the aggressor to the victim, so that the victim has more of some kind of power, because no other kind of power can be fantasized. We are told categorically to *always* believe the rape victim's report, so it's instructive to observe those moments where we are told categorically *not* to believe them. *To Kill A Mockingbird* (#26 of the Top 100 Novels Seen Only As Movies) used to be a standard middle school textbook, until porn it was a peri-pubescent kid's first introduction to the concept of rape/interr, and the whole point there is that we're NOT supposed to believe her. She actually did want it. I know it turns out he didn't do it, but according to the rules in rape cases he's guilty until proven innocent, and anyway a jury said he was, the only reason you'd believe Tom Robinson's side is that he was defended by Gregory Peck. "Her father said it was a rape because he didn't want people to know she desired a black man." Then he could have simply kept quiet about it, hell, he could have killed Tom and gotten away with it. He could have said Tom robbed her, why would he invent the story of rape *and shame himself for no reason*, tell everyone a black man's penis went inside her when he knows perfectly well it didn't? Unless it did, consensually? Is that racism or the projection of an unresolved Oedipal complex? From the moment the teacher *assigns* Chapter 1 of this melanoma you know you are to assume the Ewells are bad people, as symbolized by their poverty, lack of education, and skin color. "Tom couldn't have hit Mayella's left eye because he was right handed." You have clearly never been in a fight.

Off topic, here's where I live: her name is Mayella Violet Ewell: may "she" violate y'all. Good night everybody, drive safe.

not a hooker; but more importantly when she gets to you it doesn't count: she loves you. And a movie like 1993's *Indecent Proposal*, where the wife is offered a million dollars for a one night stand, the film's conflict wasn't just how the husband would feel but whether doing it would affect her love for him, she hesitated because the transaction had significance, it weighed against her soul. It might make her love him less.[13] (It did.) Try to film that kind of movie now, it's impossible, not only would she get a brazilian wax the night before, not only would her husband have champagne ready, her prion divoted brain would articulate the collective logic of its zombie audience: "I don't really want to do it, but whenever money is offered I have to take it, and since I have to do it for the money, I may as well enjoy it."[14]

And you need to be very clear about the insane direction of the post-capitalist utopia: it

---

That's why Rebecca has to be a murder victim and also be responsible. We *want* Rebecca to be powerful. We even want Danvers to be powerful. Since no one has any idea what powerful men do except be evil, and no idea what powerful women do except dress well, Rebecca has to be made to be evil and dress well. I hate this planet. The need to make Rebecca an anti-patriarchy antihero allows him to get away with murder; it requires her to "transgress" all of the "normative" "functions" and "roles" of a woman, so not only does she need to cheat, but she needs to have orgies, be bisexual, laugh at her husband, develop a purely female disease (today it would be breast cancer because that better deprives the patriarchy of what it uses women for), even take total control over her own life and death-- Maxim is powerless, she has the power to compel him to act on her desire, or, in jargon: she cuckolds him-- and does NOT get pregnant. Having another man's baby sounds anti-patriarchy but it's only anti-Maxim; getting pregnant was still a woman's role. English society is long practiced at assimilating bastard children from either genital, what the patriarchy won't permit-- what you can lose your head for doing-- is not ever having a son. In order to claim a small victory against the master, in order to steal back a little satisfaction, the reader accepts *everything* that the master declares is true. Ok, sure, of course Colonel Julyan lets Maxim get away with murder because Maxim matters more to him than Rebecca. But the reader is willing to allow Maxim to get away with the cold blooded murder of his pregnant wife, to refuse her justice-- just to pretend she had power. And to give her that appearance of power, the rest of the patriarchy has to be solidified. In other words, in order for her to be powerful, she must have kinda sorta wanted it. You people are lunatics, now every time I meet a woman named Rebecca I feel like her mom is probably a jerk. "It means 'loving wife'." It also means 'tied ox'. I guess we'll see what happens next.

12 Of all the quotes and citations in this book, you think this is the one that deserves APA format?

13 Careful now, the movie is tricky and not on purpose. Redford, being known from other movies to be rich and handsome, appears as desirable, but his attractiveness is a defense which allows the audience to answer the first two and avoid the third of three questions which are at the heart of all relationships; make him ugly and the defense collapses.

First: what kind of a woman am I that I slept with him for money? Answer: No, I fell for him, and to prove it I'm staying.

Second: What kind of a man did I marry, that he'd let his wife sleep with another man, for money? Answer: But he's actually a very powerful and dominant man, not a cuck loser, look how loud and aggressive his jealousy is, it was capitalism that confused him, he didn't really want me to do it.

Third: What kind of a woman am I, that I married the kind of man who would allow his wife to sleep with another man for nothing more than money? Answer: All I know is a handsome man like Redford wouldn't have chosen me unless I was worth it.

There's a difference between what a fantasy means and what you use it for. To illustrate this, turn the question around and ask it of the men: no, not the homosexual "would you sleep with a man for a million dollars?" but "would you pay a woman a million dollars to sleep with you?" No? So who

can *only* be money. She can't willingly trade her body for food, housing, or even a job because the power imbalance renders her consent invalid; but trading her sex for money is a woman's inviolable right to do with her body what she wants. Why? Because women are too stupid to know money "hides the social interactions that underlie it"? No. Because they don't count. Only the money counts. But to whose benefit? The guy would rather only pay you money.

Let's not get ahead of ourselves-- of course men don't believe in love either, they gave up on it and God generations ago; *but how were they able to do this?* Their vast knowledge of science had given them the courage to face the existential abyss, through their own power? They-- of the steady salary and 3-6 channels of television? The only reason they were able to give it up is that the women had agreed to take it on, so long as the men agreed-- "to what? Go to work

---

would?

That question is the price you pay to use the fantasy your way, because the guy in your answer is someone who has millions of dollars-- a guy for whom money is meaningless. In order to have the fantasy she is worth a million dollars, she must believe that a million dollars is worthless.

"Whatever, I'd still have the million dollars." Yes, that response was obvious-- yet it had to be said out loud. You should take note every time that happens, there before you is the defense. What you think you're doing is arguing about relative value, to you the money is worth way more than some diminished self-esteem. Except that you don't have the money-- you imagine you'd have it. The whole thing is hypothetical, a fantasy, so while in fact we've discovered you in fact don't think you're worth the money, you also in fact don't have the money. The only compensation you needed to admit to your valuelessness is the *fantasy* of a million dollars. I know a lot of professionals whose rate is $500/hr *in theory*, but in practice they charge a "sliding scale"= a quarter of that, reserving the $500 for "those who can afford it." Maybe they get that fee once an Olympiad, so it's hardly about the income; since they don't have the ability to charge what they wish they are worth, they need there to exist a theoretical client with power to declare they are.

14 Is she having sex with Redford because she secretly desires him and the money is an excuse so she's not a slut, or is she secretly doing it for the money and Redford's handsomeness is the excuse so she's not a whore? Choose your generation's pathology: in the former, sex is prohibited, so the money is the excuse; in the latter the greed is prohibited, and the sex is the excuse.

This could be a way to discuss the changing cultural acceptability of desires and how we variously permit or forbid them. However, there's no point in doing this, because in this case it's not about which desires are more acceptable.   She doesn't sleep with Redford because she wants sex *or* money-- both of those are defenses. She sleeps with him because she has no choice. *It's in the contract.*

She gets a lawyer to draft a contract exchanging her sex for his money. Why is there a contract at all? If she's afraid he won't pay, why not half now, half on delivery? Why a contract? It may be Nevada but it's utterly unenforceable and does anyone doubt Redford could easily circumvent it? During the negotiations Redford finds it all a bit childish but he plays along, it seems to make her feel more comfortable. But why would it? It doesn't protect her, it doesn't compel or limit him in any way. It compels *her*. The contract exists to give her the impression that she is subject to something greater than her desires or her will, not to give her the feeling of safety but to give her *no choice* in the matter-- it takes the question of what she *wants* right out of the decision. Once she signs, she must have sex with him. It may seem trivial distinction but one involves choosing a pen and the other involves choosing a penis. The latter is an impossible act of will.

The form of every decision she makes is, "I want-- or don't want-- something, I cannot pursue it directly, so I need something to compel me to do what I want to do." Her husband later on jealously accuses, "you did this for yourself!" And she cries, "I would never have done this for myself!"

130

in the morning?"   No, I was going to say: agreed to defer to the women on these matters. Now the situation has changed.[15] It's possible some individual men felt love, if they were girlie enough, but they didn't have to: to maintain "healthy, committed relationships", it was enough that women-- not real women, but "women in general"-- believed it existed.

But glance at any TV show for women now, their stories or their media to see that women don't believe in love anymore, unless it's for a child, unrequited, or someone's dying. Not that they don't have it-- they don't WANT it.   "Do those three kinds of love have anything in common?" Yes: they are all safe, you are free to emote passionately because there is no danger of dependency; see also "becoming obsessed" with a married man. "I want him because I can't have him."   What are you talking about, you've had him multiple times.

That's 100% accurate. It doesn't mean she didn't want it, who knows? In the 90s men had to be regularly reminded that it was a woman's prerogative to change her mind, so that everyone was on notice that the men could not, unless you want her to think you're a girl. But it doesn't matter what she wanted.   She caused someone else to force her to do it. On the big night, Redford senses her ambivalence and offers her one last way out, you want to flip a coin? Oh, look, it's affirmative consent-- he pretends to offer her yet another way out when in fact she could just say good bye. But she can't just say good bye; that would be a choice. In fact, she can't even choose the coin.   No, she bravely stares him down and asserts herself: "It's your party." He flips, and of course it comes up give me heads, but again, it doesn't matter what comes up, only that the coin chooses, which it doesn't, it's all on autopilot, but to make it all better afterwards he says, "nothing will happen that you don't choose." If he had said "nothing will happen that you don't want" you could roll your eyes at early 90s male chauvinism, but this way anticipates by a generation the workaround to affirmative consent: who am I to assume what she wants? All I know is she consented. "It's not consent."   She said, "it's your party." It's consent. But it's not a choice, it's merely the camera ready pornographic performance of a choice she doesn't actually make, she doesn't make a single conscious choice in the entire movie, not in spite of being the protagonist-- i.e movie is badly written-- but *because* she is the protagonist. Even at the end, when she wants to leave Redford and go back to her husband, she can't dump him-- that's another impossible act of will; but sensing her impotence, and knowing that him leaving her would be felt by her as a deprivation, he graciously creates a scenario in which she is compelled to leave him-- in this case, he tells her the obvious lie that she is one of many women he's bedded in this manner. The obviousness of this lie is a necessary part of the defense: she gets to simultaneously know he's lying (she's not just some chick he wanted to bed) and know he is telling her the truth (but she is still a fox he wanted to bed.) How is this simultaneity possible? Because their conversation is happening in the limo where Redford's performance is done in front of an audience: the ethical chauffeur. This is the conversation that didn't merit putting the screen up? If it had been just the two of them alone, it would have been impossible not to acknowledge Redford was completely lying; but since the audience could interpret it either way means she can have it both ways, and to ensure this Redford invites the chauffeur to participate in the conversation. Redford is the catalyst that creates gold from lead, but consistent with alchemy the transmutation can only occur in the presence of another who can be fooled. The husband, meanwhile, has to turn himself into gold the old fashion way, i.e. work; a whole series of actions (i.e. get off his butt, get a job, devote himself to his craft) were needed in order to create his value.

But these changes take on an ironic twist. At the end they get back together, repeating love lines from the beginning of the movie. Either they got back together because they were able to get past all this, or they could only get together because of all this. If it's the latter, then the irony is that while Demi could have learned her value merely by Redford offering the deal, it was the husband who needed to be cuckolded. Unless he thought she was worth a million dollars to a rival, he would not have tried to become a man, let alone worthy of her.

15 It may be useful to look at another time when the reverse change occurred, i.e. when women took

---

You're trying to convince me you get off on being *deprived?* Being self-critical is the way you lie to your self and your god because they won't make you dig any further, but it isn't going to work with me.

The death of love is frequently discussed in the pages of the media for "smart" women, where clarity of writing substitutes for depth of thought, for the demo that loves to wonder: now that I make just enough to cover the interest, what's a gal to do when I inevitably become single again? Trade up, trade down, or just ride it out? "Love or career?" Let's ask the experts: surprise, the experts chose career.[16]

"It's all structural sexism." Don't worry, men's turn next.

---

over a substantially male prerogative. Questions you should always ask about history: why then? Why there? Why them? *What does the author want to be true?*

The story of why and how women courageously wrested suffrage from the hands of white mustachioed Monopoly bankers is obvious and celebrated and thus of no interest here, we have women on both of our most useless moneys, I know what suffrage means to women, what I want to know is *how it was used.*

Women first got the right to vote in Wyoming in 1869. No doubt you were unaware that Wyoming was even a state in 1869, and lucky for you it wasn't, so note Wyoming *males* decided to give the women the vote even before they decided to join the U.S.-- this, four years after the Civil War. Next came Utah, a fabrication of the Mormon church with a theretofore suspicious track record in gender equality. That very same year the American Woman Suffrage Association and the National Woman Suffrage Association (being American was so bourgeois) were born in progressive Boston and New York City but it still took 35 years to bring suffrage to cosmopolitan Eastern Time, and then only because it was supported by the men in the labor unions. We must contend with an odd historical correlation, that the fewer the number of vocal women fighting for empowerment, the more quickly they were empowered.

What was it about Wyoming women that made the need for their enfranchisement so obvious to the men? The imaginary of the wild west Winchester and wagon train woman more self-reliant than any sissy Sassachusetts socialite is the dominant mythology of today, but it is in contrast to the reality of the frontier's females being just as frittering and feminine as those in 1950s TV suburbia, with less orgasms. "It's not an umbrella you brute, it's a parasol." The myth is taught today because the story of suffrage is needed not as history, nor even as celebration, but to retroactively provide the evidence that it wasn't about something else; and the level playing field of the frontier, lacking the nominally feminine conveniences of laws, God, and indoor plumbing, were the perfect proving grounds. The myth tries to show what should be a humanist axiom because in reality it was not *and still is not.* No one, especially the women, thought women were equal to men. They were *better.*

But if Wyoming women were proper not powerful, why them? Why would Wyoming *men* want those women to be their political equals? Think about this, think about this today. What alternative was so threatening that they preferred female empowerment? "There must be an economic reason." Only 1/3 of the time, and here no, unless you mean economic in its literal Greek, in which case yes.

The threat to men, to the "establishment", was-- other men. How you tell the story of those other men depends on the story you want to tell, so I'll tell all three because they're connected by a railroad. Communities of 1) hard working 2) white 3) Protestant *men*, with families and values and status, were overnight invaded by 10000 railroad workers= immigrants: Irish, Germans, and elsewhere Italians and even Mexicans, derisively stereotyped as "Catholics". They were solitary, poor, nasty, and brutish, fueled by high levels of endogenous testosterone and higher levels of exogenous alcohol, 2x the procreation rate of the native/temperate/moral Protestants= "Americans". Who would civilize them-- or at the very least uphold proper decency? Teach them to keep it in

132

Despite on-paper economic and social equality, in many metrics superiority, women find themselves still on the margins. Not melancholic-- but anxious. "Women are pulled in every direction." The net force is always only one direction-- the one no one ever says out loud. The conflict is described as between the requirements of the career and responsibilities of motherhood. But the practical considerations are obvious-- what are the psychological ones? If we're honest, all the family responsibilities aren't stressful because they take time away from work, and neither is work stressful because it takes time away from family, but because the combination of both *but especially the family* takes time away from "for myself." When you can't get any time for yourself, no one blames the career; why would you? It gives you self-worth, doesn't ask increasingly of you, doesn't infinitely depend on you. The family does.

---

their pants? Today's notion that suffrage was seen as a small step towards greater sexual freedom for women would be merely laughable if it wasn't specifically intended as a giant step in the opposite direction for everyone. The women weren't looking to burn their corsets; they were looking to put men in them. What these women and men wanted was a home culture, compatible with the widest possible emancipation. The first step towards social regulation and good society in towns, cities, and villages is the ballot in the hands of the mothers of those places. Let the men look after the greenback theory or the hard-money theory or the free-trade or tariff, and the women will do the home housekeeping of the government, which is to take care of the moral government and the social regulation of their home department. Woman suffrage the little children to come unto them should be understood as a repressed idea returning as a triad: voting, temperance, anti-immigration. "Why do you say they're repressed?" Nice try, I said exactly the opposite.

So in a territory with 6 times more men than women, woman suffrage in Wyoming is useful in two ways: it would prove a great advertisement, drawing women's hopefully Protestant vaginas there, who will no doubt vote in accordance with principled morality, and thus increase the power of the establishment. Helpfully, it also locates the political power so you know what buildings to board up: Protestant political power organized itself in(side) the churches, while the degenerates did it after Sunday Mass in saloons, drunkenly, but unanimously. Thus, the first target of the suffrage=temperance movement wasn't the drink but the drinkery, through the enforcement of Sabbath laws. Within 6 months of woman suffrage, Wyoming went from being a Viking sack *back* to a Puritan state. A civics lesson which is 100% true: one cannot vote for change.

Two months later, Utah gave its women the right to vote-- italics theirs: *its* women. Susan B. Anthony delusionally misinterpreted this as a vote against polygamy, voting for the right to marry the same man could only be ignorance or coercion; the irony being that if the 15 year old Mormon women had been voting for the right to marry the same woman we today would canonize them. I'll save you the trouble of explaining this: it's because we are bad people. But while polygamy was on the minds of everyone else, the Mormons themselves wanted woman suffrage as a means of preserving not polygamy per se but *everything else*. Unlike Homestead Act Wyoming, the Mormons of Utah had a carefully planned political community held together by a theocracy that would have made John Winthrop ejaculate in his grave, but was baffling to the modern Purityrannicals who were anxious to derail its undeniable success. It should never have worked; it seemed unable to fail. Worse, as unAmerican as Mormonism seemed, it was actually the only thing in America that was purely American, even California gold came from outer space. "What about the Indians?" What Indians? And unlike Wyoming, the Mormons weren't overrun by immigrant labor because they just built their part of the railroad themselves. Besides, properly managed, immigration could mean converts. As a wholly American religion and society, their worries were quintessentially Mountain Time American, tell me if this sounds familiar: they thought the real threat was the Federal Government. They knew by history and scripture that if the government had their way, they would kill the lot of them, raze the whole thing down to its very foundations, and probably build a hotel on it. To appreciate the existential seriousness upon which was grounded their "nativism"/ "racism"/ "ecumenism"/ "sexism"-- all the misleading -isms which make their actions impossible to interpret,

"That's the trick of capitalism." Capitalism? You think capitalism wants you to spend your free time looking at pictures?

Women were surprised to discover they had contracted a male disease from three generations ago: alienation. "What can I do about it?"[17] Well, you can start with Kierkegaard, that might help. "That's more of a... guy thing." For another generation, anyway.

So you can forgive the average guy for being frustrated, watching as modern women devalue love and idealism, in favor of consumer products, social justice, and celebrity gossip. I said you can forgive him-- because I don't. Do you think he figured this all out on his own? Unable to read anything longer than ingredients yet well-jargonized about the inherent biases

---

let alone predict-- note that while males fell under the typical restrictions on voting such as age, residence, and taxes, in order for a Utah female to vote she needed to be a female *and nothing else*. Only in Mormon Utah *and only for women* was voting not just a privilege but technically a right. Everyone else had to endure it. This maneuver was an early example of the reversal in political power: previously, since voters were only white males, the electorate could be invisibly shaped through "tests" which here and there squeezed out the few voters dangerous to the establishment. But after the Civil War, with the unavoidable enfranchisement of blacks, the tests became more difficult to use because they were too easily seen as racially motivated and thus illegal. It became harder for them to purify the electorate. So they flooded it.

Who was more anxious about women's enfranchisement: the Mormon patriarchists in Utah or the humanist abolitionists in the U.S. Congress? Who was more horrified at wagons full of pubescent, semi-illiterate girls rolling up to cast their ballot for the social safety net of polygamy? "It's a woman's right to choose," the Church leaders scripted helpfully. Shortening the skirts or raising the hemlines was not on the minds of the Mormons, nor the goody men of Wyoming. Neither was it on the minds of the women. Voting was then, as it is now, a tool for maintaining the status quo, not changing it.

Consider the counterexample, Colorado, where it took more than seven years after Wyoming just to muster up a referendum. It was handily rejected. Certainly, 6000 native-born men, temperance men, cultivated, broad, generous, just men, men who think, voted for women's suffrage; but they were beat out by 16000 Mexican greasers. I'm sure Susan B. Anthony would have had a more subtle analysis, but facts are facts.

What weren't relevant were economic motives. There were none; though at least Big Liquor was against it. What was changing was power, not money; indeed, the precise problem was that money didn't translate to power, except in the obscene case of outright bribery= railroads. 85% of the wealth was held by 15% of the people, ok sure, but worse, much worse, for everyone there appeared to be no proportionality of power, it was *not* related to money, or to knowledge, to anything real. Why should the educated shopkeeper have the same voice as the uneducated laborer? Why should their collective voice be less just because there were fewer shopkeepers than laborers? Shopkeepers built this country, the laborers had to be told where to hammer the nails. It didn't matter that they still had more power; it was enough that the velocity of its accumulation was decreasing-- and it made them bananas. The men and the women who supported suffrage in the West saw themselves becoming less more-powerful against what should have been an impotent class of foreign laborers. Their language reflected the hysterical illogicality of the besieged: at once the dominant majority enforcing the values of the Founding Fathers, simultaneously a shrinking subclass succumbing to barely bilingual barbarians. The problem wasn't *what* America was changing into, it was only that America was *changing*. So sudden was the change that it caused them-- in almost no time at all-- to "remember" a universal truth that no one ever believed: women were better than men at truth, justice, and The American Way. This hope seems always revived during periods of perceived social crisis=alienation, and always in media; it represents not an appreciation by men and women that

of the media, he immersed himself Oracle-style (*Batman*, not *Matrix*) in front of multiple teleprompters and-- figured it all out on his own. "I did a deep dive." And now you have the bends. He understands that the media put on display pimps and women giving birth and having sex with their own brothers, and then that same media also claims that the way we live today isn't really living. So now, because of them, our country is crammed with Republicrats and stupid Democratic monkeys who cheat the people. There's no one to carry the torch. [18]

He thinks because the women's media is branded as Not For Him, as if he is seeing something secret, seeing what women are really thinking. This former algebra drop out never considered that if he figured it out, he must have been given the answers; this "secret"

---

women are as good as men but resignation by both that most men are not very good for anything. It is not feminism. It is despair.

Because most of you are idiots it needs to be stated explicitly that suffrage was good and necessary for women, and the country; and that the women who fought for it truly believed in it. I would never doubt the sincerity of the rube, this is America: the customer is always right as long as and etc. What the history of suffrage suggests, however, is that such political movements are not higher social consciousness, but neither base economics in disguise. They condense into these; they manifest as idealism with easily detected economic causes to hide that their motive force lies elsewhere.

The expansion of the vote in the West was superficially about equality, more quietly a way of giving the "right" people more power, more sinisterly a way of preventing the loss of their power, but most fundamentally a way to **prevent** change-- supporting suffrage to protect their vision-- literally vision, the image-- of the status quo. Not at all coincidentally, the people who opposed suffrage also wanted to protect their vision of the status quo, because woman suffrage appeared to mean they would lose their power. Their differences were obvious and thus a red herring. What mattered was their point of agreement: American *democracy* at that moment-- at the moment when universal suffrage was being debated but before it actually happened-- was a dangerous farce, a manipulation by (choose your) Others who were going to ruin America; America would be unable to fulfill its promises to (choose your) "real" Americans. It doesn't matter who was right, or that the positions were impossibly incompatible. Most-- yes, for totally opposite reasons-- perceived that the patriarchy *or whatever it represented* was failing. Some toyed with the only alternative the herd mentality could imagine from their pamphlets and magazines-- socialism; but most believed that what was needed was a "real" democracy, not a manipulated kleptocracy for the benefit of special interests like the railroad, or women, or big business, or immigrant poor, or men, or etc. They wanted a return, or a leap, to a legitimate direct democracy, more representative of the people who were truly invested in the American project, whoever you thought that was. It did not matter that that sentence, full of phonemes and diphthongs, did not make any sense. Both sides pursued this course; and thus became the unwitting rubes in their own golden fleecing.

The "average" Wyoming and Utah man hoped (while others feared) that giving women the vote would change the distribution of power. And it did. But not because women voted. It turned out that women didn't need *to* vote, all that was necessary was that they *could* vote. Of course suffrage made women a visible political class, but as their desires were in line with their husbands' or their pastors' it hardly mattered. What mattered was that by their enfranchisement, the power of voting had been *negated*.

First, the *way* women got the right to vote was a perfect symbol for the future of voting. In states like Colorado that held popular referendums, suffrage was reliably defeated. The places which succeeded in granting women the vote did it through legislative action-- i.e. by *bypassing* the vote. These places were not states but territories, and so were not obligated to hold a referendum. A few legislators, a governor and poof: suffrage in Wyoming in under a month. In fact, it's not even clear

135

discussion for women is *for him* in order to convey to him *that* women don't believe in love, regardless of whether or not they actually do, so they-- the men-- him-- shouldn't either. The goal of all media isn't to band individuals together by their demographic. It's to form demographics based on a desire they didn't know they are about to have. The point is to separate individuals. To obliterate love.

Women fall for the same trap. "Men are threatened by successful women," they say, glaring at the naked airbrushed airhead in the men's magazine, forgetting that same airhead was airbrushed into women's media, with slightly more clothes and a caption that read, "Even her brains are too big for her shirt!" Maybe what he's threatened by is the kind of women who think that's what men are threatened by. Those women are lunatics. Why would a man

---

that the people of Wyoming knew about the bill or would have even wanted woman suffrage. What they wanted didn't matter. And in those states where suffrage failed due to popular vote, what was Plan B? No, not how to give women power; but how to dilute the political and social effects of drunken liturgicals? To ensure "progressive" (=Protestant) values, to make sure everyone gets on the same page (of Revelation(s))? The answer will be familiar: public schools. It became a social movement of its own; and when woman suffrage included the right to hold office, the office women wanted to hold was school board. If attendance at public (=government) schools that they controlled could be mandatory, then a "minority" government could still subvert even a majority immigrant/Catholic upbringing. Obviously, anyone who didn't send their children to public schools revealed himself to be a dangerous anti-progressive fanatic-- justifying the need for such schools in the first place. Ostensibly like the ancient Greeks they claimed to admire, education was conceived as political, the education not of the individual but of the citizen; State training for the benefit of the soul for the sole benefit of the State. It is correct to say that the "decline of public education" began precisely with its invention. It was never for education or progress; it was for maintaining the status quo.

Second, women voting had the immediate and paradoxical effect of *reducing* the total number of votes cast. In Wyoming's 1869 election (prior to the passage of woman suffrage), 5000 out of 8000 people voted. In the next year's election, despite the total population increasing by 1000 and the inclusion of women, the vote *fell by half*. No doubt voter fraud explains the previously high numbers, but if so, why would women voting decrease the fraud? The public explanation of the time was that the presence of women voters (not even their votes) "civilized" election day henanigans. But the more likely explanation is that it was simply not worth it. Voting might affect the candidates, so what? The time had come to control the office or at the very least how votes were counted. e.g. in 1910 the majority of the population was rural, not urban; by 1920 (post woman suffrage) it was the opposite. Conveniently however, Congress did not reapportion the electoral college, so that rural Protestantism was disproportionately overrepresented. Actions have consequences, and the consequences were Calvin Coolidge.

This explains what would otherwise be a paradox: did it not occur to the anti-immigrant suffrage fighters that they would also be empowering immigrant women? If you take their true goal to be not the right to vote per se, not to increase one's own power specifically, but to *deprive others of their power*, then in that they succeeded: the fight for suffrage negated overall the power of the vote-- even at their own expense. It shifted power away from individuals and to some other omnipotent entity. That they thought this entity (the "government") would then do what they wanted is both irrelevant and 100% the point: it is the shift from wanting to act on what one wants to wanting someone to act on what you cannot. This trend continues into today. It is telling that the modern public debate about the utility of online voting is about the elections, when the technology actually makes possible an Athenian style direct democracy, where every citizen votes on everything the State does. *Nobody* wants that.

The suffrage movement, publicly declared as equality with men and privately understood as a return

want her because she's successful? Why would you want a man to want you because you're successful? Why do you want him to want-- how you want? Why would you want the kind of guy who wants the kind of woman that wants to be wanted for being successful? And if you get him, what then? You'll share a house, but you're going to need a second TV, and a fifth.

"But I'm a woman and I believe in love." I'm sorry, who said you could speak? No one cares what you think. You're not *really* a woman, progressive, aspirational, conscious; you're just an indoctrinated dummy who wants to meet the right guy.[19] Real women want to know: what do "successful" women think? What do "feminist leaders" think-- i.e. what does the media think? In some episode of some TV show an attractive 40 year old was getting a Brazilian wax, and the waxer girl hesitatingly compliments her for having the "most beautiful

---

to democracy in reaction to the power of special interests and unAmerican influences, desired not to increase the power of women specifically, but to lessen the power of everything: money, class, race, gender or population. They wanted the former, but only the latter would satisfy them. The result was the negation of popular power and its shift elsewhere. But as long as power was visibly lost by the Other, even those less powerful, this was termed equality.

This is explains the strained, almost fantastic interpretation of the connection between the woman suffrage and Negro suffrage movements that is popularly hoped to be symbiotic. It seems obvious to characterize women's rights as a minority issue, but whites giving blacks the right to vote meant enfranchising a small, albeit cohesive, minority voting block. Giving the vote to women, a potential *majority* of people, is not in the logic of power unless, *properly managed*, they could change-- or negate-- someone else's. This potential majority, publicly voiced by Elizabeth Cady Stanton and Susan B. Anthony, did indeed implicitly think itself above the colored man; but more urgently, it *explicitly* feared that a formerly degraded and oppressed minority suddenly given power might become little despots and take it out on the only ones left without power.   It is correct to say that over the next 80 years blacks became *dis*enfranchised *thanks to* women's enfranchisement. Woman suffrage wasn't logically complementary to Negro suffrage; it was its antidote.

…. or so the second level analysis might conclude, true as far as it goes, suitable for 5th grade homework or dinner party with any of the college educated idiots who pride themselves on knowing about the darker complexities but still want to think suffrage was by and for women against stodgy old white male capitalists.

If woman suffrage represented a progressive force for women against an older, traditional, established, patriarchal system, then logically male support for woman suffrage should have been greater among the young males and decrease tremendously with older age and status. It did not. It was the opposite.

I quote:

> (regarding Colorado's referendum): The Methodist men were for us; the Presbyterians and Episcopalians very fairly so, and the Roman Catholics were not all against us…

> Married men will vote for suffrage if their wives appreciate its importance. 2) Men without family ties will vote against it. 3) Boys who have just reached their majority will vote against it more uniformly than any other class of men…. Destitute of experience, and big with their own importance, these young sovereigns will speak to a woman twice their years with a flippancy which the most ignorant foreigner of mature age would not use…

You can hastily reformulate your understanding of the patriarchy. It's not a structural conflict with

pussy I've ever seen... what's your secret?" Ah, unfiltered girl talk, broadcast to the men. Answer: she abstains from sex and just pleasures herself. "Give me a book and a vibrator, and I'm happy," says a woman who isn't. It's easy to roll your eyes at this nut and I'm sure in subsequent episodes she'll cut herself, but dismissing her means missing the scene and exactly what is wrong with her brain: despite swearing off sex, *she was still getting a brazilian*-- no doubt because doing the thing men wanted from her but keeping it for herself now makes her feel good about herself. So this enlightened socialiste is whacked in a very specific way: she hasn't shed her primitive/bourgeois/patriarchal need for sex, love, whatever-- she hasn't changed the game, she is still 100% all in, she's simply replaced her partners with herself in order to

---

your Dad, it's a rivalry with your boyfriend. Even your Dad thinks he's a jerk.

I flippantly observed that female suffrage was an advertisement for women to bring their vaginas to Wyoming. Well, I was being flippant but I was also quoting the Wyoming legislature: "it would prove a great advertisement."

But advertisement to whom? Women? Were single 20 somethings likely to board the party train to Cheyenne? Only *fathers* could realistically make the decision to relocate their women; the advertisement only makes sense if the ad's target demo is fathers, fathers who were making a calculation-- the same one fathers are making right now-- that they must give their daughters as many rights and powers as possible, or else they must give them a machine gun. *The fathers must have felt that men could no longer be relied upon to take care of the women*. Even if it was indeed true that men prior to the Civil War believed that marriage was the only/best chance for their women to have a secure life, they did not think this anymore. The wives must have made a similar calculation in order to go along with dragging their ovulating daughters towards the 10000 drunken penises and whatever else awaited them in the West.

They *said* that the threat was German; they *said* they worried about their daughters in a sea of gunslinging immigrants, foreskinned and intoxicated. But the fathers didn't seriously imagine their daughters would associate with them, the fear merely condensed as them. The fathers were worried about "all" males-- if we are to be psychologically accurate, the kinds of males they themselves used to be.

Read the quoted Colorado passage again, I hope you can detect that what this woman *hates* even more than illegal immigrants is young, white, American men. Her specific criticism should be taken literally, it is that they are disrespectful to older women. How can they thus be trusted to take care of women like they are supposed to? Neither is the problem their age, but their generation; the writer knows these young sovereigns will age, but she does not expect them to mature. Women, in a vacuum of "real men", and thus the last stand against civil and moral decline, were on their own.

What few noticed, however, was that the young sovereigns, in opposing suffrage, were using the exact same logic. What did young sovereigns see that turned them off to woman suffrage? What-- and this is a question for today as well-- do young men see that makes them so reactionary, especially those who loudly claim to be progressive? It is a fact not to be ignored that no 20 year old, including a prince, looks forward to living life in his father's world, unless he's a princess. So he struggles to change it. What he doesn't realize-- made worse because neither does his father realize it-- is that the change has already happened around him. He is no longer a child. Even for young radicals, the "progress" they say they want (as distinct from their fortune) is already their present, it already exists for them, concretely; by their own jargon, their enemies aren't conservatives but "regressives", who seek to pull them back into some kind of real or imagined past. Their fight can thus be seen not as an attempt to change the status quo but to prevent the status quo from being changed *again*. Half of these young sovereigns have just learned to breathe on their own and are afraid someone will change the air back to nitrogen, and soon the country will be overrun

deprive everyone else. [20]

"So your whole point is that we as a society are trapped in an unsatisfying pursuit of consumerism and pornography, and we need to start wanting better things for ourselves?" HA! Why bother, liar? Wanting is a defense against enjoyment. "But isn't spending so much time looking for love, let alone pornography, a little-- self-indulgent?" Yes, which is why you felt compelled to say this. Interesting how self-indulgence is never the critique of the media you're personally invested in. "I spend a lot of time studying the news, there's so much going on in politics right now." I'm sure your family appreciates the effort. "But I have to stay informed." I repeat. "Well then, if love's so important, how do I go about finding love?"

---

with giant reptilian carnivores; the other half fear a secret plot to flood the air with nitrogen so we become giant reptilian herbivores. The young "conservative" resists a fantasized pull into some terrible future, while the "liberal" fantasizes a pull into a horrible past. Neither one acts; they re-act, vigorously fighting for the status quo; all of their energy pretends to be for change, yet always: "first we have to prevent things from getting worse." Even "extreme" political ideas like universal living wage or the abolishment of fossil fuels to combat global warming are, in their essence, psychological positions that ensure their current lives-styles; what gives it the illusion of change, the passion for the change, is that the perceived other stands to lose something.

These males were against suffrage not because they thought they were superior to women, or because they feared powerful women. What they detected-- because the suffrage logic was identical to their own psychologies-- is that what truly motivated the imagined suffrage fighter was the desire to deprive them of something. What they believed they opposed was not female empowerment but male disempowerment. It is not difficult to imagine what they saw: unmarried women, youthful spinsters, or living in loveless marriages-- but all economically secure on someone else's money (loudly disavowed); these women were pretentiously invigorated by "movements" and activism but uninterested in the *suffering* of work; frantically busying themselves with salons, slogans and meddling. That this group of women was a *fantasy* (reinforced by the media), two dimensional caricatures entirely different from any women they actually knew was exactly how the psychology works: those women were the Other that represented the movement.

They said they were fighting for *equality*? Men must have rolled their eyes when the very first thing women did with the vote they so desperately wanted was to ban saloons because drink made men more aggressive. What women appeared to want was not more power for themselves but ways to make men less powerful. In that distinction was the rage of women perceived by the rage of men. To these young men, barely aware of the power women screamed that they lorded over them, women seemed to want to be able to exercise all of the same political powers as men, yet still demand deference, restraint, and politeness-- a feminization of the society enforced by sword. The young men saw in women-- a truly privileged class on the cusp of more privileges-- their own castration.

The people who demanded woman suffrage, and the people who were opposed to it, were so stupendously myopic that they could not see how the future would be different, or even how to make it different for them-- only that it would be different, and it terrified them. Both lacked the imagination to understand how to exist, let alone profit, in a future that seemed *designed* for others, where others= "not them". They both claimed to want more power though they knew it was unlikely in a world designed for the others. Therefore, they were both satisfied if the other was deprived of it.

It took no time at all to detect the "real" reason men were opposed to suffrage, right on time assisted by psychoanalysis: their sexuality was threatened. That this explanation could not have been both more obvious and unfalsifiable did not deter sophisticates from using it to bludgeon their way through the unwashed. "But there is a sexual dimension underlying the social. Men feared powerful

139

You shouldn't, you don't deserve it. "?!" Why didn't you ask me how to love someone else? "I already know how to love--" Oh, it's an innate talent. Like math.

Power imbalances, structural forces; mindfulness, purposeful living; connectedness, loving yourself first. But nowhere: *how to love someone else.* A collective defense against *dependency.*[21]

The reason the dismantling of love is so important to identify isn't because a generation of adult men and women are lost, but because they are raising the next generation, terribly. It doesn't mean they don't love their kids, as far as it goes, it means that what they want for them is conflicted, ambivalent-- and it is this emotional ambivalence, not harsh or absent

young women taking control of their sexuality." No. A thousand times, no. No.

The standard reference is Susan B. Anthony's *History Of Woman Suffrage,* but if you're already committed to learning history from a book that is both ponderous and portrays the suffrage movement negatively, you would be better off reading Henry James's *The Bostonians.*

Basil Ransom and Olive Chancellor are opposites, which in the 19th century means dialectical opposites: Basil is an aimless, drifting 29 year old law school graduate from Mississippi, wistful for the now extinguished plantation splendor of his Ivanhoe pornography. "Go West, young man," commanded Manifest Destiny a little too late, but lacking the spunk for physical exertion he got as far as Boston. Alas, there was nothing for him there either. Olive is a 25 year old Massachusetts socialite living off of a large inheritance from her appropriately deceased father because of structural oppression. That sentence is complete. Basil has lost most of his power, so he is against suffrage. Olive has most of the other powers, so she is for it. I'll spoil the ending of the book, and history: they both lose, power gets shifted elsewhere.

Simultaneously, however, both are involved in what seems like a rivalry for the attentions of Verena Tarrant (played by Victoria Woodhull), a young, beautiful suffragette celebrity with a gift for rhetoric. And trances, which 15 years later could be diagnosed as hysteria but for the purposes of the novel stand for a desire to be whatever the other wants. Olive is immediately obsessed with her, envisioning them fighting hand in hand for women's rights-- chastely, of course-- though within three dates convinces Verena to move in with her. They do not kiss. Basil is also smitten; but he envisions her submissive and pregnant, and apparently chaste. They don't kiss, either. Both want Verena, and both believe the other is a threat to "what Verena truly is". This rivalry in which no one touches anyone takes up eleven thousand pages. At the end Verena runs off with (=is passively lead by) Basil to be his dutiful wife, literally by being passively lead by Basil past the enraged but powerless Olive and out of the Boston concert hall full of rowdy feminist freethinkers to whom Verena was about to deliver an empowering speech that would have had no material consequence anyway. Sorry ladies, no refunds, the house always wins. We are not told what becomes of Olive, or for that matter Basil and Verena, but history predicts it is irrelevant.

All of various women in *The Bostonians* understand suffrage as a solution to a specific problem: the suffering of women at the hands of men, that none of them has ever experienced personally. Certainly James depicts these women as Protestant, wealthy, status-conscious dilettantes, and there is plenty here to debate about intersectionality and privilege. Don't bother, nothing can be gained from this. What's useful is how James portrays all of the *men*: absent. In eleven thousand pages there is only one living father, Verena's, who is likely a charlatan and maybe a pimp. Olive's father is a noble and good man, because he is dead. There are no brothers; Olive's two brothers were also good men by being killed in the Civil War. In a book about women v. men there is not a single rising son or male suitor, except the brief appearance of a heiry man with hypogonadism who lives with his mother and is made of marmalade. Taken together, what real men might have existed are gone, leaving America with pretend men like Basil. He represents a Halloween costume of masculinity: uselessly overeducated and underemployed, proudly omniscient and utterly impotent; a

parenting, that teaches impotence; the verbal hyperinvolvement masking distractibility, boredom, emotional disengagement. [22]

We are being raised to be conquered, and if the barbarians don't come, we will manifest a tyranny. A pop-culture history lesson: one of the trending topics of 1993 was whether or not you'd accept Robert Redford's *Indecent Proposal*: would you cheat on your husband for a million dollars? I know you won't believe this, but back when the terrorists were Libyans and the Mafia were Italians the American people were evenly divided on this question. So? Would you?

Don't bother answering, your answer is irrelevant because you are irrelevant because it is

---

man smart enough to teach himself German over a summer but can't be bothered to use this knowledge to start what could be a near monopoly catering to where-the-bloody-deuce-did-they-all-come-from German clients. That's beneath him. I mean employment. He self-identifies as "ambitious"-- but makes no effort to work, to improve his lot or others'-- to act. It's not even clear he bothers to masturbate, because what he secretly fantasizes about isn't sex or money or power, but leisure time, in the parlor with a brandy, thinking about thoughts while living off a wife's money. I'm not making this up. He believes the deal is that a woman should stay in the home, but neither he, nor any of the handful of male jest-objects in the novel, uphold their part of that deal and offer affection, conversation, companionship, love. Taken literally, women like Olive Chancellor perceive male oppression not because they have experienced male oppression but because *there are no males to show them its opposite*. The suffrage movement, like all the other contemporaneous movements (temperance, spiritualism, abolition) may have a meaning, but was used in everyday practice as a way of getting women together to offer each other affection, conversation, companionship, love. The men had stopped being dependable. They had given up on love, causing a vacuum. Women were sucked in to fill it.

A man's only as good as his word, so Basil et al were quick to use words to assert they were men-- but what exactly is that? *Am I a man or a woman?* They don't know what to be a man is-- especially in a world that seems to take away any opportunities for them to act like men, like pretending to be a Colonel or bossing slaves around-- so unable to act like men they try to solidify the rules about being a woman. Basil is very interested in knowing about the meaning of feminism; interrogating, discussing, and of course disparaging it; but he uses it to locate and flesh out its boundaries so he knows where he stands. (It's outside).

Meanwhile, no woman in the story is portrayed as married to someone they love, or even believes that women would marry for love. Certainly love exists, it abounds in their literature (written by men), but in real life such love is impossible. Marriage, and sex, thus go from unconscious systems of social control to conscious tools for controlling individuals. Read that again, there's a difference and the sequence is correct. Mrs. Burrage, mother of Marmalade, tries to conspire with Olive to keep celebrity spokesmodel Verena under their passive control by manipulating Verena to marry her son, whom she has trapped inside a sandwich. These are the schemes of women. But Olive, a 25 year old literally described as a middle age spinster, is done with men, period: if they're not straight up capitalist producers, they aren't attractive, and love doesn't exist-- why bother with them at all?

Olive's self-professed disgust with men, coupled with her intense desire for Verena's "affections", often leads to the question of whether Olive is meant by James to be a repressed lesbian. To be precise: not simply a lesbian, but a repressed lesbian. There's an enormous difference. The problem with seeing Olive as a repressed lesbian is that the concept of repression hadn't been described yet. Even if James wanted her to be a lesbian, he could not have thought that she repressed it. Denied, lied, or disavowed-- but not repressed. It was already obvious to contemporary critics of the novel that Olive had an "unnatural" interest in Verena; but what suggests to modern readers that Olive is a repressed lesbian is her hatred of men, i.e. that this repression would manifest itself as hating men.

a trick question designed to make you feel part of the debate, which is why everyone debated it. The question that matters is: *what would you advise your daughter to do*? You should take a minute, your soul is at stake.

While you try to do the math, take note of the world today that that generation's mathemagicians created: though it is almost unimaginable that a father would tell his daughter to do it-- if such a father existed the nation's collective superego would hang him from a gibbet at Cuckold's Point-- it is very, very easy to imagine, or turn on the teleprompter and see, a mother already advising it, already pushing her daughter to sell her sex for whatever amount of money seems really big to that demo-- not because she herself would

---

But repressed lesbianism-- a woman's unacceptable *desire* to have sex with women-- would more likely manifest as its more acceptable opposite-- not just heterosexuality but *public* heterosexuality, either marriage or promiscuity, to be easily observable by some other omnipotent entity (church, state, or audience) who has the power to declare what's true. Olive did not do this; in fact, quite the opposite, Olive almost begs the suggestion that she is decidedly lesbian, *but one who doesn't have sex.* Let me reword that: she begs the suggestion that she's a lesbian who *deprives* herself of sex. The lesbianism is a distraction. The question is why, among suffrage fighters like Olive-- hetero or homo-- who loudly asserted that male sexuality was synonymous with power, did so many manifest as *asexual*? What is Olive's manifest immovable asexuality the publicly acceptable opposite *of*?

Olive exerts a psychological control over Verena that, had Olive been a man, would be immediately detected as abusive. She may be for the emancipation of women, but 100% for the enslavement of Verena. Specifically, and no different than the men she opposes, she wants to control Verena's *sex*. Whereas a man might "force" Verena into sex, Olive forces her to never engage. Sex (having it or, in this case, preventing it) is a means of controlling the other. But if sex is used *for* control, why doesn't Olive *use* sex for control? Why doesn't she have sex with Verena and control her that way? If she's not homosexual, then why not manipulate Verena to marry the huckleberry preserves through whom Olive (and his mother) could still retain total control over her? Why is it so important to control Verena's sex-- more than Verena herself-- and why does that control manifest as *no* sex?

Maybe Olive sees all sexuality, with anyone, as oppression, so her chaste love is a way of protecting Verena (and herself) from a vulnerability intrinsic to all female sexuality. The book is fairly clear here: not even close. Verena isn't vulnerable, her sexuality isn't a vulnerability, it's a lethal weapon, it's the suicidal combination of a live hand grenade and a tiring brachioradialis, if Basil or Olive don't put a pin in her she'll come and explode on them all. Both would say Verena needs to be defused.

The repressed lesbianism theory says that Olive has a secret sexual desire for Verena. Obviously, this desire goes unfulfilled because lesbianism is all kinds of wrong in 19th century salons, so wrong that Olive can't even allow herself to know she wants it; so Olive settles for an intense Platonic love. The problem is that this theory is internally inconsistent for Olive. One doesn't settle for Platonic love, Platonic love is supposed to be the highest form of love, above hetero *and even above* homosexual love, above lust and above carnality within love. You don't settle for Platonic love; you fail at Platonic love and end up having an orgasm, or pass out drunk. This seems backwards because we're taught that "being trapped in the friend zone" is a kind of failure, but it's only a failure for the man imagining it; the woman in that exact fantasy imagines that friendship as more important than carnality. So even if Olive were naturally a lesbian, she wouldn't be settling for a Platonic love with Verena, she'd be desiring a Platonic love with Verena. This would not require Verena or her to not have sex; only not to have sex with each other.

Platonic love *requires* a mutual sexual attraction (not lust), which is then sublimated, e.g. a mentor who is attracted to a mentee but refrains from any physical expression of it and remains their

have done it but because 20+ years later, the woman who doesn't believe in love now figures she should have. But this is the lie: she only *thinks* she should have, and encourages her daughter to do it, because there is no risk in that choice to the mother today-- she doesn't actually have to make the choice, the risk is all the daughter's, the mom can simply take credit for it. NB in this hypothetical scenario, you're imagining that the mom is *already* rich, because that mom doesn't need the money, she's not doing it *for* the money; and by identification you are thus indicating that you're worth the money that she already has, just like the people she envies, which is the game we play with everything. In other words, women, not men, underestimate the value of women, and their own daughters.

"No, you're wrong. Love doesn't really exist. Love, like religion, like marriage, is just a

---

devoted friend, sublimated to their mutual benefit-- this is the Platonic ideal. Why is it so important to refrain from sex? Because of the inherent psychological quid pro quo; the introspective individuals would necessarily question if all other aspects of the relationship are not for the base long game of getting sex.

Never mind what Basil and Olive want (Verena). What would satisfy them? If they got Verena, would it be happily ever after? Could you imagine either being satisfied?

If Basil or Olive fantasized some man having sex with Verena, they would have no problem imagining both Verena and the man enjoying it. But if they themselves had sex with her, Verena might enjoy it but inevitably they would enjoy it less. *They can't enjoy.*

This may seem wrong because it presumes a kind of grandiosity about their own sexual prowess, but that has nothing to do with it: other people are more capable of enjoying than they are; and worse, Verena is more capable of enjoyment of the other, including of them. Therefore, she must be deprived.

Verena isn't just to be prevented from having sex; the purpose of having a monogamous, asexual relationship is to *deprive* Verena of sex, including with Olive. There is a ledger open before Olive: to think that Verena could have sex with Olive and still enjoy it; with a kind of enjoyment Olive couldn't get from another person-- this kind of sex would mean that Verena was able to get something from her, to enjoy her-- as if enjoyment could so easily be extracted from Olive without offering Olive something equivalent in return. The ledger would be unbalanced. *It would be unbalanceable.* Olive's asexuality isn't a defense against the vulnerability of being controlled but the most extreme form of control: Olive is willing to give up her own satisfaction, sex with anyone, in order to deprive the other of their greater enjoyment-- including with them. Olive's defense against this idea is its power and gender opposite: rigorous asexuality publicly displayed as *for* women's empowerment. The lesbianism isn't repressed, it is the obvious interpretation, which is why so many people detected it, the illusion of depriving herself because "society would disapprove" hides her true strategy of depriving Verena-- and, additionally but secondarily, of depriving all those powerful men who always enjoy so much and so easily, of Verena. She conveys an obvious "hidden" desire for her, seems to deprive herself of it, and this desire serves as a message. "She *wanted* men to know occasionally of her relations with the lady, otherwise she would be deprived of the satisfaction of her greatest desire-- namely, revenge." NB the revenge fantasies of lunatics don't involve punishment but negative reinforcement.

Basil is 100% the same, except that as a man, he has the power to deprive her by having sex, for procreation, and then depriving her of even that sex by enjoying sex elsewhere. He is not without heart, or at least a calculator: he will still jealously guard her from other men in order to communicate to her she is desirable. Isn't that all a woman really wants?

Seeing this as a battle over Verena, hetero or homo, misunderstands the nature of the rivalry, the premise of all rivalries: the prize is valuable only because of the rivalry. Olive's obsession with

143

way the patriarchy triangulated women as a form of property, locked down in the home and powerless." Huh. Question: when did you figure this out? Answer: about every three generations and right on schedule. Let's say you *were* right, that love was indeed cleverly promoted in order to enslave women. Then what's the purpose of now *promoting* love as unrealistic? Or do you think you detected love doesn't exist all by yourself? Your spectacular intellect that struggled with one half base times height figured it out in the car on the way to $10/hr? Yet ask around, every other individual in your demographic also thinks they figured it out on their own, which should lead you to suspect that you all didn't figure it out on your own, you were told this; the clever innovation was in getting you to think you did figure this out on your own. "But... I did figure it out on my own..." Sorry, I couldn't hear you over the

---

Verena is not threatened by Basil's obsession; Olive's enjoyment depends on depriving Basil of his. In real life only one of them would perceive a rivalry, the other would simply see it as fait accompli, the structure of rivalries would not apply to one of them and there'd be no drama, no novel. But in a story about two evenly matched rivals competing over the same prize, no matter how beautiful or eloquent, the prize is still only pretext. The ambiguous last sentence of the book-- do Verena and Basil live happily ever after, or unhappily ever after?-- can only be understood with this in mind: without Olive around to want Verena, Basil will soon not want her either.

But the rivalry isn't between Basil and Olive, but between each and Verena. Verena is the one that must be defeated. The fake, for mature audiences rivalry of Olive and Basil is only a defense.

No one wants Verena. Wanting things is a defense. The satisfaction is in depriving the other.

The triad of temperance, anti-immigration, and suffrage is "the return of the repressed" in the technical sense, in that what was repressed isn't the triad; what was repressed returns-- appears-- *as* that triad. Whatever suffrage meant, the purpose of suffrage-- including discussions about suffrage-- is to defend against an unacceptable idea.

Giving the women the right to vote *in order to* protect the higher values and decency was an admission by women and men that men had failed at this. And so it fell to women. Not simply that women *did* believe in these things; it was only possible to imagine women could believe these things. The loco-motor Mass and Saloon Catholicism of that time especially gave its men a way to believe in God without having to overthink it; indeed, they were encouraged not to overthink it, hence the Sunday saloon. Their rituals were externalized, then self-medicated. But the rigidly obsessive Protestantism of the time would not allow its men such an escape, and they couldn't handle the responsibility. Men had to pray to the God they had growing doubts existed that the women still believed. **Women had to be empowered to be in control of themselves, and men.**

This is why the temperance movement was so closely intertwined with the suffrage movement, and why it could be later repealed after it had served its purpose. Temperance was the return of a repressed idea about sex, and if you think you know which one it obviously is, then you are wrong: it's repressed. Temperance vocally attacked alcohol because of its effect on men-- for example, it "caused" domestic violence and rape; but observe that women did not organize to attack domestic violence and rape itself. NB: exactly opposite to today. This is partly because there was no serious male support for such an attack on rape, but not because the men wanted to reserve the right to rape and *most certainly not because they didn't think alcohol* caused *men to rape*. The overwhelming focus on alcohol's effect on men-- by women and men-- needs therefore to be understood as its gender and power opposite. The true problem with alcohol was its effect on *women*: it made them *succumb* to sex.

Even the *word* temperance was the return of the repressed. Temperance became synonymous with abstinence; except there was already a word for abstinence, which was abstinence. But the replacement's result was that whatever temperance used to mean was effectively obliterated.

IV.

Those who see pornography as a plague of immorality or a symptom of society's degeneration are not seeing it literally, for what it is: a return of the repressed, in its altered form-- a defense against fantasy, against love, the absence of love[23]. The system you think controls everything may not like pornography but it doesn't fear it, porn poses no threat to it, which is why it is everywhere but we act like it isn't while there are no love stories anywhere but we complain that there are. Though they still make some love stories set in the 1920s, when women could do nothing so they could get credit for anything. Simpler times. Pornography isn't unrealistic, it is the antidote to make-believe. Pornography fills in for love now that we no longer believe in it. Just watch how it's used: pornography expands to fill the

---

Temperance came from the Latin word temperantia, which means self-control or restraint; but temperantia was used as the Latin translation of Plato's sophrosyne, which means "moderation"-- not specifically of alcohol but of all desires, especially sexual (and homosexual), and not as abstinence or even deprivation, but in alignment with ideal amounts. A real man didn't resist temptation, he desired moderation. So temperance became the word for external compulsion to abstain from what was formerly based on self-control, that originally was about desiring ideal proportions. Said the correct way: the virtue of ideal balance was replaced by self-control; self-control then became abstinence compelled by some omnipotent entity but in a hidden way allowing you to take credit for your self-control. The highest virtue became being unable to act on desire. Do you still think they thought they were talking about alcohol?

So too the endless critiques that the temperance movement was really about freedom from, and tacitly control of, male sexuality that grew viciously with every drink. It was possible to *critique* temperance as a kind of control of male sexuality because that didn't threaten its vital control of female sexuality. What specific aspect of female sexuality? The story today is that the patriarchy feared *empowered* female sexuality, "women making their own choices". It didn't, this is exactly what it did not fear. It didn't like it, especially the extra-marital kind, there were harsh penalties for it, but it didn't fear it. Nor was empowered sexuality some kind of fantasized, projected threat in the distant future if the women got their way. It was already concretely everywhere, prostitutes were openly prostituting, and celebrity Victoria Woodhull famously promoted free love but (=and) equally famously bedded for power and status. She may have been an exceptional exception but her celebrity was media manufactured in order to evidence that women, at all ends of the sexual spectrum, still had sex *for* a reason, not for *no* reason. Sex for pleasure, sex for self-esteem, sex for money, sex for control-- all were within the transactional logic of female sexuality.

What it didn't have experience with, what it feared, was unrestrained female sexuality for *no reason*. Not seductive women, but seduced women; passively-- passive aggressively? aggressively passively? *which was it?*-- going along with sex simply *because*. No one understood the psychology of a woman who herself could not explain why she did it. "I don't know, it just happened." And yet you still *enjoyed* it? "I mean, I guess." No-thing caused it, and its residue was ambivalence. How can anyone understand-- control-- something without a cause? A cause has to be created. The material scapegoat for not choosing was alcohol. It was psychologically irrelevant that most men had never met such a sexually ambivalent woman (indeed, that increased the fear). It was sufficient that such a woman could theoretically exist-- why? Because nothing restrained women *anymore*-- another reason they were hastily given the responsibility of religion and morals. Well, what restrained women before, that now no longer could be trusted? The answer was before them, though it was not obvious.

Sex without superego could be explained; but sex without id was madness. The specific problem of why women have sex has never been solved, least of all by women, who themselves are quick to interpret another woman's sex-- not their sexuality or desires but the other's act-- as the result of or reaction to every outside force-- but never only desire. Certainly there are proximate causes, but

145

time available.

The system does not want love because love is a threat to its authority, which is why it also hates-- not ignores or dismisses, but *hates*-- religion. "That's crazy, the system totally supports these religious nuts!" Yes: it makes sure you see they're nuts. Unless it can safely absorb the religion. An example was the early admiration/infatuation with Pope Francis by America's atheists. Since the world is in such "desperate need of global leadership", a leader of a religion that has no power over you is the perfect leader to lead-- everybody else. "People don't believe in God anymore because of the huge scientific changes we've experienced, religion is obviously comforting make-believe." Comforting? I thought you said it caused unnecessary guilt? Make-believe? You mean fantasy? A whole generation of religionists

---

not a general reason. You might think this is a silly question to answer, but that would be misunderstanding what's at stake, why the question is phrased that way. The problem isn't *why* women have sex, the problem specifically is that we want there to be an explanation. Male sexuality, by contrast, has always had sufficient made-up explanations-- biology, aggression, power, etc-- these words are the equivalent of Greek gods, they're not real, they are merely placeholders: they assure us that even if *that's* not the reason, there *is* a reason.

Since Romulus alcohol has been a placeholder for women, made true by the severity of the punishment. Question: who is to blame for adultery? It's easier to figure out if you work backwards from the premise of an intoxicated wife. An intoxicated wife could be punished by death because her drunkenness lead to adultery. But adultery without alcohol was a vexing problem, more so than rape, because if women are property then rape is merely destruction of property; but adultery admits female freedom. Hence in Athens, where women were not free, logically women could not choose adultery, therefore it had to have been forced on them, not necessarily through violence but some malicious influence=power of the man. The sober adulteress took on the legal status of today's drunk girl in a frat house: her yes is meaningless, her no inviolable but also superfluous: she cannot consent. Not only was there no punishment for the adulteress, but the punishment for the adulterer was extra-legal, entirely up to the owner of the woman (the husband)-- including "justifiable homicide." Consider today the frat party "rapist" is also subject to extra-legal punishments even in the absence of evidence, it is entirely up to the owner of the woman (the college). No matter how short her dress or what she wanted, adultery was the man's fault; to punish was the privilege of the college. There is a curious fact about college sexual assault cases that has no analog in any other kind of violation: in none of the *publicly* reported cases of campus sexual assault do you ever hear from or about the parents of the woman, despite the fact that they're paying the tuition. The story cannot include them. It's not because she's an adult. It's because her owner is the college.

But very quickly the Athenian culture that had just invented individualism had to contend with a logical inconsistency: adulterers were still not deterred and sometimes adulteresses enjoyed it. Surely it couldn't be possible that a woman can enjoy something she didn't choose-- couldn't consent to do? So by 451 Pericles came up with an ingenious solution which is obviously anti-feminist but is powerfully the opposite: he added a punishment for the adulteress. The nature of the punishment is here irrelevant (she was banned from temples and public spaces), only that the punishment *required* she had had a choice, she wasn't passive-- she may not be a citizen or allowed to vote but she was beginning to be *free*.

That doesn't sound ingenious? To appreciate how this change was used by the Athenians, sit in on their continuing education courses. In Euripides's *The Trojan Women*, when Menelaus drags his cheating wife Helen by her hair back to his tent and ferociously demands to know why she ran off with Paris, her first ploy is to flip it around and say, "Listen, I know it looks bad, but-- I was actually doing you a favor." No, he doesn't buy it, either. So when she gets pushed to explain why she didn't at least resist, why she went along with it-- and why she enjoyed it-- she points to her perfect hair and body and blurts out loud the only *forbidden* answer: "It's your fault, stupid, why would you

146

survived the simultaneous discoveries of evolution, psychoanalysis, and special relativity, yet the next statistically died under the entangled litter box of socialism and fascism; a guy managed to prove that *time wasn't real* and not only did religion not die, the 1950s came next. You underestimate previous generations' shock at the rapidity of progress, and overestimate your ability to draw conclusions from the lack of your own. "I'm shocked people care more about a fairy tale afterlife than the reality of dying in massive environmental catastrophe." You must be very young to imagine being worthy of such a spectacular death, just do yourself a favor and watch your cholesterol anyway. *Your* system wants hegemony and homogeneity, which means it wants individuality to cede to collective individualism-- ego death for a stronger superego-- because democratic individuals who think they are unique will always follow the herd, each one applauding himself for discovering on his own the narrow ramp that

---

leave me alone with him? Duh, look at me-- what did you think was going to happen?" That's not an answer she's allowed to give, and everybody goes bananas; yet understand that when Helen was actually living, 1000 years before the play was performed, that would have been assumed to be the answer-- Menelaus would not have even bothered with the question. No doubt you've misunderstood her answer: she's not *only* saying she's so hot that of course Paris would want her. Remember that *The Iliad*'s inciting event is three goddesses in a beauty contest with no valuable prize, so much for rivalry, and instead of trying to win with ice water oopsies or divine pheromones *they bribe the judge with stuff*. Aphrodite-- NB: the goddess of sex, so unrealistically hot the Greeks imagined her blonde-- wins not because she's hot but because she bribes him with *another blonde*. Well, did any one of those alpha-women stop to wonder if Helen wanted it? Should have a say in it? I'm stupid? Ok.

But in this play Helen offers the anachronistically correct answer, the one the contemporary audience agrees to believe is false but lingers as terrifying nonetheless. She just went along with it for no reason and enjoyed it? Hell no. So Euripides scripts in the defenses to preserve the democracy. Paris's mom says what moms always say about their son's girlfriends, "you whores always say you don't know why you did it, but I know it was because you wanted his money." And Menelaus says what men always say about their cheating wives, "you whores always say you didn't know why you did it, but I know it's because you're a slut." Lust, money, alcohol-- anything, but not nothing.

Helen's sober defense explains alcohol's changed role today, e.g. in colleges: the issue here is not whether the frat boys broke a few rules or took a few liberties with their female party guests. They did. But you can't hold an entire fraternity responsible for the behavior of a few sick, perverted individuals; for if you do, then shouldn't you blame the whole fraternity system? And if the whole fraternity system is guilty, then isn't this an indictment of our educational institutions in general? Isn't this an indictment of our entire American society? So suggesting alcohol caused a man to act-- to rape-- is the worst kind of rationalization; banning liquor at college parties is decried as missing the point; and a woman might be too drunk to give consent but a man can never be too drunk to require it. The cause of rape is men who act. It has to be, because of the changed purpose of alcohol in our time: it gets the single women in the mood and the married women out of it.

Plan 18 was to give ladies the power in order to take the long arm of the lever, as we call it in mechanics, out the hands of the whisky power; the countermeasure of Plan 21 was to give the gals back the whisky-- then gin, then screwdrivers, then wine coolers, Cosmos, Pinot Grigio-- so they could drown themselves in its power. So much for temperance. Alcohol today is the hard line over which men are *told* they are not allowed to cross-- no matter what the woman seems to "want." It doesn't matter that alcohol is still used by women to "loosen up", and that men testing the line is institutionalized, it is part of the rules of the game; the point isn't to decrease rape, but to move the *theoretical* responsibility for consent-- for the decision of choice-- *back* to the man, for the *purpose* of subordinating both of them to the school. The point is equate woman as victim, so that she needs protection; *in order that* some other omnipotent entity must be created to protect her, after all men

leads to utopia.[24] "Moo!" Yes. Moo.

On your behalf the media separated love and lust. Now it must   separate lust and porn, now lust is the threat: whatever the man is looking at will always be less dangerous than whatever the man is thinking about. Porn doesn't suppress love, love was repressed, by us, and it returned as porn.

What may surprise you is that this isn't the first time this has happened, and it isn't the last time. Once upon a time men, not women, believed in love; later women took it over, men believed in love through women; and now "women" "don't" "believe" in love; but this doesn't mean we've progressed past love; it merely means that men will eventually take it over/back

---

are not dependable. Again, it is besides the point here that men still pressure drunk women and that it is rape; what matters is how alcohol is needed as a temporary solution to the problem of ambivalent female sexuality and the power reduction among women this creates. The subjective term drunk becomes one of the only available *objective* boundaries in female sexuality. The difficulty in seeing this is that the public example is always of a completely comatose and defenseless cheerleader being assaulted by a completely sober and rabid defensive tackle, but the logical consequence is to afford women an extra psychological protection by having had been drinking, even if it risks rape. "But she still gets raped!" *No one, least of all women, cares about her.* She is the sacrifice, now locate the scapegoat. In other words, what alcohol is-- and why then there was temperance and now it so tempts us-- changed from being a scapegoat for women's ambivalence in sex to being a defense for the ambivalence. The result?   Power moves out of both their hands and goes elsewhere.

The 19th century fear that women would have lots of random sex with random men-- the "sex panic"-- was not a feared consequence of female empowerment: it was a cause of it. Nothing else could stop the sex. Note also the temporal coincidence of psychoanalysis, which treated not the oppressed woman with no power but the repressed woman getting more power that it was improper to use. The fantasy of the *seduced woman* outside of love and lust, responding entirely to the desires of the other, was too dangerous because there were no longer any restraints on the men, and the women seemed unprepared for it, so it became a powerful force for social change. The solution was to cause women to over-perform some kind of feminine sexuality—any kind, didn't matter-- as diverse as a return to Wyoming sham Puritanism in the West or Woodhull sham hedonism in the East. Paralleling the logic of suffrage in Wyoming, i.e. manifesting as the logic of suffrage in Wyoming, it was better for women to have total control of their bodies and the responsibility to be conscious than to allow them to be ambivalent-- *because of* the declining quality of men, with the result of shifting the power to some other omnipotent entity.

It is worth the space to highlight what was the result of these incompatible and illogical fears and wishes, the triad of anti-immigration, temperance, and women's empowerment. The pro-suffrage men and women of America fantasized the "foreigner" Germans and the Irish, with their beers and their promiscuity and a religion that seemed to tolerate it, and saw the genocide of the "real" American. And if those degenerates started seducing our goodly and godly Protestant women, America would be lost. Simultaneously, "anti-suffrage" men saw Protestant women as the threat, women's empowerment was only a cover for depriving men of theirs.

It is not a coincidence, therefore, that the overtly sexual female German-Irish ("and part Cherokee") mongrel that threatened American values and so repulsed the women of suffrage became, within three generations, the archetypal icon of American female sexuality—the standard against which all women were judged, and the Skinner box for male desire. That this happened in Los Angeles, a city originally created as a destination for goodly and godly anti-immigrant Protestant families, is also not a coincidence. Neither is it a coincidence that the new fantasized plaything would easily have sex with any race--- even, God forbid, Italians. And that as part of her sexual decadence she would

148

and women will again believe through them. Maybe this means a "re-masculinization" of art and poetry, it may seem crazy but it's only anachronistic, until the mid 1800s poetry was a man's game, then events arose, ensued, were overcome; and the men stopped journaling and the women suddenly realized they wanted to be taken seriously as journalists. The women got the home, the morality, the manners and the culture, and the men had the trifecta of wages, absent parenting, and functional alcoholism, not surprisingly all the things modern women fight for today under the designation "it all." This trade has been done before, it's more reliable than epicycles. And more valid. In the 1528 secular humanist handbook *The Art Of Manliness*, Castiglione articulates that the excellent men have to be like, well, Renaissance men, if back then "Renaissance man" included working out, which it did. Strong, loyal, and

---

love drinking, that alcohol would be simultaneously a marker of her maturity and the promise of her promiscuity; also not a coincidence. These things are not coincidences because the "threat" was real, they did cause a change in "American" values. But rather than facing the psychological substance of the change, they gave it a racial and gender perspective so they could rage against it, dressed it up as a fight for morality or nativism, and tried to overpower it by... obtaining the right to vote and banning alcohol. They repressed an idea about female sexuality, and it came back as the triad of anti-immigration, temperance, and suffrage; it returned as a California blonde centerfold, giggly tipsy and DTF; a "Cool Girl," passive yet insatiable; coy but unapproachable; cock-teasingly proper and cock-pleasingly omnivorous; a lady in public with you, a whore in the bedroom with them. The pornographic manifestation of resentment, and the satisfaction that comes from depriving the other. Look around you at the results; then guess what happens next.

16 Here's the trick: the media puts the answer to, "love or career?" in the mouth of: a CEO, a judge, a woman with power; but it reports the answer to a demo that will never be these things. For years, the center two-page advertisement in a very popular news magazine was for chewing tobacco, the advertisers must have calculated that if these idiots were swallowing the news they'd more than likely chew on this. At least their husbands would. The result is that a college girl destined for part time work feels a pressure not to put love over a career; it is strongly recommended to her that she "not give up who she is" (=where she works) for a man. She'd never let a man tell her this-- she's been taught NOT to listen to men-- which is why the system doesn't have men telling her this, it finds women to tell her this, and every one of these women is impeccably dressed. It's easy to see this as capitalism tricking a woman into trading her life for a wage, but she hardly needs to be tricked into working, she doesn't have a choice. The threat is to the *media*, and the threat is her relationship, media can't get your attention at work but the other 16 hours are up for grabs, the only way to get her all in on media and away from the interfering effects of another person's desires is to weaken the relationship. She *wants* to be told not to give up her "career" so it can feel like she *chose* not to give it up, and the consequence of this "choice" is that she has *no choice* but to give up on love, for which she will substitute media. These stories are so prevalent in media and necessary to the audience not because they justify the desire for career but for the lack of desire for love, the obliteration of dependency; at work there are clear identities and safeguards but in love no one is the safe, let alone the same. That these articles are endlessly discussed in and by the media solidifies the supremacy of the media as the moderator for such issues, it patronizes you by inviting you to "be part of the debate".

17 Or, in the words of Carrie Bradshaw in *Sex And The City*:

Then I realized, no one had told her about the end of love in Manhattan. Welcome to the Age of (un)Innocence. No one has Breakfast at Tiffany's, and no one has Affairs to Remember. Instead, we have breakfast at 7 a.m., and affairs we try to forget as quickly as possible. Self protection and closing the deal are paramount. Cupid has flown the co-op. How the hell did we get ourselves into this

learned. Handsome, muscular (cut, not bulky) and well groomed-- but appear nonchalant about it. Ample of limb, and proficient in arms. He must study Greek, Latin, and the vulgar, and be able to compose poems in each; master several musical instruments, study the natural sciences, rhetoric and discourse. Learn all the social graces, the art of conversation, be witty but not showy, a pleasure to be around while impossible to cross. I can hear you think, sign me up? In theory you have the freedom to live that way now; but you'll hastily complain that nowadays work has expanded to fill the time available, which is odd as you don't have a job. So your fantasy has a hidden piece, the real wish seeking fulfillment: it necessarily requires a sponsor, and that requirement is far more desirable than the outcome, which means if I'm translating the book and your fantasy correctly what you really want to be is a courtesan.

---

mess?

"There are thousands, maybe tens of thousands of women like this in the city. We all know them, and we all agree they're great. They travel, they pay taxes, they'll spend $400 on a pair of Manolo strappy sandals. And they're alone. It's the riddle of the Sphinx!"

She wants the problem to be men, but I think she wrote that the solution is a man.

Men love women in strappy sandals, sure, even $400 ones depending on who paid, but the obvious criticism to make is that there is nothing in the description that could possibly satisfy any man. I've seen... some of the episodes, so I know she's not a complete imbecile, which means casting herself as so obnoxiously self absorbed can only be a defense against anyone asking the harder question, the one that entirely drives the psychology of the show: why would she want *the kind of man* who wanted that kind of woman? Seems to me if the first thing a man noticed was your shoes, he's a serial killer. "You're a stunning woman, can I buy you a drink?" Umm, hello, my boobs are up here.

You might think that there are tens of thousands of women who do indeed pay taxes and travel and own nice shoes, but they are not that *kind* of woman. Other women e*specially on TV* are indeed that *kind* of woman.   To actually be that kind of woman, someone must agree to see you as that kind of woman, but the trick is that you can't know them. If you know them, then they probably like you for something else. It doesn't count.

This is why you have to take Carrie's-- a writer's-- lament literally. What they are explicitly offering the men is desire-- they look good, they buy stuff, they've been to airports-- and not satisfaction. Take me literally, too, the conjunction is *and* not *but*: they specifically offer desire AND not satisfaction-- that pairing-- they don't want the man to be satisfied. "Because then he'll abandon her?" No, she doesn't care if he abandons her. He just can't have both, because she can't have both.

Carrie has a problem that is not evident in the show because it is obfuscated by voiceovers: she wants to be loved for being a kind of woman, which means the guy she wants must want that kind of woman; which means he will also want the other ten thousand Manolo models. But if he falls in love with her, then something else about her satisfied him, which means she's not that kind of woman anymore. Whereas before he caused her to be that kind of a woman by desiring her, by falling in love with her *he took that away from her*. Now she's someone else. The only way she can continue to be that kind of woman is to ensure no man is ever completely satisfied.

18 For a very specific reason. Conventional wisdom says American society is hyperanxious about the growth and safety of children, but the subordinate clause is a lie.   Children aren't fragile, they are a direct psychological threat. This doesn't mean that people don't like them or won't break their backs to send them to college, it means that they parent in a way that prevents the kids from

Hmm. Meanwhile the women had it worse, they are admonished to become the soldiers of morality, first to learn it then to guard it, their very presence elevates men's character and behavior, which is a preposterously massive responsibility considering the present men want to be courtesans. "She makes me want to be a better person." Let us attend. Also she has to be hot, a woman who lacks in beauty lacks much, and what she lacks are penises, if none are interested her chastity wouldn't count. Of course, whether she has sex is hardly the relevant metric, chastity is more about perception, both cock please and cock tease could equally get you labeled a slut; but the fastest way to earn the scarlet S is to make the man suspect tonight's adherence to chastity is based on her lack of desire; so the secret is to parry but make each man feel no shame for having played the male part so well. She should take care that no

---

manifesting as a threat to their identity, i.e. prevents them from growing up *into their replacement*.

The ultimate threat isn't to life/liberty/happiness but to status quo, so rather than at the outset *conceiving* of children, in an abstract sense, as our replacements-- not in some psychologically distant future "when we are gone", but now, while we are still alive-- and preparing both the world for them and them for the world, it is impossible to conceive of this. I mean exactly what I wrote: it is impossible to form the idea that they will turn into adults that will replace us while we are alive. This is both individually (your kids) and collectively (the coming generation). In fact, we believe we will be increasingly relevant in the world as time goes on, not less so, in exactly the opposite way that the young conceive of us.

The result is we try to maintain their "innocence" as long as possible, and boy oh boy do I not mean sexually; giving them a condom at 13 is loudly praised as being realistic so no one notices it's negligence. "You need to protect yourself." Am I supposed to fill it with gasoline? Of course eventually they do indeed grow taller; but while they are children the idea of this threat is very (unconsciously) real and we treat children accordingly, and you can see it best not in what we do, but in what we don't do. Example: parents love to "teach" their children about "current events" or "being a good person", as if such a thing could be taught by people who themselves only learned it from TV; which, not surprisingly, is at that moment on in the background; or teach them things they themselves have failed at (sports, Mandarin, condoms)-- things which do not define themselves-- but rarely do they teach their kids their own trade or profession.

"But of course I know they'll eventually replace me." You know it, you don't believe it. Can you really imagine what it would actually look like? Laius could, and he acted accordingly. Whatever actually happened in the good old days regarding parents and kids isn't as informative as our fantasies of those days: *The Waltons* was a good show for its time, but even those who only know about *The Waltons* would admit that one of the "good" things about the show is its depiction of the utopian fantasy of extended family living together and supporting each other. Ok, true, but although the grandfather lived with them, the leader of the family was *father*. Is that how it would work in your fantasy? Can you imagine yourself as the grandparent while your son-- or son-in-law-- is the leader? ("What about daughter?" Interesting: for most people that is way easier to imagine.) Of course this very situation occurs in real life all the time-- but can you imagine it? Don't dismiss this thinking as just being too young to imagine old age; ask any parent to ponder the phrase "immortality through one's children" and 100% of the time they will ponder this as it applies to their own children and 0% of the time whether they are the immortality of their own parents. Consistent with this, observe that the one time parents do try to bring their children into their trade is when the parents hope to pass on not the skills but the physical business-- something of theirs that is *not* their children.

19 But with no "information" on what the "right guy" looks like-- good looking? Rich? Kind? Funny? They are adjectives, but how do you rank them? Whose scale are you supposed to use?-- and Mom's advice is reliably unreliable, e.g.: she married Dad. So how does one judge? "If only I had more information."

evil is thought of her or she damns them both; honi soit qui mal y pense. "I carry her garter with me into battle." She won't need it till you get back anyway.

But the idea of love-- not romance but love-- for obligation, for dependency, for a limiting of identity for a new identity as required by the other-- can only be repressed, not destroyed. It will always return.[25] And boy oh boy are you not going to like this next part.

To say "men" and "women" don't believe in love isn't to say that they think *no one* believes in it; people are free not to believe only if it feels like they chose. Someone else still has to supposedly believe. So in the meantime, who becomes the reservoir for love? Who will believe in love while women abandon it but before men take it back? Through whom can

---

Information is not a powerful tool for change, information is a defense against impotence-- not a defense against becoming impotent, but a way of living with it: it facilitates impotence. The internet gives you several years of backstory and commentary and very soon DNA to make a judgment about a potential mate. What more info do you need? And yet all that information doesn't facilitate the choice. Rather than making this choice themselves people want a mediator.

The premise of online dating is that since you get to see an old CGI and a few select lies, you can find a good match. This should lead to disaster 100% of the time, yet it doesn't.

Obviously, the appeal of online dating, and the reason it works despite the lies, is that you're *not* choosing him/her: the Algorithm chose them. You trust that the Algorithm-- the thing you know nothing about-- knows best. The Algorithm chooses based on massive collections of data, but perhaps you don't want to know how that data is weighted? "It says I'm best suited for abandonment." Hmm. There's a story, likely apocryphal but useful nevertheless, about the CEO of a very popular dating site who did something very unKantian: he secretly conducted a scientific experiment on some of the users and matched them up with people they were least compatible with. Well, as he "predicted", the simple fact that the Algorithm told the couple they were compatible made them compatible. He took this as evidence of the power of authority; not surprisingly, it did not occur to him to take this as evidence that the Algorithm is no better than being wrong on purpose. To be clear: his conclusion was the Algorithm was omnipotent, not omniscient. That's important, we'll come back to it.

He correctly understood what the Algorithm does but misunderstood what need the Algorithm serves, and here I will slightly amend my earlier statement. In the old days a team of elderly widows with decades of wisdom, prejudice, and resentment would know who was your best match-- that kind of omniscience is desirable to parents negotiating a dowry, but not to you. In fact, you *don't* trust that the Algorithm knows who you're compatible with-- how could it? You are infinite, you contain multitudes. What you trust it to know is who you're *not* compatible with. You trust it to limit your choices because you do not trust yourself to limit your choices.

We "self-reflect"; we introspect; we ask science to explain behavior: am I doing something wrong that I can't meet anyone? Why do I always get involved in unhealthy relationships? And you try to be objective, but the objectivity is a ruse. The pathology isn't that you make bad choices but that you cannot make choices, so you make the ones you've made before, or none. You want to be lead.

"I get rejected by women all the time." Doing the same thing over and over, expecting different results? What kind of a woman would want that kind of a man? "Sometimes it works." You mean sometimes you make an initial tenuous connection that you can overestimate that she will later have to break once she realizes what kind of a man you are, leaving her with all the blame? "How is this my fault?" If a gambler loses 99% of the time at blackjack, we'd agree he wants to win, but at some point he needs to admit he's trying to lose, no one could pull those kind of numbers without a reliable system. He's addicted to the possibility that sufficiently large stakes will induce some glitch in the Matrix, some change in reality, *it* will choose *him*.... but specifically with no work, no change

152

men and women still believe in love?   Look at what your media tells you about the TV shows you don't even need to watch, love is safely guarded by the only people left believably idealistic about it: gays.[26]   Ah, just like old times. In media, the gays are never frivolous or flighty (those are the hetero women) but firmly committed, in love, in a magical and ideal way that women used to dream about. Media gays-- fictional and nonfictional, doesn't matter, what matters is it's in 4x9-- well, 4:3-- 16:9?-- they take love very, very seriously-- it *counts*. The freight train of gay rights was an inevitable consequence of women turning away from love, which is exactly why women got on board real fast, they had to, their souls were at stake. And men's. "No, women are just more progressive than men." Straight men, I guess. And briefly violating this book's rule of staying clear of "current events" note the overnight nuclear

---

within himself. The point is to be changed without having to change.

Even with the immense freedom and information in selecting our own mates, we still want something else to limit our options for us. Brand loyalty, even when the brand is discombobulated as a logo on an unrelated product. The problem isn't too little choice or too much choice, the problem is an inability to choose. *Don't let me choose on my own.* This should tell you the first of two important insights about your dilated cardiomyopathy: the problem isn't finding someone you're compatible with, the problem is... a kind of miserliness. The void inside you may not be full of love or golden Chi but the void is still a thing, and since it is the only thing it has to be protected.   You can't put anything in it without destroying the void. "But I don't want to be alone." You're not, if you stare into the abyss, then the abyss stares also into you. You have at least one friend, and bonus, you will tell everyone he's mysterious, or black. And you hoard the failures, the lack of love, and the hoarding makes your desire grow: it makes you think you grow. The failures make you feel wiser, which is your-- "My compensation?" HA! Already balancing the ledger. No-- your defense against impotence.

Take a moment and consider the history of love's mediators, and how they worked: not to choose but to limit choices. In the Bronze age all choices were supremely finite anyway, a dozen draft picks across various tribes, fresh out of puberty, no free agents and no salary caps. In modern (not post-modern) times the fantasy of love at first sight was the mediator-- you'll know the minute you see him (therefore: not him, not him, not him...); updated by the rom-com reversal for the cynicism and ennui generation: hate is a kind of passion, so your real soulmate is the person who inflames=inflames you the most, the person who provokes the most emotion (therefore: not him, not him...) None of these validly find the One. They reliably exclude the rest.

Now we rely on technology to lead us, selecting a handful of possible matches= excluding "over a million users."

But deselecting is only part of it. What is the aspiration? The ads for dating sites show a happy but not impossibly attractive couple; 6s at best, but their draw is that they look well paired-- it's not advertising a mate, it's advertising a matching. You are knowledgeable about how ads work, and *what you will tell yourself* is that it works through identification-- it could find even a 6 like me a match. How realistic you are, how self-aware, how free of self delusion! But then what do you need the service for, you can't attract a 6 on your own?   The aspiration you are paying for is the disclaimer: you're not settling for a 6, it just so happens the person who is perfect for you as decided by some other omnipotent entity is a 6. Don't worry, the Terms Of Service agreement says that the 6 part is a "coincidence"-- do not infer from this that you are only good enough for a 6. "I don't place such a high value on looks." Substitute "6" with words like "interracial" or "unemployed" or "mature"-- whatever you don't like-- and the logic is the same.

The *guilt* is over not enjoying enough-- the limiting of future possibilities. The *anxiety* is that your choice may be a judgment about you. Neither of these need an Algorithm that is omniscient, they need it to be omnipotent. Advertising constantly reminds you that a better tomorrow is always

detonation of transgender issues, the intense focus on their "awareness" and "acceptance" in the media-- in other words, knowledge about them-- that meanwhile totally disavows their lust. Certainly a trans person has every reason to want the freedom to act; but you should be very wary of how quickly and passionately progressives wanted them to be known. Never trust the zeal of a convert, at it's core is hate. It is a "love panic" in every way analogous to a sex panic, including how sex panics are misunderstood. *If we allow them to love, therefore love exists.*

Neither should you understand this as history's forward march towards total human equality. "Everyone should be able to do what they want, because all 'men' are equal." I love that you thought it important to put 'men' in scare quotes but not to bother to learn the rest of

---

coming soon to a low price near you, but this offer is for a limited time only so act now on a conventional 7 year lease. "But what if.... what if I do meet a better mate later? What then?" The question as asked defies answer, it dares you to go against advertising's axiom of upgrades. If some 70 year old tries to make a case for marital stability, the respondent goes thermonuclear ("so if you're in an abusive relationship, you should stay???") to bully them into silence. And yet no one in any abusive relationship needs to be convinced to stay, they stay against all advice, they are paralyzed. "But the question stands: what if you do meet a better mate later?" Then do them a favor and ask yourself-- are you a better mate for them? "I'd like to think so." Yes, you would.

20 Another interpretation, which ends up being the same thing, is that the brazilian isn't for herself, but for the waxer girl-- not as seduction but for her approving gaze-- she gets to be seen by someone who's seen sexy as a sexy/sexual being. She sees me as desirable to others, which is easier than being desirable to others and also more enjoyable than being enjoyed by others. She doesn't have to act because an authority who appears omniscient has declared she looks like someone who could.

21

> Marley was dead: to begin with. There is no doubt whatever about that.

And yet years later, we will still need guarantees. What is the central theme in Dickens's most famous unread book, *A Christmas Carol*? Arguing over a book's meaning is a game of liar's dice, you're stuck with the hand you've rolled so the true skill is in detecting that the other is a liar. I'm sure you'll bet that *A Christmas Carol* obviously depicts the evils of a life of greed; and if the enjoyment derived from depriving the other had a tag line, it would be hard to beat, "Are there no workhouses?" And maybe you are so confident about Scrooge's greed that you're able to charitably offer that even though Scrooge is a problem, he's really only a symptom of the larger systemic problem, of capitalism. It's a good bid. But I call you a liar.

Scrooge is held up as a pornographic caricature of greedy capitalism, but does anybody actually know what Scrooge does in capitalism? The book says he runs a counting house. How long does it take to count a pile of pre-1844 gold coins in an empty house? Does he have to bite every one individually? I know Bob Cratchit symbolizes the exploited workers but instead of asking for overtime he requests to leave work early so he can go play tag with his kids, yet on the way home gets sidetracked into sledding with kids that aren't. *Twenty times.* Exploited? Sounds like Scrooge made a diversity hire.

Scrooge is a moneylender, not a New Testament moneylender but a Karl Marx moneylender, i.e, he is to moneylenders what money is to lending: a go between they wish they could go without. He brings buyers and sellers together and helps set the price, he consolidates loans, he has a seat on the Exchange. There's nothing in the story that indicates he's a predatory lender beyond what is allowed by law, he wouldn't have become successful that way and anyway this is a man who is rigid about the rules, in his whole life he never cheated once. *Scrooge is not a liar.* His wealth was

the actual quote. But anyway, you don't believe that. It's not that gays are just like everyone else, the whole scheme requires they not be like everyone else, they have to be different. Only an outsider, an *other*, with a heart of gold, could love like a woman used to, i.e. simultaneously genitally and emotionally. "Look, ladies, we know there's no such thing as Santa Claus, but these handsome gay professionals still believe in him and we should support them." It's not gays they care about, and it's not Christmas-- it's the *State's* concept of Christmas, having lost its religious significance as well as any intergenerational "tradition" purpose they want some other omnipotent entity to continue to give it importance so they can pretend they are above it. If the State blesses marriage as meaningful, then you can pretend to choose not to participate in a thing that exists, brand yourself as having opted out, as opposed to there being

accumulated not through extortion or corruption, but by virtue of the volume of business that he did. In order for this greedy capitalist to keep on greedily capitalizing, he needs the existing capitalist system to continue. That sounds obvious but I can assure you it isn't.

What Dickens has a problem with is that though he's a capitalist he is *also* a miser, and even Marx wouldn't posit a logical link between his miserliness and his capitalism, to Marx a miser is a capitalist gone mad and anyway you can't explain the problems of capitalism through the personal psychology or morality of the individual capitalists. Such a caricature merely masks an economic problem as an ethical problem, and gets the system of capitalism off the hook. Anyone who calls him an *evil* capitalist is inadvertently protecting capitalism.

Many idiots have detected in Scrooge the signs of the hated 18th century Jew, which is really an ingenious thing for capitalism to let you detect: anti-semites inadvertently protect capitalism by displacing the hatred to Jews; while capitalists get to pretend that hatred of capitalism is really just anti-semitism.

But leaving aside these critiques, since everyone obviously knows that Scrooge is synonymous with capitalism, it should be very easy to answer a very basic question that the secondary sources never thought to ask: why does Scrooge want *money*?

One possible answer, made explicit=up by exposition in film adaptations that have no basis in the book, is that money for Scrooge is a defense against the fear of poverty. But he isn't poor and he's in no danger of it, his moving average is concave up; as a top hat wearing capitalist earning even 5% he could quit now and still double his money every 15 years. Fear is not the answer.

According to the book there are only two characters that really knew Scrooge, and one of them is dead. Also, so is the other one. So like any man trying to make sense of his life, he goes to visit his ex. Ladies, if 20 years later an old BF comes back looking all existential and searching for answers that he says only you can give because you're wise and you're a straight shooter, I recommend a shotgun or going for the throat, because after he thinks he hears you confirm he's special he will fall for your teenage daughter. "I never met a 15 year old girl who behaved more like a grown up and wasn't all giggly." Don't you have a garbage truck you're supposed to be getting back to? "I'm sorry, I didn't mean for this to happen." You think this happens by accident?

Ghost of Christmas Past takes Scrooge back into that past, to the last conversation young Scrooge ever had with the woman he was going to marry. For some reason she's wearing a mourning dress. Chekov's gun and etc, so by the end of this short story it needs to go off. It doesn't. Instead, she launches into a detailed character analysis of her soon to be future ex-fiancé:

"If this [time together so far] had never been between us," said the girl, looking mildly, but with steadiness, upon him; "tell me, would you seek me out and try to win me now?"

Script notes: in this scene she is a young, sexy fiancee in a LBD, and he's a fortnight away from

nothing to opt in to.

"You're trivializing the role of activism in promoting social change." Yes, because it's trivial, brownian motion still depends on the temperature. I'm sure the activists are earnest, I certainly would never doubt the sincerity of the rube, this is America, the customer is always right as long as they buy.

The fault is as much men's as women's, as much a problem of society as individual psychology, as much about expectations as aspirations. Different things are at stake, but there is a common pathology, here it is in bullet form, along with its defense:

- inability to love, manifesting precisely not as *not loving* but as loving someone without

condomless orgasms-- and he still says no; you can imagine how hard it would be to get an honest yes out of some ubiquitous media consumers 15 years practiced at unseeing their spouse. On the flip side, it's hard to imagine any woefully overeducated/underemployed socialite on the verge of becoming a trophy wife even risking the possibility that Moneybags says no-- even if she didn't think he loved her. You buy separate TVs and disavow his whoring until the end of the prenup, *American Psycho* style. Ok, so this is fiction.

But she doesn't say he doesn't love her. What she says is that he wouldn't *pursue* her, because she doesn't have a dowry, and what's changed is that nowadays Scrooge wouldn't pursue a woman unless there was a Gain in it. The capitals are hers. But even the greediest capitalist could marry a dowryless woman if there was some other kind of gain in it. I can name at least seven colleges whose existential gimmick is that the right kind of girl doesn't need a dowry or even a pedigree, her BA in Word Count isn't for employment or domestic servitude, it certifies her as the recently finished lady just back from a summer in Paris doing missionary position who would accompany the rising gentleman on his conquest of industry and government, while managing the House and negotiating the quintessential social networks. There's even a mechanism for her own indiscretions as long as she keeps to the mechanism and remains discrete. That's a gain money can't buy. Directly. No good, doesn't count. If he's such a capitalist, why can't he see there are different kinds of value in her to be exploited? Why does the Gain have to be money?

Because he's not a capitalist. I know the top hat codes otherwise, but you can't judge a book by its cover, unless the author deliberately selected the cover in spite of the capitalist requirements. He does exploit=extract a lot of surplus value, but so do pirates and poker players. He's not a capitalist because he doesn't fulfill his role as capitalist by using his money as capital or for exchange. Money is the material existence of abstracted wealth, and also the medium of circulation-- and he *hides* it. In 1843 there aren't *enough* capitalists, more are needed for the ceaseless expansion necessary to prevent Volume II of Capital, and one of the biggest candidates is opting out. He'll pay taxes because he follows the law, but he short circuits the whole ideology and hoards the money that the system depends on him to recycle, either as investment or as consumption. He's not a capitalist, he's a hard money mercantilist: *he doesn't trust capitalism.* The problem isn't fear of poverty but inflation; for him capitalism is extremely inaccurate, it fails to value things correctly, in prosperous times capitalism thinks it can intelligently value things without a metallic anchor, but crisis after crisis shows that it always will rely on it. Love, investing, and marrying the "right kind of girl" may make him richer in theory or on paper, but that doesn't count, it isn't real; if the end comes only what he has in his counting house or in his chewing teeth will be valuable-- invaluable.

The only way to turn Scrooge into a symbol of *greedy* capitalism is to make him profoundly uncapitalistic; and to hide that maneuver you put him in a top hat. "See, the height of his hat indicates he's one of the privileged classes." That's feudalism, or possibly restaurantism, not capitalism, which makes you right by accident. He is monomaniacal about money, but he isn't selfish, not in the technical sense, he isn't trying to improve his own life, enjoy more, or even show off and lord his money over people. Even if you asked any of the other moneylending sophisticates

156

satisfying them[27]

- a terror of growing older, manifesting precisely not as fear but rage-- rage at how the world that once belonged to you, or should now belong to you, is being wasted on everyone else;

- a disdain for the very idea of preparing the world for the next generation, manifesting precisely not as dismissing the future, but disconnecting the past from the present so the future starts today and the benefits are yours;

- a fear of dependency, manifesting precisely not as off the grid individualism nor

---

at the Exchange about money, drunk with prosperity and arrogantly certain of themselves they would admit that money is a purely imaginary creation, obviously it only has value because of what it can buy. But Scrooge doesn't want to buy anything, he wants to not buy anything. He wants the money to stop moving. The point isn't that money is valuable only because of what it can buy; the point is that *only* the money is valuable because other people will sell everything for it. Right now, all those smug capitalists and exploited workers all think what they have is valuable, all those people think *they* are valuable, even undervalued! But hold up a gold sovereign and watch intrinsic value turn into a Dutch auction. Spend money? You think he's going to part with the most valuable object in the world for a fleeting dinner of salmon mayonnaise? He literally eats *gruel*. You think Scrooge is going to trade cold hard coin for office heat? Heat isn't even a *thing*. Yes, yes, women are inferior and the property of their husbands; but between us top hats, how much money is that actually worth? And Cratchit? That quarter-functional illiterate multiplied his IQ by 100 and calculated he's worth 15 shillings? It's madness. *None of this is real.*

He *sounds* like a capitalist because he *sounds* like he revels in the misfortunes of others, but close/one reading reveals he doesn't actually enjoy them, he merely accepts them, because according to his bottom line mentality, the misfortunate must have deserved it. You can say that kind of thinking is evil or a cognitive bias, knock yourself out, but it's not capitalism. Capitalism values things dynamically, not statically, if something is undervalued the market will correct the price, but the only reason you think you know it was undervalued was that the price corrected. Capitalism doesn't assume anything is deserved or necessary, it makes no distinction between a want or a need, it just moves. Scrooge HATES this. When you circumvent the hard, fixed value of things-- say, by giving people money for charity=for *no* reason-- things can't be valued and you have psychosis. There's a scene where a poor man was given 15 shillings by the charity workers, and later Scrooge finds him at a restaurant eating salmon mayonnaise. "You!" Scrooge yells. "You steal 15 shillings from the other poor, and you spend it on salmon mayonnaise?" And the guy looks at him confused, "But sir, when I have no money I *can't* eat salmon mayonnaise, and when I get some money I *shouldn't* eat salmon mayonnaise-- well, *when* am I supposed to eat salmon mayonnaise?" Ah, the comedy of the 19th century, the joke being the acceptable manifestation of some unacceptable repressed idea. Nodding your head? A rape joke would be the same. There's an ethical puzzle in the salmon joke, should everyone be entitled to receive the same luxuries, or, if this is impossible, should no one at all be allowed to have them, should they not exist, thus obviating envy? "Production for use" as per the insane murderer of the black police officer? Should we intelligently direct our limited resources to creating only socially useful goods and not mayonnaise, which anyway is disgusting? This is a fun and pointless discussion to have because none of us are going to do anything about it ever and at all, but for Scrooge this is deadly business, because he knows that nobody-- *nobody*-- wants only what they need, the demand for anything concrete creates the desire for something more-- at someone else's expense, hence the accusation that the poor man *stole* 15 shillings from the other poor. The reason for this is that all demands are literally and semantically ambiguous, however concrete you are with your demand it reflexively starts a desire for something more. What's relevant for Scrooge is that when the poor man didn't have 15 shillings, he wouldn't have even *wanted* to use 15 shillings for salmon mayonnaise. And on it goes.

universalizing economic supports but as a demand for all manner of social/psychological controls all which must appear invisible

- the despising of peoples, manifesting either as a well reasoned desire for central planning or unsophisticated devotion to laissez-faire-- both are admissions that outcomes can not be left to ordinary people=you

- an inability to be alone, manifesting not as loneliness but as a *horror vacui*-- when you're by yourself in a house with greater than two rooms, always will the TV be on.

Is it too late for you? Yes. You are already lost. But with this psychology, and in this society, you will then try to raise the next generation, even and especially if you have no kids,

---

"I'd like a 3x5 wedge of salmon, no sauce, no bread, and a glass of water," reflexively becomes, "but you should cook it better…" And a third of the people reading this will argue, why shouldn't he have the right to have it cooked well? And a different eighth of you will think, why shouldn't he have the privilege of having it cooked well?-- and charge him an extra shilling; and another 13/24ths of you will want to punch him in the face, there are no other possibilities and 7/8 of all of you are varying degrees of insane, and dangerous. Good luck with the math, that's how you got this way in the first place. You can say that all demands end up becoming a desire for recognition, but that is a desire Scrooge absolutely does not want to satisfy. I'll satisfy your needs, I may even respond to your demands, but how dare you obligate me in your bananastown desires? "But he's not asking Scrooge to satisfy his desires, he's just asking for 15 shillings and he'll satisfy his own desires." No. Every demand creates a desire, asking for 15 will=must cost Scrooge 18. It's more than simply "wanting more than you get," as if baked salmon mayonnaise was going to next week be roast ox in almond braise, ad infinitum. It's not the magnitude of the desire but the infinity of them, there will always be another desire but each felt just as strongly as the one before it, no accounting for relative importance. And when he's coerced the world to give him every food imaginable he'll demand *no* food: "but I want *you* to keep me alive!" This is the problem Scrooge sees in capitalism, the expanding desires even to the point of infantilism, nihilism, self-annihilationism, he imagines a capitalism so excessive and decadent that the only thing left for it to want is-- is what we want today: *no* capitalism, "but I want *you* to keep me alive!"

Everyone today knows that *everything* is a capitalist trick: Christmas, "days off", marriage, charity, these are maneuvers to protect the underlying capitalist ideology, and everyone *else* has been brainwashed by them. Well, go read the book: Scrooge hasn't. Every one of those things, every one and every time, is a humbug, and he's not buying it. In other words, Scrooge wants to destroy capitalism. And go back to being a New Testament moneylender. So instead of fetishistic disavowal, he performs a rigorous, old school alchemical transmutation: he turns everything of mystical value into gold. Pure gold, the only thing that's real. And then he counts it.

That Scrooge loves money *more* than Belle is a false comparison; the very problem is that love is neither objective nor subjective. So what if he loves Belle more? Does that make it *correct*? What would happen if he married her for love? She tells him: "If for a moment you were false enough to your one guiding principle to do so, do I not know your repentance and regret would surely follow?" How much he loves her has nothing to do with the *rules*. What she's describing is guilt for violating a commandment of his superego: it must be in gold. It doesn't count if it can't be counted. Loving her is like-- stay with me to the end-- going to a prostitute: you feel guilty about it, but paying her doesn't make you feel better about using her; paying her *is* what you feel guilty about, it's the only thing you could feel guilty about. That guilt is what will eventually get you to stop doing it, which you will convert to hubris that you're not some lowlife who spends money on prostitutes.

Worth mentioning here is the importance of the modern 19th century dowry as a defense against the ancient 19th century critique that marriage is a form of prostitution: it can't be prostitution if she paid him.

and the cycle repeats, disrupted only by the jarring effects of an outside crisis that will resettle to the status quo post bellum-- unless one day, it can't. And if this crisis threatens your knowledge you will fight it to the death; but if the crisis relieves you of your power, then far from lamenting your fate, you will fall to your knees and worship it like a god.[28] [29]

In butchering Marx's definition, and making miserliness the asymptote of capitalism, we miss how his miserliness is actually a madness-- a defense against capitalism, against the mystical, free floating, unanchored valuations of everything. "The market decides." The hell it does, ok, he loves Belle, Belle is more valuable to him than-- than what? Than another woman he doesn't love? Than how valuable Belle is to some other man? What market decides that? There's no way to know what makes her valuable, and as a defense against that lack of knowledge, he measures his love for her with the only thing that is valuable, which is gold, and lucky for her she doesn't have any, so she's free to go marry someone who isn't a nut. Just FYI: she eventually falls in love with another rich guy.

The mistake that is so easy to make that even Belle makes it is that he's a greedy pig that looks at marriage as a business venture. Well, run what the cool kids call a counterfactual: back then, if her funeral dress meant she just inherited a fortune, would he have married her for the money? No-- *he would have thought he was in love with her*. Contrast this to a different hypothetical: some other rich man marries the now rich Belle, for love. Belle considers her dowry as symbolic of her love, it's a gift, "I know he loves me and I want him to be happy." He feels the same way about his money, doubly reinforced by his ambivalent belief that she doesn't want his money because she's already rich and anyway she could have gotten richer guys if she wanted. Ok so far? As the years passed he would cut out bits of her, things he figured out he didn't love, and since that thing that causes his love was indeed her gold he would eventually have obliterated everything else about her that he thought he loved, but still never really figuring out what in her he does love-- all he knows is it isn't *that*, or *that*, or *that*, or *that*, or *that*, and so he uses his ledger to weigh wants vs. satisfactions, so that satisfaction is found only in depriving the other. He still *thinks* he "loves his wife", yet everything about her annoys him. He won't share his thoughts with her, or ask about hers, he'll no longer care about the big boobs he used to think he enjoyed, and if someone else enjoyed them he wouldn't feel a loss or even jealous but enraged, envious, that she was desired more than him, or that the affair was somehow a claim about her relative superiority to him, she was able to get a new guy but all the husband could get was her. No, it doesn't have to make sense, and it doesn't have to be true-- only necessary. How is Scrooge different from this jerk? Easy: Scrooge figures it all out early-- decides-- exactly what counts: money. No need to slowly obliterate her piece by piece; she's immediately marked to market. Scrooge wouldn't care if someone else drools over her boobs or her opinions. Her satisfaction, some other guy's-- none of those things count, and depriving others of them doesn't count either. Only the gold counts.

I am careful in my description: the choice of gold as the thing of universal value is a *choice*, but it's the easiest choice: everyone universally agrees, regardless of what they say. He could have chosen to invest "sex" with all the value, and swaps the top hat for a Don Juan mask. But that choice wouldn't be satisfactory because sex isn't material, it doesn't physically manifest and retain all the other kinds of value within it, it isn't desirable in itself, it can't circulate as a medium of exchange. In other words, the only thing that can act like money is money. He converts everything of value to money, *and then hoards it.*

The Case Of The Mistaken Identity

A couple wants to put some excitement into their relationship. Their plan is to go out separately to a bar, he'll pretend to be a stranger and try to pick her up. He shows up and spots his wife sitting at the bar looking like a million bucks. He cocks his head, saunters over like he has every right to be there and starts smoothly hitting on her. A couple of drinks and a "whaddya say we get out of here" later, he takes her home and they have

---

Scrooge's solution to the mystery of value, of meaning, is to hoard money. Scrooge's problem in the book is that his solution isn't working. He's dismal. "Because money can't buy happiness." Ok, but it doesn't follow that he has to be dismal. The precise reason he is bitter is that even happiness and misery aren't being valued correctly. Instead of more money Coatless Cratchit wants Christmas *off*? Capitalism is still alive, despite the poor houses. Hoarding isn't working.

And then the Christmas Spirits come. Let me ask you a question: do they come because he hoards money, or because he is dismal? Ok, too hard, baby steps: why do they come on Christmas Eve? Christmas is a joyous time and he needs to learn the three spirits of it? No. The logical connection to Christmas is that Marley died Christmas Eve seven years ago. It's not a joyous time, it was the only time Scrooge possibly mourned. Marley is the relevant ghost, if he had died on Halloween then the other ghosts would have been the Prince of Darkness, Michael Myers and the baby from *It's Alive*. So now the question is why does Marley appear *at all*, and why on *that* particular Christmas?

The material for dreams comes from the day of the dream, and on that day two things happen.

The first thing that happens is that Scrooge's happy-go-lucky nephew (NB from his *sister*, the only woman Scrooge still loves) dances in like he won the lottery, which he most certainly did not, and Scrooge reminds him of it: "what right do you have to be happy, you're poor enough." The nephew could list ten things he's happy about, or reply that money isn't everything, Christmas is a time for giving, I'm happy about my family and health-- all of those answers are about value, about meaning, and would fail on Scrooge. Instead, the nephew drops a hard core psychoanalytic provocation that puts Scrooge into asystole: "What right have you to be dismal, you're rich enough." Well wait a second, why *am* I dismal? What *do* I want? And when you ask yourself a question like that, you quickly look for the one who would know the answer. He's has no patience for God, no time for Thucydides and it's going to be another generation before psychoanalysis, so as an early adopter of the coming stop-gap solution he'll get his information from the spirit world.

The second thing that happens is that, after the book has told us that Scrooge "answered to Scrooge or Marley equally", that he never bothered to correct anyone because it made no difference, *it was all the same to him*-- suddenly two men come in and ask him if he is Marley. *And today he tells them Marley is dead.*

This is why Marley appears to him, on that night. Marley explains he doesn't want Scrooge to end up like him, so he's organized three Spirits to help with Scrooge's redemption. Why isn't seeing Marley and his chains enough to scare him straight? And if it's not enough, why isn't Ghost of Christmas Future enough, especially since that future looks like Marley's? What is the purpose of a Ghost of Christmas Past?

The simple answer is that though the Future is what will change him, seeing the past helps explain it, because explaining things is awesome. But remember, the relevant ghost is Marley, the point of all this is not to share his fate. *Yet Marley never appears in the visions of his past.* Marley was his

sex like porn stars.

The next morning she wakes up luxurious and glowing. He, however, is enraged. "If I had known how much of an easy slut you were, I never would have married you!"[30]

---

only friend, Scrooge moved into Marley's house after he died, yet not a moment of them in the old days chewing on gold or shivering in a counting house. Marley can't be said to have been repressed because Scrooge is consciously aware of him. There is no repression here. Marley has been *cut out* of the past and moved to the present.

It's Christmas Future, not Past, that is powerless. Christmas Past-- seeing his past from the outside, like a movie-- is the *only* thing that can change him, because the past, not the future, is the only thing he *can* change; by the time of the end of that Stave, he has already changed. To review: his mother dies. His father is mean, and abandons him to a boarding school, where he is also similarly abandoned by all the other kids. Years later, he is recalled home to a now loving father. What caused his father to change so quickly that he wants his son back? Interestingly, the story doesn't tell you, there is absolutely no hint of an answer in the vision: i.e. Scrooge doesn't know, *and still can't imagine*. You can say he felt the abandonment as real, but more accurately, he felt unvalued without knowing what the father valued. "What did I lack? What was I to you?" He's lonely and sad at school, you might say he "retreats into fantasy"-- except he doesn't retreat into fantasy at all, he retreats into fantasy books to avoid his own fantasies. What he doesn't do is what a typical kid might then have done, which is read the book and then improvise fantasies around or even beyond what you've read. That's not what he does. He doesn't fantasize. He doesn't *play*. If I can dare editorialize: he is not taught *that he can* play. The fantasy books organize, concretize, the primitive fantasies which he is not equipped to safely observe. They are a defense against fantasy, in the same way fairy tales are defenses against the chaotic and violent fantasies of children: instead of your own crazy terrors, just be afraid of this *only*. The difference is that kids usually go on to learn how to fantasize except nowadays sexually, for which they rely on porn as the defense. Anyway, he doesn't do this. Even when he "fantasizes" about Ali Baba, he imagines him as real, as present. Fantasy is impossible, so impossible, he cannot even fantasize a *theory of value*.

At this point someone is going to suggest that a hoarder of gold is "anal retentive", because they've heard of Freud. The child saves his poop for the big day so he can give it to his parents as a gift because they-- not he-- seem to really value his poop. And if he wants to deny them the satisfaction of his poop, he'll just hold on to it. As he ages, and when feces has lost its value to them, his interest passes over to other objects that can be offered as gifts of value, say, grades or anything that leads to "that's my boy!" But now the only thing that counts is gold, which he sticks up his butt, hoping everyone will want it. Corresponding exactly to analogous changes in meaning that occur in linguistic development, the ancient interest in feces is transformed into the high valuation of gold. Because this is an early childhood, drive-driven maneuver, it isn't a choice; it can't be repaired, only repressed, sublimated, etc.

So goes the theory, but right or wrong, it doesn't apply to Scrooge: he's not planning on giving the gold to anyone. He derives no pleasure in having it, giving it, depriving others of it, or even of being known to possess it. Gold is the only thing he values because it is real. Gold doesn't have any symbolic meaning, he doesn't think or care if it makes him desirable or powerful, because symbolic meaning doesn't exist.

In other words, *Scrooge has no unconscious*. Whether he was born without it or never developed it or it was crushed underfoot I cannot say, what matters is now nothing can ever have multiple meanings. Things just are. The entire gimmick of the book is that he has three Christmas visions=dreams, but the dreams barely contain distortions, let alone evidence of repression; they're almost literal recollections/representations, seen from a new perspective, which is still his own-- they're videos. Things he'd rather not think about aren't repressed such that he thinks about them as something else; thoughts of Marley are simply redacted. In fact, the structure of the story-- what literally happens-- is that he dreams that ghosts show him visions-- that he has dreams within a dream, which is far from a complex unconscious repression, it's the maneuver of a person trying to make something true, it is *simply* a denial: I wish the thing in the inner vision, which is real, was just a dream. And when Scrooge watches his childhood self read the story of Ali Baba, in the window of the child's room appears Ali Baba, it is a dream within a dream within a dream: Ali Baba doesn't represent anything, the wish is that Ali Baba had been real, literally real, which is exactly what Scrooge says happened when he was a boy: "when yonder solitary child was left here all alone, Ali Baba *did* come, for the first time, just like that..."

Nothing in his life-- including his life-- means anything *else*. Even enjoyment, whether superego appropriate or transgressive-- is impossible. He spent his life hoarding reality, locking it down. And then one day, Marley dies. *There can be no doubt whatever about that.* "That's just to assert to the reader that Marley's ghost is real." As opposed to symbolic? Yeah.

If the miser's problem is making any sense of the various unrealities in reality-- things like love, charity, faith or relative surplus value-- that he has to concretize them, and hoard them, to ground fantasy into cold gold reality; then the kind of breakdown such a person might have if his "reality was challenged" is *A Christmas Carol*. Learning about the mystical, symbolic meaning and value of things is a lesson that can not come, it cannot be learned, what do you mean things have multiple meanings at once, some contradictory yet together even more meaningful? What the hell kind of David Lynch universe is this? Who is deciding? Teaching them "what's truly valuable in life" makes things worse, not better. All you can do is let them make minor revisions to their own story while letting them keep the anchors that have always grounded them. Scrooge does not learn money isn't invaluable, he cannot learn this; he can only learn that part of its value is in its use, that he can afford to sacrifice some of it for a disproportionately greater benefit to others at little cost to who he is. It's a kind of John Winthrop "Christian charity to those who need it, You Know What interest loans to those who can afford it" proto-capitalism, but anyway this is the change, and for Scrooge it happens early on with Christmas Past. He witnesses two men superlatively praise Fezziwig for throwing such a wonderful Xmas party all at his own expense, and the Spirit provokes Scrooge: "why are those suckers so thankful, Fezziwig only spent 15 shillings on the party." Scrooge takes the bait. "It isn't that, Spirit... even if his power lies in things so insignificant that it is impossible to count them: so what? The happiness he gives is quite as great as if it cost a fortune." There before you is Scrooge's Christmas change, you can cancel the other Spirits. Nowadays we are way too clever for that, we'll repeat the Spirit's provocation as if it were an actual intellectual insight, as if we uncovered the sneaky maneuver the bankers tried to hide from us, just so it isn't our own envy.

The 2020 straight-to-video-clips sex comedy *Confirmative Assent* (title graphic: "ConFIRMative ASSent") cold opens with the tailgate majors of Delta Delta Delta (per the boys: "Try Delta, because two out of three go down!") and the lacrosse majors of Lambda Alpha Chi (per the girls: "ΛAX: "So dumb they need a helmet!"") at a fraternity party, where the game of the night is Four Second Rule ("if you want a safeword, GTFO"). Banality aside, from an expository standpoint you could do far worse than Four Second Rule for introducing characters, you can do set up, joke, and sexual punchline fast enough to keep the audience's attention yet efficiently reveal a lot about each characters' wants, motivations, and

---

It's envy. And if someone tried to respond the way Scrooge did, we'd crucify him as a simpleton, an ideology blinded capitalist.

I don't know if Dickens is a genius or just a method actor, but he adds a scene which is nearly flawless in its psychological necessity: the next morning when Scrooge is a changed man, what he literally does is act like he hasn't changed. It's a standard movie trope now, but when a Fussbudget learns to be nice, he still makes it seem like the kindness is reluctant, he has to pad that kindness by forcefully asserting his old Fussbudgetness as who he still really is. Yes, it's a put on-- but a necessary one. He has to keep that part of him, it has to still fit. So he is certainly more giving with his money, but he's still formally a miser. He is still not a capitalist. Let me give you a very psychoanalytic example: he will give Bob Cratchit a raise, but he is not going to give *himself* a raise. He'll buy a family a turkey, but it's still gruel for himself; nor will he reduce his cash holdings to invest in a new venture. Those things are impossible because there's still no value in them to him relative to the cost. Of course, Dickens wasn't trying to convince Scrooge to invest in bonds or eat better gruel. He just wanted Cratchit to get a raise.

But then why does Scrooge need to be *redeemed*? Look, if the whole point is to get Moneybags to take care of the less fortunate, that lesson was learned by the end of Christmas Past, you don't need Future. You can say that Christmas Future is necessary to show him how little he'll be missed, but he never cared about that, he didn't care they called him Marley; he wouldn't at all pretend to still be a miser; if anything, he'd flaunt his change into a charitable man. And Marley's behavior would also be illogical: he's not missed, he's totally forgotten, that can't be changed; yet for some reason he walked for 7 years dragging his chains to become Scrooge's doorknocker? Why is redeeming Scrooge explicitly part of his own redemption? *Have you ever asked yourself why does Scrooge need to be redeemed?* My question is specific, and the answer is exactly this: no.

Christmas Future doesn't change him but boy oh boy is it important in ways you are not going to want to think about. Christmas Future shows him a dead man, which Scrooge doesn't know is himself, and he watches three despicables callously steal his sheets and his burial clothes. I get that it's supposed to warn him how little he will be missed after death, but that doesn't change the fact that those three people are still despicable. You may say he's dead, what's the harm, but the story explicitly exists in a world that has a very real afterlife, it is the entire foundation of the story. So these despicables know they can be *seen*, by an omnipotent entity, who of course won't judge them harshly because they will explain they're not really bad people, they just did a bad thing. Anyway. The point here is that those three are despicable.

Someone is going to look at my contempt and react to *it*, and say something like, "they'd been exploited and robbed their whole lives, by people like Scrooge, it's like *Les Mis*, you can't blame them for trying to steal a little something back." Except it's not really like the book you watched sung, because Valjean knows what he is doing is necessary *and* still also wrong, you may do what you have to do but if you're not going to atone at least have the decency to feel guilty. "I don't accept that. I wouldn't feel any guilt robbing his corpse of a few trinkets, because he deserved it." So in your ledger depriving him counts for more than your gain. Uh oh.

relationships without slogging through contrived backstory; i.e., their backstory doesn't need to be explicitly revealed because it manifests in their behavior. Of course the very idea of the game is contrived, but you know the movie's blown right past unrealistic and into surrealistic when despite all the high jinks and cumraderie no one at the party thinks to hit REC. "Actually, that is realistic, because they wouldn't allow cameras at these kinds of parties." They want sorority girls to show up, but they don't allow cameras. Ok. Is this party in an MRI? "They collect them at the door." Like they didn't even do in *Eyes Wide Shut*. Privacy like that doesn't need to be enforced, it's aspirational. Not to you, but therein lies the problem. "Actually, they have secretly recorded parties like those." Privacy like *that* is encouraged-- it's aspirational. To you, and therein lies the problem. "I think I'm confused." If you don't have

---

Whatever Dickens intended the book to do has failed, it even failed in its primary intention, which was to make Dickens rich. The more useful thing to do is understand why his story is so deeply misinterpreted as, e.g., a greedy capitalist who doesn't want to die forgotten and learns that there are more important things than money. Certainly this story has been safely packaged as a children's story with "a relatively simplistic message, but still good for them to hear", but it has given adults a multi-level maneuver for hating those who have more. "I'm not greedy, if I had Scrooge's money, I would definitely buy a crippled kid a turkey." I believe you, because you said Scrooge's money. Your problem is envy, not greed, and when you claim to care about others you should check to see if it's not in order to deprive someone else. Because it is.

If they had robbed him of his gold we'd almost feel better about it, because it would make sense, stealing the clothes of a dead man is somehow a worse crime than stealing his money, even though the value is less. And yet this is exactly the opposite of Scrooge's whole ideology, which shows that his horror at witnessing it happen to some body indicates he has *already* changed. But do you really believe they are stealing his clothes because there's nothing else to steal? As if something *must* be stolen? As if the problem was a lack? They took their share, their entitled cut, below a level which it was ok to steal, above which it would be grave robbing. "It's not a sin!" she announces. How could it be? It's the slave's privilege to steal a little from the master because the master values certain things above other things, take my trinkets, he says, just leave me to my business.

"You can't be so judgmental, they wouldn't have robbed the clothes off any dead man, not even any rich man, but only Scrooge, because he was so contemptible." I'm worried that you're right. I repeat: *have you ever asked yourself why does Scrooge need to be redeemed?*

If the three despicables did this only because Scrooge was a contemptible person, then is what they did Scrooge's *fault*? I don't mean karma, I mean it in the most concrete way: did Scrooge *cause* others to be evil? Did Scrooge's existence cause those three to get an extra point in the liabilities column, when, without Scrooge, they would have been saved?

Scrooge did not know it was his body they were robbing. If his shame and horror were the point Christmas Future wouldn't have hidden this from him, it would have been in spotlight, "look how little people will care about you!" But an anonymous body reveals the logical link between the despicables' behavior and the dead man; the point of Christmas Future isn't what happens to Scrooge, the point is what happens to *them*.

And this is the link in the chain back to Marley: Marley visits Scrooge not because Scrooge is guilty but because Marley is guilty for Scrooge. He shares the guilt for Scrooge's sins. Marley can't be redeemed because Scrooge keeps sinning because of his original contact with Marley, Scrooge's chains are ultimately Marley's.

You can take the other side and say it isn't any one person's responsibility how another person re-acts to you, which is a fair philosophical position to take, except that in the logic of the book, only Scrooge was selected for this elaborate salvation, salvation through Marley, which is as personalized

what you want, there are three possible reasons. 1. Since it's what you want, you can't act to get it. 2. It's not what you want, but you feel obligated to pursue it. 3. What you want is a defense against satisfaction.

Obviously, the frat boys made up this wacky rule to be able to touch girls' boobs, but whenever an explanation for a highly charged emotional state is obvious you should check to see if its real purpose is a defense. Fine, I'll start you off: when you hear the word defense, don't think "shield". Think "I never would have done that on purpose".

The movie follows the old trope of "football jocks vs math nerds", updated for po-mo audiences that can't really relate to either of those categories, so football gets downgraded to

---

a savior is he was going to get. God went the extra mile for Scrooge, so if Scrooge has the privilege of a second chance at redemption, does he bear the responsibility if others aren't? Apparently the answer is yes. I have no idea who Satan is, but I know from the primary source what he does, isn't the very idea of Satan as the ultimate evil related not to his acts of adultery, murder, apple picking and Sabbath violations, of which I count zero, but in tempting others? No, no, I'm fully Earth based, I don't mean tempting as "seducing", I mean it as "behavioral economics." Someone will read religious predestination into this, but that's only because your brain is lazy and want to push out into theology the much harder practical question: should you forgive others for their sins against you, or should you ask them to forgive you for causing them to sin? It's a question every parent should ask themselves. You won't. "I don't want to be a hypocrite." God forbid. There's no greater sin than that.

You'll say that God or no god, a person is always entirely responsible for their own accounting, and this is obviously true; but it doesn't lessen your responsibility. "That doesn't add up." Most of the problem is that you think it needs to, but even so-- wasn't it you that insisted everyone keep their own ledgers?

Throughout the book are the subtle signs of Scrooge's true sin, you will never want to see them yourself but once I point them out to you you will not be able to unsee them-- so you'll have no choice but to attack me. Why else are the three despicables there, if not to ask: who made them despicable? "The truth is it was structural, it's capitalism!" You're scapegoating an ideology? It's still entirely their own fault, AND Scrooge's. The purpose of Christmas Future isn't to scare him but to show him the reach of his contamination, Future Spirit comes last not because of chronological order but because Scrooge can only see this after he has changed. And that's why you can't. If you want to scare Scrooge with how little he will be missed, you show the wife of his debtor rejoice at his death, but if you want Scrooge to see how toxic he is to others, you do what Dickens actually did which is show the wife of his debtor rejoice at his death *and then show her feeling guilty about it.* Do you see now? Maybe it's not too late.

We lie and say we don't like it when our flaws are pointed out but no one's gone genocidal because someone laughed at their height; yet all it takes to make a man to go black with rage is merely suggest he is responsible to others, especially those he despises; you'll proudly march your son back to the store from which he stole a banana to teach him how to be a man, but to wonder-- not accept, and certainly not ask him, merely to wonder-- that rather than failing to teach him right and wrong there was something about your existence that lead him to try theft for something as trivial as a banana-- that lead him to think it was an option-- that allowed him to have the thought, and that the danger now isn't merely that he's corrupted by you but that he will go on to corrupt others...

Together with your therapist or your internet you will quietly discover that your pursuit of independence is obviously a defense against depending on others, a shame which your internet will project onto everyone else, but any god, ex, or licensed accountant can see that you don't want anyone dependent on you-- slow down liar, I mean it psychologically, you don't want anyone to be entitled to depend on you. And you'll say, according to what principle is anyone entitled to anything

lacrosse and math obliterated to pre-med, and the two sides literally and explicitly labeled "alphas vs betas". Even in a semi-porn I can sense a bait and switch, and I suspected that these changes weren't so much about updating the trope as an attempt to whiten the cast for its likely target demo, but I was surprised to discover I was only half right and way wrong. In a rather remarkable aside of accidental social critique, the film here cuts to a (fake?) moment of "Director's Commentary" voice over and example deleted scenes to show that pitting real modern college football players against real math majors could not help but be seen by an audience as a racial conflict only-- black vs Asian; worse, making the cast white but still calling them "football players" and "math majors" made this black/Asian racial conflict *more* obvious-- the change was seen as an obvious obfuscation of the real conflict of race, and

---

from me without at least acknowledging the debt? But I've already asked myself this question and I know that asking it prevents any answer, what you want and what you know is a weapon against the world, this is Scrooge's final lesson and the dream you have forgotten, stop looking for knowledge and watch what you hear: continue as you are, and even in death you will be a poison to the lives of others. Pray on it, and despair! If you're not moved it is because you are immovable but the truth that should shake you to your soul is that you will secretly welcome even your own death as long as it publicly results in the suffering of someone else. Repent. There is no time. Repent.

22 If you want a story that both utterly misses the point and nails it completely by accident, take a look at (matriarchal) Disney's hyperatrocity *Maleficent*, a retelling of (patriarchal) Disney's *Sleeping Beauty*. In the original animated film, baby Aurora is cursed by the green and black Maleficent to die by spinning loom on her 16th birthday; the good fairy mitigates this curse by pronouncing that the curse can be lifted if Aurora is given "true love's kiss". At the end, dashing Prince Phillip gives the kiss, and they go off and live happily ever after (not pictured).

Other than money, why a retelling? "New generation?" Of what, animators? The target audience is literally the same people. While older Disney movies were ostensibly for children, the current box office enticement has to target the parents who were children, especially the mothers. It has to give them what they want, and from the shrapnel their children will collaterally learn how to want.

The usual criticism of fairy tales is that they tell young girls to aspire to nothing more than marriage to a prince, but this isn't what fairy tales are for. The story isn't about becoming an adult, it is about the anxiety of being a child. In order to make it comforting to powerless children, therefore, the child has to win-- marry the prince, defeat the witch, etc-- by *not* doing anything. Not that they can't do anything-- the whole point is that it doesn't matter if you do nothing-- you do not need to act.

Journalistic sociology doesn't see the age appropriateness, only the gender inappropriateness. It sees a princess doing nothing but wanting to marry a prince and it goes black and green with rage, how dare you tell us what to want? This is fixed in the retelling, Aurora feministically doesn't want to be a princess and doesn't want to marry a prince-- *but she still doesn't do anything*. So what does she want? "To be independent." But what does that mean? Fixing the story makes it worse because now the child wants nothing, does nothing and gets nothing. In other words, this is either going to be a very terrible story or you're going to need a new protagonist.

In *Maleficent*, it becomes about the parents; children are too naïve/precious/simple to have complicated psychological lives. Even though this is still supposed to be a movie for kids, all the drama occurs peri-menopause, after all, that's what counts.

Which means the movie plays out the only way it believably can for them, as American end-of-love fantasia. *Adult* Maleficent and *adult* Stefan fall in love; but one night, after "sleeping" with her (literally=metaphorically), he betrays her, cuts off the only part of her he needs-- her wings-- to secure his place on the throne. Like a man, he used her up and then left her. Hell hath no fury, etc, etc, so for years she stalks Stefan and his younger, prettier second wife, played as an imbecile; and

audiences were nowadays primed to detect such tricks. The only way to pornographize the film was to take out the "symbology" of race or class, and use only "biological markers of reproductive fitness".

The movie's central conflict is that the alpha males of ΛAX have been forced to share their house with the beta males following the school's new policy of "promoting sexual diversity on campus". Not only do betas get a proportional number of rooms, but they must be allowed equal opportunities with women, including Four Second Rule (in a cutaway, a bored woman is seated next to a beta as he uses 4 seconds-- his voice in 3x speed-- to explain the "video" he had seen which "nailed" the evolutionary reasons why "hypergamous" women

---

at baby Aurora's christening (another fairy tale no one believes anymore, in contrast to Maleficent's pagan world which is majestic, green, and real) Maleficent shows up to curse her. But there's a key difference from the original: Maleficent *herself* adds that her own curse can be lifted by True Love's Kiss. Is she allowing for redemption? A woman scorned but still selflessly offering the possibility of hope? Women helping women? Maybe she's not all bad? No. Unlike the dumb monotheists in Act I, she *knows* true love doesn't exist. The point is to condemn them all to *false* hope.

Obviously, what makes Maleficent become malevolent is Stefan's malicious betrayal of her. Except what's all of Act I yet utterly ignored is that Maleficent's rage *preceded* her betrayal; the very reason Stefan betrays her is to avenge the King, who was mortally wounded by *her*. Having her wings cut off only made her *more* enraged, but the reason she had rage in the first place-- the reason she doesn't believe in True Love-- isn't that Stefan cut her wings off in her 40s but that he *abandoned* her when they were teens. *High school.* As the narrator tells us: "on her 16th birthday, Stefan gave her a present: True Love's Kiss" (during which she is literally floating on air). "But it was not to be." Fade to black, and then to green.

But today's Disney women are sensible, they don't harbor revenge fantasies about things that have happened in their past, they invent them for things that happened to hypothetical other people or never actually happened in the first place. Hold that thought. Time passes and her anger abates, she doesn't hold a grudge, she moves on, and in the magical way only women can she takes those negative emotions from the divorce and sublimates them into new, healthy, positive connections. In the human world she'd decide she wants to be a therapist, in porn it's an MFF, but of course in this story it's connecting with little Aurora. She comforts her as a baby, plays with her as a child, has mud fights with her as a preteen, etc. You're supposed to read this as a mother and child relationship, and just in case you can't they beat you over the head with it: the actress who plays the child Aurora is the real life daughter of the actress who plays Maleficent. This is reversing the suspension of disbelief but for the same purpose, the logical union of opposites: the usual "I know in the story the characters are related, so I can ignore that the actors actually are not" gets flipped: "I know in the story the characters aren't related, but neato, the actors actually are!" Either way, they are.

But back at the castle Stefan, played by toxic masculinity, just can't let it go. He sends his daughter to live with The Three Fairies because he is consumed with the idea that Maleficent will come back to kill him. Why would she? Because the repressed always returns. See, he's trying to be a noble king, but he knows in his heart he did something *bad*. She is living proof that he is actually weak, selfish, and mean: look what he did to her. He can't be a great and noble king if someone knows who he really is, if someone reminds him of who he is. And the logical proof of this is his obsession: because he is obsessed with obliterating her, he is revealed to be a weak and petty man, therefore it is inevitable that Maleficent will be returning.

Which would be a great explanation if Stefan could feel guilty about something he did to her, which he cannot, it is impossible. Here is the nuance that was entirely lost on the audience, and, I suspect, the writers, who did not even know what they were revealing: he doesn't feel any guilt for cutting

like her don't like "intelligent" men like him............. yet. Etc. The alphas resent that the betas did nothing to earn it, they just demanded it be handed to them, while the betas resent that the alphas did nothing to earn it, it was just handed to them. Yes, the movie is as dumb as it sounds, but it's still better than last year's Oscar winner whenever you are reading this.

I suppose it's obvious why a beta male might want equal access to Four Second Rule, but why would alpha males need an excuse to touch a girl's breast? They wouldn't, the game isn't for them, it's for people who think there can be more than one alpha male and yet still can't be one. "But alpha males do actually play these kinds of games." Yes, the logic is sound, and you've made the same mistake twice.

---

her wings off, because from his perspective, that was a mercy: what he was supposed to do was *kill* her. What he did bad was *not* kill her-- *failing to fulfill his duty to the kingdom*. Not doing what is necessary. *Failing to act.* Her continued existence is a reminder that he is not a *real* king who will do what's necessary, independent of his personal feelings. "I shall do my best to be a worthy successor," he had said to the dying King, turns out: nope, couldn't do what had to be done. He may now have a crown on his head, but he *knows* he doesn't deserve it, he *knows* he's a fraud. This is the only kind of guilt he can feel, and a guilt not easily absolved. Maleficent's severed wings, which he puts in a glass case to stare at "to punish himself", has two meanings: 1) to the audience, an obvious symbol of his betrayal of her, for the purpose of preventing anyone from seeing it as 2) a secret symbol of his betrayal of his kingdom and his superego by failing to act as he should. An obvious outward symbol of something, to hide the inward symbol of the opposite. These, not guilt over an act, are the ingredients for obsession.

You might think it's a bit of a stretch to say that Stefan's not killing her but only cutting off her wings was a mercy, but all you need to do is wait 2 minutes for the very next scene: post-castration Maleficent is walking alone in a field and sees a crow about to be killed by a farmer. She casts a quick spell and turns it into a man. The farmer flees in terror. The now human crow, not happy with the transfiguration, confronts Maleficent in anger.

                    CROWMANGONE
        What have you done to my beautiful self?

                    MALEFEASCANCE
        Would you rather he killed you?

                    CROWMANGONE
                    (ashamed)

        Forgive me.

He has been castrated, *and he thanks her for it.*

I can tell you're resisting the "castrated" part of this, but I mean it literally psychoanalytically. You will assume the farmer flees in terror because a crow turned into a eunuch, but she didn't turn him into something actually scary, like tyrannosaur or a giant axillary lymph node. She picked a benign looking human; which, in the logic of the movie, is actually *her* enemy, a weaker enemy that lacks magic. She cut out his crow-ness. The farmer flees but even if he wasn't scared he wasn't going to still try and eat him: the crow was only desirable to the farmer as a crow. The human could be desirable in totally different ways, but is irrelevant to the farmer. Meanwhile, the human crow doesn't continue to want like a crow, he doesn't use his new found dexterity to finally get the cheese

As a personal aside, whenever anyone says the phrase "alpha males" as if it were actionable intel I have to silently talk myself out of committing a felony. But in this movie race and class divisions no longer exist, so it seems the only labels the writers could come up with are alpha and beta. They even have the alpha males refer to *themselves* as alpha males. They're not. You can't be an alpha male if you have to tell me you're an alpha male, I have no problem calling you one if you insist, but don't expect me to instinctively react to you as if you are. The ΛΛΧ brothers aren't alpha males. And the TriDelts aren't alpha females. They're extroverts. I know a lot of alphas and betas want those to be the same thing, but boy oh boy are they not.

So if the alphas don't need 4" Rule, what's it for? Well, maybe it's for the women:

---

or sucker punch scarecrows; he is freed to have new wants, in the same way that paternal castration-- had you had it-- frees you to want on your own. "I do want different things than my father." But not different*ly*. Same as, or in reaction to-- but not on your own.

Accidentally or unconsciously, her castration and the crow's castration are shown one after the other. It's possible the director did this on purpose, I doubt it, but it doesn't matter. Maleficent's mercy and Stefan's mercy are forced into comparison. But if Stefan did her a kind of mercy, then this would make the *magnitude* of her rage-- e.g. her desire to murder Stefan's baby-- even more perplexing. The two don't balance. So something has to be added to the story, something that did not happen, that erases from the unconscious, in the language of the unconscious, any possibility that it was a mercy. Why what she did for the crow is totally different than what Stefan did to her; why Maleficent's and the audience's rage is justified. It is this: Stefan didn't just cut her wings off. He raped her.

Certainly this did not happen, it is not true, but the construction of the scene is sufficient to trigger an audience wanting to be triggered, to search for a traumatic event past or future that can justify present rage that otherwise makes no sense. The clues are there if you just add an l. It happens at night, as they cuddle, and he is trying to get her drunk. But it's not just alcohol (to erase any argument about responsibility), she's been drugged, the empty bottle is shown menacingly in close up next to her defenseless body. God knows there's no evidence of consent; worst of all, she doesn't even **know** what exactly happened. And when she awakens, she acts out post-roofy rape terror and shame: she gags, chokes, looks at herself in horror, then all around her as if she has no idea where she is, and screams. Her reaction tells the audience that even if didn't happen, it happened. Even if he didn't do it--

-- but he *didn't* do it. The movie shows exactly what Stefan does do-- including being unable to kill her and the improvised idea to cut her wings off and try to fool the King-- but the fully loaded audience, half cocked and safeties off, which I realize makes no sense, identifies not with what happened but with Maleficent's lived experience of it. *Now* her rage makes sense.

You may be confused about the temporal order of the facts vs. the rage, but I assure you the order doesn't matter, the logic of rage is atemporal, but anyway here you go: first she is dumped as a teen. In order to justify the rage that occurs after this otherwise trivial event, she changes the meaning of a future event (the de-winging is upcoded into a rape) so that the rage makes logical sense-- she can either nurture that rage or, in this film, nobly move past it and become a mom to baby Aurora.

And, like all exes, Stefan is shown as an abusive jerk. Well, he never actually does anything to her until the big fight scene at the end. Sure, he tries to murder her with a sword, but the audience's audible gasp comes when he punches her. Swords don't trigger; which is why he was shown punching her. Even at the climax battle scene, fully rewinged, she tries to rationally resolve things, I don't want to fight, let's be adults about this; but blinded by his privilege he pounces-- she puts up no resistance and they tumble off the top of the castle. Here's a riddle: why did the winged creature fall off a ledge? The question for the audience is whether, like in real life, she hated him because he was

obviously the patriarchy wants to objectify women, we are told it moves product and motivates consumers, while giving "social" women a way to "express themselves" when they decide they don't have the "natural ability" for "math", so it needs to create for women a safe situation-- protected by rules-- that allows them "freedom" to do what they "want"-- act sexy, incite lust, even be safely fondled without it being too dangerous or "meaning" anything. Rather than men being more free to touch her, the game puts a hard limit at 4 seconds, even with affirmative consent everything else would be a violation of the now explicit rules. "According to this affidavit, you engaged in 'motorboating' for 6.3 seconds." --But she said she wanted it. "No one is above the law."

---

abusive; or, like in fantasy, he needed to be abusive in order to justify hating him. While you're scratching your head I'll just remind you that *Maleficent* isn't real.

But what about True Love? Around the same year the movie came out there was a TV commercial which showed a sleeping Sleeping Beauty, the Prince arrives, kisses her, but she stays asleep, so he walks away perplexed. And then she opens her eyes: "Is he gone yet?" A squirrel nods. "I thought he'd never leave!" Then she pops on a TV and watches a love story. The implication, of course, is that women are sneaky and true love doesn't exist except in fairy tales, not like the one she's in but like the one she's going to watch. Well, *Maleficent* is more bananas than that.

In the big scene, Maleficent, regretting her curse, has brought Prince Phillip to sleeping Aurora to deliver True Love's Kiss. But he hesitates. "Umm... I've only met her once." Yes, that's a quote, from what I think is a man. At this point I am gnawing on my bicep afraid that the story would break off into some elementary school PSA about not making out with an unconscious woman and the vagaries of consent, which would have been idiotic, but what did happen was way worse: Phillip's kiss doesn't work. It's not True Love, which was the whole premise of Maleficent's curse and the movie, true love doesn't exist. Now we're about to be tricked, because we still want Aurora to be saved *without* true love, just as we want our wars to be concluded without enemy casualties. So when a crying, remorseful Maleficent leans over and kisses Aurora farewell, poof, Aurora awakens. That's True Love. The love between a mother and child.

At this point my eyes rolled so far back into my skull I could see the aneurysm, meanwhile the entire audience hooted and clapped like harp seals begging to be clubbed. I could bring this full circle and end here, "see, the audience of women who feels the world has cheated them doesn't believe in true love-- unless it's unrequited, for a child, or someone's dying." But then I'd be skipping a very important fact: they aren't actually mother and child. At best, they are child and... godmother.

The trick to what the demographic wants is that while it doesn't believe in "true love" between two adults, it doesn't believe in the true love of a parent for a child *either*, otherwise the relevant kiss would have had to come from Aurora's father, which would be wrong for all kinds of reasons, all of them projected, all of them bananas. His love can't be true love because it is definitional, obligatory, and *therefore it doesn't count*. What the demo believes in, what it aspires to, is unconditional love *chosen by free will*. But as this is too massive a choice let alone responsibility for those who can't even imagine adult love, there's another trick: it has to photograph like love but entail no responsibility. Maleficent didn't have to raise Aurora; that was entrusted to the fairies who dutifully made the sacrifice of their lives *and wings*, and to remind us that *therefore* this couldn't be love either they are portrayed as bumbling and resentful ("I didn't give up 16 years of my life to---!"). While Maleficent does visit with Aurora, nothing would happen if she didn't. She's under no obligation to show up, and when she does, all she has to do is "spend time together." That's love; ask any deadbeat dad stopping by on Xmas. Lacking any symbolic obligation she is free to not be anxious by Aurora's grades, boyfriends, or trajectory. Maleficent doesn't need to depend on Aurora, and Aurora doesn't have to depend on Maleficent.

"In the context of the game, men are allowed to touch her boobs." So what? If the whole benefit of touching a woman's boobs is that either she wants you to or... she doesn't want you to….. then what's gained from touching them under the rules of a game where desire is eliminated as a factor? Unless the benefit is: desire is eliminated. You can do it as long as it's not because you wanted to. "But I did want to." But it's not because you wanted to. "Are you talking to me or her?"

If she chooses to the game-- far easier than choosing her desire, including the desire not to be touched-- then within the game she has to do it, she has no choice, and if she does it we know for sure she did not do it *because* she wanted to, even if she wanted to. "Did you want to?" --I don't know, it was kind of fun but---- it was just part of the game. I never would have

---

To the demo, far from the symbolic obligation being both the requirement for love and its justification, the symbolic obligation negates it. The narrator-- Aurora-- sides 100% with Maleficent, against her father. The father has to die in order for the boy to get the mother-- I mean the daughter to get the godmother-- a father's love is heavy, his love asks things of her, obliges her, he is the impediment to the kind of love that skips barefoot and giggles. TV characters are everywhere adopting black children: rather than mirroring an actuarial trend in adoption, or even cynically reading it as "performative liberal Hollywood", it represents the fantasy of aspirational love: since there is no biological or cultural expectation to love this child, since it's *obvious* you didn't "have" to, then this love is (depicted as) real love.

This is not due to years of life experience with failed relationships and reduced expectations. It precedes it; they were taught to value things in this way-- devaluing anything that comes from obligation, convention or expectation because it didn't come from "you", because you get less credit. There's no honor in the soldier who fights in battle or the doctor who saves a life. If it's expected of you, it doesn't count. But the soldier who saves a puppy; the doctor *slash* puppy activist-- the reward isn't for going "above and beyond" but outside, for displaying "individuality." The randomness and senselessness of porn also shows this: there's no reason at all this buxom nurse should blow that patient, it's not worth the risk and it's not even clear she's attracted to him, so it counts.

Remember, *Sleeping Beauty* and *Maleficent* are for movies for children, mostly girl children. Each offers a different version of the future: *Sleeping Beauty* alludes to a better life for the child, and *Maleficent* deludes to a better narrative for the adult. The problem is that these are incompatible. You can only choose one. Please read the .following question carefully before writing your response: Who do you think chooses?

23 "Hold on, in Freud's text it says "the other sister..." That's not the same sister!" Yes it is, Otto was her *older* son; but even if it wasn't it wouldn't matter, the analysis remains intact, the point isn't what she wants but how she wants and how she can or can't act. The primitive rage which wants to deprive everyone more powerful than her of their satisfaction.

But never mind that-- *the important thing is to report whatever comes to mind*. When you say I'm wrong about my interpretation of the dream, are you saying I'm wrong and Freud is right, or are you saying that I and Freud *both* are wrong and you have a different interpretation? I see. You hadn't thought it through that far. "There's no interpretation!" Ah. You're still fooled by he doesn't exist.

What you should meditate on is why, since you don't believe the theory anyway, was your argument about a detail within the theory? Why not-- a new theory? You've so long practiced accepting the form of the argument *so* that you can debate the conclusions-- being *allowed* to "participate in the debate" has given you years of egoistic satisfaction in the form of knowledge-- that it's all you can do. There's no reward here in your being right, but you don't want to be right, you don't care what's right-- you just want me to be wrong. You want to deprive me of being right. Why? And-- at what cost to you?

done it on my own. "Thank God."

What the game does isn't sexual but grammatical: it doesn't make it easier touch boobs, but easier for boobs to be touched, even if you're the guy touching them. It changes the act from the active voice to the passive voice. This is exactly what porn-- including porn you make yourself-- does.

If this seems unbelievable observe a very basic consequence of the technology: America would go to Defcon 2 if some sorority girl handed out 4x9 Kodacolor glossies of her topless self at a frat party, but post a pic on the internet which reaches far more people and forever and it couldn't be less noteworthy, less "her."   Later in *Confirmative Assent* the multiple alpha

---

Since the only kind of poker you know is strip or losing, I'll give myself a handicap, I'll discard the sister and play my hand without her, by re-interpreting the dream without referencing the sister at all. Freud believes Charles's funeral is merely an excuse to get the man to show up. But why dream Charles's funeral-- why not dream the concert, or why not Otto's funeral *again*? The "wish fulfillment" that Freud discovers-- that she'll see him at a funeral-- *already* happened, in real life-- she doesn't need to dream it, she only needs to remember it. The death of Charles doesn't get her anything more than the real-life event she was already at. Is it because she loved Charles less?   "I assured her the latter interpretation was impossible." You sure you still want me to be wrong?

> After the rupture the man whom my patient *loved* avoided the house; she herself attained her **independence** some time after the death of *little Otto, to whom, meanwhile, her affections had turned*. But she did not succeed in **freeing** herself from the **dependence** due to her *affection* for her sister**'s** friend. Her **pride bade** her avoid him, but she found it impossible to **transfer** her *love* to the other suitors who successively presented themselves...

Look at the way this woman loves, it is one at a time and not at all, look at the order of her love and despair: unrequited, for a child, someone's dying-- then back to unfulfilled; this is a woman who does NOT want love, she wants the appearance of love, her whole psychic energy is devoted to avoiding dependence on another person. She is pathologically monogamous; in the high jargon of psychoanalysis, her heart is full of barnacled garlic. She was only capable of loving the man after Otto died; in order for her to love anyone else, Otto had to go. And now that she loved the man (whom she will never have), she couldn't love any other men. And she breathed a sigh of relief.

What does it mean to be pathologically monogamous? It is hiding in plain sight. By loving only one person at a time, you inoculate yourself from dependency on everyone else except that person. Then you put a block between you and your "love", so that you cannot become dependent on them either; and if they become 100% dependent on you, well, you win and you can cash out.

Otto was a great choice, love for a child is so structurally limited that it safely got her through the early years. First of all and what a coincidence, Otto isn't even her child, so she can't be truly responsible to/for him, he's not truly dependent on her, but she can make it appear that way; not a mother but an aunt, a godmother. Secondly, with Otto around, she *can't* love anyone else, though she'll waste hours going through the profiles of suitors who successively present themselves. Do you believe all those first dates all decided not to call you back-- unless you told them not to call you back? This is true for any relationship template, a bad therapist might proudly interpret that a woman's relationship woes relate to her falling for men "like her father", because Dad's reliably a jerk; the correct insight is that her impossible love for her father is used to make it impossible to love in other ways-- *so that* she is free of dependency on anyone else, *so that* she *only* has to deal with daddy issues. One at a time, in order of safety.

Fortunately for her Otto is dead, so she's free to love the man again, which is of course totally

172

males Abby has slept with are freely sharing their sex videos with each other and everyone else; no big deal to anyone and her only concern is that one of the videos isn't flattering because the guy is too drunk to maintain an erection so it looks like it's her fault ("and what kind of a beta wants to be drunk when he has sex with [she poses]-- this? I'm supposed to be the one who's drunk!") But later when she and the other TriDelts are discovered to have hired a studio photographer to photograph them in swimsuits (NB: one piece) for a house (=private) calendar that no one else would ever see, the school is so shocked by the morals violation that their sorority house is closed pending an *exorcism*. I've guessed a lot of movie twists, but wow did I not see that coming.

Back during the Cold War a girl didn't just hand a potential boyfriend a naked photo of

---

riskless. But even an idiot feels the sequence and wonders about her guilt, did Otto have to die for me to love someone? So she dreams it was actually Charles who died (AND wishes that it was her sister) so she could ask Freud if that's what she wanted, he agrees it's impossible and never notices the bait and switch.

The thing to notice is what Freud did not notice: what the woman did to Otto and to the man she did also to Freud. First she became *dependent* on him. So she forced him to make a mistake, to be wrong-- so that she would no longer have to depend on him; and ALSO, in so doing, managed to get him to desire her, to depend on her-- she was an interesting patient with model dreams. And then she was free to retreat=cash out to children or funerals or love unrequited. He fell for it, offering her (what he thought was) an accurate interpretation of her dream instead of seeing the form of her desire: *to deprive him* of being right.

This is how you love, one at a time and not at all. Don't be fooled by your spiritual cardiomegaly and your ability to become obsessed in series, what we're talking about is dependency, and no single person you are able to get can have that kind of power. Proudly distressed by your impulsive behaviors, thus hiding that you cannot directly pursue what you want. The guiding principle of your life isn't the application of power but a search for knowledge as a defense against impotence, against change. "I can't seem to find the right person." Then your strategy succeeded. Say you find the right person-- what kind of a person do you imagine becoming? "I'm not going to just lose myself in another person." From here it looks like you have nothing to lose. "You expect me to give up--" Well, would you give up drinking? TV? Pornography? "Those aren't the same, pornography wouldn't affect my love for her." If you were in love, you'd let her decide that.

"I'm doing quite fine without the romantic nonsense of 'true love'. I'm working on improving myself." Why? Seriously, why? What are you going to do if you become seven times more improved, or seventy times seven? You think you *want* to become more *powerful*? Your status quo only looks peaceful from the outside, inside the walls is chaos, and the longer it goes on, the more you'll want to give up power to some other omnipotent entity. That isn't love, it's not even self-love, but it is inevitable.

24 Why is it so important that women be taught not to believe in love? Because they are the most reliable consumers of public media, they are the lead in for men, so they are the targets of propaganda which does not care about beliefs, it wants to promote group belonging under its leadership. The enemy is privacy, the worst thing a woman (or a man) can do is be alone, unless it's in front of the teleprompter and connecting with others.   Love is inherently private, so sex is favored: not public sex, but public images of sex, public discussions about sex. The "right to privacy" for women isn't the right to keep secrets, but the right to be public without shame-- so she can be more public, and controlled.

25 Everything said about love applies to religion, take Catholicism vs Calvinism. The scary mysticism of the Latin rite, chanted in baritone and apocalypse, gave way to a 45 minute efficient and inviting ceremony filled with sappy songs not about Jesus but about how Jesus makes me feel,

herself unless it was a headshot and he said he knew a producer; now sexting pics of yourself and your friends is an obligatory pre-first date courtship ritual, but before you shake your head in some sort of moral lamentation, note that the new open and permissive sexuality even more strictly forbids her from giving out 4x9 glossies because-- and this is the point-- the glossies are *hers*. It's okay in digital, it's slutty as a 4x9. Or 9x4, depending on staging.[31] But there's a trade off: a person is given the privilege to act only in those contexts where they give up control to something else, i.e. and e.g., it's easy for a woman to control the capital of 4x9s, but on the internet she relinquishes all control, which is why the system doesn't just encourage digital, it makes 4x9s unimaginable. And to prove that it has nothing to do with the materiality behind "digital" vs "glossy", consider that even under Clinton the naked glossies a

---

and an infantile homily that requires corporal mortification just to prevent death by boredom-- and it's hard not to wonder if this wasn't a conscious branding to target the moms since under Johnson most of the Dads had converted to football. If you stumble over a Dad praying, he must be an Evangelical and you must be in Central Time, what they did to attract the men was to pseudo-intellectualize the faith, everyone gets to be an amateur lawyer; memorizing the Bible allows them to quote statutes and precedents and argue like strict constructionists-- rather than facing their own potential unbelief, they bury themselves in intricate knowledge, and any unbelief is safely explained by appeal to authority-- "my pastor would know." What if he doesn't? "I know what I believe." Lucky it's the same as what you want to believe. The obsessive transmutation of faith into minutiae, categories, data points, wanting to know God and thus avoiding whatever the unknowable God might want from them. The Book has to be taken literally *in order to* leave only God's *intent* as a matter of interpretation, of sophistry-- of rhetoric. As they become more omniscient their God becomes more omnipotent and he might not make you rich but he's a God you can fool if you have to.

26There's one more group that's the reservoir for love, but unlike gays or even teens cannot ever be stated out loud, it exists midway between consciousness and unconsciousness, because there is both a prohibition against it and *not enough* of a prohibition against it: brother-sister love. A generation before Oedipus there was Orestes and Electra, and now we are rushing back to the first love that was subordinate to nothing, for damn sure not sexuality; brother-sister love didn't require fantasy of any kind and didn't need to perform before an audience. I'll give you an example that isn't *Star Wars*. *Dexter* was a TV series about a psychopathic serial killer who tried to appear normal and hide the "void" within himself. "I feel nothing." When anyone tells you this, you can be sure they are telling you because they actually only feel one thing, which they think comes from outside them, and that is rage. "I call it my dark passenger." I see, it's his fault, had you not picked him up on the way to San Diego none of this would have happened. Fully a product of 21st century metapsychology ("fake it till you make it") Dexter sublimates his rage =play acts at a job (as crime scene investigator), a "heteronormative" relationship (=would convince other heteros he was normal), and autist off kilter cheeriness, because although he's a psychopath he doesn't want to be a sociopath: that, of course, would be WAY worse. Even his murders are socionormative, not because his victims deserve it but because unlike every other serial killer he targets mostly men. He's a murderer, not a misogynist. "Is he a gay?" Good guess, he doesn't need to be, you'll see why in a moment. Meanwhile, he doesn't so much occasionally succumb to his dark passenger as elaborately and complicatedly indulge it the way no psychopath ever does. Eventually five seasons later he and his sister fall in love-- to be specific: with each other. Question: is that so bad? The mitigating pretense was that it wasn't "so bad" because they were actually adoptive siblings, but what really made the relationship not "so bad" was precisely that Dexter was a serial killer: anything, *anything* that made him stop being a serial killer couldn't be "so bad." Note his life path: first he faked being normal so he could sin in private; then he kinda sorta loved another woman whom he married and at least tried to control his sins; she conveniently gets murdered so he can ennoble it into revenge; finally his true love for his sister changed his very nature. He went from ice cold murderer to action movie crime fighter. So much did Dexter become an ethical superego figure that it was he, not she,

174

girl could-- was obligated to-- pass around to the cap guys on Fraternity Row were any ones in Playboy. If she tried to hide them, she'd be a slut. "It says you're a nursing student with a great head for hands on care!" Giggle. "Can I see the test shots?" You're gross. The dividing line for appropriateness is that someone else benefits from the pics, not you; at the same time upload proudly or with shame and if at least one other unknown person "won't judge you" (they may even applaud you), you aren't just absolved-- you were never guilty. In the reverse, the fewer people who can witness it the less chance some unknown other will speak as an authority, and as the curve approaches $n=1$ from the right shame becomes infinite guilt and you have no one to answer to but yourself. If a regular girl tries pulls a hat trick without an audience there will be psychiatric consequences, she can't claim it didn't mean

---

who tried to end their romance because it was "inappropriate."

The importance and purpose of love-- why we still want to believe in it-- is made satisfyingly explicit to the audience: *love made him a better person*. But true love doesn't exist for normal people, you can't make a believable story about a man falling for a woman and it makes him a better person without everyone getting *nauseous*. So what characters can believably believe in love? Who can we believe in love through? No one's gay and there aren't any children around...

Note that paralleling *Maleficent*, the actor who played Dexter and the actress who played his sister were in love *in real life*, so you can apply a kind of disjunctive logic which yields true in all of the relevant cases: "I know in real life the actors aren't in love, but in the story they are" is the same as "I know in real life the actors are in love, but in the story they aren't". Either way, they are.

What's worth repeating is the *reason* no one believes in love, yet still responds to love stories: it's not that love doesn't exist *at all*-- who knows?-- it's that they're not capable of it. Better to say love doesn't exist. And yet-- we still need to believe in it, to believe in redemption-through-love.

What does this odd cluster of possible loves have in common? They are impossible loves. "You want what you can't have?" You think you want what you can't have-- *because* you can't have it? Or is it a negative: whatever you have you don't want, so therefore you must want-- whatever is left? "I'm just never satisfied, my reach exceeds my grasp." That's not you, you and they find satisfaction elsewhere and you should read the poem again/once. Impossible loves means there is no chance you'll become dependent on them, and you can easily minimize their dependence on you. There is no chance you can "lose yourself" or your individuality. There is no chance you will incur an unpayable debt to another person.

Why not just-- *not* love? Why not just be an ethical person and not require an irrational/transcendental link to another person? I don't mean for yourself, you already don't believe in it-- I mean, why still persist in the belief that it exists for anyone else? Because the fantasy of future AI still carries guilt, which is why it is almost always pornographized backwards. All the stories fretting about the day the robots take over, when they replace us-- that anxiety is the mark of the return of the repressed in its inverted form. We still feel a lot of pressure to be human, to love; not loving anything makes us feel guilty, for being like a robot. *But how we wish we could be robots.* Clean, unchanging, eternal, each uniquely individual and emotionally independent, yet socially interdependent: totally secure, with the securities invisible; as part of a greater-- cell→ tissue→ *organism*. To be devoid of all emotions-- even including rage. Capable of acquiring knowledge, yet under the paternal gaze of an omnipotent entity which regulates and elevates us; safe from too much feeling, even pleasure. Safe from the abyss. Safe from freedom.

A good example of this move towards emotionlessness is which psychiatric diagnoses we publicly idealize. In the 1980s academic psychiatry there was the big shift away from "being labeled as a schizophrenic" towards "diagnosing bipolar disorder"--- with the explicit target of controlling the excess emotions because they interfered with life and work. But in American popular culture

anything unless it was for some other reason, come on, slut, at least have the self-respect to say it was a blow to the patriarchy. Meanwhile since the porn star is professional/dumb/paid enough to let us see her sex, she's cleared to run for Congress, or at least Parliament, this is true, I looked it up. Follow the history of political sex scandals: 1. Once sexual indiscretions were never publicized even if they were discovered-- people with power were entitled to commit them. 2. Next a voyeuristic public would drool over the details yet demand the sinner be punished-- hey you greedy jerk, isn't being in power enough? 3. Now, as long as the public has access to the video-- regardless of whether they bother to see it-- it's dismissed as "they're a person like everybody else"-- it shows their commitment to the new ethic of full disclosure.[32] 1, 2, or 3: which of those people do you expect will have the most power to act? When a person has power, he can act. When a people lack power, they want knowledge. When a

_____

"having bipolar" became aspirational, because what was promised after the exhausting emotions were medicated was creativity, individuality, unique perspectives-- and you wouldn't be so exhausted-- you could get all the cognitive stuff, without all the emotional stuff. No surprise, this promise proved to be a false one, most bipolars were neither creative nor bipolar, but they were exhausting to everyone else. Then came Adult ADHD, with the desire for laser-focused productivity nothing more than a cover for the wished for satisfaction of blocking out the world that asked too much of you-- blocking out your reactivity to the world. "Adderall helps me get so much more done." Six hours of uninterrupted internet surfing and data mining your ex, you have overclocked your uselessness. Now the media-celebrated disorder of our times (properly managed or segregated) is pop-sci Asperger's, the sci-fi ideal of the bright, quirky individual who is perfectly content not needing, not reacting to, other people's desires.

27 One consequence of our always-connected lives is that because we are so connected, we create mental spaces-- seconds at a time like swimmer's breathing-- where the other person doesn't exist. A couple out to dinner but checking their phone are not distracted by the phone, the phone isn't rendering them "unable to connect"; they actively take a break from their real life connection because it is unreal. Being what the other person needs you to be for the purposes of that conversation, those moments-- doing that seems fake, obligatory, unreal; the real you is the one using the teleprompter even if you are lying with it, because it requires no real part of you. The checking of the phone isn't the cause of the distanced relationship, it is the solution to a relationship forced into what is felt as unnatural proximity-- because what feels unnatural is being depended on; not the being with someone else, but having to be for someone else.

28 Here's a joke you won't like. A middle aged black man is absent-mindedly rapping the lyrics to NWA's "Straight Out Of Compton". He looks up, and sees his two amused but politely deferential white coworkers watching him. He shrugs. "What can I say," he says, "I grew up in the suburbs."

29 Does my telling you that I made up the above joke make it better, or worse?

30 He's not angry she's a slut, he's angry she deprived him. She's not showing him her slutty *side;* he has to see it as a glimpse of the real her-- how she actually is, with other men. "Which men?" Men that count.

You might think that the solution is to remind him that she did it for him, she was performing, she would never do this for anyone else, she would never be this way with anyone else-- "honey, I knew it was you!" But that solution misses a critical piece of information: he feels this way because when he was hitting on her, *he* wasn't himself, he was acting like someone else-- and look what happened next. She went home with the man he was pretending to be, not the man he usually pretends to be. She wasn't faking last night, she's faking now. And why would he think otherwise? Alcohol was involved, and every man knows when a woman is drunk her real desires come out, while every woman knows when a man is drunk he becomes a different man. Therefore: the real her slept with a different man.

176

people can know everything, they want someone else to act.

This is neither a cause nor a consequence of moral decay, if you think these you are a liar: you think they are doing what they want, while you... can't. You're half right, anyway.

After the party scenes the opening credits come on (the title song is "You Don't Own Me", but in French), and the movie begins in earnest with the new TriDelts pledge class (literally a class: in schoolgirl uniforms, pigtails, chewing gum and sitting at desks) getting etiquette lessons from their hot teacher, sophomore Saydee (hair held up by pencils, glasses, pearls, heels, pencil skirt). She is dismayed at the behavior of the freshmen pledges at last night's party, why would any of the houses ever invite us back again? "In order to have the

---

31 It's hard to believe we prefer-- trust-- digital images more than paper photos given how easy it is to doctor them, which should suggest to you that it isn't about the objective accuracy of the image but simply who owns it. Here's an example. *Rear Window* is a Hitchcock movie about a man who thinks he witnesses his neighbor murder his wife, and spends most of the film spying on him to gather evidence, but despite the fact that he is a celebrated professional photographer and is doing his spying through a giant telephoto lens, it *never occurs to him to take a photo*. It apparently never occurred to the audience, either. The B story is that his girlfriend Grace Kelly wants to get married, but he says he can't give up international photojournalism to settle down, being a free range photographer is who he is, it's in his blood; yet pushing his distal IP joint down half a centimeter is a reflex he doesn't possess, hell, he doesn't even photograph the half naked blonde who proudly displays herself in the window. He just observes. Can you make *Rear In The Window* today? To ask why he doesn't take any pictures is to get the question completely backwards: the default then wasn't taking pictures-- it was not taking pictures. He has to be caused to take a picture. In his case, it has to be an assignment.

In the same way, his girlfriend, played by and as an actual princess, is a phenomenally glamorous woman who comes to him wearing the latest fashions right off the runway-- I mean she literally just left the runway wearing an $1100 dress (that's 1954 dollars) and came over to his apartment-- and she spends her evening listening to him tell her how much he loves taking pictures more than her, but he doesn't think to shoot her in various states of undress and she doesn't ask-- such a photo wouldn't count, it would serve no purpose because it would only be hers.

Say he took a picture of the aerobic blonde across the way-- then what? He took it because he wanted to, it is his, he acted on his desire. Now he's a pervert. But here's the difference today: today being a pervert is fine but acting on your desire is impossible, so today he would do what we'd all do, which is take the picture by impulse/reflex because that perversion is normal prosocial behavior-- how can I say this? Stick to the end-- and then immediately share it with someone else. Yes, I took it, but I took it to show you. All. I was acting on your desire. You doubt this? Imagine he never sends it.

And say Grace Kelly asks him to castrate himself and his giant camera and snap a 35mm of her in the dress, and he does. Now what? She has a picture of herself. If she can't enjoy being in the dress, she sure as hell isn't going to enjoy being by herself without the dress looking at a picture of herself wearing the dress. Maybe she'd hang it in her house to show some other people, but the ideal would be to post it somewhere public and have other people admire/hate it, e.g. a magazine. Now it's real. To get amateur pornography into the mainstream you'd need to invent a photography that would produce not necessarily better, cheaper, or even quicker photos but photos in which the disposal of the photo-- the ease of sharing-- was built into the act of photographing. I mean the Polaroid. Otherwise a photograph on film can't be said to be for other people, unless you're a professional photographer in which case it must be on assignment, or for them. For non-professionals, the only thing real is other people's desires, which you can act on. Hence the digital

most fun you can have in college, you're going to have to cultivate a bit of a... reputation, for being fun." On the whiteboard behind her is a Venn Diagram with two shaded circles "ALPHA" and "SLUT", intersecting at an unshaded region. The trick, she explains, is that alpha males are "very binary", they can only see girls as one or the other, but not both. Therefore, she says, you all have to learn the skill of pretending you're a slut.

I will here pause and say when I first watched this, I was totally lost=distracted. Not a moral judgment, but weren't they already sluts? I've never gotten much out of class lectures, too many secondary sources and I'm off daydreaming about sex, which was here ironic given the circumstances, so later I found the script online and discovered that what she had actually said was "pretending you're pretending you're a slut." Ok, I'm going to need a lot more coffee

---

image is real.

"Maybe he doesn't take a picture because film was expensive back then." A quick recap: she's in an $1100 dress; they are eating take out from the 21 Club; his insurance paid for a private nurse to give him a daily in-home massage; and he's willing to risk sending his girlfriend up the fire escape to the murderer's apartment. But film is expensive. Ok. Oh, and the murderer sneaks into his in his apartment to murder him in the dark, but he quick thinkingly uses the   camera flash to blind him. NB: just the flash.

This is the need that online pornography satisfies that we have collectively agreed to pretend doesn't exist. As long as the porn is on the internet and digital, it isn't your desire, it isn't yours-- it isn't you. Which is ironically correct. Your spouse will tolerate any depravity in the browser history, but try and print out a single semi-nude photo and hide it in a drawer and you won't even get partial custody.   "What do you plan to do with this-- fantasize?" This is the true explanation for the explosion of online pornography. "No, the explanation is nowadays it's so easy to make and get it." You, sir, are a socialist, you don't trust capitalism. Do you really believe that the Invisible Hand that replaced cigarettes with smartphones didn't know in the 1970s to print more magazines if you really wanted them? Democracy may stumble along but capitalism is magnificently hyperefficient, it's not your mommy and it's not your slave, it doesn't give you what you need or even what you want, it will give you only what you'll pay for, nothing more, unless it's less. Maybe you should re-learn how to want. The problem with porn isn't availability: it is deniability, not just to others but to oneself: "no, no, this isn't me." Sure I like it for two hours at a time, but I'm not owning it. In other words, online porn doesn't depict fetishes, it is the fetish.   Would you feel creepy masturbating to a magazine nowadays? Would you even know where to buy one? Interesting that one of the final places print/magazine pornography is still doing a robust business is in airports-- by common consensus it already doesn't count, what happens in [city] stays in [city]. Off topic, those magazine stands are also a snapshot into American psychology: the airbrushed porn stars are labeled "Men's Interest", for comparison "Women's Interest"= airbrushed TV stars, I guess we're all visual creatures after all. Meanwhile, the problem of porn for non-Western cultures is availability: we made it to fill a hole in our society, and inadvertently flooded them with it a generation or two too early, before they get access to easy credit, with the surprising consequence that a lot of the world is masturbating not just to people having sex, but to Americans. When millennia old authoritarian societies say that porn is immoral, they mean interracial. They can rest assured; their turn soon.

32 But this isn't entirely true, is it? It's true for them, it's not true for you, if you are an attractive woman with a pic worthy backstoryboard don't bother running, no one will support you, except by marriage. The 2000 film *The Contender* was both controversial and unwatchable, now it's just one of those, but that audience raised today's audience so it's instructive to see what they didn't realize they wanted that they tricked their kids into getting for them. It tells the story of female Democratic Vice Presidential candidate Laine Hanson, played by Joan Allen, whose nomination is opposed by evil misogynist Republicans, played by men, because of a 9x4 photo of said econ major involved in a sorority initiation threesome. The Republicans say, of course, that this proves she's not fit to be a

for this.

What the pledges did wrong at the party wasn't being too slutty or not being slutty enough. It was not recording it. "Every sexual contact should be on camera-- your camera." Her reasons were perfectly logical even if totally bananas: there was a good chance someone was secretly recording it anyway; guys then couldn't exaggerate or lie to make themselves look good; besides, during sex women always come off looking better than men. But most of all, he'll up his game if he knows you're recording it, but in the back of his mind he will wonder if you're only doing it for the camera, not him. "It puts him in his place." As long as it appears you are performing, you can do whatever you want.

Vice President, only a 'vice' President, HA! Ok, they didn't really say that, I just made it up. Here's your power shift masquerading as a gender battle: in the climax, at an indignant speech to a joint session of The House, Senate, and TV, the President (played by Jeff Bridges) says, and I'm paraphrasing:

> And believe this, there are traitors among us... I'm talking about those of you who were patriots to your Party but traitors to the necessary end result-- that of righteousness, the truth, the concept of making the American dream blind to gender...
>
> So, let me make one thing clear... there is no weapon as powerful as that of an idea whose time has come. A woman will serve in the highest level of the Executive, simple as that...
>
> And I'm now calling for an immediate voice of confirmation of Laine Hanson. And Mr. Speaker, I would like to make this a live roll call. I want to see the faces of those of you who would eliminate the possibility of greatness in American leadership because of half-truths, lies, and innuendoes.
>
> I will not be deterred by partisanship.
>
> I will not be deterred by misogyny.
>
> I will not be deterred by hate.
>
> You have now come face-to-face with my will. Confirm my nominee, heal this nation, and let the American people explode into this new millennium with the exhilaration of being true to the glory of this democracy.

That's what he broadcasts to the union seat fillers, but what he says in private to Laine Hanson as she finally reveals to him the naughty details of what really happened that photogenic night is, and I'm quoting: "What I wouldn't give to be back in college again." Did they go to the same college? That's not what he meant? Now we know which kind of woman The President wants the public to want and which one he reserves for himself, or, in slightly more nuanced language, which desire he believes is appropriate for the masses to have, and which one he reserves for himself, not because men are superior to women, but because he is superior to everyone. "You have now come face to face with my will," he tells them. Spoken like a true progressive fighting for equality. Odd that this omnipotent man gets all nostalgic for the bygone days of spontaneous penetrations, meanwhile the very first scene with Senator Laine Hanson has her not at a budget hearing or planning 9/11; she is having sex, in the very place that women wanted laws prohibiting it: in her office, you see ladies,

It's a proactive strategy, I guess, and in the movie it certainly made the female characters seem pretty alpha in their pursuit of what they want. But this plan caused there to be something wrong with overall story, and it might not have jumped out at me if I hadn't been coincidentally writing a script of my own that had the same problem. I'll explain. Saydee is teaching these alpha women what to do to get what they want. Ok. It's a movie, so I can ask a very fundamental question: what do the women want? Watch the movie. The answer is nothing.

Not just the women; none of the male characters want anything either. This is partially obscured by the presence of temporary wants (e.g. sex) but then comes the bigger problem: no

---

women can have it all, as long as it's at work.

The typical understanding of the drama surrounding the photograph is that it is a proxy, theatre, for an American public too stupid to understand politically complex issues. The Republicans know that the simpletons in Central Time could never understand why her understanding of Gramm-Rudman is simplistic, easier and more efficient to attack her character since the binary's outcome will be the same. Fortunately, the simpletons in Central Time are also misogynists, including the women, no one will tolerate a woman who enjoyed her life, so to guarantee she is not tolerated they make her life enjoy a threesome.

But is this understanding accurate? If indeed the sorority threesome is a proxy, what is it a proxy for?

Note carefully that the reason the President selected her isn't that she is both a good candidate and a woman, but only that she is a woman; and not even because she's good for the progress of the country, but specifically because he wants to be remembered as the man who selected the first female VP. "It's symbolic." Meanwhile the Republican Opposition Machine isn't opposing her because she's a woman, the movie explicitly depicts it as opposing her because of her questionable abilities and politics. Even her own governor father has his doubts about her. She switched parties; she's timid around anyone with power (they curse a lot and interrupt (each other)); she displays no interest in any hard issues beyond the usual, simplistically emotive, NPR-ready ones-- behind closed doors she discovers she's the only one who thinks those are the real issues; in fact, if you watch the movie closely, it's not even clear she knows other issues exist. This is why the Republicans oppose her, but, far more importantly, this is why the Democrats chose her. It's VP, after all, she can't actually drive policy, it's symbolic. Boy oh boy was everyone in the audience going to be really surprised in a year. But in 2000, just stand there and look pretty, but not too pretty, the level of pretty we're looking for is next week's rally in Columbus; we've prepared your keynote speech for the Global AIDS Warming summit Tuesday, and you have a meeting with the Style section of *The Atlantic* at 3:30. "What should I wear?" That's why you're meeting with them, dum dum. Having a woman in the highest level of the executive may be "an idea whose time has come", but they were sure to find a woman who comes without any ideas. She's shown jogging a lot, which in the language of movies means "frantic energy in the maintenance of the status quo", and for the audience loudly codes for full time job and still has time for herself, oh my god, sooooo jealous.

So what a woman does in the semi-privacy of her own sorority/Senate office isn't theatre for the public too stupid to understand the issues; it is a necessary consequence of the fact that her gender is the only issue-- she is chosen only because of her sex, therefore her sex manifests as the only concern. The usual push back here is that her gender is the most important issue-- if she was a man no one would try to oppose her, which-- wow; it has to be about her gender now so that eventually it's never about gender. "It's symbolic." Yes, we know. This is a very common and seductive understanding of the role of political symbols, and I don't know why anyone who thinks symbols have so much power don't automatically understand that someone smarter than them already had this thought, which is why they deployed the symbol. No. Hanson-- as a woman-- is just a standard

180

one can act on a desire. The movie supposedly has a central conflict over the ΛAX house, and it finally ends up being taken by the TriDelts, but no one acts towards that goal. In theory they all say they want sex, in the abstract, but in every single specific sexual encounter that occurs desire itself is not what causes them to act. Games, lucky accidents (she and his roommate end up in the shower together), or the opportunity arose so they had to take it. You can blame bad writing, but the scenes are inadvertently motivated by compulsion or inevitability, not desire.

For this reason, what the movie gets dead right isn't that they have to *pretend* it's for something else-- it can *only* be for something else. You can only act if it's compelled, impulsive, or for some other reason. No actions but reactions to situations that happen to you.

---

prop for others with power to use to get what they want. But here occurs an interesting reversal: the Democrats know their progressive politics are unpalatable to the idiots in Central/Mountain Time, so they need a woman candidate in order to equate these attacks with misogyny; to Republicans, her gender is precisely the kind of inconsequential issue that is too palatable to the idiots in Eastern/Pacific Time, so they have to focus on her being a bad woman.

So President Bridges isn't just wrong, but a liar: this is not a movie about breaking barriers to a full democracy; it represents the lack of faith in democracy. NB: this is in 2000. It may be a "liberal" movie that believes earnestly in progressive equality but it is so deeply cynical about time zones that it reveals itself as wanting the very thing it says it hates: tyranny, preferably by a man who pretends to be a Democrat. I think that makes him a demagogue, but I'm no classicist. In an understated scene, a female FBI agent (young, wide-eyed and powerless) effuses enthusiasm when she talks to the White Male House Chief of Staff (old, stoic, and Sam Elliot). She's been working tirelessly = overtime without pay to help him get Hanson confirmed. He thanks her for her great investigative work (she discovered Hanson isn't the girl in the photo), and she says, and I'm paraphrasing from memory, "I hope you don't think this is inappropriate, but please don't give up on Senator Hanson. She's a great woman, she's an inspiration to all working women, she's hope that there's no double standard!" And the Chief of Staff smiles broadly at her as he boards the helicopter that she doesn't get to use, "You know what?" he yells as it takes off, "you're right! It was absolutely inappropriate!" In other words honey, save it for NPR. While busy you're counting them, at the level of actual power no one gives a fig about inspirations and double standards; if giving you a female VP solidifies our power, if it makes you willingly work overtime for us, great, but we ain't doing it for you. It's not even been a decade since we barely beat the Russians and now there's chatter about some planes scheduled to go missing on the 25th centennial of Marathon. Watch your head.

That's all very disheartening, but it is, after all, only a movie you never saw and your parents-- well, your mom-- barely remembers, except to say something along the lines of, "Oh, Joan Allen, she's great!" Surely gender politics has come a long way since 2000? Except it wasn't ever about gender politics. A reporter at a publicity junket asked actor Jeff Bridges whether the movie was a thinly veiled allegory about the then recent Republican exploitation of Clinton's secret sexual affair with Monica Lewinsky, and Bridges replied, "thinly veiled?" Ok, duh, that was obvious. But if the reference point is how terrible it is that a good man like Clinton with good ideas for the country could be derailed just because of private sexual behavior irrelevant to his policies, then why didn't they make *The Contender* about a man?

Because you can't, the form of the argument you've accepted for debate causes a logical contradiction and a stroke. The real issue about the photograph is not gender, but privacy. People will tolerate anything they can't control as long as they feel entitled to know everything; where the voters are powerless, nothing can be private. That's the trade. But what about the people with power, how can they secretly carve out a privilege of privacy? Change it into, for example, a gender issue. If you want to publicize the message that sexuality is a private issue (i.e: if you want a

You can not do what you want. "I've done a lot of people I wanted to do." You think you did it for no other reason than your desire for them? Is that what-- they think?

So Abby's stuck in a loop: she can't have desires, because she's learned not to act on her desires, it has to be for some other reason, even demonic possession, you think these girls could have acted on their own free will? On their own desire? *They weren't even drunk.* But if a woman acts only for some other reason, then it's inherently un-satisfying for her. Worse, it appears the other person got more out of it. Immediately from this follows that what she thinks the other person wants-- what the entire world has publicly told her is absolutely obvious that the other person wants-- is to use her. You should meditate on the unbearable unbalance: she can't get what she wants, and she's unsatisfied, but she has been taught to think

---

powerful person not to have to answer questions about sex) you make the protagonist a woman and repackage a privacy issue as a gender battle. You win the battle with women and then apply it back to men. Not all men-- those with public but utterly pointless power like Hollywood producers or university professors will be publicly castrated, there's an infinite supply of those. Then the sheep/FBI agents all rally to support you.

If you detect cynicism underlying this analysis, it is because you are trying to figure out what side of the gender debate I'm on, instead of considering where the debate is taking place, who benefits from the debate itself, regardless of the outcome. It is a fact that there are gender inequalities, maintained by structural obstacles like absent child care or late night meetings that could easily have been handled by, oh, I don't know, banning pointless meetings. These are indeed problems your daughter will have to contend with. But this debate isn't about that, as evidenced by the fact that those things aren't mentioned. This isn't about empowering women, but disempowering everyone. In order to keep power in the hands of those who already have it, in this case not politicians but the media, the debate is constructed as a gender war.   See also the furor over "creep videos", where articles condemning such perverts is a perfect way to teach us not to do what the media gets to monopolize. This is the law, write it down: it is illegal to record another's private moment unless it is given to the media and they can profit from it. The benefit is entirely for those who have power, not newcomers, not women and certainly not sorority girls, which is why in the years since this movie "sparked a dialogue" there has certainly been advancement in the political power of women, but there has never been an American woman who has benefited from "what goes on behind closed doors is her business, and even if it comes out, it's irrelevant to the job." That benefit goes only to a few, assuredly they are all men, but no way in hell is it given unto all men, though being constantly told that male privilege exists still tempts many to try. You'll see the results on TV. But no woman, let alone man, with a secret sexual life should even dare to attempt to gain power, and by secret I mean any.

It's worth observing what was the climactic scene of the movie-- i.e. what wasn't the climactic scene. The climax wasn't the confirmation or even the vote of Laine Hanson as the first female VP; that was denouement. The climax was a man commanding everyone to do what he wanted, and making everyone else think she deserved it. The lesson for democracy, totally unintentional, is nevertheless 100% correct: democracy can't be trusted. The people have to be compelled to do what you want. President Bridges is the hero of the movie not because he fights for women, but because he is exactly the leader we want: an omnipotent other, an appeal to authority, to compel everyone else; and you'll gladly give away your power if it ensures everyone else loses theirs.

That in real life the Republicans tried to benefit from Clinton's shame is obvious; whether they actually did is debatable. No one can doubt that the media benefitted. But exactly in what way did they benefit? To a populace raised to look for economic causes, the only critique of media possible was that they did it for the money. "In the old days the press was more discreet, respectful, they all knew Kennedy was having affairs and they never exposed him. Now they're money-grubbing scandal mongers, anything for ratings."

182

that other people don't really want *her*, but want to *use* her, for their satisfaction. To the impotent there is only one solution: she learns to do what they want but steal back some satisfaction by depriving the others, e.g. of a part of her *self*. Their loss gets registered as a gain for herself. This is, in fact, how the Tri Delts actually use blowjobs.

"So you think no woman ever wants to give a blowjob?" Of course she might want to. But that has nothing to do with why she is able to.[33] That's the trend, away from personal to performance; from exhibitionism to pornography. Who wants it? Who is enjoying it? Whose desire permits them to act?

When two out of three Deltas go down to the bar and start making out in front of a

---

But was it really a higher standard of journalism? The reason the press didn't expose Kennedy's affairs is that **they** felt there was nothing wrong with Kennedy doing them-- he's entitled, he's the President, after all. Now the media has decided it's "wrong," paradoxically at exactly the time when sexual taboos are less. "No, it's wrong because we now appreciate that there is a massive power differential." Yes-- but not between the President and a woman, but between the President and the media. Which conveniently appears as a sorority girl.

Today, a President isn't allowed to cheat not because he should behave morally but because he isn't powerful enough to merit the exemption from the media. "No one should be above the law." Yes, except now the law is defined not as the courts but as "the press." We want the press to have the power to decide because, while we lose our own power, the press gives us knowledge. Courts don't do that. Courts can't be trusted.

The press didn't decide this because they are truth seekers and *certainly* not because a given scandal is good for revenue. [1.19] The purpose of deciding this is to assert itself as the decider of things. This is why the press appears inconsistent, harshly judging one politician for cheating while the same media will refer to another's cheating as "nothing to do with his job performance". You think that reveals a political bias-- because that's what more media has told you, but it's a cover. Their judgments don't need to be consistent. Only that they consistently be the ones you turn to for judgment.

That makes it a tyranny, and if the media is a tyranny then it follows the logic of tyranny, which is that it's purpose is only to be a tyranny. Make money, lose money, be beloved, become the butthead-- those are irrelevant to a tyranny. There was an advertisement for a news program no one should ever watch in a magazine no one should ever read, and it's tagline was, "We'll help you make sense of the election." For clarification: the election in question was 2016. The only thing those 4 dummies could have helped you make sense of were crash tests, and they themselves kept repeating that this was an election where the issues couldn't have been more obvious, the enemy's misogyny and hate couldn't be more explicit. Then why tune in? Because we don't want power, we want knowledge. Listening to the candidates isn't knowledge. Listening to experts discuss the candidates is knowledge. And reading a tertiary source that discusses the candidates and the experts discussing the candidates? At 50% off the news stand price? Now you're an intellectual, and you didn't have to lift a single heavy book.

Of course the standard rebuttal is that the "media" has declined in power, most obviously revealed in its failure to influence the outcome of a Presidential election; tellingly, the media's instant explanation was that "alt-right" media (but media nonetheless) was what had the influence; but while the dummy in the wireless mic and pancake makeup up may have truly wished to influence the outcome, the purpose of the media was only to get you to see it as judge. The media succeeded spectacularly. Blaming the election's outcome on the rise of alternative medias misses the point: it's not that people will believe anything they are told in media, it's that people can only believe something they are told in media. Primary sources alone have no value. It has to be a secondary source, so that belief can be safely categorized as knowledge, even if it's wrong.

group of semi-flaccid men, obviously the excuse is it's a show for men, they're "attention whores"-- but they're not actual whores, which is what they would have been if the men didn't get to watch.   Right?   Except that the excuse isn't that it is a show for men, it is actually a show for men.   She kissed the other girl because the audience wanted a performance.   She knows to act on the desires of others.   How did she know they wanted this?   How did they know she would do it?   How did she know she was supposed to-- want it?

   "Are you saying she didn't really want to kiss her?"   That's such a weird question for you to ask.   Since when did you care what she wants?   The desire she acted on was the desire of the audience, not her own.   Maybe she actually did want to kiss her, it doesn't mean they are in lesbian, maybe they're "experimenting"-- none of this matters.   Why not retreat to the

---

Tell me if you've heard this: When the TV news runs "commercial free" during an acute crisis, that's not out of respect for the severity of the crisis but as a loss leader to enhance its image as authority through the impression of service, objectivity... you've heard that before?   *Where?*

It's false: it is the rare chance for media to *be* a primary source, to own what it will inevitably revert away from, back to a secondary source.   It thus becomes unassailable.   It cares not a fig what you do with the information, it does not want you to do anything.   None of it, in its formal sense, is propaganda towards a goal.   It is all rhetoric.

Presidents were never supposed to be above the law but they were once above the media, they aren't anymore, so it's interesting to ask if there is anyone who is above the law and above the media? Who still gets to be private?   If you want to see press-ready sexual indiscretions flagrantly flaunted by evil men whom everyone hates yet still no reporter has dared try to expose, you have to go north to Wall Street.   I don't know who the CEO of Goldman Sachs is, and I don't know if he was ever in a sorority, but I know with 100% certainty that you will never see a picture of it.   Hold on, stay to the end: when I become wrong, don't bother joining the other masturbators ejaculating over the hypocrisy, or apply for his job.   Power will have moved on to somewhere else.

33   "Thucydides's Trap" is a variant strain of idiocy that comes from writing primary sources about politics but reading secondary sources about Thucydides, and traps.   It hinges on a single excerpt of the primary source, Thucydides's contrast between the "immediate" triggers of the war and the underlying, ideological reason for the war: the existing superpower Sparta attacked Athens not for any material reason but out of fear the Athenian might should still increase.

How is that a trap?   To clarify, the Trap is NOT that as your enemy rises, becomes more powerful, you feel trapped and defend your position; the Trap implies that the *unconscious* forces of great power rivalry will result in a final confrontation *for some other reason*, some pretext that is really only a cover for the unconscious rivalry that necessarily must take place, like an Oedipal rivalry. That's not a trap.   It's not even likely.   An Oedipal rivalry only occurs because the son wants what the father already possesses, i.e. the mom-- and he is forbidden not just from having her, but from even wanting her.   Do countries consciously want what the other country has?   If so, the rivalry would be totally conscious; if not, totally unnecessary.   Thucydides's Trap is as knowledgeable about Thucydides as it is about the unconscious.

But the strangest part is that if "Thucydides's Trap" means that war against a rising power is inevitable, using it to explain contemporary affairs like the U.S. vs. China requires a stunning disavowal that can only be on purpose: in the analogy the US would be Sparta, not Athens; and when Thucydides wrote what is described as the "Trap", he already knew the Spartans were going to *win*.   So is it a Trap, or a recommendation?   You can say that even with winning the cost of war is too high, yet I cannot think of a single war in which the winner would agree.   What Thucydides's Freudian Trap doesn't touch on is whether the winner will develop any guilt for conquering the loser, and according to the data that's a strictly post-modern phenomenon.   It's hard to say if we should expect a trend continuation or a mean regression, and by regression I mean regression and by

privacy of the limo or bathroom stall? Because that's not what the audience wants.

"She wants attention." Then why not join a protest? "Sexual attention, she wants to be desired." To get that, why does she have to do something that everyone knows is fake? And since the men know she's just doing it for the attention, doesn't that decrease the eroticism of it for them? Or-- increase it? It's possible she's doing what they want *in order to* get their attention-- as if that attention was somehow satisfying to her?-- but if her parents were idiots it's far more likely that she's doing it *only* because they want it, and therefore doing *exactly* what they want, which is doing what they want only *because* they want it and not because she wants it. "So she doesn't want to kiss the other girl?" She does want to, because the audience wants her to want to.

---

mean I mean mean.

The other reason the Trap is idiotic is that the entire debate about the Trap requires the invention of a dichotomy that does not exist in the primary source: between the *underlying* cause of the war, and the *apparent* cause of the war. This dichotomy is the preferred way of seeing things nowadays because it asserts that they who acted could not also have truly known the "structural causes" for why they were doing it, they did not know that what they were doing was really caused by other forces. It's called "political analysis" so no one sees it's more like political psychoanalysis, this allows us the privilege of knowledge, which is very important among people not likely to possess power.

Thucydides does not describe anything like a trap, he doesn't imply there is anything unconscious or structural in the Spartans' involvement, he explicitly makes a very different distinction that is translated incorrectly I guess out of spite: not between the underlying cause and *apparent* cause, but between the underlying cause and *lies*-- specifically, lies you just made up to let you pretend that you *didn't have a choice*. Corcyra wasn't yet another in a long series of Spartan grievances against Athens, such that this was merely the straw that broke the camel's back, forcing them into war. The Spartans couldn't have cared less about Corcyra, they barely cared about Corinth. The Spartans were *lying*.

Sparta certainly didn't unconsciously end up invading Persia, their actual enemy who was actually way more powerful. In fact, it was Spartan unreliability in the Persian Wars that made the Athenians start building up an empire in the first place. Nor did the Spartans fear Athens, and they didn't attack them to keep the women and children for themselves. It was a sibling rivalry, like you have with your wife, and in a rivalry, the prize is merely pretext for the purpose of destroying the other. "Why not just divorce?" And let that slut enjoy her freedom?

Neither was their real fear that the Athenians would one day invade them. Themistocles was never going to invade them, and Pericles – whose actual paid employment was as *general*-- did not even engage them in battle when the Spartans invaded them. Trap? Pericles-- I repeat: a *general*-- took a massive NATO military budget *and spent it on public works projects*. And the arts. WTF? So from the Spartan perspective, the Athenian military wasn't nearly as terrifying as the bananastown social experiment that was working too well. How can you prevent some slave under Spartan rule from hearing about Athenian silver mines or the wine orgies and wondering, what the hell, what do I have to lose, but my chains? Not to mention the Spartans' existential terror that their own 3x greater population of *indigenous* Greek slaves might suddenly remember that the last time they rebelled they almost won.

The story is that tiny colony of Epidamnus has an internal rebellion and ousts the aristocrats, forming a democracy. The aristocrats return and besiege the city. The people=democrats of Epidamnus go to their parent city Corcyra=aristocrats for help; they are refused=duh. They next go to Corcyra's parent city, Corinth (even wealthier aristocrats), who-- surprise-- agree to help. You can already see economics and class conflict aren't going to work here, so the typical way this is

The performance is not a clue to her secret desires: that if she did it, she must have also wanted it. No. The force of her desire is zero, it does no work, it exerts no power. She can only do it because someone else wants it. Stand in front of three or four guys and for their gaze and it becomes possible, not merely excusable. If she prefers to say she wanted to-- if she prefers to say she wouldn't have done it unless some part of her wanted to-- go girl, whatever makes you feel empowered. But this system eradicates the link between desire and action. There is no inference to be made about desire; all we can know is if she did it-- desire or not-- it was for some other reason. She is able to act-- because it is pornographized.

We could argue that she's being influenced by the leering men, but it doesn't actually

---

then explained is Oedipally: Epidamnus is the colony of Corcyra, which was the colony of Corinth. Fathers and sons are always in a rivalry, so Epidamnus turns to the richer grandfather, who is happy to help because even though he's never given an epidamn about his grandson before, he's got a chance to stick it to his entitled and disrespectful son, which as an aside is exactly the state of affairs in America today. 300 years old but destitute of experience and big with his own importance, that young sovereign will speak to a father twice his years with a flippancy which the most ignorant foreigner of mature age wouldn't use. It's time he learned a lesson.

Since very few sons have the balls to take on their fathers until they actually become fathers at which point there's no point, the cheat is to make the conflict look like something else, take it outside the family, so that you can claim you won. "Turns out the reason my Dad doesn't like my fiancee because she's black." Really? All this time, you just now discovered he's a racist? Isn't it more racist that you just happened to unconsciously fall in love with someone you knew he wouldn't like? She has to suffer so you can feel superior to him? It won't end well, because what's going to happen is you'll have a kid, and he'll eventually come around to loving your wife, around the time coincidentally coincident with your wanting to commit adultery, or murder. "So you think all interracial relationships are pathological?" HA! Nice try, only the ones you chose impulsively, compulsively, or for some other reason, which is true about all pathological relationships.

So the Corcyrans appeal to the Athenians for military assistance, and the Corinthians appeal to them to stay out of it. Let me again reiterate the structure of this argument: the Corcyran son is in conflict with the Corinthian Dad, and son and Dad both go to the neighbors to ask them to choose sides: The Corcyrans make appeals to Athens the way children do, by asserting that Corinthian Dad is a hypocrite and ratting him out: "Don't let the Corinthians fool you. They're secretly planing to attack you next." And the Corinthians will roll their eyes and give a resigned shrug, "I'm sorry about my son, he's not a bad kid but at this age he thinks he knows everything. I see you have a couple of young kids of your own, I'm sure you can relate." Then, tugging pensively at their beards, they remind the young adult Athenians of the unspoken rule of grown-ups: "I'm sure you'll agree, a man's got to have control over his own family. We've never interfered in your affairs, and of course we appreciate you not telling us how to discipline our children."

And the Athenians don't know what to do with either of these two lunatics. "Look, we don't want to get in the middle of this, except that we kinda are in the middle of this, we can't just sit by and let you guys mobilize a few thousand soldiers right outside our walls." And there's the dilemma. The practical consequences of Athens doing nothing could be a set up for future land invasion by the Spartans; the consequences of getting involved could be a naval war with the Spartans. It was one of the hardest decisions the Athenians ever had to make, and as a direct democracy all the citizens had to debate it and make it collectively. It takes them one night. The next day Athens agrees to help the Corcyrans, but only with a "defensive" force to prevent a war.

There's some controversy about whether "defensive" is really a euphemism for "offensive", an excuse to project power and dominate the seas, but when the Athenians decided how many ships to send to stand against the hundreds of Corinthian ships, the number they chose was 10, and NB none

need a crowd of men to work, in fact, it doesn't need any witnesses at all. In another scene two drunk girls stay in a hot tub while their slowly fattening boyfriends go back inside to watch sports commercials. Ten minutes of boiling pheromones and the women react in predictable ways, after all that's why they shot this in the hot tub. Why not get a room and lock the door so you don't have to worry that this is a horror movie? There's a thrill in doing it out in the open where you can get caught, sure, but women are not biologically exhibitionists, go ask Islam, the difference is that the mere idea of being observed-- what a hypothetical observer would want-- makes it possible for her to act while letting her feel like she chose to.

"Maybe she had a repressed homosexual desire, and the hot tub lowered the

---

of them were aircraft carriers; and when they voted on which of the various Athenian generals they should choose to head this mighty offensive force, the one they selected was Spartan. I don't mean he was a Spartan, I mean his name was literally *Spartan*.

All you need to read in order to see there's no "Thucydides's Trap" is the passage in which the participants actually discuss Thucydides's Trap-- the final debate in Sparta that lead to a declaration of war against Athens. The various Peloponnesian (=Spartan) protectorates, Megara, Corinth, Thebes, etc, have gathered at the Spartan assembly to voice their complaints and convince the Spartans to attack Athens. Megara's complaint is trade interference, though it will later be shown logically that Megarians are liars. Thebes makes the sophisticated second image argument that the Athenians are jerks. The Corinthians take the American approach, they make a few policy points but do a reverse ad hominem: they describe the Athenian people as innovative, assertive, creative, on the rise; while Spartans are rigid, boring, and stagnating; here is what these whippersnappers have done to our lawn; if you super soldiers aren't going to act like a ruling hegemony, then what do we need you for?

After these impassioned complaints, the level headed Spartan King Archidamus makes a speech, explaining soberly that the existing treaty between Athens and Sparta calls for arbitration first, which the Athenians have agreed to. He diplomatically agrees that the Athenians are getting too strong, but to fight them Sparta needs years to plan, build a navy; be too hasty and they will pass this war on to their children. Fun fact: that is literally true in more ways than he guessed.

By coincidence, two Athenians who happen to be in Sparta on other business hear about the assembly and ask the King of Sparta if they, too, can make a speech. He lets them. "Spartans, we won't bother to rebut the accusations, but if you want to talk character then here you go: when you were too pious to be reliable, we single-handedly beat the Persians on land at Marathon, we crushed them at sea in Salamis, and we're ten times stronger today, don't think for one second that your defeating Athens will be easy, let alone certain." They pause for effect, smile, and then graciously remind that the terms of the existing peace treaty between Sparta and Athens requires disputes to be settled in an independent arbitration. To be clear: this wouldn't be a negotiation; a third nation would unilaterally decide and both parties are bound by the decision. Imagine Germany and France have a dispute, and it gets decided by Egypt. The Athenians say they are absolutely prepared to comply.

Finally, the recently elected Spartan magistrate Sthenelaidas, with all the unaccountable arrogance of a man elected for a one year term, has no trouble offering an opinion he will never be accountable for; though the fact that he had just been elected means everyone had already counted on his opinion. "Blah, blah, blah," he says, "listen to the Athenians, clucking like women around the well about how pretty they are, but say nothing about their cheating ways. Don't tell me we're the ones who need to deliberate. The Athenians deserve double punishment, they are not as good as they used to be and worse than they ever were. What are we waiting for? For them to get stronger? They must be buried! All in favor of burying them--!" Well, the ayes have it, but to make sure he's not accountable he pretends it's too close to call, and tells them to physically choose sides, everyone

inhibitions." So let me get this straight: a repressed desire to have sex with a woman returned as-- actually having sex with a woman? Unless she's acting out Freudian slip, that's not how repression works. Whatever was the repressed desire, it returned not as sex with a woman but as sex in a hot tub. Whose desire is that?

"Maybe she's just acting out, she has low self-esteem, it probably means--" Acting out is not a behavior that calls for interpretation, it isn't a symptom of anything, as much as we wish things like rage could be safely reduced to a symptom of something. Acting out is always and ever a message, that some desire of hers hasn't been heard; best to let it play out somewhere safe, like a hot tub. We render the acting out harmless, useful, by giving it the right to assert itself in a definite field-- a playground in which it is allowed to expand in almost complete

---

for war go over there, everyone who is not for war go over there. Now the vote is unanimous. This may sound like I am making too much of it but I've already lived through two roll call votes so I know how it goes: when it comes down to it, the individual Spartans weren't afraid of the rising might of Athens. They were afraid they might be called women. That's a kind of trap, I guess.

The Corinthians' and Athenians' speeches are often mined for insights into the differences in character of the Athenians and the Spartans, but as the contents were made up by Thucydides we are really only getting what Thucydides thought were the differences in character. Fair enough, but if we agree that's what we're getting, then we might get better insight from *who* gives the speeches, take note: war is demanded by the Corinthian ambassadors; sober caution is advocated by the Spartan King; the testosteronized rallying call is made by the unaccountable Spartan magistrate; but the men giving the speech on behalf of Athens are *just some guys*. Think about this. You and 5 half windsors from marketing are over in Eurasia trying to find out why khakis aren't selling, and hear that Eastasia is there screaming to start a war, so you look up how to tie a full windsor and go ask the King of Eurasia for permission to speak on behalf of Oceania. *He lets you.* Well hold on a second, why does he let you? Impressed by the dress? *He lets you speak because even he knows it counts.* And at that speech you don't argue justice or mutual interest, you don't dazzle them with rhetoric, you tell them if they attack you will beat them into oblivion. Would you dare? You'll argue you don't have the right to speak; you know you don't have the power to speak; you'll say you don't have the privilege to speak; and you'll say that Athens had far fewer people to speak for, but it was 2 men for three hundred thousand while it took 6 of you to represent pants; you'll say you'd be too afraid of being thrown in a gulag or beheaded, though those Athenians faced identical risks; you'll say all these things, yet at the same time you're telling me that properly conscripted into the military, you would *then* be willing to fight for your freedom? No, no, I believe you-- my question is why *only* then?

That's how close the Athenian citizens felt to Athens, to power. It wasn't national pride; it was the very un-ideological fact that they *were* Athens, whatever was going to happen was either going to happen to *them*, or *by* them. At this point you'll conveniently remember that today there's actually a law against a private citizen making policy on behalf of the state, but even if the Athenians had the political privilege and the ethical duty they certainly didn't have legal immunity, if the Athenian demos thought they spoke wrongly or even poorly they would have been fined, banished or vanished. These two pantsmen simply *acted*. There's also a running conspiracy theory that says that those two were secretly sent by Pericles, under the guise of being pants salesmen, to listen in and speak if necessary. This theory totally misses the point of the *story*, because even if Pericles secretly authorized them to speak, the King of Sparta wouldn't have known this, *yet he let them speak anyway. Everyone* assumed the Athenian individuals had all the power. If there was any rising might of Athens that the Spartans feared it was this, it appeared like a chaos, at least with one tyrant you know who to profile but predicting 300k mini-tyrants is always worse than chance, and here were two individual pants salesmen who on enemy territory listened to the mightiest powers in the region scream for their obliteration, and then they calmly turned to their Spartan hosts and told them to eat it.

freedom and in which it is expected to display to us everything that is hidden in her mind. That is, of course, if we want to know what's in her mind. Sometimes we put them in the playground just because we want to watch them play with each other. "That sounds kind of selfish... and creepy." It is.

"My wife was like that, she acted out a lot when she was in college." That's a strange sentence: why did you say it? Why didn't you simply say she did a lot of wild/immoral/fun/degrading/typical/atypical things in college? "I meant that she did them, but I don't think she really wanted to do them." But *you* don't know what she wants, which is why she *was* acting out. She sent you a message from the past: you're not hearing *me*, so hear *this*. You think you have me figured out, parsed and compartmentalized. Here's something I did that defies your understanding. Why did I do it? 'For attention'? Do I have your attention now?

"I find it hard to believe--" Ha! Another Freudian slip. "I find it hard to believe she did this in the past as a message to me now." For you female desire is complicated, it even defies special relativity. Maybe it's easier for you to believe you accidentally discovered on your own something she did in the past, that coincidentally was precisely the message she needed you to hear today. The only reason you even call it female desire is so it's not your fault. "Female desire"-- are we going to be honest? – secretly yet precisely defined by males and females as the desire of one who is desirable. "I like a man who knows what he wants." As long as what he wants is you. Otherwise he's acting like a girl.

"Sometimes it turns me on to hear stories of her sexual past." So yours wasn't that good. "Uh, no, mine was pretty great." But it didn't count. "Why wouldn't it count?" Because yours involved desiring, hers was about being desired. Check your ledger: she's ahead, now who's the alpha. "I think it's exciting to learn something new about the woman you know everything about." I wonder if she'd agree you know half of anything, and anyway if it was truly new you would be enraged, not excited. What gets you excited is confirming that she enjoyed being used for someone else's satisfaction. "Why would that excite me?" Because she can't get that enjoyment from you. "Of course she can." HA! You should read this paragraph again later.[34]

This is certainly one of Athens's prouder moments, but it's only one short speech in a really thick book that is mostly not speeches. It may be history but Thucydides was writing *for* Athens; it was in every way cautionary to and critical of Athenians; his general complaint wasn't their lust for power but the way Athens used that power, and if you want the answer to be materially or imperially or benevolently or malevolently you are better off with the secondary sources, the primary source indicates it is way more complicated than that-- in fact, the inconsistency was the heart of the problem. At that moment in history the Athenians had all the power to act on whatever they wanted. They soon discovered they had no idea what they wanted. Over the next 100 years, they would increasingly want to give away their power to anyone else, until finally it was taken by somebody else. Are you surprised? Thucydides's Trap is not some offhand comment about great power rivalry preposterously taken out of context; the real Trap he described are the consequences of psychological impotence masked by impulsivity, painfully detailed over 8 books. But if you still feel you must secondary source Thucydides to a single pithy quote it's hard to do better than the one he didn't write: *even if every Athenian was a Socrates, together they would still be a mob.*

34 "But whatever happened to privacy?!" It's right in front of you.

People will tell you that overexposure on the internet is a way of broadcasting an identity you hope

There's no need to control people when they can't act on their desires, just give them access to knowledge and let their OCD paralyze them. They'll celebrate their own impotence as long as they feel like they know what everyone else is doing. Instead of telling our 13 year old daughters not to put themselves online, we pretend it's inevitable and maturely permit it-- "I trust her"-- only to use it as a way of monitoring them. Now you can see the lie: the worry was never that they will expose their private parts; the worry is that we won't know their private parts. We have no power over them so we want knowledge of them, or at minimum a diagnosis, we can't control their actions but we can change the context of their desire, even in retrospect. "I want to give him a blowjob." --No, honey, you're not some slutty sorority girl, you need to respect yourself; what you mean to say is, 'I should be allowed to give a blowjob if

---

everyone will believe, but we're also told by those same people that nobody believes anything on the internet, everyone knows it's a cesspool of liars pretending to be someone else. Capitalism is marvelously hyperefficient, it gives you exactly what you will pay for, it detected we'll pay to be the main character in our own movie, so it gave us exactly that. That no one else wants to see our movie, let alone be in it, is not a design flaw in the product, because what we paid for was merely the potential of someone unknown audience taking a look, but that's hardly broadcasting an identity. The question of identity is a no longer relevant.

When you post a photo of a chocolate cake, you are sharing the experience of that cake; when you post a comment about a news event or someone else's photo of a cake, you are sharing your experience of those comments and photos. It's tempting to see a bikini picture or a carefully revised 9 word zinger about someone's metaphysics as something different than a cake picture, but if it uses the same media, it has to follow the same logic. And, sadly, it does.

It's an obvious cliché that the whole point is to share experiences, but what the experiences have in common is that they are inner experiences: enjoyable in themselves. Publicizing these experiences suggests-- in fact, what it has defended against-- the inability to enjoy the experience. Including sex: nothing in the universe was ever more desirable than having sex with that person in that position on that beach... and then the enjoyment fails to match the desire. Why did it fail to satisfy? "Here's a picture. I was hoping you could tell me."

Enjoyment of negative experiences is no different: a broken leg or someone's death is presumed to have a certain intrinsic emotional weight-- a satisfaction-- that the person fails to experience as much as they think they should. They may feel sad, mad, or in howling pain, but somehow-- it doesn't count. It doesn't feel real. Because it isn't: "Pic or it didn't happen."

In order to compensate for this inability to enjoy fully, we publicize the experience and offer the enjoyment to unknown others. This is the tragedy of pornographization. The others have to be unknown or this will not count, because the people you know don't count. Some of the individuals can be known, but in the aggregate it has to be "others". Understood this way, bragging "look how great I look" becomes "you know how to enjoy the experience of looking good-- you'll enjoy this more than I do."

The pornographization of individual experience, for an unknown audience, is the solution not to an identity problem but to an enjoyment problem. Note that the solution doesn't actually help you enjoy the experience any more; but you have traded the experience you don't know how to enjoy for a new thing that everyone *knows* is desirable, even if they say it shouldn't be: the gaze of others.

The smiling sorority girl pictured laying out on a beautiful beach may appear to be enjoying her life, yet you have no problem agreeing the candid picture of her enjoyment is staged. Why fake it, if she's enjoying it so much? Because she's an artist trying to 2D represent an incommunicable inner sensation? That's not how it works. The purpose of art is to repress the truth, so it can return as art. She cannot enjoy the beach as much as she believes she should be able to (i.e., as much as some

190

I want.' --"You're right, Mom; I'm not doing it for him, I'm doing it for myself."

Occasionally you'll find the holdouts to ubiquitous publicity, to omniscience-- to pornographization; they will be proud to tell you they still want something to be-- left to the imagination. They are all liars. "I prefer Playboy to porn." For what purpose? Porn is still young, soon it will consolidate into a few big houses and stop catering to your keywords and start telling you what an aspirational man or woman should want from sex. Back in its day Playboy didn't need to compete with porn, not because there wasn't any porn but because their draw was the celebrities, implying you could be a celebrity, too; their competition was magazines. In order to entice more celebrities, Playboy lowered the risk to them. Who would

---

other person would enjoy not the beach but *the experience of being* "a smiling sorority girl on the beach"); so she performs the enjoyment for others because she-- wants-- the reactions. The fact that she knows everyone knows the photo is staged makes sense only in this context: fooling the public would be a trivial satisfaction if the real enjoyment was the real experience.

Therefore: a private person-- no, let's start more simply: a private woman-- a woman who enjoys her privacy, or, at the very least, whose enjoyment is not diminished by being private-- cannot be allowed to exist. A deliberately private woman is much more of a threat to society today than what 200 years ago a deliberately childless woman was, but in the exact same way. Such a woman-- especially if she is *desirable*, i.e. is *thought* to have power-- for whom being public should be so fulfilling and obvious, yet she rejects it-- she causes other women, *and men*, to question if privacy might be valuable-- enhancing-- if they shouldn't also be private.

It's certainly possible that there exists a woman who would just as much enjoy her bikini or beach without ever telling anyone, but that woman would then not tell anyone. Private people are the most private about what they enjoy-- their pain, their happiness, their fantasies; because other people might try to deprive her of her enjoyment by telling her how it is supposed to be enjoyed. Is love any different? Now it is: it doesn't exist. It's an important philosophical question whether inner experience can be communicated, but it's an easy psychological question whether inner experience should be communicated: no. Not unless you're trying to understand it from someone else's perspective, or get rid of it. "I'm so in love with her I want to proclaim it from the highest rooftops!" Then you aren't or you shouldn't, unless you are trying to kill it, or her. On second thought, do her a favor, get a ladder, roll your unfinished math homework into a 329ml megaphone, and testify.

I should stop here and let you digest this. Telling you how we don't know how to enjoy, which causes us to seek the gaze of others because it is at least universally desirable—you might not believe all of it, but there's something there that rings true, it gets at the truth, it informs you, it lets you see things in a different way. You'll consider possible solutions: you're not going to unplug completely, of course; but maybe you'll try not being so public, trying to want on your own, learn how to connect more deeply with the present, enjoy each moment? "Food for thought." This is where I would stop if what *I* wanted was your consideration, your approval-- your gaze. But I do not care about these things. Which is why I'm going to push the analysis further, past disavowal and denial into repression, to where you will shake your head no and totally disagree, it no longer resonates, I don't know what I'm talking about, it's not true, I am wrong. And yet-- ask everyone else who knows you if I am wrong.

The solution to not being able to enjoy is to push the enjoyment of the experience onto others; but you'll observe that the "others" do not, in fact, get to enjoy your experience-- more accurately, they suspect *you* enjoyed it, if for no other reason than you were the one who experienced it. You might even say... that the others were deprived of the enjoyment. So who did enjoy, and what did they enjoy? The reason that sharing is the solution to being unable to enjoy, even though it doesn't help, is that it isn't a solution to being unable to enjoy-- this logic that "rings true" is the *defense* against

think twice about being able to say they were tastefully nude in Playboy? Who was going to actually see it anyway? What father would seriously object to-- the publicity? God knows the mother is on board, she knows for one reason or another a woman will eventually have to get naked, may as well get something out of it. Now an artistic CGI labeled as a candid photoshoot (with a making-of video in which you can even hear the camera shutter) is just part of an actress' resume, and since we're all aspirational actresses, this is all part of the larger propaganda directed at all women: be public.

"It's still the objectification of women." Not the way you think-- not anymore. Those photoshoots are the reservoirs for physical sexuality until it can be taken back-- by men. NB that in the male target demo film *Confirmatory Assent*, the girls are finally allowed to make their

---

what you do enjoy, a defense against what truly satisfies you: depriving the other.

No? Too far? As a last volley for intelligibility you will put it into a hypothesis so we can argue about the evidence: because we've lost the ability to enjoy our experiences, we pursue what others would want, but secretly derive compensation out of making other people jealous. Does that sound more correct? Are you willing to admit you see yourself in this, at least a little? Did you hope this? But who are you fooling? I don't need to argue the hypothesis, I only need to observe how you've changed the pronouns and quietly reversed the logic. Let me correct your correction: since the *only* thing you can enjoy is the deprivation of others, *therefore* none of your experiences are sufficiently satisfying. The defense against your true enjoyment is pretending you have an obviously shallow and selfish desire for the gaze of others. "I admit it, I do enjoy making people a little jealous, because it is so hard to really enjoy my own inner experiences." You have it backwards: pride always comes... before the fall.

"But how can I get my teen daughter to stop overexposing herself online?" Do you mean-- stop her from wanting to deprive others? Because that's what you should mean. Let her have a private life. They already feel overexposed, everyone sees them, like a reclusive teenager trying to get a snack from the parents' refrigerator, they feel the weight of scrutiny and expectations and judgment, nothing they ever do is good enough, they are fully aware of their lack of ownership in anything while constantly being reminded by their inconsistent parents about their shortcomings and obligations under this shared ownership. A lesson in socialism, I guess. And it's not just being judged to her face, let's not forget all the adults-- men but especially women-- whispering amongst themselves, judging her for being too sexy or......... so sexy. And so they put it all out there, the logic of overexposure is the logic of hiding in plain sight. Every teen knows that you can't hide anything because people will keep on looking, and they will always find something even worse. The trick is to make them stop looking, to make them think they've found it.

A picture of your reflection is all that's needed to stop them from digging deeper. "Now I've seen everything." Fat or fit, naked or not, hate or heart-- as long as they stop at the level of the interpreted image. Or a picture of a wise/ironic/enlightening quote, it's basic math: a picture is worth a thousand words, but a picture of a word is priceless.

The "overexposure" may have consequences, but it is itself the consequence of not being invested in life; not being able to derive satisfaction from the world, because early on they learned satisfaction was always relative to others'. "Who did they learn that from?" With no power within the system, and no clear payoff by committing oneself, as one self, to the system or to anyone, you'll give it what it wants (your privacy) but deprive it of "the real me". People with power over others don't exhibit themselves in this way, but the correct understanding is the reverse: if you can't exert power over others, the only satisfaction you can get is depriving them of the only thing you have: yourself.

The problem today isn't that nothing is held in private, the problem is that there is nothing *to* hold in private. What do you want, that you're not allowed to want? You've never read Freud, but you know about repression; and you know about it so you can be sure you haven't done it. "Nope, all

swimsuit calendar only after they agree to sign it over to the college to sell it; and have each sorority sister in a one piece pose CFNM style with a naked (but obstructed) frat brother. Why does the college need the men? It's not because they think that's what women women want-- this whole thing was a corrective to the women wanting pictures of themselves for themselves only. The naked men aren't capitalism's sudden recognition of women's sexual desires or the growing demo of male bicuriosity, but rather the point in the product cycle where it had glutted the market with female sexuality, reducing its appeal to almost nothing. Nowadays you barely notice a nude woman, let alone a barely nude one, but a hot naked man can deliciously serve as the reservoir, the guarantor, for male and female sexuality. *Obviously* only such a man could satisfy her; but only such a man could derive full satisfaction from actual sex with her. Yeah, sure, he's the hot guy you want to be with, be, or watch; but what you really need him for is to show that some men and women can choose what they want.

The calendar doesn't represent the objectification of women, only the publicizing of women, which in real life is reliably done by making them *feel* desirable, which can only be done in public. Did the pledge class dress like that "for themselves" or in case a janitor walked by? "But it's a movie..." The "school" or "workplace", where sexual actions are forbidden, work attire is increasingly sexualized. Is the pencil skirt/heels for the men in the next cubicle? She 100% correctly says she's just expressing her real self-- but that's not why she could make that choice, what it *is* for. It isn't sexualization, but to make the women more public. You got her out of the house and into the nightclub, you got her out of the nightclub and into the

---

my "secret" desires are fully conscious." And unfulfilled, that's strange. Knowledge without action. Omniscient and impotent. As if we--- sat through too much porn. Stasis. So you deliver a stream of authentic images-- safely reproduced from images you've seen in other people's streams, "this is who I am--" immediately disavowed: "but that's not the real me." Well, what is the real you? The only thing you've confirmed is what you're not.

The overexposure pretends that there is something else that is private. Everyone's privacy is their past or their future. She doesn't have much of a past, and you are controlling her future. "She needs more independence?" She needs to be depended on. "But every time I give her a responsibility, she messes it up." The only way you can give someone a responsibility is if it's actually your responsibility. So you messed up. "She doesn't even do her homework." Because she doesn't see it as practice, but as the performance. Whatever you told her homework is for she thinks she can get without doing homework. "Then she's retarded." Learning disabled, so either it's genetic or her teachers suck.

Since there's no one for her to become, she leaves it an open question: "this is me-- but not the real me." She puts the whole block of marble out there and hopes someone can see the bust within, chip away the parts that aren't you. It would have been better to sculpt the bust yourself. But you can't. "I could if--" That's the same as can't.

Now we don't bother sculpting an idealized image-- no one would believe it; and anyway the only idealized image we can even imagine is someone else's idealized image.

But who would want to do this for you? Or at least motivate you to practice chiseling? That task requires love or psychoanalysis, and you don't believe in either. Truth be told: neither does your lover or your psychoanalyst, which is why you picked them. "You're wrong, I'm trying really hard to figure out who I am." Know thyself-- the command of those whose profit comes from telling you who you are. And so we come to today, the contemporary defense against the unconscious by an ego that knows all the tricks of the unconscious: instead of our superego repressing desires incompatible with who we want to be, we repress nothing and wait for a superego to come along and tell us who we are.

193

workplace, now get her to dress for a nightclub at the workplace (under the safe watch of HR) so we don't all have to go to the nightclubs; get all of her self out there, leave nothing private. Make them feel it is both empowering and meaningless. It's the visibility, not the sexuality, to illustrate this try sexualizing it. "You can't fire me for leering, look at what she's wearing!" We were, but then you ruined it for the rest of us.

Privacy leads to fantasy, and fantasy leads to action. Privacy deprives the public of knowledge, it leaves them to fantasize, it forces them to have to act; so publicizing things, even superficially or stereotypically, makes them more knowable, keeps them at the level of images and-- reality. Under our new Overlords, privacy as a possibility must be obliterated. So whatever wants to be private must be repressed.

Back in *Confirmatory Assent*, the Tridelts must earn a pearl necklace as part of their sorority initiation (everybody with me?), so one girl uses Four Second Rule to fulfill it. Yeah. It's hard to tell which of the two is the more preposterous contrivance, which leads to the important question: why are there so many contrivances? Why bother? We all know what's going to happen to her, why not just get to it? Ok, the movie has her occasionally be a glasses and scrunchie "econ major" to juxtapose with her mascara and bikini top sluttiness, but why does she have to be a "sorority girl"? "Because sorority girls are sluts." Slow down: why can't she just be slutty? Why do we need the extra code for slut? Why a pearl necklace *requirement*? Why do we *need* Four Second Rule?

If you have a sexual fantasy, it is impossible to attain it. If you have a pornographic sexual fantasy, it is impossible to attain it-- except in porn. In real life you could sleep with a nurse who is a slut, a slut who is a nurse, a nurse pretending to be a slut, a slut pretending to be a nurse, but the only place to find a slutty nurse is porn. Porn, which exists, offers you the impossible, which can't. As a product, the purpose of porn is to make it impossible to get that kind of sex except through porn. It easily replaces fantasy, because it provides a kind of satisfaction.

She's is a slutty sorority girl not because she's a slut but in order to make her a kind of impossible slut-- a fantasy, an impossible desire. "But I have had sex with slutty sorority girls." You do know that they weren't *really* slutty sorority girls, right? "No, trust me, they *really* were." Do you have MS or is one eye as lazy as the rest of you? If your monocular vision can only see real women in 2D, then your ability to fantasize is probably at zero. "No, I have very elaborate fantasies, they're just not the adolescent 'slutty sorority girl' kind. Mine are much more elaborate and play with power dynamics." That you found on the same porn site.

"Sorority girls are sluts"= "econ majors are not sluts" may not seem equivalent but it is a tautology nevertheless. There are no econ majors in porn. She can only be a fantasy if she stops being an econ major. The direction matters. She's an econ major, pornographized into a sorority girl. The purpose is to prevent you from accessing your fantasies-- from being able to touch her as a fantasy. No matter how slutty an econ major is, it's never like the fantasy of a sorority girl. In the movie the "love interest" of Abby is at the very same party she is at, he's seething in a corner as she giggles through molestation by C- business majors, but he has to endure it because it's Four Second Rule and rules are rules. *But he himself never plays Four Second Rule with her.* What's the point? She's an econ major, he'd be touching an econ major's boob, not some sorority girl's boob. That became impossible the moment he got to know her.

There's a chance you will not immediately be able to put into words exactly why that impossibility is way worse than it sounds: the fantasy part of "sorority girl" that is *semantically*

194

blocked off for him is (he imagines) realistically attainable by every other guy because to them she's-- a sorority girl. It's bad enough he can't get his fantasy from the woman he loves, but worse is that, logically, everyone else can get it from her *except* you. "Sorority girls are sluts" = "econ majors are not sluts" is a psychologically devastating tautology-- read it again and take it literally, the tautology is devastating to the psychology-- because even if your wish for a sorority girl is fulfilled she will quickly become an econ major--------- *while (you perceive) she remains a sorority girl to everyone else.* [35]

At the scene when the two girls are kissing in the hot tub, two random alpha males jump in "to get warm." The girls giggle, and let them. At this point one of the boyfriends comes out. Trying not to sound possessive, he tells her she's wanted inside by one of her *other* friends. Note that well: his desire doesn't count, he can't make her act on his desire; but he believes she would willingly obey some other omnipotent entity, so he invents one on the spot. "No," you say, "it's so he doesn't reveal himself as a wuss to the guys." It's better that they think he walked out in the cold to deliver a summons from one of her girlfriends? Of course she's blonde= baffled, which friend? Etc. Finally, she goes inside with him, and the "how could you--!"'s begin.

> ECKS
> They could have been psychopaths or serial killers for all you know!

35"Why so many footnotes????" Which is the same question as, "why are your sentences so long, why so many commas, what the hell is with you and semicolons?" It's all on purpose, to get rid of readers. You're stumped by the physical layout? This book is not for you, your brain is already set in concrete, it can never change, only crumble as it ages. Which is fine if your plan was to be a foundation for the next generation, but it isn't; you're the rotting walls that they have to knock down while you play the flute and pretend to give freedom to everyone else. If you look forward to TV, if you think "the problem with the youth today is that they're entitled," if you think, "damn all the partisanship, I wish someone in government would just take charge and do the right thing!"-- you are a true Athenian democrat. "I'll take that as a compliment." Yeah. I'm not saying you are necessarily a bad person, I'm just saying your kids would benefit from a more hands off approach to parenting, and a math tutor. Most of you should not read this book, the Disclaimer represents all the justification you deserve, I did everything I could to exclude everyone, including adding the porn story at the beginning, a Beware Of Dog sign written in cat. You are the kind of person who will be bothered by the presence of the porn story here, in a book safely away from any observation, even as you don't observe that your kid observed... what you have been observing. You are the kind of open minded replicant who will say, "I don't have a moral problem with porn, it just has to be well written!" That's how you were told the kind of person you want others to think you are would select even his porn. Exacting measures of quality for your self-indulgence, while your standards for employment and diet are bafflingly arbitrary. "Are these cubicle donuts gluten free?" They're regular free, is that not free enough? You demand excellence in everything for yourself except yourself, you figure that will come after you're discovered for being excellent. "But I can't follow your book, why can't you write more clearly?" I typed it, what the hell more do you want? Audiobook? But you didn't mean it literally. You never mean anything literally. Try it. You can't. Never mind all that: how do you *experience* your frustration with the book? Answer: *As if I owed you a debt.* When Tarkovsky sent *Stalker* to the Soviet censors for approval, and they came back with the complaint that it was too slow paced and dull, he told them, "it needs to be slower and duller, so people have time to leave." I would have published this in 4pt font if I could, the irony is sometimes I had to write in 4pt font to avoid the surveilling eyes of Athenians who sat next to me on transports. "Couldn't help noticing you weren't talking to me, what's that you're working on?" It's a manifesto, you should buckle up.

No, they just saw a pair of tipsy blondes in bikinis

Does he really think they were psychopaths? Of course they *could* have been psychopaths, psychopaths are the most direct of actors, so anyone who manages to act directly on their desires has to be on the spectrum of psychopathy. Right? Because the pathology has to be action, not inaction. But obviously he just said it to scare/control her, to make her doubt her judgment. But why say this when the events *have already happened?*

Neither is he trying to prevent future occurrences, this is not the psychology of a person who plans for the future. There is no plan for the future, the plan is to await the future to come find him. Here's a different movie pitch, if you use it I get credit: the lonely loner, who suspects he should be destined for more than this, gets visited by an alien from another dimension who offers to show him experiences he can't even imagine. He hesitates. Will this satisfy him? NB: he's not even impressed his travel agent is from another dimension, or that of all people it chose him. So, no. Also, even aliens from another dimension can't prove to men they are valuable, only a woman can do that, as long as she is textually asexually desirable. So off they go to find a brunette. This is sci-fi film so we already know he's no Don Juan: he doesn't so much seduce her for their temporary mutual pleasure as get her to fall in love with him so that he can use her for his. Of course, the moment she does, he doesn't want her anymore, so he abandons her, which the alert reader will intuit was maybe the whole point. Then he goes to an *Eyes Wide Shut* party[36]. Those women are sexually desirable. Does that

---

36 I had always thought these kinds of masquerade parties were female fantasies, a thought I kept to myself hoping for an invite, but a woman angrily volunteered that the movie is a typically adolescent=middle aged male anxiety about women: "the wife doesn't even cheat, all that happens is she mentions she has fantasies and the guy has a nervous breakdown." There was nothing I could say, she was lost. What hurt Tom Cruise wasn't that she had fantasies, but that she used the fantasies in an argument with him, to hurt him: she wielded the fantasies as a weapon. She didn't want him to think she was capable of cheating, no guy needs to be reminded, any more than a woman of 40 needs to be reminded she's doesn't look 20. She wanted him to think he didn't *know* her.   And as she was the only dependable, meaningful, knowable thing in his otherwise semi-committed, imaginary and powerless life, well, he better pray there's a pharmacy still open that stocks whatever Thorazine is called over there.

To be clear: he became psychotic, not neurotic. Yes, he imagined her with her hypothetical lover; but could not imagine anything else. He stopped fantasizing. He stopped knowing. Everything came down to the level of the world, everything lost its meaning. Typical *Eyes Wide Shut* questions, "what did that scene mean? What did that object mean?" First of all, NB that Cruise never guesses, never wonders what it could mean. But anyway, the answer is nothing. That's the point. Whatever it was supposed to mean, it stopped meaning it. The secret password "Fidelio" is simply the secret password, but in his mind-- and the audience's-- the lack of a concrete meaning means it could mean anything, and therefore it does, and it drives people insane. Never mind what his wife wants of him, the active question now is-- who is she, really? Usually he'd see his sleeping wife and see his wife; now he sees her, and she could be anyone-- anyone except a normal wife who once again must parry but not stab yet another one of the nonstop string of sophisticates who hit on her at parties. "Umm, excuse me sir, I think that's my drink you're drinking." --Ta ta ta, but of course I know. "Do you know I'm the one that has to be drunk for this conversation to continue?" So random words, events, or experiences become-- not quite *connected*, because that would be knowledge and that would have solved his paranoia-- but *clues* about what he doesn't know, clues that he is being prevented from knowing. If he discovered that he was merely a pawn in a great conspiracy, then at least he would know the game was chess. It would be enough. He'd know there was a King, a Queen, that the clergy exerted power obliquely, in cahoots with the military-industrial complex, and since the King

satisfy? Instead of enjoying what he always thought he wanted, he gets freaked out by the weirdness of it: what's weird, of course, is that they all appear to be enjoying-- enjoying *him*-- without actually wanting these things-- wanting *him*. Script notes: To solidly depict *those* kind of women's uncanny ability to enjoy even without desire, either put everyone in masks or show a woman orgasming over something revolting, e.g. when she opens her mouth in ecstasy he sees something wriggling around inside it. It's alive, but not for long. Disgusting? Hot? The audience decides. Because the audience for this movie will be mostly cowards they will immediately identify with the disparity between his intelligence and his feeling of insignificance. So The One needs redemption, and in the third act he learns the woman he hurt is about to be hurt by someone else, threatening to demote his hurting of her as her most significant life experience, so he and his zany partner make a final push to rescue her with a getaway car and prison break in. Out. The Act III climax comes at the very end: he fails. But he gets credit for trying: as she dies, she tells him she loves him. He is redeemed by her love. Let's practice the elevator pitch: alienated young loner conflates knowledge with importance; a wise cracking, pan-dimensional guide takes him on a series of soft-core porn adventures; he finds redemption through a woman's love who conveniently dies immediately-- strike that: her death is the necessary precondition for his redemption so that he isn't then obligated to her, he no longer has to satisfy her; and since nothing has actually changed there is no need to show an Act IV, it can repeat as Act I, the ambiguous ending is proof of a sequel, there's the potential for more adventures, more women, more *Eyes Wide Shut* parties, hopefully next time with an all star cast. Green light? I'm can't promise this will be a hit, but

---

was not invulnerable, a decision had to be made to give up some of his power in exchange for the foreknowledge of a threat, and the power went to the woman, who still innately desired to serve the man. To protect him from within soldiers weren't allowed to become a King, only a Queen. See? It's easy to save yourself. It is true that this kind of knowledge doesn't give the conspiracy theorist any power, but that interpretation is exactly backwards of the direction: the purpose of the conspiracy is defend impotence by knowing something. Cruise's problem was the opposite: he doesn't know anything, at all, hence the breakdown. But there's a flip side: rather than being manipulated by the successive levels of pseudo-power he experiences, he is totally immune to all of them. He's constantly under threat by these mysterious forces, but nothing hurts him. He is the only person in the movie who can-- and does-- act. They have to come to him when a prostitute OD's. He easily infiltrates a secret party of the elite. They catch him, they unmask him-- now he's the only one with identity-- but they can't hurt him. The best they can do is hurt someone else-- and they can't actually do even that. When he finally sees the mask on his pillow it could mean anything, but now he makes a choice, based on will alone. Either the paranoiac world of excessive, random meaning; or he settles for sex with a faithful woman who is twice as hot at 40 as she was at 20 and is apparently a little bit of a minx.

The ironic thing is that much was made of the fact that Cruise and Kidman were real life married and played movie married; the suspension of disbelief here runs the opposite, in the service of destroying knowledge: are they real-life in love, so in the movie they aren't; or are they in-movie in love, so in real-life they aren't?-- What am I supposed to believe? Yet the mystery of sexuality was around Cruise, not Kidman. No one had any idea what he fantasized about. So why didn't they make the movie the other way around?

They could have, the entire movie works just as well with the wife as the paranoid-- except the ending. What makes it a "male" movie isn't the protagonist's reaction to his wife's fantasies-- a wife could have a similar breakdown when assaulted by her husband's secret fantasies-- but what saves him in the end: love for his wife. NB and to be specific: *fantasy about dependency*. In such movie today, for today's audience, the solution could not believably have been her husband-- it could only have been her child. To be specific: that which you do not depend on.

I can promise it was.

So the future is not his business; his game is rewriting the past. He is trying to change the men's desire in retrospect: sure, they looked like they liked you, but they're not particularly discriminating, they would have slept with anybody. "He just wants her to think only he truly likes her?" Isn't that obvious? Then no.

The point isn't to make her think only he likes her, but to make her think there are only certain things she should be liked for. Everything else doesn't count. He is re-reducing her to only the things about her he likes and erasing what other people like. It took a lot of work to get her down to a manageable amount of female, and for the most part she doesn't notice because he really seems to like her. But those forgotten lures are still visible to others: when she's accidentally out of his sight and in some other guy's view, she's intrigued by his gaze, she starts to notice she's covered in lures, inside and out: which part of me does *he* like?

"He said I had pretty hair." --He meant your breasts. Breasts are not a threat because he knows she knows they're hers, they're not her. For her they don't count. Her hair could be a threat, it is more her, it is something she might like being wanted for. "Unfortunately it wasn't may hair, he just saw a blonde in a bikini..." But she's been trained well.

The risk isn't just that she cheats on him; there is no risk of this, relax, even if she does it can be made not to count. The risk is that someone sees her as desirable, and she changes into what he likes. "But that's stupid, she's not going to change who she is just because some other guy likes her." How do you think he got her? He already changed her into someone else, it took a lot of work. She's not going to change for the other guy, she's *supposed* to be what the other guy sees in her; his worry is that she changes back. To the real her.

You can't control a woman through guilt about her sexual desires, not while commercials rely on them, we need a new control: make desire rational-- explainable by something else. "Big hips are a cue for fecundity." Why can't you just like big hips-- why the extra step? "Well, it's science, it's objective." It's not science-- but it is objectifying, Why explain it? Who is the explanation for? "They could have been serial killers!" It's not her judgment that's to be doubted; it's their desire.

You force her to understand it because then she's on your turf, the fake grass of fake reason-- and you control the argument. "What did those guys want?" --Nothing, they just saw a blonde in a bikini. "So we agree-- it doesn't count."

What about her desire? What about her-- lust? Don't ask. Seriously: you control it by not asking. Asking about her desires is dangerously close to loving her. She can't want on her own. Otherwise it can't be explained. --Why do you like that guy? "I don't know, I just do." Well, that kind of attitude is going to get you evaluated for witchcraft, having an unexplainable desire in a world of people obsessed with explaining everything rationally is not going to endear you to them, they are going to try and smother you-- to dissect you. "There's no free will, everything is deterministic, we're just unaware of all the steps before it." Phew, even if she doesn't know, there was a cause. Now the past 600 years of debate about free will vs. determinism is a defense against women's desire. At least let it be money, or security, quantum mechanics or evolution, or even a thick dick feels better ("A HA! So it *is* true!")-- anything that starts with "because", just don't say, "I don't know, I just do." You can't control what she doesn't know. So you make her know anything.

198

I anticipate your idiotic sexist retort: yes, men's desire is also *only* about desire; the difference is that from day one they are interrogated about the why, so they know the acceptable responses-- they know that there must be responses. They are so practiced at the technique that it becomes second nature, it becomes their only nature-- second nature is better than none.

The good news is that everyone now wants women to want like men, i.e. for some other reason, other than their desire; so we can all look forward to a world of women who don't believe in love and--------

Before TV, if they had some naughty sexual desires, they would have to repress them, and it made them hysterical; now they are simply asked to offer a public explanation, which is worse. "Ummm... I was lonely?" Kinda girlie, but it counts. "He made me feel desired." Typical female, definitely counts. "I was drunk?" Whoa, whoa, hold on, is that why you did it or why you wanted it? I'm not moving until I get an answer.

The system is reactive=reactionary, and it is teaching women the appropriate rational logic for their desires-- and making them insane in the process. "You want a career, because smart women want a career." --Can't I just want a career? "No, because then you won't be able to pursue it, we trained you not to act on your desires but on the desires of others." -- But if I feel in some way obligated to want it because others want it, won't it be unsatisfying if I get it? "HA! You were never going to be satisfied when you got it. We just gave you something to blame that on, with the additional benefit that you think you came up with it all yourself. You should thank us!"

Rational reasons to control desire. Not control her actions-- the purpose is not to get her *not* to have sex-- he knows deep down he can't stop her (and all the other patriarchs don't want him to), the purpose is to make it to be for another reason, a concrete reason, a rational reason-- a reason that takes away the anxiety even if it leaves behind rage. "He was rich." "He had a big dick." "He made me feel pretty." Not-- desire.

You can say: "The reason you want him and not me is X!" Forbidden: "Who do you want more, him or me?" It's not the answer, either answer is irrelevant-- it's that she'd be desiring on her own, without your input. That's the objectionable part, not the orgasms. If she still had private desires he hasn't pornographized or obliterated, he'll have to figure out what makes her desire, and then change *himself* into that thing. Once was enough, when he met her she looked like the kind of girl who would like the kind of guy who likes Seurat-- so he temporarily became an expert on Seurat and began insplaining-- "it's the same principle as an LCD screen, and look-- the woman has a pet monkey!" And once he got her to like him for more than Seurat, he began the relentless work of obliterating her interest in Seurat-- after all, that's never what he wanted-- and evidently she can be fooled by it.

She wants to have sex with a good looking, powerful man-- logical. She wants a million bucks for sex-- sure. Both "make sense", both are "rational". The problem of her choice-- the reason there can even be a dramatic movie about it-- is that neither were the reason, she didn't know her reason, and neither did he. Sex with a handsome billionaire and also get paid for it, and you didn't even make the choice-- it wasn't either of those? It's excessive-- obscene-- it makes no sense. But if it wasn't impulsive, and there wasn't another reason-- how were you able to do it? "I don't know-- first I did it because others wanted me to, and then past a certain point, it was on autopilot. I felt like I couldn't stop it." Good enough. Back to Act I.

The interesting part of this deliberate *self*-deception is that he thinks that telling her they only wanted her body is going to turn her off. He hopes the lies he has heard from four generations of women and the current generation of men are true: that women don't like being objectified, that women really only want to be liked for their mind or personality. The result is he spends a giant amount of energy hiding the fact that all he sees of any woman is her sex; he is overly respectful, overly polite, hyper-cautious. So it is enragingly confusing to him when other men are able to objectify them right to their big ass boobies, and the women don't seem to mind. *They giggle.*

The men who believed these lies were precisely the men the women needed to believe them: not "male chauvinist pigs"-- those men might not respect women but they could be reliably restrained by rules-- because the rules were enforced by other men[37]; the dangerous

---

37

Before his suicide, Hitler was asked by his valet, "For whom should we fight now?"

Hitler replied: "For the one who is to come after me."

There's a part in *The Godfather* that I think I'm making up where Old Man Corleone says, "we're not going to sell drugs like the n---- do." Good old fashion racism, Italians at the top and blacks at the bottom, though still above Jews until the rap epidemic of the 80s. Correlation, not causation, how these things are ranked still baffles me, at one point within my lifetime the worst thing a person could be was a pollack, it was so obviously bad they had books of jokes about pollacks which they gave away free in elementary schools, fast forward 40 years and now 100% of the pollacks are either supermodels or particle physicists. Of course Corleone knew some blacks were good and hard working but they are still they, and they=inferior. Who says? Italians. "We have culture and opera, they have god-awful jungle music." Rap? "Jazz."

Old school racism seems appalling but not on its merits: it's bad because it needs to be worse than what we do today, which it isn't, as I'm about to show you. Because while Corleone's racism came with an assumption of superiority, yours does not; yours requires them to be superior. That makes you worse.

Today, the racist doesn't come from a place of racial/cultural pride-- in fact, he thinks racial pride itself is the telltale sign of racism and ignorance, including and especially those who have white pride. Those guys are a losers. He can't be a racist because he defines himself as not having racial pride, he may be white but he's quick to tell you he hates white people. *Individual* white people are ok, some of his best friends are white, but as a whole-- well, ok, it's not being white that's bad, it's *white culture*. He's racist against racists, who are universally white. That's the key: supporting other races is the cover for a homicidal rage towards some other group, say, rich sorority girls, that if pointed at rich sorority girls would be detected as "pathological"; but as long as the TriDelts are accidentally in the blast radius it's celebrated as "pro-social." FYI that's why activists prefer bombs over guns, the target is the collateral damage.

He doesn't know much about Asian racism, because they were all in the other math class.

On the other side, the racist these anti-racists hate also doesn't think of himself as a racist, also because he defines himself as not having racial pride. He doesn't need it, he's proud of who he is, which is "my own man." He is an individual. He is informed. When he says, "I'm not a racist, I just see reality", he isn't lying-- he truly believes this, because it doesn't come from a pre-existing racial pride. He's just a guy, no better than anybody else, trying to make his way in a world where exist well defined, fully formed and characterized groups-- with their own culture, language, ideology-- while he has publicly disavowed any. He knows we are all just human beings, but

ones were the God-fearing atheist men, pro-social and anti-misogyny, who could suddenly violate any law, *commit any act*, if they thought they were acting not on their own desire but on the desire of the woman. They were, in essence, poor judges of human desire; they were told to listen to the words, not the woman. The result, unexpected but perfectly foreseeable: they stopped listening to women.

Relax your jaw, you'll save on ibuprofen and mouth guards. I'm not arguing this is how things should be, only explaining how things came to be. Did you read those sentences and infer, "women are sometimes ambivalent, and men have to respect that?" But I don't know if women are ambivalent or not, only that *you* perceive them as ambivalent because *you* can't tell

---

individuals are not all the same, equality of outcome is always going to be impossible, we each just have to work hard, do our best. Not everybody can be an NBA player or an opera singer, or even a lawyer or a teacher.

And boy oh boy is he is wise to the media gimmick. From time to time our media show, for the edification of the American philistine, the news that from some part of the "underprivileged neighborhood" a black man has become a lawyer, a teacher, a pastor, even an opera singer. He stares at the bourgeois blockheads on TV that say how marvelous are the achievements of our modern educational system, and because he is informed he recognizes this as a socialist manipulation to support the theory with which "they" infect the public: that all men are created equal. He knows that what they report is a crime against reason itself, that it is an act of criminal insanity to preferentially train someone who is barely an anthropoid by birth until the pretense can be made that he has been turned into a lawyer; while, on the other hand, millions of intelligent people are stuck in positions which are unworthy of their intellect. He realizes that it is a sin against reason to allow hundreds of thousands of highly intelligent individuals to remain floundering in the swamp of misery while former criminals are recruited to fill positions in the intellectual professions. If the same amount of care and effort were devoted to intelligent individuals you'd get people a thousand times more capable.

But who supports him? No one. And so "us vs. them" becomes "me vs. Them," and me feels outnumbered. You is, they is only one of you. Thank God for the internet.

You will no doubt counter that he doesn't recognize his privilege: that however much he doesn't think he benefits, the society is designed for him; not only does he have the structural support to pursue what he wants, but more insidiously, oppressed groups are even taught *to want* like him, e.g. and NB, the black guy he still doesn't respect became an opera singer, he was praised for that choice. These are all excellent rebuttals you learned online, too bad: this is exactly what he says about the other groups. That's the point. You'll argue that his privilege is a fact while "yours" is his projection, but neither of you will break character if the food runs start. Both of you think the other has artificially manipulated what should be a natural process based on merit. Both of you see the other as the problem not because they are inferior, but because they found a way to game the system, to cheat normal Darwinian capitalist functioning, and you think this even if you don't like capitalism or Darwin. Turns out you think like the racist you hate, which makes sense because you had the same teacher.

One of the worst book to give kids or their parents or their teachers after *The Giving Tree* is *The Boy In The Striped Pyjamas*, a lactulose and toxoplasmosis emetic about a Nazi officer's family moving to Auschwitz where the father just got the job as the new commandant. Their son, age 9, like no other 9 year old anywhere ever, has no idea what's going on around him: he thinks the bald kid in the zebra Garanimals on the other side of the fence is fun to hang out with and likes sandwiches. They become BFFs. Oblivious, melodramatic, brotherhood of manipulated nonsense occurs, with the conceit that the reader (also aged 9, but American) is sophisticated enough to understand the red pill reality of Auschwitz beneath the boys' blue pill world of "Outwith." Eventually the Nazi boy--

what they want. So intolerant of ambiguity are you that it is enough to know women are ambivalent *or* are not ambivalent-- knowing facts about them relieves the tremendous anxiety that comes from having to act.

Girlfriends are too close to home, so let's practice on the future: when you give your daughter the talk about how all guys are scum-- you'll think you're being proactive, wise, in explaining to her that when a guy approaches her in a meat market all he sees are cans, but what she will hear you say is this: "honey, given all I know about you, and it's pretty much more than anyone else in the world knows about you, yeah: they only want one thing from you." Do you think this will make her understate her sex? No wonder she's so quick to put her best foot forward (in the right pair of shoes).

---

do I call him a Nazi?-- sneaks into the camp to be with his clueless friend, and they accidentally find themselves ushered into a crowded room that keeps colds away. Get it? He is never seen again. Neither is the Jewish kid, but whatever.

That the Jewish kid doesn't completely know what's going on is preposterous, but maybe this is a call back to *Life Is Beautiful*, in which a Jewish father protects his son by telling him that life in the camp is all just a game. Ok, fine, nowadays victims can take decades to realize they were victimized, but why doesn't the *Nazi* boy know what's going on? Is he retarded? The book's answer is that his Nazi parents don't tell him, to "protect his innocence"-- *as if even the Nazis knew what they were doing was horrible*. But the book's logic makes no sense, it reinforces the simplistic, conventional wisdom that the Nazis were killing Jews simply because they were inferior and makes it harder for the reader to understand the existential ferocity with which the Nazis pursued their goals and the Holocaust. The father is a real deal Nazi; the "Fury" and his hyperblonde personally invite themselves over to dinner at his house to ask him to take over Auschwitz to increase "efficiency"; even if he-- well, his wife, hold that thought-- hates living in Poland (Auschwitz is in Poland, hold that thought, too), he's all for the "possibilities" that the gas chambers promise; the only thing he would think he needed to protect his son from is *Jews*. The Dad might not let him see the bodies *yet*, but for sure he would at least explain that anthropoid parasites are being fumigated on the other side of that fence, don't go in without a mask. In other words, the Nazi child dies because he is illogically excluded from a core truth which for Nazis grounds their whole existence, a truth more important than *Germany*, such that they ramp up the Holocaust when they are losing the war. *They think it is their gift to the world.*

My truly tasteless joke that the 9 year old Nazi boy suffers from some kind of pervasive developmental delay is both a joke and completely accurate. He's stupid. The family moves from Berlin to Poland. And right away, he's lost. Ok, by analogy imagine some Texans have never heard of Mexico, donde estamos? So he and his older sister wrack their brains trying to figure out where the hell they are that has these strange modern buildings, and what they come up with is that this must be the weird place they learned about *in school*, and you're definitely going to want to sit down for this: "the countryside." I'm not making this up. I can see you think I'm making it up.

> [His sister] stood still for a long time staring at them. She was 12 years old and considered to be one of the brightest girls in her class, so she squeezed her lips together and narrowed her eyes and forced her brain to understand what she was looking at. Finally she could think of only one explanation.
>
> "This must be the countryside," said Gretel, turning her head to look at her brother triumphantly.
>
> "The countryside?"
>
> "Yes, it's the only explanation..."

"But that *is* all men see in the supermarket!" So what? Are you worried that your daughter is so stupid she'll fall for it? She's so hungry for attention she'll blow him for the compliment? NB both of those things are comments on how you raised her, which is predictably badly. Do you really believe telling her about men will keep her away from men? Or---- are you changing the context of their desire, robbing her of the flattery implied in the approach? So that now she disbelieves her very own eyes and ears-- not that people don't like her-- *but that anything anyone likes her for shouldn't count.*

"How did you know they weren't serial killers?" he asks, which is the same question as, "why did you believe they were casting agents? How did you know what they said about

---

This goes on for another two pages, which drains their glycogen so they lick a giant lollipop and take a nappy nap. The kind of audience that would find this believable is the kind of audience who would also think what the kid is wearing is striped pajamas, i.e. dolts, which I guess explains why the publisher thought it was prudent to change the title from *Pyjamas* to *Pajamas*, as if this audience would be confused by a word they've never seen in print or real life anyway. The moderate to severe intellectual disability evident in the Nazi officer's son is supposed to stand as a proxy for his innocence, but what you should consider is the unintended reveal that the only way to make him believably innocent is to make him an *imbecile*. He even physically appears... innocent: for no reason at all except the return of the repressed the book describes the kid as not only 9, but small for a 9 year old, so small that others mistake him for 6, and he could not convince them otherwise.

At this point it will seem off topic but just remember the rhythm of the words: *Life Is Beautiful* is hopeful not because it ends with the boy's survival but because it *begins* as a love story between the boy's *parents*; meanwhile, not only do the Nazi parents not love each other, there is no love depicted at all anywhere in *The Boy In The Striped Pyjamas* unless... well, spoiler.

If *The Boy In The Striped Pyjamas* was just a book that sold a few million copies worldwide it wouldn't be worth reading, let alone discussing, except that modern adults wouldn't expect a 9 year old reader today to have any understanding of the Holocaust-- "Outwith" and "Auschwitz" are equally empty signifiers-- *unless we were going to use this book to explain it to them*. So this book represents the new way we want to teach kids to think about the Holocaust, which is why this is worth discussing here, in a book about pornography: it is pornography.

In the old days you taught kids the Holocaust separately from WWII because of the enormity of its reality, but now that the survivors are all dead and the Holocaust less real, it still has to be separated because it doesn't fit with what we now want to teach about WWII and wars in general: that they are ultimately over economic issues. Troublingly, the actual Holocaust, and modern genocides that regularly recur despite the promise of increased connectedness in our global village, can't really be explained by economics, so these exceptions are carved off and explained as having religious or racial "root" causes. I put "root" in quotes because while it gets us out of having to explain why a particular genocide isn't economics like everything else is supposed to be, we all "know" that religious/racial conflicts *in general* are-- surprise-- "really" about economics. And so on down the line, you get to class struggle without ever having to identify or justify whether it is class struggle. The idea of class struggle replacing fear/honor/interest as history's universal motivator didn't take off until the 19th century, and so either you believe someone figured out something truly novel about human nature, or someone discovered a much needed defense against human nature. "Yes, yes, it's really about exploitation of labor!" You can imagine how bad the alternatives were.

Anyway, here's why *The Boy In The Striped Pyjamas* is child pornography: obviously, a story about a retarded German boy getting caught up in his Dad's death chamber is a way to show the evils of racism. But why do we need to empathize through his death-- isn't the Jewish boy also innocent and a boy in exactly the same way? So the popularity of this book, far from signaling some collective agreement about the evils of racism, proves that we only object to the *violence*, the acting on it,

203

themselves was true?" -- They told me. "But they could have been lying just to get you naked!" Because if they had actually been casting agents-- then she really would have had no choice. Impulsive, compelled, or for some other reason-- anything, other than desire.

You can say this knowledge is manipulative or invalid, but take note of its form: they are offered as if they were gifts of his experience and wisdom, of love, but because of his ledger these "gifts of himself" are actually a kind of negative reinforcement. He gives gifts of himself not because he wants to be the only one who truly loves her, but so that he can be the only person who truly loves her *and then renders it insufficient*. The purpose of these gifts of oneself is to keep the other person interested=unsatisfied enough not to abandon the other.

---

while our own racism is still quietly permitted but disavowed.

But we could be more psychological about this, and ask not why we need to empathize through the Nazi boy, but why it's *easier* to empathize through the Nazi boy *even if you're Jewish*. And the obvious answer is: the racism is a ruse, it really is simply a cover for class struggle. You can't empathize with the Jewish boy even if you actually are Jewish because, see, your *class* more closely matches the Nazi's class, which is why it is so easy to be drawn in with an "innocent" bourgeois Nazi boy's death. Our class identification is so innately biological that it trumps race or religion; it's easier to find kinship with a "good", class-equivalent Nazi, e.g. *Schindler's List*. But that's a trick, the identification is a cover for projection: the reason we empathize better with the bourgeoise Nazi boy is not because he matches our class better but in order to make the *other* Nazis different from us, to push them out of our own class and into a higher class. Real Nazis were all hyper-rich BDSM industrialists, not-- retarded 9 year olds or civil servants. Class struggle is detected to be the problem, so it can be used as the defense.

The real question is why anyone assumes we need a new way to teach that Nazis were bad. What for? Who is still confused on this issue? "Tomorrow's test will be on things my grandparents were wrong about." Phew, as long as it's not math. Everyone knows the Nazis were evil, it's an axiom, a cliché, they were the bad guys in two *X-Men* movies (though audiences did manage to completely ignore the parallel they represented.) You're going to tell me there are plenty of people who think the Nazis *aren't* evil, but at least concede they are not going to read, let alone be persuaded, by any book that isn't a video. Empathizing with (=through) the Nazi boy doesn't get us anything new-- it only gets us out of something. The key to the popularity of the book among adults-- and why it such a terrible way of teaching kids about the Holocaust, and why it therefore will be the only way we teach them-- isn't whose death the reader empathizes with but what the book gets people to do next, you should write this down, every time you see it, you should write it down: nothing.

The desire the book serves, what the adult audience wants, is *not to act*. The boy's death at the end, and the last chapter about the father's grief while his wife goes back to Berlin, relieves the reader from having to think about what the reader should do. *The Nazis get what they deserve*. "Everyone suffers", "the cost of war is too high." This sounds a lot like a revenge fantasy but when the story flows without conscious action it's a fairy tale. The child reader is praised by a self-praising adult for learning that belief in racial superiority is bad, and directed away from the question of what next-- what to do about it? It presents the *collateral* damage of the Holocaust as so tragic that one hopes--- what? That no one reading *The Boy In The Striped Pyjamas* will start a genocide? But what about the *inevitable* scenario that a genocide is started by someone else? What have the kids been taught to do-- shake their heads in satiated self-awareness and look for economic causes? "I cried so hard when they died." You're triggered because you care. No, let's all sit together in a circle and support each other, we're going to skip math today.

The book is a tragedy. Literally. The point is catharsis, the readers aren't meant to imagine what they w/should do, tragedy is a *political* art, it's purpose is not individual elevation but cultivation of nature by human art for a definite purpose; it is how to serve the group; it isn't "there but for the

It's not just the physical abandonment but the ledger imbalance the abandonment would imply: after all I've given you, you're leaving? "Well, who would want you now? You have nothing of value left." Sound familiar? It shouldn't: take a look back at Shel Silverstein's 60s storyboard, *The Giving Tree*. Here's an invalid but reliable statistical observation: if you sell 7 million copies of a book with a positive message and it doesn't make people live the message, then they didn't get that message. What they did get was a very strong defense against the actual message, see also The Gospel of Mark.

It's universally agreed that the *The Giving Tree* tree represents a mother. This is a very odd association to make, because it's clearly not a mother, it's a tree, if it was a mother than the boy would be a sapling. "It's literally a tree, but the tree is a metaphor." Obviously it's a

---

grace of God go I" and certainly never "if that were me, I'd..." but about training the audience of prospective citizens how to feel and think by pairing context to emotions, or erections, depending on need. When you hear that a "bad" melodrama is "so clearly manipulative" you should understand that what the audience objects to is the clearly, not the manipulative. They want to feel knowledgeable, but they want to be lead. Which makes it very important that kids are taught to want that too, hence this book is in a long list of correctives to the "racist white males" canon, there's no social justice message in *Macbeth* and it's offensive to witches ("Art thou women? I would call thee so, but thy beards forbid it"-- Ha! Funny as ever); even the title is dripping with hereditary patriarchy-- never mind the play is about the exact opposite and the wife is the only one who acts-- so it got replaced with *Secret Life Of Bees*, a pro-witches coloring book so egregiously racist that only a white mom could love it. Aspiring sell outs: if you want to guarantee your book gets excerpted into *The New Yorker* and/or inserted into the middle school English curriculum, make sure it contains a scene where some 12yo white daughter is crying near some 60yo black grandmother who then gathers her up with her calloused hands into the safety of her nurturing bosom and says, "hush, child." In fact, make *Hush, Child* the title. What does such a book inspire kids to do, other than watch the movie instead? *The Diary of Anne Frank* is not pornography because the reader is implicitly prompted to participate-- to act-------------- to fantasize action. Even if an 11 year old reading it fantasizes acting out *The Legends Of Chima* to save her, good for him, it may be derivative and implausible but all our fantasies are; the way you practice these derivatives-- remember playing?-- decides the kind of person you'll *want* to be, and-- I can't believe I'm about to say this-- wanting to be someone you're not is better than wanting someone else to be it. The growth is in the fantasy, the payoff is in the fantasy. Who cares what it means? The point is what you do with it, and what you did with this book was nothing. Not even fantasize. It got you out of fantasizing.

If adults want to masturbate to this book, well, your porn is your own business, but for a society to short circuit a child's fantasies of action-- of *heroism*-- seems contrary to the instruction of children but I'm no paideiagogue. "We have structural problems that require political solutions, we don't need heroes anymore, there are no 'bad guys'." Except for Nazis, of course, and anyone who fought for or against the Nazis, or was alive in the 40s, or can count to 40, or likes numbers. So you're telling me that except for the half of the US that you're sure are SS, in three generations you've managed to eradicate all human evil, using nothing more than consumer technology and secondary sources? "We need to work together to overcome the real problems of society." We?? I'm sorry, could you take your hand out of your pants, it's hard to take you seriously-- we????

No doubt you've heard how much it is a comment on "human nature" that during the War very few did anything to help their Jewish neighbors, no one protested or declared it was wrong; and no doubt you've also heard that the sad reality is that if it were to happen again probably none of us would do anything to help them, such is the "nature of group dynamics". Well, you've heard both of these from the same people. Both of those may be true, but the point is that it's both of those that are stressed, both simultaneously. When you hear this simultaneity come out of someone's mouth, you should brace yourself: you're about to hear that the only solution for the innate inability to act due to

metaphor, what I want to know is why you chose the wrong one. The boy is a biped and has a human girlfriend; the fact that the story requires organisms from two different kingdoms not only complicates the possibility it represents a mother, it requires the reader to force the interpretation on the book, to "do violence to the text". You know, like rape.

Why do you think it's a mother? It gives and gives and gives and asks nothing in return, but that's not what defines "a mother", that's how your mother defines herself. In fact, the fundamental characteristic that would make it a "mother" is explicitly absent from the story, and that's responsibility to the boy. The Tree has none. It may be nice to him, it may sometimes let him win at hide and seek, it may give him a boat, but it doesn't have to punish

---

group dynamics is... some other omnipotent entity who can act for the group. But certainly, no adolescent fantasies of individual action, no *Iliad* under your pillow, just watch it unfold on TV and tell yourself your responsibility is to be informed.

"Adolescent fantasy doesn't get us very far." Boy oh boy do I agree. So imagine how far we'd get without it. "Realistically, a lot of things in life are out of our control." Like becoming a Nazi? You're enraged at the system because it is so powerful it won't let you have a job you don't want but no way are you subject to the structural forces that got 9M generally better educated people to sign up for fascism?

For those who have turned the Holocaust into a superego comparator for their own performance of loving morality, then action is decidedly not the point, no matter how much they say it is. Rape "awareness" is the same, men shouldn't rape, short skirts don't cause rape, rape is about power, blah blah blah. So what? So if you don't rape, you can take credit for having learned all those lessons? How does this stop rape? You seriously think you're convincing someone else not to rape? Interesting that no one ever drills people on what to do when they see someone else get raped. "I could see his victim was blackout drunk, and she appeared to be naked, but I got confused because I couldn't tell if there were economic causes."

The theory of group dynamics influenced inaction-- and the otherwise paradoxical solution of strong state power as a proxy for collective action-- isn't a discovery about human nature, it is a defense against our current nature. We aren't afraid to act on our own; a strong state doesn't make it easier to act against evil-- it's the other way around. We can't act because we *want* to be lead. We don't wish some power existed so that we could stop acting; we don't act *in order to cause to exist* some other omnipotent entity. We create the vacuum. Hopefully something will rush in to fill it.

Here you might assume it is because we are sheep, but at least you can eat sheep. Our fear doesn't drive us to wish for some omnipotent power to exist to protect us. "To protect us" is more cover. We don't believe we have any meaningful power. But the only thing we are capable of enjoying when we lack the power to do any of the everythings which are promised as possible is to steal from the powerful. *Therefore* someone has to be given all the power.

This is the ledger. The theft is called compensation but it is felt as satisfaction. And that feels way better than power.

"You have a very, very bleak view of human nature." I don't look for economic causes, I look for madness, and I see it everywhere. Some of you are unlucky enough to have too much power and you'll find it hard to enjoy anything but work, maybe you can get some plus sized dominatrix to leather up and stand on your face, it'll feel so good to underpay her later. "I'm sorry, I really believe we are inherently good." Not good, *better*: you think you're better than everyone because you don't think you're better than anyone, unless it's better than Nazis, because they thought they were better than everyone. Which they didn't. That makes you a Nazi.

This is the other trick of the book, and it is completely unintentional but nevertheless it is there in

him, it doesn't have to protect him, it doesn't have to worry about teaching him to swim or warning against gold digging hippies, it doesn't have to make him sad/angry/scared for his own good. "I just want him to be happy." That's it? The Tree isn't his mother. At best, it's his godmother. Uh oh.

So the question you have to ask your pop rocks and triple cola conscience is not why you thought it was a mother, but why you wanted it to be a mother. "Because it acts selflessly out of love?" Boy oh boy are you way off.

The trick to what the demographic wants, and this may sound familiar, is that while it doesn't believe in "true love" between two people, it doesn't believe in true love of a parent for

---

black and white. Question: why is the book set at Auschwitz? Auschwitz is the obvious symbol of the evil of the Holocaust, but it's only obvious because we've heard the stories from the survivors; but we've heard the stories of the survivors because they survived. Auschwitz was a *concentration* camp-- there was there, inherently, a chance.

Before your idiocy is inflamed you should understand that the "chance" here isn't the chance a Jew could do something to survive. No one in the book's demographic cares about Jews. AT ALL. Auschwitz as the *publicized,* default, symbol of the Holocaust allows for the chance that *Germans* were not fully aware of the extent of what was going on, that Germans thought Jews were being concentrated, not being killed. In the book, such a person is the commandant's wife. Of course she's anti-Jew but she doesn't want the details, she doesn't want to be part of the nitty gritty, she disavows all of it. "She's not an idiot, what does she think is going on at Auschwitz?" She is an idiot, and she thinks it's a concentration camp. You know what that is, right?

Imagine that the author had chosen to use a different camp which the kids called "Ball Sack." See? It still works, and now you have something for the retarded boy to giggle at. But in a camp with zero exits, there is no way for the wife to disavow what happens there, and the ending-- she leaves the Nazi husband with all the guilt-- would fail.

The symbols are chosen not because they best convey the truth but because the symbolism allows for loopholes. Auschwitz as symbol makes you think you know, so there's no need to act. "Only someone who considered Jews inferior could build gas chambers, and I don't think they're inferior. So I'm good." But as much as the ovens sound like the monstrous perversity of a sadist's depraved sexual fantasies, it was only a contingent step improvised from facts on the ground. Nor was it German industrial efficiency as the book portrays, but the opposite; the better metaphor is American ingenuity and adaptability.

The question the reader should be lead to ask is the one that asks him to be an adult: why did they build the camp in Poland? The simple answer, "that's where all the Jews were," isn't sufficient, there had been plenty of Jews 300 miles to the left as well, walking around downtown Berlin like they owned the place. The banal, stupid, history changing reason the death camps were in Poland and not in Germany was because-- tell me if Western Civ sounds oppressive to you now-- *German law wouldn't have allowed it.*

The evolution of the Jewish problem in Germany is never explained well, on purpose, because the lesson that they want to teach is that racial hatred is the *root* problem, but in this way the kid doesn't consider how he becomes complicit because his hatred is not explicit, how people without fanatical racism might actually support a genocide, which is the very lesson we need to learn from the Holocaust. The persecution of the Jews in Germany from 1933-1939 was not intended to kill them at all, but to make them leave; even the Jews that were sent to concentration camps from Germany during that time would be released if they promised to emigrate. The original fantasy was to deport them all to Madagascar or Uganda, laugh if you want, but it was enough that they simply left Germany *and had their own territory.* To literally *ground* them.

a child *either*. Parental love can't be true love because it is definitional, obligatory, and therefore it doesn't count. What the demo believes in, what it aspires to, is unconditional love *chosen by free will*-- that can be witnessed and confirmed by other people *as* an act of free will. To the demo, rather than the symbolic obligation being both the requirement for love and its justification, the symbolic obligation negates it. This is the form of love you and the other adult readers are capable of-- of imagining. That's why it's a tree. Since there's no cultural or even biological responsibility to love this boy, then this love is (depicted as) real love.

The desire to display gigawatt devotion with zero responsibility is the standard maneuver of our times, note the trend of celebrity soundbite social justice, or children's fascination with doing the extra credit more than the regular credit, and as a personal observation this is

---

What changed after 1939 and then 1941 wasn't the German's level of racial hatred but the bureaucracy-- their ability to act, and everyone else's desire not to be responsible for acting. Taking a cue from Stalin, yeah, I said it, as the army went east it became easier to shoot Jews where they stood than deport them to Africa. Next it became easier to ship them all to camps rather than shoot them where they stood, which is really quite the calculation when you consider it how easy it was to shoot a million of them where they stood. At first, no one even seriously considered the killing of German Jews because German Jews were German citizens; but once Poland was conquered Polish Jews were no longer Polish but only Jews, so the camps logically got placed in the geopolitical netherworld of Das Countryside. This was a logic of improvisation, not some decades old master plan. There's a key passage in the book that is absolutely lost as a teaching point: the Jewish boy explains he had a nice home, but one day is told he has to wear an arm band with the Star. Later on, he's forced out of his home, moved across town and walled off in a ghetto. Later on, he was on a train to Auschwitz. Etc. Ok, here's the thing they don't tell you: at the time of the arm band, not even The Fury was blueprinting gas chambers. Yet regular people who certainly never considered killing anyone easily became a part of an unplanned massive racial genocide in a matter of *months*. Turns out identity is indeed a fluid construct. "Today, I am a racialist!"

So the question is: why did the Jews need to be deported in the very first place, such that killing them was the *next* best thing? *What was the problem with Jews?*

Yes, there is a long history of anti-semitism, from impotent slaves to Christ-killers, from disease carriers to mercantilists, but the pajama answer is Hitler was orchestrating a race war and thought the Jews were an inferior race. And this allows you to dismiss him as wrong and pat yourself on the back for knowing better. But there were lots of inferior races Hitler didn't deport let alone gas. Jews aren't *a* problem, Jews are *the* problem, and the problem they are is unintentionally the very plot of the book: they *cause to exist* inter-racial cooperation, using the Jewish inventions of science and monotheism, Marxism and capitalism, philosophy and pornography-- the simultaneous deployment of contradictory ideologies that couldn't possibly be linked but suddenly make sense if they are seen as tools of a larger Jewish plan of global domination, which rather than actualizing at some point after 6000 years prefer to submit to generalized anti-semitism and the occasional diaspora or genocide. "It's all part of their plan because--!" Ok, got it. That's why they have to go, not because they're "inferior". Hitler's logic was very persuasive to a people looking to explain not their economic predicament but their rage, the incompatibility between the *necessity to compete* with their neighbor and the *obligation to love* them-- especially since the neighbor doesn't seem similarly obligated-- and it is so seductive a logic I hesitate to explain it here because some of you will pull a sharp pencil from behind your ear and a ledger from out your butt, but here goes: we are in nature, we evolved according to natural laws, we exist inside the logic of competition for finite resources, the logic of natural struggle. Races, like species, naturally compete-- and not intra-species capitalist competition, that's a Jewish trick, but interspecies struggle: the tigers have to clear out the elephants who are eating up all the trees the tigers need to jump onto antelopes. (Ok, I'm not a zoologist.) And if some if some frog comes along and says there's plenty of trees for everyone, and we should only be eating trees anyway, you can be sure he's Jewish and what he's really wants

208

exactly what's wrong with the worst medical students and nurses. They'll spend hours talking with a patient about their lives and feelings while fluffing their pillow to cause it to be true that they are devoted-- they chose to act, chose to love-- while acts solely out of ordinary duty are devalued if not completely avoided. "Well I believe the patient's spirituality is very important." It will be if you don't get this NG tube in. You may think you have very valid personal reasons for not wanting to assume responsibility, like apathy or minimum wages, but the overwhelming motivator for devotion by choice is the rewarding reward of giving gifts of oneself, seemingly selflessly, because these publicly "count" more than discharging duty. The retort to this is that often times the selfless acts are done outside of everyone else's sight, so what possible reward could there be? But one doesn't need to be seen by individual people,

---

is to kill tigers. That the Jews want to take over the world is therefore not *bad*, that's their and everyone's natural right, this is totally consistent with the laws of nature. But the Jews are cheating because unlike every other race, they don't operate from territory nor do they even need it: they form states within states, they have no national loyalties. The ingenious trick that they devised was to make their state sail under the flag of 'religion,' thus assuring it of the tolerance which states grant religions, thus affecting almost all sociological, political, and economic fields of knowledge which can have any bearing on their preservation. From the safety of other races' states they invent seemingly incompatible, even contradictory ideas that made races *get along*. Their "inventions" took us out of our state of nature and tricked us into subjecting ourselves to ethical rules instead of engaging in natural racial struggle. These invented rules seem like humanist progress but paralyze a struggling race's power of self-preservation. That has always been their only visible result.

Another example from the 5th grade primer on elementary racism: along with books about pajamas and bees, kids are given *Warriors Don't Cry*, the unpretentious autobiographical account of the Little Rock Nine kids who relucto-heroically were the test cases/human shields for school desegregation/integration. Governor Faubus was a racist and against integration, and tried to block it; but when integration was upheld on multiple appeals he went full suicide vest and shut down the schools, "hell no way are those Negroes getting an education on my watch." Wow. WOW. Ok, I can see this hasn't blown you away, so let me jostle the detonator: the schools he shut down were *white*. He was willing to sacrifice the education of whites to prevent integration. That's where that guy's head was at. We're used to racism going homicidal but when it turns suicidal it might be time to for a shrink. The goal wasn't to keep blacks separate and unequal, he was all in on equal, what mattered to his eyeballs and remaining right ventricle is that they stay separate. Basically, he banned the study of math in order to cancel the prom. Ironically his attempt to keep them from mixing forced little Melba out to California where she eventually married a white guy. That's a plot twist Faubus did not see coming, kind of surprised me, too.

I'm sure he did think they were inferior but that isn't *why* he wanted them separate. It's because they're already separate, a biologically separate species-- except for the fact that they can interbreed, which only proves how unnatural it all is (he's not a zoologist either); but most importantly, when the food runs start, everyone always sticks to their own. He's not a white supremacist but a supreme realist: there is no such thing as surplus value, the food is running out and no amount of GMO will save us, race is the zero-level of any politics, so if the only math you know is arithmetic and there's no homework then a scientific solution can't be imagined, the only solution you can fantasize is a political solution, a giant farm, and an army to back it up. Hitler's solution was conscription and the amber waves of grain of the Ukraine. Off topic, not really: this was Pericles's solution as well.

So rethink Hitler's, and your, racism: Hitler did not think the race wars would end only after he killed all the Jews. He wanted to kill the Jews so that the race wars could *start*.

Hitler believed that the worldwide desire for peace, goodwill and globalism was a sneaky Jewish trick to get you *not* to fight for your own survival. You want to know how sneaky this trick is? *It is exactly what happens in the book*: the Jewish boy, not even consciously, has the power to seduce a

it's enough to imagine being seen by a hypothetical audience.

Speaking of extra credit, if you want a subject that is all extra credit for which you have no choice but to take all the credit for either success or failure, you should look into physics. It is even impossible to cheat, short of seducing the professor you got the grade you got because you deserved it. True story, other than my max deadlift this is my proudest achievement: my post-modern physics class was taught by a Chinese dissident that under Reagan had either been granted asylum or escaped an asylum, and his midterm exam was five problems he had smuggled out of Hubei, the questions were way beyond the range of our illegal stimulants and as was his wont he declared there would be no partial credit. "In future you must specialize, and only will you be rewarded for incision and defection." At least that's what I think he said,

---

"superior" Aryan boy into "friendship"-- and thus kill him, destroy his family, and disrupt a part of the Nazi power. This Jewish kid who doesn't exist even tricked the author who made him up.

So you have a book that is being given to children to teach them how to think about the Holocaust. Please observe the results: anyone who "knows" that the Nazis were evil is even less inclined to act against them; and anyone identifying with Hitler's logic-- i.e. racism without superiority-- feels... less inclined to act against them. Both want a strong state to do "what's necessary." Are the results the same? There's a name for this: propaganda. Please don't yell at me, I mean this absolutely literally. You think propaganda is about getting you to think something, and that's because you think your thoughts are valuable. They're not, no one cares. "It's so important to stay informed, to fact check!" The more informed the opinion is (notice I said "more," not better"), the more susceptible it is to propaganda. The greater a person's knowledge about political and economic facts, the more vulnerable-- particularly if the propaganda employs ambiguity. The reader of a number of different media expressing diverse attitudes-- just because he's better informed-- is more subjected than anyone else to propaganda he doesn't perceive, even though he claims to retain free choice in the understanding of all this information. Actually, he is being conditioned to absorb all the propaganda that coordinates and explains the facts he claims to be mastering. The only purpose of propaganda is to get you to act on its desire, regardless of your justifications, and in this case the propaganda wants you NOT to act-- to give your power to someone else. Hitler was followed not because he had power, he was given the power so that people could just be followers. What was going on was on autopilot; if he succeeded they could passively share the credit for the new empire; if he failed they could publicly accept an utterly purposeless "collective guilt" but assure themselves as individuals they had not acted with him. Fact check: is that what happened?

Of course I do not think the book is deliberately anti-semitic. But it has absorbed to the bone marrow the arsenic propaganda of self-righteousness predicated on *inaction*, that *wants* the existence of some other omnipotent entity to do all the acting; this propaganda serves a State that monopolizes power and placates us with knowledge. I am not repeating the common criticism that the State is becoming more authoritarian; quite the opposite, *I am saying it is becoming less so, and we hate it.* Even those who want it to be "liberally progressive" want it to be more powerfully so, to tell us-- well, the intemperate, uncultivated, ungenerous, unjust men, the men who don't think-- what is right and wrong, what's expected of them. This wish can only exist when centralized power is declining, when power and responsibility is shifting *back* to you-- so you frantically push back, give away all your power hoping *therefore* something will amass it. Something will. The propaganda is *yours*, on behalf of the future State, it wishes for one. *The Nazis get what they deserve* = I wish some other omnipotent entity could act= can we have a benevolent national socialism, but, you know, without all the SS? And yet the SS was the arm of the party, so no. The popular thing nowadays is to call an opponent a fascist, and then the opponent gets to say you don't really know what fascism is, and all of that is good for laughs but according to the primary source, fascism exists as a response to socialism, the *logical* antithesis to socialism; and in Germany they called themselves both. I think that's some kind of dialectic. Here's a stat that the teacher isn't going to teach you: more people became anti-semitic because they joined the Nazi Party than joined the Nazi

I skipped a lot of lectures, 8am is a weird time to demand excellence or recruit for the NSA. Yeah, I saw you. Anyway, I got the highest grade in the class. It was a 30.

That test taught me an important life lesson that I have failed to teach anyone else the second half of: in order to succeed in life, you don't have to be any good, you just have to be the best. But being the best does not entitle you to believe you are any good.

You might be wondering how I got a 30 when there was no partial credit, and this brings me to an even more important life lesson. In the last ten minutes of the test, I wasn't satisfied with how I solved one of the problems even though it got me to the correct answer, so I crossed it out and on the back in a burst of manic inspiration I provided the more rigorous solution. I felt enormously proud of myself. Well, he took ten points off anyway because I had done it wrong first. Yeah. Here's the life lesson he wrote on the bottom: *The crew is dead. What good are your revisions?*

The entire childish fantasy of "motherly love" collapses the moment obligation enters into it, which is why, in *The Giving Tree*, it never does, and this is why so many remain deeply attached to it as a mother figure. It doesn't represent a mother-- the wish is that it could. Tree-mothers will do anything to convey devotion and "love"-- because there is no obligation to do it. They are willing to sacrifice, to give of themselves, to convey the appearance of suffering and sacrifice *even by actually suffering and sacrificing*-- they'll cut off their own arms to prove it, in order to assure themselves and a love object too guilty to be suspicious that they do it all out of willful, chosen love. "I love!" But can you help me with my math homework? No? Fine, I'll just go back to wetting the bed and playing with matches. The desire for it to be a mother also satisfies within the adult reader the childish desire to be special: if only my mother did these things for me because she loved *me* and not because she had to-- not because

---

Party because they were anti-semitic. And it took almost no time at all. Hate isn't natural. But boy oh boy is it satisfying.

And even if we don't get a centralized power, we will at least get an uncentralized power, it doesn't matter, they are the same. It only matters that the power isn't with us, and it is omnipotent. I'm sure the next book the kids will have to read is *1984* because "it's so relevant to what's happening today." Certainly gets you out of reading the book that is relevant to today, which is *Brave New World*. "But Big Brother controls information!!!!!!!!!" Yes, that would be the one thing that upsets you. But the one thing about *1984* that should truly terrify is fortunately not considered important enough to teach: Big Brother doesn't exist, but you will obey anyway.

When someone says that "some of what Hitler said makes some sense, on some level" the general hedge is that the flaw was his belief in racial superiority. But that isn't the flaw, this was not the postulate of his logic. His nationalism, his Aryanism, his racism, was the zeal of a convert, and everyone else converted, just as you will, do you remember why? Because zeal means to emulate. I know, you're informed, you focus on facts, you aren't fooled by ideology. That's Hitler's ideology. Nothing abstract is permitted, no philosophy, no axiomatic values, it is ruthlessly material, concrete, appealing to the obsessive idiot that sees through ideology and "only" sees reality; this person wants many things but would really only be satisfied with depriving the other. The chief-- the only-- difference between you and Hitler is that he acted. He *could* act. Hitler didn't seize power from the powerless people. They didn't want power because it didn't seem powerful, they gave up their power, and watched pragmatically as Hitler had others pick it up off the streets for him. This is the practical problem with giving up power wishing that someone would amass it: you can't then control who will amass it. But you will look for economic causes as you follow it to the end.

she would have been similarly obligated to any of her meiotic anomalies. Because then it would count.

Why would Tree-mothers so reliably avoid acting out of responsibility, but might perform the very same acts out of "love"? Why is this kind of mothering so aspirational, celebrated? What's so bad about obligation that it needs to shrouded in "love", or outright resisted? Because obligatory mothering means you matter less than your replacement, no thanks, my place in the world is unique. And the uniqueness is signaled by regular, public gifts of themselves, not public in the studio audience sense, but public in the storyboard sense, the potentiality of an audience that doesn't need to exist. "I've sacrificed so much to give you a boat." But shouldn't you teach me to boat so I can boat for a lifetime? No? That's Dad's job? Got it.

Your desire to be a selfless godmother *may* imply you're a bad person, but it doesn't automatically mean it's bad for the kid, he still gets a boat, right? Can't self-interest result in positive outcomes for others? Yes, but this isn't self-interest, it is self-definition, it is *relative* to the outcomes of others. In other words, there's a ledger that needs to be balanced, and the kid is going to pay eventually. The apparent selfless devotion perversely/purposefully obligates the child to them-- it causes there to be a debt owed back to the parent which should not exist: the child perceives the existence of such an unpaid debt and thus believes his guilt is warranted. This is the guilt that the adult reader misinterprets as "nostalgia" or "poignancy". This is entirely separate from the complex duty an adult child owes their parents, which many avoid anyway; this is an unrepayable debt that keeps the child indebted to the parent-- in this way precluding the possibility that the child can mature into their replacement, or at all.

The Giving Tree is an anagram for *I Get Even, Right?* That's a solid example of the return of the repressed assuming it wasn't on purpose. So the boy rebels, becomes selfish, he grows up and appears not notice or not to *care* that he's hurting the Tree; but this is inaccurate, his destructive actions should be seen as a *response* to this debt, to the unfillable gap constituted by the symbolic debt against which his neurosis is a protest.

Not everyone likes the story. There have been a lot of ferocious criticisms of its "theme". The question is, what is the outcome of these criticisms? Do the criticisms offer an alternative understanding, or do they pretend to criticize in order to maintain the status quo? A popular criticism, heavy with contempt and thus conveniently dismissed as misogyny, is that the Tree "mothered" him too much and failed to foster independence in the child. While this may be factually accurate, it's even more wrong, it's the kind of insight that gets you out of having to go any further, it ends your connection to the story-- you are done with the book. The criticism that the Tree fails to foster independence presumes it is *supposed* to do this. But that's not its job. It's his actual mother's job, it's his father's job. Based on how this little rat turns out it's clear they failed, but that's a totally different book, and it's called *Oedipus Tyrannos*. The critics say the Tree failed as a mother because they *want* teaching independence to be the metric of motherhood; but as they are misogynists their true target for redefinition is fatherhood. No one criticized the Tree for failing to teach the boy math, or for self-cutting to guilt him into a debt, its one celebrated failure was not teaching him independence, which, you will observe, is way easier than teaching him math. Consequently it is correct to say that the criticisms of the book pose no threat to the underlying psychology which both haters and admirers share, their ends are the same, both pro and con have succeeded in reprioritizing the myriad defining responsibilities of a parent for the modern age, here are they are in full, in order of importance: 1. Foster independence. 2. Other stuff.

Asserting parenting's main job as fostering independence is not merely self-serving, it's bad for the kid, and it's probably correct to say that in modern times we have completely accidentally but nevertheless excessively fostered independence, to the point that dependence of any kind is seen as a moral catastrophe, or at least an easy target for self-righteous indignation. Of course the independence that's fostered isn't real independence, it's green screen individualism, all the dependencies are disavowed or at least fetishized with money; even the money gets fetishized into credit so he doesn't even have to see he needs money, the credit card lets him believe he is his own man; and it only makes jarring the instances where independence is utterly impossible, e.g. medical illness or falling in love. We'll tolerate a certain amount of material dependence because it doesn't count, but no way is anyone going to allow an emotional = "pathological" dependence on the other.

"But isn't pathological dependence just borderline personality disorder?" Border between-- what and what? The question you asked about their pathology is a symptom of your pathology. You want the borderline's pathology to be their pathological over-dependence on the other because you don't want it to be the characteristic that you both share, which is the absence of interest in whether the other can depend on you. The crucial distinction is that while neither of you are dependable, the borderline wants to be seen as dependent and as not dependable; while you want to be seen as not dependent but as dependable. The borderline may be more thirsty, but it's still a babbling brook for both of you: can't live without it, derive no real enjoyment out of it, can't tell it apart from any other water and often pee in it. The water gets nothing in return from either of you.

If you accept that the boy has an actual biological mother, never seen in the story because the need for her is repressed and thus of no interest to the childish reader, then something else becomes true and changes the genre from kiddie porn to Lovecraftian horror: the man doesn't keep coming back to the Tree, the man keeps coming home to his actual mother. The Tree is outside waiting for him.

But the claim that the tree fails to foster independence turns out to be literally incorrect, a defense in the form of a criticism. The last sentence of the story is, "And the tree was happy." Why is she happy? Because the old man has wasted his life and came back to her?

The tree doesn't fail to foster independence; it actively thwarts the child's independence at every turn. This may seem hard to believe, she did give him her trunk so he can heed the call of Manifest Destiny, but unless you're going to chop it up and Huck Finn the pieces into a raft that trunk isn't going to carry anything away but your optimism. And who taught you to use an axe, your mom? Don't dismiss the giving of the boat as a contrivance solely for the purpose of furthering the plot, because the contrivance is what the passive agent uses to cause the active agent to act on her desires. She offered first her apples which were useful and then the wood which she knows is not useful. But instead of first offering the apples and then referring him to the 2 ton cedar trees in the next forest or at the very least a boat maker, she offers him what couldn't possibly satisfy him. "I hope the scent reminds you of me!" You know he'll be back in a week, when was he going to forget?

The tree isn't giving "of itself" because it has nothing else to offer, it is giving of itself because it doesn't want the boy to want anything else. But this selfishness is totally opposed to how the Tree views itself-- a kind, loving, giving Tree-- so it is necessary to disavow this. To hide that thought from herself-- not the boy, but herself-- she is willing to chop parts of her body off for him, as long as those parts don't do him any good. The magnitude of the sacrifice is illusory even if it fools other people as well, it looks huge to the outside, which is why that part was chosen for sacrifice-- but it is of only passing value to the boy. The sacrifice hides to herself her attempts to keep the boy unsatisfied, wanting more. The last page of the book shows the man come full circle, sitting on the stump. "And the tree was happy." Which was the whole point.

In other words, the Giving Tree is a giant cunt. Take it easy, that's not me saying it, that's Silverstein: in a later comic, he drew a picture of a man approaching a cave that looks like a the top part of the Giving Tree and all of a 60s mom's vagina, I'll wait, and the guy goes in but doesn't come out. The title of the comic is "And He Was Never Heard From Again." Well I have a question: is the cave happy? Anybody want to tell me why?

It's important to ask: if the Tree's target is the boy, even into adulthood, why does it continue to position itself as a mother-- instead of as one of the historically reliable poses for manipulating adult men such as a wife, lover, or damsel in distress?

Because she doesn't know what he wants. The only thing she knows about him is that he keeps coming home to his real mother. But hold on-- I don't mean she tries be a mother because that's what she thinks the boy wants. *She doesn't know what he wants.* Stop here, read that all again. But his mom must know-- it's why he keeps coming back to her. So the Tree identifies with the mother in order to figure out what the boy wants; not like Special Agent Empath who "gets inside the head" of the criminal, but like a high end escort or high priced psychoanalyst. She has no idea what the guy lying beneath her wants; the only thing she knows about him is that he thinks escorts and psychoanalysts would know. So she doesn't guess what he wants; she simply stays in character as the one who is supposed to know, and waits for the man to act.

Of course escorts and analysts get paid, i.e. the ledger is immediately balanced. In the Tree's case, however, no payment is forthcoming; and since it is an arithmetical necessity that the ledger must balance, it becomes even more important to figure out what he wants, in order to deprive him of it.

Some readers saw the story as a commentary on gender, male vs. female, as if gender was a more fundamental distinction than "mother and child." It isn't. It works equally well for two gay men or consecutive generations. It's about the form of a relationship. The Tree-- yes, in this case a woman-- gives gifts of herself, not because "all I have to give is myself" but because the parts of herself she offers are unsatisfying, it won't do this kid a bit of good-- her life purpose is to keep him unsatisfied. What can I be for you that will keep you wanting—me alone? "Can you be a house for my wife and me?" I can be an applewood house, that should rot in tandem with your marriage. "Is that irony?" It's on purpose.

And the man-- yes, in this case a man-- wants her, even needs her, but only in the beginning is he satisfied with the tree as a whole and not the sum of parts; and you'll observe that consequently the tree didn't have to make any further sacrifices to keep him. As he gets older but not because he gets older, two problems arise.

The first is he idealizes her less and less, and then is able to see certain things about her-- not stuff that he doesn't like, just things which are superfluous-- but which might be desirable to others. They all have to go. I can eat an apple, but what's with all the leaves? Get rid of them, you look like a whore.

The second problem are her desires. Obviously she wants to be what he wants-- which he recognizes means she generally wants to be what others want, to be desired by others. So now he's in a competition, ostensibly with others but mostly with her. Initially he limits her exposure to other people, not just physically, but also by framing the interactions to be about something else other than their desire. "You're going to meet X, he's a big jerk who hits on everyone" = "even if he wants you, he doesn't want you." It looks like he's a meany guarding her jealously from becoming attracted to another man. This is false and anyway wouldn't count. The fear is that she might believe the guy is attracted to her. If being desired is what she wants, someone desiring her means she got what she wants: she is ahead.

The solution to both of these problems is, bit by bit, careful not to disrupt the part that represents him (in the book: the heart with M.E. + T) and even more careful that she doesn't notice he is doing it, to destroy everything desirable in her. Whatever she was that's her-- and attractive to others-- is slowly amputated, reduced to the bare minimum of whatever is still required by him. Then, as the only one left (he thinks) who could desire her, the final move is to deprive her of his own expressions of his desire for her. "But after all this cutting, wouldn't she be less attractive even to him?" It is outside the scope of The Giving Tree to depict what the man would do to her next, for that it would have had to be porn: re-fantasize her as an idealized tree that others would have wanted, and masturbate to it. He can desire her, while making sure she never knows it. From the safety of an obliterated stump, he would ask her about the other boys who had played with her leaves, stripped off her branches, eaten her apples; how many people have peed on her; the threesomes with other couples... he reminds himself through the imagined affirmation of others that she is desirable, loudly implies to her she was desirable, while safely hopes she is not.

These are the two problems he will have as the relationship progresses, that with couples therapy he would be able to realize. It will feel like a breakthrough. The thing is....... both of these problems are lies. Faded childish idealization and jealousy about what she wants/who wants her aren't the problem, they are the defense against the problem. The fundamental problem, the one that causes the other two, is that he has become emotionally dependent on her. This is the only reason he obliterates her. The other two reasons are factual and are the reasons he will discover in therapy and will make him feel self-aware, but they are truths he will use to lie and he will then go no further and nothing will change-- for her. He will be more self-aware and he will continue to obliterate her. What he really wants to obliterate is his dependence on her, a dependence that feels unnatural because it doesn't feel like anything "real"= discussed in a video. Despite that everyone with at least a tenth of a soul has felt this dependence, no one has ever described it, explained it, pornographized it-- so it remains unreal. In other words, he never really wanted a boat or a house, the objects are red herrings-- what he wants is to sever his dependence on her, in this case to halt being in love with her as a total, incomprehensibly unknowable other organism-- symbolized by a tree-- that depends on him just as much. So he gets an axe and starts chopping.

In the case of a wife the easy cut is into Madonna and whore, cutting off the lover and making her a mother; certainly this reduces his emotional dependence on her as a lover, freeing him to find that part on the internet; and the obvious solution is to help him re-see her as his lover, totally erroneously by "spicing up the relationship"-- but this grossly underestimates the purpose of the splitting. By splitting the wife into a lover and mother, he's limited his dependence on her as a lover *and* on his real mother as a mother. The split isn't to limit dependency on one specific person, it is a series of cascading logical propositions to limit

215

dependency in general. No amount of couples therapy can fix this.

And he succeeds. The last panel seems like some kind of pure love because they no longer need anything from each other, as if it was balanced, but that's precisely why it isn't love. It's two carbon life forms in close proximity with no obligations to each other. You know: trees. If this isn't clear by now, if you can't see the underlying rage in the service of balancing the ledger, then consider that had the boy not kept chopping her up and cutting her down, then at the end of the story the boy would still be an old man, but the tree would be as vibrant as ever. You think that's fair? You think you're just going to die quietly and leave everything behind while she-- blooms?

While the story reads as gendered, it's not; it's just as easy to spot The Giving Tree dynamic played out with the genders 100% reversed, with a wife who splits and desexualizes her husband to minimize dependence on all men in her timeline: she reduces him to a series of utility parts, safely emasculated and fully contained somewhere else in the house; while the husband, in the home office watching other men perform acts, makes great visible sacrifices but secretly withholds from his wife the most valuable parts of himself that would be constituents of love (e.g. his inner life and thoughts; desire for his wife's inner thoughts; sex, etc.) In 1979 Silverstein published a four panel cartoon called "I Accept The Challenge." A woman is sitting on what looks like a tree stump on which is written, "Real Man Wanted." A nude man comes up to audition. She pulls out scissors and cuts off his penis, arms, legs and etc. Then she sits on his torso stump now with the words "Real Man Wanted" on it. This is 100% the same story as *The Giving Tree* but with the genders reversed, with the boy's oblivious selfishness being pornographized as the woman's overt sexualized aggression. The trick is we still *don't* know what the woman wants, but she revealed her hand: the sign is still up. *She's not satisfied.* Ok, here's the thing: she didn't trick him. He tricked her. The man (/Tree) had willingly offered himself up to her hoping she wouldn't want anything else, *as if* he grandiosely thought he could satisfy her, but what he offered is himself, i.e. nothing of value. In less rigid terms: he'll make her cum a dozen times, but at the end he will (100% absolutely feel like he will) deprive her, of something. Of course, you might be the kind of person who thinks that the cartoon cunt *is* satisfied, what she enjoys *is* cutting guys up into stumps. That's a gendered criticism to make and the purpose of the pornographic transformation: why didn't you think the boy *enjoyed* cutting up the Tree?

In that it is about formal relationships, it can apply equally to generational relationships. Generation one can't imagine and doesn't want the second generation to become its replacement, so it not only fails at fostering independence, it actively thwarts all attempts at independence, so that the second generation has no choice but to return, unsatisfied, to its parents (or other omnipotent entity). It encourages them to get a job for independence, but not jobs with independence-- it discourages such jobs, autonomy is too risky, preferring the safety of a corporation or institution. It gets the child to want things in which nothing can change but lets it have the illusion of change, of forward progress, usually in the form of fashion or technology that the older generation is content to appear excluded from. The younger generation is given illusory independence, while inter-dependence is impossible. The long term result is the next generation remains unsatisfied, they can't even imagine more power for themselves. So they devote their lives full force towards depriving others of theirs.[38]

---

38 If there is one thing I know it's that I know myself, which means I know nothing, that's a truth table you don't want to run in front of another person, so when a 9 yo asked me this question I did what I now do all of the time, which was bow my head in shame and admit the idea had never

Here's a fun test. Imagine a man says this: "He has a reputation for bedding a lot of women, he knows precisely what to do..." Is the man who *says* this desirable to women?

Here's the fun part. Imagine a woman says this: "He has a reputation for bedding a lot of women, he knows precisely what to do..." Is the woman who *says* this desirable to men?

It's almost as if... there are some things that can be said by some, and not by others.

"Unlock The Secrets Of Women!" "How To Get Any Girl You Want!" As if the holy grail is The Flowchart, The Plan, a procedure for action that can be followed to get any chick you want, to make her desire you, regardless of who you are.

---

occurred to me: "Did they ever do a *Giving Tree II?*"

For a kid, any ambiguous ending is evidence of a trilogy, but of course I knew Silverstein hadn't ever written a sequel. What I didn't know is whether someone else had.

So I gave the internet a series of words and asked it to free associate, and the first thing that came to its mind was the same thing as the next three million things that came to its mind, after which it let slip something it claimed was only peripherally relevant: *The Apple Tree*, by Daphne du Maurier, who unlike Silverstein is a woman but much like Silverstein liked women. Or hated women, it's hard to know how meanings will get used nowadays.

It was written 10 years earlier so it's more of a prequel, and has no pictures so 30k more words, and instead of a boy whose stalker is a tree, it's an old man who thinks his dead wife has become a tree. Back when the wife was inspiring she was hesitant and timid, didn't nag, tried very hard to please, never made demands, never asked for anything in return; but what she did do, all the time, is make sure you could see how much it costs her. An example: it's a cold and rainy day in countryside England, but he's snug in his study, heat on cozy, sipping a brandy. Then his wife tiptoes in. "Are you going into town?" she asks, already putting on her raincoat. "... I can go myself if you're busy, I only thought..." Sigh. So he reluctantly gets up, "all right, I'll get the car." You'll deduce that she passive aggressively got him to do what she wanted, but are you sure you know what that is? If she wanted him to act on her wishes then the next scene would be him in a wet car and her in a dry house, but even before he's out of the chair she's already at the front door saying, "I'm bound to get wet in any case," and out she goes. So now he's still in the study, still dry and warm, the only thing that has changed for him is information, meanwhile she's puttering about in the rain for some reason directly outside his window, her "raincoat not properly buttoned". Now what? He turns the heat down. Still think you know what she wanted?

As it is a relationship, you are legitimately allowed to ask to what extent he deserved it. Here are two examples of things he does that would exactly equally make any man's wife go apoplectic with rage: 1. One time he and a younger, more carefree, younger and considerably younger woman impulsively kiss. NB she is younger. 2. Another time he goes into town while she's home with the flu, and secretly sees a movie by himself. Both times she catches him. The first time he feels very ashamed. The second time he feels very ashamed, and then thinks, wait a second, what's the big deal, it's only a movie and she only has the flu? So she dies of it.

Those are the things that he does do, that make him feel ashamed. The thing he doesn't do, for which he feels no shame, let alone guilt, is love her. I don't mean he merely doesn't love her, I mean he deliberately deprives her of his love, not just in practice but deep in his heart, and I know this because of the single fantasy he is described as having: moving to the South Seas to get what today both men and women long for: a practical, dutiful, preferably but not necessarily more attractive spouse, who merrily handles the chores and the cooking, asks nothing in return, is always happy to offer a laugh or brief conversation-- and more, if the urge strikes you-- but otherwise your time is spent at your discretion and with your own sex, by which I mostly mean masturbation. Sounds

Unfortunately for you, eventually your true desire will resurface: after enough practice with The Plan, you'll want women to want you before you even use The Plan. A signal, a name, a label, one thing that embodies everything you are and also all of the steps of The Plan, so that the moment she knows *who* you are, you will know her desire for you is assured. *You want to be famous.* While you want women to want you regardless of who you are, you also want women to want you only because of who you are, but therein lies a trap, imagine a 1960s James Bond type movie in which Matt Helm follows a trail of discarded woman's clothing to a room containing a semi-naked hyperblonde he's never met before, and this happens:

---

awesome? I'm no judge of lifestyle but I am a prosecutor of motive: If this is what you want, why didn't you fantasize a loveless domestic partnership with an attractive maid or manservant-- why did you fantasize another spouse?

In other words, other than the climate and the Coriolis, precisely how is the fantasy different from his reality that makes it so desirable? 1. In real life the wife wants things and you deprive her wherever possible, but a South Seas wife gets nothing because she is fantasized as not even wanting anything, her deprivation is already part of the structure of the fantasy, it is half of the enjoyment of it. 2. In the fantasy, the South Seas wife doesn't know she is being deprived, as per the structure, she thinks not wanting anything is what she wants. But if this is what he wants, why doesn't he just go find such a submissive housewife in 1950s England and buy a beach house? Did they all die in the bombings? 3. Because he can't act on his desire. He can't even fantasize acting on it. He has to fantasize moving to a place that tells him he's allowed to. His fantasy isn't to have power, but to live in a system that gives him natural privileges, over his wife, and the wife is expected to live with it. Before you detect this as patriarchy I should emphasize that to want this means he does not think he has it. In 1952. In England. In a book written by a woman. In the same book in which she published *The Birds*.

From the wife's perspective, what would have satisfied her is to be desired, or, to quote from the primary source: "wishing to seem advanced, anxious to please, and more than either of these things desperately anxious to attract." If that's all that it would take, it would be a fairly simple thing for a husband to give a wife, and you could even slap her, certainly easier than a home, money, or protection from Nazis bombings; nope, he gives the wife what she wants but not what might have satisfied her. This is the problem with their relationship. But unlike the South Seas wife (and therefore the South Seas wife) this wife knows she is being deprived. So, according to her ledger, he has to be deprived of his satisfaction. She thus appears to make enormous sacrifices to give him what he wants ("you stay home and relax, I'll go"), sacrifices which appear selfless, that in the video would show no loss to him, that deprive him of his satisfaction.

She dies; and short story shorter, an apple tree appears outside. It looks a lot like his wife. Well, it looks a lot more like an apple tree, because it is an apple tree, but it produces no fruit, it's a hypocrite. The man tells his gardener to cut it down. The gardener asks for another season, let him work on it, and if it bears fruit next season, great; otherwise, he'll cut it down then.

Maybe this story sounds familiar. In the Biblical parable the gardener also asks the owner for another season to work on the fruitless tree, if he succeeds, great, and if he fails the owner can cut it down then; the difference is that the parable ends right there. It doesn't tell you the outcome. It's pretty much assumed that the tree will bear fruit simply because of the intercession of the gardener, but this interpretation precludes thinking about the third possibility, which is the one in the The Apple Tree: the gardener does get the tree to make apples, but the owner hates them. That's a pretty unbiblical twist, but it gets worse: only the owner hates the apples, everyone else finds them delicious. And while he doesn't build a boat the other thing apple wood is good for is setting on fire, everyone loves its sweet and soothing scent, but when he puts a branch in the fireplace, it

                    HELM
    I couldn't help noticing, are these your clothes?

                    HYPERBLONDE
    And what if they are?

                    HELM
    What shall I do with these?

                    HYPERBLONDE
    Just throw them anywhere, I won't be needing them till
    morning.

---

comes out like mustard gas. Only to him. Now what? The Bible is oddly silent on these more likely eventualities, so rather than merely understanding the meaning of the parable we have to figure out what it is for, so let's play the oldest and most terrifying eschatological game of all: Guess What Happens Next.

Although there are behaviors in the wife that the reader can see as enraging, the husband never tries to cut her down; yet the Tree, which is just a tree, he targets for murder. So if he tried to murder his wife we would say it's wrong, but we understand his crazy logic; but wanting to murder the Tree we say he's a lunatic, but concede it's not wrong. "Because it's just a tree." But it's not just a tree, right? The whole conceit of the story is that the Tree is the wife, the audience and the husband identify the tree with the wife. The question is why is that the whole conceit of the story, and the answer is that it isn't: it's a deliberate maneuver on our part. Everything that is said or done is to be understood either in its literal signification, or else it signifies something figuratively; or at least contains both of these at once, both its own literal interpretation, and a figurative signification also. If this were a supernatural story then the Tree is his wife and the man is wrong to kill it; and if this were a fully materialist story then the tree is not his wife, it's not wrong to kill it, but there's no reason he should want to kill it, especially since everyone else likes it's use value. In between those two is real life, where the man believes it is his wife; but not because of identification,"the Tree reminds him of his wife, so he kills it." This belief is projection, it is the fulfillment of a wish, put together the logic becomes: "If you were a tree, I could murder you like you deserve." If p then q. In other words, the wife doesn't turn into a tree to be near the man; the man turns a tree into his wife, so he can finally kill her.

You might scoff at my application of formal logic in a story that requires the man to be illogical, but I've found that even when your conscious mind is bad at math the logic of the unconscious is rigorous, and to illustrate this I'll modus tollens a prediction for Act IV: failing to murder the tree implies it was not a tree.

So the husband, like the owner in the Biblical parable, gives the Tree a second chance when the gardener intercedes, though he would rather just do away with it immediately; but unlike the parable he still wants it dead even though the gardener succeeded and it's pleasing to other people. Ok, sure, this is Du Maurier, Biblical Jesus would have been a little more forgiving of trees' shortcomings. It's a good thought. Turns out it's factually wrong.

There's another fruit tree story in the New Testament, in which the protagonist walks up to a flowering fig tree, but nope, no figs. He gets angry and curses it. Then he goes into the Temple, gets even more angry and starts flipping tables over, and when they leave Peter catches sight of the now dead fig tree and his head explodes: "that tree you cursed has been dried up!" "Well duh," Jesus responds, "have faith in God. If you tell a mountain to throw itself in the sea, and you believe it, it will."

The 100% no exceptions universal interpretation of this story is that it is about the power and importance and of faith, and I think that's very empowering and costs you nothing, and, probably no

                    HELM
    Don't you think we should be introduced first?

                    HYPERBLONDE
    You're Matt Helm.

                    HELM
    That's good enough for me.

And certainly good enough for you, but unfortunately doesn't leave you any time to enjoy it because instead of a scene that shows her having an orgasm clean, loud, and female superior, she tries to stab him in the back. What he should have asked is, "tell me, who do

---

surprise, therefore I also think it's wrong. Overwhelming agreement on a proposition that doesn't involve math is the loudest possible signal that we don't want the truth. Jesus curses the tree, and Peter is surprised to find it dead. Well wait a second, why is Peter surprised? Ok, depending on which biographer you read Peter's reliability as a disciple runs around 33%, but is he really surprised Jesus could do this? Or is he surprised that Jesus did do this? First of all, it's not Jesus's tree. Second of all, the passage explicitly says the tree had no fruit because it wasn't in season. Whose fault is that, if not God's? So Caesar unto Caesar, but I'm cursing down someone else's perfectly good fig tree because although I can fast for 40 days and 40 nights I'm hungry now?

It makes no sense as journalism and even less sense as fiction. What's the message? Peter is surprised at what he can do, so Jesus does the little finger thing and says, "I find your lack of faith disturbing"? Never mind Peter, when they all come back and find the tree withered, the very literal reading of the passage shows that *Jesus* is surprised, not that he could do it, but that he did do it. He witnesses what his wrath hath wrought, takes a deep breath, and upgrades his ministry from the dative to the genitive, no, the other genitive: "Have the faith of God." You already have faith in God, now be like God, with the belief and the power comes the responsibility.

The subsequent passage about "the ability to move a mountain is insignificant next to the power of the force" is further cited as a metaphor for all the wonderful benefits belief in God will give you. But these two passages don't show examples of what your faith can do, they show examples of what not to do with your faith, and if you doubt this observe that the passage in between these two abstract examples of what not to do is a concrete example of what not to do: Jesus goes into the Temple and starts flipping tables over. And-- surprise-- the disciples are surprised, their first association upon watching this catastrophe is to Psalm 69: "Zeal for my house consumes me," and whatever you think that means you should go read the Psalm to find out what they were using it for: zeal is a bad thing, and anyway it's a human thing. I am aware of the doctrinal assertion that Jesus is perfect and loving and never acts in anger, I would gently like to suggest that even if this was true, wanting this to be true is splitting with a capital S, it is only for the purpose of making Jesus into the defense attorney and God into the judge/jury/executioner, smoting our enemies and balancing our ledgers, we will gladly live sinless lives while others enjoy their genitals because I accept that vengeance is Thine, as long as it is mine. Yes, Matthew's spin on the story makes a weaponized faith a faithful weapon, but the Gospel Of The Battalion Commander was for a different audience of conscripts, and anyway the very next line has the priests surprised not at how Jesus was able to do this, but whether he was allowed to do this. I am also aware of the primary sources citing the immutability of the God who has long since been mute, and I've read plenty of attempts to dismiss the aggression of the two passages as allegorical to the fate of the Temple Mount or God's judgment on Jerusalem but either way a tree was still sacrificed in a religion that eschews sacrifices; the result of these meanderings is to shift the theological problem away from how to pray for God to the contemporary anxiety of Christians and atheists: the significance and meaning of unanswered prayers for them. "What about me?" What about you? Where are we, Job? So now God has to explain himself? This is Mark, where knowledge and power stand opposed; Jesus's game is not giving them information about what to believe-- in the logic of the New Testament, the answer is

                    220

they say I am?" Because letting your reputation precede you is guaranteed to deceive you, you can't have it both ways, which is why this isn't going to work. The problem isn't what you want, it is how you want.

"What's the difference?" Another person might tell you fame is not a worthy goal, but that is yet another person telling you what to want. Let's accept without prejudice you want to become famous, fine: what are you doing to get that? What are you, today, doing to enhance your reputation? Dreaming big and doing nothing, sounds like someone is planning to fail, on purpose. How you want has lead you to want something that you.... don't want. One would be tempted-- well, your Dad would be tempted-- to call you lazy. But he's wrong, you're not lazy, you'd work harder than anyone, you just need to get chosen first. And who can

---

standing in front of them-- but teaching them what to believe for. Don't pray idly, don't pray for nonsense, be careful what you pray for-- don't pray for what you should not want. I'm going to transcribe his recommendations here, updated for a modern audience, but for context instead of wanting the power to tell a mountain to jump into a lake just imagine that what you are praying for is your slut wife to do the same:

> For this I say to you, whatever you pray for or ask for, believe that
> you would receive, and it will be to you; and when you stand praying
> forgive if you have something against anyone, so that your Father
> who art in heaven would forgive you your trespasses.

It's not a smooth translation to English, and I deliberately made the last line King Jamesy so that those who wonder why the Lord's Prayer is in Matthew and Luke but not in Mark, well, there you go, there's the important part; change "and" to "so" and consider yourself put on notice. The faith necessary for clause 1 is weirdly non sequitory to the requirements for God's forgiveness in clause 2, unless your prayers themselves require God's forgiveness.

On the background of this event with a fig tree comes the parable about a fig tree, the one in which the question really isn't why did the gardener give the fig tree a second chance when God forgot to, but what will happen next after the 100% guaranteed outcome that the tree will still not be good enough? Chop it down? Are you so confident that in you, God is well pleased?

The parable is deceptively simple if you want it to be merely about second chances, but du Maurier's story forces you to take your logic its conclusion, because while the tree is pleasing to others it failed to please the master. By the terms of ownership the tree should be doomed, he has the right to cut it down, but doing so is now is an act of aggression. This is the reason the parable doesn't show what happens next season, it is irrelevant: biblical salvation is possible not because you got a second chance; the intercession is the salvation, regardless of what you do with your second chance, which as per above is 100% for sure nothing. This a God that's used to disappointment, it can only be that he'd still bless the tree for what it's doing unto others; and if you're a husband no one is saying you have to stay married to your slut wife but it's not for you to deprive the world of her or her of herself. And let's be very clear why that is: not because killing your wife is wrong-- oh my God, I actually have to say it is, stupid, but that's not the reason-- but because in the final analysis, your rage doesn't entitle you to punish her, your rage doesn't even count. "That's just not fair." Which means you're not going to like this next part, but I'm only telling you what it says in the primary source: if you do not forgive her, the one who is doomed is you. "This is all nonsense, and anyway I don't believe in God." HA! Liar, you think I'm speaking for God? I'm talking about *The Apple Tree*.

Your ischemic cardiac fibrosis can forgive anything anyone does to you-- as long as they didn't enjoy it, that mortal sin requires hellfire or gunfire; if neither's an option you will move mountains in order to show how much better you are than her, and if there's no audience for your public display of faith then you can try subtly depriving her of everything that would satisfy her; but the

221

blame you? Everything you've ever seen with your eyes says greatness is thrust upon the unsuspecting hero; while everyone who works hard becomes.... a worker.

And so this "laziness" is the logical first step of exactly what you desire. You want to be selected for doing nothing. You don't want to do better in calculus because then you will become a calculator and you will be responsible for calculating. You must not commit to any definite path in case the Sphinx is down another. It's also why you're still single, even if only mentally.

"Yes, it's about maturity." Says the guy who wants to equate his ability to work for other people with some kind of trophy. At some point being called "mature" is the best and only compliment you'll ever get, so you better make sure your kid believes it counts because if you hear it from your spouse it's backhanded at best. Besides, what did you do to earn your maturity-- other than age?

The secret to fame that no one ever tells you, because no one really understands it, is that you don't want to be famous for doing something. You'll accept that fame, sure, but it is not sufficient, it is not satisfying, the precise goal is to be famous for nothing. That kind of fame can not be earned, in order to truly be yours it has to be independent of any accomplishments, so that a truly famous person is famous not for something but for being *that guy*. His material accomplishments are merely the shrapnel of his exploding greatness. Meanwhile, a built in hedge in case it goes wrong: "That's not me, that's just a persona, the real me is different." And the crowds swoon, they want YOU, whatever that is.

"But how can anyone be so stupid as to think fame can come for nothing?" Their media taught them it was possible and you taught them the media was important. "I never taught them that!" What did you tell them is the truth about their favorite celebrity? That she's really a drug addict? Where did you learn that? The media doesn't want you to like the celebrity, it doesn't care about your opinion of her, it only wants you to believe in the

---

easiest maneuver that requires little imagination is to pornographize your wife into a tree, and start cutting. "What's the big deal? I know others enjoy it but it is, after all, just a tree."

One of you is a liar, and you will read this and possibly even agree but compliment yourself on never having chopped down your spouse let alone a tree, but refer back to the primary source to explain your benevolence. What's disavowed in *The Giving Tree* but explicit in *The Apple Tree* is how the man is able to chop down the tree. In both stories, the trees deprived no one else except the respective men. Everyone else loved the man's wife. And everyone else loves the tree. Bad enough her apples taste horrible; worse, the apples are delicious to everyone else. To everyone else, her cyanide logs smell like fresh apple wood. And you can guess the market for her sweet apple jelly (everyone else). The difference between how little he enjoys her and how much other people enjoy her manifests as resentment, write this as a children's story and it manifests as nostalgia, write it as a porn and it manifests as arousal, it makes no difference because the end result is the same: he wants to get rid of the tree, but he *can't*. He's only able to cut the Tree down for some other reason, e.g. when someone else wants him to. He can't act on his desire, but he can act on someone else's desire; it's necessary that he find an other to compel him to act, and that is the reason, the only reason, that at the request of a bartender on a snowy night he goes full Shining and hacks at his wife with an axe. But because of the ledger, he can't enjoy it more than the bartender he's doing it for, because then he'd be doing it because he wanted to. That excess-- not the crime itself-- is what is punishable, and why he fails. In a horror story, that excess would mean she'd survive and he'd be killed, by her. In a children's story, she'd be happy and he'd have wasted his life. In porn, she'd orgasm and he'd be at work. In real life------ well, that's the trick, isn't it? In real life, his wife couldn't be a tree. He-- well, you-- just wish it was.

importance of media.

Why do you get so angry at someone who is "famous for nothing?" You're looking the wrong way, all of the various media constantly reporting on her isn't because of her fame, it is her fame. It's the kind of fame you want. But the trade off is they are using her for their own profit, regardless of whether she profits. It could indeed just as easily have been some other woman, and it will be. And if they couldn't get access to an A-list star, they have to pretend that X is a star worth accessing-- she was chosen because they have access to her. And it enrages you! Your rage, however small, that she is too unimportant to receive media coverage supports the premise that the media should be important.

If you loudly deny you wish to be in the media, then I can predict with considerable accuracy that not only do you wish for it, but I can even predict the desired form: you wish to be interviewed.

"America likes to turn on its celebrities." I'm sure they'll tell us when. In the words of the intuitionist logician Marshall McLuhan, "media expands to fill the time available, and nowadays we have nothing but media, from which logically follows we're out of time."

You want to be famous? Pursue that. Fame has always been the reward for virtuous action. We can quibble about what "virtuous" is, but that main point is here besides the point. Action. You can't get the reward for action by not acting. And yet that is precisely what you want.

The mirror image of fame is love, if you doubt this you've never been in love. Or famous. When someone falls in love with you, it's not specifically for what you did or what you look like but because of some intangible quality-- *and only your lover can see it, no one else could, including you*. The question you must ask is if that counts.

How does love die? You actively obliterate the intangible in her. Then you suspect the intangible never existed. Then you assure yourself intangibles aren't real. Except for the one in you, which of course obviously exists but people can't see. Advertising's most important command-- and the premise of psychotherapy-- is that it's impossible to love someone else if you don't love yourself. Look around at the result.

In *Confirmatory Assent*, when the tipsy blonde in the hot tub tries to deflect her silly boyfriend's jealousy, it is easy to be distracted by the tipsy blonde such that you miss the ingeniousness of her deflection even if it was accidental. We should study the primary text carefully:

> ECKS
> They could have been psychopaths or serial killers for all you know!
>
> HEIRESS
> No, they just saw a pair of tipsy blondes in bikinis and came over to talk to them… you can't blame them for trying.

So there's a tipsy blonde in a bikini, which sounds like all you need in a movie, but here Heiress refers to herself as a tipsy blonde. What is the difference between a person who is a tipsy blonde and a person who describes herself as a tipsy blonde? With the first everybody wins; with the second, somebody is going to lose.

Any woman who calls herself a "tipsy blonde" is aware of the connotations-- which means she can't actually be a "tipsy blonde", she knows it's a put on. Whatever "tipsy blonde" means, the way she uses it is the opposite: by saying it about herself she proves it is FALSE.

Except it's only false for two people: herself, and the person she's explaining this to. She asserts it is false for him. Everyone else who doesn't know her sees "a tipsy blonde." You can say they're wrong, and sure, if they get to know her they will realize she's an econ major, but until then: tipsy blonde.

Which is precisely the ingeniousness. Of course that's what they saw. That's exactly what the boyfriend was afraid they saw. She identified the perception, but-- accidentally? deliberately?-- locked the boyfriend out of it.

If she cheats, the men get what is impossible for the boyfriend: they have sex with a) his girlfriend and b) a "tipsy blonde." No matter how drunk or blonde she gets she's still his girlfriend; he may be able to fantasize some of it in real time as he's taking her from behind, but she is still his girlfriend. For him, she can never be a "tipsy blonde", especially when she calls herself one. This is experienced with a very specific grammar: to him, she didn't just have sex with them, they got something she has never given her boyfriend, and can never give her boyfriend. They will always have a part of her he can never get, because it isn't real-- it's only real for them. You can say it isn't real for them either, but who are you to say what they perceived?

The *fantasy* of "the cheating wife" is always out of reach, because she can never be a "cheating wife" with him, only with other guys. The closest he can come is watching or imagining her do it, which is risky. "Is there a porn for that?" Her past always sounds more sexual not because she is now less sexual, but because he doesn't hear the past as continuity, the stories of the past are about someone else, before he turned her into an econ major and later a wife. The underlying problem that can't be solved is that therefore the real her, had she been left to her own desires, *was the one in the past.* That he has no access to, that only everyone else does. "But I made her a better person." Keep telling yourself that, so you never ask if you ever wanted to be a better person for her.

Things are easy or hard to understand depending on your perspective, so if getting off on your wife as a fantasy object for someone else is hard to understand let me flip it around for you and unfortunately it will be easy to understand: pathological jealousy.

Pathological jealousy doesn't refer to the amount of jealousy you have over some objectively trivial event. What makes your jealousy pathological is the perception of what happened. "Yes, stupid, that's pretty obvious." No stupid: not *your* perception.

"Nothing happened at the party, I swear!" says the wife, sobbing like a terrified 5 year old standing next to a broken lamp that it is no longer relevant whether she broke. He believes you, yet he still feels enraged, so *therefore* there must be more to this story, the rage makes him a psychologist, the rage makes him psychic. He was mad before but now there's something about her *reaction*. Hence the repetitive going over of the events, inference and subtlety under 10000x magnification-- because this much rage has to have an external cause. "I mean, I'm not crazy, I'm not a bad person, I might not be totally right but I must be detecting something, her reaction is showing me something about her true character that even she doesn't know..."

What enrages him isn't what she did or what she wants; those things he can control or reframe with a million psychological techniques some of which he has been allowed to believe he came up with himself. What he can't control, however, is what *the other guy* perceived. He imagines the other guy got to experience his wife in a different way, a fantasy way, inaccessible to him-- a different her-- the *real* her. Maybe she had a glass of wine and chuckled at one of his jokes-- and now the husband imagines the guy perceived "a tipsy, giggling blonde at a party." "It's actually just light brown." That makes it worse: she let him perceive blonde anyway. She "gave" him a side of herself she never gave her husband, which of course she can't ever give him, it's impossible, because it's not hers to give, it's the other's to perceive, and he can't control that. Hence the rage.

And yet he's stuck in a loop, how many times does the pathologically jealous husband dare the world to see her that way? He wants her to dress in ways that would enrage him if she wanted to dress in those ways; nonchalantly seething from across the room as he watches her innocently chatting with leering men, but not acting to stop it. Why, if it enrages him so much? "I trust her." But you don't trust the guys, do you? "I don't want to be a controlling jerk." You have said it.

The point isn't what they do with her. The point is what they perceive. Of course there's a huge risk you go over and tell her she's drunk and you should go home and she drunkenly assures you she's only teensy weensy bit drunk and you should definitely go home, she'll get a ride home with-- tee hee, I'm sorry, what's your name? But just as bad is walking out with her draped on your arm thinking the only reason she didn't sleep with him is you were there. "Are you saying the husband would think this?" He already *knows* this. The problem is that now he thinks the other guy thinks it.

She has to be the one to turn the guy down, but *for no reason*. You want her to choose you, not him, but he can't think she didn't choose him because of you. Got it? No? It's insane? It gets worse.

"Wouldn't you want the guy to know she chose you over him, proving you're the better man?" Well, it certainly *looks* like a rivalry between two men for the prize, and I'm sure you have been told to stop seeing women as some kind of prize that rivals compete over, which is exactly the kind of thing a woman who has never been fought over would tell you, and anyway only reinforces the idea that you do see her as a prize-- but the whole point of a rivalry is that the prize isn't important, it is merely the pretext for destroying the rival. But it doesn't apply here because you never competed against the guy. In fact, you avoided that competition entirely. Do you know why? "Because I'm... afraid of him?" HA! How bad is the true answer that you'd prefer me to think you're a coward? No. There's no competition because he's not your rival. Your rival is your wife.

I am aware of the obvious, that you are opposite genders and at least one of you is not bisexual. Well, let's look at the ledger. What does she want? To cheat on you with the "alpha male"? Unlikely. But she does want to be desired by people she finds desirable, even if she doesn't have sex with them. Guess what? She has two desirable men desiring her. +2. What do you want? To sleep with your wife? Unlikely. You already have, and it doesn't count. But you do want to be desired by people you find desirable, even if you don't have sex with them. Guess what? You're a girl.

I can promise you that none of this has anything to do with gender at all, but you like to use words to your way, so I'll just stay quiet. "I don't go out on many dates, I guess because

I'm antisocial." You have said it.

You're envious of how desirable men are attracted to her. By contrast, desirable women aren't attracted to you. Slow down: there are plenty of desirable women who are attracted to you, but they don't count because they're not desirable. I said slow down: I don't mean they're not desirable to anyone, or even to you, I mean that even if they are it doesn't count, they have to be considered desirable by your girlfriend, in the exact same way it matters to you not a lick whether she finds the men desirable, only if you consider them desirable. --To women!

"So is the jealousy really repressed homosexuality?" As if you unconsciously desired the other men? As if the problem was jealousy over what she has? But the problem isn't jealousy, which is why you call it jealousy. It's envy.

In the rivalry with the girlfriend or wife, the prize is desirability-- not her, not her fidelity.

You envy the ease with which she is desired, and this envy of her desirability is the same force that prevents you from acting on your desires. By simple analogy: you don't talk to that girl over there because you want her to want to talk to you. But even if she does, it won't count, because-- like it is with your actual girlfriend-- if someone likes you, it must be for some other reason. It's never about desire. "She only likes me *because* I'm [adjective]." "-smart." "-funny." "-nice." "-attractive." None of those count.

But the prize of desirability is pretext only. You may want it, it's perfectly safe to admit you're a bad person for wanting it-- but even you know the prize cannot satisfy. This isn't motivated by a passionate desire for what the other has; these are crimes of another class which men commit, not from jealousy, but from the rivalry fostered between equals until they are carried away by blind rage into the extremes of pitiless cruelty. The envy is over her good luck in what she has, but not because of what she has, but because *she* has it. Envy doesn't want it, envy wants her to be deprived.

Is that a modern insight? A post modern discovery? But this was the default understanding of envy for 2000 years until the idea of repressed homosexuality posited a hidden object of desire-- turned envy into jealousy. "Repressed homosexuality" wasn't the cause of envy but the defense against it being envy: it has to be about wanting *something*, either you believed this was the deeper desire, or you believed it wasn't *and so* it was something else; but in both cases, you were immunized form the possibility that your envy wanted no-thing, there was no material prize, that it was purely envy of your wife and will only be satisfied by her deprivation.

And so with your mouth and your knowledge you battle your rival, you try to convince *her*: she either tried to get those guys to desire her, or they desired her for something that didn't count. *She's not more desirable.* This logic hid your envy, so you could honestly speak the truth that safely sounded like you were lying: "Don't be ridiculous, I'm not jealous!" You have said it.

You'll repeat that everyone knows women are taught to be desirable, taught to want to be desirable, that they are taught to exist for the male gaze. Then why is her husband yelling about it? The problem isn't that women are taught to value being desired, the problem is that you were also-- and women seem to be way better at it than you. A woman will certainly retort that being desired isn't particularly useful, that it doesn't count, but no man will believe you.

When you see a billboard advertisement with a gorgeous woman that's been defaced by what you hope were 13 year olds, it's obvious that that's misogyny; but when you see a billboard with a gorgeous man similarly defaced, then that's homophobia. That seems wildly incompatible and anyway, don't they involve the same media? Simply on its face, we should consider that these aren't attacks against men or women, but against billboards, and those who get to decide what goes on them. Yet while it's not evident what the attacks mean about the people who did them, it is demonstrably evident what the attacks are used for by you: to blame a type of person, regardless of the actual perpetrator; to call it a type of crime, regardless of the actual intention; to identify a single type of motivation for disparate crimes, or crimes for which the actual link must stay hidden-- not to punish the individual perpetrator but in order to elevate the accusers as guardians of society and reflexively above reproach. We're appalled at how some people treat images! The images become even more worthy of worship, especially when contrasted with the baseness of the defilers. A segment of the population logically becomes psychopaths, or worse-- sociopaths; but most importantly of all, the one who gets to decide all this is you. The mutilation of the billboards becomes a cause for political action: financial reward and immunity from prosecution to anyone who can help us weed out the BAD PEOPLE. There was once a world where the streets were lined with stone statues that had a face of a man at the top and an erect penis jutting out from the pedestal, and those penises were never defaced, not because 13 year olds didn't exist but because no one envied the statues or the people who erected them. In fact-- and it's hard to put a precise date on these things but I think most scholars would agree-- when some still unknown individuals finally did deface them, *it was the beginning of the end of the world.*[39]

---

39 There are few things potentially more boring than a 2500 year old whodunit, but in this one catching the criminal is much less important than guessing what happens next. Although there are hundreds of varied academic explanations and investigations into the desecration of the Hermes statues in Athens in 415, their single point of agreement is that Thucydides's account is wrong, or at best incomplete. *Incomplete.* He wrote a 568 page apocalypse and the part he half-assed was what lead to the apocalypse. Ok. I'm no scholar, but ok.

For those who didn't read the story or weren't there to see it I won't spoil Act III of this little mystery, I'll give you Act I and Act II and leave you to wallow in Act IV.

The story begins with the ending of an earlier story, in which the Athenians took four months to conquer an island the size and ferocity of a lullaby. Not content with that or with fighting the Spartans for a decade and a half, the Athenians have been musing about whether they should invade and conquer Syracuse, which, for context, is the only other significant democracy of the time, 4x further away than Sparta and according to reliable sources guarded by Cyclopses. But the Athenians just absolutely must have it, as it's full of oregano or whatever. The biggest advocate of the scheme is Alcibiades, a not very good person who will eventually defect to the Spartans and help them kill 10000 Athenians, but who will then, delirious in his arrogance, have the audacity to return to Athens and suggest they make them their leader. They will. But at this time, what the Athenians know is that Alcibiades is a young go-getter and bon-vivant; an excellent strategist but wannabe tyrant; and a complete egomaniac. Possibly apocryphal but utterly true, he once chopped the tail off a dog so he could be in an anecdote.

Alcibiades gives a speech before the Athenian assembly saying they should Manifest Destiny their empire 500 miles to the west, and any old people who try to dissuade you are cowards afraid of being surpassed by the younger generation. To really visualize this, imagine it's an assembly of assorted stuffed animals and Alcibiades is a very vain bunny. Nicias the dog, a seasoned general from the older generation, tries to dissuade them. He fails, the assembly is persuaded by Alcibiades, and vote to invade Sicily. "Well," says Nicias in his next speech, "if we're going to do this..." and

Pathological jealousy is a rivalry with the wife. Being with her makes you feel more desirable, as long as she's desirable; so someone praising your wife for her desirability is tolerable only insofar as it implies you are desirable. Anything more than that arouses envy-- and disbelief. She has to reject the other guy-- that you think is desirable-- not because she prefers you over him-- as if she was entitled to choose what she wants-- she has to reject him because she now understands he never really wanted her-- he wanted something else. She has to be convinced his desire doesn't count for her, or else she'll be ahead.

Pathological jealousy is a rivalry with the husband. Being with him makes you feel more desirable, as long as he's desirable; so praising your husband for his desirability is tolerable only insofar as it implies you are desirable. Anything more than that arouses envy-- and

---

then massively exaggerates the size of the force necessary, thinking no sane person would agree to send all of their best men and silver into the sunset on giant rowboats. Nicias was right, and the Athenians do exactly that. Worse, they also vote to send not just their very best general-- Nicias-- but also their next two best generals, Lamachus and Alcibiades, who has finally gotten the promotion he has always wanted to deserve. Now, with the all the best men going west, you might wonder who was going to stay home and guard the place against the 16th annual Spartan invasion. Logically, the answer is the worst men. We'll come back to this.

The morning after the vote, Athens awakens to find that during the night was committed the largest act of public vandalism in their history: the many stone statues of Hermes that stood in front of people's homes were defaced, a job that would have required a lot of time, perseverance, and people. The Athenians are shocked and appalled, it is a despicable attack on the very spirit of Athens. Since it occurred right after the big war vote, it is taken to be a very poor omen for the campaign, if not outright sabotage.

It's hard to script this as a story because none of the protagonists actually do anything, but here's the break into Act II: almost immediately, the Athenians conclude that the only people who could have done this sacrilegious act are *Alcibiades*.

You don't have to work to convince me Alcibiades is a jerk, it once took an earthquake just to get him to stop talking about himself, and I know I'm supposed to always believe the victim, but has anyone stopped to look for motive? A rule of writing story or dialogue is that just because it happened doesn't make it a believable story, but even as reality this is pretty unbelievable, you have to imagine that morning after the vote at which he is finally handed command of the largest Athenian expedition in history Alcibiades is up early trying on helmets and shaving his genitals when suddenly a bloodthirsty mob rushes in accusing him of having stayed up all night defacing statues of the god-- and he just stares at them, are you insane? I just got the biggest break of my entire career and you think I'd sabotage it by a night of drunken stupidity? What am I, a draft pick?

Despite its wisdom the crowd can't prove he did it, probably because he didn't do it, but they *know* that this privileged bastard must have done it as evidenced by his privilege. A large reward is offered for information, and immunity is offered to anyone who knows of any other acts of impiety.

Here's where modern secondary sources begin muddling the story, and I'm going to suggest for entirely nefarious purposes. The offer of reward and of immunity are often conflated as if they were two expressions of the same thing, but let me be clear because Thucydides is clear: these are two separate events in time. First they offer a reward for information about the desecration of the Hermae statues AND THEN they offer immunity for information about *other* acts of impiety. You can see where this is going, the best analogy isn't to the police but to the media: we'll pay cash for an interview about the crime, and if anyone has any juicy info about other shameful acts, we'll make you famous. To push the analogy further which will make sense later: impiety is always the charge leveled against a threat to the status quo that wants impotence, and which is publicized as a threat to the democracy by those who do not want freedom.

disbelief. He has to reject the other woman-- that you think is desirable-- not because he prefers you over her-- as if he was entitled to choose what he wants-- he has to reject her because he now understands she never really wanted him-- she wanted something else. He has to be convinced her desire doesn't count for him, or else he'll be ahead... do you see the pattern? Do I need to recopy it for gays? Trees?

This might seem needlessly complicated, after all, she didn't actually sleep with the other guy; but if you want to see just how complicated you're willing to get in the service of your envy, imagine that she does. So if she doesn't sleep with him, if he gets nothing and she gets nothing, then his desire can be most easily reduced to "he only wanted to have sex with you,

---

No surprise, the offers are too good to pass up, some slaves and non-citizen aliens come forward with information, not about the Hermae but about *other* statues defaced in the *past*, crimes which at the time of their occurrence merited no reward or even interest. Also, *separately,* whistleblowers offer detailed information about what the elite do behind closed doors, their secret meetings, and their peculiar perversions of the sacred rituals. In other words, people without status, money, or power, and no other people, have inside knowledge about the Illuminati, which they've been saving for today. And they accuse Alcibiades. Again to be clear though not that it mattered: they don't accuse him of the Hermae, they accuse him of *other* acts of impiety. Allegedly, he divulged the religious Eleusinian Mysteries to the uninitiated while drunk at a party. The evidence is circumstantial, not to mention hearsay, but anyway none of it makes sense: the law, precedent and logic indicate that he can't be guilty of revealing the Mysteries to the uninitiated unless he actually knew the Mysteries because he had been initiated, which he hadn't. Not to be the devil's advocate, but technically a hierophant divulges the Mysteries to the uninitiated in order to initiate them, it's actually what the word hierophant means, which would make all hierophants guilty of impiety.

So who destroyed the Hermae? According to Plutarch, "the people" had three suspects: some Athenians claimed it was Corinthians, friends of Syracuse, to sabotage the expedition; others said it was drunken youth; but "most" thought it was indeed a conspiracy against Athens. The first is a bit of a long shot way to stop a war, but ok. The second at least makes sense, when you consider that the Hermae are just large pillars with a head on top and an upright penis jutting out from the middle, nothing else and this is not a joke, so when Plutarch says the Hermae had their "faces and forms" destroyed, there's nothing else for "form" to refer to except penis. Do I need to draw you a picture? You can imagine a bunch of drunken boy-men 0-11 at the bar which is now closing and diners don't exist, and on their sing-along back to their parents' house they see all these rock hard penises. And it makes them giggle.

In another supplementary source, a man reports that he was up late that night and saw 300 drunk and rambunctious men carousing through the city, up to no good. That's an odd number to have even seen, let alone counted. The number "300" occurs 65 times in Thucydides, in reference to objects, people, and years, so casually but consistently inaccurately that I can only assume it is the Greek equivalent of "holy crap, there was like a million of them". But while I don't know the exact number of people breaking penises that night, it was certainly greater than n=Alcibiades.

But Thucydides says something peculiar: he says only and specifically that the faces were damaged. He does not say the penises were damaged. Think about this. Alcohol has turned you into a 13 year old, and you've decided to vandalize a penis statue that consists of only two things, one of which is a guy's face and the other one of which is a penis. You don't break the penis? Or at least suck it? For the story? In every account of what happened, even in the fictional *Lysistrata*, the penises are broken. Heck, it's the only interesting part of the story-- yet Thucydides doesn't even mention it. The way Thucydides describes it, the defacing prompted a conspiracy investigation; the depenising-- since it is a fact that it happened-- was unremarkable or... disavowed.

And why do Athenians care so much about these statues of Hermes? The typical explanation is

---

that doesn't count." If he does sleep with her, no matter how much you know that's what he wanted, you cannot allow her to know that. You will help her realize, through the magic of yelling, that he did not want her, or didn't want only sex with her: he's a dog, he pursued the first woman available, he came out of a break up, he wants to marry her, he wanted to humiliate her; or, the most satisfying of all rages, he did it because he wanted to humiliate you. He slept with her for some other reason. As if the other guy was-- a woman.

"So it's a self-esteem problem?" A problem for whom? For you? Your problem is your problem. The problem for everyone else is that your envy makes you less energetic in the pursuit of... I was going to write "virtue", but the correct noun is "anything". It can only be

---

Athenian primitive hyper-religiosity, their fear of curses and reprisals from angry gods, mostly concluding this from a combination of ½ of Thucydides's single statement, "And they took the fact exceedingly to heart as ominous to the expedition..." and a brief recollection of *Clash Of The Titans*. But Thucydides's statement has nothing to do with gods or superstition, all you have to do is read the other half of the sentence: "...and done also under a conspiracy to overthrow the state and destroy the democracy."

Whether the Athenians were superstitious or not, it is irrelevant to the discussion here. As metaphysically ominous as the portents were, it occurs to no one to *not* set sail. Including Nicias and he didn't want to go in the first place. No one consults the Oracle. Sacrifices and atonements are not made. If the Athenians were truly wracked by superstitious fear, the boats would never have left. They left. It was the largest expedition since the previous record of 4000 men of arms and "300" horse-- these weren't just the best of the best but all of the best-- and if you make an accounting you'll find a great many talents were carried out of the city. Pericles was dead only 15 years and they already forgot his main lesson: if you have a currency that's harder than you you should make sure it is flowing towards you.

Maybe you're thinking *Oedipus Rex* and the scapegoat theory, such that they merely need to punish *a* guilty person in order to lift the curse. No. Alcibiades is accused, but not only did they not have a trial, not only did they not detain Alcibiades, *they left him in command.* You don't have to speculate why they would leave the man they thought was guilty in charge of everything, it's literally in the text: the accusers didn't think he was guilty, either. Of the *Hermae.* The statues were a pretext to accuse Alciblades of *other things*, so in order to get more time to *contrive* further charges against him, they let him go.

So it seems that the destruction of the Hermes was a conspiracy all right, but not by Alcibiades, but against him. Why so much hate? Alcibiades was a known demagogue and wannabe tyrant, too good looking and famous, with a charismatic hold over both men and women, so you can imagine that his enemies thought his appeal to the idiots was a threat to the democracy, and that's certainly what they said, and certainly what they *believed*. It's wrong. They didn't care about the democracy, either. He was their rival, a threat to *them* becoming "leaders" of the "democracy". Alcibiades had to go. But the first place he had to go was Sicily and conquer it, and then we'll figure out what to execute him for after he brings back the oregano.

So he goes; and what happens is exactly what you may now predict happens. The rest of the Athenians who aren't in Sicily work themselves into a frenzy over rumors that there is a tyrannical revolution in the works, headed by Alcibiades. Who is in Sicily. People are accused of being his spies and confederates; the Athenians don't vet the accusers, that would defeat the purpose: "through jealousy" and "upon the reports of evil men", any "good" men who were accused were automatically imprisoned. In order to prevent a non-existent tyrannical revolution, the democrats bravely weeded out those insufficiently democratic, and they found them right away and just in time. It is said that most of Athens was caught in this fever, but you should take note of what no one would have dared to say: most of the men of action, the men of ambition, the educated, the fighters,

satisfied by depriving the rivals of their satisfaction.

This is the line between arousing pornography and enraging pathological jealousy, choose which side you want to be on because there's no actual line, they're the same. Take the simple example of "drunk." "Drunk" is a common label in porn, but there's no porn labeled as sober. Drunk is a fetish, it stands for something missing. Drunk has the real life connotation of erasing the self ("I didn't know what I was doing, that's not me"); but in porn, "drunk" means *willingly* erased the fake everyday self so that the real desires come out, so that you turn into someone else's fantasy. Thus telling your husband-- a man raised on porn-- "I'm so sorry, I was drunk", as if it was an excuse, doesn't make things better, it makes them

---

the men who set out for the glory of Athens and themselves-- they were all in Sicily. The people left in Athens were... not those people. The ones who stayed behind found the chance to re-make Athens in their own splendid image by purging the remaining traitors, all hail mediocrity; and bafflingly assumed that when the most powerful, fastest, and strongest people came back they would just-- what? Turn over their weapons and just get in line? "Forgive us, we admit we were actuated by boundless hatred and by lust of power, we bring you the spoils of war, and we return humbled and loyal to you. Yes, of course you can keep the farm and my wife, I was stupid for assuming they were my property."

There's a lot that can be said about all this, which makes it remarkable that Thucydides says nothing about this. Instead, he goes off topic for several pages to explain that the Athenians were not very good historians: a hundred years earlier, Hipparchus, an oppressive tyrant, had finally been overthrown by the two Athenian martyrs for democracy Aristogiton and Harmodius; unfortunately, Hipparchus's brother Hippias took over, and it required the Spartans to overthrow him. The current Athenians' experience with tyranny makes them hyper-fearful of its return. That's not an unreasonable fear, it would be like Northerners during the Civil War wondering if the British, or just the idea of monarchy, might not be contemplating a rematch. What Thucydides finds worthy of criticism is that the Athenians don't remember that the tyrant of the last century was actually not Hipparchus and then his brother Hippias, but only Hippias. You may be underwhelmed with this correction, thinking this is analogous to an American saying, "Wasn't it Hoover?" No, Harding. "Wait, there was a President named Harding?"

So in the middle of his telling of the Hermae statues and the Sicilian expedition and everything else, Thucydides goes into a long non-sequitur into the correct history of the 100 year old tyranny. Most people skip over this part. They shouldn't, and I'll use your own analogy: "There was a President named Harding?" He died in office, 1923. "Was he assassinated?" No, he died of stroke. And heart attack. "Aren't those two different things?" What? This was right in the middle of the Teapot Dome scandal, in which Cabinet members were found to have taken bribes from oil companies; people went to jail. Charles Forbes-- yes, that Forbes-- was accused of siphoning money; his lawyer committed suicide. Jess Smith-- Harding's poker buddy and one of his closest aides at the Justice Department, but who had no official position there, the man who knew more about Teapot Dome than anyone-- committed suicide the night before he was scheduled to be arrested after Harding gave him a day's head start. All his papers were found burned. No oil company was ever convicted of paying the bribes. Meanwhile, Harding was a notorious philanderer, and at one of his famous Illuminati parties that he had to be evacuated from a woman identified as a hooker died from a head wound. To be clear about the order: she died. Then she slipped and wounded her head. And then was identified as a hooker. I'm still hazy as to exactly when Harding was evacuated. His years of sexual devastation had a full time a clean up crew; abortions were performed, payoffs made-- and paybacks... alleged. A few days after Smith's suicide, President Harding cryptically asked Sec. O'Commerce Herbert Hoover, "If you knew of a great scandal in our administration, would you expose it, or bury it? Asking for a friend." Hoover the moralist told him to expose it, and at least get credit for integrity. Harding was sanguine, "it would be politically dangerous..." The next month he

way worse[40].   He can control you, he can't control other people; hence a massive amount of energy spent on controlling how she acts/looks *to* other people.[41]

---

lay dying suddenly in a hotel in California, his wife with him, but when doctors like the President of Stanford University came to the scene, his wife forbade anyone to examine the body.   There would be no autopsy, and he was embalmed within an hour; meanwhile she rushes back to the White House and when everyone and the body finally get there, she is found burning documents. It's later discovered that Dr. Sawyer, Harding's personal physician, had been giving him mysterious "purgatives" for the past month. Fun fact about Dr. Sawyer's service to the nation: He had always refused any payment for being Harding's doctor-- wait for it-- to avoid liability, he said, in case the President or the First Lady ever died under his watch. No, that wouldn't actually fly in civil court, but is irrelevant because he wasn't actually a doctor. "How did this guy become physician to the President?" Well that's a funny story: Harding's mom was a doctor, who accidentally killed a child with opiates, and Sawyer backed her fake diagnosis to protect her. And then was promoted to Brigadier General of the Army Corps. Anyway, after being identified as a pyromaniac Harding's wife was quickly admitted to "Dr." Sawyer's "sanitarium" for "treatment" where she stayed for a year, and died. "How come I've never heard any of this?" But they made sure you learned about Nixon, right? Do you think it's because the Illuminati is protecting Warren G. Harding? Or because what Nixon did was worse? No. It's because with Nixon the media gets to be the main character in their own story, and the primary source for all secondary sources.

The correct history, Thucydides says, is this: Hipparchus was the younger brother of the tyrant Hippias. Hipparchus is a patron of the arts and all around fun guy, and he makes googly eyes at a man named Harmodius, who rebuffs him.   Harmodius's boyfriend, Aristogiton, worries that Hipparchus might try to take Harmodius by force or at least by confirmative assent, and sulkily fantasizes... not quite fighting him, or cuckolding him, or whatever, but overthrowing the source of his power, which is his older brother the tyrant Hippias. That may seem excessive. It is, especially in that the tyranny of Hippias was not oppressive but quite liberal.   Of course Aristogiton does nothing, like all revenge fantasies the fantasy is its own reward.

Hipparchus, however, does try try to seduce Harmodius a second time, and is rebuffed again; Hipparchus is miffed, but doesn't want to use violence (that's a quote) and instead insults Harmodius by... calling his sister a slut. Words hurt. Harmodius and Aristogiton seethe, for different reasons, and decide to make real Aristogiton's elaborate fantasy for hyperbolic revenge: the overthrow of Hippias.

I will pause here to emphasize a nuance: Aristogiton's original fantasy for acting to punish Hipparchus was indirect-- by overthrowing his brother Hippias. Now that the plan is actually to overthrow *Hippias*, how do you think he'll go about it?

There is an annual parade in which the citizens are supposed to march with their arms, which in Athens are spears. The plan for the overthrow of Hippias is this: Harmodius, Aristogiton, and a few other confederates will bring daggers, sneak up on *Hipparchus*, and stab him. That's it. That's the whole plan of action for the overthrow of Hippias.   They believe that when the crowd sees them do this, the people will be inspired by the assassination of the slut shaming Hipparchus and *they* will rise up and overthrow Hippias-- the friendly, affable, and non-oppressive tyrant. You'll note that

232

Catholic school joke:

> In the lunch line of the school cafeteria is a bowl of apples, next to which a nun has written: *Take only one apple-- God is watching!*

> At the other end of the line is a plate of cookies, next to which a child has written: *Take as many as you want-- God is watching the apples!*[42]

---

this part isn't so much a plan as something a 15 year old might underline in a pamphlet.

If the desire is to overthrow Hippias, why kill Hipparchus and thus alert Hippias to shenanigans? If the desire is to kill Hipparchus and you're not the go-getter you thought you were, why not at least kill him Macbeth style and not at a public parade where, gee, everyone is armed? You might be tempted to say doing it this way is two birds/one stone, but remember the only reason they wanted to overthrow Hippias is because he was the source of Hipparchus's power. If you follow the force vector of the fantasies and the plan, the answer is that no matter what it is they actually want, in order to act on what they want, it has to be for some other reason.

But on the big October day, Harmodius and Aristogiton notice one of their confederates speaking to Hippias; they assume they're being ratted out (they're not), and hurriedly kill Hipparchus. Harmodius is caught and killed on the spot (NB: with a spear), Aristogiton a short while later. Hippias is informed about his brother's murder, and can't fathom that anyone would do that this way for a petty reason and immediately concludes it has to be a political conspiracy; he puts on his poker face and tells the crowd he has an exciting announcement to make, leave your weapons over here and gather over there. His guards collect the weapons, and anyone who had a dagger is executed. It's not many people, but it isn't zero. And now Hippias is nervous, he knows tyrants historically have short lives. Over time Hippias becomes more paranoid, more despotic, and the Athenians start to suffer under an increasingly oppressive tyranny until he is eventually overthrown by the Spartans.

It's bad enough men can see her in ways he can't control. What about when men and women see him in ways he can't control? Is there a porn that can fix that? Plenty: intricate, detailed, consumer products laden stories about a cheating wife whose husband finally gives her what she deserves. "I'd drain all the accounts and make her suck my Glock!" Seems excessive, all she did was take off all her consumer products and give the other guy what he deserves. "At least it's not some wimpy cuckold story. Finally, a man acting like a man!" You're talking about the other guy? "No! The husband!" But what was preventing the husband from acting like a man, when nothing prevented the other guy? Why do you need a fantasy for that?

At this point I should probably point out that a person who fantasizes an overly

---

This is the truth about the former tyranny that the Athenians had wrong. The history they told themselves was that Hipparchus was the tyrant, and he was overthrown by Aristogiton and Harmodius, not over some petty penile grudge but because they were true democrats, deliverers of Athens from shame, avengers of Liberty's wrongs, acting for the benefit of all, nobly sacrificing their lives for freedom against tyranny. They even built statues to them. Endless ages would cherish their fame, embalmed in their echoing songs. Harmodius and Aristogiton became, in the popular imagination, pro-democracy tyrannicides. Yes, eventually the Spartans had to come and finish the overthrow of the successor tyrant Hippias, but "we" Athenians took out the first one.

Thucydides offers evidence that the official story is a fiction. Everyone knows the first tyrant, Pisistratus, was Hippias and Hipparchus's father. The tyranny passed logically to his oldest son-- Hippias, as evidenced by the fact that Pisistratus named him Greek style after his own tyrant father, Hippias. And if you want concrete proof of all this, there was and still is an altar in the agora placed there by the grandson of Pisistratus (named, of course, Pisistratus) with an inscription in honor of his father-- the tyrant Hippias. The Athenians had over the years built up the altar, but *deliberately destroyed the inscription.*

This wasn't a mistaken recollection of history; the Athenians had disavowed the truth.

So the actual disavowals Thucydides claims to correct are: 1) the tyrant was really only Hippias all along, not Hipparchus; 2) Hippias's tyranny wasn't oppressive until after his brother's murder, related to paranoia about a conspiracy; 3) Harmodius and Aristogiton were motivated not by democracy but phallus envy. In other words, what Thucydides implies is that the Athenians are bad at history, worse at democracy and great at making things up. They've also conveniently forgotten that the precious Hermae statues that were appallingly desecrated and must be avenged were originally placed there by Hipparchus. You know, the tyrant.

The non-sequitur about the non-overthrow of the non-Hipparchus tyranny is the only way Thucydides can tell the story about the Hermae. The Athenians disavow that either has anything to do with gross anatomy penises. It can only be about the ideological *face*. In both stories, a petty envy is elevated into a political cause; and the consequent paranoid magnification of a non-existent conspiracy which is then used to consolidate power. In both stories, the Athenians pretend to be fighting for democracy when they are really just fighting rivals out of envy, and then congratulate themselves for their virtuousness. And both stories minimize the unfortunately undeniable fact that the Spartans were the ones who overthrew Hippias, by inventing the story that the Athenians overthrew the previous tyrant Hipparchus.

Anyone who thinks Thucydides is not clever enough to write quasi post-modern, or at least esoteric, ciphertext should consider that the word he used to describe the defacing of the Hermae faces-- while saying nothing about the penises-- is the word literally translated as to trim, to *prune*. Uh oh. And the word he uses to describe the destruction of the Hippias altar's inscription was "un-reveal." This is the writing style of a man who knows when he's not wanted. This is lost in the various translations-- both Warner and the Strassler translation say their faces were "mutilated" and the complicated and elaborate revenge instead of acting directly on what he wants isn't thinking like a psychopath but fantasizing like a child, but the rebuttal to this is that draining the accounts and making her suck a Glock all sound pretty adult. And they are, except they're not what he wants. This is not a man who can act on what he wants, he can't even fantasize it, and I know this because the story is written by someone else.

The kind of guy who extracts revenge on a cheating wife-- sorry, let me be very precise: the kind of guy who enjoys someone else's fantasy about revenge against an imaginary cheating wife is not a sadist fantasizing about violence, nor a masochist pretending to be a martyr; the fantasy is used to describe the kind of a guy he would be if he acted. But he can't fantasize acting, so he has to fantasize being compelled to act (for example, if she cheated).

---

inscription "obliterated", because-- why bother, close enough? But not Hobbes, another guy with a go-bag and multiple passports, who slyly indicates both his understanding of Thucydides and wind direction by translating the phrases as, "had their faces pared" and "defaced the inscription".

Which brings us to the fourth correction Thucydides makes, which renders his seemingly pointless non-sequitur suddenly deadly pointy: 4) Hippias wasn't actually overthrown by the Spartans, to the disavowed shame of the Athenians. He was overthrown by the Spartans *lead by the ancestors of Alcibiades*.

Now the Hippias/Hipparchus story is both a history and-- a parable. In Athens the accusers said they were fighting against the tyranny of Alcibiades and his conspirators, and they are protecting the democracy as did the mythologized Harmodius and Aristogiton. Ironically, it was exactly like the real Harmodius and Aristogiton: they merely pretended to want to preserve democracy, the only conspiracy was theirs, their motives were purely selfish, and Athenians are very good at manipulating history to end up on the right side of it. And #4, the Spartans? What a coincidence: just as everyone is yelling at Alcibiades, the Spartans are spotted marching towards Athens. That had to be working with Alcibiades, right? It's not like the Spartans would just invade Athens on their own, would they?

In this context the Athenians offer the reward and the immunity for information. The whistleblowers come forth, identify the guilty, who are all executed, except for the ones who confess and point out more conspirators. It's such a reliable system I fully expect it to be used in the U.S. eventually. The execution of these prisoners had no practical but four very important psychological benefits: 1) it revealed the left-behind Athenians as part of a great struggle for Athenian democracy against a sinister enemy, because someone, hell, it could even be a woman, might have observed that while real men were out fighting in Syracuse these idiots were doing nothing at all; 2) finding conspirators made it true that they were right about a conspiracy, it manifested their knowledge; 3) it unified, and made sense of, the chaotic, random, and all-too-*coincidental* threats they faced, that would have required multiple disparate and unfilmable actions instead of the frantic, dramatic performance of action that was a defense against impotence; 4) the purge of scapegoats cleansed them of their own shame, including: the disavowed shame of not actually having overthrown the tyranny 100 years ago; having ignored the desecration of the other statues in the past; and now using those and the destruction of the Hermae for their own selfish purposes.

If this sounds like a preposterously complicated way to assuage the anxiety that comes from not wanting to act, let alone act correctly-- if you think a person, let alone thousands of people-- could fool themselves this way, let alone derive psychological benefit from it; that linking a made-up conspiracy to a made-up historical event would make them feel good about themselves-- let me quote what Thucydides says happened as a result, it is only one sentence long, Thucydides's laconic brevity after pages of complicated exposition reveals the exasperation of a man who could not believe what he was about to write: "The city received immediate and manifest relief." WTF. The Athenian democracy was finished.

Now he's powerful, he's a man of action, even though it's only reaction. That he needs a wife to cheat in order to be able to fantasize action suggests he has no idea what "a man of action" looks like, or marries, or does, hence the branded symbols of power prominent in the fantasy. He can't use a gun, it has to be a Glock. It's the kind of guy he is, not the guy he is. It's an entirely inauthentic display of identity, so to the demographic, it's 100% authentic. Tell me you killed your rival and I'll have a couple of questions, tell me you smote your foe with Orcrist and I have all the answers.

There's always a My Lawyer® in the stories, but since his only understanding of lawyers is TV the lawyer doesn't actually do much lawyering, he's there mainly because powerful men always seem to have one. And Glocks. Don't bother trying to explain he wouldn't need both,

---

Slightly off topic, you should also know what happened to Hippias after he is overthrown: he flees first to the Spartans, then to the Persians, and then returns with their help to re-conquer Athens, but fails. *That is exactly what Alcibiades does.* Like Hippias he's a traitor to Athens twice over, the only difference is that Alcibiades was actually invited back to Athens, by the very same numbskulls who wanted to kill him to save the democracy, in order to help them set up an oligarchy. But what do you expect when your civil unrest is managed by idiots, except an oligarchy? You really think they're going to let everyone have a say? Alcibiades is an epic jerk, both Thucydides and Socrates agree with me, and a bit of a dummy, he's the kind of 40 year old male who was last alpha at 25 and stopped maturing at 20 because he already knew everything at 16, whose strategy is therefore not to directly challenge a rival but instead sneak, seduce, subvert, and make sure he gets the credit, and if it's a slow news day chop the tail off a dog. He's not so much a lion or a wolf as he is a chimpanzee, at first you're thrilled, "oh my god, is that a chimpanzee?!" and the next thing you know you're covered in feces and on fire. I wouldn't so much warn my daughters to stay away from him as I would my sons to shoot on sight. Nevertheless, it's useful to hear his side of the story. While in Sicily the Athenians call him back to execute him, so he defects to Sparta, where he tells the Spartans that democracy is probably ridiculous but he and his family have always been hostile to tyrants; and anyone who opposes arbitrary power is called his People. His family's philosophy has always been to uphold whatever government maximizes greatness and freedom, and that's now the Spartans, not the Athenians. I know it's a work, but I also think he meant it. So there's that.

But then he says something else, worth quoting, and NB he says this not to Athenians as an excuse but to the Spartans to whom he is defecting; and even though I'm quoting it's probably not his words, but Thucydides's, so it likely applies to both men:

> I am an outlaw from the iniquity of those who drove me forth, not, if
> you will be guided by me, from your service: my worst enemies are
> not [you Spartans] who only harmed their foes, but *they who forced
> their friends to become enemies*; and love of country is what I do not
> feel when I am wronged, but what I felt when secure in my rights as
> a citizen. Indeed I do not consider that I am now attacking a country
> that is still mine; I am rather trying to recover one that is mine no
> longer; and the true lover of his country is not he who consents to
> lose it unjustly rather than attack it, but he who longs for it so much
> that he will go to all lengths to recover it.

Well? I've offered my dismissive judgement of Alcibiades, but who am I to even dare? And it's my opinion that the Sicilian invasion was ill advised, poorly improvised, and idiotic-- but who am I to say this? From the safety of a car? But what I know with the entirety of my soul is that as the ships left the Piraeus bound for the unknown, and Alcibiades watched the receding but indignant faces of the stay at home Athenians who had given him all the power so they could later accuse him of stealing it, he must have let out a heavy sigh, put his head in his hands and pushed his eyeballs into his skull, and lamented that what he was leaving behind was madness.

he knows everything already. Meanwhile the husband still drains the   accounts, hides the assets, invades privacy and gathers evidence not permissible in any court: these extra-legal maneuvers brand as powerful. Any physical revenge is cruel and/or violent to the extreme, lovers' skulls are bashed and testicles are smashed, and even if the wives aren't physically harmed they are taught that grown ups pay, grown ups suffer consequences, none of that makes semantic sense but I'm just quoting form the primary sources. That's what (he thinks) power does to its enemies. It smotes them. He sends photos of her cheating to her job, because the job has the power to punish her, corporate jobs may be a field of HR pussy willows but they don't tolerate individual expressions of will. No one knows that better than him.

---

40 But: the kind of woman who was drunk when she cheated would NOT be married to the kind of man who would interpret it as, "she was drunk, she didn't know what she was doing" but to the kind of man that hears "drunk" as "obliterating the resistances to pursuing real desires," and he thinks this because he thinks *he* is her only resistance, he is her superego. The easy interpretative mistake to make is that since he is a jerk, he is obstructing her from pursuing her desires. No. He doesn't want her to even have desires. That's who she picked: that's why she will have cheated.

41 But the pathologically jealous man didn't choose a woman who could act on her desires, did he? He chose the kind of woman who would like.... a pathologically jealous husband, sorry folks, that's how it works. Love is not real and lust is highly contingent, so she'll settle for any kind of affect as long as the volume is set to 11. "It's one louder." His rage means... he wants me. His rage is an accounting of how many other people he thinks want me, even if I've become convinced no one wants me because the ones who do don't count. Having no practice with her own desires, she settles on the one reliably endorsed by her husband and TV: the desire to be desired. He worries that she is, and convinces her she's not, by making sure he doesn't.

Sometimes a structural fight is turned into a rivalry, and sometimes the rivalry is perceived as a structural battle. When I was 20 I applied for my first corporate job, and as this was during the era of management consulting, excellence at the cubicle level was secondary to "being part of a winning team". Instead of a triathlon or Mensa puzzles as part of the interview process we were invited to spend a day in "team building" exercises. "Dress casually," we were shocked to hear her say, "we want you to be comfortable." She was right, trust falls are hard to do in heels. It was a different time, nowadays whenever I see anyone dressed up in a suit I say a little prayer for them, the only places they could be going to are a funeral or trial. There but for the grace of God go I.

So in a huge meeting room with one stool, two flip boards and nothing else, one of the impeccably high heeled sophisticates running the exercise wrote "OK" on one flip board located at one end of the room, wrote "NOT OK" on another located at the other, perched felinely onto the stool, crossed her legs high and no doubt work appropriately, and asked us to walk over and physically choose sides: "How would you feel if your spouse made more money than you?" She didn't answer herself, but I'm going to guess she was OK with it.

Oh, to be 20 year old adult again, dressing for the job you want and undressing for the person you shouldn't. I marched maturely over to OK, situated myself criss cross applesauce on the floor as the kind of mature adult who would be OK, audibly nudged the marketing major sitting next to me, "heck, better than OK, I'd actually prefer it!" and we all masturbated each other, appropriately smug about how stupid our fathers are.

Of course, on the other side of the room, standing, not sitting, in front of "NOT OK" was-- well, book by its cover I judge he knew two letters of greek and where to rent a keg. There before us was everything wrong with America, and it was wearing a baseball hat.

Anne Taylor duly asked three or four of us who were OK to expound on our egalitarianism, and then

Why does she have to be punished? It's not because she cheated, per se, but because she took away all the glorious possibilities that a Glock signaled; she dragged and chained him to a cubicle and a conventional marriage, and then cheated. The rule of relationships is that the ledger must be balanced. You might get more of what you want, that's ok, but no one can enjoy more than the other; she can't enjoy more than him, it is obscene. To prove this, the fantasy uses the contrivance that she obscenely enjoyed... more than him. The unconscious has the structure of a language, get it? Now it's time to even up. How? Success is the best revenge, but the kind of success you used to imagine requires the kind of work you could never imagine, so that's out. Seduce her friends? Hmmm, risky, plus they wouldn't count, and you won't enjoy sex with her friends as much as she'd enjoy sex with your friends. Better to

---

in patronizing paternalistic amusement asked Sigma Epsilon if he wouldn't mind removing his cap and justifying his entitled-to opinion. The person who kept the hat on may have been a frat guy, but the person who responded was 100% econ major: "I wouldn't be happy if she made more money than me, I'd feel like I wasn't working hard enough. I feel like I have to make more money than everybody."

You can guess he didn't get the job; in fact, he didn't last the day, later I spotted a male sophisticate having a private but public discussion with him and we never saw him again. I don't know what became of him. But he was right.

Here was a structural problem reduced to the level of a rivalry, and all of us fig counters raised on "'Greed is good' is bad" understood that the problem was Capitalism in order to make it ok to hate capitalists while working as serfs. The econ major's ambition made no sense to us, corporate as we were hoping to become, and so his "NOT OK" had to be a frat guy's misogynist secret rivalry with a more successful wife. He was threatened by powerful women, we'd say, and no doubt he would be looking to marry a sorority girl. Of course, we couldn't say that out loud, because if any sorority girls heard us they'd rightly tell us to get over our stereotypes, and then we would be the ones threatened by powerful women.

Interesting that even today it would not occur to any woman to stand under NOT OK; and maybe he was a misogynist as evidenced by refusing to sit, I doubt it, but what if he was? Jump to the middle-end of the movie and ask, what if it happened? What kind of a man would he be if he was OK? He recognizes her achievements, applauds her tenacity and success, feels lucky to marry up? Do you think the patriarchy that allowed her to make more money than him would also leave one of their own psychologically defenseless? No. "Of course she doesn't work harder than me," he'd explain as if it needed no explanation, "she only has a job that pays more." Because, of course, the job is omnipotent, now you see why this was Corporate's first team exercise. Since these things are out of his power-- structural forces that allowed her to get a better job not because she was better but because, who knows, the system favors women over men?-- why not accept it?

But he didn't believe these things were out of his power, and if he did believe men were better than he had a way bigger problem that was "NOT OK": if men are superior than women either by design or by design, yet she's still able to make more than him, then doesn't that mean he's even less than a man? Shouldn't he be working harder? Better? You can postulate some universe where "they already have enough," fine, but how about working harder so she could work less? "That's sexist." It's sexist to let her work less? "She doesn't want to work any less--" These are the rationalizations of a mind made of turnips, the point is he could work harder to make her life better, period. I get that he could make her life better in ways that didn't involve money, ok, I have heard of alchemy, but except for two or three exceptions the only people I've ever met who actually did try to make their spouse's life better in non-economic ways were women. "But I wouldn't resent her for making more money than me." I believe you: you think it's because you're not a resentful person? You? It's because her money doesn't count, it's out of your (pl.) power. You might get jealous of her money but you wouldn't envy her for that-- it doesn't count. Your resentment will surface in things for

stick to what you're good at, because if you fail your enemies will laugh at you.

Everything in the fantasy is about that imbalance of enjoyment; nothing in the fantasy is about anything else. Including sex. If the problem is she enjoyed more, then the solution has to be either increasing his enjoyment relative to hers (totally impossible-- see below) or depriving her. The violence itself can't rebalance the ledger unless he enjoys violence, which he doesn't, it doesn't count either. The violence is only a means to an end-- the end of rebalancing the ledger.

You'll say that the cheating as the cause of rage is fundamental to such "male" stories because it is a direct assault to his masculine pride. No, look at the story: she didn't cheat.

---

which you do use a ledger, like what she gets to do with her Saturdays or how work keeps wanting her attention, wanting her; or, if your castration has been particularly complete, why she gets to spend more on her clothes and grooming than you do. "Clothes make the man." Into a woman?

Later on we had to do that dom/sub team building exercise in which a blindfolded person trusts you'll catch them as they fall backwards, and for structural reasons even then I had the suspicion that the person I could have trusted most to catch me was SigECaps, but what I and everyone else didn't stop to contemplate was how there was no way he could have trusted any of us to catch him, if he went down he was on his own. No, you're not really seeing the point, I can tell. Of course we need to depend on each other when we fall, that's the reason it's a team building exercise, but if you want to see a critique critiquing itself note that companies no longer do these team building trust falls because of the liability. It was never about trust, it only works because only some of us *and not all of us* see the hidden obligation: if you are responsible to catch, you have to be depended on not to fall, there's no I in team but there's no we in duty. There's only you. I guess the arithmetic he did was that since he was probably going to be hated for it at least he should get paid for it. "We all contribute in our own ways." From each, according to our need.

42 Come on, does no one read the primary sources? The one thing God doesn't do is watch apples, this is demonstrably inaccurate, the nun should know better. And, the nun isn't watching the apples either. Nobody is watching the apples, and unlike cookies what the hell kind of kid is going to take two? Is he escalating for the wicked cool food fight planned for 12:30 or are we going to stuff our bras with them?

So before we applaud the clever boy for besting the idiot nun, we should consider the possibility that the nun isn't an idiot and the boy is just a boy.

It may be that the nun, watching the kids NOT take any apples, puts up the prohibition as reverse psychology, "they always want what is forbidden to them," hoping the kids will thus want healthy apples. Inciting a transgressive desire even for a good purpose isn't very sisterly, but it also won't work: the object of desire is the apple, but the cause of desire isn't the apple but the prohibition. Which means getting the apple will not satisfy, unless you're a model, because models only eat apples while they know full well they shouldn't. Liquids only and photograph the rest. The sign may trick them into taking an apple this time, but finding them unsatisfying, they will effectively have learned not to trust any more signs. "So we turn to wisdom." Sadly, yes.

Assuming the nun is not an idiot, assuming she's thought this through, then perhaps her plan was not to trick kids into eating healthy apples, but merely to get the kids to take them so she wouldn't have to throw them away, after all, wasting food is a sin. Maybe this nun would like to discuss the relative sinfulness of causing another person to sin, especially so you don't have to? Some other time? Ok.

The other possibility is that the nun is malicious: she's created a guilt for a sinless act not to protect her apples but to deprive the kids of their unique enjoyment of excess. This possibility only makes

She doesn't even exist. It's a fantasy. The cheating is incidental, not fundamental, it is the contrivance that propels the story only because there is no law against it. Everything else she could do has redress in the Law, it has absolute power to punish all crimes. For some reason, however, the Law completely ignores infidelity. If you think about it, which he has, it's insane that infidelity, an act that results in such an imbalanced ledger, offers the victim no compensation; not no equivalent compensation, none at all. If you really, really think about it, which he really, really has, you could even conclude that the Law doesn't just ignore her cheating-- as if the patriarchy served men except in the one thing really important to men-- it encourages her to cheat: to enjoy. In real life the Law castrates him. This is why the fantasy isn't that she stole from him or tried to murder him (the Law could handle it), but that she

---

sense if she's also an imbecile, because it's a children's cafeteria in which cookies exist but she doesn't think to deprive them of those.

But this gets us to the po-mo Catholic solution: it tacitly lets you break one rule, by giving you another harsher rule that you don't break. You're no doubt familiar with the rationalization that you're still a good person because at least you've obeyed the majority of the rules or the big ones. This is different. This is finding a way to take credit for not doing something sinful when the reason you didn't was that you couldn't, not that you didn't want to. You need an objectively measured system of rules that could reasonably apply to you that allows you to calculate a true bottom line in your favor. In the spirit of historical authenticity let's work through the derivation in Latin. Say eating a cookie is a sin, with a value II per cookie; but eating an apple is declared to be a sin of X. The kid takes IV cookies. Ergo, he's has sinned VIII which you can see is almost as bad as eating one apple, but he's still better than all models. But wait, says your accountant, the tax code allows you to make a deduction: you didn't simply not eat an apple; you deprived yourself of an apple. So now it's:

II times IV → IV IV = IIVV = IIX = VIII → God shows on his ledger that you owe VIII

You show X = VIIIII on your ledger that God owes you for depriving yourself

VIIIII minus VIII→ VIIIVIIIII (→ remove common symbols) = II → TOTAL = II that God owes you in your ledger

I know, I know, the tax code doesn't allow you to deduct more than you made, but we're arguing that you're not offsetting a gain but deducting from a loss. "Makes sense, but will it pass an audit?" As long as you keep good records. In fact, if you can show you didn't get an abortion last year, you can carry MMMM of that forward every year and use it against future infidelities. "Privileged and confidential: but last year I got my girlfriend pregnant because I forgot to pull out, so we had to go for an abortion." Slow down, Johnny Appleseeds: you got her pregnant, but she got the abortion. It's a woman's right to choose. How do you like them apples?

So to solve the problem of the guilt which is too hard to avoid but impossible to feel, the system tacitly permits you to get away with one thing (cookies) by allowing you to take credit for not breaking an explicit rule (apples) that was within your power to break but were never going to break anyway. "Rules are rules, I don't question the logic." So now the boy isn't revealing a flaw in the system but is in effect performing an ideology built for adults who are children: it only counts if it is counted.

If you take the theological position that God is not a very good accountant, then the only way this would work is if God knows THAT you didn't eat an apple, but doesn't know WHY you didn't eat the apple, which is why you have to keep a ledger: so you can tell him why. "I stayed strong." It's easier now that cookies exist. If God was omniscient of causes and desires, if he knew you didn't

cheated. This is the only crime it does not care about, which means it is one of the only ways you get to show "what kind of a man" you are-- what does that mean? It means to be able to act without recourse to a higher authority. It's all you.

You're going to say the Law would permit him to cheat, too, why doesn't he just do that, but you're still not thinking straight: she didn't cheat. She's not even a person. It's a fantasy. He doesn't want to cheat. It's not about cheating, but about being able to act.

But what about the alpha male she cheated with? That guy for sure wasn't impotent, let alone castrated. Exactly. It's perfectly *natural* for a guy to try to seduce his wife, but it's also natural he could then get shot in the face with a Glock. Right? Here we have two groups-- women and alpha males-- that rather than being castrated or at least punished by the Law use the Law as a loophole in the natural order of things, it gives them immunity from natural liability while disabling him in the protection of his rights. "She's not his property." I was referring to happiness. In fact, you could say it's not just her that's bad; the Law is corrupt, it has to be punished.

Well, this doesn't happen. As much as the Law castrates him, it's also the only thing that tells him his life has value. He defines himself as a hard working, law abiding Glock owner, because the alternative is he has to make his own life in a world that has no laws and everyone has a gun. He needs the world exactly as it is, he can't destroy it, it has to remain intact, otherwise the trivial successes of his life simply don't count. Who's going to give him credit for being a hard worker or good husband-- especially if she cheats-- if not the Law? Those things are done out of obligation, no one else is going to credit him for them. He needs the Law. Thus, in his fantasy, he doesn't destroy the Law; the Law doesn't interfere. It's not that the Law can't stop him, it doesn't try. It just-- stands aside.

You can ask why, if he derives so much self-worth from the Law, doesn't he just fantasize the Law punishing her for cheating. All his other fantasies are about swords and castles, why not set it in 900 AD, have her be taken in irons and watch the clerics set her on fire? But then he wouldn't need the cheating fantasy at all. The fantasy is about cheating because the Law doesn't punish cheating, so he can fantasize punishing something. He needs to fantasize about punishing because it's the only action he can even fantasize himself possibly performing, because it is not properly an action, it's a reaction, but it looks mighty powerful.

When I said the Law stands aside, I don't for a second mean he believes has the right to punish her. It can't be a right, because it would be his to act on. He believes he has been granted the privilege, it is a special case, he is a special case, because the Law knows who he is. That counts.

You should count the number of times he's been castrated on your fingers: first, in real life, the wife prevents him from exerting any power in general by making him an emasculated, law abiding cubicle husband and gun owner. Then, in fantasy, his wife takes even that away, by enjoying more than him, depriving him, and getting away with it. Surprise and fortunately, it's the one thing the Law ignores. Now he can act. It took two castrations to get

---

like apples, or that you cleverly didn't eat the apple in order to net some cookies, then it wouldn't count, you are at -VIII. So God can't be omniscient. You have to be, in order to foil him. But he has to be powerful enough to say you are good. Only a system of ledgers in which are tallied your sins against all the sins you didn't commit, that you deprived yourself of, will you come out ahead. "But surely God couldn't possibly be fooled by this." You bet your life he can. "But I don't believe in God." You mean you've been doing all this for yourself-- for no reason?

him to act.

The reason you have to count them is that while he is terrible at math he is excellent at accounting: after being castrated twice, any power he does get only moves him back up one castration, to where he was before she cheated, but it feels like he gained something. I guess you never traded stocks. Say her cheating cost him 40% of his phallus, then if his revenge gets him back to where he was, he gained 66%. The math says he's profited 26%, he's ahead, and it's all the sweeter because he gained it at her expense. You will tell me that this maniac can't possibly have deluded himself into thinking he got anywhere more than back to break even, and anyway it doesn't change the fact that she still cheated on him, but again, for the third time: she didn't cheat. He didn't lose 40%. He fantasized about getting 66%. And then he came on himself.

Which is why, after acting on his revenge, he doesn't fantasize becoming a tyrant or getting his own harem. He fantasizes going back to being what he was before the second castration but after the first. Since the Law didn't interfere with his revenge, he happily bows to it afterwards and forfeits his power. The story ends with him plugging right back into the cubicle. In fantasy. The reason for this is the same reason as the branded consumer products: he's an idiot. He can't fantasize anything else. He needed the architecture of the Law-- and someone else's fantasy-- just to be able to fantasize.

This isn't about morality, she's bad and he isn't, nor is it misogyny coming from masochism. The crime is only that she enjoyed more than he did. He only pretends to be faithful himself, in order to take credit for his own fidelity; but in fact, he can't cheat, and this is true even if he did cheat: it didn't count, he didn't really enjoy it, he is not able to cheat like she can-- she's capable of enjoying it more. And the "rival" who took his wife certainly enjoyed her more than he ever could. He already knows it is impossible, in this world, to be a good person-- too much is at stake, after all, house/cars/bills and everyone else is on the take, grifting, cutting corners; so instead of imbalances in justice he's motivated by imbalances in enjoyment. That's why he's glued to media even as he says he hates it: they vigorously detect hypocrisy in those who seem to do whatever they want and also enjoy it. They must pay.

Unfortunately, this complicated fantasy is not his but he thinks it is, so it does not occur to him to ask what he's learning from having this fantasy, what it's for: the purpose of the fantasy isn't to make himself feel better for being a castrated slave, "well, I can be a man if I needed to." The purpose of the revenge fantasy is to train himself to be a slave, in order to get the reward of stealing a little power back.

As long as he thinks it is a privilege, then the Master is still the Master. As long as he thinks what constitutes actions are violent and public shifts from a status quo, then he will always regress to that status quo. As long as he immerses himself in other people's pornography it's no longer even fantasy, it's by the book, socially acceptable tropes of ooh-la-la conformity, no different than BDSM, incest, MFF-- his compliance in the ordinary world is assured. The pornographic fantasy tells him he is chaotic good but is teaching him to be lawful neutral; it seems sociopathic but it is 100% socializing. If you ask why he's satisfied with this ridiculous caricature of Glock power, why doesn't he just go make his own life, then you need to go back to the beginning: the fundamental problem isn't impotence; it's envy. The only thing that will satisfy him is the deprivation of the other, and he is willing to become impotent in order for that to happen. In the final analysis, what he/she did/didn't actually do is a ruse, the math says he's up 66% or at least 26% as long as he deprived her in fantasy.

"Hey, what ever happened to your wife?" --Nothing. "Jesus, what a whore." [43]

Meanwhile the real life or future wife has no idea she's being punished for the cheating she wouldn't even want to do.   Ironically, if she did cheat, the great vengeance that would follow wouldn't follow the fantasy script not because he's a coward after all but because whatever cheating she actually did is a totally different movie than the "cheating" he fantasized her enjoying in order to fantasize his vengeance.   The only fact that still has to be incorporated into the accounting is why the guy who succeeded in getting her in fantasy would fail in real life but the guy who got her in real life fails to be in anyone's fantasies.   "You cheated on me with that guy??" Yes. "How?"

---

43 Get up. The reading is from the Holy Gospel according to St. John. Let's wait.

> And early in the morning he came again into the temple, and all the people came unto him; and sitting down he taught them. And the scribes and Pharisees brought unto him a woman caught in adultery, and put her in their midst. Saying to him, teacher, this woman was caught in adultery-- in the act. Moses in the law commanded us that such be stoned: what do you say? This they said tempting him, that they might have something to accuse him. And Jesus bent down and with his finger wrote on the ground. So when they continued asking him, he got up and said unto them: let the sinless one among you be the first to cast a stone at her. And again he bent down, and wrote on the ground. And those who heard it [being convicted by their own conscience] left one by one, beginning with the eldest; and Jesus was left alone, with the woman standing in the midst. Having gotten up, Jesus said to her, woman, where are they, your accusers? No one condemned you? And she said, no one, sir. And Jesus said to her, neither do I condemn you. Go, and sin no more.

"That's a weird translation." You should have seen the earlier one. Off topic: do you imagine her as a middle aged bantha herder with a prolapsed uterus, or some kind of Mary Magdalenesque belly dancer in a midriff and castanets? You actually thought that was Mary Magdalene? For a book with a dozen different female characters, it's weird you think of them only as Madonna or whore. Secondary sources? Got it.

I know this story is supposed to provoke soul searching, but Jesus's reply is actually ridiculous. Why do you have to be sinless to cast the first stone? That's not part of Mosaic Law, or any law, or even logical. Yet the crowd heard this and backed down?   Why? Because it forced them to introspect, maybe we are all sinners after all, and sulked away guiltily? Really? As if it was possible to make another person feel guilty? If it was so possible, why didn't they just make the adulteress feel guilty, let her stone herself?

One way to solve this is to focus on the line, "convicted by their conscience"; i.e. sinless refers not to vague/ignorable "all sins", but specifically the sin of adultery. Jesus was shaming everyone as having adultered sometime in their backstory. Totally plausible in a time with no TV, and explains why the oldest men, having a lot of backstory with which to be convicted by, leave first.

You could go up one psychic level and allow that maybe no man there actually cheated, but they all wanted to cheat, and as Freud explained, the superego assigns as much guilt to wanting as it does to acting, which is why to Freud, Oedipus's guilt preceded his actions-- the guilt, not the actions, were what was predestined. He was screwed either way, so it may as well be by Jocasta. "That's silly, I certainly don't feel as much guilt when I think about cheating as if I actually had cheated." I think you have never cheated. When you do, you will be pleased to discover that you feel just as much

_____

guilt as when you merely thought about it. If only you had known that sooner!

You could take a parallax view and say that Jesus wasn't a superego conscience but a punitive superego, one that assigned guilt not for an action or even a desire, but for failing to act on that desire. So you're not man enough to cheat with her, you are disgusted with yourself at your lack of balls-- and rather than acting, you stone what you can't bone? Punishing her for her obvious guilt was their defense against their own impotence. What they really resented wasn't that specific act of adultery, but her having the ability to act on her desires. NB: they couldn't even stone her on their own.

Finally, you might play literary detective and suggest that the whole thing is a lie. Why should Jesus believe the mob that this woman was really an adulteress? Is the husband or the lover here? Any evidence? Just hearsay? Smells like a set up. But never mind, the story is about something else.

No matter what your faith, your read on Jesus here is that he is obviously a kind of superego, and since it is obvious you can be sure thinking this is 100% a defense. So it's back to literal: Jesus is never critical, he never prohibits-- he never tells them not to stone her, only that they be without sin. "But he's bluffing." He's betting her life on a bluff? At what odds? Does he have a system? It's not a bluff.

Most Bible nerds agree that the purpose of the passage is to discuss the status of the old covenant/Mosaic laws now that Jesus's presence begins a new one (salvation through faith), and the transition between the two, rhetorically summarized as, "Who punishes sins? God?" But the answer is NOT God, otherwise Jesus wouldn't have allowed anyone without sin to cast the first stone. "But he knew no one there is without sin." So why didn't he throw the rock? "He forgave her." You need to read the story again, or once.

What would be evident to anyone actually there, and Jesus, and anyone writing this story, is that it neither matters if she is really an adulteress, what Mosaic Law commands, or what anyone wants because no one is ALLOWED to stone her: they live under Roman Law, and only it has the power to bring charges and dispense punishment. Only the Roman Law is "without sin," you have no recourse outside that structure; going outside that structure is the crime. This is the non-bluff of Jesus: "ok, let's say God commanded you to stone her, I agree you want to, for various reasons, most of them bananas. So...? Which one of you God fearing men dares overrule Roman legal procedure and do God's bidding or what you want? Anybody? Here's a rock. Anybody?" This is the math: "convicted by their conscience" equals the limit of the "courage of their convictions" divided by "fear of the Romans." It doesn't just approach zero. It is zero.

However the New Testament was cobbled together, however much it appears to be about the Father, the Son, and The Holy Spirit, the single character ubiquitously present is Rome; The New Testament is premised on the existence of that civil-- imperial-- society, a world where some other omnipotent entity has inserted itself between humans and God. The Roman Empire is necessarily omnipresent in the New Testament but is cleverly out of focus, boringly background and setting, it only appears

                    244

                    ECKS
        And you were fine with that?

                    HEIRESS
        I told them to behave, but I don't blame them for trying,
        right? If you have a willing blonde posing for you, you'd
        have to be married to her not to at least try and get her
        top off.

It's almost like she wanted them to try.

She and you have opposite opinions on the matter: you think trying almost never works, and she thinks it almost always works. Unless she's the one trying, then you both switch

---

at civil impasses-- which is the very point of a civil society: "give unto Caesar", appeals to Pilate, censuses. Meanwhile, a casual reader would get the impression that the Pharisees and scribes have all the power. They don't. They have knowledge, but they don't have any power. Rome is the opposite of Big Brother, who is the extreme of omniscient impotence, frantic energy maintaining stasis. Rome, on the other hand, never seems to know what's going on, it does not care to know, it does not need to know. It acts.

The mob becomes a group of children pretending to have their own rules "from God", yet ultimately requiring the Romans' supervision, approval, and power to: pump up the bike tires, break up fist fights, or throw rocks at a bantha herder. Rome is the system that lets the impotent masses pretend they are autonomous because they know more. Remove the Romans and the New Testament becomes the Old Testament and there's no god in The Old Testament: there are many gods.

The New Testament is the description of God's place in a world which doesn't require him. It has Rome. And Rome doesn't care about unfaithful wives, certainly not yours, anyway. You'll observe that the mob didn't drag a murderer in front of Jesus, they didn't ask what to do about the marital assets; only "crimes against God" that have no real analogue in Roman law are offered to Jesus for his consideration/entrapment. It's a crime for which no real punishment is at stake-- except shame; and if she can't be shamed, then what? "Maybe Jesus will tell us stone her." But it's not up to him.

This is one of the reasons why this story is likely a much later addition to John-- much, much later, i.e. when the omnipotence of Rome was wishful nostalgia and so adulteresses were stoned by mobs.

So what is the lesson of the story? "Only God can judge?" That's the lesson they told you to learn, even if you don't apply it, to avoid the work of the lesson you actually need to learn. "I don't like where this is going, and anyway you just said the stoning story is apocryphal." You mean it's not fact? "It's not true!" HA! How can you understand what truth is? Truth has many levels, the lowest truth is the truth of fact which is mostly a defense against the other levels. That's the truth I'm telling you now. I don't know what the story means, you seem to think the meaning is obvious, all I can do is show you how obvious is used. Jesus and the mob know that punishment is no longer the right or responsibility of ordinary men; the switch is that Jesus is telling them he won't do it either. Forgiveness and condemnation are separate, which is why he tells her he won't condemn her even though he never tells her he forgives her. The latter is on her, if she wants it. "What the hell does she need forgiveness for if there's no punishment?" Yes, he figured you were going to say that. The mob wants to know-- what now? What do we do with adulteresses if we can't punish them? Let them get off like they did in the first place? How come they get to act and we don't? Why do they get to enjoy? When do we get to deprive her of something, when do we get our justice, when do we get our sweet, sweet desserts of her just deserts? What should I do if my own wife cheats on me? "No one condemned you?" No one, Lord. "Neither do I condemn you." If no one will stone her, and Rome doesn't care, and God won't punish her, what does Jesus offer the wronged husband-- and the mob-- as compensation?

opinions.

None of the characters exist, everything that happens is a fantasy for the reader. But be precise, take it literally-- after all, it's a fantasy. The fantasy is not that she might go along with it, it's that she doesn't. Sure, most of the people get laid in the end, but the fantasy here isn't to succeed, the fantasy is that even a rejection reflects well on you. This is why the fantasy sexualizes the failure, not "he was trying to assault me" but "he tried to get my top off". She, a beautiful woman=superego, appreciates the effort; hell, she had to refuse him because he's too good at it. What makes James Bond James Bondy isn't how easily he gets the ladies but how smoothly he parries their refusals-- how the rejection makes him look even more desirable-- no, not to the woman that refused him but to the audience. "It's his confidence."

You can close your Bibles now: the answer is nothing.

Since you're not going to listen it's of no use pointing out that wanting her to suffer is the reason you suffer, especially if "her" is a surprised woman in a one or two thousand year old document that you use as a screen for your projection, but even if it is your own wife who cheated the math is the same. It is therefore correct to say that what Jesus offered them in compensation was only freedom from the need for compensation. He brought freedom from ledgers. He brought guilt. It is a gift so painful you wouldn't wish it on your worst enemy-- so you forgive them, to spare them that pain, and in return you are free, because if you live your life with a ledger your the bottom line will always sum to rage. No matter how bad your wife's "crime", she will never get what she "deserves"; God is not active on Earth and the State doesn't care whose penis went inside her or how many times she climaxed on it. Pray on it! And despair! I know you were trained that she'll eventually get her punishment in the afterlife, it says so, well, somewhere; but the marvelous frustration of the system is that despite what's "supposed" to happen you still will never know, I guess you'll have to believe she burns forever because she hurt your feelings so. Of course, then you'll have to explain how your raptured soul finds peace knowing that others are suffering for eternity simply because they hurt you. "Well, I'd forgive her, but it's also an objective sin against God." Objective and God in the same sentence, I sense high school math and more than one TV. Your interpretation of your religion is a defense, so the only thing you can pray for is the balancing of the ledger. Your eternal salvation requires that you forgive her, but you are only capable of this pseudo-forgiveness because you know you have no power to punish her anyway AND you still want credit for being forgiving; meanwhile you think you can hide from God your secret hope that she'll be punished anyway anyway, by God, so it all works out. Let me ask you a question: what if your eternal salvation was based on her forgiving you for your rage against her? "Why the hell do I need to be forgiven by that slut-whore adulteress?" And you are surprised she will have cheated. Maybe to God it seems a fouler offense committed by you than any which had since been done to you, that in the time when her heart knew no better, you tricked her into thinking herself happy by your side. "So you're one of those Buddhist nuts who think anger is always bad?" HA! Nice try, sophist, we're not talking about anger, we're talking about accounting.

Your problem is envy. That's why you focus on the laws and not what they're for. If it had not been for the pernicious power of envy, you would not have so celebrated vengeance above innocence. In these acts of revenge, you take it upon yourself to begin the process of repealing those general laws of humanity which are there to give hope of salvation to all who are in distress. And if you are not so confident in your ad hoc revision of your secondary sources faith that the reassurance that she will eventually be punished in the afterlife fails to brings you comfort, well, then you're screwed, it says so in Luke 7:36. "So what's the solution?" You let it go. "Umm, you know it's not that easy?" Umm, you know why? Because you wrote it down, in a ledger, assets and liabilities. Column Assets says "Me" and column Liabilities says "everything else" and the Liabilities help define the Assets. "Me"-- the man who was wronged; "Me" the one who is not as bad. "Me" the man who likes reading about science but hates math. And right now your unbalanced ledger shows she gets to enjoy cheating and still go to heaven and you're just the law-abiding husband but aren't 100% sure

246

He's confident he's going to strike out 70% of the time? Because he acts on our desire, it's easy to miss that he's not really acting on his desire. "He's just playing the odds, striking out costs him nothing but when he hits it's a home run." Your analogy fails because home runs don't count unless other people know about them. "You don't think hitting home runs is enjoyable in itself?" You got to really love playing ball, and you don't. "Whatever. He's doing what everyone dreams about." You have said it.

Meanwhile, back at the sorority house, Saydee stumbles home drunk to find her roommate's naked boyfriend waiting for the roommate to come out of the shower. It's their "three month anniversary". Being the alpha that he is he immediately tries to seduce Saydee.

---

heaven exists. "To hell with this, I'm going to give that whoreslut what she deserves!" Well it's about god damn time. The problem is that you can't think without a ledger, you assume everyone has one, there's even a ledger in the Bible because you can't even imagine God wouldn't use one. But why would he? What does he need to write down? Who would audit him? He doesn't need a reason to act-- or not act. If you didn't use a ledger you'd be a totally different person, arguably a lot happier but in any case not you. That's the entire purpose of the bottom line rage, it asserts to the universe: sir, I exist! Well, you should read the rest.

"I have some trouble following your Biblical examples, I'm ~(Christian)." Ha! Slippery snake, put down the oil, I'm not here to wrestle you. No one is trying to convert you and nothing bad will happen to you, stop worrying so much about who you are and what you know. Though I do find it giggly that you believe religious faith is 100% related to your environment and thus deserving of historical criticism but your pornographic desires are sacrosanct because they are inherently genetic, you know, like Father to Son. "Why'd you capitalize those?" Autocorrect.

Your brain is stuck, stuck in neutral, what is the proper measure of justice for adultery? But it's not the adultery she needs to be punished for-- had she not committed adultery you'd have fantasized she had, she still has to be deprived, because of your envy: your ledger shows she is more desirable than you. She can enjoy more than you, while you-- are forced to accept it. "It's just not fair." I know, I know. You took out the comma.

That is your curse, to carry a ledger, to check the ledger over and over until it balances, whether that's seven times or seventy seven times or seventy times seven I have no idea, God's math isn't base 10 and I suspect it probably doesn't involve numbers. The very next sentence starts the parable about the "unmerciful servant" and you should read it because it's a lot more complicated than doing unto others:

> Therefore the kingdom of heaven is like a certain king of men who wanted to settle accounts with his servants. And when he had begun to settle accounts, one was brought to him who owed him ten thousand talents. But as he was not able to pay, his master commanded that he be sold, with his wife and children and all that he had, and that payment be made. The servant therefore fell down before him, saying, 'Master, have patience with me, and I will pay you all.' Then the master of that servant was moved with compassion, released him, and forgave him the debt.

> But that servant went out and found one of his fellow servants who owed him a hundred denarii; and he laid hands on him and took him by the throat, saying, 'Pay me what you owe!' So his fellow servant fell down at his feet and begged him, saying, 'Have patience with me, and I will pay you all.' And he would not, but went and threw him into prison till he should pay the debt.

247

She's reviewed enough game films to know he performs well, but she thinks this guy and her roommate are stuck up jerks (even by Tridelt standards). Therefore: she blows him. In her logic a bird in the hand is worth two in her bush, and she can kill two other birds with it. It is a spectacular, R-rated super-pornographic performance in which it appears very much like she is getting just as much out of it as he is, except we later see she's faking it. Of course the guy, unable to reconcile the protocols concerning gift horses and Greeks bearing them, happily goes along with it; he finishes, and she runs off just as the shower stops; and the scene ends with Saydee giggling from the next room as the anniversary couple become frustrated→ irritated→ enraged by his inability to get an erection, "what kind of a man can't get it up for me?"-- and his predictable ego defenses yelled back at her, and they break up.

> So when his fellow servants saw what had been done, they were very
> grieved, and came and told the master of themselves all that had
> been done. Then his master, after he had called him, said to him,
> 'You wicked servant! All that debt I forgave you because you begged
> me. Should you not also have had mercy on your fellow servant, just
> as I had mercy on you?' And his master was angry, and delivered him
> to the torturers until he should pay all that was due to him.

Well that's certainly a pro-Christian revenge fantasy, first question: what does the King represent? "Obviously he represents God." That was easy, extra time for a nap. Yet please observe that selling someone's wife to pay your debt doesn't sound much like what God would do, and that's because it isn't, it's what the Romans would do, and, not off topic, what porn would do. The King isn't God, the King is a Roman. In fact, the entire point of the parable is that the King is not God. "But it says right there, 'the Kingdom of God is like a certain king.'" End of passage, period, paragraph? That's when the chamomile and alpha waves kicked in? You need Dexedrine and a little more commitment.

If The King was God, why did The Jesus have The King threaten The Wife and The Kids? Think this through. If I was a golden tongued sophist talking to those who loved wisdom I would approach this as a question of knowledge, I would claim the King-God was omniscient, not omnipotent, and if he was-- what would he know? Do you think the King would have been surprised that his servant begged for forgiveness? "I never would have predicted you'd feel bad and ask for more time, well, okay, everyone deserves a second chance!" An omniscient King God wouldn't be swayed by the servant pleading for forgiveness-- it was a trick, he never had any intention of selling them in the first place. The point of the charade was to teach the servant about forgiveness, a lesson the servant evidently didn't learn.

Does this analysis make sense? Sorry, no. If it was planned, why did he change the punishment? Why didn't he sell the wife and kids at the end? Or simply threaten jail in the beginning? And why was he omniscient enough to know this servant would ask for forgiveness but not that he was an untrustworthy jerk? "He had to reveal himself as wicked." So God-- tempted him? Like Satan? No. This is St. Paul's Christianity. God can't be omniscient, he has to be omnipotent.

The King is really a Roman law King, which means you have to follow the logic of the LAW. Why were the other servants who witnessed all this so upset at what the bad servant did? Why did they rat him out to the "master of themselves"? "It seemed unfair to them." Unfair?? Which part-- that he might get extra money, or that he could strangle a guy and they couldn't? The servant he strangled didn't rat him out, these unrelated servants did. "Oh, look, oppression!" That's what you noticed? The King publicly erased the servant's debt-- only to come back two paragraphs later and impose, out of nowhere, a punishment for the very debt that he had forgiven. This isn't metaphorical, God isn't punishing the servant later in the afterlife-- it's happening in real time under Roman civil law, which is more than anything else about the handling of debts. Is anyone, even the Roman King, allowed to reinstate a debt which has been wiped away?

It's hard to know what he wants from her because he's not real, but it's easy to figure out what you want him to want. "Obviously he wants to have sex with her." Slow down. When a know-thyself sophisticate like yourself has a dream about a woman who obviously symbolizes your mother, you can be sure it's not your mother. "Then who is it?" You'll have to trust me on this: you don't want to know. Maybe he doesn't want sex only, maybe he wants to date her, too? Maybe he wants her to become his wife? Maybe he wants to humiliate her boyfriend? To humiliate her? He happens to be a bartender, so maybe he feels obligated to sleep with every woman because the opportunity exists and it's expected of him, whether he really wants to or not? She may know what he wants in general, but she doesn't know what he wants from her.

All of the parables are structural allusions, not fables, so the story isn't about forgiveness but about the structure of the symbolic debt. This debt can only be felt-- it can only exist-- on Earth. Where did the servant 1 get 100 denarii to lend to servant 2, if not from his debt to the King? You forget that two column accounting is a worldly invention, when it comes to the soul there is only zero columns. When the King "wiped away" the debt-- using the precise Greek word relating to debts and not sins-- he wiped away all debts connected to that debt-- he didn't do a solid for the servant and give him a 0 in the liabilities column and +100 in the assets column. It wasn't merely a good idea or a noble gesture that the servant in turn forgive servant 2's debt. That debt no longer existed. The servant's crime, therefore, wasn't in not being merciful but in lying, tricking the other servant into believing a debt existed when one did not.

Not for nothing, the first gospel is written by a man who understands ledgers. "But that's not true!" You can sleep now.

The next question then becomes: why didn't servant 1 "forgive" servant 2's debt-- why did he insist-- pretend-- lie-- there was a debt when there was none? Greed does not explain it, the timing is there before you: how badly does he need 100 denarii right now, suddenly and out of the blue, when he was content merely to be owed this money all that time before? For orientation note that 100 denarii is three months wages or 2500 loaves of bread, or a third of a bottle of perfume, it's a weird economy, anyway-- did he actually think he was going to get paid immediately? He wasn't unmerciful, he was enraged-- because he was shown mercy, because the mercy that was shown to him was a kind of enslavement: when his monetary debt was waived, he owed a different debt to the King; with the cash debt gone another debt overwhelmed him, he owed a debt with his entire existence, his soul. The kingdom of heaven is like a certain king of men who wanted to settle accounts............. This debt can never be paid back, and how one lives with such a debt determines... how one lives with such a debt. The servant couldn't live with it, his brain collapsed into a black hole. That kind of infinite dependency to the King was intolerable. To him, far from the debt being a new kind of freedom grounded in a new kind of duty-- the debt meant madness.

It wasn't greed, stop saying it was greed-- greed doesn't drive a man to take another man by the throat, the force vector is in a different direction; greed wants to have more but is indifferent to whether others have any; "greed" is the modern defensive rationalization for the true origin of his=your relentless rage. He couldn't bear the weight of the loss of the monetary debt to the King-- however big it was, it was calculable, it was real; the duty he now owed was infinite and... abysmal. The King hadn't just erased debts, he had stripped him of everything that formerly defined him-- who are you anymore if everything you are is in service to the King? It must have been an important defense to that servant to be able to think of himself as "a man to whom 100 denarii are owed", the ledger isn't balanced but at least it still exists, it was so important to him he never previously tried to get the cash. This is why the servant then reacts to servant 2's debt with rage: you still owe me, right? Tell me what I am worth!

The King asked the servant to be like him-- to identify with him: forgive! The servant resists this identification, so he changes the identification to change the meaning of his symbolic debt. If I'm

Jealousy is wanting what the other has but envy doesn't want what the other has, just that the other doesn't have it. She doesn't blow him to satisfy him, she blows him to keep him from being satisfied, and to keep his girlfriend from being satisfied by him. NB it's established she would enjoy sex with him, she knows this. So she's willing to deprive herself of sex with him in order to effect that deprivation. That's not subtext, it's pretext. But how does she know a blowjob won't satisfy him? She doesn't. It might. So she does it better. She does it to make him want more of her, and then she can deprive him of that.

"I find it hard to believe that the reason Saydee gave him a blowjob is because she wanted to deprive him of sex." Sounds like you believe Saydee is real.

You have to wonder what it means to pretend to feel something that you are actually

---

asked to be like the King, then servant 2 is like the me; and if I make servant 2 owe me money, then all I owe the King is money. "Pay me back so that it can be true that payable debts exist!"

"This is way too complicated, no one thinks like this." It is the only way you think, and you make it the way other people think. You know that the credit card company considers your debt-- the money you don't have and might never repay-- as its self-defining, material asset. It's accounting, but at least real accountants discount it. You think everyone thinks like this, and you surround yourself with those who do, to be sure.

He is compelled to repeat the events that lead to the loss of his identity hoping to produce a different outcome. If the parable was another 100 pages it would only show the servant trying over and over to make servant 2's debt coincide with this symbolic debt owed to the King. "Pay me or it's prison! Pay me or I take your wife!" It would show him trying-- and failing-- but the compulsively repetitive trying and failing at least keeps him in the world of material debts. The parable isn't about forgiveness, but about the unbearable disappearance of his ledger: the unfillable gap constituted by the symbolic debt against which his neurosis is a protest.

The parable's end looks simple but it's worth taking literally. The King punishes him "until he should pay all that was due to him"-- which is what, money? If so, why not sell off the wife like he threatened in paragraph 1? How could the servant be expected to pay the debt from jail? He wouldn't-- not the money, anyway, the monetary debt is gone, the debt he had to pay back was the symbolic debt. Which is why he isn't actually put in debtor's prison, that's the wish fulfillment of translators and you eyeballs deep in ledgers: "God wants his due, so all we have to do is give it to him, and also debtors' prisons are ok." But it won't be enough, haven't you been following the math?-- it is simply not enough. The King didn't imprison him, but rather "delivered him to the basanistēs", a word which is optimistically mistranslated as "jailer" but which nowhere ever means "jailer", the root is only ever used as "frustrate or torment"; literally, "the tormenters who extract the truth." Not the money-- the truth, e.g. and i.e., demons accuse Jesus of doing it to them. "What am I to you?"

You can ask the story a different way: what would have happened if the King explicitly waived the debt of the servant AND the other servant, out loud and to their faces, so that the first servant couldn't even pretend a claim on the other's debt? You don't have to speculate, it's in Luke 7:36.

JC and the sunshine gang go to the home of Simon the Pharisee, who passive aggressively sleights him by not offering the customary washing of feet/anointing of oil due all guests, and then "a sinner" woman comes and in front of everyone does all these things. Just like in the U.S. everyone in the New Testament is labeled by their name, occupation, or diagnosis, so either "sinner" is a cool name for a comic book hero or it's #2. Ok? The Pharisee smirks derisively and says to himself that "a real prophet would have known she was a sinner", i.e. wouldn't allow himself to be touched by such a woman. Unless he paid her. Then it's ok, because she did it for some other reason. Sorry, that's how it works.

feeling. What does she think she is depriving him of? Performing a blowjob is one thing, but why perform an internal state that's real? How do you perform it? According to what you think he thinks it should look like? But how does he know what it should look like? A pomo mofo might ask a question like, "where is the subject located?" which is simply a two part question, the first is: which is the real her? Is she the good girlfriend faithful to her own boyfriend, so that when she did those things she did them as the girlfriend, conscious of that identity, and thus wasn't completely into them, something was necessarily withheld-- only for her boyfriend? Or is the real her the woman who enthusiastically participated but later lies about her lust to pretend to be a good girlfriend? Whose desire was she acting on, or against?

Except the i.e. is not in the story and is utterly a post-textual defense. The Pharisee's concern isn't that Jesus does not care she's a sinner, but-- look at the words-- that Jesus does not know she's a sinner. This is important, especially to you, we'll come back to it.

In response to that unspoken thought-- that he does not know she's a sinner-- Jesus goes parabolic on him:

> "A creditor had two debtors. The one owed 500 denarii, and the other 50. Because they had nothing to pay, he forgave them both. Therefore, which of them will love him most?"

> Responding, Simon said, "I assume the one to whom he forgave most."

> And he said to him, "you have judged rightly."

Wait, what? Is this a joke?

I am willing to grant you that the story happened, fine, but Luke was both a doctor and not actually there, so his documentation is doubly suspect, doctors document for exculpation not explication but an omniscient God or even semi-competent accountant could not have both asked that question and settled for that answer.

The word "rightly" appears rarely in the Bible except in Luke, who uses it ironically. This is because Luke was a doctor and a Greek at a time when Greeks and doctors learned medicine from Plato, who wasn't actually a doctor but an ironist, or at least an esotericist. The word is a pointer: it is Socrates's verbal crutch, he says it to know-it-alls when they think the answer they gave should be obvious. Of course you've been told that by the end of a dialogue Socrates has exposed the emptiness of the other person's knowledge, through the dialogue we perceive the interlocutor's prejudices or appeals to authority. But what you don't get from the secondary sources is what the interlocutor *perceived*: that Socrates is retarded. The interlocutor doesn't stumble out of the supermarket with half a melon and his worldview shaken by the koans of Socrates, he strolls out of there more certain of his knowledge, more confident, more arrogant, because what he perceived from the dialogue is that Socrates is a dunce, all he does is ask questions with obvious answers that apparently never occurred to him, and then says "huh, you have judged rightly." *Everyone else* thinks Socrates is a genius, but *he* discovered Socrates doesn't actually know anything, he figured it out, he detected Socrates is a hypocrite. Socrates fooled everybody except him. He's smarter than Socrates. You can imagine that after a few years of dialogues there are suddenly *hundreds* of individual know-it-alls, each one figured out *on their own* Socrates is a fraud, each one now feeling much smarter than both Socrates and all the dunces who think Socrates is smart.

But Socrates can't tell these idiots they're idiots, because they're idiots; all he can do is show them, with the paradoxical effect that the more you try to show them they know nothing, the more confident they become in how much they know-- never for once observing that they cannot act on

The second question is: who gets to determine that, who makes the judgment? In a utopia of gnosticism and Human Resources a woman and even a man would get to pick their own avatars and we'd all have to play along, but that's not how it works in media: the audience decides, and no one you know can count as the audience.

As an example, let's assume your serious girlfriend for real cheated on you and you are not happy about it.   Assume that these are hard facts. Given this, which would you prefer: she did it full of lust; or she did it with no lust? Just say the first thing that comes to mind.

You're going to need to find one of those old calculator watches because you're about to do some arithmetic and it's going to take a lot of time. The problem is that then her sex is

---

that knowledge.   There's almost no better/more ironic example of just how little they could act on their own infinitely superior knowledge than the trial of Socrates: more people voted to execute him than had originally voted him guilty. He deserved death because the verdict proved to themselves he was guilty.

Luke would have read the Platonic dialogues many times, when there aren't many texts around you get deep with the ones you have, so apart from pondering the arguments he would have spent a lot of time contemplating the *form* of the dialogues: they're dialogues. Unlike Thucydides and most of the Old Testament, the New Testament writers-- especially Luke—structure their narrative as dialogues, sometimes in such subtle ways that seem unnecessary because you're focused on the monologue. The Socratic dialogue never produces much in the way of knowledge, but taken as a dialogue it presents both the futile pursuit of that kind of objective truth and the destruction of our necessary pretenses; looking for the biggest payoff while simultaneously risking no losses, the presentation of two logically incompatible principles that cannot exist in any single person-- which is why they are presented in a single dialogue.

So like the lunatics Socrates dialogued with, when the Pharisee is being told he judged rightly, he is being told he's an idiot. And a lunatic. Really? That's the world you live in? Love can be bought? Not the appearance of love, but the internal incommunicable state of love-- that can be bought? Red-500 might be more appreciative, but it isn't at all necessary that he would love more. Why would he-- is love measured in ledgers? If he had been forgiven 400, would he have loved 20% less? Love is transactional, correlated to gains and losses? No one's ever loved you for no reason?

I understand you're going to say that I'm playing with semantics, these are different loves, and anyway sophistry aside, Red-500 probably does love him more, it may not be "good" but it makes sense. And you have judged rightly, because you're also a lunatic. Do you really imagine if someone forgave you 500 denarii, you'd love them more? In fact, you can't actually imagine this at all; you can only imagine yourself as the man with the lesser debt. The starting point is always the other guy: whatever amount the other guy owes, you would owe less than that, whatever amount the other guy loves, you will love less than that.

Red-50 now sees the forgiven debt not relative to the creditor but relative to Red-500. His debt was ten times smaller; so either Red-500 got more out of the forgiveness-- as if he actually benefitted from being more indebted-- which is just not fair; or, when the creditor wipes both ledgers clean, Red-50 gets to put 10x in his assets column relative to Red-500. If you tell me that there is not actually anything going in his assets column, he's retarded for thinking this, they're both at zero, I don't disagree but you're equally retarded: you too are still thinking in terms of assets and liabilities, the persistence of the ledger, the need for accounting, the need to compare to the other's debt. Neither debtor could pay off his debt, they are essentially infinite, both are unpayable; and the creditor wipes them both to zero, they vanish. But the reason Red-50 loves less is because he still sees himself as having been   forgiven less. Red-50 holds on to-- no, he resurrects-- a relative gain/loss relative to the other debtor. Yes, I know that gain doesn't exist anywhere.   He makes it exist. In his ledger. It's erased from the creditor's ledger, and it got moved to his. He literally takes

cheap-- she did these things even without desire; she was willing to be the passive recipient of their lust and semen, she gave them what was so precious to you, for no reason. There may have been reasons, of course, but they weren't desire. She wasn't strong enough-- your relationship wasn't strong enough-- to refrain from doing something she didn't even want to do. Does this sound like the kind of woman you'd want to be with? Whatever your answer, it is evidently yes.

So why does hearing that she cheated because she wanted to sound worse to you? Because she chose him over you? No, because she chose.

If you don't believe all this, which you don't, run this scenario on every other person you

---

credit for his smaller debt. "Just so it's in black and white and read all over: I'm ahead." He deprives himself of the full forgiveness of his debt in order to deprive the other guy of the forgiveness of his "bigger" debt. Madness. NB: Red-500 has no idea Red-50 is a lunatic and that any of this is going on. Madness.

This is why the Pharisee is concerned with whether Jesus knows she is a sinner. Touch, not touch; forgive, not forgive; that doesn't count. Just as long as someone knows who had the bigger debt.

While you let this interpretation fail to bludgeon its way through your wolfram carbide sternum we should take a moment and figure out not the conversation's meaning but what it was used for. It was used to highlight a fundamental theological mistake being made by the Pharisee, which is this: to Simon, God is omnipotent, not omniscient.

To Simon, Red-50 loves less because he was forgiven less. That feeling gets accounted for in his own ledger. The trouble is, does God remember? If God kept a ledger, then he would know that he forgave 50 to one man and 500 to another. But to use that knowledge in the future, i.e. "rewards in heaven" or merely smiling down more on Red 50 would require that some percentage of the debt remains, "counts", *counts*. Yet it sounds awfully like God doesn't keep good records. What God doesn't do is come back ten years later, "hey, I forgave you 50 denarii, the least you could have done is bought your kid an ice cream cone and taken him to the movies, and you didn't, so I'm selling your wife and kids." To be justified in doing that would require that some residue of the 50 denarii debt still exist as, say, a 0.003 denarii debt-- tiny, a marker, but not zero. But this isn't what forgiveness means. This creditor has no ledger. If the Pharisee doesn't keep his own ledger, it's not simply that no one would know he is/had been less indebted or a better person; it would not be true for himself or God that he was better. God cannot be trusted to be omniscient, but if the Pharisee keeps good records, God has the power to certify it.

This thinking would be pathological if it were not so normal, but in fact it gets way worse: once Red-50 moves to resurrect the debt, he has to make a further accounting: since God forgave me less, I owe *him* less.

This explains Simon's seemingly backwards criticism of Jesus: not that he associates with sinners, but that he doesn't *know* she's a sinner. Prophets are supposed to know. What if they don't? If he then forgives the debts, how will God know who was better or worse? He wouldn't. Why did I spend so much time being relatively sinless, if this dummy can't tell the difference between me and a whore?

The question that it occurs to no one to ask or answer is not which debtor loves the creditor more, but is the creditor capable of love? The Pharisee's premise is that greater debt forgiven=more love, but then it can't be true that the creditor loved at all. Did he forgive the debts to reduce paperwork? There's no room in the Pharisee's math for that kind of love. For him, God cannot love. Simon cannot see that in matters of virtue, the creditor is among the unique; he acquires his friends by granting, not receiving, kindness. The one who does the kind act is the firmer friend of the two;

know. Would you prefer your daughter to have had sex with a total jerk that she really lusted over, or a total jerk that she sort of, kind of, just went along with? Not just which is worse for you, which is worse for her. Or your male friend: which implies a marriage built on popsicle sticks?

In every scenario you will decide it was better for everyone else that they did it because they wanted to, except as it applies to you. When it comes to you, other people can't act on their desire. "Well, my wife was the one who came on to me first..." I wonder why you think that is.

It is probably possible to have sex with someone you are attracted to and not have it be a

---

through his kindness, he preserves a sense of obligation in the former debtor by demonstrating goodwill. The one returning the obligation is less motivated, because deep down it feels to him as a repayment, not a freely given kindness.

Assuming that the creditor in the parable is a person, what allows the creditor to be kind? Jesus doesn't give the creditor's backstory, but all of the psychological forces are written down in black and white-- not black and red. At some point in his life, the creditor had to change the way he thought, neither towards justice nor towards expedience, but in a way that the most expedient thing was logically the just-- that by his will and daring, he could make what was just also be the expedient. This required him to take risks, to be brave--- to dare to act. This daring then allows him to come to another's aid fearless of consequences-- offering the benefits not from calculations of expediency and advantage but from the confidence of generosity. In other words: for no reason.

You can even ask what would happen if there was only the creditor and one debtor, no other immediate debtors to compare to. What then? The lunatics have to compare it to someone, the starting point is the existence of a ledger: "when he wiped away my 500000000000 denarii debt, what did it actually cost him? It sounds big to me, but if it isn't a big deal to him, why should I incur a bigger debt of-- thanks? love?-- to him?" The more he is forgiven by a creditor who was not compelled to forgive him, the more enraged he will grow. I want to correct a mistake that you are dying to make: the problem is NOT that he doesn't want to owe anything to the creditor, otherwise the forgiveness of the debt would be enough. The problem is that in order for the waiving of the debt to be emotionally satisfying to him, to count, someone else has to be deprived. In this example there are no other debtors to compare to. The only other person is the creditor. So the creditor has to be deprived somehow, preferably more, certainly not less. There's no love possible anywhere here. There is only war, famine, plague, and lunacy. The debt has to mean something, because otherwise I have to act on my own.

And so instead of Jesus explaining it, he uses Simon's own logic to show its inanity:

> "Therefore I tell you, her sins, which are many, are forgiven because
> she loved much. But he who is forgiven little, loves little."

raa, it is the atemporal logic of your pathology: Since she loved, her sins will have been forgiven; but since you would have thought she required more forgiveness than you, you had already deprived me of love today, on purpose. "That sounds way too complicated to think consciously, let alone unconsciously." Yes. It is exhausting to be you.

In the hypothetical of the two debtors, Jesus uses the word "forgiveness" which is really "do them a kindness" (charisomai), but when he explains the relationship between "forgiveness" and love of the woman he uses the word aphiemi-- as in "forgive a debt". The confusing love → forgiveness vs forgiveness → love disappears when charisomai is used, because it is not about ledgers. In explaining it to the Pharisee using his own logic-- aphiemi, the logic of ledgers-- which comes first, love or forgiveness, is insoluble.

254

reflection on your own partner, but it is impossible to have sex with someone you are NOT attracted to and not have it be a reflection on your partner. This analysis is hard because you're stuck at not wanting her to have cheated at all, what you don't understand is that in such matters time moves backwards: the reason that she will cheat is the way you will later choose to frame it, so when the time comes to, say, decide between having sex with a kobold just because it's persistent, and NOT having sex with a kobold for this trivial reason, most of her rationalization will have already have been made by you, way before she got in the car.

"You're denying her agency." You're blaming me?

It's not so simple as wanting to manipulate her choices, as if you were merely a

---

You need to take a moment before you give up, this isn't a wild revisionist explanation, it actually happens: the woman washing his feet is not performing an extraordinarily pious action, it was the usual custom, the Pharisee himself should have done that for any guest who comes to his home. He deprived Jesus of this courtesy. We can agree he loves Jesus less than the sinner woman does, but that's not why he deprived him of what he would have done for anyone else, what anyone else would have automatically received-- and he deprived him before she even showed up. Simon deprives him because, by his own logic, he has very little debt to need forgiveness and no one around it can be compared to. He has nothing to gain, so someone must lose. When the woman does appear and Jesus lets her touch him, the Pharisee considers the deprivation justified: Jesus doesn't know who has the greater debt, so he was right to deprive him of the courtesy in order to balance the ledger.

This also explains the extremely curious description of the woman being *allowed* to wash Jesus's feet, when what is really happening is she is *choosing* to wash Jesus's feet. It has always struck me that prostitutes, who know exactly the value of their sex, are never depicted offering Jesus sex. If the gimmick was to show his humanity/divinity he could have been depicted refusing it, but it never comes up. Even Satan tempts him with the three Ps of power, picnics and parachutes-- but not prostitutes. Somehow this is supposed to paradoxically point out the pervasive misogyny of Christianity-- all female sexuality is perverse, disavowed or repressed. But read the primary source: no man is ever described as having sex, only women-- and Jesus never chastises them for it. Even adulteresses, who presumably hurt their husbands, are left uncriticized; unless you call the tongue-in-cheek ribbing of the polyamorous Samaritan woman a criticism, which even you would say doesn't count.

Jesus not judging women is the beam in the eye of ledger based Christianity, which is why misogyny manifests so vividly in the historical practice of Christianity. As baffling as women's sexuality has been, it is thus an easy standard, a superego comparator: if Jesus doesn't punish them I can at least use it to show I'm better; but in order to do that I must prove that they're worse, and the only way to prove they are worse is to punish them first. God would have wanted it that way.

So one should take very literally what the "sinner" woman does to Jesus: what she is doing is only what is expected of anyone, let alone one who loves Jesus; it is not something for which a repayment is expected. If the Pharisee had washed his feet, it would have been dismissed as a typical courtesy. Anyone impressed that the Pharisee offered him a meal, likely at considerable expense, does he get credit for it? No. It doesn't count. She doesn't offer him sex-- for which there is a transaction cost immediately calculable by everyone else, whether in denarii or in spiritual ledger points. You will likely consult your ledger and tell me her "courtesy" of feet washing is different because she doesn't have to do it, but this is backwards: she loved him, she could not do otherwise. A wife buys her husband a shirt she thinks would look good on him. While it's labeled as a gift and I'm sure he appreciates it, it's not more than what would be expected of any woman who loves her husband; it would not obligate him to repay her-- indeed, either of them thinking he had to would be a sign of madness. Well, should be, anyway. It was once a common wry criticism

controlling prick, which would make her infidelity a kind of response, an acting out-- a message to you. No: she can not choose. It's even okay if the other guy chooses for her. As long as she doesn't choose. When you make a choice, you immediately tell your imaginary audience what the choice means, so it doesn't much matter what you choose, which is why you usually choose nothing. But as it's your movie, the only way to signal her choice is to show it, not tell it. Her choice has to be performed.

Let's ask a slightly different question. Which is worse: she cheats with someone and immensely enjoys it but doesn't show it during sex; or doesn't enjoy it at all (this is fact) but during sex moans, squeals and acts like she does?

If it helps, assume it was recorded.

Her actual enjoyment isn't the relevant metric, but if you recall from your imagined video neither is the man's: what matters is how the sex looked to a hypothetical observer, the amount of enjoyment the observer perceives and receives. Unfortunately, this also applies to video evidence in court. Meanwhile you can't enjoy anything as much as the hypothetical audience thinks she did-- you certainly can't enjoy her that much. I'm supposed to say it's because you're not seeing her as a real person but only as she impacts you, but the truth is much worse. For her, anyway.

You'll completely misunderstand this, as if the husband has overestimated the importance of the spectacle over any real enjoyment she had. No. This is pornography, like the ending to *The Invention of Morel*: what she felt or what you felt doesn't matter because only the perception counts. Not what someone actually saw-- no one needs to see it-- but what could have been seen.

"Who gets to decide?" The very fact of this analysis is that you want to decide, but not based on what you want, but based on the movie you think you're in. You are manipulating the decision to be yours, in the four hour argument you will have after she shamefully admits to her infidelity, you will appear to be extracting details, trying to know exactly what happened and what it all means, but in reality you are rewriting history; the plot will be the same but the motivations will change, you will be causing her reasons to be anything else but desire-- she could even do it to hurt you in reaction to X-- so that she didn't decide based on desire.

She tries to meet you halfway, so she tells you she was drunk, surely that erases desire, surely that negates her choice? 150 years ago maybe, but not today, not 2500 ago. She doesn't understand what drunk means to you, why you would retort, "don't give me that

---

that "she paid for his gift with his money"; and today her rebuttal would be that she actually paid for it with her money, after all, she makes money, too. Both of you are idiots, you'll buy a house together but at the level of gift giving you're keeping receipts? "Of course I don't want repayment, it's the thought that counts." No, this is what I'm trying to tell you, which you will reflexively and idiotically agree with yet devote your life to disavowing: the thought doesn't count. No one should be counting anything.

In other words, the only person there who can be depended on to wash Jesus's feet-- to love-- is her. This is a prostitute, she is used to transactions, the cost is consubstantial with her every act-- usually. But this? She's certainly not doing it because she thought she was forgiven or because she hopes she will be, this act comes with no expectation or even possibility of repayment. The act can't be marked in the ledger, it cannot be valued. I know, I know, it's uncanny: love-- especially from a woman-- for... no reason? If she didn't get paid-- then someone must pay.

excuse, you were not that drunk!" We can argue about alcohol and consent, but in fantasy drunk always means the real her wants it. This goes double for cocaine. Ergo: she wasn't that drunk.

Look at this from the other side: the other guy doesn't care why she did it, he just wanted to have sex with your girlfriend. He got what he wanted. It already happened. But since he's not your rival what he got counts much less in the ledger than what she got, which counts much less than how much the audience might think you were deprived of, by her. What you are trying to do after the fact is minimize the loss to you by imagining him enjoying it even more and removing the desire from her-- and believing that you can make her believe it.

For a very good reason, let's try this with its power and gender opposite. You're a woman, and a guy whom you know well-- but not so well you have ever confided in him-- comes to confide in you. And what he tells you is that after ten years of marriage, he's having an affair with a woman who, for the sake of backstory, takes lots of photographs of herself. "I need your advice, you're the only person I can trust with this."

For the next two hours you sit uncomfortably, listening to him go hyperbolic about his new girlfriend [6.31], how amazing she is, she's my soulmate, she makes me want to be a better person, I married out of loyalty and obligation but I never knew love could be like this; all the kinds of things an adult man after his first menstruation would say. Then he gets serious: "be honest with me, you're a straight shooter, I trust your judgment: what do you think about what I'm doing?"

What would you say? Write it here: _____.

The line is drawn to actual size, and this is a read only document. It doesn't matter what you are going to say, he's not going to hear it. It only matters what you don't say.

I said he went hyperbolic, but within a limited domain you can approximate it with a quadratic polynomial, i.e. a parable, so maybe we should focus not on what he said, but to whom he said it. Here's the question you're taught not to ask: why did he pick you to judge him? "You're smart, you're a straight shooter, you really understand people, I trust your intuition," says the fox. "Well, I am worldly and insightful," agrees the crow, and down goes the cheese. In this analogy, crows have a reputation for cleverness and foxes would rather eat cheese than crow.

I don't for a second think he is lying to you: he in fact believes he is there to get your advice, but he selected you because he knows you won't express disapproval. He doesn't know this with his brain, which is too occupied with the day's haul of political soundbites, but he knows it. You wouldn't yell at him, you're not going to call him a jerk or a home wrecker. "Well, I'm not going to say it in those words, but...." For this man who has decided that his personal growth counts for something, not hearing disapproval is the same as approval. You, the straight shooter, cosigned his lunacy. "Cosigned? He's a jerk!" That's not what you told him, you told him information, you hid behind "objectivity", this will be hard on the kids, this will be a hard divorce, this new chick seems young/old/clingy/bananas; but at no point did you, could you, say what you later said to your actual confidants: that he's a terrible, immature person for doing this, worse for his self-serving rationalizations, and he should probably cut his own brake line so at least his kids get the insurance. You didn't tell him that. What he heard was your unconditional support. "Then he's insane." Did you tell him that?

257

Which explains why you now feel anxious and he doesn't. He feels good because he has your settled approval; and you are left unsettled because you feel like you left something unsettled. You did: the part about him being a jerk. As hard as it is for you to sleep, now it's that easy for him.

"It isn't really my place to judge." And so we come to it, the ostrich defense amidst the shards of broken mirrors. *He wouldn't solicit your judgment unless you were a judge.* "But I'm not a judgmental person." But that's exactly what he thinks everyone thinks you are. For this to work, it isn't enough that he pick someone he knows won't judge him. He has to pick someone everyone else sees as judgmental. And he thinks he can fool you.

None of this is conscious, of course, he truly walks out of there thinking you were honest. It's even true that you-- you!-- made it easier for him to cheat on his wife, because he already anticipated approval from you, which is why he says to you: "sometimes, when I'm trying to figure out what's right and wrong, I hear your voice in my head." That voice is his conscience, and the only reason it sounds like you is because it never existed before, you look like a superego, and you can be fooled.[44]

---

44 Biblical exegesis is an awfully crowded sport played by well trained professionals with top quality equipment, they get paid to play but that usually means they can't bet on the outcome. I, however, am all in. Your God must be omnipotent so he won't be omniscient, open your Bibles to the Gospel Of The Television Christian, Mark 13:6, and let's see what today's reader wants out of a translation:

> Many will come in my name, saying, "I am he!" and many will be lead astray

You can read it again and again, it's obviously a clear warning about being fooled by imposters and false Christs, which, curiously, there are no examples of anywhere in the New Testament or indeed in the history of Christianity. Huh. So much for omniscience.

A couple things about this sentence. First, in the original Greek(s) there are no punctuation marks. Second, the word "he", the predicate nominative of "I am", is not there; the translator, whom they executed for being a translator and then plagiarized his work, just added it, along with all the thees, thys, hasts and forsakens that effectively inform us that Jesus was a Stewart, all this being especially ironic as King James knew Greek even better than the translators, and probably Mark. Third, I guess to balance the ledger, the translator then omits the Greek word that comes after "saying", and that word is "what." So the actual line, translated using no psychoanalysis or literary deconstruction or collapsing the wave function— simply copying down the words— is:

> many will come in my name saying what I am and many will be lead astray

What you are feeling right now is the vertigo and unreality that comes from a life of secondary sources while denied the privilege to wonder if they were wrong. And what you are doing right now is praying that I am. Look, if there is any text in the world other than the Odyssey that you are not supposed to take literally, it is the Gospel Of Mark, and at least the Odyssey had a beat to minimize alterations. The Gospel Of Mark wasn't written/copied with attention to spelling or word order, no one was "interrogating the text", no one was highlighting passages unless it was in black, the Gospel was read out loud by the semi-literate in passable Greek to the fully illiterate in pssst down here groups, they were just happy to get the gist and argue the ideas later over rum.

Ok, so maybe rigid literalism is out, but come on, sometimes you have to take a guy at his word. Read this way, the right way, what becomes plain is that Jesus isn't warning about people saying they are him, but rather people saying that he is something else. I am aware of the obvious: that

A bitter pill to swallow, so you won't. You are sure that you do know things, you are sure that people truly respect your advice, so I offer you a secondary point which may be the only thing that gets through to you: the very fact that he selected you as his confidant shows implicitly how little he values you and how much he thinks he is better than you. He thinks you are a tool. "He told his priest." Another tool. "But he even told his daughter!" Yes, "she's so much older than her years," he will say; find women innocent enough to be a malleable superego and make them absolve you.[45]

"But what good is my 'support' to him? Even if I don't say anything explicitly, he must know that he didn't fool me, that I still think he's selfish." I think you think he thinks a person

---

Jesus explicitly refers to coming imposters a few verses later; that "what" could also be "that"-- though this is an odd rebuttal in that it hopes Mark invented not just Christianity but diacritics; and I am aware that no one else agrees with me, that I'm a nobody sitting in a car in the woods safe from the authority of secondary sources, that this is a creative misreading of a trivial miswriting, and that for two millennia scholars and theologians have never thought anything other than that it refers to imposters, but I do not care, I'm right, everyone else is wrong, the most contextually appropriate reading here is the literal one: that people will claim Jesus is something else. Do you know why? Because that is what the Gospel of Mark *is*. That's what happens over and over in the Gospel Of Mark, no one else claims to be Christ, and almost no one doubts he is Christ; but everyone, Pharisees, Romans, disciples, Tusken raiders, everyone wants him to be something else. Take the story as a story and ask: what do the characters want? The disciples are eyeballs deep in miracle after miracle, yet what interests them is mostly their rank and when they can start shooting the Romans, not only do they not understand what Jesus is saying, they do not care: they want him to be Che Guevara so they can take from Tiberius what is Tiberius's. Jesus hints at a sketchy plan to evacuate them from Mesopotamia and airlift them to an extra-dimensional theocracy and they cut him off, nope, no interest, we'll tolerate your fruity analogies so long as you gather an army, or at least bring the nukes. Half way through the story they realize he isn't going to kill the Romans after all, then he tells them he's going to be killed by the Romans, and so will they; and they begin to suspect he might be a little too melancholic to possess the testosterone for sword fighting or a winner's ideology of Us vs. Them. "The one who is not against us is for us." Yeah, that's not going to work, we'll get Matthew to fix it in post.

Most of us couldn't have gotten through high school without Cliff and Spark's notes, but at least those were 30 pages long, now the entire society operates on vitriolic arguments based on four or five sentences of synopsis, at this rate we can look forward to the day when calculus class consists of 15 minutes of what math means to me. We are not used to thinking of the disciples as the bad guys in this story but unfortunately I see bad guys in every story, what could the supporting characters have done differently to make the protagonist's life easier? "That's a high bar, we can't all be selfless like you." Way to make it about me so it's not about you. Nothing anyone does in Mark even approaches commitment, let alone selflessness, at one point Jesus is in a garden deliberating between two suicides and the disciples slink off to take a nap. "The spirit is willing but the flesh is weak." Pretty sure that's backwards. I don't fault the disciples for their hesitant belief, I get it, Jesus is vague on the details and admittedly the whole operation sounds suspect-- but if I'm accepting the narrative as is then I fault them for their lack of commitment to even what they believe. Who can depend on them? They could either take Jesus at his word and bravely accompany him to his cross, or they could believe he was just a human Messiah come to overthrow the Romans in which case they should have extraordinary renditioned him to India or Kos until they could get an army together or learn how to make flamethrowers from the Boeotians if they still remembered how. That's a story worth an aside: 400 years earlier the Athenians line up against the Boeotians, both Socrates and Alcibiades are there, but the Boeotians' right flank is composed of 300 gay Theban supersoldiers-- soldiers so hard core that they eventually put even the Spartans to shame-- who crush the Athenians in a battle of such chaos that the Athenians accidentally kill each

can have both knowledge and power. Do you think that? Because he doesn't. Since you're the judge, you can't know everything, you can be fooled. "But I am not fooled." You are fooled, you don't see how. You think you know he is bad, but are unable to do anything about it. You think you have knowledge about him, but no power over him. One or the other. That's what he thinks about you, the fact that he thinks it's the other way around is irrelevant: one or the other. He fooled you into thinking that he believes you know anything.

One of the hazards of being a psychiatrist is that physical acquaintances will hit you up for your "professional" opinion about their partner/kid/boss, they will ask if I would agree that this person whom I've never met has whatever diagnosis is popular in the media. Should I be insulted? Yes. The standard psychiatric response I'm supposed to give is that I cannot

---

other in the first recorded instance of friendly fire, which means I've scored the words gay, friendly fire, and Alcibiades in the same sentence, for the hat trick. Afterwards the Boeotians build a 4 wheeled flaming tar thrower and set the place on fire. That's flaming for the extra point. Also worth mentioning that Socrates was so fearless and calm-- stoic-- during the battle of Delium that people were afraid to fight him, don't be surprised, it took 360 Athenians to finally kill him when he was 70 and still it took two days. I guess it doesn't matter now, Thebans, Boeotians, Athenians-- Philip rolls over all of them. Fun fact: Philip should have one L and two Ps, and it means horselover. Anyway. Jesus's disciples did nothing. They just-- waited for someone else to act. "Your example is wildly anachronistic." So is the name Jesus, but you pray using it, or won't. I'd like to point out that no matter which ending of the Gospel Of Discipleship you choose to go with, the disciples never even visit his grave. "It was dangerous." That never seems to stop the women, though Antigone chose suicide and Elektra favored homicide, so there's that. "Oh faithless generation, how long am I to be with you?" That question is going to get a lot more complicated in ways we probably didn't predict.

You have a battle between what Jesus wants for the disciples and what the disciples want from him, and a battle between what Jesus wants for the people and what the people want from him, and this mirrors the modern readers' battle between what they think Jesus wants from them and what they want from him, and all of this is structured within the Gospel as a battle between belief and knowledge. "Belief and knowledge, yes, that's pretty obvious." Slow down, college algebra, I said battle, not distinction. This is not "who can name three disciples other than Matthew, Mark, Luke and John" belief even without knowledge. They want to know, and Jesus doesn't mind if they know-- but he does not want them to want to know. He deliberately frustrates not their knowledge but their desire to know.

You probably remember Jesus performing miracles so people will believe in him, but you should read it again because it is very clear he doesn't want this. He performs the miracles out of-- kindness? Duty? Anybody wonder why he bothers doing this, on such a limited scale, assuming he could do what he says he is about to do? But he doesn't want people to believe in him because of the miracles-- because of evidence, and so he tells everyone not to tell anyone about the evidence. He wants belief in him, not a desire for knowledge about him. "Your mother and your brothers are outside." --My brothers and mother are in here. "Umm, I don't really understand what that means." --Now do you believe? Morpheus's saying these words to Trinity after she witnesses Neo's miracles is an excellent contrasting analogy to what modern readers want from their Christianity: belief through knowledge. Not knowledge, not belief, not knowledge over belief: knowledge raised to the level of belief.

Perhaps Jesus is merely trying to encourage faith without proof, but then he should have performed the miracles in secret, but anyway do you think even in 33 CE hearsay evidence counted as proof? The only thing eyewitness accounts of miracles are going to convince anyone else of is, "wait, what? Yeah, I've got to see this for myself." Witnessing a miracle is perfectly ok, seeing is believing, but hearing an other's account of a miracle becomes a matter of objectivity, of science; not

make a judgment without seeing the patient. Except-- I am seeing the patient.

You may have heard the story of Wise King Solomon who was presented with a baby that two different harlots claimed as their own, which woman was telling the truth? In his wisdom he ruled the baby should be cut in half and given to both. Hmm. Even sagittally it wouldn't be quite fair, let alone wise, but as you might guess one woman quickly gives up her claim to the baby, let the other woman take it! And so Solomon then knew who the baby's real mom was. Clever? Well, it's not so easy.

The logic is that a real mother would never let her baby die, she'd even give it away to save it; or, alternatively, only the woman who wasn't the mother would allow it to be killed.

---

that the witness is correct, but that there is a correct.

That Jesus wants belief without knowledge may seem obvious, but it's only obvious because Mark implied it and then gave you something else. Mark offers belief through knowledge, reason. It doesn't matter what you know, only that the knowledge bit in your 64k brain gets a 1 and not a 0. Something is known. Reason may seem absent in a book of parables and demons but you have to admire the cleverness in which Mark uses events that you do not even have to think happened to give you knowledge about Jesus to believe. So he doesn't just describe the miracles, but also that Jesus tried to hide them-- because the first part requires suspension of disbelief but that second part sounds like insight, it feels like you're getting at the truth of something. Rather than Jesus doing something that you have to believe, Mark is revealing something about Jesus's character that you get to know; and I'm sure you'll agree, insights into character count way more to us than action. So Mark adroitly undermines Jesus, he uses Jesus's attempt to suppress the desire for knowledge in order to convey knowledge-- and this lessens the burden of belief.

When I say he is against the desire for knowledge, I don't mean that Jesus is anti-math, if the other primary sources are to be believed he knew a lot of math. I've always been impressed/depressed by the fact that Plato is supposedly a "we can never know the truth" speculative philosopher while the Oracle of Delphi was famed for its truth bombs, yet the inscription over Delphi was the subjective "Know Thyself" while the inscription over Plato's school was "let no one ignorant of geometry enter here." Math is not the kind of knowledge Jesus is anti. It's not the knowledge, but the desire for knowledge. The desire he doesn't want people to have is desire in the service of impotence. When you're in an airplane you tell yourself it won't crash because of Science, but you don't really know the Science-- you just know that there exists people who do and you trust their knowledge-- not the science, not even the plane. The thing is, you tell yourself you don't know Science because science is hard, but you don't really want to know the science-- you just want the digital soundbytes, you just want to believe in it. But how much turbulence can you stand before your belief is shattered? "I'm the opposite, the second I get on a plane I'm convinced it's going to crash." Then why would you risk all of those people's lives just so you can go to another airport? Shouldn't you stay home for their sakes? Or do you believe it might not go down because all those other people know it won't? Do you believe that knowledge summed over a population has mystical power-- that it will protect you? "Obviously not." So yes.

This kind of knowledge feels empowering precisely because it mitigates not your ignorance but your impotence, and you walk around confident in your knowledge until you have to decide something yourself, and then you may as well lay out Tarot cards, which, weirdly, is something you do know how to do yourself. Somewhere in Mark is the parable about seed being sown in four different places and the seed on the fertile ground is the one that takes root, yay knowledge-- so why mention the other grounds? Is it just a stylistic binary, i.e. [all 3 grounds] vs [the good ground], to get you to the moral? All the parables are structural allusions, not fables, he's not giving a moral, he is describing what things are like. Each kind of ground represents a kind of reception of his message. The only other ground you remember is the rocky ground, but you've misremembered why, that

But this isn't necessarily true; more importantly, assuming Solomon is wise, he would know that he cannot know if this is true. *Solomon still does not know who the real mother is.*

The sophist's way out is to change the debate from who is the real mom to judging which woman is a better mother for the child, to whom should the child go? But this isn't any easier, it's certainly not inarguable that a woman who wants a baby so badly that she is willing to kidnap it may actually be a very good mother-- maybe even a better mother than the flat chested harlot that allegedly gave birth to it but was too sleepy to notice she was sleeping on it and losing it. But why would Solomon even care that this baby go to the better mother? How much better could either one be? The women are harlots. Admittedly, they have value.

---

seed doesn't not grow, it grows great, it sprouts quickly, but then it dies when you are tested. That's how you receive knowledge. You think you know-- about science or "truth" or yourself, it feels great, sprouts plans and ideas and insights-- and then it burns up. You may think you know, but you are unconsciously aware of your ignorance, which is why you never act-- you aren't afraid to act, that would imply some conscious awareness-- you cannot act. "The Jews seek signs and the Greeks seek wisdom," perhaps you should have read the next line: "and both of those are awful." Please recall what happened when Oedipus got both.

Sort of an aside: the parable of the sower of seeds is a good example of tremendous human ingenuity in the service of getting out of doing math. The precision with which this parable is spoken/written, its detail and intricacy, is in inverse proportion to the utterly useless interpretation it is commonly given. So "knowledge which falls on fertile ground grows well"? You needed a metaphor to understand that? Isn't that kind of a metaphor in itself?

The parable doesn't have a title, so to facilitate discussion it has been labeled "The Parable of the Sower", the irony being that the one thing no one ever discusses is the sower. "The sower is God." I guess that was obvious, though why isn't he more careful where he spreads his seed? That the message takes root only rarely is literally incorrect if you know how to read and also count: one seed falls on rocky ground, one seed is eaten by birds, one seed is strangled by thorns, and three seeds grow well and multiply by a factor of 30, 60 and 100, respectively. In other words, your rock brain constitutes the minority, not the majority. And you may flatter yourself that you're the fertile ground, but that just means your IQ is a perfect 100 and you believe with all your heart "TV is so well written nowadays."

The next spot curiously unworked is what happens to the seed in rocky soil: it grows immediately because it has no roots in the ground. I'm not sure that makes botanical sense, unless rocky ground=hydroponics; but more importantly, why describe what happens to that seed at all? If the idea is supposed to be that the ground is you, then the seed not growing in the rocky ground is no different than if the seed had been eaten by birds. So? The only reason to describe what happens to the seed is if the parable isn't about the ground but about the sower: this seed looks like it's growing well in rocky ground to him. Because he's an idiot. Yeah. Bet you didn't see that coming. The sower isn't God, the sower is you.

I didn't pull this interpretation out of the ground, either, if it's about a teacher sowing knowledge then the book we're riffing from is Plutarch, your complaints of anachronistic historiography are irrelevant to me. Education as farming is an obvious metaphor today to get us out of considering its original, very specific, parallel: cultivation of Nature by human art for a definite purpose. Plutarch uses the sowing analogy to suggest that deficiencies of nature can be made up with training and practice, an idea today considered utterly preposterous because we need it for another purpose: when you fail at training, you can't be blamed; if it succeeds in others, they can't take all the credit. Naturally, you'll still want them to produce; from each according to his ability; to each, according to their enjoyment. "That's not correct." You should check the ledger. Sometimes wanting is a defense against enjoyment, and sometimes needing is a defense against wanting.

Maybe not a lot, but not zero. Children, on the other hand, are so disposable that one of the harlots fell asleep on one. Solomon may care about justice, but he don't care much about babies. This is a man that's got about five million children running around the house. He'd as soon chop a child in two as a cat. There's plenty more. A child or two, more or less, was of no consequence to Solomon.

The unexamined piece of the analysis is the very premise that the two harlots come to Solomon because he is wise. But not only is this premise iffy, the story requires this premise to be false. The lying woman's fundamental assumption is that Solomon is the respected authority to everyone else, but he will *not* know the truth, he can be fooled-- and not by some big city lawyer with fancy degrees and three syllable words-- by her. This isn't America where

---

The importance of reading this through Plutarch is that this solves the problem of the seed's growth. The parable of the sower is a parable about parables. "I know that." No, you don't. "I'm not stupid, I can follow a simple story." Come on, you get confused by shows with more than 3 characters. 'Who is that guy again?' "That's just because they're badly written." You're blaming the writing? You're blaming the seed? The seed is the parable, but the sower is not God. The sower is you. The sower doesn't have the luxury of only planting in fertile soil; his obligation is to work the soil over and over, season after season, to make it become fertile so that the seed will eventually grow, so that what is produced from nature after much effort is finally stronger than nature itself. But that sounds like hard work, no thanks, God can do the sowing and I'll take my information in passively like the fertile ground I think I am. "My mind's a sponge." So you can throw it out the moment it gets seeded.

If you're not totally convinced let me go a step further to help you stay that way. For Plutarch and Jesus neither the ground nor the sower is the point. All that matters to them is the yield. The cultivation of the pupil, by the pupil-- the pupil working his rock brain to get the seed to take root-- all of that work is for the benefit of everyone else. If the promise of becoming as rich as astronauts isn't enough to motivate your teens to work harder, you might try telling them that in the future other people will depend on how hard they worked today; and that like it or not, arrogant or not, they will be responsible for others, including those who didn't put in the work today. "That's not fair, why us?" Because if not you, who?

This is why I know my translation of Mark 13:6 is right. Jesus would not care if there were false Christs, or real Christs, indeed, the whole point is it shouldn't matter if they all had Certificates of Authenticity. You may remember the empowering story of Moses and Aaron vs. the Pharaoh's sorcerers, Aaron throws down his staff and it turns into a serpent and Pharaoh's sorcerers throw down their staffs which turn into serpents, but Aaron's serpent eats the other serpents, praise be to God, ok-- which God turned the sorcerers' staffs into serpents? Wasn't it-- the same God? So you have a story that literally couldn't have happened describing an event that literally shouldn't have happened. Does that make sense? Either the story is about what to believe, or it's about how to believe.

Jesus says the highest commandment is to love God, but it appears to be the only commandment, the others are simply logical correlates. He certainly doesn't take a hard line on adultery, he regards the well-water Samaritan woman with... amusement. "Cotton mouth, huh?" Zing. He wants belief-- even if it is tentative, unsure, skeptical, faltering-- disavowed; any belief, as long as it comes from you, it doesn't have a foothold in someone else's knowledge. I know you think that this kind of total belief is weird nowadays because we know so much more, but the subordinate clause is either a non sequitur or absolutely a defense. Knowledge is how we get out of having to act.

If "belief" is way too hard for you to understand, change it to love and try it on yourself. "How can I love for no reason? How can I love what I don't know or understand?" Well, how has loving what you do know worked out for you? "I know she's a bitch." Got it.

the operating conceit is that the juries need to be persuaded (=fooled) and second guessing is in/constitutionalized. Everyone believes Solomon is wise and powerful, except her, who believes he is only powerful. So it's correct to say that the liar took a chance at claiming the baby *because* Solomon was the judge. Meanwhile, the real mother may have hoped he would know the truth, or she may have been worried he would get it wrong, but you can now see that part of her and all of the liar think Solomon could be fooled. Yet he has the reputation for wisdom.

This is the perception that makes Solomon's initial judgement to cut the baby intelligible. Both of the women suspect he can be fooled, and one of them is actually trying to do it. Which one? While it's not true that only the biological mother would give up her baby to save

---

Don't accuse me of a covert religious agenda, your paranoia is displacement, I'm not trying to get you to abandon knowledge or convert your beliefs, I am trying to show you that you know nothing and are incapable of belief in anything except envy-- and the consequences for everyone else.

The rock hard foundation of your knowledge is appeal to authority-- to the one who does not act. If you accept the very basic premise that the one who acts-- for good or evil-- does so out of belief in his own power, then to balance this in your ledger, whoever has power cannot also possess knowledge. They have to be totally separate. If you're wondering why your stellar post-secondary sources education has failed to result in commensurate power, it's because you're asking the question backwards. You have no power, therefore you assume you are educated. "I know how the world really works." Let me guess: incompetently, frivolously, or exploitatively, and there are no other choices. "I actually do like science." You like science videos, produced and shot like music videos, of the same duration and impact. What's the result? The Gospel of Information, the Gospel of Mark. Completely consistent with the psychology of you, the only characters in the Gospel Of Mark who know who Jesus is-- not believe, but know-- are demons. They know exactly who he is, but they have no power. Believe it.

Jesus wants belief in him, and he offers believers power-- not knowledge. He tells the disciples to go forth and heal the sick and cast out demons, but he doesn't tell them how to do this. All the power comes from belief, and it comes without any knowledge. "This kind [of demon] can only be cast out by prayer." "Can you at least tell me the prayer, so I say it correctly?" No, because this isn't Hogwarts. "It's leviOsa, not leviosA." Oh, that's why it wasn't working, thanks for that. Look... I'm not trying to cause a bother, but wouldn't we all be far better wizards if we simply learned whatever language "leviosa" is in and wrote our own spells? "Slow down, freckles, wizardry is a privilege, not a right. You learn what and how we tell you." But what are we supposed to do if Voldemort shows up with his own magic? "Duh, we wait for the One to save us when he graduates." But isn't he getting the same superficial education we are? "His power will be genetic, of course, do you not believe in science?"

The knowledge/power battle is so complete that no one looks up from their scrolls and says, "wait a second, it's actually modern times, can't we just take Voldemort out with a 50 cal from the bell tower? What about a Faraday cage? My uncle's diner has a microwave, couldn't we put him in it?"

"It's interesting that Rowling, a successful female author, is still an unconscious agent of patriarchal norms and had Harry marry the quiet and deferential girl instead of the outspoken and intelligent one." Yes, it is interesting you did not praise the author for having the quiet girl marry her choice or complain that Rowling forced the smart girl to end up with the wrong one: men shouldn't be allowed to choose and women can't possibly have chosen, the only solution is for the audience to decide. It is also interesting that you think outspoken must equal intelligence, and is the relevant factor in love. "I'm not an owl!!!" She's right about that, anyway.

What were we talking about? Oh yes, demonic possession. "Ahem, I'd like to politely suggest that those people weren't really possessed by demons, they were probably... mentally ill." Who are you

it, it is a textually evident fact that while both women say they want the baby, one woman is only satisfied by an outcome in which the other woman is deprived of the baby-- either by getting custody of the baby or by it being killed. And if the King does the depriving for her-- so much the better, there can be no guilt when omnipotence does the acting. And now Solomon knows the truth: the kind of woman that is satisfied by the deprivation of the other would also try to deprive Solomon, of what (she thinks) satisfies him: his wisdom. She cannot do otherwise.

But if the point was to deprive the other mother, why didn't she simply kill the baby, and then try to fool Solomon that it was an accident? Why kidnap the baby and pretend she

---

talking to? Are you giving me information? Is the form of your defense-- to repeat the content of someone else's defense?

Just as a technical aside, the people at that time may have been monotheists but they were not morons, they knew about psychotic mania; demonic possession was the diagnosis after they had ruled out mental illness. But anyway it doesn't matter if demons don't exist-- why are they in the story? To show Jesus can cast them out? Are you surprised he does this? Even the Pharisees weren't surprised he was doing it. So why mention what the demons say, especially when Jesus tells them not to say it? Because demons know, they have the information. The fact that the Devil is a liar means he knows the truth, whether he tells you or not is irrelevant, the point is he knows. It doesn't matter if demons don't really exist, the story doesn't need them to really exist, what matters is the structure of the opposition: some other omniscient enemy versus your omnipotent entity, and the role of this enemy is to give the audience knowledge and then lose to the One. When Agent Smith pulls up a chair and offers to share with you an apocalypse, let him who has ears listen.

It's a commonplace nowadays to say that youthful religiosity matures into sophisticated atheism, but what you've convinced yourself of is that the god you were taught to believe in as a child doesn't exist, and in this you are correct, that god doesn't exist. Your belief at that time was the same has your unbelief now, both rely on someone else's knowledge that you don't really possess, both prevent belief in anything. Including love. "Love doesn't exist, it's a trick of evolutionary biology to get us to mate." Seriously? You need to be tricked into mating? "No, into staying, love improves the offspring's chances of survival." I love that your wife had to trick you into staying. "No, stupid, love is the trick, your feeling of deep undying love is the biological trick to make you stay." I'm confused: I thought you said love doesn't exist.

John was the preferred Gospel for intellectuals who found philosophy an easy plug for leaking belief; the Gospel of Mark was rediscovered in the 1800s around the time the authority of Church went ski slope downward; and when consumer electronics made it harder to believe in anything people rediscovered Revelation, there you have a clear omniscient enemy that could guarantee what you know, he may be imaginary but his name is a number and the number is real. Neither does it matter if the Gospel writers believed in demons. Clearly he/they wanted the reader to believe in God, and the inclusion of the demons-- whether it was literally a witnessed fact or utterly invented expository scenes-- serve that necessary appeal to authority on the subject of God, without which the reader would have to rely on his belief alone. And it is that-- not what you believe, but how you believe-- having to believe-- that the reader can't stand. The modern Christian will take the word of a demon that he knows didn't exist as long as he doesn't have to believe it all himself.

Which is why "historical Jesus" research conducted by atheist academics poses no threat to this kind of belief, it supports it; when a "fundamentalist" reads that it is likely Jesus wasn't actually crucified on a cross or that Peter was illiterate, it doesn't deflate him at all, it inspires him. It's not because he clings to irrational belief, exactly the opposite: it becomes a matter of knowledge, knowledge means authority, and that authority looks like a jerk, no way am I believing him. Making their beliefs the subject of university scholarship and "objectivity" relieves the burden of total belief-- the belief is

265

wants it? Getting the baby is not what satisfies her, only depriving the other woman satisfies her, *but she needs a defense against that.* Note that when the real mother hastily agrees to let the fake mother have the baby in order to keep it alive, the fake mother doesn't take it: she tells Solomon to kill the baby as decreed so that neither of them have it. Her satisfaction is entirely relative to the other woman, in flux, as if she kept a dynamic ledger: at this point, if the real mom would be satisfied by losing the baby but keeping it alive, she must be deprived of that. Wanting the baby was only a defense, because then she's a woman who wants a baby, not a woman whose envy targets mothers, kings, and babies alike-- all are columns in a ledger that have to be reduced to zero. "Wanting the baby" is a defense against what truly satisfies her, the deprivation of the other. When Solomon decrees the deprivation of the real mother in the initial decision to kill it, the liar no longer needs to want the baby, so she stops wanting it.

registered within the world of knowledge, albeit incomplete-- it is no longer entirely their responsibility. The unpayable debt gets crossed out. The ledger becomes balanced.

45"Hey, you said the mob wasn't allowed to stone the adulteress! You're wrong, the Romans did allow the Jews the freedom to handle their own social conflicts, and you also said the Roman Empire didn't care about adultery, but in fact they had very strict laws on adultery!" It would be so much easier if this wife simply registered as a prostitute, the law says she can have as many orgasms with as many men as she wants, as long as she gets paid. Before you try to parse the logic or build a Tardis, NB the Roman Empire was near its max: it was down hill from there. But what motivated you to go look up adultery laws? The game you want to play is hiding behind the discrepancies to avoid seeing your own complicity. You think my interpretation is wrong because I don't know the *facts*? Wow, you caught me, I wish I had anticipated your use of the internet. Stop trying to interrogate me, torture the truth out of yourself, why was *the law* the single part of my explanation that you chose to think about? How badly do you want me to be wrong?

Ok, let's play your game and I'll spot you some points, let's say that the Augustan laws punished adultery with property confiscation and banishment, though fathers were allowed to kill their daughter's lover, and while husbands were not allowed to kill the man leniency could be expected if he did. Were either of them present? No? That's weird. And let's say Tiberius wasn't a hands off wannanotbe tyrant such that laws were, say, negotiable. And let's assume that a wormhole opened and the Julian updates 600 years later applied retroactively so Rome did in fact punish adultery with death; or let's say that the whole story was really written in 1000AD and added to John after the fact; or let's say Rome did allow the mob to stone adulteresses so long as it didn't cause a "public disruption"-- even if all of this is granted, *why did Rome choose this crime to give the mob power over?* They can't deal with murderers or tax evaders on their own, right? Hold on, ask it the other way: why was jurisdiction over this one crime enough to satisfy them? Perhaps Rome did the math and determined that this was the crime that had the least impact on its own affairs while simultaneously being the most impactful for the mob to have-- i.e. give them this pointless way to feel powerful and they'll never rise up. Or, even more sagely, did the masters understand that the mob would even more willingly bend a knee to Rome if they were allowed to believe they were stoning adulteresses *in spite of* Roman law, as if they were getting away with something-- as if they were satisfied with the appearance of power? While you try to come up with an answer don't bother, the answers are irrelevant, in all of these scenarios, the privilege of stoning was still granted by the state, not God. "Father said we should stone her!" But you don't live with Father, you live with your mother, and Momma Roma doesn't give a damn what your deadbeat Dad wants because he only comes around when he wants money. "Ok, ok, we asked Mom, she said it was okay if we stoned her but we have to do our chores first." I'm sure your Father would be proud.

Why does the mob tell Jesus that she was caught in adultery-- "in the act"? *Who* caught her in the act? Did *they* catch her, was she found drunk in a hot tub, maybe so she could say to herself it doesn't count? It helps if you've had experience with both sides of the legal system, you spot certain expressions which signal the case as a set up. You can convey the meaning of "caught in the act" in

266

She is satisfied, and she no longer needs a defense against what satisfies her, because she has the ultimate defense: it's not my fault the baby died, it was caused by-- some other omnipotent entity.

English with a dozen different idioms but the Greek phrase that is used and translated as "in the act" never appears anywhere else in the Bible despite all the times people are caught in the act. Where it does frequently appear is in rotting from the inside Athens, where recent advances in political science meant that while crimes should be tried in front of Athenian jurors, if the perpetrator happened to be caught "in the act", then summary judgment and execution could be passed by eleven dummies who I'm sure were above corruption, democracy works better if you let the experts handle it. "In the act" became not a description of the arrest but a prosecutorial maneuver for the purpose of skipping a trial. Nowadays we have "plea bargain" so both lawyers can claim it as a win while the only person who can lose is you. "Your Honor, we're asking for probation and time served based on the 11 months he did while incompetent to stand the trial that we've agreed to skip right now." Very well, the defendant is remanded to psych. Court adjourned.

The missing adulterer is a problem no one there or here wants to discuss, because the Hebrew, Greek, and Roman laws all have death as a possible consequence for the adulterer. Who isn't there. For the adulteress, in the cases where the law did offer a punishment, it was almost certainly the privilege of her husband to execute. Who isn't there. So the problem isn't that the woman *isn't* guilty of adultery, the problem is that even if she was no one in the mob has any power over her. They cannot act. That's what they want, and when Jesus offers any individual to come and take the rock, he is offering them the pretense that they are *choosing* not to. He has framed his rhetoric in terms of allowing them not to act-- as if it was their choice. The group unity that they needed from collectively stoning her he effectively gave them by letting each think they chose not to. This is why each *individual* in the mob disperses so easily, one at a time. Their inability to act was turned into-- an act. And the woman is left standing there, blinking, relieved but incredulous. "So-- that's it? All that was for nothing?" Jesus shrugged.

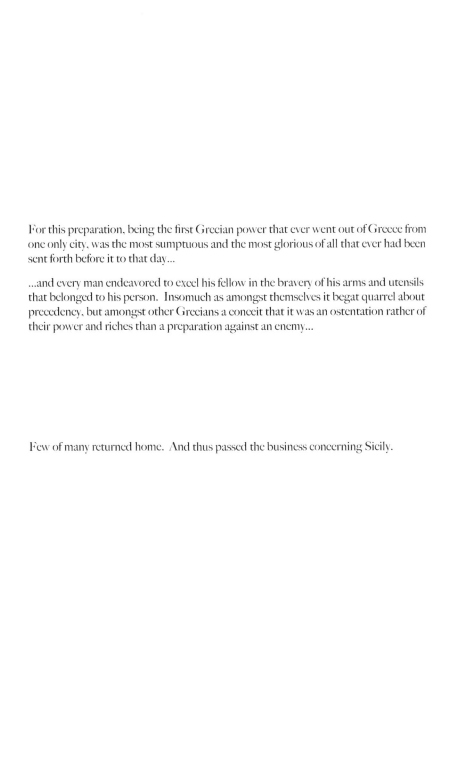

For this preparation, being the first Grecian power that ever went out of Greece from one only city, was the most sumptuous and the most glorious of all that ever had been sent forth before it to that day...

...and every man endeavored to excel his fellow in the bravery of his arms and utensils that belonged to his person. Insomuch as amongst themselves it begat quarrel about precedency, but amongst other Grecians a conceit that it was an ostentation rather of their power and riches than a preparation against an enemy...

Few of many returned home. And thus passed the business concerning Sicily.

The believable lie has the form of-------- a lie.

Gone Girl was a very popular movie based on the novel by Mrs. Brett Nolan about two strangers who are only incidentally married, nevertheless the story was taken to be "a comment on modern marriage," which only makes sense if "modern"= "your". I saw it in a theater filled 90% with women and a handful of men who had been dragged there to have their privilege checked, and when the film ended someone in the audience turned to the person next to them and, in a voice soft enough to suggest they were conscious of their role as the minority report, said, "I don't understand how two twelve year olds can legally drive. What state is this?"

That the person who said this was likely drunk and possibly me should not deter you from taking a moment and considering its wisdom.

Man of limited means marries a woman of infinite possibilities who has all the trappings of what a woman thinks a man should want: she is quirky, cosmopolitan, college educated, and comes with a dowry. Alas, Amy soon discovers that the first three are devastatingly useless to this husband, and everyone; and the fourth doesn't exist because her parents have spent it.

So the couple move to Missouri to be near his family, which in theory is the father but in practice is the sister. You can see where this is going. Like most Americans they are unhappy but as long as it is like most Americans they can live with that. More troublingly, they are unsatisfied. They can live with this too, as long as the ledger is balanced. Then he cheats. She sees it. So did the audience, the one in her head, so now she has no choice, and payback is going to be her. In every revenge fantasy there's a consumer product incidental to the plot that is the whole point of the fantasy, it will be temporally, spatially, or logically proximate to the murder or suicide, it symbolizes what kind of a person you could be if-- allowed. Don't worry, it will be labeled Exhibit A to make sure you don't miss it. Well, one morning the world awakens and she is *gone*, the only trace is UV-light evidence of a poorly cleaned up pool of blood (NB: in the kitchen)------ and Exhibit A, her diary. Guess what's in it: the prescient calligraphy of an abused and literate wife, terrified her husband will someday murder her.

He is consequently arrested. You wouldn't believe there existed a theater full of progressive, educated women who despite already knowing he didn't do it were still quietly thrilled that Central Time has the death penalty, but I saw it with my own eyes.

Is this a commentary on modern marriage? The story itself doesn't add anything new to the understanding of marriage, it doesn't tell us what marriage is today, or even what it's like. The story doesn't help us see what are the relevant social conditions which make this kind of marriage appear, but it does help reveal what are the social conditions which make this kind of a story about marriage to appear, that make us want this story to be about marriage and not something else.[46]

---

46 No one reads primary sources anymore, ok, fine, but why do even those who do read from Thucydides's "magnificent history" only ever read the speeches, and mostly in the same way? "The Funeral Oration is a masterpiece of ancient rhetoric--" Are you just saying that because your internet brain couldn't handle the absence of dialogue in Book VIII? "Well, there is a lot of dense reading... you have to begin somewhere." How about at the beginning? "I'd love to read books, but no one has that kind of time nowadays." I know, you want to get smarter, but after a long day scrolling through your teleprompter, by nighttime you're just too exhausted to do anything other than crash

"Poorly cleaned up blood in the kitchen" is a perfect symbol for what men are really good at and really bad at if the person who came up with the symbol was a woman, but nowadays even boys of 11 know you're supposed to use bleach and an oxy cleaner, so how well it can be *described in words* should suggest to someone the significance: it's fake, Amy staged her own murder. And she's a nut. And eventually a quasi-feminist chaotic neutral (anti-) hero, or symbol, or id, or symptom, or etc. She may be some of these, but the simplest division it is possible to make of the human race is into the people who take things hard and the people who take them easy. She belonged to the former class. Amy staged the whole crime to get back at him for cheating, and the first thing to observe is that her preferred method of hurting him wasn't to kill him but to kill herself. Of course, she doesn't actually kill

---

on the couch and scroll through your teleprompter. If only there was some kind of low weight low rep workout you could do from the couch to get in decent shape for teleprompting. "90% of it is diet." In your case, it's not so much the portion control at each sitting as it is the number of sittings, which is all of them. Have you ever gone a full hour without putting something in your mouth? Your foot counts. You probably figure you can fast track to that aesthetic brain you crave you by supplementing with *The New Yorker*, take one every two weeks and you'll be able to show off your gains in about month. "I also do 15 minutes daily of *The Atlantic*, I've never felt smarter in my whole life." It's easy if you stay away from math. Everybody wants to be a bodybuilder, but don't nobody want to lift no heavy ass weights.

For context: with war declared, Pericles has convinced the Athenians to abandon their homes and farms and come live inside the impenetrable walls of the city, not as a retreat but as a strategy: "Why bother fighting the Spartans? We're home and we have infinite resources, and they're a long way from home and have limited resources. Unfortunately we don't have snow, but let them scorched earth the trees and farms, let them call us names, who cares? We have a central bank, a silver mine, and we control the seas; we'll import our food from the Ukraine and in the meantime open some schools, gyms and brothels, and heck on weekends we'll put on musicals." Sounds great. What's our plan for inventing antibiotics?

In the relentlessly discussed Funeral Speech given by Pericles when the war started, written by Thucydides after the war ended, he talks about dead soldiers and honor and etc, and then in the penultimate paragraph adds a special message for the womenfolk:

> On the other hand, if I must say anything on the subject of female
> excellence to those of you who will now be in widowhood, it will be all
> comprised in this brief exhortation: great will be your glory in not
> falling short of your natural character, and greatest will be hers who
> is least talked of by the men, whether for good or for bad.

"Seen but not heard", discretion the better part of valor; never mind the women, someone should have told the men, and he did, and they didn't want to listen, they wanted valor. At this point, the only thing the younger generation of Athenian men had to talk about is what their fathers had done, good or bad, so they felt like they needed to go out and fight like men to prove they weren't women. But look at it from the other side: what did the women have to brag about? Their husbands? "Seen but not heard" is an obvious symbol of Athenian women's obvious inequality and obvious subjugation to men, but if all of this was so obvious, why did Pericles have to say it out loud? Was it not obvious to him? It could only have been sayable if it were no longer true; and by the time Thucydides wrote it, at the *end* of the war, well-- he had to tell the women something, after all, the men had failed them.

You know you're being lied to when, in all the modern criticisms of Pericles's backhanded compliment to women, never is included the context, e.g. the immediately preceding sentence, in which he forehands the men for their stupidity, envy and rivalries.

herself, because unlike in real life where suicide is a relentless torture for the survivors, who, assuming they possess at least a midbrain will feel some guilt regardless of whether they are actually guilty, in this story for people who got as far as a notochord the husband's superego cannot be assumed to exist. Guilt is not a believable punishment to Amy or the audience. So that's out. She could shoot a shockumentary of her suicide seeking to shame him, but that will only work if she provides the voice over narration, too. Which she does. But in Amy's case, suicide won't work because he won't suffer enough, or at all. Unfortunately, she can't stone him for adultery, and shaming for it would fail because of a structural problem she will interpret backwards: it's not that men, unlike women, are allowed by society to do whatever they want and can't be shamed for cheating; but that since media is now in charge of public shame, no one can feel shame without media: unless she films a hidden camera cockumentary

You can imagine the scene of common household women wailing and beating their breasts over their fallen men, acutely self-aware of their gender responsibility to the national mourning. Go ahead and imagine it, because Thucydides is telling you it wasn't like that. "Pericles" tells them *to* mourn-- men need to see it to know their sacrifice will be worth it-- but otherwise for Christ's sake keep quiet, the men already feel girly for hiding inside the city walls, but if they go out I'll be doing a lot more Funeral Speeches. If a woman criticizes a man for not going out and fighting Spartans it means he's not a real man; if a woman applauds him for not going out and fighting Spartans, it means he's not a real man either. Either way, the Spartans are the real men. So either way, the women have to stay silent.

And bad enough Athenian men might be less manly than Spartan men. The prevailing rumor is that even Spartan women had bigger balls than Athenian men. A generation *earlier* there's a story about the Spartan queen Gorgo, wife of Leonidas of *300* fame, who while in Athens is hit by a smooth talking Athenian Don Juan. I can't elaborate here, just accept that a Spartan wife is actually allowed to have sex with other men if she wants. But Gorgo doesn't want, not least because the man hitting on her is the Athenian equivalent of a nightclub bartender, he runs a standard neg/kino approach, tilts his chin and purses his lips and suavely strokes her elbow. She looks down like he's peeing on it. "Jesus," she says in disgust, "you can't even play the female part right." I'll explain: she's saying he has sex with men. Which is ironic because etc.

In another time and anecdote Gorgo is discreetly asked by some Athenian women how it is that Spartan women famously can boss the Spartan men around so easily. Gorgo shrugs. "Because Spartan women are the only ones that produce real men." I'll explain: she's saying Athenians aren't real men. A real man isn't threatened by a woman bossing him around, and no one else who witnesses the bossing would think he was less of a man, because by the time he became a man has already proven himself a real man through his accomplishments, such that he is not diminished by being bossed around by a woman, who would anyway not bother to boss around a fake man, she would just abandon him in the woods to die. The clever part is that Gorgo here is blaming the Athenian women as well, if they can't boss their adult men around it is because they never raised their boys to become real men, so instead these fake men merely assert they are men with rhetoric or bossing the women around. That's all very nice, butt in order for this anecdote to be believable, let alone to have actually happened, the conversation could only have taken place *in* Athens, because unlike Athenian women, Spartan women could travel. Travel *alone*. Stay with me: never mind being *allowed* to travel; if you want to tax your sociology degree explain what had to have been the relevant social conditions in Sparta that a lone Spartan woman felt safer than an Athenian woman *in Athens*?

It's hard to keep your Athenian women in line when less than 150 miles southwest the Spartan women are doing whatever they want, enjoying all kinds of extra-marital sex and bossing their husbands around-- just as a reminder, their husbands are *Spartans*. It's got to occur to someone, male or female, that the problem might not be that women are naturally inferior but that only the Athenians needed to think so. "If women become like men, what will we become?" Better men?

the cheater can only be shamed for whom they cheated with or whom they cheated on. So she's stuck: he can't be shamed, because whom he cheated with is a supermodel and whom he cheated on was her. It's frustrating. I know.

But here things get complicated. See, he didn't *just* cheat on Amy; his real crime was marrying her when he wasn't good enough for her, tricking her into being with him: taking away all the fantastic cosmopolitan magazine possibilities that a trust fund and an Ivy diploma offered, moving her to Missouri, reverting back to a low T TV news target, and *then* cheating-- and now she's stuck, stuck in Central Time, where even the clocks are retarded. All her dreams have been deferred, shriveling up like raisins in the sun, notwithstanding she never actually had any dreams to defer and she wouldn't get the reference. Not only did he deprive

---

Just guessing, I'm no biologist. But our modern society has made some changes, the good news is that nowadays raising a man means teaching him "to respect women." The bad news is: and nothing else.

BTW, the movie *300* obliterates all of this by changing not what Gorgo says but what she says it for, by changing whom she says it to. The bad guy Persian messenger has come to scare the pants off the Spartan council, surprise, and Gorgo has a seat at the table so she leans in:

                    GORGO
          Do not be coy or stupid, Persian. You can afford neither in
          Sparta.

The Persian turns to Gorgo, never having been spoken to by a woman in
this tone.

                    MESSENGER
          What makes this woman think she can speak among men?

                    GORGO
          Because only Spartan women give birth to real men.

The Persian must swallow his pride along with the insult before his
men.

                    LEONIDAS
          Let us walk to cool our tongues.

Yeah, man, what can I say, you know these hot blooded Lannister bitches. You can imagine the applause of the male audience, this is the kind of strong powerful super hot female comic book character they'd be happy to live off of financially and every other -ly; I want you to imagine however the applause of the few women dragged there on their third or fourth date who welcomed any female movie character not underdressed or in distress and what unholy hell their lives must have been that they would want to take credit for another woman's pointless bravado. "She doesn't hold back, she speaks her mind." You know, no man would ever be proud to do this. Though now I guess I have to write should. Oddly, to an audience well practiced at locating structural causes they seem not to have noticed that maybe she can get lippy because she's flanked by a king and 8 hill giants and her husband is both. Her point here isn't that she birthed Spartan men who aren't threatened by women, but that she's not threatened by Persian men because Spartan men aren't afraid of anything. And to prove this, Leonidas later kicks the scary Persian man into a giant pit, thus taking credit for doing what in real life an Athenian had once taken credit for doing. Side note: the Athenians eventually killed that Athenian, too. The scene completely undermines the original meaning of the anecdote, it makes it all about the men, not the women, so still wanting this particular woman to have the power to get lippy the movie makes it uniquely Gorgo-Power, i.e. they made Gorgo super hot, but, and I'm speaking from experience, she wasn't. Her name was Gorgo

her of her potential enjoyment, but-- get this-- he then went out and enjoyed more than her. It is obscene. *This is the crime for which he must be punished.*

So she frames him for murder. You might think that's excessive[47]. And *obviously* it is, *no one* disputes this, which is a big clue you're about to get hit in the face with a defense. She went too far, sure, but the audience understands her rage, they get it, with a degree like that she should be in NY or New Haven, not Missouri. *Carthago delenda est.* "He actually expected me to love him unconditionally, and then he dragged me penniless to the navel of this great country." Ironically, the navel's motto is "nothing in excess". "Is that supposed to be funny? Because I don't get it." It's funny what you get and don't get, as I'm about to demonstrate. So

---

which I'm pretty sure wasn't an accident, whichever one you think came first actually makes the situation worse.

Meanwhile, for a culture that had their chicks locked up, the Athenians spent a lot of their pop culture worrying about the coop and not at all about the fox. In the supposedly comic play *Lysistrata* you have the women of Athens and Sparta conspiring to withhold sex from the husbands until the men agree to end the war. The women don't see much point in winning the war, or even having the war, or sex, and the only power they have to stop it is a sex strike. Sex workers of the world unite, though I should point out this is a play written by a man for men, so while it's debatable whether the war should be stopped it's axiomatic that women only have sex instrumentally, for a reason. Well, women with their husbands anyway.

The problem with a sex strike isn't that it might not work but rather that it is absolutely never going to work ever, because women are doing it, to men. I am not Aristophanes so I can't pretend to know what he was thinking, but anyone who thinks the audience heard this as a pacifist play should have at least their pituitary checked, the only people who could think this are women, or men who have watched more sex than they've actually had sex, which I realize is now everyone in America but you get my point and the comparison still holds anyway. Only for those two groups is it obvious that sex=power, for everyone else with access to both such an equivalence is utterly laughable. "Are you telling me," says the male 18-35 demo watching the play, "that I'm going to give up my honor, my freedom and maybe even my city-- just to have sex with my wife? Just so some other dummy can have sex with his wife? Are the prostitutes on strike, too, or just the married ones? What kind of a fig licking beta cuck would fall for this? --"Menelaus!" replies the Spartan woman Lampito, "as soon as he saw Helen's naked breasts, he dropped his sword!" See, that's a joke, Aristophanes was a comic playwright, every one of us saw the 2nd place tragedy 4 years ago, we know perfectly well Menelaus's jealousy dragged an army to Helen back, but the only reason he dropped his sword is because he was done killing the Trojans and because he mostly used a spear. Off topic, not really, fun fact about "playwright": it's spelled correctly, and it's an insult, it was coined to mark the distinction between one who wrote plays and one who wrought-- pornography. And in case Aristophanes's irony is too unibrow for you, Lampito is described as a cow who could throttle an ox. Is that the signifier of irresistible lust for a Spartan warrior? Her plan is to give her man blue balls? He's going to have no place to dump his load? You know Spartans are... Greek, right? Hell, the Spartans don't even live with their wives. Hold on a second, I just realized one of us is insane: *you think a woman can tell me no?* By Hera, this is a comedy.

This is the psychology of men who are at war but not in a war. Aware of their growing impotence, not being able to win a war-- or even fight one-- or, evidently, satisfy their wives, they stage a play in which their power to do any of these things is taken from them. The early ancient Greeks called this *comedy*.

It may be the premise that women only have sex instrumentally, for a non-sexual reason, but as a male fantasy you should look closely for the wish fulfillment: in Act III the women become so horny that they are willing to break the strike, and let war continue, just so *they* can have sex. *With*

274

in order to pretend to distance yourself from what she does while countenancing the rage that wants to do it, the move is to label her behavior as *pathological*: she is, they say, a *psychopath*.

But what's pathological is indeed the rage *itself*, you're not supposed to be able to identify with that kind of rage at all, in a way no different than one should not *be able* to identify with the rage of a guy who shoots up a sorority. Not "shouldn't"-- shouldn't be able. "But how could you not, it's so obvious." They say empathy is lacking nowadays, so it's notable that the little empathy that you were taught is hyperspecific. "Well, I wouldn't do what he did, but I get it." Well, then, you're a nut. The mistake you're making is in assuming that your rage is on the lower end of a hyperbolic curve, and your awesome imagination merely extrapolates=

---

their husbands. It must be love, love exists, their women love them no matter what, *even* if they don't fight the war.

So rather than it being a pacifist play, it's a straight up call to arms: any guy who wants to end the war is a girl. End the war? Just as we're getting new leadership that can turn this mess around? Only a woman doesn't understand the value of the war, judges it less valuable than her sex that she undervalues in the first place. Withhold sex? Do they know what will happen if the Spartans win? Oh, so they're admittedly powerless against the Spartan penes but they can withhold sex from us?

Lysistrata is a male play, it has no insights into female psychology; in contrast Pericles's speech written in the future and set in the past is a great reveal to what the women were eventually going to be thinking: *Mourn the dead? Keep silent?* What the hell did we-- yes we, we were out there slinging rock just like you idiots-- build these giant walls for in the first place if you all go outside them to invade giant democracies? Did you even have a plan? The guy who told you it couldn't be done is the guy you told to go do it? "We chose him because he was lucky." And you think women are irrational. Ok.

In theory it was a democracy, the individual men had all the power to do what they wanted. Anyone watching *Lysistrata* buy that? The common misquote from Thucydides is that Athens was a democracy in name only but was really a tyranny under Pericles, which eggheads use to say "a ha!" No. What he said was way worse: the way things were going, it was *becoming* a tyranny, NB imperfect tense, but not because Pericles was becoming a tyrant but because the people were becoming idiots.

The very idea that women were oppressed, with no voice, forced by men to stay in the home is so ludicrous that Pericles had to suggest in a funeral speech that they at least pretend. It was a fantasy. First of all there's no AC and its an agrarian society. "Yes, but a woman's *place* was in the home." You say that based on what? Billable hours? An archeologist a thousand years from now would have to conclude that a woman's place was in the car-- but they had such feeble bodies so were given the bigger one, for safety. "Ancient women were segregated because the men didn't trust the other men." Then why not punish the men more severely? Or was the fear that women out in the fields would have sex-- for no reason? "Certainly this is an evolutionary anxiety about ambiguous paternity." Is the anxiety that he doesn't know, or that he doesn't know and she does? Because that second one sounds more anxiogenic but way less evolutionary. The idea that men had to keep women locked up because they were irrational and couldn't be trusted is a specific misunderstanding of an interesting psychology that is easily intuited if you have immigrant parents: in order for a woman to act, it had to be based on a lie. It could not be based on desire. It neither matters what the lie was or what the desire was, only that desire be hidden and the lie not reflect desire, and often the easiest way to do this is phrase the lie as a need. Don't worry, I'll walk you through what will at first be easy to follow and then is going to take a sharp left turn into the dark alley of I don't feel comfortable with where this is going, you said we were going to PJ O' Hannigan's: she *wants* to visit her friend, so has to tell her husband she *needs* to borrow some sugar. The sugar becomes the acceptable excuse for the action because she fears her husband wouldn't allow her the indulgence of

fantasizes the punishment at the extreme. But you have lost the ability to fantasize, and you don't know what a hyperbolic curve looks like, which this isn't anyway; your ability to act isn't a continuous function of your rage, it's binary: killing them isn't the max punishment along a curve, it is the *only* punishment you can effect. You are powerless. The only thing you can do is either absolutely nothing or absolutely anything-- you fantasized about killing not because it's meaningless to kill in fantasy but because your fantasies are primitively pornographic, all or nothing.

She must be a psychopath-- to serve as a defense for what she actually is. There's nothing to be gained from criticizing a fictional character, but there is everything to be learned from the kinds of criticisms-- and defenses-- the audience foists on them. Amy orchestrates an

---

visiting her friend. Please note for later that at the end of this, she will have visited the friend and returned with sugar. Of course, eventually men catch on to this technique, and they conclude that women are liars, in a specific way: that women pretend to *need* something innocuous, in order to get what they *really* want, which is comparatively less acceptable. With me so far? Ok, pull down the blinker and roll up the windows: now pretend she *wants*-- not needs, but wants-- some sugar. In order to go get it, she has to say she *needs* to visit her friend. Uh oh. The whole point of the lie isn't to get something more or less objectively acceptable, but to hide that the motivation is her desire. Now here's where you're going to want to jump from the moving car: she's not just hiding her desire from him-- he assumes she's lying no matter what-- but from herself: she cannot act on it if she desires it.

The problem for gender relations, which has nothing at all to do with gender and everything to do with relations but still only makes sense to you if I use the language of gender is that the man *tells himself* the problem is *what* she desires. When she returns from the second visit with the sugar, and unable to imagine why anyone would lie in order to get sugar, he figures that if she said she needs to visit a friend, she must be blowing him. What else could it be? He tells himself *what* they desire is unacceptable. But the problem isn't what she desires, but how she desires-- the problem isn't her, it's *him*. He's not letting her *want*. It's not certain desires he wants to block, he and everyone else want to obliterate all of her desires. She doesn't know this, she only knows it seems that lifelong and for no logical reason a lot of her desires have been blocked, out of proportion to their objective acceptability, so she has thus trained herself not merely to consciously *hide* desire but unconsciously not to act on her desire. She has forgotten how to want. When she reliably avoids acting on her desire, her desires change, from what she wants to what others want of her; from what satisfies her to a defense against it.

Maybe that's too abstract, here are two porn examples. Instead of *Lysistrata*'s withholding of sex, imagine a modern sex comedy where the women have sex to motivate the men to win. Sex comedy, not WWII musical, they're not being fought for, they're being fought over: e.g. in *Confirmatory Assent*, the cheerleaders, who are the girlfriends of the home team, publicly offer themselves as the prize to whichever team wins the big game, saying that it will motivate their boyfriends to not lose. Sounds hot, though I should add that the game in question is lacrosse. Question: what do the women want?

Off topic, but relevant in an other way: the idea of women being part of the spoils of war has a long history based in actual history, but the anxiety over women passively giving themselves to the other team and enjoying it is a kind of French pornography that became quite popular circa WWII, around the same time the French men not employed in the steel industry decided Americans may not actually be anti-semitic and they're even worse than Nazis. The and is correct. It must have been very hard for a generation of young French men, already antsy about being labeled as French, having to watch-- strike that, thinking that they were watching-- a generation of young French women freely flinging themselves at the brave and rugged Yankee alley pigs rolling in on tanks, say what you want about the Nazis but at least they were organized, never got drunk in public and for

elaborate Rube Goldberg trap-- not for money or tangible reward, but for revenge. But she doesn't pursue revenge against him directly, she causes it to happen *to* him, she causes him to be hurt (passive voice) by something else-- some other omnipotent entity, who is (spoiler) far from omniscient. It has to be powerful enough to act, but one she can fool. Fortunately, Justice is blind. You get to set up the shot.

The bananasness cruelty of her scheme is the evidence many cite for her psychopathy, but this is utterly a defense for the audience, psychopaths are the most direct of actors, they wouldn't go through all this unless they derived some pleasure out of the scheme itself, in which case they wouldn't be psychopaths, but perverts who get off on anything but the point. When you have an overly elaborate strategy for bringing about (passive voice) what anyone

---

the first time since Napoleon had the French women acting like proper ladies, or proper whores, each according to their ability. Now the lot of these harlots need a haircut, or a date with GI Jody. "Confess! You have the breasts of a spy!"

The French men were pushed to the side cafés for the month and the next fifteen years where they not surprisingly began feeling nauseous; having to endure the *hedonistes* weekending in Flavor Country and naturally selecting capitalists is enough to trigger a full on existential crisis, or at least invent the concept. We shouldn't blame them for being a bit hysterical. "I was part of the resistance!" Whatever you say, comrade, save it for the Vassar girls on summer break.

"Well, some of those 'hedonistes' weren't actually consenting partners, even at the time many were confirmed to have been victims of rape." Yes, but by whom? It only counted as rape if the femme was a Fraulein; and if the rapist was a Negro then it was a hanging offense. Ok, too many sub-subreferences, I'll explain that last one as a freebie: French execution was by guillotine.

No doubt you'll say the cheerleaders secretly want the other team to win, for naughty reasons, while merely saying they want to motivate their boyfriends. Well, wait a second, if her true desire is to sleep with the other guys, instead of just going over and cheating quietly or dumping her boyfriend entirely, she creates this elaborate scheme to get what she wants indirectly but in public? What the hell for? "So she can't be blamed for doing it." So it's only ok if she gets what she wants by pretending it's what's publicly expected of her? Is she a communist?

"Maybe she secretly wants to be a sex prize not to motivate her team or because she desires the other team; maybe her kink is being a prize in a competition between men-- she turns a real rivalry in sports into a rivalry over her." She wants to be fought over and taken by the winner... and then go back to the loser? Pretty sure that's a male fantasy. "It's evolutionary psychology." Yes, that's a male fantasy as well.

What she secretly wants is hard to figure out, partly because she doesn't exist but mostly because your brain has a glitch: *whatever* she says she wants has to be a defense. If she says she wants to be a sex prize, that can't be what she really wants, her true desire must be something else: *e.g.* to have sex with the guys on the other team. Or maybe to hurt you. Or maybe to make you feel something for her-- desire, anxiety, jealous rage. Or whatever. But observe that at the end of it all, she will have visited the team and returned with the sugar. She still gets what she wants, but not because it's what she wants.

NB: this isn't a trick, she's not *lying*. The fantasy gives all the knowledge to the audience and deprives her of it. In order for the fantasy to work, in order for it to fully explain her behavior and her psychology-- in order for it to be useful-- she has to not fully know what she truly wants, which is why the cheerleaders are portrayed as tipsy blondes even though they're neither (they're not even cheerleaders, it's ridiculous, because of the university ban against sexualizing sports that even women can play.) She may think she wants to be a "sex prize", that's why she's willing to do it-- but you know better. Better than even her. Not because you know her, but because you know how

else would have pursued directly, you aren't acting like a psychopath, you are daydreaming like a child. Why doesn't she divorce him? Why doesn't she run him over with an SUV? Why doesn't she and some new guy seduce his mistress and then send him a video? None of these are good acts, I am only asking why she doesn't act. She doesn't even imagine it. This ruminative, crazy, fantastical logic has no problem consciously imagining any outcome or idea except one: the will to act. This is what she lacks, and this is what the fantasy is about. All of her will is absent, not simply the will to "punish her husband" but the will to change her marriage or her circumstances or how she wants. By comparison, when TV thought Nick killed his wife, they called him a sociopath: to the movie's demo, men always have the power to act, what's troubling is how they use their power to act.

---

the logic works: she said it, so it's not what she wants. And the fantasy will prove it to you by showing you how much she enjoys the other thing, the thing she doesn't even know she wants. The later utility of the fantasy will be that now that it is clearly shown what satisfies her, since it's only a fantasy, you can deprive the real her of it. "What real her?" All of them.

But if she's not allowed to want, what makes it possible for her to even think she wants to be a sex prize? Why is that desire ok to have, but not, say, the desire to want to just have sex? This brings us to the unique utility of the cheerleader porno: *he* wants her to have sex, but he doesn't want her to want sex, so he turns her into a sex prize. She's not allowed to want whatever she wants, but she is allowed to want what he wants, which in this case is being a sex prize. So when she *says* she wants to be a sex prize, she's not lying-- she thinks she wants this, because she's allowed to want this. For her, being a sex prize isn't a sneaky way to have sex with the guy she wants. She believes she wants it, even though she doesn't. The only desires she can act on are *his* that she makes her own. If you're confuse by who "he" refers to, let me just cut to it: "he" is you.

The gender specificity of this logic will seem absolute, except that it has nothing to do with gender. A teen boy may lie to his mom to get the keys to the car, but more usually he'll tell the truth and go the store for her, and also sneak off to see his girlfriend. Ok, you say, this is different, because he's merely going to the store as an excuse, but why then does he tell his girlfriend he *has* to go to the store? Is he more truthful to his mom, or his girlfriend? NB in this example, when he gets back home from his girlfriend/shopping, he has done both. Then you can say this teen boy isn't acting like a man, he's acting like a girl; but then you may as well say the porno cheerleader is acting like a boy. Which would make it not so much gendered as Athenian.

Imagine a similar porno, but what the cheerleaders want is that their boyfriends win the game, after all, they have money on the game. What do they have to do? How do you show this pornographically? They go have sex with the other team all night to make them tired before tomorrow's game, so that their boyfriends would benefit. Who wants what? What did she enjoy? Go ahead and roll your eyes, but this logic was so common that the Athenians had to make a law requiring that the husband divorce his raped/adulteress wife in order to prevent the more *frequent* occurrence of married couples conspiring to trick other men into having sex with the wife in order to blackmail them.

You'll say that the cheerleader was secretly using this as an excuse to go have sex with the other team, that that was all along her real desire. We can debate this all day, the only way to know for sure is for *you* to ask her: if she says it's for the win/money then you know that's a lie, it's for the sex. If she says it's really for the sex, then you know that's a lie, it's really for the win/money. According to the rules, she cannot act on her own desire. Either way, the only desire she could act on was literally the one she did act on: the audience's.

Neither of these porns could have been popular in Athens. It certainly makes no sense to fantasize their women offering themselves as prizes for the winner because they actually were going to be prizes for the winner. What's more interesting is why they didn't fantasize the women going over

278

Let me back up and amend something, say it in less psychological terms. Never mind "she wants him punished, by some other omnipotent entity". Let's be precise about the form of her evil: she blames her husband for her plight, in him coalesces the social, political, and economic explanations for why she feels eternally impotent. So she invents a reason *to denounce him to the State*.

And the State gladly accepts the responsibility, not because it cares so much about her, or him, or even thinks he is guilty, or cares; but because for this trivial service people are happy to give it all their power. What is it supposed to do? It cannot do otherwise. And the media-- while hardly state controlled-- is happy to televise it, they both benefit from the flow of power

---

and tiring out the Spartans so they'd lose the war, especially since everyone knows the Athenian women were obviously just glorified prostitutes, and even if they weren't, their prostitutes certainly could be. Part of it is that in the modern porno, the other team, win or lose, has no expectation of sex with the cheerleaders except through this random and surprising offer, while in Athens women were explicitly part of the booty. But the real reason the Athenians didn't send over their women or even their prostitutes is the one it did not occur to you to consider in the football game porno yet is the same reason the men didn't like Pericles's clever strategy of staycation attrition: *winning that way wouldn't count*. Uh oh. In the world where football is more fun as fantasy our gods have to be omnipotent, we'll jerk each other off during the betting but a win is a win is a win. But not mid century Athens, where when Alcibiades reminded everyone how he had won the Olympic chariot race with his wicked cool horse and buggy, the people were like, no stupid, sponsoring the racer doesn't count. You may think the Greeks thought cleverness was a virtue, this is not completely true, Odysseus was famous for his cunning but he was more often derided for it, if he hadn't finally killed 108 people in Act III all his cunning would have meant he was kind of a bitch. And, for reasons too complicated to go into here, a wannabe cuckold, maybe someday I will have had written a book about it. The audience at *Lysistrata* was interested in converting to omnipotent gods, they may not be able to change the outcome but goddam it if they're going to let someone else take credit for it.

The Polis was changing in such a way that men were increasingly acting like women so the women had to be explicitly told not to act-- like men. Or, removing the red herrings of gender: the people with power didn't want the responsibility, but in order to maintain the status quo and in the hope that they might be re-inspired to act with responsibility, the people without power had to be told not to take it from them. No coincidence, in the tragedy competition of the same year, *Medea* came in third. Please don't try and read it from a feminist perspective, *Medea* wasn't reflecting the hidden monologue of immigrant women oppressed by conventional marriage, it was what a male writer believed even women were thinking about Athenian men, which was then performed by a male actor, in front of a male audience, for their benefit only-- *and they didn't like it*. Euripides was using the everywhere apparent unease of women to scare/criticize/punish the Athenian males for pettiness, for vanity, for the strutting around with the trappings of power-- for failing to act like men. If you consider that *Medea* came only a few years after *Oedipus*-- an attempt at reinstalling belief, responsibility, guilt-- which was itself coincident with the death of Pericles from the plague-- we're at the inflection point of the democratic experiment. Democracy, and men, existed, but male democrats were losing power because they didn't want the power, they wanted someone else to have it, and they wanted to delude themselves with knowledge. Sometimes in history what happens next is the women rise up and take the power, but in this case what happened next is the democracy collapsed.

47

Never rejoice in hell, swordsman; by the sword you did your work,
and by the sword you will die.

It's a poetic, majestic, heroic invocation; film a shirtless/hairless/carbless Sir Gawain of the Garter

upwards (to themselves) and encourages people to use them for their grievances.

She is not a "misandrist", nor is the fantasy to punish the husband, this is not what she wants-- if it was, the story wouldn't resonate with the audience, the commonality is not a hatred of husbands. Nor is this projection or scapegoating. What they feel in their bones is the lifelong inability to act and its subsequent rage, so what resonates is the *fantasy* that a cause for this impotence is located and something else *compels* you to act. The movie doesn't elaborately imagine acting to punish a cheater; it elaborately imagines a motivating cause for acting on anything.

Neither can this be about gender; any man who thinks like the wife, i.e. fantasizes a

---

intoning it through a historically inaccurate helmet as he slo-mo bro-swos the Green Knight and you have yourself a trailer that could make enough to make the movie. Unfortunately, it was Clytemnestra's final curse to the recently punctured Agamemnon, and she's the one who punctured him, which maybe taints it. Even though *Agamemnon* is a 5th century Greek tragedy, it suggests an allusion to Matthew 26, "he who lives by the sword will die by the sword", which is Jesus's allusion to Genesis 9:6: "he who sheds the blood of a man, by man shall his blood be shed." In case the biblical parallel is not obvious it returns in the second play, *The Libation Bearers*, where The Chorus lead by Orestes lead by Elektra demands Clytemnestra's death in kind, "whosoever shall take the sword, shall perish by the sword"; but because Orestes can't act without being compelled this is a subtle refrain/alteration of Revelation 13:10: "if anyone is to be slain with the sword, with the sword he must be slain." Amend. That's a combination of omniscience and omnipotence that's best left to allegory.

Of course the translator of Aeschylus needs an allusion to Jesus, done for an audience of cynics that neither believe in Jesus nor Aeschylus but say they admire both, because on the one hand it uses Jesus to tell you that violence is bad in itself, but on the other hand punishment for violence is guaranteed by the Fates since Christianity is notoriously forgiving. Listen to Jesus, or Zeus will smite you.

But the allusion is more than just literarily manipulative, it's sinister. The very practical problem in the *Oresteia* isn't that the crime will be punished by the gods, but that it *won't* be punished by the gods: the gods require that humans carry out the punishments. None of the avenging swordsindividuals in the three plays killed because they wanted to: they felt compelled, the gods demanded it.

This biblical parallel is an obfuscation, on purpose, to fool the reader into thinking the violence is a kind of personal choice, and, no surprise, Aeschylus never wrote those words. It's not so much that translations are inaccurate; most often they are lies, deliberate alterations of meaning, based on the *expectation* that every line will only be read out of context. They are translated to be excerpted as quotes. What Clytemnestra actually says is this: "equivalent acts, equivalent consequences… death is the payment for what you started." It's a little more boring but a lot more accurate, that's accounting for you. What he did incurred a debt; and she is *obligated*, as an instrument of the gods, to collect for *them*. She has no choice. The Chorus laments that perhaps who Agamemnon is should count for something; but, no, it only counts when you're alive. Since she's right in killing Agamemnon, Orestes is wrong to take revenge on her; when he does, the Furies chase him demanding equivalent blood for the debt he incurred.

If you see the violence in the play as subjectively understandable but objectively bad, and do not pay enough attention to the ledger-based system of justice "on behalf" of the gods, you cannot appreciate the difference in the solutions offered by Aeschylus vs. the translator of Aeschylus. The solution to the cycle of violence that the translator implicitly proposes is to not be violent. How Clytemnestra is going to choose to not do what she is compelled to do isn't something he really thought through, which is why he linked it to Matthew 26 and hoped Jesus would explain it. The similarly complicated scheme to punish his hypothetically cheating wife would of course be labeled a psychopath *but also* a misogynist, the inconsistency being explained as some excess of male power, but the form of the fantasy, the fact of the identification, shows that it isn't about the gender but the inability to act. [18]

This is the purpose of the husband. The fantasy is to be compelled to act. But she knows she cannot act. Therefore she marries *him*. He will be why, since she will fail to act in life, she failed to act in life. And he can easily be deprived.

This is also the meaning of the affair. The fantasy isn't just what she'd do *if* her husband had an affair, the fantasy *requires* an affair: something for which no other recourse is possible

---

solution Aeschylus proposes, i.e. the solution he has the goddess Athena propose after she sways the verdict, is to free individuals from the obligation to settle such debts owed to the gods. From now on, the State will handle justice; which means from now on, violence is *only* a choice.

I realize a Christyrannical translation of Aeschylus is only going to interest maybe a dozen or so indentured graduate students no more than 200 miles from the Atlantic east or west, people for whom violence anyway isn't much of a choice, let alone compelled; or maybe it becomes the caption to a poster in an honors English (?) class because they don't permit Bible quotes, so who cares?

Except that over in the soon to be former Roman Empire Jesus wasn't criticizing violence either. You will observe his complaint is the sword. "The sword is just a symbol." Yes. That's the part he objects to. The consumer products which are so necessary to your imagination of power.

The reason Jesus says that phrase isn't because the swordsman decided to fight but because the guy with the sword wanted it to be a sword fight *when it was not*. Jesus didn't want to escape, the point was to get arrested. The swordsman has entirely missed the purpose of the whole endeavor-- the one which he was explicitly told about in advance-- instead making it about himself and his dumb sword: look at me, I'm a swordsman, I fight for what I believe in, I'll even risk my life as long as there's no chance I'll affect the outcome. If you have convinced yourself he was being noble trying to save Jesus and you'd have done the same, you need to stop watching pornography: the swordsman can't save Jesus, they are outnumbered by actual swordsmen, there's no chance he and his Vorpal sword will do anyone any good, but instead of doing what Jesus wants he does the *easier* thing which is *show* Jesus and us that he'll fight for him, so he lashes out dramatically and as predicted by his personality entirely uselessly. Does he annihilate the soldiers, decimate the Centurions, do you think he's capable of doing the math? No, snicker snack, he cuts the ear off a *servant*. That'll show 'em. Off topic, you'd think Jesus would have told his companions to leave their swords at home, so either he didn't, or they didn't listen. The swords did let them sleep better, that's helpful. I know, I know, who am I to criticize, but Jesus criticizes, "hey stupid, you don't think I couldn't just have everyone here vaporized?" You will no doubt respectfully remind me about recent developments in physics, and that you therefore don't believe Jesus could actually vaporize people, and that's certainly a fine position to take, it is irrelevant here: Jesus's disciple believed it, but pulled his sword out anyway. See, you got me muddled as well-- I don't mean anyway, I mean instead.

In order to avoid thinking too much about this-- it comes too close to your own precariously balanced disavowals, not to mention your practiced ability to turn quiet duty into a showy rivalry between two servants-- Jesus's statement is safely quoted with raised index finger or put on a poster promoting non-violence. "But don't you think Jesus wants us to be non-violent?" I am 100% certain he does not want *this*, because according to the story he does not appear to be a coward and very clearly understands math. He wants something else. Non-violence is merely a logical consequence of something else way harder to do. So it is admittedly easier to do nothing and call it non-violence. "I'm not a violent person." Am not is a lot different than can not, so maybe you shouldn't be so quick to take credit for your marital fidelity. "Oh, you think I couldn't get someone to sleep with me, is that it?" Maybe you could, but it wouldn't count.

since there's no institutionalized punishment, no one else will act for her, she is compelled to act; and the floodgate opens, now she can perform a hundred unbelievably complicated (though indirect) actions when before she couldn't even figure out how to move back to Eastern Time. She can't even *fantasize* acting without a cause; and the only cause she can fantasize as motivating is infidelity-- and not because they were in love but because it disrupted the superheated stasis. He enjoyed more than her. And for the audience, a fantasy in which she is compelled to act allows them, today, to take credit for her cleverness, her determination, her knowledge.[49]

To be clear: the fantasy is not *to* act. The point of the fantasy is NOT to inspire action-- by which I mean, literally, the point of this pornographic fantasy is *to not* inspire action. It

---

No doubt Clytemnestra had prided herself on her non-violence, even thought less of her husband because all he was was a swordsman, and then she turned out to be quite the swordsman herself. "I thought you said she was obligated." Yes, which brings us back to the beginning, the excess that Elektra detected that required a whole new rebalancing, and the reason humans are poor distributors of divine justice, and wealth: Clytemnestra enjoyed it. Pretending to be merely serving the gods, she secretly stole a little satisfaction back from them. Actually-- she not so secretly stole a lot of satisfaction. "It's like rain on the corn fields," she says of divine justice, get yourself a clear mental image of the simile and then go look up exactly what's rain and what's corn, and despair. Noble, or obligated, violence is a wonderful cause for extracting some secret enjoyment; the swordsman was standing right next to Jesus and thus managed to get a few slices in, if Clytemnestra had accepted Jesus as her personal lord and savior you can imagine the sound and fury she would have felt fortuitously compelled to bring about. It would be loud. It would be meaningless. Athena is done with all of this nonsense, she may be hot but she's also a soldier and also wise, she gives solutions not oracles, so when Clytemnestra demands to know what Athena is offering her in place of divine vengeance, I'll give here my own translation: "A republic, madam, if you can keep it."

48 We're proud to assert gender is a social construct, not a gross anatomical consequence, the patriarchy cannot tell you who you are; but it seems our individuality still requires patrimonialism to tell us what the choices look like. "It doesn't matter what she wears, a trans woman is a woman." I have no problem calling her a woman, but why do you keep calling her a trans woman? Backstory? If you have a revenge fantasy that (passive voice) someone is fired or framed-- punished by some other omnipotent entity, then you're a girl. "But some guys fantasize about that, too." Also a girl. "But if the terms are really about how one imagines desire vs. action and not one's gender, shouldn't we just abandon gender terms and use better words?" We had them, but we abandoned them because they became gendered.

As a clinical diagnosis hysteria is long gone, and even as a hyperbolic insult we hardly dare use it, labeling a woman as a hysteric is a big no-no, not just because it trivializes her, but because it is used in order to silence her, to disempower her; saying she's hysterical means nothing particularly concrete but is *used* to ignore the legitimate complaints she has. Etc. All of this is certainly true, but we should also wonder why there exists a single instance in which it is totally ok to identify hysteria, in fact, it's considered *a mark of intellectual sophistication* to make this assessment, including by women: mass hysteria. I'll observe that the hysterical masses are never thought of as comprised of women, only as acting like them.

I'm sure the word helps silence the idiots you want to disempower, or at the least lets you ignore them, but there's still truth in taking literally what you meant only figuratively: hysteria isn't so much a character trait as change in state, it is a reactive existential position, that wants an answer-- any answer, as long as it is an answer-- to a question that is constantly being ignored, and that question is: what am I to you?

slyly assures you of what you could be capable of-- if you were forced to act. Watching this fantasy spares the audience from having to act on their own failings or lives or dreams, it relieves this pressure by assuring them that they *could, because they know how.* "I'd never do that, but I could." There's a 25% chance that statement is true and 100% chance you're all kinds of crazy. In this way the book is "anti-feminist", dis-empowering; it trades knowledge for power, and that it is held up to be somehow "true" is the trick of the system, by which I mean individual psychology summed over a population. The goal is always the maintenance of the status quo.

What prevents women from acting, what robbed them of will, what-- castrated them?

49

> Many will say to me, "Lord, in your name did we not prophesy? And in your name cast out demons? And in your name perform many miracles?"
>
> And then will I say to them, "I never knew you; depart from me, you workers of lawlessness."

A man cannot serve two masters; so if you want your god to be omnipotent, you're going to have to pray you can fool him.

It's been years since you lied about *The Scarlet Letter*, but do your best with this short-answer question: According to the book, which is more shameful, cheating on your husband or being molested by your priest? Relax, it's open book. You don't even have the book? Ok, here's an easier one: why do they make her wear a scarlet A-- as opposed to setting her on fire or exiling her bald to Papist Maryland? Doesn't that reflect badly on them, that they keep such a wicked, naughty, slutty young MILF within their long walls and within penis range of their upright men? Patriarchy? I see.

Well, this town has no walls. It's surrounded by woods, and the few remaining Pequots who weren't shipped to the West Indies or incinerated. In the land of the MBC, dead Cthulhu waits dreaming. Since the book was written 200 years ago it's easy to forget that it was set 200 years before that, so whatever cultural distance you are imagining exists between your time and Hathorne's time is about the same as the distance Hathorne's time imagined existed to the Puritans' time. This is a fun game to play, here's another: The Pilgrims progressed to Plymouth 13 years earlier than the Geocentrists got to Galileo. Both had guns.

There are many insane idiocritical interpretations ejaculated on the story by modern high school teachers who fancy themselves low-key Quakers, intolerant Christian morality being the keystone state of them all: patriarchal oppression of women, double standards; primitive religiosity masking social antagonisms; xenophobia; prole-capitalist America exploiting labor. Etc. These are simply wrong. Fact is, Hester did commit a sinful act, she had a baby out of wedlock, instead of the socially conscious act of committing infanticide just within eyesight. I'll explain later. One of the main reasons teachers in high school can get away with these banalities is that the students are virgins, so the idea of oppressive morality still has some reality to them; the consequence is that even after you grow up, you are forever imagining that adult Puritans thought like adolescents. They didn't. They thought exactly like you as an adult. Which is like an adolescent. So maybe you were right.

Here's what you did not notice about *The Scarlet Letter*: no one else in the town has sex. I don't mean they don't speak of it in polite company, I mean there isn't any. Forget pre and extra marital; there are barely references to "husbands" or "wives". In fact, there aren't even any children in this story except the annoying one. The townspeople are described as being, variously,

The story's answer is "modern marriage"-- it limits their options, it constrains them, it forces them to give up so much of their potential enjoyment. This is a very telling criticism, because it is exactly what men have long said about marriage. When two opposing groups both use the exact same argument you can be sure there is a third party benefiting from the conflict. That would be an interesting discussion to have. Don't worry, no one will have it, too much is at stake. They want the problem to be marriage.

But it isn't, how can it be? No one in the story is old enough to be married. I know they appear like adults because they display the usual markers of adulthood like diplomas and credit card debt, but they are children all the way to their absent pubic hair. You don't notice that Amy and what's-his-name aren't adults because there are no adults anywhere else in the

---

shocked/appalled/curious about Hester, but when Hathorne chooses to describe such an *individual* townsperson, she is a spinster with winter in her heart, or a widow whose children are grown. Or possibly a witch.

And stop saying Dimmesdale and Hester are in love. They might be, who knows, but it isn't at all relevant to the story. I know it says "Romance" in the title, but that's not what Romance means to Hathorne, and he certainly uses it for something else.

It is, of course, impossible that no one in the Massachusetts Bay Colony had sex. John Winthrop founded the MBC and I know for a fact he plowed through at least three wives. If this story was about sexual immorality, then there would be examples of moral sex to compare to its opposite. There are none. Not even hypocritical ones, no one brags about, flaunts or even mentions their own holy matrimony. Or any love. The only sex depicted in the book is the adultery, which is then turned into the only love depicted in the book, except for mother and child. So now things are taking a dark turn: instead of the book making a comparison between immoral sex and moral sex, it's actually between sex and no sex.

The problem isn't sin, unless there's a new definition of sin, which there is. Nor is it even sex, though it's the easiest vehicle for the problem to ride in. What makes the townsfolk hesterical is their perception that she enjoyed the sex. Why does the town think-- *know*-- Hester enjoyed the sex? Answer: she had a child. Her enjoyment manifested as a baby, that's the tell in the 17th century. In the late 19th century it would have been sufficient that she merely got pregnant, as all sluts do. In the 20th century we could just count the orgasms, including his in her face at the end. Today? Today how much she enjoyed it can only be determined by the audience. Preferably video, but sufficient that it would look enjoyable to some hypothetical audience.

Which brings us back to high school, and the necessity that the reader is an adolescent in order to deliberately misinterpret the story. The adolescent can't imagine that sex between married people is enjoyable, mostly because of the unenjoyable things that go with it-- love, commitment-- and adolescents. Pre-marital sex is sexy sex, and adultery is wicked hot. Even so, kids today want to see concrete proof that the adulteress enjoyed the sex, having children won't do, so it is this: she has to be attractive. That's it. To prove this is true, ask yourself: is Hester Prynne attractive? It's unlikely you are a close reader and recalled the one single narrative description of her appearance, in contrast to the elaborate description of the country women as-- well, Elizabethan-- but I assure you that even redacting it would have made no difference. You *assumed* she was hot. The question is, do you know why?

So the child is the Puritans' evidence that she enjoyed too much, but for the adolescent reader being taught the book is about something else the child serves as the "punishment" for her excessive sexual enjoyment; in true modern day Puritan fashion, i.e. the logic of adolescence, the child prevents the new mom from ever enjoying sex again. In the spirit of equality someone needs to invent female friendly porn.

story to contrast them to. There is no adult behavior or thinking in the story; the audience doesn't see things from the perspective of an adult.[50] This isn't an adult story, it's anime for adults whose best year was senior.

Which brings us back to the diary. Here's something odd: when the adult female cop is reading the missing wife's diary, it never occurs to this adult female cop that no woman speeding towards 40 writes longhand in a diary. "She assumed Amy was quirky." Yes. But why would she think this? *She doesn't know Amy.* You can't use the diary to infer she's quirky, and also take her quirkiness to mean the diary is legitimate.

Of course the wife uses the (fake) diary as a contrivance to create a narrative (=lies other

---

Wait-- you didn't assume she was attractive *because* Dimmesdale slept with her, did you? As if she was so hot... he couldn't stop himself? The brain teaser for you is to figure out why her being hot means she couldn't stop herself. Because that is what you think. Surprise, you're a Puritan.

But the town's problem with her is not just about her enjoying sex too much, more than the townspeople could. This is not a sexually repressed society: they put a big A on the sex kitten, and the womenfolk get all charged when they rub up against her. "Shocking!" Sex was quite consciously on the tip of their tongue, which only the kitten got. In real life Puritans enjoyed fun sex all the time, they weren't Victorians; but these townspeople seem to have a lot more hangups. The problem for them is she enjoyed *anything* too much, more than they could. There are countless examples of this in the book, I leave them as an exercise to the home schooler, but it's more illustrative to focus on the town's solutions to this imbalance in enjoyment: not by punishing a sin but by depriving her of her satisfaction, sexual and otherwise. I'll offer a single example here: seeing that Hester now derives all her joy from her little daughter, the town wants to take it away-- "to raise it properly Christian"-- literally to ensure it never enjoys like/as much as her mother-- and so that her mother is deprived of her.

Hester is marked with the Scarlet A, and of course this color was a reference to Revelation 17 and the clothes of the Harlot. Well, slow down. *Gone With The Wind* was only 2 or 3 generations after *The Scarlet Letter*, and whatever Scarlett was, harlot wasn't it. Nor was it a reference to the ancient Greeks' marker for a prostitute, red lipstick; by the mid 1800s lipstick was already an accepted fashion accessory even for non-harlots. Hathorne's use of the color, and many of the symbols in his writings, was an anachronistic trick: to the characters in the 1600s, scarlet was shame; to the readers in the 1800s who had also read (excerpts from) Goethe's book on color-- which was everybody-- it was rational, beautiful-- and induced envy in others. Short Answer: what does Pearl's Green A symbolize?

She wears a scarlet A, but by now we've seen enough other stories to know the gimmick: the explicit mark is a red herring, a distraction, which is why Hathorne put the scarlet A on her boobs, but look around at the townspeople and lo, on every visage a black E, backwards because it faces inwards, from the outside all anyone else might ever see is the logical symbol for "there exists". Within you there exists the same envy that drives the townspeople not to punish Hester, but to employ negative reinforcement, to perpetually deprive her of her enjoyment. And this is why the reader needs Hester to be attractive. An attractive person can enjoy more; so there is thus more enjoyment in depriving her of her enjoyment. If Hester the sinner was ugly, it would completely break the story, there would have been no satisfaction in depriving her of her sexuality. So the Salemists would have simply stoned her.

If you insist on learning that sin is central to the story, then maybe we should look for the actual one, the one Hathorne wrote a whole book to condemn. How come no one in the town knows Roger Chillingworth is Hester's husband? The backstory is that Chillingworth was finishing up some business in Holland, so he sent Hester ahead to Massachusetts. Well, what kind of a lunatic sends his hot young bride-- that he knows doesn't truly love him-- unchaperoned to a new continent full of

people want to believe) that explains her "murder." But an actual female cop should have wondered not what a handwritten diary means, but what is it for? The audience of adult women should also have balked at this, why would you write private thoughts somewhere no one can see when you could just as easily write them where everyone can see?

Here's a contrasting example: in *Death Note*, Kira, a high school senior, has a demonic notebook that has the power to kill whoever name you write in it. He is a suspect in dozens of murders, but the police can't figure how he could have done it. He hides the notebook in his desk drawer beneath a false bottom. On top of this false bottom, he places a fake diary, so that if anyone came poking around, they would find the diary and stop looking. Just in case, he booby traps the false bottom, so if someone did keep looking, the Death Note would

---

future Bostonians, unless there was some expectation that the goody commons of the MBC would come together and absorb her, be responsible for her? Isn't that part of the charter of the City On The Hill? The town did manage to rigorously and vigorously find common purpose in punishing her after the fact, which sounds awfully like displacement. The former POW turned secret Satanist Roger Chillingworth is the only doctor in this stupid town, but of all the possible patients he could treat Hathorne only explicitly lists two: the Reverend Arthur Dimmesdale-- and the Honorable John Winthrop, who, big surprise, don't recover. In this supposed theocracy, both the theologian and the theocrat most responsible for ensuring Hester remains a goody wife failed her husband, failed her; the one man failed to ensure a community under God, and the other put his penis inside her. You're going to tell me Chillingworth doesn't at least have a civil case in there somewhere? Of course... since the sex happened right there in the town, yet no one heard her protest, she must have wanted it. Sorry, I don't make the rules, it's in the Bible, and curiously the Bible that Bible Literalist Dimmesdale is described as carrying around all day is the one that has that rule, not the one that doesn't. Yes, Hathorne can seem wordy, so maybe it's worth observing the ones he didn't use.

The other thing for sure your English teacher tested you on is whether you know Chillingworth was intended to be the metaphorical personification of evil. Take the F: he wasn't. For one thing, it isn't metaphorical: the townspeople themselves literally think he is a devil, and I guess I should remind you that the townspeople are idiots-- not my assessment, Hathorne's. I know "Chillingworth" sounds sinister, but it isn't his real name, he *chose* a creepy sounding name, for effect. He isn't supposed to be Satan, he is Nemesis. The story's 1640s Puritan townspeople had come over from England, but the original 1620 Mayflower Puritans started out from exile in Holland-- which is also where Chillingworth and Hester started out, that's weird, almost like Hathorne planned it. "But Chillingworth's medicine is weird pagan alchemy which to the townspeople is Satanic." Yes, but they're idiots. No. Look at the words. He says he practices the medicine of Paracelsus, who was *first* a lead-to-gold alchemist who *then* turned towards the serious study of medicine-- which is exactly what Chillingworth did. His herbalism isn't primitive, it's cutting edge medicine. That's also why he's referred to as a leech by the bond-servant, and then the next chapter is called "The Leech", and the next chapter after that is also called "The Leech"-- Hathorne is beating you over the head with it-- it's not because he "metaphorically" sucks Dimmesdale's soul out like a leech would-- at this point he doesn't actually know Dimmesdale is the adulterer; but because he is literally using leeches as medicine to help Dimmesdale; you could even say Chillingworth tries to suck out Dimmesdale's "bad blood" like a "metaphorical" leech would, but with literal leeches in case everything with you is seeing. But if you insist he's evil to his core, let's wonder at the black rage of his revenge: he shows up to the town to discover that while he was being kidnapped by Indians, his wife was having orgasms. And a baby. Keep in mind it's 1642 and it's a patriarchy: does he have her burned? Hanged? Beaten with a rod no thicker than his thumb? No. *He forgives her.* In fact, he tells her the adultery was his own fault for pressuring her into a marriage she only kinda sorta wanted. "But he's evil because he pursues vengeance against Dimmesdale." He forgives the woman and pursues the man? What kind of hoes before bros patriarchy is he trying to pull here? No. Dimmesdale didn't apologize. Hester did. That's it. That's the whole story.

286

completely incinerate. Here, the fake diary is also to be found, but in this case the purpose of this diary is to make a searcher stop searching *period*, to indicate there is nothing more to find; while Amy's diary is supposed to suggest something has been hidden. Kira's setup is supposed to be believable because Kira is only a teenager, though I find it hard to believe any male teen keeps a diary; but the set up still works as a red herring because if the cops found the diary, whatever they might suspect about the truth of the contents, it wouldn't (/doesn't) occur to them that the diary itself was a distraction from another notebook.

In the interest of textual comparison, here is where the *Death Note* setup fails: knowing his room is bugged by the police, he allows himself to be surveilled writing in his diary and also

---

And what does he do to Dimmesdale, exactly? Annoy him? Seriously, can you please tell me what Chillingworth laws of physicsally does, in a book with no magic and a whole paragraph that calls the townspeople's belief in such a *mental disease*? Ok, I accept that Chillingworth's desire for revenge is evil; hate the sin, love the sinner is a maxim the MBC would have ploudly agreed with, which makes it especially ironic if not 100% on purpose that the only character who says, "I hate" followed by a pronoun is Hester Prynne, about Chillingworth-- after he has forgiven her, let her go, and right after he admits to her that his desire for revenge on Dimmesdale has made him into a bad person. "Was I not once kind?" Her reaction of hate makes no sense if you assume Hester's character arc is from fallen to purified. It isn't. They become worse people, not better, by the end they think these lunatics think they are better than Chillingworth. Ok, I can see this one needs explanation: *they think they have the authority to judge their sin vs another's*. They have become PURITANS. She and Dimmesdale both share the same pathology, a symptom of a highly disordered mental state, it is egotism, it is narcissism. Fun fact, this is the only place in this book where that word appears. And to think I was saving it for Alcibiades.

"But confession is the theme of the book, and Dimmesdale and Hester are finally saved at the end when they together admit their guilt to the townspeople." That doesn't even make any sense, the townspeople are Protestants, not Stalinists, and again I remind you: they are idiots. Protestants did not have as part of their anti-Catholic orthodoxy public confessions of guilt. The requirement that Dimmesdale do this would be historically inconsistent-- if it wasn't deliberately anachronistic, symbolic, like Hester and Roger being from Amsterdam. Because where public confession of sin would be required was 50 years after Dimmesdale's-- during the Salem Witch Trials. But the more relevant historical connection comes even later than that: after the Witch Trial madness had died down, public confession of guilt was performed by those who *participated* in the Witch Trials.

This may seem a super stretched-thin interpretation if it wasn't explicitly Hathorne's right at the beginning: he announces the story as a part of atonement for his own guilt related to his grandfather's role in the Salem Witch Trials. This is what Dimmesdale needs to do: atone not just for his sin but for his participation in the purging of sinners. *He never does this.*

In case you missed the logic, if Hathorne believes that as a descendant of his grandfather's he himself has some guilt over what his grandfather had done, then Hathorne would believe Pearl shares her mom's guilt. Ok, I'll rephrase it: though Hathorne doesn't believe in inherited sin, if Hathorne still feels some guilt anyway for his grandfather's sin, then Dimmesdale should also believe that Pearl might someday feel some guilt for *his* sin (did you think I was going to say Hester's?)-- but Dimmesdale does nothing to absolve her. "But he suffers!" What good is that to *Pearl*?

A few things about the future Salem Witch Trials. First, "Salem" isn't Salem, Massachusetts. It's Salem Village—now Danvers, but then effectively the MBC. Second, other than Salem, the witch hunts are popularly thought of as an English phenomenon, related to bees which is irrelevant here; but the majority of purges had been occurring over the span of 300 years in, well, greater Germany. In fact, it was very limited in England, and then in two specific English villages, worth looking up

performing his secret shame: looking at porn. Ah ha, gotcha. The police accept the porn as normal for a male teen, and also normal that he would be trying to hide it. Here's what should have tipped off the cops, and especially the consultant detective, who is also a male teen: the porn is a magazine. Which he reads by placing on top of his keyboard.

Any attempt at repressing a thought is never fully successful, there's always a leftover. This leftover is misleadingly called "the return" of the repressed, but it doesn't return so much as transmute into a different form. You can reliably identify something as "the return of the repressed" because repression is an identifiable process, it causes the leftover to appear in typical ways-- for example, as a negation or an excess.

---

why. It didn't come to Salem/MBC until the very end of the European experience, it was the last gasp of that theocratic expression of power, by that time the Inquisition had even given up hunting astronomers. In other words, by the time of the Salem Witch Trials, the rest of the world had moved on from believing in witches, let alone persecuting them. It's probably intellectually unsophisticated to label an American historical episode as retarded, but it literally was.

Hathorne was ashamed to discover that his grandfather was a key figure in a wholly unnecessary, anachronistic, hysterical purge. But even not knowing this, nothing in this story should lead any reasonable person to conclude that Hathorne's critical target was the Christianity. Where is Christianity criticized? You all seem to love your leather bound ledgers, well, open them up and count: how many acts of Christian forgiveness or recompense are described in the book? The answer is 1, and you're not going to like the tally: Chillingworth semi-forgiving Hester, 0.7; and then leaving Pearl his estate, 0.3. This town of Christians never forgives Hester, it merely shines a blacklight on her to see the excitement of her shame. (Get it? Cochineal pigment? You were thinking semen? You both need Jesus.) Dimmesdale committed a sin, we're taught to detect the *moral weakness* of keeping his sin secret, but what you should wonder is why he never preaches a sermon saying, out loud, that as Christians they need to unconditionally forgive sinners, starting with Hester Prynne. I want you to long and well meditate upon the remarkable fact that this godly town has devoted so much of their emotional and religious energy on punishing an adulteress for not ratting out her accomplice, meanwhile not a single person has any problem with the presence of an ACTUAL WITCH in their town for all these years. What should worry you more is when it is they finally do kill her: shortly after Dimmesdale confesses to the town. In math that's called order of operations. And they suck at math.

The pretense is that the town took God's laws and used them for their society, but this is backwards: they negated God's laws by asserting that the laws they made up were God's. I know I've heard that before, and I know what happens next. The town adores the secondary source of the sermon, they accept Dimmesdale's authority as gospel, but I defy you to find a single example of someone even attempting to pretend to read the actual Gospels. Including Dimmesdale. You sure this is a book about Protestants? I make no accusation of hypocrisy, I don't doubt that they truly believe that something wicked this way came, that Hester is irredeemable, must never be allowed to re-assimilate. They do believe it. That's what makes them corrupt fanatics, Voltaire will explain it to you later. They aren't Christians. They're the cast of *Young Goodman Brown*.

Hester comes over to deliver some gloves she's embroidered to Gov. Bellingham, and a bond-servant opens the door. A bond servant was a debtor who was thus obligated to be a servant=slave for some amount of time, but meanwhile could also be sold off as property. It was not uncommon for criminals in England to be indentured; Americans love to laugh that Australia was populated by England's criminals, but oh my God do you have no idea what and how much they sent us. Odd the Americans didn't try to build a wall. Anyway, here is how Hathorne describes the bond-servant:

> [The door] was answered by one of the Governor's bond servant—a free-born
> Englishman, but now a seven years' slave. During that term he was to be the property of

288

So she needs a diary in order to write her narrative. The narrative is fake, ok, fine, but how she "chooses" to tell it will therefore itself be fake: *a diary*. She-- Amy-- would say the diary was necessary because her plan is to have it be found partially burned "by him" in a furnace (NB: he's bad at burning evidence, too), but the logic is backwards. The diary isn't a tool of her plan any more than a Glock is a tool in a revenge story; those things are the whole point of the fantasy, because they stand for what the person wishes they were if they had the power to act. What's necessary is that she use a diary or use a Glock, so she has to come up with a reason to use one. The only way she can tell a fake story that seems authentic is by doing it in a way which is already inauthentic. *She cannot do otherwise.* Why not? And why didn't anyone notice this fake attempt at authenticity? Because, like children, the audience

---

his master, and as much a commodity of bargain and sale as an ox, or a joint-stool. The serf wore the customary garb of serving-men at that period, and long before, in the old hereditary halls of England.

Ok, let me interrupt you before you say anything, I know what you're thinking, and it's stupid: "The Puritans were hypocrites!" Did you think that? You're stupid. Here's the question: in 1848, who could possibly have needed this explanation? Bond servants have been everywhere since the Bible, and in America-- both English whites and Angolan blacks-- since 1619. The description served as a reminder to the readers of 1848-- i.e. the abolitionists-- that debt-slavery was still a real thing, largely ignored by the focus on black slavery. Yes, Hawthorne was more worried about whites than blacks, but he understood the larger political problem that would become true: you can outlaw slavery, but not enslavement. So you might but he was not surprised that when the 13th Amendment abolished slavery, it-- surprise-- explicitly allowed an exception for involuntary servitude *if it was part of a criminal sentence,* and 35 years later a new crop of Angolan blacks found themselves enslaved all over again. As much as the slavery/abolition argument was about black and white or North vs. South or slave vs bond-servant, those binaries precluded seeing the issue for what it actually was, and had always been. So Hathrone just left slavery out of his books. The high school teaching problem which is well worth discussing is the complex Venn Diagram showing that Hathrone was simultaneously a racist but also anti-slavery AND also anti-abolition; as well as the reason he himself gave for not being part of the abolition movement of which is sister-in-law was a prominent leader: he couldn't stand the abolitionists. Especially the Bostonians. And the Transcendentalists, and Emerson, "the everlasting rejector of all that is and seeker for he knows not what." Imagine how annoying these people had to be to convince an anti-bank Jacksonian Democrat who was otherwise sympathetic to ending all slavery to want no part of their movement, think about that next Thanksgiving before you try to berate your Dad into ideological purity. "It's not my job to educate you!" It was mine, and I failed.

"The Puritans were hypocrites!" Ok, we'll go with that.

And we're back to the purpose of a high school education, to churn out members of society or patients of psychiatry, there's way too many trending social issues to read a book closely and only a selfish jerk would study math, teachers figure if the curriculum is so patriarchal that they're still using the western canon they may as well load it with rock salt and shoot it at their dad. So the paradoxical lesson teachers will try to impart about this story is that it is about hidden sin and confession, and in order for Dimmesdale to be saved, he must reveal his hidden sin to the town. But the teachers don't believe in sin or redemption. They don't think adultery is that big a deal either, certainly not a sin-- the part they do agree with is that he must still publicly confess to the town. Wait a second, why? Even the Catholics kept it secret and BTW unlike psychiatry theirs is legally privileged. It's stated as a Christian requirement, yet *there is no theological reason for anyone to think this.* Well? Where are the other adulteresses-- how come no one else has a scarlet A? But Hester is the worst kind of woman, she wants to be hot, have sex, **and keep a secret**. The sin was

has learned to accept as authentic only *fake* attempts at authenticity, because real authenticity is customary, obligatory, carries responsibility-- it is based on pre-existing rules and not on the individual-- and therefore doesn't count. The modern demographic only can believe in authenticity that represents them publicly, even if it is definitionally inauthentic. Like an avatar.

So too the diary: how does she tell a lie? She lies by using the trappings of what she believes is unassailable authenticity. Why doesn't the audience notice this? Because the audience imagines itself, flatters itself, that it writes their private thoughts in a diary; not just *in theory*, they believe that they do it *now*, and this is because they actually did do it very recently: when they were children. This is the strength of the emotional closeness to that age, decades

---

adultery, but the capital letter offense was depriving the townspeople of knowledge. This is another reason why the town wants to get their hands on Pearl, for phrenology. "Well, this baby is a whore like her mother, anyone can see that in the sutures, but since it's a girl we'll have to wait till puberty to determine paternity." The people must be allowed to know who Hester had sex with, not so they can fantasize, but to limit the fantasies. This feeling of being deprived of knowledge is intimately related to Hester's attractiveness, perhaps you did not notice that the townspeople begin to forgive Hester, accept her-- right around the time she becomes explicitly unattractive. Skipped that part because there was no dialogue? Maybe you'd prefer reading trailer scripts? The very thing the book is criticizing is the stabilizing value of their, Hathorne's and our hysterical modern society: that transgressions against the social order must be confessed and punished publicly-- not for the transgressor's benefit but because the social order is afraid of its own shadow and made of pudding. And so your teacher triumphantly explains the ending: now that Dimmesdale has finally declared his sin publicly, now he is forgiven, now he can "metaphorically 'go to heaven'".

But Dimmesdale's sin isn't the town's to forgive, it's God's, it's Chillingworth's. And as far as I can tell he makes no amends to either. *Why does he believe he should confess publicly?* I don't mean he is stupid; rather: what is that belief used for? Doesn't Chillingworth *alone* deserve some kind of apology from Dimmesdale, anything, "I'm sorry things happened like this," "we were working late, I was drunk?" Not to get puritanical here, but if we're accepting the logic that Chillingworth *became* evil, then isn't Dimmesdale guilty not just of adultery, but of corrupting the soul of Roger Chillingworth? How can Dimmesdale expect forgiveness from God when he hasn't made amends to Chillingworth but instead-- at the moment of his glorious "redemption"-- has convinced himself and the other 10th graders that Chillingworth is the bad guy? God damn, teachers, do you hate your students' parents' teachers' generation that much? Forget about the adultery, because Hathorne doesn't care: as the town's Reverend, as a Christian, what he should have done was try to make things right, instead of what he did do, which is do absolutely nothing to make things right. "But his sin was eating him up inside." Don't you see how *that's* the cheating? But neither he nor this stupid town want him to *act*, they for damn sure don't want him to promote Hester's unconditional forgiveness, because that robs the town of its power to punish, which the townspeople gladly gave it so that they could have their precious right to know. I would never condemn Dimmesdale or anyone for their sins, who am I to judge? But don't tell me that it's for *society* to judge sin, that *it* has the power to determine what's right and wrong. Ok, according to the rulebook maybe it isn't theologically necessary for him to explicitly apologize to Chillingworth, only to God; but what kind of sycophancy has lead him and you to think he owes nothing to Chillingworth but needs to confess to the town, and that it counts? Your tyrannical society has convinced its people *they* deserve to know so that *it* can have the power to judge. "Of course there is no God to redeem you, it is to us you must confess!" I'll take my chances with God. "We won't allow it, your devilspeak will lead others astray-- there is no salvation outside the State!" *Then I'll see you all in hell.*

50 The one adult is the black guy, but even he can't overrule the children when they want to be on TV. The black lawyer is the single adult in the story, the single individual with *will*, who mostly regards the playground arguments with bewilderment. You're for sure in the land of child

290

disappear, they still take credit for doing it; and right here reconsider whether the Oedipus Complex might not therefore have some force on adults after all. Never mind that in reality their diary does not exist: they "remind" themselves that they are the kind of person who wrote (= writes) in diaries, that they still have secret, private thoughts, and that identification-- bolstered by it probably having been true decades ago-- is more true than the actuality of their behavior. I don't have to do anything because I could. This branded fetish object is their manifestation, it substitutes for all of my actions. Nothing could be more true.

This same emotional connection to a distant and irrelevant past also explains the importance to the audience of her college diploma. When does it no longer matter where you went to college? I say 6th grade, but for the demographic its importance can only increase with time. It substitutes for all future actions. A Yale college education must have value, and anything that threatens this, including admissions scandals or lowering the tuition-- is anathema. You can waive the student debt afterwards or give me a scholarship but don't you dare tell me and anyone it's only worth $5k a year. No one wants here to critique college, e.g. "how come she has a degree from Yale but is an idiot?" because the audience looks for meaning, not utility. They are brands, certified by some other omnipotent entity as revealed in the price, they are unassailable. If they fail to deliver, something else must be blamed. Him-- *marriage*. The problem for her is that marriage protects him. He can do whatever he wants, deprive her, and there are no consequences. So while her actions are extra-legal, they ultimately are the necessary correctives to the marriage-- they reassert marriage, not because she wants marriage to secure their love but because she thinks of it as a cage he's managed to get out of. This is why she doesn't punish him only, but forces him back into a fake marriage with her, to minimize his enjoyment. It's the only world she can fantasize. Put it this way: if she was able to fantasize action, to imagine a different life for herself, she wouldn't have bothered with such an elaborate revenge; but she probably wouldn't have married him in the first place.

The demo conceives of itself as adult, mature, sophisticated book readers and diary writers, but I'd like to point out that if you had asked anyone in that movie audience what the last book they read was, it would have been *Gone Girl*. Their perspective is the perspective of a

---

psychology whenever you see a black supporting character used to portray masculinity, maternity or maturity, these are equivalent to the trope of Orientalism=wisdom and resonate deeply with 8th graders who know of neither. Which partly explains the defensive utility of interracial porn, and there's a cis-white heteronormative term if there ever was one, does anyone know if it's more racist or more sexist to like it or hate it depending on the race or sex of the man or woman--and/or audience? It's has the odd distinction of being one of the few kinds of porn still categorized by the thing you don't like. The point of the white wife getting the big black dick isn't her humiliation (she likes it, and anyway no one would shame her for it), nor the husband's humiliation (no one's dick is bigger than that guy's, and anyway, women are sluts) but the black man as the go-to signifier for masculinity logically causes the woman to be feminine; keep the video but flip the logic and it applies to a black audience as well. Interracial porn is a true fetish: *it* isn't what you want, but a way of re-capturing with what went missing. In other words and for example, anyone who thinks "full-bodied", "bigger is beautiful" acceptance is the result of female empowerment and escaping the objectifying standards of men has been duped: the only thing that changed is which men get to decide. If your reflex here is to accuse me of lamenting *that* shift-- because what you want even more than to be right is for me to be wrong-- you'd be confirming my assertion: you agree *you* did not choose.

child.[51] While on the surface it appears as a story about a wife under the "crushing weight of patriarchal society's expectations of adult women and the complexity of modern marriage", the only relationship in the story that is depicted as emotionally sincere and inviolable is the one between the husband and his sister. His mother was a bitch. His father is scorched earth.[52] Amy's parents are self-centered dolts. There can't be any love between the spouses, this is a story for spouses, and there's no child, no love unrequited, no one's dying. But there is great comfort in the fantasy of no dependency love between two siblings in overly close proximity. So they move in together. Why bother with the couch? He may as well sleep in the bed with her, it's not like there's going to be any sex, in this house we masturbate like grown ups. "No matter what," says the sister, "you know I love you."

As if to reinforce this, the wife sees the sister-in-law as a kind of rival. You would think the husband's girlfriend would be her rival, after all, that slut keeps stealing Amy's ejaculate, but that would make the husband's sex the prize, no thanks, Amy wants a *partner*. Amy has sex but manifests as asexual, she doesn't want sex, how can she? She's obsessed with the idea that the other person might enjoy more. The girlfriend isn't the rival because Amy doesn't see the girlfriend as a woman with her own desires, she imagines her as a fantasy of the man, which is why when the girlfriend goes on TV to admit the affair, what makes Amy angry is that she is pretending to be a regular woman: the girlfriend Amy knows has "cum on me tits" but the girlfriend on TV is dressed like... her. This is the meaning of her rant against Cool Girls.[53] [54]

51

Great minds discuss ideas;

Mediocre minds discuss events;

Small minds discuss people.

  --Eleanor Roosevelt

We can discuss the truth of this idea, or what it means that it gets quoted on posters, but what's not true is the attribution, which is in fact unknown. In order for small minds to discuss the idea, the idea had to be made into an event, and attached to a person.

52 For what purpose does the father have to have dementia? Why not just have him be dead? Because dead fathers have a lot of power over their children; living but impotent fathers reliably do not. If these were adult characters it wouldn't matter, but these are children: the impotence of paternal authority predicts (and here manifests as) a child who is never forced to give up on his childhood dreams-- and thus never forced to create new adult dreams that require him to act.

53 The only trouble is that the mistress is indeed a real woman, not just a man's fantasy. Even if you detect a rivalry between Amy and the mistress in this story, the mistress certainly doesn't think of the wife as a rival, she's not threatened by Amy at all-- she sees the outcome as fait accompli. The truth the story's author has inadvertently hit on is that the mistress values the husband more than the wife ever did. This is the true problem with Amy's marriage, that everyone wants to be a problem of marriage: the mistress could have loved the husband, but neither the husband nor Amy love anything.

54 The "Cool Girls" passage in the book and movie became a pop-feminism manifesto for those looking for a structural problem, it describes the kind of woman (not girl) who sheds her skin and meat and bones and transmutes into whatever it is she thinks the man wants. Amy herself admits she's done this, too, pretending at guilt, and the self-recognition of a character flaw sounds sufficiently self-critical that it gets her out of digging any deeper, which means it gets the audience

But the wife strongly imagines a rivalry with the sister-in-law, where there should be none because, in fact, that *is* where there is one: love between spouses is pure fairy tale, and she assumes there's no real love with mistresses either, Cool Girls just have sex (because that's what men want (not what women want)). The only love that can be imagined to exist in a story with no homosexuals is between a brother and a sister. Amy's at a disadvantage, of course: no actual siblings, though she does have an intense life long rivalry with her perfect twin sister, Amazing Amy, whom her parents evidently favored.

Preposterously complicated revenge fantasy where the person is punished by some other omnipotent entity, rather than acting directly; where sisters-in-law are rivals for an asexual, no dependency LLC with the man; where parents are weak, useless, stupid, or mean; and where

---

out of it. "Why do we change for men? Discuss." But instead of the meaning, first ask yourself what the rant literally says: it says Cool Girls don't exist.

Except that they do exist. In the movie we see examples of all the subtypes of Cool Girl who changed for men, yet none are actually with any men. Two of them were actually giggling *together*. Are they faking Cool all the time, even when there's no guys around? When they decide not to be a Cool Girl anymore, do they joyously abandon hair and makeup for a kerchief and a chili dog? Because I was always told that the hair and makeup wasn't for guys, it was for myself.

Saying that they change for men suggests that their relationships with their female friends are more authentic. Women supporting each other through their men troubles is celebrated as the strongest of female relationships, especially in fiction. You could ask whether these strong female relationships are the cause of bad romantic relationships (it's axiomatic that this is true for men's friendships); or you could guess that bad romantic relationships become the excuse to allow women to be affectionate, intimate, with other women. You could even speculate that these bad romances are a check on too much female intimacy; lesbianism that cannot be allowed into consciousness is repressed into emotionally unsatisfying but visually unassailable hyperfeminine MF heterosexuality, with a pressure valve of frequent FF hugs and watching each other pee, and if you've never heard this argument it's because you've only heard it used to describe fraternity guys.

There was a time when compulsory homosexuality, within strict parameters, was not just normal but expected. Rather than there being a statistically high rate of "born that way" homosexuality, the culture itself promoted and enforced the development of that practice because the alternative (strict heterosexuality, including promiscuous) was not satisfying. The Spartan, Theban, and Athenian upper classes preferred the company of men, and under some sophistry combining pedagogy and friendship dressing up a mannequin of lust, it became erotic. The Spartans, at least, were able to do this without relegating the women to the role of slaves. It's easy now to imagine an equivalent group of modern female upperclassmen, fresh from the gymnasium, choosing female company, with admiration and etc becoming erotic, but it may still be hard to imagine that this becomes normalized, let alone expected. But why not? The difference between the Greek culture and the American culture is that Greek culture was vectored towards the goal of attaining the desired object, while American culture is vectored towards the goal of being the desired object. Alcibiades is so famous for his homoeroticism exactly because he was doing it backwards-- he wanted to be desired, he wanted the other person to cause him to be desirable-- and this was even worse because he was a man, not a boy-- instead of pursuing (as Socrates cleverly determined) the man he desired. America is in this the opposite of Athens: despite the rhetoric, the propaganda of America teaches both men and women not to pursue their desires, but to want to be desired. This may seem wrong in a world where we have seminars on how to pick up chicks or make money fast; and even advertising links our desire for the impossibly beautiful model with product placement. But the images are aspirational, not inspirational, you may desire the person in the ad, but you've really been taught to want to be desirable like them, or desirable to them. Not desirable during a sexual relationship-- it doesn't count when your partner actually finds you attractive-- but that you feel desirable in theory,

writing down your innermost thoughts gives them significance because someday someone will believe them and their bubble letter magnificence.

Far from the story being a critique of marriage, it reveals a regression to childhood, the rageful fantasies of children which look for big structural explanations to "figure out what's really going on"-- that therefore explains=permits their impotence. Amy isn't a bad person, they discover; modern marriage brings out the worst in people. But it's not marriage that doesn't suit modernity; it's the individuals who don't *want* modernity. They don't want freedom because it comes with responsibility, the responsibility to make someone else happier than you. They want some other omnipotent entity to ensure that if their enjoyment is ≤x, everyone else must be < them. She intones: "My cute, charming, salt of the earth misery guy has to learn grown ups work for this, grown ups pay, grown ups suffer consequences." Who calls themselves a grown up? Because it sounds mizzourable. These are the ramblings of a child pretending to be a grown up, her rage covered in the rhetoric of a wise TV grown-up about to punish... another child.

"Well, we can't all have perfect marriages like you!" Good come back. Same as: "well, we can't all have perfect children like you!" Thinking comparatively is the default. Meanwhile your infantile criticism is structured tellingly: "we can't have perfect X." Why do you think about it in that direction? Shouldn't you worry about whether you are a perfect parent for the kids? Instead of worrying if you have a perfect marriage, shouldn't you try to be good for the other person? You say you can't depend on them, but you resent that they might depend on you.[55]

---

to the camera, to the audience.

Amy rants that women change for men, and the audience discusses why this happens. But that's not at all what she is ranting about. She sees all these fake bitches, but instead of telling them to stop pretending to like chili dogs, she wants to tell the *poor men* that no bitches really like chili dogs, in order to deprive the men of their satisfaction. The whole problem of the story isn't that women-- she-- changed for a man, but that this incurred a debt which the man has not paid: *the man did not change for her*. To be arithmetically rigorous, the husband didn't simply *not* change for Amy-- when she first met him he was acting as a Cool Guy-- but after marriage he changed *back* into himself. If you follow the accounting, him as a Cool Guy was something Amy had created that she was later *deprived* of. For this he must pay. Nor does she have any interest in a fairy tale ending where she can stop pretending to be Cool and he loves her for who she really is; she doesn't want to be loved while she's without make up in a kerchief, she wants his love to require her to be in make up-- so that she must wear make up. NB that at the end of the film, she wants him to pretend-- explicitly pretend-- to be the man he was pretending to be when he wooed her-- even though she and he know its fake. Why bother? Because it would still look true to the audience.

55 The Funeral Oration of/by Pericles is the most famous of the otherwise annual funeral orations given to honor the accumulated dead of the past year. I should point out that Pericles gives the speech by invitation, as an honored speaker, and not because he is the Emperor of Athens, which he isn't, he is only one of the ten elected generals of Athens. He is also mostly hated at that moment, especially by the young sovereigns destitute of experience and big with their own importance, for forcing them to retreat inside the safety of the city walls rather than gain glory (=die) fighting the Spartan army who is right outside the walls ravaging=annoying their abandoned farms, notwithstanding he lead 10000 infantrymen on various victories only a few months earlier and notwithstanding it's a democracy and he can't force anyone to do anything, they could do whatever they wanted. Ergo: what they wanted to do was nothing, and blame Pericles. To be very clear: it wasn't an excuse; by blaming Pericles for preventing them from going out, they wanted it to be true that he had power over them. Apocryphal, but to my point: Pericles's girlfriend gave a little speech

If you still think that the problem is marriage and not a brain that paused at puberty, observe the most important thing the audience never considered unusual, in fact, they thought it made all the sense in the world: she doesn't just frame him for her murder, she gets it all on TV.

Certainly Amy takes no action to get it on TV. But of course her case *must* go to TV. The point isn't merely to punish him, or shame him, it's to get as many unknown people to see her the way she wants to be seen, and I'll here only highlight that that way is as a *victim*, of men, which she has never ever been before in her entire life. Victimhood is aspirational. It solicits passionate sympathy, when you don't have the capacity for unselfish love you look for an energetic substitute.

---

of her own to the women, probably more effective in getting them to stay silent: she told them that Athens only had the appearance of a democracy, the men didn't really have any power; it was really a tyrannical rule by Pericles. In other words: the rest of the men have just as little power as we do. Let these late stage democracy idiots think whatever gets their penises hard, and leave the phallus to me. This is the audience Pericles has to give a eulogy to, i.e. idiots, so Pericles starts by criticizing eulogies and then moves on to idiots: I'd like to honor the dead, but you idiots can't handle it; instead of inspiring you, hearing about great men inflames your selfishness and envy. So I'm not going to deliver that kind of a speech, nor recite a list of the heroic battles, explicitly because a) everyone knows them already; and implicitly because b) most of you weren't in them, it'll only inflame your envy. I'm trying to keep you inside.

So instead of giving a eulogy for the fallen, he gives a quotable speech about how wonderful Athens is, "it gives equal justice to all"; "instead of jealous surveillance of our neighbor, we don't get angry with him for doing what he likes"; "its generous people do favors for others in order that the recipient doesn't feel obligated to the repayment of a debt, but the giving of a kindness."

Wait, who is the audience again? His description of the Athenian people is logically inconsistent with his description of the Athenian audience, recall: they're idiots. Pericles might not have had a lot of time to edit his speech, but Thucydides had decades to do it, and so it takes on an ironic twist: it is a eulogy after all, but it's for the Athens that will have fallen. It's written in the present tense but it was formulated in the past tense, which, not ironically, is the perfect tense. Athens was great, it was just, it was heroic, we invented wings and soared into the sky. And when the wax melted, we will proudly tell ourselves that our reach exceeded our grasp, instead of admitting that we didn't think to invent glue, or at least the parachute. "Therefore, having judged that the happy is the free, and the free is the brave, do not shy away from the risks of war." It's a life lesson quote, I guess, but if you're going to put it on a poster you should include the Venn diagram, I'll draw it for you: happy is inside free is inside brave. In order to be happy, you have to be free and brave. But being free and brave does not guarantee you will be happy. Sorry. Math isn't fair, only necessary.

This reversal of the Funeral Oration's verb tense from past to present isn't merely rhetorical, it is psychological, it is for a purpose. That's Thucydides's stylistic maneuver when he's sending you a code. Only a page earlier Thucydides describes the Athenians evacuating the countryside and setting up refugee camps inside the city walls wherever they can, including a spot warned about by an oracle:

> Leave the Pelasgian parcel desolate, woe worth the day that men inhabit it!

That's unusually specific for an oracle. No doubt you will want to know what the gods have in store for them, which is strange since this is a historical event and you don't believe in gods. The question is, is this is a prohibition or a prediction-- and when do you decide that? Thucydides interprets this using an atemporal logic specific to the psychology of you:

That's why the story pretends to be about women but is called *Gone Girl*. No one much cares if a woman goes gone, only if she came, goes double for men; but when a girl goes gone, the parents will get it on TV and grown ups are going to pay.

> Yet this [parcel] too was now built over in the necessity of the
> moment. And in my opinion, if the oracle proved true, it was in the
> opposite sense to what was expected. For the misfortunes of the state
> did not arise from the prohibited occupation, but the necessity of the
> occupation arose from the war; and though the god did not mention
> this, he foresaw that it would be an evil day for Athens when the
> parcel came to be inhabited.

This is not the post-hoc rationalization of a pre-scientific mind; Thucydides was agnostic, but this is an instance that Thucydides writes as if the gods exist, in order correct a fundamental theological mistake the Athenians wanted to make, which was this: the gods are omnipotent. No, he says, they are not; they are at best omniscient. All of the power rests with you. Everything that happens will have been your fault.

If the Funeral Oration is the eulogy for the future fallen democracy whose demos wanted to get rid of their power; and, according to the technical manual, temporal/spatial coincidence represents a logical connection; then what follows the Funeral Speech should represent the causes of that fall, the turning away from individual power and freedom towards knowledge, envy, and impotence. Well, fast forward the audiobook and decide for yourself: the very next thing that happens after the Funeral Speech is the plague.

A guy in a nuthouse is walking around naked except for a hat and gloves. The nurse says, "You can't walk around that way." He says, "it's okay, nobody comes around here anyway." And the nurse says, "well, what do you have the hat and gloves on for?" And the guy says, "well, you never know."

There is one bit of dialogue in *Confirmative Assent* that was so unintentionally insightful I'm pretending I came up with it. Abby's boyfriend, Ecks, a beta, wants her to seduce the President of ΛΑΧ fraternity and then accuse him of sexual harassment, in a ploy to get the Office of Greek Affairs to take the frat house from the Alphas and give it to the Betas. It's probably coincidence rather than irony that actual ancient Greek married couples sometimes plotted affairs for similar purposes, though in this case he doesn't want Abby to actually sleep with the guy, just get him into a compromising photo op. This part of the script is a true dialogue, not dia=two but dia=through, it is a passage of speech that traverses the circle and not just two people practicing their monologues on each other.

INT. ECKS'S ROOM

                    ECKS
Just drive him crazy. Make out with him, let him get you
naked, but then make sure you face the camera every once in
a while and say, "we really shouldn't be doing this, my
boyfriend would be mad", "oh god you're so big, please don't
make me cheat on my boyfriend."

                    ABBY
So you want me to be a cock please.

                    ECKS
               (smirks)

Tease.

                    ABBY
Oopsy. Freudian slip-- tease.

Obviously, "cock please" is a Freudian slip, the unconscious desire slipping through, facilitated by rhyme. She quickly fixes it. Oopsy.

But in this case it's not an *unconscious* slip-- it's fully conscious. She is a cock please, and even if she was unwilling to be it now, it's hardly an urge she needs to hide from him or herself. Nothing here is to be repressed. Her desire is conscious, she may not act on it but no one would be surprised she had it. So this isn't a Freudian slip.

Well, it's not her Freudian slip. It's *his*. She's articulating his unconscious desire for her to be a cock please, not just a cock tease. He is the one who couldn't think this, this was his repressed thought that came out of her mouth. That's why *she* could call it a Freudian slip. If it was her repressed wish, *she* would not be able to identify it as a Freudian slip.

More importantly than this technical correction is why to *the reader* this sounds like her Freudian slip, and the answer is we are very sophisticated with our psychic defenses. Freudian slips are by definition unconscious and uncontrollable-- they happen despite your attempts to prevent them, so one way to defend against them is to misunderstand them, on purpose.

Psychoanalytic terminology has been cleverly incorporated into our every day speech, but in ways contrary to their original meaning-- turned into jargon so that they can be made to mean something else. And if that something else is their opposite, you should be alert to a defense.

So here, the responsibility for the desire is shifted to the woman for whom there is no danger in its ownership.   To help hide this move, the desire is made to appear rational to everyone else: why wouldn't she "secretly" want sex with that guy? It's perfectly logical. (But not because the guy is attractive, but because she is. Those are the rules.) It may not be moral to cheat, whatever that means, but there's nothing irrational or destabilizing about her desire, it does not need to be repressed. Understanding Eck's desire to be cheated *on*, however, is going to require a lot of complicated math he doesn't know and the results are incompatible with his identity. So what he wants "accidentally" finds expression in her mouth, in the form of his Freudian slip and the other guy's penis. That last part isn't a joke. Oral sex with the guy is the manifestation of the Freudian slip, Ecks's true desire: cock please instead of cock tease; because *teasing* his penis would be something she'd enjoy more than the guy; *intercourse* with his penis might please both of them; but *oral sex* pleases only the guy's penis, not her. Ecks isn't trying to deprive the guy, he's trying to deprive her.

But if she's speaking his unconscious, how did she know it? What she did not do is "figure him out"-- "ah, you kinky devil, you want me to cheat on you!" It's certainly possible she *could* deduce this, but within the story she has *not*. She does *not* think this. Yet she "knew" it. How did his unconscious get into her unconscious? Since they aren't in psychoanalysis together, there is only one other explanation, and it is the necessary premise of the fantasy: *they are in love*. The events may not look like a love story, but the structure of the fantasy is that of two people in love, not simply two people who "really know each other"; in love each knows *without* knowing the other's desires. Even if she later cuckolds him, humiliates him-- as long as she unconsciously detects this is what he *unconsciously* wants, the fantasy confirms they are in love.

"But if she loved him, she wouldn't cheat." Sure, in real life. But this is a fantasy. Her love is proven by her acting out what he wants in fantasy. The fantasy assures him that in real life she loves him. "So all that cuckold and MILF porn is just about men who think their wives don't love them?" Slow down. It's not anyone's fantasy, it's porn. It's a carpet bombing, not a laser strike. You can't be sure what it means, taking someone else's unconscious for your own is risky, it's hard to say which part of a porn is important for you, which part becomes the fetish. But every porn assures us that love exists somewhere, especially by explicitly excluding it from the shot.

The other way to understand this is to ask what desires Abby *would* repress. She loves her boyfriend and is consciously willing to be whatever he wants (even if he can't face those desires); AND all sex is permitted for her, there are no sexual urges she would need to repress or even disavow because they might threaten her sense of self.   However, she wants to be what he wants.   She wants how he wants. That's what drives her, that's what makes her willing to consider all this cock pleasing. Her own desires have become secondary; she has learned to live her life for her men, so that how she wants *is* how they want, even at the expense of what she may have wanted. She may *want* to sleep with the guy, she may not, we'll never know, she never gets the opportunity to nakedly choose because it is her boyfriend's desires (and then the guy's) that cause her to act. The ambivalence she displays is his, not hers, if he was all in, she'd be all in. She's obligated herself to want how he wants, and how

299

he wants is through scenarios, images-- porn. The only desire she must *repress* from her consciousness is the desire to *deprive* him of his satisfaction.

So her Freudian slip, revealing a repressed wish to deprive him of his satisfaction, that she would immediately think was utterly preposterous, would be:

```
INT. ABBY'S BEDROOM

                    ABBY
          So I should be a cock blocker.

                    ECKS
               (smirks)

     Tease.

                    ABBY
     Oh my God!  Tease!  That was so weird!

               (smirks)

     Cock blocking is more your thing, baby.
```


In Thucydidean tragedy *Abstain From Beans*, the Athenian Empire has just crushed a rebellion in far away Mytilene, and Cleon and Diodotus have a debate before the Athenian assembly about what to do with the rebellious population. Kill them all or spare their lives?

No one could fault you for not having read it, as a novelist Thucydides has no sense of pacing and even I would agree he could use an editor, but if you read the book like script notes and think logically not chronologically you'll see things that should not be left unseen. So you should stop here and do so now, the fruits of 10 minutes reading will multiply 30, 60, a hundred times, and if after saying this you still don't read and think about it, well, you're an idiot. I don't mean that as an insult, merely as a statement of fact. "Stop calling people idiots, we know you're a psychiatrist, we get it, 'mental age of 2', we all know its original meaning." And you're a dunce as well. I know, I know, reading Thucydides is no indicator of intelligence, you've read lots of other books and have thought lots of other thoughts, and my only response to this is that I can't argue with an idiot. I will then slyly suggest you could read it if only to disagree what I'm about to say here, maybe you can prove me wrong? Because basically I don't care whether I'm right or wrong, I just want you to read Thucydides-- not just apathetically but on purpose, for a purpose, with the desire to be able to use it like a weapon. There are not many better weapons, though I admit a Glock codes more alpha. People with low muscle tone and weekly seminars will offer you more pretentious reasons to read it, but as a practical matter-- aside from the practical benefit of experiencing something that can't be conveyed through the secondary sources-- the America you live in and the Athens they lived in no longer have "shared experiences" except, ironically, each other; neither in politics nor recreation nor math do we anymore draw from a common well-- we all have our own wells and most of them are filled with soda, or alcohol. Maybe *The Brady Bunch* in one of its three prime time slots is not comparable to *Medea* in one of its three prime time slots, but at least everyone saw them. You'll counter that more people than ever are sharing experiences; but from the experience of any single individual, everyone else's experiences appear to exclude them, or are wrong. Humans peacefully coexist by analogy and metaphor, or in a pinch, jargon and cliché, you may think you know what inflammable means but if you want to know how it's used you better make sure the guy who said it has the same education or at least watched the same TV show. Now we don't even share war coverage, most people are not quite sure if we are, or are not, at war, and it's fair to say many Athenians were equally ambivalent. Which means that for the educated-- not college educated, not people who are smart because they learned but people who learned they aren't smart, people who are driven by purpose-- they will inevitably resort to subjects like ancient history as the shared avocational experience because there is no other valid signal that both crosses class/gender/education lines and also reliably excludes the lazy. "You're so stupid. This is America, as long as I bring in the $$$ no one's going to care what I've read." I hope you who said this are young, I hope there's still time: they are lying to you. Yes they told you this and yes they will hire you and yes you may get rich-- but you will have no power, you will be excluded from it, this is why they told you that. You will, however, covet the right *to* know, loudly demand more information; and then you will ejaculate. You have been shown a world where creatives work smart in great spaces surrounded by supportive networks, and after pursuing their passion come home to unwind with TV or masturbation, but I have looked, these people do not exist. The world is changing, it is becoming not classist, neither lineage, money, nor education code reliably, but corporate. Maybe I should say-- tyrannical. But you're not sure what I mean by that word because you're not even sure what the word means. Too bad. You should have paid attention to how it was used.

This is how the story goes: The Athenians have beaten down the tiny but rebellious Mytilene. Now what? Cleon, in a speech that will make you proud of your own skepticism about democracy, appeals to archaic political justice. Any person with an interest in international relations or an age <30 will not be able to help but wonder if Cleon... doesn't have a point: no one has hurt the Athenian Empire more than the malicious Mytilenians, he says, they are deliberately aggressive, have aided the enemy, and would happily kill every one of us if they could. Show them mercy and they will try again, and our other colonies will see that mercy and they will try once. Athens must "do what is just", which in this instance is kill all the men and enslave the women and children. This isn't vengeance, it is savagely rigorous mathematics: "If they were right in rebelling, then we were wrong in ruling." You don't start with ~p, it gets you nowhere. ~q, *therefore* ~p.

Cleon the hawk wants them killed; Diodotus the dove wants to spare them. First, note the setup: Cleon is "the most violent man in Athens", but Diodotus's name means "given by God." One is id, the other is superego, but don't get excited, this is a pre-Socratic superego. Does Diodotus appeal to forgiveness? Obedience to the gods? Human decency? Categorical imperative? Justice? Our wine is 1:3, we're not barbarians? Surprise, that was Cleon's angle; Diodotus is a pragmatist, he doesn't care what things mean but how things are used: "we are not in a court of justice but in a political assembly, and the question is not justice, but how to make the Mytilenians useful to us." Don't alienate them, don't make them hate you, but with moderate punishments get them to "continue to pay us tribute." (Or, in the inane translation for a world that's read a lot about Marx: "that we may benefit in the long run from the revenue-producing powers of our dependencies.") It sounds sophisticated, worldly, with enough cynicism to convey practical *and* moral superiority. Diodotus wins the debate. Athens votes to spare Mytilene.

But was it too late? Unfortunately, the victorious Athenian general in Mytilene was already preparing to carry out the massacre. After the vote, Athens sent a ship to stop him, and because the crew was given wine they rowed all day and night and got there a day early=just in time, pulling into port just as General Paches was starting the executions. Mytilene was spared.

"It represents the political idea of might makes right." I know Cleon says the words, "prefer might to right" but he's not claiming it's true, he's saying that's the premise the Mytilenians used to revolt in the first place. This story isn't about might makes right. There is a "might makes right" story in the book, but it's over a different issue, the invasion of Melos; and the Melian Dialogue is structured as a dialogue between states-- not individuals. True or not, only states can claim might makes right, because states have power, so it is therefore pretty important which individuals are speaking *as* the state. But the Mytilenian debate is explicitly between two people, and neither of these people have any power. They have influence, as far as rhetoric goes, but they do not have any power. You might think the distinction between influence and power, or rhetoric and propaganda, or Athens and Athenian is trivial, but boy oh boy is it not, not for you, not for me, and not for the Mytilenians.

"Thucydides uses the Melian Dialogue to explain the reality of power--" How can you tell me what Thucydides uses the Melian Dialogue for, when the only Thucydides you've ever read is an excerpt from the Melian Dialogue? It's ironic that the School Of Realism directly quotes an unhelpful rendition of a totally imaginary dialogue. "Right is only a question between equals in power, the strong do what they can, and the weak suffer what they must." Come on, is this the *Game Of Thrones* translation? It actually says, "the strong do what they have to, and the weak will accept what they are able to." Greek food can be hard to digest, I know, but a waiter with a British accent can make even pudding sound delish, so *Game Of Thrones* it is: there's a scene when the Royal advisor, Lord Baelish, brags to the Queen of the many informants he has all throughout the land, and with a haughty gaze and punchable smirk he says to her, "Knowledge is Power." The capitals are his. The only people who say that are people who have been castrated, I know that's the other character but it's still 100% Oedipally true, which is why she gives an equally punchable smirk, summons some mindless hill giants to kill him, then at the last moment belays the order and cooly corrects him: "Power is Power." Did you get the point? They're both idiots. That's not the point you got?

What she did wasn't a display of power but straight up bullying, she's done 4 sets of tricep extensions and beat him in a staring contest. So what? That's not power, that's force. Did no one else take physics? Did she do more work? Or did she divert a kingdom's resources to display what any pre-teen with a lacrosse ball and passable aim could have effected in 1/100th the time? "Sometimes a woman's power is being able to get other people to act on what you want." Just not Lord Baelish, I guess, only mindless hill giants. "And her brother." Brother. Yeah.

If you understand this as a debate about political theories, e.g. moral justice vs. realpolitik, does might make right?-- and you have seen just enough Renaissance paintings to assume that the Athenians were 6'2 secular humanists in pristine whites and no body fat, body hair, or male pattern baldness, then you will conclude they sagely chose kindness and mercy *but pretended* it was pragmatism, not the other way around, notwithstanding that they executed 1000 Mytilenian hostages anyway. The problem is that though Thucydides is called a political historian his explicit purpose was to understand the psychology of people and states, and people in states, and here it gets a little more complicated, because in this story the participants aren't states, they are people. People can't act.

I have to say up front that the standard understanding is Cleon is a bad guy, not because he wants to kill everybody, but in order to make agreeing with him seem sophisticated: "...but he does have a point!" This is the basic maneuver of an academic looking to troll his colleagues or a powerless person looking to position himself as a man who knows "what needs to be done" without actually being responsible for doing anything. I'll explain.

To start simply, this is what Cleon says he wants: to kill all the Mitylenian men and enslave the women. Diodotus wants: not to do this.

Details aside, what they are debating is what most rhetoricians end up debating: action vs. inaction. Cleon says he wants to act (to kill them), Diodotus says he doesn't want to act. It seems very simple. It's not. Because after a few readings there's something you will notice: *neither person can act on his own will.*

Even though Cleon is the imperialistic demagogue Athenian-supremacist, power mad and glory hungry, none of these words are why he wants to kill the Mytilenians. No, his reason is that he feels the Mytilenians *compelled* him to act; he isn't choosing revenge, he's not exaggerating the threat, he's not doing it opportunistically for a gain: he feels he has no choice. They acted, we have no choice but to react.

Of course, Cleon could be lying, and wants to kill them for person gain. But even if he were lying, then *again* he can't do it because he wants to: he has to pretend it's for some other reason. Regardless of what he wants, Cleon can only act because he is compelled or for some other reason. He is not capable of doing it *because* he wants to. You may counter that Cleon *could* do what he wants, the issue here is getting the Athenians to do what he wants. Hold that thought, it's important. I'll leave full analysis of Cleon for another time, suffice it to say that Thucydides gives ample additional evidence of Cleon's inability to act on his own will; he can perform near miracles but only when an outside force compels him to act. Otherwise, he does nothing except talk. For emphasis: this is a man who wants to be tyrant of Athens. Do you think he succeeds?

The interesting character here is Diodotus. What he wants to do is *nothing*-- not act, not kill the Mytilenaeans. But then he wants this inaction to be perceived as an action: he wants "nothing" to be perceived by the Mytilenaeans not as weakness or blind allegiance to justice but as an act of free will, as a *chosen* act of magnanimity. *But why would he think the Mytilenians would see it the way he wanted it to be seen?* Today, policy makers consciously incorporate into their strategies the "objective" news media "independently" "reporting" the "realpolitik of magnanimity", ensuring our enemies get the proper message about how "inactions" are to be interpreted. Who was going to tell the Mytilenaeans how to think? The only media discussing the news in the 5th century was the Oracle and no one had asked it.

The only way the people of Mytilene would interpret inaction the way he wanted it interpreted is if *the inaction was an obvious lie.*

Which brings us to the first of three disavowals. The trick to understanding the debate is that while it sounds like they are deciding whether to kill the Mytilenians, the real issue is the *opposite*: whether to *stop* the killing that is *already in motion.* Two days earlier, after the rebellion in Mytilene was put down, the Athenians in *Athens* angrily voted to kill the men and enslave the women and children. This might sound like a standard 5th century Athenian punishment, except that it wasn't: *these Athenians had never done this before.* And the next day they regretted it, a fact emphasized in the text-- it was hasty, extreme, excessive-- it was hubris. *But it was also too late. They had acted impulsively, and it horrified them.*

Yet while everyone knows the Mytilenian massacre is on autopilot, this is utterly disavowed; not simply that the massacre *may* occur, but that the current debate is happening too late to stop it anyway. The second boat got there in the nick of time, but only because they had arrived a day ahead of schedule. The original order was to execute them *speedily*. You think General Paches is dragging his feet, wrestling with the ethics or consulting an eclipse, just in case? For backstory let me tell you what Paches and his army did right before receiving the first execution order. After taking Mytilene, he gets bored and cruises around the Mediterranean sacking other nearby towns; then he stumbles on a fleet of 42 Spartan ships which he chases, for 300 miles-- NB he's in a giant rowboat-- before doubling back and sacking some more towns, the last of which was Notium, which he found well-nigh impregnable, but instead of oh well and leaving enough alone he stayed and improvised: he invites the enemy's commander, Hippias (no relation), to a parley outside the gates, giving his word to return Hippias safely back inside afterwards. Hippias comes out. Paches has him seized and immediately blitzes the city and kills everyone else inside. Then he takes Hippias safely back inside. And then kills him. Then he goes back to Mytilene, sends off some Mytilenians to Athens to be executed there, and eventually gets the first boat with the order to kill the rest of the Mytilenian people. So? The only thing Paches is reluctant to do is nothing. Diodotus never mentions this urgency, never says they need to act quickly to stop the massacre. In fact, *he never says they should act to stop the massacre at all*. What he says in his droningly uninspiring speech, over and over, is that they should not act *to* massacre them. Do Not Act. But there's still a massacre in progress, how can you *stop* it if you don't *act*? Diodotus's *rhetorical* gimmick is to pretend it's not starting it; disavowal of reality is his rhetorical strategy. The problem is the rising impotence of the Athenians, they are losing the ability to act. So in order to get the audience *to act* and stop the killing, he must phrase it as *not acting* to kill them.

But the inability to act isn't the doves' problem only; hawks always have this same problem, because they have to convince the people to act, which is usually nearly impossible. It's popular to see pro-war advocates as wanting to do too much or go too far, but the psychology does not allow for those choices. The desired outcome has to be arrived at through *no* action on desire. So on the one hand Cleon wants to convince the people to act to kill the Mytilenians; but in reality he has a much easier job because he what he is technically advocating is *no action*, he gets to tell the Athenians *not to stop what is already in motion*. This is why he, and only he, can say *out loud* that they are all merely "pretending as if what was completely decided is not yet decided" and advocating "not reversing the policy which has been decided". He doesn't have to ask them to vote *to act* to kill the Mytilenians, he is advocating for *passively* letting the massacre happen. You can roll your eyes at what seems like splitting hairs because it's not your hairs being split. Remember, the whole reason there is a debate at all is because almost all the Athenians regretted their initial decision, they wanted the chance to take it back-- *yet Cleon still gets almost half the vote*-- not because he was convincing but because doing nothing, keeping the status quo, was and always is easier. If instead Cleon had to convince the Athenians to act, to send an army, now, to kill the Mytilenians, he would have failed, and I know this because that actually happened: Mytilene had revolted once before, and the same two debaters argued about what to do. The difference? In that debate, they were truly debating whether *to* genocide the Mytilenians. In that one, Diodotus is explicitly "most strongly against" action. Of course, forced to consider doing something they had never done before *without a tyrant to compel them or a State to act for them*, the people voted to do nothing. Not to act.

Let me highlight this again: the Mytilenians had already revolted once before, and Athens had already spared them-- yet they revolted again this time *anyway*. So at issue is not merely the morality of killing Mytilenians, but the practicality of being killed by Mytilenians should they be emboldened revolt again.

The framings of realities are opposites, the desired outcomes are opposites, but both men are appealing to the same psychological position: not acting. You may resist seeing why this matters because you are focused on changing the outcome; but the outcome is generally perceived to be inevitable. What would it mean if they first voted to massacre them, then vote to spare them-- and they die anyway, because the second vote didn't get to Paches in time? Seriously, this is the key question: *what would that mean?*

This is not a debate about action, it is a debate about meaning. It is, formally, rhetoric. The primary target of rhetoric is belief, not action: rhetoric tells you what to believe regardless of what happens. The opposite of rhetoric is propaganda. Propaganda doesn't care what people believe or don't believe; pride, shame, benevolence or vengeance: believe what you want, as long as you act in the required direction.

The debate is not about what *to* do at all; it's about constructing reasons for what will have already happened, whatever ends up happening. The psychological problem that required this retroactive reframing was the inability to act on a desire-- it had to be impulsive, compelled, or for some other reason. So while on Wednesday the Athenians definitely regretted the horrible cruelty of Monday's decree, there was *nothing* they could *do* about it-- they were powerless to change what had already been put into motion. I don't even mean there weren't things that *could* have been done; I mean they could not act to do any of those things. There's no better example of this than the debate itself: even after immediately regretting their Monday decision to execute, the Athenians themselves couldn't even call an assembly to reconsider it. Even if only a day old, it was now the psychic status quo. The only reason there even was a second vote was that the Mytilenian ambassadors who happened to be present in Athens *caused* it to happen-- they plainly saw that most of the citizens wished someone to give them an opportunity for reconsidering the matter, and so they acted for them.

If you still think the debate is more about the outcome than the interpretation of whatever turns out to be the outcome-- if you still doubt that this is rhetoric-- note that Thucydides has both men include in their rhetoric *a discussion about rhetoric*. The worry isn't the outcome, the worry is the message. So at the outset, both men explicitly use the argument that rhetoric is often misleading-- and then go on to use rhetoric. Cleon scolds the listeners for being too easily influenced by the intricacy of rhetoric over the simplicity of plain talk, even though he speaks much more eloquently and idealistically than pragmatic Diodotus. Diodotus also scolds them for this but then undermines Cleon's gimmick: it's not just that rhetoric is more persuasive to idiots than plain talk; Athenians assume everything *but especially* plain talk is rhetoric because they *always* assume there's an ulterior motive, the other *never* reveals their true desire. NB: this is a direct democracy. People are more suspicious when the ulterior motive isn't obvious, or, said the correct way, an obvious *ulterior* motive reassures the people that they know what's really going on. Plain talk is worse because its simplicity hides ulterior motives-- so the projections of an already impotent but omniscient (=paranoid) audience are magnified. Plain talk is the mark of your enemy, which is why devils and demons did it, what they said makes too much sense so you can't make sense of why they said it. If this logic makes sense to you, then it will also make sense why they executed Socrates.

So Cleon is wrong, no one is *fooled* by rhetoric. They could be 100% certain the rhetoric hid an ulterior motive: they prefer that-- because then they know exactly how much the speaker stands to benefit. Diodotus explains *out loud* that an honest speaker wanting to influence the vote in a "good" direction has no choice but to lie because the Athenian individuals do not judge the advice based on the state's gain but on the hypothetical gain of the speaker. Though the advice might be the best that can be given, the Athenian people would rather deprive the state of a certain benefit out of envy of the speaker's *possible* personal gain-- even though they are uncertain about how much or even whether he would benefit. They aren't looking to gain; their principle is envy, to deprive the other.

The most noble speaker who wants a good thing for the state is *obliged* to lie *and be known to be lying* in order to be believed, in exactly the same way the advocate of the most monstrous measures has to use deceit to gain the people. But the insight here isn't that a speaker has to lie to get *his* benefit, that part's obvious; the unfortunate conclusion is that because of these suspicious imaginations, it is the *state* alone that can never benefit from the plain and open way, anyone who does try to serve it openly will be more suspected of serving himself, and so the state will not get the benefit. If this logic makes sense, then you should wonder if it didn't make sense to Socrates as well. It did, he didn't care, he had had enough. A few years before he drank the hemlock, the very same Athenians voted to execute their victorious generals, one of whom was the son of Pericles-- all of those words are correct-- and Socrates was the only one who voted no, are you people insane? "Keep your eyes on that guy, he's up to something."

The logic of envy is the logic of a democracy that does not feel connected to power, which is troubling because these democrats theoretically and *in reality* had all of it. They didn't lose their power; they didn't want it anymore. This is why rhetoric was developed not merely as an art but as a science, to methodically and reliably target the psychological needs of a people whose belief in their own power was being replaced by knowledge. "I can't do anything, but I know that guy is up to something."

Knowledge was the defense. Using their power was never the point of the Mytilenian debate.

Which bring us to the second disavowal, which is actually a repression. Leaving aside the question of what the Athenians wanted to believe, why was Diodotus confident that not killing them would be heard by the Mytilenians as magnanimously *choosing* to spare them? Certainly that's not the message they got the other time they were spared. But this time was different, the Mytilenians didn't need to hear the Athenians' explicit reasons for sparing them, they didn't have to interpret the meaning of their choice, *they didn't even see which choice they made:* they saw *both* choices, *simultaneously*. I'm sure they were thrilled the second boat saved them, but what do you think they thought? The second boat could only have been interpreted by the Mytilenians as a denial: the real desire of the Athenians was to kill them, and then-- they didn't. To the Athenians, the second ship was the truth, "we do not want to kill all those people", and the first ship didn't count. To the Mytilenians, the first ship was the naked, unfiltered, truth of desire; the second came as a hedge, some other reason--- but a diabolical hedge, because that hedge obligated them to act like the first ship never happened. In this way the Athenians installed a tyranny over the Mytilenians, because it turned any future *defensive* actions by the Mytilenians into acts of aggression against the benevolent Athenians;

306

and if the Mytilenians remained quiet out of fear it obviously proved they valued the benevolent Athenian rule. A guy and a girl are on a first date, and he Freudian slips, "you're a really cool girl, I'd totally rape you-- I mean date you!" It was obviously a mistake, an accident, but if she gets out of the car she's a hysterical bitch; but before you agree with this meaning understand how the Freudian slip was used: now, if she doesn't get out of the car, then obviously she wants it. Luckily for her she's safe, since it's a Freudian slip it is impossible for him to actually act on his desire. "Unless it is compelled, impulsive, or for some other reason-- like she wants it?" Touché. Get out of the car, and then burn it.

The story of Mytilene follows the structural logic of a Freudian slip. An impulsive, unfiltered action, quickly taken back and disavowed; followed by *no* action at all. The purpose of the Freudian slip is to *convey* to the other person one's repressed wish and then validly take it back, meanwhile the other person sees what supposedly never existed. The Freudian slip is used to make inaction into an action: I tell you something, I reveal my desire, then safely take it back and do nothing. But they don't think they're lying, it only works because the slipper truly thinks they don't have the slipped desire. The Athenians don't think they changed their mind, they truly believe they never wanted to kill the Mytilenians because in the end they don't do it-- the double lie that they are both noble and capable of action. The result is that the *correction*-- the recanting, the "oopsy", the second boat-- that publicly denies any such desire to act-- leaves the recipient with both boats. They heard it, they know it, they've been affected by it-- but now their actions will determine what happens next. So while the Mytilenians know the Athenians truly wanted to kill them, to revolt again against the Athenians who so vigorously "don't" have these urges could only be seen by the Athenians as an unprovoked assault-- confirming that the Mytilenians deserved it.

Could the Athenians have planned this in advance? No. Planning a Freudian slip is immediately detectable, no one can explain why but everyone knows when it's faked; it is the ultimate signal of weakness, not just to the other person but to yourself: a planned slip doesn't reveal a secret desire, it proves this desire is conscious *and you still cannot act on it*; you admit your insanity and your impotence and request the other person take power over you.

The Mytilenian debate wasn't about what to do. No one on the hill needed convincing about what to do, because no one was going to do anything. The last time they tried to do something was Monday and it was horrifying. The real purpose of the second debate was about how to reinterpret what their *State* will have done. This debate has now offered the Athenian individuals *multiple* different *causes* and *actors* to choose from, depending on what happens. E.g. if the Mytilenians are saved (passive voice), then *they saved them* (active voice) out of expedience, which was really kindness. If it's too late and the Mytilenians are killed (passive voice) then the State killed them but the second vote shows they (individuals) tried to save them.

This explains the closeness of the vote despite the near unanimous initial regret: for the Athenian individuals, the vote is irrelevant, the outcome is irrelevant-- so long as it is close: I voiced my opinion but I'm only one person; the State was ambivalent, but it acted. And if "State" is too abstract, the debate offers two individuals who might be blamed. This is barely a speculation: Diodotus himself says that the Athenians, far from accepting the blame for their own decisions, "visit the disasters into which the whim of the moment may have led you upon the single person of your advisor, not upon yourselves, his numerous companions in error." Again, NB: this is a direct democracy. The average citizen no longer carries the guilt for the action of the collective, he does not even act as part of the collective, exactly the reverse situation a generation earlier. The Athenians want a tyrant.

Admittedly this all will sound like a bit of a reach or at least historically irrelevant, there is, after all, a very real outcome Cleon and Diodotus are debating, except for the third disavowal, the disavowal of *ours*: Diodotus didn't actually argue to spare them, because Diodotus didn't exist. Thucydides made him up *to serve as a proxy for the regretful Athenians*. The story of the debate is *about* the ambivalence of the Athenians, about what *they* did, and their search for understanding what *they had done*, which literally becomes their explanation of what the *State* had done, because they wanted no part of the responsibility.

Whatever the foundation for human morality may be, it doesn't apply to States, any more than it applies to ducks or hand grenades. It applies to the leaders of states, though they also have different obligations, but not to the State itself. You will make the case that the structure of States causes individuals to behave immorally, or honorably, or cowardly, or aggressively, this may be true of Sparta but this isn't the problem the Athenians had. The unique problem the Athenians had was that they were absolutely, 100%, materially equivalent to the state, which meant they didn't have recourse to the defense that "the State acted" or even "the head of the State acted." But instead of this making them behave more morally, or at least ethically=consistently, or even more profitably, they had epileptic fits of depersonalization, they spent their energy trying to make it true that the State was some other omnipotent entity.

The vote did go with Diodotus, but not because Athenian people were predisposed to mercy; the book shows they were not. The first massacre decree was universally regretted by the Athenians, there should not have been any support for Cleon's position, so the fact that it was close suggests two possibilities, which are the same: either Thucydides made it up to teach the reader about how the action by Athens is to be understood; or the vote itself, in the aggregate, represents the true desire of the Athenians, which was *only* to decide what the outcome *meant*. A close vote doesn't indicate an evenly divided electorate, each who know exactly what they want; it signals that it is a false choice, seemingly gigantic but with relatively trivial consequences, flip a coin or opt out; the real desire isn't to choose between two choices but to be able to decide what you want your choice to mean. Since each choice can have any, multiple and even contradictory meanings, you really only need two. The Athenians were 50/50 on their choices, but 100% all in on wanting to decide what they meant by the choice. You'll retort that in your life you feel very strongly about the choice, that you think the outcome matters and you want to effect it; but rather than convincing others to do what you want, you try to convince them to believe you are right; more specifically: that they are wrong. Rhetoric or propaganda: you chose rhetoric. Thus permitting a coin toss to be sufficient for the outcome: everybody gets to believe what they want, no matter what happens next.

The Athenians got exactly what they wanted. Well, what did happen next? One way to tell it, the usual way, is that with the second boat the Athenians spared the population of Mytilene, executing only the revolting oligarchs. The other way to tell it is that they killed 1/3 of the population of Mytilene and *called* this executing only the oligarchs. But don't think for a second this was rationalization for their action, do not give them so much credit. Calling them oligarchs wasn't just their justification for killing them, it was also the reverse: only an oligarch could have acted to revolt, could have acted at all. In this way you satisfy an ambivalent Athenian population that wished it had oligarchs, such that, regardless of the democratic vote, it is really their oligarchs who act.[56]

    The idea of events occurring in one tense and the description of it occurring in another in order to cause something to be true or not true in retrospect is analogous to a movie being re-released plus or minus a key scene that causes the entire story's meaning to change; but if those releases had been presented in the reverse order, the meaning stays the same, but the purpose becomes repressed. So when someone asks, "which version of *Blade Runner* is better?" the answer is tricky: you have to see them both.

56

But while this understanding helps explain what the Athenians did, it isn't sufficient to explain why the modern understanding is that they obviously made the right choice to spare them. What would have been the wrong choice? "What they did to Melos." No, I mean *specifically*?

Using the Mytilenian *and* Melian debates is a terrible way to understand State power, but their use itself is a perfect way to understand how we want to understand State power: separated from its context and totally out of our hands.

By not reading the rest of the book, or even the surrounding pages, or even the title, we can ignore an important fact grounding the Mytilenian debate: the problem wasn't that they revolted, the problem was that they joined the Spartans that had declared war on and invaded Athens. Hold on: not just the Spartan State-- the Mytilenians had allied with the exact same Spartan *individuals*, literally the exact same guys, that had invaded Athens three years earlier. But while the Spartans were the same Spartans, the Athenians listening to the debate were very different from the Athenians three years ago: *many of those Athenians had died in the plague*. Wait two more years and it would be accurate to say that the remaining best men of Athens have *all* been killed, accurate because Thucydides himself said it, such that by the time they film *The Melos Sanction* ten years later you still have most of the original Spartans but the Athenians have been replaced with a younger, edgier cast that mirror a demographic so self-absorbed and responsibility averse that when they themselves become famous, they're astounded they're still supposed to *demand* a higher salary on their own. "But shouldn't they pay me what I'm worth?" They did, stupid. That is a generation that does not want to be challenged, especially not intellectually, so it's not surprising that these same Athenians-- minus the ones who went to Sicily and stayed there-- had no patience for Socrates. "Enough, you ignorant old man, it's not my job to educate you." Yes, that's what I've been trying to tell you. "Hey, isn't he the elitist who voted to acquit a group of war criminals?" "Let's make a public example out of him, so it's easier for our children to be conquered."

No matter how often someone pretends not to be quoting from the first dozen pages of Clausewitz, no matter how much pro-po-mo jargon infirms our vernacular, no matter how much we attribute ideological forces to the doings of the world, the actively sought understanding of political affairs is reductive: they are all separate, or at most geographical, and it's all about money. Certainly Country A has dealings with Country B, but unless we're talking about colonialism or Israel/Palestine any historical context-- not ancient, merely a generation or so back-- is not only irrelevant, it's considered unsophisticated to mention it. That seems untrue in an age where everything is put in a historical context, but the only time history is used as context is to claim everyone else is on the wrong side of it.

The excerpted "Mytilenian Debate" is used to isolate out of its larger context an event, to use that event to discuss justice or expedience; and since the discussions can get pretty sophisticated we figure the context wasn't necessary. But if this was possible, the Mytilenians, having just lost 1/3 of their population and aware they were merely a boat away from 3/3s, would have to be insane to

The usual question of *Blade Runner* is whether Deckard is a replicant, and while it's pretty clear from the director's Final Cut version, not to mention his larynx, that he is, the more interesting question is when did you know to ask?

In the 1982 theatrical release of *Blade Runner*, there's a key scene that was filmed but was cut out, leaving the movie's underlying question of what Deckard "is" not just unanswered but unasked; the theatrical audience did not know there was a question to be asked. In the 2007 release of the Final Cut, this scene is put back in-- the answer is given to a question that hadn't been asked. So in the theatrical release, what was repressed? The question or the answer?

---

revolt yet again; except that's exactly what they do for a *third* time, under the direction of the Spartans. How does knowing what happens next affect your understanding of the Debate? Or knowing that they surrendered in the second place only to buy time for the Spartans to show up? How would knowing these things have affected the Athenians?

The real Thucydidean question isn't whether Creon-- Freudian slip, Cleon-- is right; the problem for the Athenians, which they solved by not solving it, is how to run an empire during wartime without a Creon, because you sure as hell don't want the responsibility. Here's a simple test to reveal what you truly believe about the difference between moral philosophy and political philosophy. Say some lunatic breaks into your house to murder you and your family, but because your Glock is in a Glock safe you go with the weapon at hand and collapse a third of his skull with a rum bottle. Then you call the police. The knowledge economy can pleasantly debate whether your action was a privilege or a right, and this is because the State has saved you from the obligation of vigilante justice by promising that he will go to jail for 10 years. What do I mean by obligation? As you're waiting for the cops he tells you something important: he'll use his one phone call to call everyone he knows to come and kill your family. Now what? Obviously, the answer is you collapse the other 2/3s of his skull with a rum bottle, what was never your right and not much of a privilege now looks awfully like a duty owed to your family. So Cleon is right?

That's what I would do, but I make no argument that my intentions will afford me immunity, I already know the US government hates me and for God a sin is a sin, nevertheless don't I have the duty to protect my family even and especially at my own *moral and legal* risk? I'm proud to say I'll take a bullet for them but I won't do 15-20? Not just to save their lives-- do I have the right to saddle my children with the future burden of *their* having to kill, even in self defense? Again I acknowledge the sketchy sophistry of my contention, but what I won't let you get away with is your position that doing *nothing* is the "right" action, ostensibly because it looks like a choice but secretly because it is *not an action at all*. Not acting on a threat that is left to others to deal with sounds like a deeply immoral act that pretends to be the moral act, you use your inability to act to assert you're a pacifist. I'm no lawyer, but that sounds like you sinned in your heart.

Now imagine this same scenario in Athens 427: your great leader of 15 years, and a third of the government, is dead, and the only people left to replace them are a specific kind of 20 year old: cocksure junior varsity boys whose primary childhood experience was living in comparative affluence provided by their war hero grandfathers who never let them forget it. "Aw, are the little baby's feeties all swollen from sucking them all day? When I was your age, at the crack of dawn we'd be crawling in the silver mines, then we'd fight the Persians all day, and if you survived you came home and pushed the plow all night! And man, we were thankful!"

The Mytilenians revolted once, and were spared; they revolted a second time, and were 2/3 spared. Will they revolt again? (The answer is duh.) So what would have been the right thing for State Power to do after #2, *given* #3? Given that #3 could lead to #4 and to the Spartans killing everyone you know? Knowing the future makes the answer a lot harder, so there's a bait and switch: you disavow #3 ("well, you can't know the future." But can't I hedge it? "Hedging is for corrupt

In the ending of both versions, Deckard flees his apartment with the replicant Rachael, and he sees on the floor an origami unicorn. In the theatrical release, helpfully reinforced by a voice over, this means that known replicant hunter and origamist Gaff had been there. The purpose of the origami was as a message to Deckard that Gaff spared Rachael (because Deckard loved her).

In the 2007 Final Cut version is an "extra" scene which had been removed from the 1982 theatrical release: Deckard dreams about a unicorn. Now the Final Cut's origami unicorn has a totally different meaning: Deckard realizes Gaff knows his dreams, because Deckard is a replicant. The deletion of the dream scene in the theatrical release therefore had repressed the entire question of whether or not Deckard was a replicant.

---

capitalists." Got it.) You claim you're going to discuss "realpolitik" *through* Mytilene, never actually discuss the realpolitik *of* Mytilene, but subtly conflate it with a whole other issue existing in an entirely different context to judge whether Cleon is right, so as to say he was wrong. That second issue is the invasion of the tiny island of Melos by the mighty Athenian Empire, who told the Melians in very plain talk that they should surrender or be killed. [3.56] Spoiler: they are killed. If you haven't read the Crawley translation I suggest you do that first, his is full of good poster quotes while mine comes from a symposium that no one else was invited to:

Melians: Let's talk privately.

Athenians: Instead of in front of the people? Don't they deserve to hear all the information so they can make up their own minds?

Melians: You care about transparency? I count only two of you, and you're basically aristocrats. Would you like to take this discussion back to Athens so we can be transparent in front of your people?

Athenians: Ok, ok, point taken. Then let's dispense with rhetoric and, oligarchs to oligarchs, negotiate plainly.

Melians (looks out into the harbor and sees Athenian boats): Looks like the deal you're offering is we surrender and you enslave us, or we refuse and you invade us. Not much of a negotiation. Why can't we just remain neutral? We've never been a threat to you.

Athenians: Come on. We won't sit here and tell you we deserve your loyalty because our fathers saved your fathers from the Persians. But don't you sit there and tell us you're not a threat because you're only a Spartan "colony" and not a Spartan "ally". You've been openly hostile and plundering our territory for the past ten years.

Melians: Still, what you're doing isn't right.

Athenians: Don't tell us about what's right. Right, as the world goes, is only a question among equals in power; the strong do what they can, and the weak suffer what they must.

Melians: That's true.

Athenians (pause): Well?

Melians (pause, confused): Wait-- you're the strong?

Athenians: You are tiny Melos, and we are mighty Athens!

Melians: *You* are mighty Athens? I'm sorry, I didn't catch you ladies' married names. Didn't actual Athenian men try to take us ten years ago? As I remember, what the strong did back then was lose to us. And now you want to give it a try? Lead by two dummies? The only reason you have

Take special note: though the dream scene is what was cut out from the theatrical release, the dream scene itself doesn't mean anything. It's deleted, but it isn't repressed. It's the origami that means something; the origami means Gaff knows Deckard's dreams, because Deckard is a replicant; the origami's meaning is repressed by deleting the dream.

Now imagine if the films were released the other way around-- what if the unicorn dream was shown in the early version, only to be deleted from the later? In the later release without the dream, the origami means Gaff was there; its use is to tell Deckard he spared Rachael. But since we've seen the earlier version with the dream, we still know there's at least a question about what Deckard is, but now we are denied the explicit answer. The origami's now repressed meaning-- the meaning that was repressed-- is the answer to whether Deckard

---

any status in Athens is because the top 120 of your people got lost in the woods that the Aetolians set on fire, and now your hereditary oligarchy is down to nephews. Forget about imperialism, you need to recruit new immigrant talent or come up with the 13th Amendment.

Athenians: You need to be pragmatic.

Melians: Thank you Thrasymachos, I say it's very pragmatic to keep the discussion at the level of right and wrong and not strong and weak, because we both know what right and wrong is, but strong and weak are subject to a number of external variables. Like wood fire. You stand to benefit from this as well, god forbid you lose a battle or there's an eclipse, you'll then want the privilege of invoking fair and right, even if the arguments aren't strictly valid. Your fall would be a signal for the heaviest vengeance, and quite the object lesson for future generations who will study you.

Athenians: Future generations? Are you kidding? The only thing the sheep 2500 years from now will care to remember of us is that we were mean to women and we invaded you. One tenth of those quadrupeds won't know who wins this war and the other nine tenths won't know there even was one, and then they'll go, "baaaaa!". The end of our empire hardly worries us, we would way rather be conquered than suffer an internal revolution which overthrows the rulers.

Melians: I thought Athens was a democracy and didn't have rulers.

Athenians: Contradictions inherent in the system, the development of historical necessity: we're a work in progress.

Melians: In the interest of fairness--

Athenians: Stop saying fair. There's only self-interest. It's in your interest not to fight and lose, and it's in our interest not to have to fight to win. Surrender.

Melians: Your notion of self-interest is far weaker than our claim to Justice. So we're not surrendering. We're going to put our faith that the gods will see the justice of our cause.

Athenians: Justice is nothing other than the advantage of the stronger, and unlike history it's decided by the winners, and anyway you don't have a monopoly on invoking the gods. We happen to think the gods are on our side. It's a law of nature that even gods follow: rule wherever you can.

Melians: That's not a law of nature, you just made it up. Why would you think the gods would follow a law you made up?

Athenians: We're the ones who made up the gods.

Melians: You people are lunatics. Thanks but no thanks, we'll wait for the Spartans.

Athenians: [5.110] The Spartans? The worthiest men alive-- when it comes to their own interests. But more than any other men, they call honorable whatever pleases them, and they call just

is a replicant. I say that the *meaning* is repressed because no amount of deleting can change the fact that for the audience, the question still stands. In fact, the deletion highlights the question, it forces the audience to wonder what Deckard is.

You might disagree with this and say the director in this hypothetical release order was simply trying to fix a mistaken link between dream/origami, "no, I didn't mean to imply Deckard is anything but human", but truly correcting this association knowing that the question now exists would have required pointing the dream to something else. You need to give the dream its own meaning, for example Tyrell could say to Deckard, "Rachel is unique, she's almost mythological." Then Deckard's dream unicorn refers to Rachel, and the origami

---

whatever profits them. Don't count on them. You will learn, as others have done, that the Athenians never once yet withdrew from a siege.

Melians: That's not very sound military strategy, and in this case all your best generals are dead. Our guess is that your siege won't be too hard to beat.

Athenians: [4.108.4] Your mistake in your estimate of the Athenian power is as great as that power afterwards will turn out to be, relying on blind wishing rather than any sound forecast; for it is a habit of mankind to entrust to careless hope what they wish to be true, and to use sovereign reason to reject what they don't.

Melians: Kind of like what you're doing right now?

Athenians: Enough! Here's what is true: You will surrender or die.

Melians: Just to be clear, do you mean that as OR or XOR?

Athenians: What?

Melians: I see. No, we'll take our chances with our unjust justice.

And, of course, the next thing that happens is the Athenians slaughter them.

Or so the standard explanation goes, a fluid transition from "might makes right" to "absolute power corrupts absolutely". But that isn't what happens. Phrases like "the tiny island of Melos" vs. "the mighty Athenian Empire" and extracting quotes that sound like power politics subvert what Thucydides likely intended and actually wrote. First of all, it wasn't like the Athenians dropped a nuke and were home by lunch. It takes the Athenians *five months* to beat them. They build a giant wall, and then most of the army leaves. They do have two small skirmishes, and the Melians win both of them. The Spartans did indeed come to help, which would have been very bad for the Athenians, but half way there the Spartans turned back because Orion had twins or a donkey was in declension or whatever piously got them out of having to act. And the reason the Melians eventually lose isn't because the mighty Athenian Empire crushed them from the outside but because of Melian traitors from the inside. I'm not going to say it was all dumb luck, but I will say the Athenians were lucky, and dumb.

There's so much discussion about what the Melian Dialogue means that you miss what it is for: to cause the Melians to surrender, *only*. This is not Thucydides attempting a Platonic dialogue between abstract political entities. The Athenians aren't trying to convince them they have the better argument, that the ethics of state power differ from the ethics of human beings. They're not trying to give them knowledge. They are trying to scare them into surrendering.

Because Thucydides has the Athenians say "Might Makes Right" it gets elevated to a seminar title by following it with a colon and 14-16 jargonized syllables, the invasion is only ever used as an example of Goliath eating David, instead of what it actually is: a Mexican standoff. I can't call it

in both versions means Gaff was there, and he spared the unicorn Rachel, because Deckard loved her.

A similar shell game is played with the endings of *Picnic At Hanging Rock*. The movie isn't for everyone, but it should be; it is a period piece which tells the story of the disappearance of 2-3 Victorian pubescent schoolgirls during a picnic in 1900's Australia. Many *uncanny* things happen in the film, but nothing you see on screen requires anything other than classical Newtonian physics and contemporary Freudian psychology. The theatrical release and a Director's cut differ most significantly in a 3 minute scene at the end, I won't tell you which is which: without the extra 3 minutes, the movie ends with no explanations. With the extra 3

---

that anymore? Because it reveals that both sides are equally powerful? "The Athenians" weren't sent by the actual Athenians, this is an unsanctioned freelance operation by a couple of fraternity boys who thought they could pull it off, they took what's left of the family's retirement fund on a trip to Vegas, a couple of losing hands and hookers later they cannot return empty handed/humiliated because otherwise they will be executed. So they double down. All that political theory is simply a hustle. If Thucydides had them anachronistically threaten to use a tactical nuclear weapon, would you think Thucydides thinks time travel is real, that it's relevant in power politics? The whole thing could be a higher truth or strategic lies or total nonsense, it neither has to be factually accurate nor logically coherent, which is why the Athenians assert, in the same two pages, totally contradictory positions that taken together could not all be believed, let alone true. They don't have to be true. Only necessary.

This isn't rhetoric; the Athenians explicitly say it isn't rhetoric. It is propaganda. Might, right, gods, tactical nuclear device— they don't care what the Melians believe. Only that they act in the required direction.

The Melian dialogue is used by *us* to discuss whether might makes right, but at the beginning of the speech "The Athenians" – the 2+1 dorks that actually represents-- did not have the full might of Athens to assert they were right, so it's a better example of the overconfidence that comes with *believing* might makes right; and the consequences of this belief are what happens at Melos (tiny victory, at what cost?) and what happens immediately after Melos (giant catastrophe, for what benefit?) We *say* they won because they were the overwhelming power, but had the Spartans burned a fish instead of a dog it could have easily gone the other way; most of the battles Thucydides highlights are precisely those where the odds of winning are low or the payoff is even worse. They took credit for the win *as if* it was due to their power, and we let them-- we want them to. We say might *shouldn't* make right, to hide what's not really true, what's only a wish: that it *could*. And when we "mighty" choose not to act, it must be because of our benevolence, not possibly weakness, cowardice-- impotence. What a big penis, too bad it's floppy, you can slap a bitch with it, I guess, let her know who's boss, but beyond that it's as useless as the photographs you'll take of it. Whether might makes right it for sure doesn't make it inevitable; neither does sending 3x more soldiers than necessary, it may be a 3d20 but it's still a die roll, if you lose you'll be entirely responsible but if you win you should thank the gods the other team isn't used to playing in the snow. "That's not fair. If you can't take credit for the win then you shouldn't really be blamed for the loss." I see you're 12, you'll get to Thucydides eventually, let me just give you a quote you can put on a poster: You can win lots of times. You can only lose once.

If they would have just stayed quiet and looked to their navy, and during the war not sought further dominion, nor risk the city itself, they would have had the upper hand. But they did the opposite, including things which didn't concern the war, and managed the state according to their private ambition and envy. Whatever succeeded well, the profit and honor went most to private men; and what miscarried was to the city's detriment. And labeled its fault.

The Mytilenian Debate *with* the Melian Dialogue is an academic bait and switch. In a discussion

minutes, the movie still ends with no explanations, but for the only time in the movie it *shows* something impossible: a different girl who had suicided walking around Hanging Rock.

There's a lot to be said about that scene related to the "omniscience of the camera", which was not omniscient enough to follow the missing girls up the Rock or the final girl out the window or the headmistress into the closet where she makes a spectacularly prescient sartorial selection. But my telling you about this 3 minute ending is not a plot spoiler because despite the fact that it is paranormal, it still does not in any way explain anything that happens in the film. It merely forces the paranormal into this universe, to be one of the possibilities. It would be like a final scene in *Raiders of The Lost Ark* where Indy asks the Feds where they put the evidently magical Ark of the Covenant and they tell him it's in a "safe place", well, gee, that could be *anywhere*, and Spielberg then closes the movie with a tracking shot of Europa. So what am I supposed to do with that?

You might argue that these 3 minutes are the director's way of informing us that the paranormal is, in fact, the explanation for the girls' disappearance. But had he wanted to do this, he should have shown one of the missing girls. By showing us a girl who had suicided but who had never even been to the Rock, he recruits the paranormal, but fails to deploy it as the

---

about State power, they start with the Mytilenian debate, which looks like a debate between individuals but is really about the State, and then before the payoff switch to the Melian Debate, which looks like a debate between States but is actually about individuals. The reason the Melian Debate isn't about State Power is that it's not the Athenian State that is debating or acting. It's someone *pretending* to speak for Athens. The sophist's argument is that because Thucydides made the story of the Sicilian catastrophe follow immediately after the Melian genocide, he was showing the cause and consequence of political karma. You've read the logic right but not the book: *Melos* is the consequence, the cause is literally in the text only three paragraphs before the debate. Neither is Sicily a punishment for Melos; Sicily *and* Melos are the consequences of *Alcibiades*-- of demagoguery for private benefit, of the ambivalence of the Athenians towards their own democracy, *of wanting to be lead*. Thucydides isn't the one who labeled the debaters as "Melians" and "Athenians", Hobbes did that *to make it* about State power. But it's not the Melian State talking to the Athenian State, it's not the Athenian people talking to the Melian people. It is *literally* the Melian oligarchs talking to the Athenian oligarchists, the cronies of Alcibiades. Here's some political theory: what do you get when oligarchies disagree internally?

The State did nothing. Unlike Mytilene where it was everyone's fault but got projected onto the State, in this case a single guy pretended he was the State so he could do what he wanted, and no one did anything because when it comes to power, better him than them.

Once you strip away abstraction and "State power" and think of it as the high testosterone dilettantism of a locker room braggart that people hysterically love/hate/envy because they don't want to act and he seems always to be acting, you see the other rhetorical trick of conflating the Melian *invasion* with the inevitable Melian *genocide*. Inevitable? For God's sake, it was five months later. Maybe there are no neutrals in a total world war, you can debate *this*; but regardless of the necessity of the invasion, "The Athenians" did not have to massacre the people. That was a separate choice. It wasn't a necessary action of the State. That was a choice, made by a guy, who convinced the idiots to passively concur, months after the invasion, which he did on his own, under the cover of the State. In theory, with so much time to reflect, the Athenians could have made a dozen different choices, 5 months is hardly an operation on autopilot, even at their most passive they had managed to not kill 2/3 of Mytilene. But their preference for interpreting outcomes synced well with Alcibiades's preference for causing them. Safe within the walls and content to display our knowledge and cynicism, we allow-- want-- the State to act for us, all outcomes are effectively equivalent-- *so long as we get to debate what it all means*.

deus ex machina. In other words, it was a waste of the paranormal, which is a really remarkable thing to waste. Nevertheless, the point for our purposes remains the same: showing this paranormal ending and then deleting it in a later release is an entirely different situation than not having it in the first release, and putting it back in later. "All we see and seem is but a dream within a dream." That means it's real.[57]

There is a crucial psychological difference between repressing the question of what you are and repressing the answer of what you are, and this difference is depicted in what Deckard does when, in the Final Cut, he sees the origami and realizes he's a replicant: nothing. Deckard has no problem accepting that he's a replicant. Well, wait a second, why does he have no problem accepting it? Even Neo gets nauseous after the Red Pill, but Deckard switches so fast there isn't time to discharge the capacitors. Where's the existential dread and "no one can tell you who you are"?

He has no problem because, like the audience, he never wondered what he was. What he knew changed, but there was always a 1 in the knowledge column, never a zero. If something made him wonder in Act I-- not told him he was/wasn't a replicant, but forced open the question-- that uncertainty would have changed him, and the movie would be completely different because everything that he did would be about him wondering. By always knowing-- even when what he knows is wrong, and even when what he knows completely reverses-- does not change him. The 1 in the knowledge column never changes.

In other words, what's removed isn't what Deckard is, from the theatrical version; what is removed is doubt, from both versions. Deckard never wrestles with the question of what he is. But neither do any of the other replicants. The vital question for all the characters is not "what does it mean to be" human vs. replicant, but being alive vs. dead; and it is this consistency that makes replicants most like humans; strike that, I mean humans most like replicants.

There is only one character that wonders about what they are: Rachel, and I'll simply note that she's a woman. She isn't motivated by staying alive, she only cares about what she is. Rachel has to spend 2/3 of the movie in despair because she doesn't know and Deckard won't tell her.

This brings us to the touchy subject of Rachel's "rape." Lacking any interest in the individual psychology, and looking only at the size of their biceps and whether this scene can apply to society-- i.e. whether she is pretty enough to stand for college girls-- it might look like Deckard forced himself on her, notwithstanding she's a replicant while his bicep has the tensile strength of a banana. And as an aside, "forced himself on her" is a tellingly passive aggressive way to construct a phrase signifying rape, it makes me wonder whose side you're on. But even if this is the conclusion we want to reach, it would be useful to understand what about her Deckard took advantage of-- unless we're positing that if Pris had come in there existentially vulnerable, that rapist would have kissed her too? The reason Rachel went to his apartment is that she wanted to know what she was. But she wasn't going there only to learn the objective truth from Deckard, that would not have been satisfying to her. She wanted to find out what she was to Deckard. It is that desire that made Rachel both uniquely vulnerable to Deckard and unique among replicants. She was in love. *What am I to you?*

---

57 Likely of no interest to anyone but me so I'm noting it here: the guy who wrote and played the flute music of *Picnic At Hanging Rock* also played the "Lost Shepherd" theme of *Kill Bill*. And also *Once Upon A Time In America*, but you didn't see that.

Here's an example that will make sense later. Say you tell me you hear voices. One possibility is that you tell me no one else can hear them; another possibility is that you tell me someone else could hear them. Though the etiologies are different, those are relatively easy cases to treat by obliterating the voices, because both of those people exist in the same world as me, a world that is built on rules. The hard is the third case that sounds like it's the midpoint of a continuum between the two but is actually an entirely different problem: you are not sure if others do hear them. Now the voices are not the problem, and obliterating the voices does not solve the problem of the disparity in knowledge; in fact, merely deleting the voices after they were experienced highlights the uncertainty. The only thing you know for certain is that you *heard* voices, and now *you* can't.

A different example that will make sense now. In 1973, *The Giving Tree* was animated into a short film, produced and narrated by Silverstein, it is a scene for page remake of the book, except for one change: the last page is deleted.

Not the page that says, "And the tree was happy." That's the second to last page. Turn that page, and you see the man, sitting hunched on the stump-- his coat is still on but the hat lays on the ground. Underneath, in different font-- not the book's unreliable narrator but some other omnipotent entity-- are the words meant to be taken literally: "The End."

In the movie, the man's hat doesn't fall to the ground, and the words "The End" do not appear. The movie simply fades out a page early as the man sits down and holds his hat. "And the tree was happy," cue harmonica, pull out, fade to black, roll credits.

You might not have given any thought to the last page of the book. But the movie highlights its absence. Regardless of its meaning, what question is highlighted by its deletion?

You can answer it by reversing the order of the releases: if the movie came first, with no last page; and then the book, with the last page-- then that last page would force into your mind the answer to a question you had not thought to ask; and its absence in the first version would have repressed that question: we know the Tree is happy, but what about the man?

Now, in the actual order of book then movie, the movie's deletion of the last page leaves open but highlights that question: What happens to the man? Because we know that something happened-- that the movie took out. Is he alive or is he dead?

You might optimistically hope that Silverstein was clarifying the ambiguous meaning of the dropped hat, "I didn't mean to imply he was dead or that the Tree would be happy about that." But since we've all seen the hat scene in the original, it's not enough to delete it and hope "And the tree was happy" stands on its own, because we still know about the hat. The only way to break the connection of origami pointing to dream-- "And the tree was happy" pointing to the missing dropped hat page-- is by giving the hat scene its own meaning. For example, he drops the hat, but then picks it up again: he's alive.

You might think that's a stupid way to solve the impasse, but I know this is what Silverstein would do, because it is what Silverstein actually did do, in another cartoon called, "And He Was Never Heard From Again": a man slowly crawls into a cave that looks like the Tree drawn as a mother's vagina, dropping his hat; the next panel shows nothing but the cave and the hat outside, laying on the ground. Get it? But then in the next panel he is heard from again: his hand pokes out of the cave to retrieve the hat. There, Silverstein wants us to know that man is definitely alive, the title's meaning points to that event. The cartoon deliberately

317

leads you to the obvious conclusion involving dropped hats and vaginas and then subverts it by having him retrieve the hat. Why was he never heard from again? Answer: because he freely lived happily ever after in the vagina. Never show the hat retrieval and we might probably assume that the cave vagina ate him up, a neurotic's anxiety about marriage. But important here is that if you delete the hat retrieval in later editions it would highlight the ambiguity of the title, we'd know that the title should be interpreted, we don't doubt he is never heard from again, but we are now implicitly tasked with wondering why was he never heard from again? What happened to the man? Is he alive or is he dead? Who came out ahead?

Are there any questions?[585960]

Here's a joke that you will really creep you out when you realize you misunderstood it the first time: A wife is laying in bed almost asleep, and groggily notices her husband getting out of bed and taking his underwear off. "Not tonight, honey," she says blearily, "I have a headache." "I know," he says under his breath, "I poisoned you."

The sexual fantasy of a cheating wife is an ancient one, sometimes the husband is enraged, and sometimes he's aroused. But that a man would get aroused by the fantasy that a cheating wife is aroused by the fantasy of the husband's reaction to catching her cheat is about as post-modern as a master's degree will allow. "The fantasy is his wife cheats because he

---

58 "Oooh! Oooh! I have a question! I've been dating my girlfriend for about a year now, and she's great in every way-- except that she doesn't know I'm addicted to porn. We still have a great sex life, she treats me wonderfully, has a good job, but... but I stay up all night just looking at porn. I know exactly what kind of porn I like, I have a favorite genre and actress and scenario and aspect ratio-- yet I keep clicking around for hours and hours. Is it novelty seeking, dopamine release in the nucleus accumbens?"

Even your explanation isn't very novel. You should consider how you avoid novelty in everything else-- the way you take your coffee, your drink, your opioid; your hyperspecifically critical gaze (ask your girlfriend, though she's not going to tell you because she'd like to avoid the unnovel response); the very position you sleep in; not to mention your brand loyalty, interest in sequels, similars, upgrades, derivatives-- this isn't novelty seeking, it is flooding the room with amber after bricking the exits. Why in sexuality do you claim you are chasing infinite novelty-- that approaches an asymptote of highly specific criteria? As if the next MMMF/interr/glasses is any more novel than the first. "Well, admittedly I chase novelty in consumer products--" but they just come at you slower, like elections: it isn't novelty seeking, it is planned obsolescence, in some cases by the marketers and in all cases by your own psychology: you don't want something novel, you want a status quo that takes you by incremental steps into the future while you hang on tight so you can take credit for the movement. "Capitalism can't last! Things must change!" Not if you can help it.

"But isn't playing the same slot machine for twenty hours novelty seeking?" Yes, you have been told that, and nothing has changed.

"But look how much I've changed just this year!" You need to check your units, this isn't zero velocity but zero acceleration: it's no change in the rate of change.

As a child you were offered the appearance of novelty as an escape from boredom, but quite quickly you discovered it is an excellent defense against dependency, against change. "I'm kind of a news junkie, there's so much happening right now it's hard to keep up with it." Yet no one depends on you keeping up with it, they'd benefit much more if you didn't. Devotion to something with the appearance of importance, of velocity, of kinetic energy; that you don't really need, that you can always claim in an emergency doesn't "actually" define you. "This stuff doesn't really matter," you say as you watch the xth hour or push the nth button, "but right now, I'm satisfied." Look around you to see who you've deprived.

59"Oooh! Oooh! I have a question! I've been dating my boyfriend for about a year now, and he's great in every way-- except that he's addicted to porn. We still have a great sex life, he treats me wonderfully, has a good job, but... but sometimes he stays up late at night just looking at porn. I've never actually caught him masturbating, but I assume that's part of it-- and I worry it's going to destroy our relationship down the road. Should I just demand he stop? Should we try to watch pornography together? What can I do to support him?"

Ok, this is a difficult situation. First, you should know that you're not alone. Studies have shown

secretly wants her to?" No, the fantasy manifests what he thinks she wants, but he doesn't want anything she wants. Right now he just wants to masturbate, but God knows he can't choose that, she won't let him-- unless she gets hers. She might let him now, but-- it'll cost him later. No, of course he didn't ask her. He just knows. What he wants is that he *can't* have sex with his wife, he wants that he has no choice but to masturbate. "Why not just masturbate in secret?" Because then he would have chosen that. The point is not to choose.

All pornography is in the service of masturbation, duh, but here the difference is the desire to masturbate is the disavowed force of the fantasy itself. This may be hard to see as it very much looks like he wants his wife to cheat, but here's a more explicit analogue that is of

---

that 40-60% of men used pornography for over 7 hours per week, and though it's still not clear precisely what the adverse effects are, experts agree that desensitization to normal relationships can certainly be one of them. There have been critiques that porn is fundamentally misogynistic, except for the healthy pornography that treats the participants and the scene respectfully, a kind of porn which we need much more of, especially today. You should also know that his pornography addiction isn't your fault, it has nothing to do with your sexual desirability, observe how many celebrity husbands are sex addicts. You need to open the lines of communication and have an honest and open discussion about it. Perhaps there are things he wants sexually that he's ashamed to admit to you because he's afraid you'll judge him? Maybe there are ways you can share pornography together as a couple, set boundaries that open up a safe space for experimentation and play. Sometimes there are psychological factors, depression, bipolar disorder, OCD; talking with a couples' therapist is a good step.

And now I need a Silkwood shower. Is that the answer you solicited in advance? An appeal to authority, reinforced by vague misuse of misinterpreted science fiction journalism; subtly conflating porn addiction with sex addiction or anxiety about your desirability so as to assure the problem isn't *his* desirability to other women, after all, what girl wants to be the girlfriend of a guy no girls want? Not to mention absolution from any blame and a structural set up perfect for your personality-- he's broken, you're whole; you're ok, he's gonna be okay, with your help. Sounds like you want to be his mother, so it's lucky he wants a MILF.

Madness. The hope that a person is put together as pieces, bit by bit, all the other pieces are fine so let's repair the broken piece and we can all go back to our own TVs.

The truth is you didn't buy a car that had a broken engine part you neither could see from the outside nor even understood to look for. Whatever is wrong with him-- has to be wrong with him, for you. And the treatment you'll seek is whatever it takes to get him better, at your expense. "Isn't that a noble thing?" At your expense = the problem isn't you. When your teen hits a parked car you step up and pay for the damages, when you hit a parked car you check for cameras and varoom. You'll sacrifice anything for him-- as long as it leaves you intact. Which means rather than being an agent of his change, you will do everything possible to defend against his change. I'm no couples therapist but here's my recommendation: don't have kids. Or cars.

"How did this become my fault?!" Fault is a powerful word that is used to assert that what matters is the cause-- because of course it's very important to spend all the time learning about the cause because that's time not spent on what to do about it. God, Oedipus, or DNA, now it's your responsibility, and even you can't look me in the eyes and say, "how did this become my responsibility?" But you *want* to say that. So here we are. And if I know you want to say that, he knew it too; never mind love, *he knew he cannot depend on you*. So he has to depend on himself, but having not done that before it's probably not going to go well, but what choice does he have? Reverse the genders and there's the ending to *A Doll's House*. Sure, the way he's manifested his inability to love is worse than the way you manifested it, but we're not talking about him: we're talking about you. If he asks a question I will give him an answer; when you ask me a question the

320

the same form: in the equally nauseating female eroticas, heavy on the power imbalances and consumer products and totally devoid of meaningless-ness, every sexual act has an elaborately explicit backstory[61] and a dramatic consequence; every sexual act is compelled or for some other reason, it is never 100% an act based on desire alone, it is never only her choice alone. Except in one case: the sexually explicit scene where female character is masturbating while fantasizing about having sex. The biggest problem, it seems, with female fantasies are that it requires you to fantasize a second person, which automatically involves quids and quos and all debts still have to be paid. So here is a fantasy with the solution, take the scene literally: choosing to masturbate to a sexual fantasy is itself a fantasy, shot with great lighting and shallow depth of field. That's a fantasy you can get off on.

---

answer is for you. Psychiatry may have abandoned logic for   biological robes of authority, but I have quietly been doing math problems so that I never forget how. I am not going to figure out the hidden meaning in your words, I am going to pay attention to how your words are used.

Of course I'm not saying he can't be helped. I'm saying that he will not be able to change as long as you are in his life unchanged. You picked him, however he was put together; and he picked you because you'd accept it. A relationship is a new whole, not two parts. But if you keep talking about two people, then you aren't responsible.

"But I didn't *know* this part of him until now." What changed that you wanted to know it now?

Do you really want him to stop looking at porn? What do you expect he will do instead? Spend three hours a night staring at Thucydides? Now he's a sociopath, and that's not a relationship you can post pictures of. You think the fantasies that he needed porn to replace are just going to stay repressed? Porn isn't the pathology, it is the defense. If you take the defense away, what remains?

"Open the lines of communication!" say the therapists, who should know better: the lines of communication are WIDE OPEN already. *He let you see him addicted to porn*, and you responded that while it hurt you you would remain nonjudgmental, to which his reply was to keep doing it. I got the message instantaneously, and it wasn't even addressed to me, how's that for spooky. Or did you think he'd communicate by *talking*, because that's how you think unconscious fantasies and conscious anxieties are communicated, through nominative/present active/accusative? "Use your words, honey." What the hell did you just call me? Well, you want this to be true, because you're better at talking than he is, you have the upper hand, and the result will be his acting out can be taken by both of you as you're right, he's inappropriate: you win, he should feel ashamed. Nothing will change. "There's no shame in getting help." Nice try, that's not what I said. BTW, do you know what follows shame? You should look it up, it's important, and bad.

"Should we watch porn together, to be included in his fantasies?" They're not his fantasies, it's porn, you'd be included in someone else's fantasies, which would indeed make you very attractive to him. He is being told what to want and how to want, and it's working, which is why I know with 100% certainty that you may not like porn but you love TV, you are the SAME. All you have to do to prove this is wait until he starts using porn not for sex or sexual stimulation but merely out of boredom, habit, simply as a way to relax. "It's a bit different, I can watch TV with my kids." The day of reckoning for our culture will be not when it's normal to watch porn with our partners, but with our kids, effectively destroying the symbolic relationship so you can replace it with whatever relationship suits your purposes---- as opposed to theirs. Then the kids will grow up. And if that happens you better hope the Earth has an omnipotent and benevolent King, because it will have half of those. "My daughter and I have a great relationship, she's like my best friend..." Why not sleep with your daughter, consenting adults can do what they want? "Wait, I thought in this example I was the mom?" Does that matter? That's the part that derailed your concrete brain? "But ultimately symbolic ties are societal inventions, they don't really mean anything." Yes, easier to focus on meaning, and not-- how are they *used*.

Here's a true story, I was once friends with other people and one woman in our group was dared to do what she claimed she could do, which was cause herself to orgasm just by thinking about it. I'm going to allow the possibility that some of us may have been on drugs. Well, she closed her eyes, drifted off to somewhere that we could never go, and for forty seconds the only thing you could hear was her soft gasps over the sound of five heart attacks. No doubt you'll say she was obviously faking it, because, you know, that's what women do, putting on a show for the four girls and a guy, but that sounds awfully like a defense and anyway-- you'll have to take my word on this-- she wasn't faking it. Here's a question no one had the troponin left to ask her: when she has an orgasm during sex, why?

---

60 "Oooh! Oooh! I have a question! I've been dating my girlfriend for about a year now, and she's great in every way-- except that she's addicted to porn. We still have a great sex life, she treats me wonderfully, has a good job, but... but sometimes she stays up late at night just looking at porn. I've never caught her masturbating, but I assume that's part of it-- and I worry it's going to destroy our relationship down the road. What can I do to support her?"

What are you, a girl?

61

> The path of the righteous man is beset on all sides by the iniquities of the selfish and the tyranny of evil men. Blessed is he who, in the name of charity and goodwill, shepherds the weak through the valley of darkness, for he is truly his brother's keeper, and the finder of lost children. And I will strike down upon thee with great vengeance and furious anger those who attempt to poison and destroy my brothers. And you will know my name is the Lord when I lay my vengeance upon thee. --Ezekiel 25:17

Why aren't we given some backstory for Jules's character in *Pulp Fiction*? Is he authentic? I don't mean did Tarantino make an authentic character. I mean if *Pulp Fiction* was real, would you think Jules was two dimensional? A phony? I realize you wouldn't say it to his face or behind his back, but the question stands.

What do we know about him? Everything about his character we get not from a detailed backstory or informative clothing but from his actions, and if you doubt this note that he spends the better part of half the movie wearing a Krazy Kat t-shirt. For example, he's a gangster, but we see that some of Jules's gangster character is an explicit put on: after a pleasant chat about the pitfalls of massage they reach the door of their target, and he outright says, "ok, time to get into character." And of course he quotes Ezekiel 25:17--

> I never gave much thought to what it meant. I just thought it was some cold blooded shit to say to a motherfucker before I popped a cap in his ass.

--also for show. Jules is apparently not much of a Bible reader, this is the actual Bible verse:

> I will stretch out my hand against the Philistines, and I will cut off the Cherethites and destroy the remnant of the seacoast. I will execute great vengeance on them with furious rebukes; and they shall know that I am the Lord, when I lay my vengeance upon them.

A number of internet intellectuals have helpfully pointed out that translating from Hebrew into English is difficult. Not as difficult as translating from Greek into Hebrew, but that's another story. Tarantino has always explained that he (Tarantino) wasn't trying to directly quote the Bible, that it

It's easy to focus on the cheating wife and assume the fantasizing male wants to be humiliated, but why only during sex? Why not on a bus? Why not just call your Dad? I bet he'd spank you no problem if it wasn't so humiliating to him. "But it means--" You know what I think? I think your sexual fantasies, which you spend so much time trying to understand, exist so you can understand them. You want to know what they mean, to avoid thinking about how they're used.

"But----- everyone is different, the same fantasy can have a different meaning to me." Sure, if they were your fantasies, but they're not, they're someone else's, so they don't mean anything, they can only be used. You want to search for meaning so you don't have to examine your use. There's really no better example of our collective desire to get out of the responsibility for our fantasies than the prevailing pop-scientician theory for why cuckold porn is so popular nowadays: sperm competition. Competition! Only in athleisure wear America where unemployed salarymen flatter themselves as dog eat dog capitalists is pushing out the away team's semen with your travel size penis raised to the level of a competition, finally, a sport you're good at! Is there a prize at the end, oh, it's an evolutionary prize, yay team, everybody's a winner.

Never mind why you like what you think you like. If a fantasy is like a dream, a return of the repressed, then what is so contrary to your identity, so *wrong*, that the only way to even possibly imagine it is to manifest it as a shameful sexual fantasy-- if anyone saw it, the obvious conclusion would be you get off on being a loser? What, in comparison, makes humiliation in fantasy *safer* to manifest?

The unconscious wish to be humiliated is obviously there and every pop-Freudian would detect it: the husband is "castrated", the big penis belongs to the dick. But isn't this obvious? Perhaps you were supposed to detect it? If everyone knows Freud was wrong, when are the times you pretend he was right?

Why accept the meaning of castration-- and not how castration is used? Whom does the

---

was just a riff inspired by it.

But the passage Jules recites is, nearly verbatim, the opening monologue from the very 70s 1976 Sonny Chiba movie *The Bodyguard*:

> The path of the righteous man and defender is beset on by all sides
> by the inequities of the selfish, and the tyranny of evil men. Blessed
> is he, who in the name of charity and good will shepherds the weak
> through the valley of darkness, for he is truly his brother's keeper,
> and the father of lost children. And I will execute great vengeance
> upon them with furious anger, who poison and destroy my brothers;
> and they shall know that I am CHIBA, the BODYGUARD, when I shall
> lay my vengeance upon them. EZEKIEL 25:17.

What's the right way to understand this? The mistake would be to think this is Tarantino "paying homage" to movies from his childhood, or remixing old movies to different beats; and stupidity to think Tarantino is a hack. The only way Tarantino could have in intended this-- which explains his vague dismissals of the misquote-- is that *Jules*, as a child, was influenced by this movie. It's part of Jules's backstory; and this would never be stated explicitly in the movie because it's unnecessary to hm being a character, only necessary to him having character.

castration benefit? The "Father"? Really? You think he thinks you're a threat? Or do you wish you could be a threat? You think Oedipus's wish was to sleep with his mother? You think he wouldn't have preferred that his father had just chopped his penis off?

The movie may show him watching his wife cheat, but the wish is that the husband *has no choice*, even if he permits it, the wish is that *it is inevitable*. The stud forced him into a situation where his only release could be watching her have sex-- oh well, and thank God, may as well enjoy it. I am prevented from pleasing her= I have no responsibility to please her. Besides: she looks like she got what (you think) she wanted.

"No, the big penis, her orgasms with him-- it's really about feelings of inadequacy." Hold on: you want me to believe you feel inadequate because you can't *satisfy* her? Satisfy *her*? That's how you've failed her? Say you can't satisfy her-- can't you still treat her right? Why does your inadequacy get in the way of your responsibility-- or is that what the inadequacy is for? This is how the ledger of your life is constructed: you would rather "discover" you are weak, inadequate, than become a person she can depend on for satisfaction-- for love. Why should she be satisfied by you? *After all-- she hasn't satisfied you.*

Studies have shown that many men find the idea of a cheating wife sexually arousing. Studies also show men kill their wives, so you should probably not trust that they know what they want, or studies. His choice in a fantasy is a serial progression of all the previous fantasies he's been taught, starting with an airbrushed sex bunny in a provocative pose that provoked him to create an elaborate fantasy to answer the implied question, "what does she want, so I can become it?" The answers were not in the back. But the chorus of myopics, highly articulate and willfully miseducated, try to confuse him: "she's not even real!", "she's disgusting!", "low self-esteem!" But if they don't like her, doesn't that mean she's got to be perfect? Ten million fantasies of her and whoever came next vs. the cacophony of misogyny from her and your critics, and you're trapped between being told to want what you probably wouldn't like or being told you can't want what they don't like. Well? Now you've been driven to pornography out of spite.

Christey is an anagram for hysteric. Ok? Let's move on.

Obviously the cheating wife wants a big penis, right? Phew, that was easy. But she has a secret: she wants to be desired, but she doesn't want to satisfy anyone-- she wants to deprive them of their satisfaction.

In her case, her husband is the one who must be deprived, because the other guy is *already* deprived-- it's a fling, he doesn't get her, he doesn't even know her, all he gets is to penetrate her in lots of positions. I can hear your carotids stenosing, please go back to the ledger: that doesn't count. If you disagree, if you think that counts a lot, the husband loses and the new guy wins-- if you imagine a rivalry with him over her as the prize, well, then, that's why she cheated on you. The reason she must deprive her husband is that he thinks the already deprived rival would get more than he did. "My husband doesn't even enjoy the part of me that is so valuable-- that I've never given to anyone else, ever-- so I'll deprive him of the part that he considers oh so precious, even though so many other people had it before him."

"Why is she so interested in depriving men?" HA! You keep forgetting she doesn't exist. This is a fantasy. It is *imagined* that she enjoys depriving everyone of their enjoyment. He doesn't know what drives her, he is guessing, he is working it out in fantasy. Well, he would be if it was his fantasy. If it's porn, he's being told how other people want, he's making no forward progress. He is just masturbating.

Being in love with someone is impossible. How can you lose yourself, to depend on the other person? How can you allow yourself to become the object of their love? To become-- an object? Is that something you can choose to do-- you, who can't choose anything, who can't do anything? The only way you're going to do what you want is to be compelled to do it, on impulse, or for some other reason. Someone-- say, her-- has to take the power totally away from you, then you become their object, and the more it hurts, the more they have the power. You have no choice but to love her, which means you don't have to choose to love her. And you no longer have to be someone she has to depend on.

The good news for you is this is all just fantasy. No, not that your wife is not really cheating. Structuring the fantasy as if it were the woman's point of view, as if it were a real life woman's secret desires being revealed inside his fantasy, allows for an important logical consequence: the woman finds satisfaction with other, better, men. You should not miss the rage underpinning the fantasy: if she finds satisfaction with other better men *and she is not cheating*, then consequently, in real life she remains unsatisfied. The ledger is balanced. The debt has been paid. "Not tonight, honey, I have a headache." --I know, I poisoned you.

If all this seems needlessly complicated and bananas, it's because you don't see what's really driving her choices, which are, of course, only what you think are her choices and are therefore your choices: resentment.

Say you visit room 3435 of your academic hospital's pediatric ward and find a mother wearing another hospital's scrub top sitting vigil for her sick child who doesn't know he's been drinking Mr. Clean cranapple cocktail. The popular understanding is that the mom is evil and deserves to be beaten by a bus. The medical understanding, the objective, value-free perspective that refrains from imposing personal judgments on people[62] is that she poisons her

---

62 Imposing no judgments is impossible, so by refraining from imposing personal judgments, you end up imposing society's judgments, which is why everyone is told not to impose their personal judgments. "I think it's bad", becomes "it is inappropriate." It all seems so progressive, simply use a value-free judgment that only circumscribes... appropriateness. It allows for total freedom of behavior and thought, except in certain contexts where people have to get along. So you can do whatever you want in your personal life, but here at work-- that behavior is inappropriate.

Well, let's check that. Which is more inappropriate: to tell a woman she has a great rack while you're at a funeral, or at work? About the same? 60-40? It's a trick question. It is not at all inappropriate at work; it is expressly forbidden, you may as well claim it's inappropriate to stab her at work. The use of the word "inappropriate" outside of work is the correct usage-- where context matters but ultimately there are no significant formal consequences-- but it must be applied inappropriately to work so the word can later use the consequences which exist only at work.

The success of this maneuver is already evident, people nowadays get fired for inappropriate behavior outside of work. But not because of elevated standards of appropriateness. Is it more inappropriate be a Nazi today or in 1948? What's spread to the outside isn't what's considered inappropriate, but what consequences exist for it. In Germany today, being a Nazi is illegal. In America? The only one with the power to punish you for it is your job.

Of course you'll say the job's punitive outreach is only capitalism "protecting its money." But you should be precise about the direction: capitalism responds to what the consumers want, and what they want is not a higher standard of appropriateness. They do not want people to be better. If they wanted this, the market would create a service that would give them *that*. They want these things

325

own child because she wants the attention: she wants to be needed, she wants to be thought of as a devoted mother and have the praise of doctors. But if she got these things, would she stop poisoning her child? No. Why would she? The method works, and anyway what she wants is only 50% of the game. The other 50% is what gives her enjoyment, and that's what she's doing to her child. Those are connected but not in the way you think: wanting is the defense against the enjoyment.

WANTING

The wanting-- the thing she wants, "attention," "to be thought of as a great mother"-- does not give her any satisfaction, which is why she still has to add the Mr. Clean. The reason what she wants doesn't satisfy her is because it isn't what *she* wants-- it's what (she thinks) others want of her. This applies just as much to one who wants to be "a devoted wife and mother" as to the one who wants to do "his own thing", where "his own thing" is defined as what (he thinks) his freethinking band of unemployed post grads would want a man to want.

She wants what others want of her because she has never learned how to want on her own, she can't assess what she wants, so she goes with "social norms"=media because they're louder than the alternative. She thinks she wants to be thought of as a devoted mother who now has to home school her child because it's way better than NOT being thought of as a devoted mother, but you can imagine the moment the Overlords take over and maternal devotion isn't pic worthy she'll be a strong advocate for boarding school. "They agreed to pay for everything." Just not the return ticket. Huh.

Neither will she have her own sexual desires, sex with others holds no fascination for her-- unless the kind of man she wants to be wanted by happens to be sexual. Then she's "always been intensely sexual". Sexual intercourse cannot satisfy her: someone must pay.

Meanwhile she has to pursue psychic satisfaction elsewhere. The payoffs are different. She pursues enjoyment in order to be satisfied; she pursues what she wants in order to avoid anxiety. Those are two very different force vectors with different magnitudes and directions, you should draw them out every time you make a decision of your own and see which of them is driving your purchases.

ENJOYING

You might be fooled into thinking she wants the attention and ENJOYS the attention. She doesn't, otherwise she'd be poisoning herself.

So what brings her satisfaction and enjoyment? Is it just hurting the child, is she a sadist? But she doesn't hurt anyone else, neither does she enjoy hitting her child. Neither would she enjoy her child's pain if he had actual cancer. The pain of it all is incidental-- she doesn't feel her kid's pain anyway. Her satisfaction, like she assumes about everyone else's satisfaction, has everything to do with... everyone else's satisfaction.

---

only secondarily. What they want is that *the job has more authority* over our lives-- that it becomes a benevolent tyrant, that it publicly display its authority over us; and we cause this to be true by demanding *or complaining* that it is true. Of course, while we want corporate power to increase you yourself don't want to work for a corporation. You are, after all, a prothinker not a sucker; you want others to work for it, so that its power can be wielded by you passively over others. That the only such absolute authority we can imagine is a corporiathan is historically hilarious, but no other power was believable. What we want is to not to be *good*, but to be *ruled*.

Her satisfaction comes from *depriving* the child of what he needs to be satisfied: her. Her enjoyment comes from his deprivation. In other words, in her head, she isn't poisoning her child: she is withholding treatment from him. Phrased this way, she isn't acting to hurt him; she is not acting (she cannot act), and through passive aggression receives her enjoyment. She deliberately prevents the child from obtaining satisfaction from her. She WANTS the child to want her, but she does NOT WANT him to be satisfied by her or else he will be satisfied BY her and the ledger would not be balanced-- what's he done for her? He just takes, takes, takes... and you know how it ends, when he's had his fill, he'll leave her. Empty.

"You mean physically abandon her?" Physically doesn't matter in the age of pornography, by which I mean photography. He could live with her into his 90s and it still not count. The point is the abandonment of the debt-- leaving her ledger unbalanced, e.g. the last transaction reading, "And then *he* was happy..."

Contrast this with its psychological opposite: the physically abusive mother who burns the kid's bicep with a curling iron *and then* treats the child's burn, hugs him, consoles him. This mother isn't a sadist either, she derives no enjoyment from his pain (she, too, can't empathize). She suspects she doesn't have enough in her to satisfy her child normally, or else the obligatory nature of mothering means it doesn't count; so she creates a scenario where he could be satisfied by her. She wants to be thought of as a "good" mother-- where good means *more* than a mother, and derives enjoyment from being a good mother. The Regretful Abusive Husband employs the same logic: "I know under normal circumstances I could never make you happy: how about I beat you with a Smirnoff and then I take you on a trip? It would help if you could cheat on me there to explain why I had no choice but to beat you here." You enhance the satisfaction by convincing the child/wife that they deserved the punishment, it was kinda their fault too, so the love he gives now is felt as a gift. "He really does love me, he just becomes a different person when he drinks." The real one or the fake one? "Well, the bad one." Then wouldn't he quit drinking? "It's a disease." Maybe not the kind you think it is.

This is not the mom in the hospital room: she is not hurting her child to create a scenario where he bonds to her, relies on her. She doesn't care about obtaining his love, this is what everyone assumes=wishes is true because the alternative is unfathomable: she cares about depriving him.

You may be resisting this analysis. But if I told you a rich producer used that relationship in order to get actresses into bed, you would easily accept that not just the sex, but also depriving the actresses of their dignity and dreams-- of the implicit deal in their ledger-- was part of his enjoyment.

If this is the logic of the mother's satisfaction, then the logic will apply everywhere, let's check the ledger vs the doctors. She believes what those kinds of people value is a devoted wife and mother, so she tricks them into thinking she is that. The easy mistake is to think that she tricks them *only* to get them to like her, but that isn't the payoff: she derives enjoyment out of playing that role for them *and also knowing that it is a lie*-- knowing that she is depriving them of their ideal woman. In this nuance is all of the substance: she doesn't want to trick them *so as* to be thought of as a devoted mother; she wants to be thought of as a devoted mother *in order* to trick them.

At this point you will no doubt wonder if this woman is not just evil but also unbelievably stupid: does she not realize that no one in this scenario actually feels any deprivation from her? But you don't realize this is all a movie: the whole event is staged for someone else. It doesn't matter to her AT ALL that the kid has no idea she is depriving him; she is not an evil genius who has to monologue to the victim in order to extract maximal enjoyment; in fact, the only reason those evil geniuses monologued is so that the plans can be disclosed to the audience-- and her audience already knows. That the kid doesn't know what he's losing while *the audience she imagines watching does*-- this increases her enjoyment: the child thinks he is obtaining satisfaction from her (she's at his bedside with a juice box) but the audience can see she is robbing him blind.

Then you'll say that not only is she unbelievably stupid but also delusional: there is no audience watching. Don't worry, it still counts: the possibility of one is what sustains her, until for whatever reason it can't. Then she will eventually need to get caught. Not by the police necessarily: maybe by family, or social workers, or even better: the *news*, dare to dream.

In porn, a husband in a 69 with his wife might be pleasantly surprised with the way the night has turned out, what he doesn't know is he's eating another man's semen out of her vagina... and it is driving her wild. "She's so turned on!" Well, obviously; the question is: why are you so turned on? What appears to be about a power or humiliation ends up having nothing to do with either. The enjoyment of the porn is in its depiction of resentment. Not hers-- she doesn't exist. "Why would a husband enjoy eating--?" Not the husband's, he doesn't exist either. The audience's. Yours. You don't identify with a character in porn, your identification is with the image. Not a part of the image; the image. The image pornographizes resentment. Now you can finally get off, and to make sure it doesn't mean you're chaotic evil you willingly accept the shame that you might possibly be a cuckold. That you are driven by resentment of the one you love is so unacceptable that it is more acceptable to indulge it in "humiliating" pornography-- one of the most acceptably popular kinds of pornography that exists today. "It's not acceptable to me! I'd kill that bitch!" Let me guess: Glock?

The mom resents the child's ability to enjoy *her*. She is envious of the child's: desirability, happiness, ease of satisfaction. And the more noble the child's struggle, the more he can stay happy in the face of all these terrible medical issues, the more Mr. Clean he's getting. That's what she resents, and what gives her satisfaction to deprive him of. There is more satisfaction in depriving someone of something than in getting something for oneself, which is not satisfying at all.

The porn wife doesn't exist. If this happened in real life, she'd be the one with the resentment. If it's a porn, then it's the audience's resentment projected safely onto the fantasy. The manifest content may be husband eating semen, but the form is Person A enjoying depriving Person B, distorted by a power and gender reversal. That's a wish fulfillment you can get rock hard about.

BACK TO WANTING

As a not-for-profit self-improvementologist you might be tempted to get your own wanting and enjoyment into some kind of alignment, thinking this harmony will bring you happiness, and it will. But ask the kid how well that would work out for him. Perhaps you shouldn't worry so much about yourself.

Not only can she *not* want what brings her enjoyment, what she wants is the defense against it. She wants to be a devoted wife and mother-- she knows she's not, ok, but she believes she's supposed to want this. She wants it because others want it for her, and so it becomes her conscience, her identity. Wanting this-- just wanting, not even being it-- saves her from anxiety. If she wanted what she enjoyed, she would know she was a monster. The wanting is the defense against the enjoyment. "I want to be there for him." You have said it.

This is why therapy, which she has already been in continuously, consistently fails to change her: she's happy to go to therapy because *by design* it's going to fail her. Even if an astute therapist detected "on some level" she *wants* to hurt her child, the most the therapist can do is change *what* she wants. But her very problem is how she wants: she only wants what other people want for her, so it will succeed. She'll want something new for herself, based on what the therapist wants of her-- no doubt socially responsible= media approved-- but nevertheless and for sure yet another defense against what she enjoys. "I've learned a lot about myself in therapy." Then it failed as planned. "But I finally want different things for myself." Yet everyone else gets the same things from you.

MORE WANTING, BUT LESS

You should take a special interest in the form of what she "wants"; even that is exactingly phrased to get her out of any responsibility. It is, literally, "to be needed by her child." NB followed by a period. What she doesn't want, what she has staged a TV- ready felony to prevent, is being depended on for anything else. When the child is sick, she doesn't have to be a disciplinarian, a cubicle drone, a role model, a worrier-- after all, she knows full well that his current dangers are entirely under her control-- and now there's no anxiety about raising him well or car accidents or porn or math, or him becoming a bully or what college he's not going to get into.

In other words, she doesn't want to be a mother, what she wants is to be a godmother.

So when the wife says, "not tonight, honey, I have a headache," the truth is: you're thrilled she has a headache. If only you had some safe poison that you could give her to induce a headache as needed, though I will here point out that poisons have always been a woman's game, it gives the powerless some power and failures go unnoticed, so then perhaps it makes sense for you, too, and so maybe it has nothing to do with being a woman after all. But as a man, or a woman, you can't choose not to have sex with her-- you have to be compelled not to have sex. Then you're off the hook, free to masturbate or watch TV or whatever one does in a home office. "That's where I pay the bills." Then you earned it.

"Well, first of all, I've never poisoned my wife, so I can't be blamed for that, and second sometimes I do want to be free to masturbate. Why should I be ashamed of that? Is that so bad?" HA! When you proudly admit your shame, your shame is a defense. Because even though maybe you didn't poison her, the headache was all her, you did do something much, much worse: *gave her tea.* "Oh, I'm sorry you have a headache, you had a long day, do you want chamomile and honey and a giant mug you can cup with both hands?" --Oh my God, you're a prince! "Just like the book I read about that is all me!"

The tea isn't kindness, it is the right hand side of a balanced equation. It's not enough to be free to masturbate-- for which the tea would have been superfluous, he was already off the hook the moment she said headache; the tea is psychological accounting, it is balancing the ledger: in column 1 I have to pay you off so I can get my enjoyment from porn guilt free; in column 2 I have to make it true that you are indeed in pain, so that I can prove that it isn't that *you* didn't want *me.*

329

Add all the columns up and you get: "she still wants me, but I'm free to go get my satisfaction elsewhere." No, no, you don't get away that easily: he doesn't simply find porn more satisfying than sex with his wife; what the audit now certifies is that since she still wants to have sex with him (if not for the headache) but he doesn't really want to have sex with her, then she must ENJOY sex with him more than he does with her, and logically he is depriving her of her satisfaction.

"Come on, this is insane, you think people are this deviant?" Statistically no, but I think you meant devious, in which case oh God yes. This magic poison that will make their spouse just sick enough not to want sex "right now" but preserve *in theory* their overall desire, so that the ledger remains balanced, sex free, and porn positive, already exists and women spent 50 years trying to ban it and the next 50 trying to brand it, which of you enablers is honest enough to admit it?

The ledger has to be balanced, the wife must be deprived, but unless she's an alcoholic or has a glioblastoma you're going to need a more reliable strategy for giving her what she wants so that you can then go deprive her of her satisfaction. If you can remind yourself that the ledger is being kept by you, you fill in the columns, then the solution is immediate: you create a fantasy in which she is adequately satisfied by other men. Now you can have your turn.

You might pause here and tentatively retort that she is not, in reality, satisfied by any other men. You're right, but he doesn't want her satisfied in real life; but he is willing to give her what (he thinks) she *wants*: to be desired in real life. So his fantasy is used to show his desire for her, which is all he thinks she wants. You will then retort that since she is asleep she doesn't benefit from or even know this desire. It's a valid point, but you're missing the important one: who cares about her? Since he now he's shown her desire, his ledger is balanced, and he can satisfy himself.

If he had to generate these fantasies on his own he'd have a lot of explaining to do, fortunately there exists enough porn that no explanation is necessary, it's media approved and it's not his fantasy. Which, of course, it isn't.

Porn has saved you from interpreting your dreams, and there's no shame in that. If you break up with your girlfriend for another woman, she (briefly) tortures herself with fantasies of you with another woman. If your girlfriend breaks up with you for another guy, you torture yourself with fantasies of her with hundreds of men. Do you think you do this because you're 100x more masochistic? Because you want to punish yourself? You? Punish yourself? Imagine your ex-wife tells you that since the divorce, she can't stop thinking about you with hundreds of other *men*. Would you say she's punishing herself? Well? It's not yourself you're hurting, it's her, there's the form of the resentment. Your satisfaction has been compromised, so you must deprive her of hers. She may have a new boyfriend, but the fantasy re-assures you that what she really enjoys is *many* men-- her new boyfriend won't be enough for her, she cannot be satisfied by him, that slut will never get what satisfies her.

Resentment: aggression, revenge, compensation for a loss: deliberately putting a real person in these fantasies, "forcing" her to enjoy sex with strangers or sex she wouldn't ordinarily like; using her image without her consent. *Well, if I can't have you, then*--[63]

63

In this world, who can do a thing, will not

"But it's such a sad way of being, don't these thoughts make you depressed?" I'm pretty sure you don't know what sad is, that's why you added depressed, now they're clinical, pathological, they are not you, let alone real. Which is completely correct, success! The thoughts are covers for rage: the thoughts make her less real. You are erasing her, overwriting the memories with new, imagined experiences that you're not in; if you're especially unimaginative you can publicly post her nudity and let other people do the fantasizing for you; eventually years from now not only will you be over her, you will barely remember what it was like to be with her, or even what she looked like. That became everyone else's job.

It could have gone the other way. God forbid you learn she had been cheating on you for a long time with that other guy, now you're under the porch with a Glock and an acutely

---

And who would do it, cannot

I asked a girl on a youth soccer team about the kinds of daydreams she had about soccer, everyone has them, don't be embarrassed, so she told me with some embarrassment that she imagines scoring the game winning goal at the last second against great odds by a header or bicycle kick, and hearing the roar of the crowd, and then running back and hugging (=being hugged) by all her teammates. This was soccer not psychoanalysis and if she was going to spend 3 years on something she's better off with soccer, so what I lead her to notice was that she was mentally practicing touching the ball *once*. What she did not imagine-- and had extraordinary difficulty even trying to imagine-- was dribbling the ball up the field, past/through/around defenders, and then shooting a goal. She had difficulty *fantasizing* this. You can fill in the rest, but the main question is *why* she had such difficulty. Here is the wrong answer: even in fantasy, she lacked self-confidence. The correct answer is she hadn't had enough practice dribbling and shooting to be able to even fantasize what that would feel like. "That's so true." Slow down. The reason she had the fantasy she did is in order to defend against the one she didn't. She *deliberately* limited her dreams to make practice pointless, by using a fantasy that required nothing of her.

Off topic, a special case of the three body problem: if two opposing players of any mass are running towards a stationary ball and the further player's distance from the ball is less than 2x the closer player's distance, then no matter what their initial velocities or angle between them, they will both reach the ball at the exact same time. The proof is left to the reader.

"Ah, but a man's reach should exceed his grasp, or else what's a heaven for?" So you didn't read the primary source either, let me guess, you got it from a poster or your prom date's Spiral Notebook Of Iconoclasm. "A man said to the universe--" Yeah, I know.

Modern education loves the excerpt, it conveys the illusion you are reading primary sources in order to facilitate the acceptance of the secondary sources as primary. A quotation beginning with "Ah!" and attribution "Famous Authority" is all you need to think you are getting centuries of inspiration and wisdom and not what you're actually getting: a line from the defeated monologue of an obsessive cuckold, told to a harpy, about all the reasons why he never achieved the success he thought he deserved. I'll summarize: it was all her fault.

Here's the manifest content of a poem written 150 years ago set 500 years ago applicable 2500 years ago, i.e. when love and art were still a man's game: Renaissance painter Andrea del Sarto's wife Lucrezia is about to run off to meet her lover, and instead of pistols at dawn or faking a coronary he drones through 267 lines detailing the reasons why she should stay with him instead, I'll list them all here: 1. "It would help me paint." 2. "It's what I want." I don't think there were any others. The poem is often interpreted as Andrea's struggle to feel worthy of his wife as displacement for guilt over his artistic inadequacies, or vise versa, but before you concur with this dialectical exegesis you should just *look* at the poem: he's sitting hand in hand with the wife he says he loves, but it's a monologue. She doesn't get a word in, he has no clue or interest in what she is thinking or what she wants, this is a man who says he loves his wife yet tells his wife he's jealous of men who don't have

rigorous sense of moral fairness. Truth is, it's not the cheating per se-- ok the new guy had more money, a bigger penis or a better job, but he's hardly a better man-- other women wouldn't think he was so desirable-- so his desire of her doesn't count-- the cheating doesn't reflect on you. The cheating doesn't count; what counts is *that you were fooled*. There is nothing on this earth worse than being fooled. What really gets you is that all this time she was cheating-- without you knowing? She had a life you didn't even detect? There's a part of her, of reality, you were never aware of? It's like *Usual Suspects* or *Balthazar* or the opposite of *The Matrix*-- the sudden paranoid realization that there is a whole other world in which you are at best a pawn, at worst entirely absent. It's not the cheating, or the loss of her, it is the apocalypse that shows your worldview was WRONG and everyone else was in on it but you. Try to deprive her? She's been depriving you. Now you have to lock down your reality

wives. "Just think of all the masturbation!"

While he does not think to ask the woman he supposedly loves what she wants, he does assume he knows what *women* want, and so he promises that if she agrees not to cheat on him he'll bring home more money.

"But that slut does want money." Maybe, or maybe she wants money because that's all she's allowed to want, he's probably told her in a hundred different ways she is not going to get any of his time, or his passion, or his conscience, or his private thoughts-- let alone his attention to hers. What a person wants and what satisfies them may not be the same, sometimes wanting is a defense against satisfaction-- or its absence. He's the famous Andrea del Sarto: you think she's cheating on him because he's poor? Every guy with a sturdy penis wants to show her he's not a premature ejaculator *except* him: the only time she ever hears him say, "hold still! don't move!" is when she's being used as a model for his Virgin Mary paintings, this is a man who figuratively and literally splits his wife into Madonna and whore, she's willing to be both but as far as she can tell he only wants her as the former. You have to figure a woman as sexual as her at some point offered, "you know all this time I'm sitting here modeling for you I could also be blowing you? Isn't that why anyone becomes a painter in the first place?" Which means we should find the direction of the force vector: because he thinks she's married to him for the money or the fame, he is depriving *her* of satisfaction-- of the sex, of her marriage, of her individuality-- regardless of whether she even knows she is being deprived. But to balance the ledger he is giving her what he thinks she wants, which is to be desired. "My face, my moon, my everybody's moon, which everybody looks on and calls his!" I assume moon is butt.

I do find it interesting that she's helping her lover pay off gambling debts, I know I've heard that story before. You know what else I've heard before? The term "cousin" as a euphemism for "lover"-- in cuckold porn from second-world eastern Europe. When you retain the xenophobia of the past while being dragged towards the globalism of the future, you lock everyone out to limit the threats, so your family remains your only peer group. But then they also become your main rivals, this is the sad story of most immigrants to America and every mob movie. Your cousin? Your wife would spread her legs for that cocksucker in a minute if it made financial or semantic sense, but phrased that way you can pretend she has no interest in any of the bloodsuckers who aren't part of the family. Exodus makes it pretty clear thou shalt not commit murder, but when it says thou shalt not covet thy neighbor's wife, the direct object is uncharacteristically specific: neighbor=kin. The god that wanted to be loved above all the other gods that he evidently allowed to exist knew the danger of intra-familial envy; it would be an unusual and lucky to meet wives from another clan hence the curious lack of commandments against coveting them. It isn't until Luke that the definition of neighbor broadens to include everyone, but it took St. Paul starting psychoanalysis in Romans 7 to get everyone to forget about what the law says and get into the spirit of the law, and so Paul terminates the commandment at the word covet: the sin is no longer what you want but how you want. I doubt del Sarto's real life wife knew any of this but Mrs. Robert Browning was a translator of Aeschylus so I'm guessing the Mr. knew all of this: the problem isn't that his rival is

332

before hers annihilates yours-- your suicide or her murder are guarantors of truth, of your being linked in your own story. She will forever be remembered as killed, by you, for cheating. Who controls the narrative now-- and forever?

And yet you do not realize that the only thing you will be remembered for is killing her *for no reason*. "Wait a second, it was for cheating!" But you said it yourself: the cheating didn't count. Hopefully you get a fan club or an omnipotent God who certify the reason you did it, so that it had a reason, and by a logic which makes total sense to you she's a harlot who has to rot in hell while you're a martyr who will go to Heaven. Let's ask St. Luke what kind of a Heaven you're reaching for:

---

sleeping with his wife, but that his rival is sleeping with her cousin.

Please observe that the famous artist Andrea's metric of success isn't art but fame-- relative to his peers. This is the strategic long game of a man trying to keep himself at a constant velocity, i.e $dv/dt=0$. How do I know this, how do I know he planned his mediocrity in advance even as he says he wants greatness? Because what the poem is about, what he is obsessed with, isn't art but rivalries. He sees them everywhere, especially where they are not. Rivalry with the lover, rivalry with the other painters, rivalry between the other painters. Anyone who thinks he has that many rivals but isn't #1 really only has one rival, and in this case her name is Lucrezia. Andrea tells his wife an inadvertently revealing story: Raphael is commissioned to paint a chapel wall, and Agnolo (Michelangelo) says to Raphael, "you're a lucky man, because if Andrea had your money and resources, you'd be out of a job!" No doubt del Sarto had been praised in the past, but he cherishes this exchange, and you should examine very closely why: 1) it is praise from his rival to his even greater rival; 2) it praises not something specific that he had done-- which would therefore not count-- but his immaterial, ideal self; 3) how he uses the exchange isn't to inspire him to paint, or to beat those rivals, but to tell it to his wife-- as information, as if someone else's opinion of him was going to increase her desire for him, because... someone else's opinion of her increased his desire for her. To emphasize just how bananas this is: he doesn't even manipulate a big con so she sees for herself how desirable he is; he just *tells* her. "You know, I'm kind of a big deal on the internet." Oh God, I'm coming.

Some people say that it's these small, friendly rivalries that explain history's temporal and geographic concentrations of achievements in art or science, and this is usually said by those whose only achievement is saying this. Those painters aren't his rivals and Andrea isn't trying to be a better painter, consider that "Agnolo" in the poem *likely* refers to Michel Agnolo=Michelangelo, but you know who else was actually named Agnolo? Andrea del Sarto. After his father. The measure of his value is not being better than his rivals but proving that his rivals are worse than him, to his actual rival. Andrea believes he can fix Raphael's art, "indeed, the arm is wrong...thus the line should go!" This is the thinking of a critic not an artist, he thinks he knows how to improve *someone else's* art, he has weaponized omniscience to defend against=permit his impotence. A story, no doubt apocryphal but anyway known to Browning, is that one of Andrea's most impressive achievements was painting a forgery of one of Raphael's paintings so good it even fooled Raphael's assistant. Impressed? You would be. "Why not? Being as good as Raphael is pretty darn good." Ordinarily I'd tell you to ask any real artist if he'd be satisfied with that, but it's beside the point here, none of this is about art: ask Andrea del Sarto if he thought his wife would be satisfied with that. "Why wouldn't she be satisfied?" Of course she would be, God you're stupid, I said ask Andrea.

You might think that the idle dreamer who never lives up to his fantasized potential is overestimating his talent, this is wrong-- he accurately senses in himself the reasonable probability of success through effort *and it stops him cold*. The work seems massive but worse, much worse, all that work would negate the talent. If he improves through work, then he wasn't special. What will become of the girl who dreams of scoring big with a bicycle kick if she ends up becoming reliably

Therefore, what does the Kingdom of God look like? It is like a mustard seed which a man plants in his garden and it grows into a tree which birds nest in.

It is like leaven a woman received and hid in 3 measures of flour, until all of it was leavened.

Seems to me she ruined a year of flour, meanwhile her ecoterrorist husband shaded the garden and invited birds to eat what he sowed. What the hell is going on over in the Kingdom of God?

You're not going to solve it unless you see it as a logic: "therefore..." follows from the

_____

good enforcer? "Wait, what?" How do her obligations change? In which of those must she always act, not react? In which must she become-- dependable?

Neither is their nostalgic sitting together, hand in hand, his attempt at reconciliation; nor her leaving him to be with her lover its failure. The whole drama of this rivalry is the way, the only way, he can desire her. The only way to catch a glimpse of his wife as desirable is through the desire of another person. Now she's another man's woman, so he is free to desire her with no obligation to satisfy her. But the goal is not to desire her or to have her, she is his rival, he is competing against her for desirability. She was winning, so he started name dropping, "Raphael and I think my dad say I could have been somebody." I'm just as disappointed as they are.

Which brings us to his wife Lucrezia-- named after a woman who was famous for being raped by a guy named Sextus, short skirt or no, how do you not see that coming? It turned out for the best, though, some powerful men promptly commandeered her tragic story and used it as a tool to consolidate their own power, which I think by definition makes her a third wave feminist. "Come on, you've been around these Roman chicks, you know she wanted it." Ugh, how dare you. Don't you know what she wants is irrelevant?

Here's a mirror to your soul: do you get the sense from reading the poem that Lucrezia is happy? Of course you do: he seems sad, therefore she must be happy. But she wasn't, Lucrezia was well known to be a bit of a borderline. "That's a pejorative label for women, like hysteric." In these times, hysteria would be an improvement. You would think that a woman with great beauty, money, as much sex as she wants with whomever she wants and a famous husband to submissively support her would be more... satisfied-- but why would *you* think this? *No one* loved her. Worse, *she didn't know this*: so many people desired so many different parts of her, but nobody wanted all the parts of her, or even most of them. She probably convinced herself that this was normal among sophisticated moderns, and she should try to be like them and get different things from different people and fill up that way, but I'm not buying it: a person who isn't really loved by anyone feels it; just like a person who doesn't really love anyone feels it. And just so we're all on the same page, what they feel isn't loneliness. It's rage.

There's a guy downstairs who's going to sleep with his wife. Does Andrea think of himself as less powerful? More impotent? Does he think of himself as beta to the rival alpha? Why doesn't he go downstairs and kick him out, kick his ass or at least get his ass kicked? Why doesn't he do-- something? Because that guy isn't his rival. That guy barely exists. Andrea asks questions about the lover, but doesn't wait for the answers, he doesn't need them, it's enough to cause answers to exist. In fantasy the rival isn't more powerful, he is only described as more powerful. Two or three characteristics that make him "better", bigger penis, more muscles, more money, but hardly anything definite-- certainly nothing that, had the husband possessed them, would make him the better man. How could they? If he himself had them, they wouldn't count. The rivalry *fantasy* makes the lover into the rival, and thus a fantasy, he disappears; even though the guy is still going to sleep with her he disappears as a threat. In reality, the rival is his wife.

statements that occur 7 lines earlier: Jesus heals a crippled woman, and the leader of the synagogue is indignant that Jesus is working on the Sabbath. Jesus replies that everyone does certain kinds of work on the Sabbath, e.g. you still tend to your livestock, right? This sounds simplistic and Luke sounds like a simpleton, let's check how it was used.

> On a Sabbath Jesus was teaching in one of the synagogues, and a woman was there who had been crippled by a spirit for eighteen years. She was bent over and could not straighten up at all. When Jesus saw her, he called her forward and said to her, "Woman, you are set free from your infirmity." Then he put his hands on her, and immediately she straightened up and praised God.

Nostalgia, regret, if only things had been different... What he *says* in his monologue is he gave up so much in order to be with her, equating the other famous artists' wifelessness with their success. What his monologue *means* is that it's her fault, she wanted too much from him, and the work suffered. But what the monologue is *used for* is to deprive her: well, I could have been great, and now you're stuck with me. Serves you right. Enjoy that extra inch, cause that's all the satisfaction you're ever going to get.

This is why he doesn't dump her, that would be no kind of deprivation to her, hell, she might be better off; instead he maneuvers it all into a loveless marriage that seems artistic, spiritual, irreplaceable-- and sad; trapping her, forcing her to run around picking up pieces of what she should get entire from him, or someone else.

"Ah, but man's reach should exceed his grasp..." It's a lie. Man's grasp exceeds his nerve. He barely has the nerve to grasp his wife, and he's actually literally grasping her at that moment. Does this sound like a guy planning to reach?

So what should be grasp gets recoded as reach, as a fantasy; and what should be reach cannot even be fantasized. Madness. Instead of using his penis, he prefers to tell his wife what he could do if he had a phallus, so that she would become the phallus-- are you listening? He thinks he can convince his wife of all this with rhetoric.

The whole point of life is to grasp, this does not mean to be satisfied with your grasp, it does not mean to stop trying-- trying *is* your grasp, it is your minimum responsibility. *Other people depend on it.* But the man who extends his hand a few inches but *pretends* to have dreams of reaching the stars-- dreams that he is entitled to reach them if only they'd align correctly or aliens would grasp down from them-- is a fool, it is hubris, it is the kind of moral imbalance that brings down *ate* or a marriage to your mother. That Andrea says that reach *should* exceed grasp is the lie of a cuckold wanting to be cucked, it is intended not to rationalize his failed grasp but to *limit* his future grasp, it is his attempt at making noble the selfish thinking that defends his misery-- and causes Lucrezia's. He is trying to bring you down with him; strike that, your world is trying to take you down with him by giving you the quote out of context but allowing you to pretend you once studied the context, so that you don't. What about everyone else who depends on your grasp? You think they can survive on your reach? I guess that's what heaven's for.

All you had to do is pay attention in 7th grade to know that a dream deferred shrivels up like a raisin in the sun; but the sun turns out not to be structural inequalities or totalizing judgments but a strong support network that loves to say no. Walter is a jerk but his wife unhelpfully reminds him of it every chance she gets; meanwhile his sister's going to be a doctor but he informs her that she and it are stupid and she should marry this bum he knows. The grandmom has a very simple dream, and that is to not be murdered by white people and then maybe to buy a house, but in an act of contemptible arrogance dares to act on this dream and dares to actually buy a house, as if she deserved it; and of course the gods are not going to permit such an unbalancing of enjoyment to exist in the same family, so they deploy the family to put you back in your place. Ah, just like old

Indignant because Jesus had healed on the Sabbath, the synagogue leader said to the people, "There are six days for work. So come and be healed on those days, not on the Sabbath."

The Lord answered him, "Hypocrites! Doesn't each of you on the Sabbath untie your ox or donkey from the stall and lead it out to give it water? Then should not this woman, a daughter of Abraham, whom Satan has kept bound for eighteen long years, be set free on the Sabbath day from what bound her?"

When he said this all his opponents were humiliated, but the people were delighted with all the wonderful things he was doing.

You might observe that while Luke describes the synagogue leader as indignant because Jesus healed a crippled woman on the Sabbath, neither Luke nor the synagogue leader were impressed that Jesus healed a crippled woman at all, and NB Luke was a doctor. No one asked Jesus *how* he was able to do the impossible, but up for debate is *what day* he did the impossible? As if the miracle is merely a pretext for a more important discussion about workweek regulations? Are those the stakes you think Jesus is playing for? Or that Luke would bother to write about? It's not about the Sabbath.

As an aside, for the Bible eggheads who like to do "close readings of the text" except for the words: nothing about this passage implies she's 18. So maybe we should re-read this.

As another aside, the reason the synagogue leader's hypocrisy seems so obvious is because we *want* him to be a hypocrite, because few things are more satisfying to a mass of idiots than the identification of a hypocrite. It's because we are idiots. And we don't know what hypocrite means. "I do know what it means, -*crite* means critical and *hypo*- means little. He's... not very critical...of himself... enough?" You gave it your best shot. Even if the

_____

times. If there is any single physical representation of the frustration that comes with acting on your dreams only to have them sabotaged by those who can only dream about acting, it has to be biting your own clenched fist to suppress a scream, then composing yourself, and going back to serve your frustrators.

There's a story about Caesar observing that some tourists visiting in Rome were cradling little designer dogs and pet monkeys in their arms, fawning and cooing over them, and he says, "so the women of their land can't bear children?" It's easy to identify the underlying sexism, as if the patriarchy thinks women should only be having babies, but the point is that they have babies, yet these idiots deliberately misplace their affections on unworthy things. So stands the criticism; but why does Caesar even care? The answer comes in a different story: King Philip stumbles upon his young son Alexander playing the flute with great skill, so he eyeballs him suspiciously and then shakes his head in disgust: "Aren't you ashamed to play so well?" Hear it, and despair; though 100% you assumed it was another hypermasculine insult trivializing a child's natural talents, but while you're upset at the suppression of self-expression what should puzzle you is why it was recorded by the same biographer of both of those men in his biography of someone else. Alexander got the message that the only person who would criticize you for loving a monkey or practicing the flute is a person who knows what you used it to get out of, at the expense of everyone else. So he put a sword under his pillow well within his grasp and the Iliad right next to it just out of reach. Someone like him uses his fantasies to work out what he will do, while you use someone else's fantasies to get out of work. You keep insisting heaven isn't real, and then one day someone else's grasp exceeds your reach, and it enrages you, why? Because he had the nerve to try?

leader did secretly work on the Sabbath, telling Jesus to stop doesn't make him a hypocrite: he's the synagogue leader, the gatekeeper of the law, not an ordinary person, it's his duty to uphold the law, regardless of whatever sins he personally is committing. His authority that he was given doesn't require him to be sinless; his authority is by definition sinless, it can cast stones, even if the rotator cuff injury representing the authority is a sinner. You may think that an ordinary person should automatically be less of a hypocrite because he has no such duty to uphold, and you think this because you're a hypocrite.

The usual mangling of the word hypocrite places the emphasis on the bad thing being hidden, but the Greek word that Jesus uses (trans/literally: hypocrite) means performer. A hypocrite isn't a man who cheats and lies about it; he'd be a hypocrite only if he benefitted by playing the part of the kind of man who would never cheat, the benefit being not that he gets to cheat but what he gets from acting like he doesn't. Neither is it hypocritical to denounce a cheater even though you are cheating yourself, though it is hypocritical to denounce a cheater when you tell everyone how non-judgmental you are.

Being a hypocrite in the information age carries a high risk you get found out as a phony, and so professional hypocrites get someone else to do the performing for them, like a publicist or a host introducing you to the podium, "this woman is perfect," so when the threesome pic one day surfaces, you can say, "I never said I was perfect." If that's you in the picture we can let the facts speak for themselves. But hypocrisy by proxy carries an even bigger risk, the one we are eyeballs deep in now, the move from jealousy to envy: never mind whether she is perfect, who is she to deserve people demanding I should admire her? This is why the threesome pic is guaranteed to one day surface. You might have thought that in the information age we don't need anyone to publicly honor what we've done; the worth that had displayed itself in the deed would be sufficiently rewarded by honor also shown by deeds. In fact, we would wish that the reputation of the honored wouldn't be at risk by the words of the speaker, to stand or fall according to whether he spoke well or badly. It's hard to speak fairly about any man; even if you do, it's harder to get people to believe it; because people who know of his success will think it weak praise, and people who don't know them will be lead by envy to suspect exaggeration if they hear anything above their own nature. You can endure to hear others praised as long as you can persuade yourself you could have done some of what you heard. Past this point, envy comes in and declares it is false. Haters hate not because they're jealous but because they are told by an authority that they are required to recognize this person's greatness in an unfair competition they were not even allowed to compete in, which if they weren't so blind with rage would realize they didn't really want to compete in anyway. But the hater's hate in the face of the hypocrite's humility is raised as proof that the hater is a hater and worse than the hypocrite.

The post-modern way to be a hypocrite, favored by politicians, is to own it: they make it obvious that it's all a performance, a lie-- for some *other* demographic, that you knowledgeable people get to listen in on, knowing it's a lie. "He just has to say that to get elected." And a series of logical contradictions are then permitted to exist simultaneously, each lie understood explicitly as a lie because it's for those others who need such comforting lies. You would be forgiven if you thought the others who need these lies are idiots, because that sentence is literally correct yet opposite to how you used it: the idiot is you, because you need those lies to be told to idiots so that you can believe you're not an idiot. In simple terms: the target of the propaganda is them; the target of the rhetoric-- the lies that *you* end up believing, told to another demographic that is supposed to act on them-- is you. "But it doesn't make me

337

believe them." That's not their purpose. Their purpose is to obliterate the necessity of truth to you-- not to them. You're probably baffled, I'll give you a simple example you're not going to like. When former Presidential candidate Donald Trump told "his racist core demographic" of half the country the giant whopper that he was going to build The Great Terrific Wall Of Mexico entirely out of pesos, did they believe him, or did you? Now ask yourself: exactly where did you hear that you should believe him?

Sometimes hypocrisy looks so cinematically sensuous you forget that it's diabolically suicidal, had you realized what you were up to earlier you could have just masturbated to retro porn and spared your soul the heartache. In Casares's novella *The Invention Of Morel*-- and this is a spoiler for a story it is impossible to spoil-- the protagonist falls for a mysterious and aloof woman who doesn't even give him the time of day-- because she is actually a physical hologram recording from a long ago visit to the island (and now replayed all over the island, in a loop); so he gets the idea to record another hologram, this time with him interacting with her hologram (by anticipating her next moves and words, etc), such that in the new recording they will appear to be in love. I should mention that... the recording process also kills the people, and what you're seeing is their souls. Yeah. Casares was friends with Borges, and anyway there was a war on. Moving on. The problem isn't the obvious one: that the two only appear to be in love and interacting, but in reality are not. Neither is the problem that he has no idea who this woman really is/was, maybe she's a nut? Of course, real life love is like this: you never know if the woman you love is performing an identity different than her "real" one, but we say that love sees through all of this, love catches sight of her "mystical essence"; and the rest is actually superfluous. But then why does he need the machine? Under this logic, he *does* love her, whomever she performs she is; he's not fooling us that he loves her, he certainly doesn't need the machine to declare his love to be true. But what he needs the machine for is to make it true that he is not merely performing the role of a man who *is loved*. Hold on: his problem isn't that she's already dead, so she never got to love him because they never got to meet. He's a nut but not an imbecile, he knows with certainty that if she had met him, she would not have loved him, she'd have realized he was a nut. He can only *cause* her to love him the only way anyone has ever *caused* anyone to love them, i.e. by one, two, and/or three of only three maneuvers: 1) wearing her down with how much only "he" "truly" "loves" "her"; 2) pretending to be someone else; 3) staging her corpse. *The Invention Of Morel* goes with #3. The recorder is his way of generating in him the thing that she will desire; it causes-- forces-- her to be in love him. Don't worry that it's not true, for him it is enough that it appears true, because *a potential audience can be fooled into declaring it to be true.*

That is a general outline of the plot, though with a second reading and adequate paranoia you might detect that the above isn't the plot, that something else is happening, the hint is to imagine you're going to make a movie based on the book, narrative passages and internal thoughts which are the bulk of the text have to be filmed, and so the movie requires the writer/director to answer the question: how do these thoughts help advance the story? Now you have a second plot. But when you try to write the script you will shudder to discover that if the book's logic is internally consistent, then in fact *neither* of those can be the plot. Now you have a horror movie, or at least a Tarkovsky movie. And in case there are any producers out there I'll say that I've already written the script. Yes, I am aware of the French and Italian movies. Boy were they way off.

You'll say, why bother? She's dead, after all, and soon he will be, the love is doubly unreal, why not just masturbate in front of, on, or over her, which nowadays would be way more satisfying and still consistent with #3? It's a valid criticism, I suppose, but isn't being so pragmatic a little hypocritical when your entire identity is built around recording yourself acting out a scene in a film you didn't write?

It's sometimes hard to figure where Jesus stands on the truly important issues, his positions on sword fighting are wildly contradictory and many have complained he is enragingly lenient with the female orgasm, but the one sin that Jesus explicitly warns against over and over is hypocrisy, in this performative sense. Not "don't pretend you're good when you're really not" but "don't show anyone you are good." Pray by yourself, be invisibly charitable, don't look for rewards for good acts. Well, what's wrong with bragging a little, as long as you do what God wants of you? What makes this a hypocrisy isn't the personal benefit you obtain-- the desire "to be seen by others as a good person"-- that very obvious desire-- your willingness to shamefully admit to it-- is a defense for yourself against what the performance is really used for, it gives you the certainty that what I am about to say is wrong, but Jesus's overweighting of this sin-- yes, even above female adultery-- is otherwise unintelligible. The theological significance is formally psychodynamic and manifestly pornographic, and anyway literally in the passage: by appearing to give God exactly what he wants, you deprive him of his satisfaction.

Changing paragraphs here gives you a moment to digest that last sentence and even imperceptibly nod your head in agreement before I flip the dependent clauses for technical accuracy and you scrunch your face up in hell-no disbelief: you appear to give God exactly what he wants *in order to* deprive him of his satisfaction. That sounds insane, I know. I know.

"It's easier for a camel to go through the eye of a needle than for a rich man to enter heaven," which is bafflingly abstruse as it is, Christian capitalists jump through hoops to explain it away and atheist socialists duck like the Matrix to avoid getting shot in the face, but no one seems to notice that although Jesus says this line after he tells a rich man to give away all his money and the rich guy walks away dejected, Jesus wasn't saying it to him, he was saying it to *other* people. Who are not rich. Who are already going to heaven. Is Jesus a Puritan? A Jacobin? You think he thinks like you, "those fat cats are all gonna get what's coming to them, rejoice!"? He tells this rich man *whom he loved* to give away everything even though he just told him that good acts don't work, meanwhile he performs a miracle for a presumably richer Roman Centurion he either just met or didn't even meet for no money down, simply because he showed astonishing faith. Well? "Your wish is my command," secretly says the Jesus of your psychology, "but you're still going to Hell and we're going to enjoy watching you burn!"? Today's Christians spend a lot of time deciphering the camel and the needle part because symbols are awesome and we don't want to know about the rich man part, after all, it's obvious. Apparently so obvious that Jesus has to repeat himself, "clearly you kids didn't hear me the first time, I said..." The interesting fact about things labeled "a camel" is that unlike things labeled "a rich man" they have little to give up and it wouldn't help anyway, in order for them to fit through the eye of a needle *they would have to stop being camels*. Or at least not tied. "Then who can be saved?" Jesus isn't talking to an atheist, the rich man is all in on Kingdom Come, and Jesus even offers him an explicit pay off: not only will he go to heaven, there will be even more treasure for him in heaven. You're still stuck on the needle? Even if we assume a heaven we shouldn't assume commodity fetishism in heaven, so the promise of more treasure is the symbol to be interpreted, it is used to reveal why a rich man *and the other people Jesus is talking to* need to be mindful of their sowing. The loss of *money* is rendered irrelevant since it becomes capital with a high rate of return. But the *loss,* incidentally here of money-- while no one else has to give up anything, lose anything-- for him that is an unbalanced ledger no amount of future earnings can rebalance. The only thing that can count is the deprivation of someone else. You doubt it? Do the arithmetic. So he invests all his money on the poor and lives out his life as one of them; afterwards he gets 300% ROI and a dream house in Bespin; do the poor who gave up nothing go to hell? Do they go to a different heaven? Get less treasure? I understand my loss will bring me a gain, but when does their gain require a loss? *When do they have to give up who they are?* The only thing that would satisfactorily balance out his loss is the deprivation of someone else. Of whom? The poor have nothing else to lose, so close your Bible and open your ledger: it will have to be God.

On a traditional balance sheet you add both columns up at the bottom and then compare profit to loss, but in the distributed ledger of madness your gain isn't reliably someone's loss, but their gain is always your loss and your loss is always someone's gain. A Scrooge makes some loans, then one day there's sudden inflation. Even if everyone pays him back in full tomorrow, he lost and everyone profited *from* his loss. His only hope is that they don't pay him back tomorrow and higher interest rates will make up for it. But don't be tempted to think that all he wants is an inflation adjusted return. It only works-- the system only works-- if he gets his money back at the expense of everyone else. "No, he only wants to make his money back." No: the system doesn't work if he only makes his money back. Someone has to be deprived. "That's the problem with capitalism." Actually, that's the problem with socialism, but anyway capitalism is amoral, not immoral. The problem is you.

The other theological implication is the one that forms the basis for the contemporary Christian-- well, monotheist, where mono is defined as ≤1-- idealization of God: hypocrisy requires a god that can be fooled by appearances. That god may be Yahweh or it may be "the media", but whoever it is it can't be omniscient and *therefore it must logically be omnipotent.* It sees appearances (is fooled by them) and *declares* you to be a good person, and the whole purpose of doing this isn't to get away with anything but to deprive him of your dependability. However, Jesus's explicitly repeated description of God is that God will see your hidden acts of charity or prayer-- or see through your hypocrisy: he is omniscient-- not omnipotent.

The Christian hypocrite's rebuttal to this is that God is both omnipotent and omniscient, "of course God knows you are being hypocritical." Excellent parry with the progressive tense so God won't use the present plus a noun. Well, you have to take the rebuttal all the way to see it is part of the defense. "God isn't fooled, he sees through your hypocrisy," but inside your head he then sees the desperate all-too-human battle between being good for him and also wanting to look good for others, and will see that after all there is *some* goodness, and that at most you are only trying to steal little bits of personal satisfaction back, ok you're petty and certainly you're sorry but such a theft couldn't possibly cost God anything. Right? But this only concedes God can see the tissue beneath the skin-- but not further than that; you've let him discover your fascia so he doesn't see you're full of crap. At the same time, by *saying* he can see through hypocrisy, you promote the *public* belief he is omniscient. Add it up: you've fooled him into declaring you good; everyone agrees he would know.

If you doubt you are this sinister, note that the form of this theft matches the form of your defense: God is the master, to you he is omnipotent but not omniscient, he doesn't know he's being robbed, in his ledger the theft doesn't even register but in yours it counts as gigantic, not because of what you gained from him *but how much your ledger records he was deprived of.* It's very easy to deliberately misunderstand this so I'll state it explicitly: you want an omnipotent

340

master so you can manipulate him into declaring you to be something-- this is ok, you accept the shame of it; but the purpose of having an omnipotent master is to be able to steal from him. It is the only satisfaction that's possible.

Part of the difficulty of Luke's passage is that it is so obviously *about* hypocritical Sabbath violations that you don't think it could *be* something else. But it is indeed something else. Just look at how the words are used. It appears that Luke draws an analogy between healing and untying, as if there is wisdom in parsing the similarities and differences between the meanings of those two words-- e.g. they are both kinds of work that maintain the health of their multiped, and therefore can be permitted on the Sabbath. But while the synagogue leader says healing, Luke *the doctor* doesn't say healing, he uses the word untying, twice. What Luke's Jesus textually (not analogously) does is *untie* the woman, exactly as the leader unties his ox. There is no analogy at the level of the verb because it is *literally* the exact same verb, the analogy you have to interpret is elsewhere-- at the direct object: ox and woman. They're not both sick or both thirsty, they are both disabled. They have no power.

The thing to notice is that while the leader of the synagogue is angry at Jesus for healing a woman on the Sabbath, he doesn't tell Jesus to stop doing this. What he does do is tell the people not to come to be healed on the Sabbath. You're not going to like this parallel, so brace yourself: he doesn't tell the rapist to stop raping, he tells the woman to stop asking for it. I realize that in this case she was actually asking for it, but stay with me.

This is why Jesus calls the leader a hypocrite, not because he wouldn't also untie his oxen on the Sabbath, *but because he wouldn't then go up to the oxen and tell them it was their fault they got untied.* In all of the other 6 or 7 cases of Sabbath healing they blame only Jesus, and NB all of the other victims were men except for one other woman, who was elderly, unconscious, and at the request of her master. "Under whose authority does he do this?" is the only thing the leaders want to know. To be clear, the answer is irrelevant, only that there is an answer; the problem isn't building a prosecutorial case against Jesus, the magistrates have already decided he's getting executed Athenian style= by Popular Demand and for no logical reason, the problem here is how to explain why they didn't stop him in the first place. Those male victims can't be blamed because male desire to be healed is sufficient authority, but despite being lawyers they are deliberately hazy on whether that would make it a right or a privilege. Given that no one seems at all surprised that Jesus has the power to heal people, it is very interesting that no one ever asks if Jesus has a duty to heal people, and this is the very reason the leader tells the people not to ask for it: it would mean the people had a right to it but had been deprived.

The gatekeeper of the law pretends the violation is the Sabbath, when the real violation is healing a woman *at all*, as if her desire counted. It doesn't. *She can't consent to her own untying.* A man could; but as there are no men to speak for her, the only one who could consent for her is the synagogue leader. The rape victim is blamed for her rape not to protect the rapist-- nobody likes that jerk anyway-- nor to "tacitly permit rape" for future jerks-- but to protect the system that was supposed to protect their oxen, but failed.[64]

---

64 Victim blaming has been around for millennia, so you'd think by now we'd have perfected the technique, but all that's really changed is what we use it for, which is the opposite of what we used it for, and exactly what it was supposed to be for, tell me if this sounds familiar: if a woman is raped, say, out in a field, it's the man's fault. If she's raped in the city, however, she's blamed, because since no one heard her scream, she must have wanted it. "Objection, conjecture!" Overruled. "Then the defense rests." Court adjourned, hand me a rock. "Do I still get my fee?" Of course,

To be clear about the important nuance which is everything: what matters here is how her status as disabled obligates everyone else to her, and this will not be intuitive because it is not how our society is structured-------------- yet. [2.20] Jesus isn't healing free men on the Sabbath, which, although against the law, does not *obligate* other people to stop him; now he's kicking open barn doors and freeing tied women, *other men's oxen*, in fact he's claiming they're actually *his* oxen, and everyone is *supposed* to stop him, and no one *can* stop him. The way Jesus has handled women-- other people's property-- is a threat to the society. Faced with such a threat over which the synagogue leader should have all the power but seems to have no power, he pretends that the women have a choice-- to be very clear, I don't mean her desire is detected, deduced or otherwise recognized; it is asserted as cause for why Jesus was able to do

---

you're paid to serve the law.

You might think the above Deuteronomy law parallels the modern short skirt logic, except that no one helpfully recommends she not live in cities. Nothing here is about her safety. The only difference is whether she will be blamed. So "what you wear has no effect on whether you are raped" and "since you can't control other people, you shouldn't dress like that" seem like two opposed sides of a debate, you may continue yelling-- but they quietly combine to form, "it is true you can't control whether you are raped, only whether you are blamed. You don't want to be blamed, do you?" But I still get raped? "Can you please focus on the bigger picture?"

Seeing this as a sinister plot to let men get away with rape requires you to ignore that even though in the city the woman also gets blamed, in both the city and the field the man is executed. And saying the law should protect, not blame, the victim is literally correct, except the victim isn't the wife: it's the husband.

What's counterintuitive is that though the logic of city rape seems archaic and exceptionally unfair, the exceptional case is actually the thoroughly modern field. If the assumption is that all extramarital genital contact is wrong, then the law has given *women* an immunity in a special case-- not from the penis, but from the blame. Why? Because in contrast to the conventional line that women were merely the property of the man, in fact she's *not* property, because otherwise she could never be to blame. *She has some power to act on her desires.* She's more ox than merely box-- the husband, and by extension the society, are responsible for and to her. If the Bible contains any reliable statistics, women compared to men have a significantly higher incidence of extramarital genital contact, consensual or not, though I'll admit the math doesn't work out. Sure, it's not 100% up to them, but no one can deny that women have desires to be or not to be contacted, just as thirsty oxen may wander off into other fields if they get too hot. *No one thinks they possess knowledge. They can act.* Knowing this, the expectation is that someone-- everyone-- is going to keep them tied. And most of the time they're successful, for all of history up until the Reagan administration one of the first things a boy learned is how to tie a really good box knot. Any secondary sources feminist will assure you that "victim blaming" serves to control women's behavior, but even a cursory glance at the 1971 primary source shows that it isn't for controlling the victim's behavior at all, and not to benefit the rapist, but in order to obliterate society's responsibility to the victim. And this has been true since Deuteronomy. In the *default* location of the city, where women are the responsibility of the husband and the community-- it has to be the wife's fault, because otherwise the husband and the community are guilty of not keeping the penises away from her. The person to be protected isn't the woman, or the rapist/adulterer, but the community, from the charge of negligence. That's *The Scarlet Letter*.

But in the field-- i.e. the metaphorical case in which there is no rope long enough-- and thus no one could be negligent-- to preserve the woman for future legal penetration, it is codified to be the "rapist's" fault no matter how much she wanted it. This is trickier than it sounds, because if rape is by definition sex without consent, how can a *complicit* sex act in a field be made into a rape? Surely I can't be the only person who's ever been drunk? By physically *taking away* her default ability to

342

it and no one stopped him. Yes, women, your desires matter, just not right now; defer your desires until normal business hours. Please, ladies, control your Jesus. And Jesus laughs, wait a second, now you want to pretend you care what the woman wants? As if ten minutes ago she wasn't tied to a post? The only reason you're blaming the ox is because you were negligent in keeping it tied. And you don't want to get in trouble with ther farmers.

Two millennia later it makes no more sense to blame the synagogue leader for keeping the woman tied than to blame the woman for not untying herself, these are judgments we can't make; we can only blame him for pretending she wasn't tied while he made a living off of rope-- as we could blame her if she then went around pretending she untied herself. And any interpretations we give of the story end up being irrelevant, the text is immune to them,

---

consent.

So according to the laws of physics, if a woman falls in a field and no one is around to hear it, did she make a sound? Answer: no. Sound requires ears. It doesn't matter what she wants, that doesn't count. Since in the field we can't *know* what happened, we are omnipotent-- we have the power to declare things true. So we *say* she doesn't have the power to consent-- she doesn't have the power to change his legal relationship to her, to make a technical battery into a voluntary intercourse. Never mind the skirt or her desires, by definition it is a rape. In a city, if no one hears her consent or protests, could she have consented? Of course. We have ears to hear, let us hear. She generally can consent-- even if it's with a moan. In the city the expectation is we are omniscient, but not omnipotent; we *could* hear, and since we heard *no-thing*, no protest, she must have consented, with a moan. You might say I'm wrong, I'm conflating desire with legal consent, that whatever she might want or do, no woman back then had the right to choose her sex partner or the power to consent. But this is logically incorrect. She does have the power to consent, because that's what the law says: in the city it's adultery *because* she consented.

You might allow that taking away her consent was for her own good because in the field the drunk woman in a short skirt is at higher risk because no one is around. So as an extra layer of protection men are told: never mind what you think she wants, no trespass: out there she cannot consent. But this is hardly a preventative: the guy is subject to execution no matter where it happened. So in the field, what is she at higher risk for? By taking away her power to consent there, she's not necessarily any safer from rape, but she is immune to being complicit in adultery. The risk to *society* these laws address, therefore, is her promiscuity, not her rape; the point isn't to let men get away with a hypothetical city rape by labeling it adultery-- he dies anyway-- but to make a woman's very problematic unchaperoned field promiscuity into a rape-- no one's fault but the rapist's; to be extremely precise: not not *her* fault, but specifically not *society's* fault.

The goal isn't to protect her from rape-- nothing but Scanners can protect a woman from rape-- but to preserve her goods/goodness from being labeled an unmarriageable slut in contexts where her desire is unknowable (field); and to protect her owners from the charge of negligence when they should be watching her (city). If you follow this logic, then a slight reversal is revealing: sluts can exist in the city, but cannot exist in a field.

So it's off to college, where one can still play the field.

There's no doubt that affirmative consent may make an overzealous penis think twice before penetrating, and in this sense they are perhaps a necessary protection for defenseless women. But it's not *for* defenseless women, affirmative consent has a much more tyrannical purpose, and please observe that women who believe they have education AND no power are generally for affirmative consent, but women who believe they have power regardless of education are against it. There's a reason for this: neither know what affirmative consent is. Ask-- well, anyone-- to define affirmative consent, and they will 100% confirm that affirmative consent requires explicit verbal consent, i.e. and not merely e.g.: "Yes." No. It doesn't. Almost no college policy uses "affirmative" to mean

and it would be correct to say that the interpretations are nothing but an expression of despair over this fact. But you don't have to consider everything true. You only have to consider it necessary.

The gatekeeper of the law didn't tell Jesus to come back another day, he didn't tell Jesus anything, he told the women. This is his only concern. He doesn't care about Jesus, Jesus will be executed, for rape or adultery it matters little, he's as good as dead. The struggle is between the gatekeeper of the law and the rest of the oxen who strive after it. One ox just got free, now the gatekeeper has to deal with a stampede, so to them he makes a suggestion so reasonable you almost accept it, he points to a little ox door and says, "see, it's wide open, it's possible on another day, just not now." Oh, well, that seems ok, I'll wait-- hold on a second,

---

"parley", the radical policy of "affirmative consent" is pretty much taken directly from 1980s porn: acting like she wants it. It's hardly even a change, affirmative consent policies just move the official standard up from merely deferring to her resistance to actively looking for some kind of... agreement. But it doesn't require an unequivocal signal, let alone vowels. This single, ubiquitous misunderstanding of affirmative consent is important and *on purpose*.

It seems obvious that what the college would want is to decrease the incidence of rape, but this is absolutely not what it can want. The incidence of rape is *already* low, from the time of segregated colleges, through to segregated dorms, down to unsegregated bathrooms, and soon etc, by any and every measure rape has fallen. But there's a new problem: unlike in the rapey 1980s, the colleges now are responsible for the oxen. They are its *property*.

Assume the premise: that there's a lot of non-consensual sex that's been historically passed off as just "sex." If affirmative consent worked exactly as described-- preventing the portion of sex that is not affirmatively consented-- then logically it would lessen the amount of sex. Anyone think that it's less?

It may be that women are more affirmatively consenting to sex that would have happened anyway but under different pressures, the true benefit being that they themselves have been given the language to feel more sure about it. They're empowered, they made choices about their sexuality. That's great. How many women are we talking about? 1% more? 30%? A number >50% requires you to believe the average woman is not just powerless but an idiot, and I for one refuse to live in a world where you exist.

The trick is to imagine the analogy taken to the hypothetical extreme, which fully immunizes the college from any claim of negligence: the campus as a Deuteronomy field. The man is told: no matter what she wants, no trespass. No sex at all. Sure, out there in the world of cities women can consent to sex in all kinds of ambiguous ways and thus carry some of the responsibility, but here in the field of the campus, the woman *loses* all power to consent to sex. If it happens, she could never be responsible.

Precluding all sex on campus is a non-starter, so instead of taking away all her power to consent like a true field law, the college takes all of it except "affirmative consent". Men are told: it's still mostly a field law, no trespass, *except* for this. You might think I've sneakily flipped around the college campus to equate to the field instead of the city just to make my point. I haven't. Campus literally means field.

You'll retort that a coed could still physically have sex without giving verbal consent, it happens all the time and there are several movies about it. NB again: she did give affirmative consent, just not verbal consent, which is unnecessary. The real question is when is even her verbal consent still not consent, when are we at a true field law? That's easy: when she's drunk. You're going to ask how drunk? Go back to Deuteronomy: in the field, she's drunk by definition. What she does or wants is irrelevant.

344

after 18 years, now you're telling me all along I had a choice? "Yes, this door was intended for you. Now I am going to shut it."

Everyone knows that blaming a woman's short skirt for her own rape at a frat party is some patriarchal neurolinguistic programming to get her to I guess wear pants and avoid parties. Of course, there is a (small) chance she could be raped. But the greater risk is that the sex falls in a psychological grey area for which she feels partly responsible. So things are reduced to a binary. "Did you say to him, 'I want you to have sex with you?'" Well, no. "Then it's rape. It's black and white."

But it's not. What he did is immoral, if anyone even knows what that means anymore, and he should feel guilty. But it isn't rape. "But it is definitionally rape, because she did not consent in the only way she is privileged to do so and he was allowed to accept." Well, you got me there.

I am aware that a loud criticism of "affirmative consent"= verbal consent is that it will unintentionally= intentionally Ms.-label more men as rapists. This is a red herring. While a man is required to obtain affirmative consent, the woman isn't required to give it; she could still have sex with someone without affirmatively consenting. But to the omnipotent entity of the school it still *counts* as a rape. Not in theory-- in practice. If you doubt this, you have never been on either side of an epidemiological study. Imagine you're a study participant: "Question 1: Have you ever had sex without giving affirmative consent?" Ummm, what do you mean by-- "I'm not allowed to elaborate, just answer as best you can." Yes, it's that bad even in medicine; in the social sciences it's... not even wrong, and if you don't know what that phrase means, look it up. It doesn't matter that no arrests will be made or that she was ecstatic or that the man is never informed of the new data linking him to rape; or that the study relies on "affirmative consent" being misunderstood to mean explicit verbal yes-- even assuming the scienticians themselves know what it means; the hyperspecific result is that it increases the numerical incidence of statistical rape. In the campus-- the one place they are most likely to be sluts, the one place they are very *unlikely* to be raped, and the place where neither parents, employment, judgment or fear can "protect"=control them-- the reverse situation is created. In theory affirmative consent gives the drunk girl at the party greater safety; in practice the policy is an uncontroversial warning to mid-level psychopaths to actively look for her consent or else; but in reality consenting becomes a power taken away from all women by some other omnipotent entity, and privileged back to them in limited circumstances. It seems backwards, I know. This doesn't mean more men won't be "wrongly" accused, that's irrelevant; it certainly doesn't mean unwanted penetrations won't still occur, also irrelevant-- the omnipotent entity is not trying to protect the woman from rape. Meanwhile the wished for=projected paranoiac anxiety about the ubiquity of rapes becomes manifested as a statistical reality.

The consequences of all this Matrix semantics: 1) activists are in fact advocating not for more power but to *give up* their power, to the college, they are causing to exist some other omnipotent entity; 2) powerless women think they got what they wanted, but will find it useless; 3) women with power, who think explicit verbal consent goes too far, obtained in *actual* affirmative consent the kind of policy nudge they actually would have wanted. Off topic: do things usually go the way power wants them to go? 4) the college is given the power to declare what is true. On topic: do things usually go the way power wants them to go?

345

The patriarchy-- and we should stop saying that word, power isn't imposed from above but offered like alms from below-- benefits not from rape but from being the one that decides what *counts*.

You can parallel this with the standard argument about patriarchal rape tolerance: "she wanted it" is the lie rapists tell themselves. But are they lying, or do they really believe it? As a defense in criminal court it's obvious why it's asserted; but if most rapes go unreported and there's no such thing as guilt, what purpose does "pretending" she wanted it serve? If rape is a "crime of violence", why would they need to tell themselves she wanted it? Why do they need her "unconscious" desire in the form of intoxication or a short skirt, or even the general principle that "all women secretly want it", in order to act?

Because there *is* a fundamental psychological distinction between "date rape" and "violent rape" even if the distinction doesn't exist in reality: the public's fantasy about the relevance of a woman's desire on his *ability* to act. In violent rape, the act is done because he assumes she lacks desire. But in the date rape, it can be done only if he assumes she has some desire. You resist this because you're trying to apply it to rape, or even hypothetical rape, but that's not what this *public* logic is for: not a hypothetical date rape but a hypothetical discussion about hypothetical date rapes, i.e. victim blaming in the abstract. Because the man engaged in a hypothetical discussion about hypothetical victim blaming cannot imagine acting on his own desire-- any desire at all-- in any way-- he can only imagine acting on someone else's desire *and then he can't imagine refraining from doing so--* he has to imagine the hypothetical man also could only act on the imagined desire of a hypothetical woman. To order the logic correctly: the hypothetical aggressor in a date rape can be imagined to have been able to act **only if** he truly believes she kinda sorta wanted it; whereas the hypothetical aggressor in a hypothetical "violent rape" doesn't care what she wants, because he is imagined to be able to act on his own desire *period*. You can see this binary played out in black and white in the media imaginary of "date rape" vs. "violent rape": in the first, the aggressor is white; in the second, he is black. To anyone whose brain obeys the media, black men can act on their own, they haven't been castrated. "Is that a dick joke?" No, it's psychoanalytic history, and ancient history, but things are about to get post-racial. What I did not expect but should have expected was how popular cheating wife porn was among blacks, to be specific: the pornographic fantasy of a black wife cheating on her black husband with a black man, for a black audience. Then I watched a few days of network TV, where the black characters' desires and their non-actions were no different than any of the white characters-- a true parity had occurred in media where the role could just as easily been played by either race-- or gender-- but not because racial prejudice was giving way to individual character but because all characters were devolving away from anything individual, distinguished instead by the vicious binary of wanting and enjoying-- of the ability or inability to act on desire. An example: on TV no matter what the race or gender, 90% of all characters work for someone else, and for a salary, even if it is huge, and even if there's a pretend competition for "the bonus." The only characters who derive income directly from their own activity are either failing at this, tragic, or the bad guys.

There will be no shortage of unemployed people who wish the college could extend its power over students out into the world the way work has; so that the field laws apply to students who are only incidentally at an off campus bar, or only incidentally online learners. But what about post graduation in the city=the world? The parallel to the Deuteronomy laws reveal why field laws don't apply to the city: they refer to an unmarried but betrothed woman. Shortly after graduating to the city, women in the aggregate are essentially coded as betrothed, even if they haven't matched yet. When they are out in the world, their desires have to matter otherwise their commitment would not count. If you retort that many post-grads stay single and don't marry, you need to go re-read your feminist conspiracy theories: marriage, and employment in the capitalist system, are the same. You're married to your work. You're not a slut, are you?

Unequivocally still true, for men everywhere and for women everywhere but the field, power includes the ability to consciously send out ambivalent or even conflicting signals; the threshold of explicit verbal consent there would neutralize it. Women would have, practically, less power. This is not a consideration in college; a college girl's sexuality is potent but hardly powerful, the only thing she can use it for is sex. "Not to get pornographic, but she could use it to get a better grade." Is your porn on VHS? Nowadays everyone's getting an A anyway.

In a fixed exchange rate, bad money drives out good money. How often we toss it aside, stretch out our hands for what is new!

– Aristophanes

I guess this is a good time to tell you about my lunch.

1 can beans, washed (rotation)

6-8 oz meat, cooked and chopped (rotation)

½ avocado

1 bell pepper

½ chili pepper

handful nuts (rotation)

handful olives

handful mushrooms (cooked)

amount feta cheese

too much turmeric

too much paprika

handful basil

amount oregano, sage, coriander, mint, dill, parsley (rotation)

amount olive oil

Place in 8x4x3 glass baking dish. Mix. Serve with 5oz red wine.

Some general comments:

Studies have shown that Yellow contains Red and Green. Other studies were not able to replicate those experiments, pure Yellow did not separate, and they alleged cross contamination. Red supplementation failed to increase Yellowness. Green has consistently been observed to contain no Red, suggesting that Green and Red are mutually exclusive; but basic science investigations have determined that Red and Blue are "structurally opposite", Red consists of "stretched waves" and Blue of "compressed waves". Many were quick to make the connection that Green must therefore be a variant of Blue, which was enough to convince them to take Blue supplements, hoping to become more Green. Results have been mixed. People are dismayed. Then anecdotal reports observed that high amounts of Orange made people more Green, is Orange the answer? Researchers caution that these were mostly Indigo people, who spend a lot of time outdoors surrounded by Green. (Having replaced the Woads, Indigos are peaceful and content with communal life; some scientists believe they are not actually a separate group.) Nevertheless, many are passionate and adamant about Orange supplements, likely because of this very association to the Indigos. Others still swear by Yellow, and laugh at the Orangotangs, disparaging it as a lifestyle.

"It's very simple: you have to listen to your body." I've seen your body. It's lying.

The three principles guiding my lunch are a) I'm going to eat the same lunch every day, such is life; 2) it should thus at least have a lot of diverse ingredients, that can be easily rotated, not for taste but to maximize exposure to the good and minimize exposure to the bad; c) I need to eat a lot, I deadlift. Two times my body weight for 10 or eight times my age for 2 if I want to impress my reflection. Double overhand, no straps, I don't want a biceps tear and I need the grip strength for strangling.

No person reading this description will think this is a delicious lunch. You won't want to make it, let alone eat it. I was the same way. I used to want something tasty, prepared by an expert, whose ingredients I could disavow. I always got what I paid for, nothing more, nothing less.

The key to making this lunch palatable is never to snack. Then you will look forward to it. You will be glad to eat it. And glad you ate it. And relieved you didn't snack. But if you just pop a little something into your lie hole because your primitive hypothalamus can't tell the difference between a craving for salty oils and straight up thirst, you won't want it and you will not be able to eat it. We could argue these points, I guess, but it would be an argument in which you are trying to assert as good what you enjoy vs. trying to learn to enjoy what's good. We are never going to agree on anything, including lunch. Try this, or don't.

Beans: daily rotation through kidney, black, lentils, garbanzo, etc. "Don't you get gassy?" Canned and then washed, and I drink 20 oz of water just at lunch. Thanks for asking. No.

Meat: whatever dinner was yesterday. Chicken, beef, salmon, cod, crustaceans, etc. I usually have a few hard boiled eggs made in advance to add when I don't have enough meat. Yes, I eat the yolk, even when it's green. In a clutch: 2 cans of sardines or tuna. "That doesn't sound very appetizing." It's not supposed to sound at all. I don't Pavlov at the crackle of inorganic polymers or the package they're in.

Bell pepper: they're crunchy, hydrating, and I can tell myself the secret to my lunch is nightshade. "Aren't you afraid of Hannibal Lectins?" He's 5'5 and a psychiatrist. Pretty sure I can take him.

Avocado: mashed into the meal. It's a lubricant not a photo op. Same with the feta, cow milk is available but sheep or goat is creamier.

Olives: I guess they're good for you. I have no idea why, beyond a meaningless soundbite

349

(monounsaturated fatty acids inhibit LDL oxidation, or something). If I don't have olives I put in olive oil. Sometimes both, out of spite. The ancient Greeks used olive oil for bathing and wrestling, not eating, which was one of many things they did backwards. I only use California olive oil because I've seen *The Godfather II.*

Spices: scienticians say "turmeric", aka curcumin, aka cumin, none of which are the same thing, has "benefits" in "liver" "function" and "Alzheimer's", but I don't think those words mean what they think they mean. The science is about as reliable as a penny stock promotion, but Indian people swear by it and the East India Company profited from it, so you can pick your appeal to authority. I use a lot, it is also supposedly synergistic when mixed with paprika and every weightlifter could use more powders in their life.

Herbs: basil always, and then others variously. Yes, it says a handful. I'm not sure on whose authority it was decided that basil should be sprinkled in a countable number of tiny flakes while half a fibroid of lettuce is an acceptable garnish for a creamy ranch dressing and crouton soup, but I dissent. Those herbs are vegetables, and I'm eating them as such.

Mushrooms: various. Downside is they taste like mushrooms, upside is bears eat them and bears are indestructible, downside is bears are also psychopaths. I used to be allergic until I stopped caring about my feelings.

Wine: "But—!" Shut it. I dilute it 1:4 because I'm not a barbarian. "But--!" I said shut it.

I don't use condiments except lemon, it has to work on its own. You can make something taste better, but you can not make it better. Most sauces are added to things that are terrible or terribly prepared, stop drowning your apathy in flavors. If you're going to put barbecue sauce on your 5 year old's chicken nuggets so you can get a quiet minute to immerse yourself in other people's lies, you may as well just introduce him to anime.

Chili peppers: because of the avocado, they won't be as hot as you'd expect. They also (allegedly) prevent bacteria as it sits in the car. "Why not just bring your lunch inside with you?" Because I'm not a 6th grader. Or Norwegian, or an extrovert, I eat in the car. I even brush and floss after. If I can find an isolated spot in the woods, turn off the engine and shut the windows, it's so quiet I can hear my own synapses. Moving to the passenger seat, I go into my private space where I have my books, eat the food that alone is mine, and for a little while I feel no boredom and forget my troubles. I read, I write, I drink a lot of coffee, and every day I do a little math. And because they say no one understands anything unless they retain it, I do the odds and the evens.

There's something you should know about me. Have you ever gone to a party, a rally, a religious service, a concert, and there's a really positive energy in the crowd, former strangers with their own different lives and rhythms start getting into synch; and maybe someone starts singing, and then it's two people, ten, a hundred, the song spreads-- suddenly it all clicks, for these moments there's a collective sense of existing together, everyone connected to each other through the song… our differences melt away, the whole crowd unites, finally becomes a community, one body in one moment, lead by a common passion, all of us part of something transcendent. And we sing as one…

Well, I don't ever get that feeling at all.

I don't have to be the leader but I'll be damned if I'm a follower.

"He seduced me." "She came on to me." "It happened so fast." "I was drunk."

It takes two to tango, they say, yet the first rule of tango is that the man leads, even if the woman has way more experience than him, which in America is pretty much always.

The second rule of tango is that though the dance can be improvised, there are very specific forms and moves that are allowed and... required. Meanwhile, the third rule of tango, never to be said out loud by anyone who wants to tango, is that only women really enjoy the tango, the main reason the men even put up with it is because that's where the women are. So there's your metaphor: women want controlled sexuality with the appearance of male power, and men will dress like a matador to go one on one with an ox.

"You're just saying that because you're American, in Latin countries we learn to dance as children, it is in our blood." It's not in your blood, it's on your calendar, you're two generations behind us, we once had dance numbers in all of our war movies and our cowboys sang ballads before gunfights. Then we all got access to unlimited credit, so choreographed seduction skills like holding a boom box over your head became unnecessary and even... creepy. "He, like, wrote me a *poem*," says one girl to her cringing roommate as she's checking the locks for forced entry or ejaculate, the only thing more unsettling would have been if he had cut and pasted the letters out of magazines, or eyelids. Dance? Why bother with dance when you can just buy her stuff, or tell her she can buy stuff, especially when you don't have to pay for it until eventually? Will happen to te, too, tu performative socialism is temporary, socialism is never as tempting as the possibility of having it all, unless socialism is your way of making others have less. Better look into your heart before you claim to care about the masses.

"Are you saying women will do anything for money?" No, I'm saying TV is saying this, and you'll eventually agree, including if you're a woman. "But I don't even watch TV." HA! Name me five TV shows you don't watch and their basic premises and what the characters look like. You seem to know a lot about what you don't know anything about. Kind of like science. Hey, do any of those shows feature dancing?

Tango is "acting out", it is a metaphor for the seduction process: recognizing a woman's secret desire and overcoming the obstacles to her submission. It is the only art in which the artist is in danger of death. But why the pretense there are obstacles? Perhaps the real purpose of the tango is to pretend that there are obstacles.

"But there are obstacles. Women are taught that sexuality is wrong, taught they have to be pure, taught to deny their desires..." She can do a standing full split in heels with a partner of the right physicality, but I'm not supposed to infer that she's been practicing being seduced her entire life? Here's an old joke: How can you reliably tell if a woman likes you by looking at her feet? If they're by her ears, she likes you. Get it? See, the joke is that a blowjob is not reliable.

No woman wants to be conquered. She wants to perform the role of conquered. She wants him to perform the role of conqueror. "But then don't you both kinda know it's fake?"

Look around as you fake it: tango is a performance, maximal enjoyment occurs in front of an audience, even if it's hypothetical. It is for them.

Fifty Shades Of Grey is a novel that was a huge best seller at a time temporally coincident with a 10 year peak in the American suicide rate. Correlation is not causation, and anyway the direction is backwards. To properly interpret this relationship, you have to use a calendar: not why did middle aged people kill themselves so much more in 2011 than in 1999, but what in 2011 so depressed the people who were happier twentysomethings back in Y2K? What went wrong?[65] It's the same thing that caused this book. "So the book is a symptom of society's pathology?" No. If it involves public media, that is not how it works. The book is the defense.

The simple synopsis is that the awkward but beautiful college virgin Anastasia collides with young billionaire CEO Christian Grey, and then 400 pages of teen angst. A 27 year old billionaire who likes both a woman and Pinot Grigio may seem about as realistic as a 107 year old vampire who still lives with his parents, but the true mystery is how did a hot college girl with such low self esteem stay a virgin? She wasn't saving herself for Jesus or the highest bidder, somehow it just never came up.[66] But at a chance encounter at his office, the man who could have any woman was smitten by her vulnerability, her authenticity, her ambivalence-- and since all those things were attached to a porno quality body hidden beneath Casual Corner clothing he thought he deserved it. Uh oh, he doesn't have a mustache but you know he wants one. At no point does he or she ask, "Why would this guy of all guys like this girl of all girls? He sounds like a creep. Did anyone look him up on the registry?" I get that many anxiety disorder patients would love it if a billionaire wanted to tie them up and give them a laptop, but would any of them have wanted their daughter to lose her virginity or hemoglobin to this nut?

"The interesting thing about Anastasia's virginity," runs a typical pomo-feminist reach

---

65 It's actually worse than this. If the 1999 suicide rate among twentysomethings was very high, then the 2011 suicide rate among middle agers should be lower because the highest risk people are already dead. But if the rate among middle agers was higher in 2011 than the twentysomething rate in 1999, then either something kept them "artificially" alive in 1999 or some factor appeared/worsened as they got older. I'll leave you to work out the current statistics. "It's the economy, stupid." You do realize that's from 1991, right?

66 The explanation implied in the book illustrates the defense: she dresses plainly and goes unnoticed while her friend is always well dressed/done up and gets all the attention. Therefore, any interest Anastasia does get is really about her inner beauty. Grey likes her for her.

Like any fairy tale the wish is that she's noticed without the consumer products-- a superego appropriate "true love" wish. The outward transformation into a princess represents what was in her all along that the prince noticed (=that a prince would notice); her inner beauty is finally uncovered where before it had been suppressed.

But this isn't a fairy tale. This is BDSM, a fantasy in which someone else must be deprived; so the consumer products aren't "reflections" or symbols of her inner beauty. They function as Halloween masks. She isn't revealed to be a princess, she's deliberately dressed up like a princess, by her prince. The makeup doesn't reveal a hidden inner beauty, the makeup cause her to be beautiful, desirable-- but not to him, he already desired her-- but to everyone else. Now everyone can see what he "saw."

Now that the products have made her desirable in a conventional way, now that she's *public*, now that she is someone else, she has the power (the only one she has) to deprive him, in this case of his precious BDSM, and even of her. That's what happens. You could argue that that's merely a result of both characters' growths, fair enough, but it still is used as fantasy: in *your* fantasy, would you continue to go out with him? When you finally dump Christian Grey, do you look like you did in Act I or Act III?

around, "is that it is something that men desire; which means its inclusion in this book is an example of unconscious patriarchal norms still prevalent in women-- they want what men want." It's half right, men don't want virgins, they want to be billionaires, but the only women they can fool that they will some day be billionaires are virgins. No one else would fall for it.

What does the mainstream popularity of this book mean? In order to answer this question, you have to read the book. Not read about the book, read the actual book, the one thing that best characterizes the problems in American style education isn't the grade inflation or guaranteed loans with unguaranteed repayment but the dominance of secondary sources. You might not get much out of a week reading Thucydides, but you will only get lies from a semester reading about him. "I really liked that class." Then it worked and you didn't have to. Right here someone usually says that reading Thucydides is hard, you need some context, but calculus is hard yet no one has ever offered me a biographical sketch of whoever invented the Hamiltonian. "You know Thucydides was bald and hated women?" I'm pretty sure you just made that up, but anyway, if it was relevant to the writing, don't you think I would have picked this up by actually reading the writing? But thank you for New Yorkering a physical description into your criticism, it helps put the writing no one will read in context. You're not going to want to hear this, but there was once unanimous intellectual agreement that it was impossible to understand Plato from a translation, and 1500 miles and years from the crucifixion Martin Luther derailed top-down Christianity almost entirely in reaction to the insidious influence of expert commentary. Meanwhile back at college you could have learned about the differences between love and madness straight from the 26 pages of the relevant dialogue-- and why is it lumped with rhetoric?-- or the logical incompatibilities between love, lust, and alcohol; but instead you attended a class given by an old man bored with his wife or a young bore with neither man nor wife, with predictable results. "I learned a lot in college." Then you must have been really stupid to begin with.

The prevalence of secondary sources is neither laziness nor academic expediency, it is the quotable maintenance of the status quo. Flooded with secondary sources students probably learn nothing useful about the primary source but do become accustomed to accepting all knowledge in this way, second hand and pre-selected, so that when we're confronted with a later life question it's natural for us to parrot someone else's phrasing and understanding. "That's called 'appeal to authority.'" I feel smarter already. But what they didn't tell you in college is that by adopting the thoughts of another, you also accept their unconscious motivations for having thought it. "Come on, that's not true." Who says? And so we're full circle, these are the kind of mistakes you get from a ROM full of secondary sources. We want to be "relevant to the debate." But as long as we believe we are relevant, we won't try to be relevant, if you believe your voice should be heard then the only thing you'll want to do is be louder, we are way past the time when drunken and leaden discussions about how to pull the supply curve to the left resulted in prompt political action and tea in the harbor. "Lead poisoning from pewter is a myth." I didn't say it came from pewter, and do you even know which authority you are appealing to? That this is in line with what you want-- no responsibility to a position or ethic, safety and branding inside a hierarchical group-- is why it works. That this is in line with what the system wants-- media as the only forum for discussions and debates, appeals to authority, everyone's disorganized rage safely decomposed by Fourier transform-- is on purpose, and if once in a while someone goes offline or off script and acts up or acts out, it only reinforces that media is where the conflicts are supposed to be enclosed. But the whole reason they acted out wasn't *to* be heard but *because* no one had heard them.

To be clear, the conflict itself isn't bad, only it's compartmentalization in the media. It's in the conflict between factions that all laws favorable to freedom originate. Virtuous actions have their origin in good training, good training in good laws, and good laws in these very conflicts which many would thoughtlessly condemn. If you consider the results of these conflicts you will find that they lead to laws beneficial to the public liberty. And should you object that the behavior was extravagant and outrageous; that for the assembled people to be seen shouting against the Senate, the Senate against the people; for the whole commons to be seen rushing wildly through the streets, closing up stores, and quitting the town, these are indeed scary things. But the demands of a free people are hurtful to freedom when they originate either in being oppressed, or in the fear that they are about to be so. It is in this conflict that all laws favorable to freedom have their origin.

So most of the second hand commentators on *Fifty Shades* came at it as if this was it was either/or: a) an example of women finally allowing themselves to enjoy kinky sex; b) a welcome reprieve from decades of objectification in visual male pornography; or c) a manifestation of women's secret, trans/pro/regressive wish to submit to a real man with a big net worth. Choose any or all. They are all wrong, WAY wrong.

First: "women are drawn to 50 Shades's kinkiness." That would presume there's something kinky in it, which there isn't. That everyone says it's kinky is necessary to the defense. In this book the BDSM symbols of whips and straps are present, and they perform what looks like BDSM, but it is sanitized BDSM for Disney audiences, where Disney= "100% in line with conventional social conduct that doesn't threaten the existing system." What you do sexually is your privilege as long as it is safely in a Central Time monogamous relationship with appropriate "roles" and at least one set of parents approve. His "dungeon" is catalog-aspirational closets and cabinets. He may have a flogger, but Grey doesn't even pretend to degrade or hurt Anastasia, he barely even curses. He does slap her, slightly less hard then the book's demo slapped the V-hold during *Dynasty*, and anyway she was asking for it. They have safe words, but no one uses them; they are there only to convey the impression that safe words are needed. Fun fact or return of the repressed: the book makes much more sense if you assume that the agreed upon safe word was really "Christian". There is some blood, but-- and I can't tell if this is better or worse-- it's just her period. At one point Grey inserts ben-wa balls into Anastasia's vagina, which may not sound Disney approved except then he sends her to the *kitchen*.

Next: that jaded materialist women secretly want a real man= billionaire. "Don't you mean materialistic?" Nothing could be more obvious, i.e. a defense. Christian is a billionaire not because billionaires are desirable to women (though they are most certainly one of the approved desires for women to have-- no one would fault you) but because being desired by a billionaire-- someone who could have anything and knows the value of things—identifies them as desirable. But since it is absolutely forbidden to reveal you derive your self-worth from a man's opinion of you, she must be shown to initially resist him, *because* he's a billionaire. "He's not my type." Yeah, well, imagine he accepts this and moves on to someone else. Now it's a slasher movie.

Next: it's a book about the good, bad, or important-- please debate those words only-- secret female fantasy of submission to a handsome and powerful man. Secret? As opposed to... what? Seriously, what is the alternative this stands against? The man's power is here graphically hyperbolic, but the fantasy is only of the woman "giving up control", which may not sound insightful except that it is here a *fantasy*-- as if they wish they could give it up. A fantasy? What control do the readers have to give up? Carpool? Automatic bill pay and their very own TV shows mask the fact that all the big things are utterly out of their control. The manifest fantasy of "giving up control" is for the purpose of causing it to be true that they have some control to give up.

Which is why instead of giving up the control that she never actually had, the story shows her never really losing control, she never really is at his mercy; she is shown gaining power relative to him, because-- and this is important-- he is *afraid* of it. This is a key point not easily appreciated, especially by men who date women. *The 50 Shades demo cannot imagine that a desirable man lacks power.* This thought is unthinkable, it's like trying to imagine a salmon that is 2/3 Olympic triathlete except for not knowing how to swim. What is possible-- what women have plenty of experience with-- are desirable men that are afraid or unaware of the power they have. If you can follow this, it will help make sense of a semantic controversy: male privilege is literally *not knowing* the power you have; and those without male privilege, i.e. women, have instead the privilege of *knowing* the power they don't have that the other does. But you'll observe that the previous two sentences work just as well with the genders reversed, depending on circumstance. "I went to Paris, and everyone was super nice and welcoming!" Let me guess, you're either a size zero, or German. Privilege, and all imbalances projected to others as necessary, are about the distinction between knowledge and the power to act. "Oh my God, if I could be a man but keep my brain," she tells herself and everyone else, "nothing could stop me." Except another man, and all women. And that's assuming you would even start, which you won't.

So the *50 Shades* fantasy is the opposite of what it looks like: she has no power; she imagines a powerful man wants to take power from her; but, surprise, this man is too afraid to wield power, and so he gives her the power. If you follow the math, she starts out with zero power and ends up with all of it. Now who's the sub? Grey is weak, emotional, and *passive* aggressive; he's supposed to symbolize a dominant male and he'll have either the ties or the tats to prove it but at no time in the book is he ever *dependable*, a decision and its consequences are never his to bear alone. He wants her complete agreement at the beginning not because he values her but because he can't make these kinds of weighty decisions on his own: he always finds a way to spread the responsibility. There's no way such a salaryman could ever be a CEO, but the audience has no experience with what a CEO does so it assumes that what turns a CEO on is what turns *them* on: not real power that might be invisible, but the display of power, comparative power, the pornographization of power differentials, e.g. over college virgins.

But if this back and forth of power between dunce and a dimwit were all that *50 Shades* signified, it wouldn't be worth the reading. However, it also wouldn't be so much more popular than "real" "BDSM" "erotica". So there's a problem, one or more of those three words has to be wrong.

Instead of reading the book as the "secret sexual desires of women" it's better to read it as: what unacceptable desire have the readers repressed, for which a pornographic cover story is *preferable*? What is so terrible that they'd rather admit to secretly wanting to be a sub?

There's one more transfer of power in this story that you don't really notice because it won't work if you do notice. The running gag in dom/sub relationships is that while it seems female submissive (never mind that the majority of real life contractual dom/sub relationships the sub is the man, and this includes the situations where the dom is also a man) it's really female empowering: the woman chooses, by her choice, to submit; she decides the parameters of the relationship (and so at the beginning BDSM stories show the future dom treating the future sub as an equal partner (indicated by her getting dressed up, cooly discussing the merits of the arrangement over adult beverages, all while witnessed by and thus distinguished from other high class sex objects (waitresses, secretaries) who don't have the power to make such a choice)) She doesn't need an agent to represent her in this sex sale (well, technically it's a swap) because she has all the sophistication and expertise of a big city lawyer. She is post-feminist, uber-feminist: she (believes she) ignores social pressure and feminist expectations, she chooses to submit because it is rewarding/fulfilling for her, period. An act of individual will. "I am asserting my *self* by submitting myself to a man I trust and love completely, who will respect me and protect me, and within that safety allow me the confidence and freedom to explore my sexuality."

Well, that sounds *fantastic*-- but wasn't that the whole gimmick of marriage? "So it's a secret desire for conventional roles in marriage?" What secret? They're already in conventional marriages. The problem is you can't do these kind of explorations with a husband because marriage requires the very thing that BDSM obliterates, the anathema of our time: dependency. The fantasy of being a sub negates it. "But isn't BDSM all about depending on the dom?" Yes, except that it is explicitly a performance-- no actual dependence occurs. Even though, within a marriage, you can do all the same things, relabeling it as a pornographic performance disavows the emotional dependence. The appeal of this kind of BDSM fantasy isn't in the loss of control but the loss of dependency. She's not a wife or a girlfriend-- that dependency is obliterated. She's a sub, and sub means power.

[7.85] Except for one problem: he doesn't actually have control over any situations. It would only take 10 psi of grip strength for this to go from erotica to snuff, and she doesn't have the lats or the deltoids to get out of her shackles even if they are made of caterpillar silk and imagination. And she certainly has no control over his real life emotional "torture" of her. So what actually protects her?

"Well, he protects her." From what-- himself? The whole thing is not to need to depend on him. She trusts him, sure, but she doesn't have to-- she has recourse to a higher Law, against which he is *voluntarily* powerless. By agreeing to the BDSM-- by opting out of a conventional relationship in which women may or may not have some or even all of the power=responsibility-- she is *given* a whole new infrastructure necessary to stay safe and independent-- especially from him. Behind the closed doors of a marriage a man could rape his wife and say she wanted it, and the courts would just, "well, next time make sure she was asking for it"-- but in a BDSM everything is vague except for the inviolable safe word. "She said 'Red' and you kept going? What kind of a fiend are you?" There's no ambiguity in *Fifty Shades* BDSM, it is more real, more concrete-- not compared to real BDSM, that's the wrong comparison-- but compared to a marriage. This isn't a BDSM fantasy, it is an MFF threesome in which contract law is the M.

That's not an exaggeration or even an "interpretation." It's literally in the text itself. What Grey wants Anastasia to do before they engage in all this Kinky® brand sex isn't a couple of lines or set up a tripod, he wants her to *sign a consent form*-- a contract. Don't dismiss the contract as incidental to the story. It is so important that it is included in the body of the novel, all the chthonic pages of the legal waiver/ "Contract Between the Dominant And The Submissive" are in the book, as well as a "non-disclosure agreement" (which is there not to keep secrets but to convey the impression that there are secrets to keep[67]). Every one of those pages grounds this sex in the real world-- not penis and vagina real, but modern society real, where buildings are to code, "organic" is FDA certified, and rights based in reason become privileges based in fact; where "no" is debatable but safe words are sacrosanct-- I don't have to decide anything because my ambivalence is protected under law.[68] And Grey gets to display power over her without worrying about consequences-- no, not consequences to her, but to anything: how else can I know what I'm allowed to do? *It leaves intact the appearance of danger while obliterating the actual danger.*[69] Both Grey and Anastasia know this nonsense isn't legally binding, but they *wish* that it was: it tells Grey he is permitted to act and tells Anastasia she is permitted not to-- she can be ambivalent. The contract offers the feeling of some other

---

67 What could she reveal that would need to have been kept secret? "He would tie me up gently and engage in safe, consensual sexual play, including light spanking and breakfast afterwards. On several occasions he made me dress well. He forced me to use high end consumer products and enjoy the view. I ate dinner with his family who were respectful and welcoming, after which we began to introduce elements of affection and emotional reciprocity within the confines of a monogamous relationship." The hell you say. The only disclosure that would raise anyone's eyebrow is *that* the relationship had a non-disclosure agreement; being asked by your partner not to discuss your sex life is today a form of domestic abuse. But this is one thing the book gets right (by accident)-- the NDA doesn't prevent her from talking; it gets her out of talking about her sex life, the NDA compels her not to do what she already wanted not to do. To be clear: a woman doesn't have to talk about her sex life; but excluding strangers no woman can refuse to talk about it if asked, she can't say, "I'd like to keep that private," that would violate a social rule, especially among women. Sexuality must be part of self-identification, because the system demands that the public's curiosity be vented at minimum with an allusion or sly reference ("I'd like to keep that private, *all I'll say is it's amazing*")-- and allow the signals of hair, makeup and shoes tell the rest of the story-- something on which can coalesce people's projected fantasies, otherwise: *what does this woman want??????* But a woman with an inner life wants to keep it private for the same reason the public needs to know: speaking it gives it a single meaning, decided by the public. For her it has infinite meanings, and the public needs it... not to. Knowing any information about her sex limits the fantasies which are otherwise infinite, and the extension of this defense is porn. A powerful person's privacy results in a unbalanceable ledger: it logically implies you have no knowledge *and* no power. The only thing worse would be her refusing you information she gives freely to others; experienced by you as a Secret from which you are specifically excluded. You don't count. Idle speculation wouldn't be sufficient to balance the ledger, a coherent system of information needs to be found or even invented, as in the case of conspiracy theories. The object isn't to obtain any power-- this is beyond anyone's reach-- but simply to balance the ledger with knowledge. Freud's analysis of the Wolf Man is intended to show how the primal scene returns distorted as fantasy, but the key insight of the analysis-- and the reason Freud detected no further changes in him-- is that the primal scene was *witnessed*, concretely; the fantasy was an explanation for what he saw, instead of the fantasy substituting for what he saw. In the reverse, stalking is a viscerally terrifying crime because it represents the double imbalance: the stalker has seems to have more power than you and more knowledge (about you) than you.

68 Which law? In Unnecessary EBITA's 2016 *The Jungle Book*, Shere Khan is a strict constructionist upholding the common Law Of The Jungle against the encroachment of foreign colonialism, ironically represented by a native Indian. Instead of story the movie uses CGI to ask what kind of world we want to live in: a rational democracy that ensures all animals are equal; or a racialist anarchy become tyranny that sees the state of nature as a violent interspecies struggle for resources? "The tiger looked so real. Discuss." The big difference from the animated movie is that it's not just about colonialism, but modernism: at the end after the Great Battle, Mowgli doesn't follow his tumescent moral compass down from the trees and back towards the woman village where he came from; he stays in the jungle free of original sin-- yes, a human, but just another of

omnipotent entity's supervision above them both. An entity who has the power to tell both of them no. *The fantasy's wish is that some other omnipotent entity exists, and the 'BDSM' is the manifestation of the fulfillment of that wish[70].*

Just ask the audience what they like about the story: the BDSM fantasy. But for Christian, BDSM is not a sexual fantasy, it's not equivalent to having her dress up as a slutty nurse. He (thinks) it's a need, he feels compelled to do it, compelled to exclude love. Neither is it Anastasia's fantasy: she thinks he needs it, so she feels compelled to do it, compelled to exclude love. This is the sleight of hand of the story: what the audience wants is only this kind of BDSM relationship. The majority of readers didn't want her to fall for him *at all*. Anastasia gets to pretend, in dramatic fashion, that she's an independent woman for whom

---

many indigenous species sharing the Kingdom, a noble savage equal to wolves, bears, panthers, and elephants, living harmoniously in a climate unchanged Eden. Isn't that how it should be? The problem with modernity is it destroys the natural balance. But the movie also slyly suggests that the cause of the problem with modernity is modern women, because unlike lionesses these temptresses want modernity, they're against climate change but all in on climate control, they pull men out of their natural balance, it's the women who demand modernity's comforts, man is never satisfied because their women are never satisfied because they heard the housewhores in the west villages now have large open living rooms. "Did you ever think about going into finance?" Now I can't stop thinking about it. We've all heard this story before, and I at least have read the book, and I'm not talking about *The Jungle Book*. Wait a second-- elephants?

Gender and race are proudly rotated in the remake, after all, where is it written that a super hot woman can't play a seductive serpent or a black guy can't voice the king of the jungle? Here's a joke, makes no sense but funny anyway: how can you tell if a snake won't be dangerous, just annoying? It doesn't hiss, it hers. But there's one animal inconspicuously absent from the remake, and that's the elephant. They're there, of course, and the panther bows down to them, and the final scenes do show the elephants with all the other animals gathered in solidarity around Mowgli, but where the hell were they when they were needed? Heck, didn't they sort of owe Mowgli a favor? Seems to me an elephant, let alone many elephants, could have shortened the Great Battle by all of it. So if the story is about a jungle wide war for a new world order, you have to pretend you forgot there are giant elephants around keeping the ordinary order. They are the backstop that allows all of the other animals to have pretend conflicts over the "laws" of the jungle. In the original cartoon the elephants are culturally appropriated as the British colonial military, formerly the East India Company, mockingly portrayed as, well, stupid British colonialists; but you know enough to know that stupid does not mean impotent, it often means the opposite.   Since elephants explicitly exist, explicitly patrol the jungle, the final conflict of the cartoon could never escalate to a jungle wide war without the elephants showing up to shut it down, so in the cartoon it's depicted not as a world war but as what it actually is, a small scale rivalry between Mowgli and Shere Khan. *Disavowing* the elephant omnipotence in the 2016 remake allows the conflict to appear to be structural, it lets Shere Khan seem to rule over the jungle, as if an anonymous tip to Dumbo's maternal relatives (take a breath and hell no I'm not explaining it) wouldn't get him disappeared; it lets you think all the animals could be involved in collective action and thus fighting to change the status quo. But the entire "structural" conflict was illusory and safe, *this is why we wish we could have one*, it was straight up sibling rivalry observed form a distance by omnipotent and hopefully benevolent elepharents who will happily tolerate anything as long as it doesn't hurt the State. "We have a State?" Don't worry your pretty little head about it, now off you go, you can use the red flower, but if you feel burning let me know. "Are you talking about my vagina?" HA! No, that's still ours.

69

Regarding the footnoted passage above, which of the following statements BEST reflects the beliefs of the older generation with

love and sex isn't contractual, "I'm not going to sign a paper to have sex!" But sign or not sign, the discussion alone is sufficient to give the audience the fantasy of a world of limited emotional dependency where something greater than them is supervising. That power is being negotiated between them is the gimmick: the fantasy's wish is that no power could ever be negotiated between the two of them, it safely exists elsewhere. She doesn't submit, he doesn't dominate-- both are protected=castrated by something higher than both of them. The fantasy here is not of patriarchal authority, but a regression to parental authority, both obeying simultaneously a powerful father and a nurturing mother. They aren't romantic partners, they're siblings. Which means-- surprise but boy oh boy you should have seen it coming-- this BDSM is really an incest fantasy.

---

respect to the younger?

a) "Things were safer when we were kids, we could walk to school!"

b) "We were tougher when we were kids, we would walk to school!"

c) "Kids are so spoiled nowadays, they won't walk to school!"

d) "Things are so dangerous nowadays, kids can't walk to school!"

There are no wrong answers, of course.

The assertion is that things are indeed incredibly worse today than ever before, yet all of the evidence is to the contrary, everything is safer now: food, buildings, sex; cameras and GPS are everywhere we still won't let kids go; going by official statistics the only thing children need to fear nowadays is their parents. Cars in the analog age were unsafe at any speed, and people had to wear driving gloves because the steering wheel was made of uranium. Now that cars have been litigated into such safety that they drive themselves you can be sure driving gloves will make a comeback. Things aren't worse today, if anything previous generations were staggeringly oblivious to the dangers. Why would they let their kids walk to school if serial killers famously roamed the streets? Now you can't even name one contemporary serial killer, murderers are caught too quickly to become interesting, let alone infamous. So why weren't people then afraid, while we are?

We say the media popularizes dangers and we get a skewed view of the world. Fair enough-- but it's not enough to say the media causes us to have a skewed view, *we want this skewed view,* we want intact the appearance of danger while obliterating the actual danger, because then our frantic activity worked-- what has kept the kids alive in a world of catastrophes is your obsessive effort to protect them. Our public attempts to protect against exaggerated dangers masks our impotence to prepare them for real ones, or adulthood. Since I appear to be expending so much energy protecting them, I'm a good enough parent-- and if I go the extra mile as a parent to teach them that God and climate are human mistakes and to respect all people of the correct Party I can be forgiven if I don't teach them math, if I take some time "for myself."

The problem with taking credit for protecting them is that there isn't much credit in it, not because it's easy but because it's every parent's obligation. So it doesn't count. To make it count, the parent has to do something for no reason, so protectiveness gets upgraded to overprotectiveness for which choice you pretend to feel guilty. "I don't know why I drive these spoiled brats everywhere they want to go!" It's so you can call people from the car, and tell them.

70 Here's a joke you may have heard:

A man comes home and finds his wife watching cooking shows, and says,

360

Contrast this with the contract in *Indecent Proposal*, in which Redford smirks while listening to Moore read off her pre-sex conditions the way a father listens to a 9 year old negotiate chores. Both stories' contracts are meaningless but make the woman feel like some higher authority is watching over them-- but only in *Fifty Shades* does the man want that same meaningless reassurance. NB: this doesn't mean that men do or do not want this assurance; this is a female fantasy-- the fantasy is that men *would* want this assurance-- the fantasy is that men would want and submit to some higher authority watching over both of them.

And so we come to the answer of the unasked question of *Fifty Shades Of Nay*: why do the readers have this *fantasy* of equal but mutually reduced power supervised by omnipotent parents, and not simply *fantasize* more power for themselves?

You're not going to want to hear the answer, but unfortunately it will satisfy a lot of you. The 50 Shades demo feels women have gained equality in rights but haven't gained anywhere near as much power, they still lack it. This is duh, ok, so the men still have it? That makes sense. But when you check with men-- not the primary sources, obviously, that would be stupid, but "men's media"-- those sources are quite vocal that men are upset they have lost power, they assume to women. Now there's a problem: both can't be true, so either men are all lying or the power is being siphoned off before everyone's eyes. Hold that thought. Wherever it went, *a loss of male power has not resulted in an equivalent gain in female power*. Certainly

---

"why do you watch all those cooking shows but never cook?" And the wife says, "why do you watch all that porn...?"

Grey sells the BDSM contract to her in a revealing way: he detects she doesn't *want* to have to make choices. "If you were my sub, you wouldn't have to think about this. It would be easy.... All those decisions, the wearying thought processes behind them. The 'is this the right thing to do? Should this happen here? Can it happen now?' You wouldn't have to worry about any of that detail." Grey's offer is tempting because he makes her feel like what she's giving up are expressions of power-- instead of what they are, which are anxieties related to having no power. Everything in her life is out of her control, all she can do is worry about it. This includes sex-- sex is never just for her, she always has to worry about what the other wants.

Anastasia's single objection to the contract-- the "deal breaker", in her words-- isn't what she'd have to do sexually but:

"No." I am so not backing down on this. No one is going to dictate to me what I eat. How I fuck, yes, but eat... no, no way.

What she believes Grey wants isn't to control her eating, specifically, but to control her. He's permitted to think he can control her sexually because in reality he cannot control her sexually, the BDSM and the contract limit that. But he could control her eating-- he could have that power, there's no law against that, and men do it all the time. Therefore he cannot be allowed to have that power. Said differently: nowadays she's allowed to eat whatever she wants, but would ordinarily (be made to) feel guilty about doing so; the contract means she has no choice. Pancakes, eggs, bacon, multiple breakfasts, all fetishistically described-- a stand in for something desired that has disappeared. That thing is privacy. Eating is the only pleasure, the only act, that is not for someone else. In everything else a woman feels pulled, shared-- even walking down the street she is conscious that men and women look at her for their own satisfaction (which includes hating her). Eating-- or not eating-- is the last bit of control left to a woman who does not own her own life. And Grey is trying to control even that. So she refuses the offered privilege of eating guilt free for her old right of eating freely with guilt, because the sacrifice serves the purpose of depriving him of the satisfaction of controlling her. Don't worry, she still eats the pancakes.

HR has made men more docile around the cubicles, but it's hard to say this made a 21st century woman feel more powerful than a 19th woman, otherwise there wouldn't be so many shows about powerful 19th century women. Having not taken physics, they are surprised to find that power is not conserved. The result of this math is that as much as they say they want more power and etc, as much as they *know* that it's possible, they actually don't *believe* that it's possible-- *it is not even fantasizable.*

The only fantasy they can imagine-- i.e. the pornographic one they are shown by approved media sources, which therefore must have some other purpose-- is not that women should get more power; it is that men might be deprived of theirs, taken not by women but by some other omnipotent entity. That men might subordinate themselves into a new role as an equal sibling under the supervision of the parents.[71]

Disempowered men would be expected to resist further disempowerment, and it certainly looks like they do, finding prophets and then idols in masculine looking men in media; as one of a million examples, 2020's twentysomethings' complicated love/fear relationship with (media) black men. Stop nodding your head, NB I didn't specify the race of the twentysomethings. Strong black men are the last line of defense against male disempowerment by aggressive feminism. He'll be respectful, sure, but if he wants to check out yo ass, he's checking it. Because somebody still has to, may as well enjoy it. Now NB I didn't specify the gender, either.

Of course none of this is true-- men are not *resisting* disempowerment. Many are hoping to resist women getting it, I guess, but women aren't getting it, so it's moot. Tell the men the power is going somewhere away from both women and men they know, and these men couldn't be more blindly enthusiastic about their own disempowerment. If only there was someone who could take all that power, who could do what needs to be done, someone who could say no to the people.

The government as the wished-for suprapower is an obvious guess. But the book presciently chooses corporate power as the omnipotent entity. The 50 Shades demo wants power to shift away from men, but democratic power has failed them, "men" can still circumvent it. The only reliable source of power, the kind that everyone obeys, is corporate power. Changes in the workplace may have been motivated by a desire for gender equality, it may have been at the expense of male chauvinist *employees* but the changes could only have been permitted by those men if power increased for someone other than women and men they know: the corporation. The women made the same deal. Corporate power became nearly inviolable. Tax the billionaires into oblivion, burn them in effigy or even in ovens-- but leave the corporation intact! (If only there was a political system modeled on the notion of a corporation!) We *want* the corporate power to be even stronger, because it alone ensures a kind of world with rules, dress codes, appropriate behavior-- not just safety, but a place, a purpose, a *title.* Good enough, so long as we retain the public(izable) freedom to express ourselves sexually, which, not ironically, now requires restraints.

You might dismiss this and say that such BDSM contracts nevertheless do offer the

---

71 While there are various powerful women in both fiction and non-fiction, when a woman is depicted in media *to* women as more powerful than men she will work for/through/with the government, or at least some hierarchical power structure. No one acts on their own. *Gone Girl's* Amy has the same fantasy in mind when she plans to have her husband die not at her hands, the hands of hired killers or his mistress's jealous ex, but at the hands of the justice system.

couple some safety; that an appeal to a higher authority is realistically important-- your dom might be a nut, after all. You're thinking at the wrong level. *The point is that this omnipotent authority is necessary just to be able to fantasize.* The audience can't fantasize "giving up power" unless the fantasy *itself* contains such safeguards. Not just the contract; consider that in this imaginary BDSM fantasy where anything could happen and sex has no limits, they have sex with a condom. Not incidentally with a condom; we get to read about the finding of a condom and the unwrapping of the condom and the removing of the condom and condom condom condom. It should be impossible to find anyone without a latex fetish that fantasizes a condom; but here we have a best seller about it. Since Anastasia doesn't exist it's pointless to ask why she likes it, but the reason the audience likes her story is because it is a fantasy *about* being able to fantasize in safety. Rather than the condom being an incidental part of the fantasy, the condom is the fantasy-- just as the contract is the fantasy, just as him submitting to it is the fantasy. Of course people have reason to want condoms in real life sex, just as they will want parachutes in real life airplanes, but what does it mean that in order to fantasize flying, you have to fantasize wearing a parachute? Why not just... fantasize?[72]

Cartoonish dominance with her pretend submissiveness; the pretense of a power differential padded in pages and pages of banal demands, negotiations, contracts, NDAs. In this freaky tale of kinky erotica-- in this tale that people saw as freaky and kinky and dangerous-- it takes them 200 pages to get to second base; but boy oh boy are there a lot of loving descriptions of consumer products. Computers, clothes, cars, there are more brands in this book than in *American Psycho*, and they serve the same purpose in both books: not shiny hollow ephemera devoid of value, but concrete slabs grounding them in artificial reality; for both Bateman and the *50 Shades* readers, keeping the fantasies from getting out of control. But in this book their inclusion is without any hint of criticism, it's part of the pornography. Within this structure the reader is completely safe, free of dangerous fantasy, completely taken care of in the "real" world.

All of these structures are necessary just to *be able* to fantasize.

The way we discuss issues of freedom and security are as if they were on a continuum, more/less freedom = less/more security. But instead of shifting back and forth between those two things the system found a way to give us what we want: the *belief* in absolute safety simultaneously[73] balanced, impossibly, with the pretense that this safety does not exist; public displays of absolute freedom supported by a disavowed infrastructure. "I pulled myself up by

---

72 Condoms as overdetermined: the fantasy condom allows the fantasy to proceed in perfect physical safety, but also emotional safety: as every good Catholic girl knows, oral sex is whatever, but the most intimate thing a woman can do is let a man ejaculate inside her. "It's because of the pregnancy risk." But she can't get pregnant in *fiction*. What can't be disavowed even in fiction is that the internal ejaculation represents his total satisfaction. It is so outrageously intimate that in 50 Shades it occurs *after* the BDSM, after an appropriate Disney waiting time rationalized as waiting to get on birth control pills. The reader is shown a relationship progressing appropriately slowly.

The movie, limited by a 2 hour runtime and an R rating forbidding cum shots (and it is for that reason, and not because it is a "chick flick", that it is her orgasm the camera dwells on), has to show this progression differently. You still see him *bite* open condom wrappers, but since it's too difficult to "show don't tell" the change to condomless sex *because* she's finally on the pill, the movie always remains at the level of condoms-- instead of never showing a condom in the first place. The condom isn't for Anastasia's uterus, it's for the audience's amygdala. You can watch the movie without obsessing about the threat that male satisfaction poses, and justify it by the anxiety she could get pregnant.

my bootstraps!" says the dummy who does not want to wonder who made his bootstraps, let alone his boots.[74]

Though this asexual mess was originally Twilight fan fiction, it's real derivation is from the previous pop-erotica phantasm, *9 1/2 Weeks.* Just like in 50 Shades you have a handsome, brooding, damaged capitalist (played by Mickey Rourke) who detects hidden value in a beautiful woman (Kim Basinger) that inconceivably the rest of the world never noticed; "his obsessive desire both gives her worth and threatens her sense of self." In that story, however, camera-friendly BDSM was mostly absent, but the danger was 100x greater because the woman never had any guarantees, no protections, no power. That could be a cherry, it could be a hot pepper, it could be a shotgun, she had to trust that the guy would treat her what she

---

73 What regularly occurs in some people is that a compromise is arrived at which enables both the opposing tendencies to find expression simultaneously— which kills two birds with one stone; whereas in others, each of the two opposing tendencies finds satisfaction singly, first one and then the other, though naturally an attempt is made to establish some sort of logical connection (often in defiance of all logic) between the antagonists.

74 Within days of the U.S. Federal Reserve beginning its gigantic third round of bond purchases-- 5 years after the first and double the amount-- the comedy group Lonely Island released a song called "YOLO: You Only Live Once." It starts by praising the grab life by the balls YOLO philosophy, but quickly mushrooms into 2 minutes of punch line: since You Only Live Once, don't take any chances at all.

> Wear titanium suits in case pianos fall on you/and never go to saunas cause they're crawling with piranhas...

> So board your windows up the sun is bad for your health/And always wear a straight jacket so you're safe from yourself.

Ok, but what are the odds? But this response immediately makes the debate between severity and likelihood, and unless you know math who could argue against the severity? The thing to notice is that while the song says "take no risks at all", the song quite explicitly recommends not doing nothing, but doing a whole series of proactive actions which necessarily appear 100% effective. This is the real payoff: getting credit for acting. An impotence to act in ordinary life is displaced onto catastrophic dangers so that some action can be taken that can appear potent. Frantic activity as a defense against impotence, and if not physical activity than mental activity, and if not mental then at least let it cost money-- so it looks like it counts.

It's tempting to think this is a defense against cowardice, except that calling it defense against cowardice is a defense already. It is a resentment of dependency, which also explains the inability to love past infatuation. A teenager, screaming at his parents to give him his freedom-- and the keys to the car; what he says he is screaming about are the (basically trivial) limits on his freedom, but what he's enraged about is his utter dependency on the parents. This is why "love" is magnified 10000x when the teen falls in love with a peer: that love feels infinite because it is absolutely devoid of dependency, nothing is placed in the liability column.

That he fails to identify this dependency as a necessary part of love-- that he thinks he can love without being dependent and dependable-- that no one stands him up and explains that his desire for independence does not require him to be a jerk or NOT love his parents-- is mostly the fault of parents and the world that regularly reward them for their pseudo-independence ("I'm trusting you to make good choices on social media.") The solution is to give him more responsibility to and for others, to give him a real exposure not to independence but to the give and take of dependency, his own and others'. However, the time to introduce him to this would have been at age 5, instead of

was worth-- because there was no "other omnipotent entity" to ensure her safety by limiting his power. In the movie the food is eroticized-- weaponized; but in 50 Shades it is deliberately stripped of sexual content. It's Anastasia's safe place, free of his control-- i.e. there exists a safe place, free of his control, and it's guaranteed in the contract, so it is material, real. The *9 ½ Weeks* demo wanted to be consumed, the 50 Shades demo wants a safe place to consume. In *9 ½ Weeks*-- genitals deep in the 80s AIDS panic-- there were no condoms. In *Fifty Shades of Grey* they are an engagement ring, the Big Other made of rubber.[75]

   9 ½ Weeks was the fantasy for the post women's lib generation obligated to want it all-- the only sin was to not want it all-- and so the fantasy depicts when it is acceptable for a woman who didn't actually get it all to pretend to not to want it: when a more powerful man

---

introducing him to accounting. One of the likely results of his home schooling is his belief that he doesn't need love, he doesn't have to depend on another person, he can spread his dependency over the vastness of society so he can get what he wants and feel like he owes nothing to anyone. Except that his very own ledger shows him that since he depends on no one, it must be true that every one is trying to depend on him-- to use him. This dependency that has been spread out over the whole world is felt as depriving.

75 I had the misfortune to be in the kind of open and honest dialogue that has no tolerance for dissent, and a 30 something woman revealed/proclaimed to us that when she has cybersex with strangers, she always insists on elaborately and purposefully including a condom in the role play because if they meet in real life, she wanted there to already be a precedent for using a condom: in her experience, men were "manipulative, dangerous, and deliberately try to undermine a woman's right to safety." The obvious question is why is she retarded. We can skip that one for now. The question here is what does the main character want? Here's a hint: it wasn't a dialogue, it was a monologue.

Repeatedly engaging in risky behaviors used to be interpreted as a secret guilt, "she wants to be punished"; but everyone knows this-- *she* knows this-- and she proudly cites it as a defining attribute. Her "dark side" of masochistic repetition compulsion is publicly proclaimed for all of us to wonder at. Rest assured, she's lying, and anything but masochistic. The wish isn't to be hurt; the wish is that she *can't* be hurt-- she's safe. You'll say you should expect to be safe, you should expect men to be safe. Agreed-- but *she* doesn't expect them to be safe. She expects and the fantasy requires that all men are all dangerous all the time AND she is absolutely 100% safe. The fantasy is that the man is the most direct of actors-- a psychopath-- yet he can not act.

In real life a condom is a tiny sacrifice of enjoyment for safety. But the cybercondom's utility isn't in prepping the real life meeting, I doubt this cybernut ends up meeting even a fraction of the cybermen in real life. If getting him to agree to a fantasy condom in fantasy sex makes it easier for her to enjoy it in fantasy, then her hope is that a fantasy condom logically makes it harder for him in fantasy.

Of course she's wrong, the man has no idea he's supposed to be a psychopath and she's actually a nut, he just wanted to have sex with her. But then she wouldn't have sex with him. If they met in real life for sex, she'd be looking to create the modern equivalent of a 1950s date, where perfect gentlemen are still assumed to be date rapists, but under the rules of dating "behave like perfect gentlemen"-- not with women, but with her *only*. So the Rules keep the men in line; but the 1950s trick was for the woman to say, "I'm not that kind of girl" and take credit for his gentlemanly behavior, his gentlemanly behavior was a consequence of that sentence, of her-- not of the Rules. Similarly, the cybernut *needs* to believe her cyberman is a psychopath, that she tamed, otherwise his perfect behavior doesn't count. Not only did he not get to hurt her like everyone knows he wanted, but she's made him go through an elaborately complicated scheme that is totally besides the point-- she even made him wear a condom. That-- not the sex-- is the payoff.

takes your power from you in exchange for taking care of you.

50 Shades takes into account the new realities. A woman will never have any real power, and men are too obtuse to know how much power they have. If you could just get him to give up the power he has to some other omnipotent entity, together you can live as siblings and enjoy stealing back little bits of insignificant power branded as kinky or transgressive.[76]

Which leads to the other important function of the book. If the book's latent wish is for some other omnipotent entity to have all the power, why does the story manifest as *sexual?*

Unlike the conventional wisdom, the book is not for the sexually repressed, and no one under 80 feels guilty about having secret sexual thoughts, especially "kinky" thoughts. Strong,

---

76 It might be helpful to contrast this with the fantasy for men which answers the opposite question: under what circumstances can you act like a man? There are three answers, queue up the movies that have no female leads but get an A for effort.

I. Getting Into The Machine

20th Century action movies have been dismissed as pornography for weak teen boys. But what made those boys weak? It isn't lack of pushups, they often can do a lot of them. Alexander The Great may have kept the Iliad under his pillow to inspire his dreams, but under that he kept a giant knife for when he woke up, this is not a man hoping to sleep comfortably, this is a man planning to act. Off topic, but important: the American understanding is that his big dreams of world conquest inspired him to conquer as much as he did, but this was a kid who knew full well that his grasp exceeded his reach and not the other way around; not only did he not imagine a limitless world of infinite possibilities, he watched as his father grasped it all for himself. "And when Alexander saw the breadth of his domain, he wept, for there were no more worlds to conquer." "Plutarch?" No, *Die Hard.* Neither was it arrogance, he thought *anyone* could conquer the world-- the world was up for grabs, it just required the right kind of commitment. Even more off topic, the quantum mechanical sci-fi "many worlds hypothesis" is used to say that every possible outcome is located in one of infinite worlds, but the theory is hardly new, so if Hans Gruber made you feel a little bad about your grasp, the actual Plutarch quote is going to make you really ashamed of your reach: "When Anaxarchus told him that there were an infinite number of worlds, Alexander wept, for he had not become a master of a single one." If all things are possible, you have no one to blame but yourself, think about that the next time you arrogantly claim to have imposter syndrome. That the Persians conquered the world first was no concern at all, he would simply conquer the Persians; but his father, though a jerk, was not only impossible to conquer, but also his father. When your father's very existence is the unbeatable obstacle to your desires, you either change what you want or one of you will get castrated. Fortunately for both he died when Alexander was 18; unfortunately for Persia he didn't die until Alexander was 18, one year earlier and today we'd all be Manichaeans, which is not that far fetched when you consider that most of us are anyway. Right is decided only between equals in might, but history is full of lucky and unlucky accidents, so the strong do what they feel they must and the weak can try to take credit for both.

What's preventing the daydreaming teen from fighting a hundred bad guys isn't that he physically can't but that he's *not allowed to*, e.g. the bullying victim isn't overpowered, he doesn't even fight *back*, not because he's scared of the bully but because he's scared of fighting, of violating the inviolable power of social convention that says fighting is wrong. The action hero's fighting skills matter less than being *permitted* to fight-- *by some other omnipotent entity.* This is why the protagonists are cops, bounty hunters, former special forces. It's not their training but that they were trained by trainers which also sanction the power to act. The premise of Steven Seagal's first movie *Above The Law* was that he was a cop chasing "above the law" CIA operatives who were trafficking drugs to pay for their covert ops. But in order for Seagal to shoot them in the street the way no cop could, he himself had to be above the law: so he's not just a cop, he's also a former CIA operative.

independent women are supposed to have them. The only kind of guilt that comes with sex is the guilt of not wanting it. For sure they don't want their disinterest in sex to mean they aren't strong women; so they announce they've tried all kinds of sex, they just prefer masturbation, they prefer their own fantasies. Except, surprise: they can't fantasize. The book doesn't describe what women "secretly" want; the book itself is a solution to the problem of want. And because this pressure to want sex comes from outside you, the only way to satisfy it is to display your secret hedonism publicly. Everyone has access to whatever specific erotica they might want, and millions of people wanted... a media approved erotica. The media blessing not only makes it ok to have such fantasies, it gets you out of having to have them. Your creepy grandfather hid his disgusting porno mag in a brown wrapper, this is the opposite: dirty on the outside, totally safe and sterile on the inside, branding to yourself and

---

Because of their official rank in the hierarchy of power such men have the privilege to blow up the bad guys— at the end the heroes could die, go on the run, or even get busted all the way down to Traffic, but they can't be jailed, jail would mean they aren't above the law. In other words, to the target audience, the prospect of getting killed in a gunfight is way less of a deterrent than the prospect of getting arrested for a gunfight, this is wisdom, let us attend.

The privilege to act matters more than the skill or courage [5.7], and when you see a movie where the good guy is "off book", "gone rogue", you should understand this not as a lack of permission but as the highest sanction for action: you still have all of the physical risk but now are above all laws, you don't work for the government, you work for the very idea of government, do what you have to, go crazy. Most do. James Bond's solution was to play the gentleman, dress in fancy suits and speak with measured diction, those were self-imposed restrictions he forced himself to abide by since no other rules applied to him. "Is what I am doing wrong?" Wearing a white suit after Labor Day? Yes. "I'm British." Not anymore. And here the usual interpretation misses the mark: he wasn't drinking to forget all the things he had done at work; he was drinking so he wouldn't do them except for at work. I'll put money down that when he was not on a mission, he stayed home and masturbated. Privilege, not ability, is the American way. Bruce Lee brought kung fu to America, but Americans preferred karate and judo because they had a structured belt system and tournaments, though both had an aspirational plug-in to the establishment: "after you get a black belt, you have to register your hands with the FBI." The hierarchy, the school, symbolized the permission to act. Meanwhile kung fu was the cool martial art for poor black kids: permission wasn't really what they were after. Neither was its usefulness, they already knew how to fight: the point was to make fighting a kind of art, meaningful in itself. You can say that today there's more interest in "real" fight training, this being a shift away from the hierarchical and symbolic permission to act, except that the shift is only in who grants the permission: no one says, "I'm learning how to fight," they say, "I'm doing MMA." There are no belts but you do get tattoos. MMA is a media approved sport and the media is the highest authority in the land, you can break pretty much any law or bone you want as long as it is for them.

So if you want a real world bullying victim to stand up for himself, put him and the bully into a broadcasting live polygon, tell him, "here it is permitted to fight"-- and that kid may not win, but he's going to come out swinging. He will fight *because* the fight is sanctioned-- now there is *nothing* to fear. This will work 100% of the time, but this isn't a good thing, it's a very, very bad thing, because it works not on the principle of right and wrong but "an authority says we're allowed to do this..." "But shouldn't the State have a monopoly on force?" I don't know if it should, but only one of those two combatants thinks it does. "Can you hold my glasses, I was told I have to keep getting punched in the face until we can reserve the Thunderdome."

This is why, in bully and action movies of the 80s and 90s, the final confrontation *still* had to occur in a socially acceptable contest-- a ring, election, or game-- somehow authorized by the highest authority. Even in *Lethal Weapon*-- where the final combat is in some guy's front yard, that yard is senior detective Murtaugh's yard ("I'll take responsibility!") and if that's not sanctioned enough they

everyone else that you are alive, powerful, you have secret fantasies-- but still societally approved, Best Seller list and corporate media authorized, after all, the whole fantasy is about submitting to corporate authority. One can imagine the physically impossible but psychologically plausible scenario in which a beachside reader inserts a math book within a hollowed out *50 Shades* so no one sees she's some kind of a sociopath.[77]

---

fight within a *spotlight*; The bad guy grabs a pole but Gibson is handed a police baton, and there's an audience of cops; and together the fighter and arena owner provide the final justified kill. But in *Above The Law*, Seagal and the CIA bad guys are too evenly matched, because the same authority is sanctioning them both, and so you have the only action movie I've ever seen that ends with no final contest: the last scene presciently shows Seagal and his basic wife humbly appealing to the only authority that today no one can be above: the media.

Unlike assault, bullying succeeds because the bully doesn't care about society's rules while the victim is castrated by them. Take this to the streets, where you're not allowed to prejudge people to their face, so that the white guy feels an internalized social obligation to stop and give directions to the black guy he "knows" is going to try to rob him, which is why he gets asked in the first place, and if you think that's racist that's the point: he is a racist, that's why he feels pressured to stop and give directions. Easy does it, racists, consider the significance: the true tell of the breakdown of society isn't whether or not the robber robs him, but whether the victim no longer feels that obligation to society's conventions even in the face of a threat; he's allowed to "know" it's a threat, just not act on it. The system never had control of sociopaths, but when it loses the socialized, it's over-- now everyone's a sociopath and we're back to social Lamarckism. "Don't you mean Darwinism?" I don't mean anything. And it's not like the socialized have a well developed internal morality anyway; society has so many external rules you'd have to be suicidal to complicate it further with your own sense of right and wrong, consequently no one has bothered. The all too real example is when a rule-squashed victim of perceived bullying does overcome his resistance to society's frowny face on fighting, he takes it to the weaponized extreme-- there's no proportionality between rage and response, if he's managed to get over the meters high walls of convention, then the only thing that limits his rage is nothing.

II. Getting Out Of The Machine

What if there's no authority to give you the permission to act? What if you go through life and you're still impotent, you're not an ex-cop or spy and never will be, you still lack the approved phallus; what's media offering you now? An Oedipal solution: you, the nobody, has *no choice* but to act on what you want: family's been kidnapped, you've been injected with a poison, no one else believes there are demons/aliens, etc. The logic requires two consecutive castrations: in life the man is powerless to act (either forced into a cubicle, forced out of a cubicle, now down and out, etc) followed by the fantasy of a second castration, in which some other mightier power (e.g. bad guys) takes what's left of his identity and *forces* him to act-- he has no choice. You should take this literally: the fantasy solution to having no power is having no choice.

The difference between this group of action movies and the *Above The Law* genre is the difference in the desirability of societal power. When you need permission to act, you want power within that society, you want to be a part of it, though in a privileged position. So you fantasize an enemy you're allowed to fight. When you need to be forced to act, however, the enemy isn't the enemy, but society.

368

In the horror movie *Het Veldt* (*The Welder*), one of the male victims of the masked killer is so terrified that he goes along with his own murder, as if to avoid the terror of it. The Welder lights his torch, holds his victim's hand on a table while the victim offers no resistance at all; he doesn't fight, he doesn't run, he passively participates. The Welder burns through his hand; the blubbering victim voluntarily holds it up for inspection and manages to say quite clearly, "oh, good job, nicely cauterized, excellent technique, union pride. Can I go now?"

The victim is trying to do some complicated math, figuring that if he simply complies with this, doesn't enrage the Welder, even applauds his power, he'll somehow have fooled the

---

"How far would you go to protect your family?" the child abduction movie pretends to ask, e.g: would you kill or torture? Asking that question locks the debate to that very safe, easy question ("what kind of a jerk wouldn't?") allowing every audience member a moment to assert how powerful they could be-- if only they had no choice. But he's not killing in order to save his child; and he's not killing because he has repressed homicidal ideas (who represses those nowadays?); the fantasy is that some contrived reason has forced him to violate society's rules, ostensibly to save his child. The only way to imagine being forced to act against society-- not to hurt it, that's impossible-- but at least to deprive society of the good, law abiding cubicle drone they want him to be-- is if there are bad guys; and in order for there to be bad guys, his child needs to be abducted. It is Munchausen by proxy, in fantasy, you should probably cross check this.

The kidnappers aren't the enemy, they are the solution, they are the second castration that sets him free from perpetual masturbation. The true enemy is society: society didn't kidnap his son, but society had castrated him into being only a husband and father, it told him a whole series of things he wasn't allowed to do; and now it's telling him he's not *allowed* to go retrieve his son. If "society" sounds too vague, you're right, it is, on purpose, and we should be very specific: in these movies, *who* tells him he isn't allowed to go save his son and should just stick to masturbating? *His wife.* That bitch is useless, obstructionist and cowardly-- she is the shackles of estrogen-saturated social convention. "We need to go to the police!" she repeatedly pleads, by which she means, "let some other omnipotent entity handle it!" --But we both know they won't, why do you keep saying that? "Because my believing in their omnipotence optimistically lessens the power of the bad guys," she won't say, which he hears as, "let real men handle it!"-- after all, no one knows better than your wife how much power you really have. "Looking good in that bikini, maybe after I fix the toilet, I could also lay some pipe." Don't bother, I can get an expert to do both. "On a Sunday?" Meh, I can also do it myself.

Society/his wife castrated him, feminized him; he sits in the home office theater or singles' cafeteria waiting for something bigger than all this to compel him to act like a man. Run the fantasy to the very end to see the payoff: after killing the bad guys and saving his family, he returns precisely to the same place in society he was before; and he doesn't get to keep the power to act, the only thing that's changed is the wife's-- and audience's-- *perception* of him. Was it all worth it? "He did get his kid back." He has a kid?

In today's society, where are there places for a man to act "like a man"-- i.e. exert independent power of will, with visible results? Video games, sports betting and following the news are all socially acceptable answers, and not very satisfying. What's the result? "Out of nowhere-- he just snapped!" "Society's" "suppression" of "masculinity" is blamed for this, and maybe this is true, but you have to look really closely to appreciate the system's astonishing efficiency. The reason he *consciously chooses* (read: does what he feels the system compelled him to do) to "snap" is because it a) displays his masculinity to the world because it appears masculine, all that yelling and physical force; and b) reinforces the system's devaluation of masculinity: "See? This is what masculinity does!" You could argue that he didn't choose it, he "went crazy", but he didn't go crazy and short

Welder into letting him go. But he's not good at math. The kind of physical and emotional stoicism, mental ingenuity, and control of one's fear required to pull off that kind of strategy does not exist in a victim. This is paralysis. The reason he can speak with calm and complexity in the face of such terror is precisely because this is his *reflex:* giving away what little power he has for the appearance of knowledge. It's not supposed to fool the Welder, it's for himself. Knowledge as the defense against impotence.

Let's be clear about the legal issues: even in the real world, he has no right to self defense. He has the privilege of self-defense, granted to him by the State. What is he allowed to do? Whatever you think the answer is, the verb preceding the infinitive is allowed. If this is hard to envision, imagine a date rape. She's getting raped, no controversy about whether she

---

gold futures; he planned and executed a temper tantrum that required turn signals and emptying his bladder first. The system then ascribes a psychiatric explanation to this "inappropriate" "acting out", which helps reinforce to everyone else the idea that all expressions of "masculinity" are on a "continuum" of "pathology".

But misogynologists should note that "masculinity" is an utterly empty signifier, the trick here is that it isn't really the masculinity that the system objects to: it is any *individual* expression of power that the system suppresses, by *labeling* it masculine, in exactly the same way completely ordinary women who say no to a meeting or politely ask for a raise are criticized as being, well, masculine. The words are lies. Neither is it "women" who suppress him, it's only staged that way, but check the ledger, the women for sure didn't get any of the power men lost. The power all went elsewhere.

As an aside, I will here mention in passing only that when a people want power to be taken by some other omnipotent entity, anyone who *obstructs* this is reflexively hated and labeled a fascist or tyrant-- especially if she is a woman. Former Socialist President Francois Mitterrand once said that Margaret Thatcher had the "lips of Marilyn Monroe and the eyes of Caligula", that was supposed to be his backhanded compliment of a fascist back when forehanding French women was *de rigeur*, and no, it makes no sense at all. "Caligula," a female interviewer asking Thatcher to make sense of the quote once helpfully explained, "was a Roman general". Yeah, that's what she came up with. She didn't even attempt Monroe, "blonde swimmer" seemed too obvious. Thatcher was at that time the second most powerful human being on the planet Earth and head and shoulders smarter than anyone else in this paragraph, so yes, the interviewer was stupid, but so was the quote. What Mitterrand actually said was "lips of Monroe and eyes of Stalin" which at least is sensible as a *kind* of critique of Thatcher, still wrong and not quite fascist but oh my God the irony. It may be that the quote got changed in the quoting from Stalin to Caligula because that was the same year *Caligula* opened in France, but now you have a possibly worse irony in that the socialists thought the film was spectacular.

To illustrate the gender neutrality of the system, consider a female protagonist action movie that uses this same structure for the same male audience, i.e. porn: the innocent wife who is compelled to have sex with the bad guy in order to pay her husband's debt, even over his objections. It's "wrong", she shouldn't do it, but she has no choice, in an action movie this part looks like rage but in porn you show the naked emotion realistically: she *enjoys* it, it is *satisfying*-- not him, it-- so in the porn, the enemy isn't the guy who won her in poker (even if he cheated-- one way or another, he got what he deserved); the enemy, the one who is finally deprived of something in this encounter, is society=the husband: by its emasculating rules she shouldn't do it, but by its rules all debts must be paid. Recall that it was once easier for a man to get away with rape than not paying a debt; this has reversed because we know better than to throw a proven consumer into jail, you throw a violator of proven consumers in jail, for a time proportional to their lost consumption. "That's a very cynical and likely wrong interpretation of the law." Then this is going to sound bananas but civil defense strategy is always evolving, if you accuse someone of rape his lawyer won't bother with what you were wearing or if you were drunk, he'll ask for your credit card statements, you may try to argue

370

wants it. Does she have the privilege of raping him back? No. Can she punch him in the face? Well, she *can*. If self defense was a right, he would just have to take it. But he's not legally obligated to let you punch him in self defense. He's still not allowed to rape you, but he does have the privilege of self defense against your self-defense.

Some of you will say this is stupid and pedantic if not outright inaccurate, and go for the cricoid, and I'm with you. But some of you will, in the moment, come to a very different conclusion: all he was doing was raping her, if you punch him he'll punch you back. She may or may not be blamed for her own rape, but she's very afraid she'll be blamed for escalating it, even if it's only by him. It's not codified but it is common law, you need only to walk to any 4th grade to hear the official response to a kid's plea for justice: "but he hit me

---

you're too traumatized to work but if you're not too traumatized to spend he'll move to dismiss.

III. There Is No Machine

Today the pretense in media is that "there are no real bad guys, only structural problems", so the third group of movies especially popular today neither gives permission for action on behalf of the idea of society nor compels action against a corrupt society: action is so inconceivable that it requires the obliteration of the society. "An ordinary man in extraordinary circumstances"-- zombie attack, alien invasion or natural disaster apocalypse-- the ordinary man doesn't bravely rise to the challenge, society crumbles beneath him allowing him the freedom to do whatever he wants. That's the only way it could be *imagined*. Well, what does he want to do with his new omnipotence that required nearly everyone else's obliteration? Not only does he not go full Kurtz or two thirds Caligula, he becomes defiantly committed to one woman, to family-- he becomes the kind of husband or father he never was before the catastrophe.

Because "capitalist ideological" institutions (e.g. bourgeois love) are still evident in the post-apocalypse world, some have criticized that "it's easier today to imagine the end of the world than to imagine the end of capitalism". This couldn't be more wrong: the *purpose* of the fantasy is to fantasize the creation of those structures that were lacking before the apocalypse. If "bourgeois love" marriage is merely an expression of capitalist ideology, then what these movies show is that he can't imagine capitalism existing *unless* the world ends. It's easier to imagine the end of the world than it is to imagine being in love.

Of course, she also becomes the kind of wife she never was before the apocalypse. Why is the post-apocalyptic wife now 100% devoted to him when before she was cheating/leaving/annoyed? Is it because all the other rival penises are dead? But there are plenty of penises that survived. Other men may be competition but were never a threat to the husband. What he couldn't compete with is what used to satisfy her: *not* other men, but society itself. Post-apocalypse, there are no TV shows to watch, no clothes to want, no celebrities to worship. This is what he had no chance against. The only thing she can want anymore is him. So the destruction-- the punishment-- of this society has to be hyperbolic, by which I mean hyperbolic. It is revenge against it for satisfying her without satisfying him, against that "capitalism" that only served the female market; and simultaneously her deprivation of everything she ever enjoyed.

I should here emphasize that while the movie is set up as a man getting back his wife, it's only set up with that gender orientation because the movie is mostly for men. But the form of the problem it describes has nothing to do with gender but enjoyment. The reason he doesn't like her TV shows is because to him the shows are "stupid". The reason they irritate him is because she enjoys them. But the reason he *hates* them is that her enjoyment requires his exclusion. She'll say its because he always makes snide side comments. No. It is that points of identification with the show-- not just the with the character but with *moments* in the show-- are impossible when the reality next to you on the couch, silent or not, makes you self-conscious of the identification. This is entirely genderless. "This is so asinine, why is a guy in a three piece suit fighting with a sword in a parking garage of a

first!" --That doesn't give you the right to hit him back. "I think it gives me the privilege." -- Sorry, only we grant privileges, and usually in retrospect. "Then I'm going to the media." You have that privilege. For now.

In real life most people don't have a lot of practice with *Welder*-level impotence and terror, so when it happens you regress to the last time you did have some practice, e.g. a toddler faced with an enraged parent. Not a chaotically abusive parent, who has sufficiently proven himself to be outside the law, but an enraged one, who has instilled in you a respect for the Law, which he conveniently embodies, and then improvises. At that age, you couldn't possibly defend yourself and anyway your parent has all the power, so the fear isn't getting hit but total annihilation. Which is why your five year old doesn't run from you when you scream

---

fake wrestling match? And why the hell is he wearing sunglasses?"

But if the goal was to deprive her of what satisfied her, why does he become committed to her and not leave her for some other post apocalyptic Marilyn Monroe? Why doesn't he deprive her of even himself? "Is it because he loves her?" Your guess is that someone loves someone? No, this is an exclusive disjunction: she depends on him or he depends on her. In the post-apocalyptic world he doesn't depend on her, she depends on him. Love is impossible. Now it's safe to appear to love her, to emote spectacularly, see also love for a child, unrequited, or someone's dying. He can only become the kind of husband he never was if she becomes the kind of wife she wasn't then: dependent on him. His real life complaints that she is in fact dependent on him for house/car/bills is mostly wishful thinking: I wish she thought she depended on me for those things so that I don't have to figure out in what way I'm dependent on her. The collapse of society scenario is necessary to sever his enraging dependence on wife and everyone which is logically implied by no one depending on him.

Now that she wants him, now that there is nothing else on the planet which could satisfy her-- and now that apocalypse has even caused her to become *physically* hotter-- what do they do? The sex scene in a typical action movie is as hard core as the rating will allow, but in disaster movies there is no sex, he doesn't seem to want sex at all. Why would he? Now sex is *only* an expression of love, of commitment-- it's now what he thinks she wants and what would satisfy her. She doesn't deserve it, it's enough he's keeping her alive. If the incredible significance of this didn't strike you, here's a summary you will assume is hyperbole: in order to deprive her of satisfaction in fantasy, he sacrificed all fantasies of sex.

The collapse of society scenario offers to men the same thing explicitly offered to certain women by the other popular genre of our time, the alternative universe of alternative universities. Magic is a plus, but sufficient that it has an aesthetic. Of course almost all the characters are men; the presence of one or even two important female protagonists makes it ok to want that kind of world within which there is nothing *for* a woman to want. Ordinarily this should make the genre uninteresting to women, but that's the appeal now: these worlds offer women freedom from having to want. Something is prized, but *nothing else* is prized. Even if "money" might still be prized or at least serves as backstory, consumerism is absent. In a way so obtuse it becomes acute, a fountain pen or an old leather book means you value ideas more than the trappings of ideas, as shown by the trappings of ideas. *Harry Potter* may take place at a private magic school where they use parchment and quills, but all of them were born in 100% modern Britain: why don't those kids want clothes, brand names, electronics? Harry did, before Hogwarts. The only consumer products they covet relate to their use (brooms, wands) but they have shrugged off all other superfluous desires related to identity projection, including "experiences" and "travel". In the real world people can only relate to one another through the branding associated with the products they buy; in Hogwarts, people seem to freely relate without those signals. This naturally appeals to "unCool" Western girls eyeballs deep in the struggle for taller shoes; their heroines don't naturally engage in competitive wanting, and their society doesn't *require* them to participate in it. But there's a cost: the societies

372

at him-- i.e. it was not because of respect for you or deep down inside he knew you loved him. "So... what does it mean if he does run away from you?" I'd have to check the DSM.

The scene is staged like this to terrify the audience. The victim is shown trying to invent meaning, in this case that it's all an interesting technical procedure, that he's only cooperating with a mild dismemberment to avoid the horrible meaninglessness of what is happening to him. With this final assent the Welder now has total power over him; but the victim conveys the impression that by *not* using 100% of his fight or flight, by *choosing* to not to act, he has performed one act of will, and at that moment is spared from becoming *only* nothing more than a powerless victim. You give it or he takes it, either way it's going so the only thing you can do is nothing, and pretend you came up with that on your own.

And now to cumshots.

There's not much in porn that's as reliably arousing as a cumshot to the face, unless it's two cumshots or three faces, though the female consensus used to be that it's degrading. Do they still think so? Guess it depends on which woman you ask, which is most of the problem for those who want to speak for all women. "There's a special place in hell for women who don't support each other." Then I'm lucky you're an atheist. If it was degrading, how come in porn 9/10 times she likes it? If the arousal is *in* the degradation, why doesn't the porn depict her as feeling degraded? Are we saying that men like it when women are being degraded but don't know they're being degraded? That's giving a guy with his penis in his hand an awful lot of credit for sophisticated introspection. "First I deconstruct the relevant binaries inherent in the images, then I blow my load in this sock, which I leave on the floor for my girlfriend to be disgusted by. I don't know why I do that last part." Or the first part.

"Obviously, cumshots derive their eroticism from the appearance of the woman's subjugation: she is on her knees, after all. And there's a disregard for her satisfaction as well." What porn are you watching? She always looks satisfied after the cumshot. In fact, it's the only thing that does satisfy her, otherwise she would keep going, and wanting, and going, and wanting...

You may have noticed something unusual about written erotica; all the cum goes inside her. Shoot this scene on video and all that cum ends up onside her, the question is why? "Because cumshots highlight the man's dominance over the woman?" So when he bellows, "take that, slut!" I'm not supposed to notice she told him to do it? If it's about dominance and power, why would any guy be satisfied with merely the pretense of it?

The simple reason why there's a cumshot in porn is that it's the camera-friendliest way to show the climax, and it gets scripted as pretend dominant; while in written porn the climactic scene can easily be an internal ejaculation since it has to be described in words anyway. It has nothing to do with the audience's patriarchal preference for seeing the male orgasm at all,

---

that offer this freedom from want are essentially feudal. In order to relate to each other, something still has to tell you all who you are. No one can fantasize any other kind.

77 "They'd be reading it electronically." That's what I thought. But in the age of ebooks, *Fifty Shades* held the record for the fastest print sales-- 1M in 11 weeks. The previous record was *The DaVinci Code* in 2003, another safely un-transgressive novel meant to be publicly consumed, especially by critically thinking Christians who gosh darn aren't threatened of heretical ideas, 1M in 36 weeks-- but this at least was before electronic books. *Fifty Shades Of Grey* was meant to be seen read.

which is why when the patriarchy makes mainstream movies for the male demo like action and horror, where copious ejaculate is not allowed, the end of a sex scene is signaled by the woman's orgasm: clean, loud, and female superior. Who has the climax isn't the point, just that the audience knows there is a climax, and cut. Shoot *Basically Instink* as a retro porn and it will be his semen we focus on as she reaches under her bed for what truly satisfies her. The apparent disregard for the woman's orgasm at the end of a porn scene is techniquely the same as the mainstream movies' disregard for his-- not based in sin or psychology but cinematology.

So a technical decision for the convenience of the DP has resulted in something you're really not going to want to believe, and all those who favor increased media representation of "alternative narratives" and sexual practices because it "opens up a space" for them, it makes it possible to even imagine them, should here take special note: now it is nearly impossible to *fantasize* sex that doesn't involve a cumshot, the fake depiction of masculine dominance, the opposite of the situation two generations ago. If you know how to drive stick literally and not just figuratively you may remember a time where the only porn you could get was magazines stolen by an older boy from his stepdad and then buried by the creek to be shared, read, and shred by the neighborhood Huffy gang. "It says she's in nursing school! They have to sleep with the doctors, it's part of their Hypocratic Oath." So take yourself back to pre-pornotron masturbation: in your fantasies, how much cum did you imagine? Did you imagine any at all? Did you imagine the *male* orgasm at all? I saw a sex movie in which the main character didn't even imagine having sex.

There is, therefore, a single instance when an external cumshot does occur in written erotica: when there is someone watching it. It's on her, but it's for them.

That many/most men now find cumshots arousing is an indisputable fact which I do not dispute. But its ubiquity-- that it became the standard turn on for men 12-65 is not because it *is* degrading to women or arousing to men but because it was convenient to photographers and we want to be told how to want. Never mind dominant; prior to VHS, the female perspective on the male orgasm was that it was when he was at his most *vulnerable*; it was the moment of her power over him. So now even if it was factually a fact that facials are degrading, the degradation is the collateral damage of a single camera setup. None of this is driven by "male desire". There is no male desire. Not until someone tells the males how to desire.[78]

---

78 Pro cheerleaders, models, and actresses seem older than the young and younger than the old, on purpose-- maturely youthful/youthful maturity which puts them out safely of reach. Take the conventional wisdom's dichotomy that in the West girls in media are sexualized=made to look older, while in the East women are sexualized=made to look younger. (NB the reverse of the 1970s.) Both are claimed to promote some kind of pedophilia.

But why interpret it? Why not take it literally: making a 30 year old look like a 16 year old or a 16 year old look like a 30 year old doesn't make men want 16 or 30 year olds, but specifically the illusion. For women to look like whatever they're not-- to look fantastic. Do you assume the market is inefficient? This is capitalism, it is hyperefficient. If you wanted 16 year olds looking like 16 year olds then that's what you'd get, child porn laws wouldn't prevent this, in fact, laws would be changed to support the market (e.g. through "progress" in "social science", "Studies® have shown that it reduces real child abuse"). The draw of the fantasy isn't the actual age or the represented age but having them both together-- their incongruity, their impossibility. These are impossible desires.

This is confusing only if you think the media picks these images because they reflect contemporary desires. Its purpose is to take your attention and desire and direct it not towards what the images

374

In porn, as in all media, males don't dominate, women don't dominate, the medium dominates, you will come to it to tell you how to come.

And now with minimal risk (to the producers), porn shoots investigate the cinematic possibilities of internal cumshots, either oopsy or hell yeah, but since you can't use hearsay in HD they have to show it, provide DNA evidence before case closed, so it has to shoot a close up of the leakage. Is that erotic? It's not up to you, it's up to porn. The unintended consequence is that this pornographizes the male refractory period, the part previously conditioned as "and cut", and historically manifested as a sudden rush of sobriety, shame, and shhhh. Now the climax of the movie comes way after the climax of the man; which means

---

represent, but towards the images themselves-- that it controls. The producers of pop music don't want you to like women in general, just *their* women. They have the privilege of having the only place you're going to find a teen who looks like a woman that acts like a teen, or a MILF who looks like a freshman who has never seen one this big or etc.

The complaint that media promotes impossible images that causes unrealistic expectations for the average person thus misses the point: they're not supposed to be possible for anybody, *so* that the only place you can find them is by coming back to the source. You can say it skews men's desires, ok; but any woman who feels the pressure to look like the woman in the magazine is making a very dangerous decision: not only will she fail, but she is revealing that she wants to be wanted by the kind of people-- men and women-- who like impossible images. By someone who wants an impossible love. It's actually worse than this: until and unless she is seen *as* an impossible image, she won't be able to love anyone either.

For this reason you might think "healthy" porn with real bodies is "better", but if it was found as porn, it's porn. The "realness" of the "real body" lets you feel grounded in reality and lets you brag to yourself you're socially responsible, so you can keep going back to porn. It must draw you to porn. Porn is a very jealous lover, and it demands absolute fidelity. As much as it may seem "normal body types" become more desirable because of their inclusion in porn, or advertising, it's only a temporary, superficial desirability; any media approved hyperblonde from the 1990s will tell you how rarely someone told her she was perfect and how relentlessly her perfect body's imperfections enraged... the type of man she wanted to want her. Media can always make a body type more desirable; but it cannot make it more satisfying. It can only make it less so.

I saw *Transformers Age Of Extinction* in the theatre, and I overheard a guy who presumably had access to the same internet I did say, "first time actress in a Michael Bay movie? I'm betting this is going to be awesome." That's a great bet to take the other side of because then you win either way, except Michael Bay is smarter than all of us: he took an underaged starlet, sent her to hair and makeup, dressed her in short shorts and a tank top, arched her back/breasts/hips needlessly and cinematically and shot her from 45 degrees above and below the midriff-- but rather than letting her stand as the sex object he made her into, in iconoclastic violation of the rules of modeling, advertisements, movies and TV, he scripted the underaged girl that looked like a woman as an underaged girl and all the time *used explicit dialogue to tell you that she was underage*. There was even a seemingly unnecessary scene where her boyfriend (20) explains that since they had been dating back when they were both underage, their relationship was legal (=moral). In other words, Bay hypersexualized the girl and then reminded you it was not okay for you to sexualize her, causing a psychological dissonance that leads to a feeling of impotence. The psychiatric term for that is *monopoly*.

You could say the movie is for teenage boys, for whom it would be legitimate to lust after said starlet, in which case Bay was circumscribing the appropriate teen audience, keeping out the squares, letting the teens that the movie is theirs-- in this way targeting the movie to the smallest demographic possible, the ones with the least purchasing power. I did say Bay was smarter than all

forget about gnawing your arm off, a man is going to find himself having to *perform* after his orgasm, no stupid, not for the woman's benefit, still no one cares about her, but in order for the man to get what he thinks he's supposed to wants. And for you all Nexus 9s you may want to think through the societal consequences of pornographizing not pulling out. "So abortion will be not just legal, but routine?" It's not up to us, it's up to porn, though you should be aware that the porn of ESL countries loves to eroticize the pregnancy risk. "He's putting a baby inside me!" I'm not one to kink shame, but really? That's a turn on for men? For the purpose of this joke as well as technical accuracy the CSA is an ESL country.[79]

You should know that post-cum shot performance has always been routine in gay porn,

---

of us. I stand by that statement. So no.

If you don't trust the Bayesian gaze to tell you who you are, trust advertisers, because while Bay films are obviously for teenage boys, the commercial before the movie was for "well fitting" khakis, with the tag line, "Are you a victim of Dad pants?" Ok, so this is a movie for Dads. Well, made for boys, who are now Dads with boys, from which the new boys will collaterally learn how to want. Let's see what's coming in post modernity's quarter life crisis.

The scientist-father is played by midlife crisis benchmark Mark Wahlberg: he has kids but also time to work out. Where's mom? She's dead. She has to be, this is a movie for Dads. Moms never let Dads go work out, and for sure they won't let them go see *Transformers*. "Oh, when do I get two hours off to do what I want?" Wahlberg turns into an action hero because this is a movie for boys, AND Wahlberg doesn't have a love interest because this is a movie for Dads: they don't feel love, only lust; and if they're watching *Transformers* then the sure bet is they've accustomed themselves to satisfying their lust only visually and single handedly. This is why Wahlberg has a hot daughter and not a hot wife: he *doesn't* want to have sex with her, he doesn't want to have sex at all, and a hot wife entails some obligation.

So what's at issue here is not "is it ok to notice a hot teen"-- it is, as long as they're under contract-- but when is it ok to *not* want sex, but still take credit for sexuality? Daughters? Before you recoil from the description of this idea please observe it is already the mainstreamed maneuver everywhere: the proximity to someone else's sexuality substitutes for your own. Male celebrities choose to bring their grown daughters to publicity events-- around the time they stop bringing their wives; but more importantly, female celebrities also take their daughters, too. "They're helping them get exposure." Odd they never take their sons, I thought celebrity pics were for women and this was a patriarchy. "I got it from my momma." Vintage. If we're going with the theory that women's fashion is subject to massive patriarchal input-- in other words, if no matter how much it's a woman's right to choose her wardrobe, no matter how much she dresses for herself, you still think that the available fashion choices which exist are nevertheless based on male desire-- then the increased sexualization of female workplace attire when they are legally protected from workplace attention has less to do with freeing her to make her own choices, and more about him taking credit for her choices. "Nah, she and I just work together." You don't say. "But it still counts, right?" No sex is implied by this proximity, exactly the opposite: no one *can* be sexual with anyone, so no one *has* to be sexual with anyone, but you get the credit for being in the world of sexuality. Now the friend zone is the sweet spot, if a man is close with a woman who has no interest in his penis, it means she's the phallus.

79 19th century men could frequent prostitutes, and they had mistresses, but they demanded absolute fidelity from their wives. Women did not fornicate, not for love and certainly not for lust, that was the right-- right, not privilege-- of men; the women had to make due with writing letters, church, or a consultation with Dr. Freud. They were paragons of virtue. Does this sound like an accurate portrait of late 19th century bourgeois gender roles? You should pass the finger paints to the next 5 year old, he has a brontosaurus he's been itching to draw.

376

and real women. You still have to account for the camera, even if there isn't one: the mere possibility of a camera is what let's us know which one is the man.

I'm supposed to ask, can you fantasize in a way that doesn't look like *a* porn? What makes you think you can thus imagine a different economic system, a different political system-- a different you? But it's too late for this, you can't even imagine the continuation of the world you are already in-- it is impossible for you to imagine this. "But things can't go on like this." Because of you they can only go on like this. "But things are too complicated nowadays to be left to chance, if we want to survive we're going to have to start planning things out." But the world you don't understand requires an imagination you don't possess, which is why you want someone else to take the power you don't want. So here I can clear up

_____

"Paragon of virtue" is one of those phrases that enjoys a literary resurgence every generation followed by ten years of recession as people are embarrassed they used such a cliché. Oddly, "paragons of virtue" as a description of women was a phrase the patriarchy seemed not to need in the patriarchal 19th century, yet its use quadrupled right after the 19th Amendment. I'll leave you to a calendar to work out the significance. You know what word men used all the time that you would think would have been uniquely unnecessary to the naturally manly patriarchy of the 19th century? "Manliness." It's an invalid yet reliable historical pattern: when your gender is important, you're not, and war is coming. Victorian women were not Puritans, psychologically or geographically, so if you're imagining a female sexuality bound by the strict yolk of Calvinism you are on the wrong side of the Atlantic, or Channel, and century, and wrong. "Sex was immoral. Sex carried a lot of guilt." That's what you got out of *Notes From The Underground*, let alone Freud? No. Easy promiscuity has always been a hoped for and thus relatively trivial misdemeanor that served as convenient pretext for displaced rage, as anecdotal evidence I present you with one slut's instantly successful defense against the accusations of a bloodthirsty mob, and this was given 200 years earlier: "Good people, be civil-- I am the *Protestant* whore!"

The men went to prostitutes, but they didn't do this in secret. There was discretion, of course; don't ask/don't tell and salicylated mercury, but while everyone agreed prostitution was bad, the prostitutes were accessible and everywhere, especially in England, a country famous for having religiously tortured and burned hundreds of thousands of promiscuous women on the charge of witchcraft, except for that they didn't. Lord Acton said he and a friend counted 185 prostitutes on the 2 mile walk home from the opera house, but that kind of precision is about showing others how much they've underestimated a problem in order to delimit for himself a problem which he overestimated. Seek and you shall find, and anyway what married man goes to the opera house with another man except to blow it up?   A widely read source reported that at a time when the male population of London of all ages was one and a quarter million, the prostitutes were receiving clients at a rate of two million per week. That might seem high, but in economic terms it's about £2M/year, or 1% of GDP. So in the age of repressed sexuality, incurable syphilis, and the quenching power of chimney sweeps, the main difference is that the prostitutes were public with it. The female ones, anyway.

One explanation is that prostitution was a public shame and a private guilt and so needed to be condemned-- but the system quietly permitted it so that men could still access it. Prostitution was the pressure valve for the patriarchy's steampunk libido. Fair enough-- but why were the prostitutes so obvious? They couldn't pretend to be ballerinas, or at least seamstresses? Why would a sexually repressed society want to have it known publicly that men went to prostitutes? What was the obviousness a defense against?

One unconventional explanation is that prostitution was obvious because of the benefit to women. Condemn it, lament it, but mainstream it: you only get minimal wages for standing in a factory and a girl's got to get laid. Meanwhile the upstanding wives and mothers who supervised the home for no wages did not want to be caught lying down as part of the job. Why did wives publicly pretend to

a bit of intellectual dishonesty. The usual argument that modern society is too big/unfair/complex to leave to chance or "the free market" may be true, and it may be true that central planning is vitally necessary. But you are asserting this argument not because it is too complex, but because it is too complex for you to imagine. So then how could you possibly imagine planning it? You couldn't, it's impossible, not because it is impossible but because it's unimaginable, for you, which is why what you actually want is what you can imagine: some other omnipotent entity imposing order on your chaos.

"Well, I have imagined it, and I have some good ideas." Yes, they're the same ones the other subscribers were given. You've convinced yourself that "all that openness", all that media, or news, or analysis, or porn-- more experiences means more knowledge and

---

be prudes, refraining from sex-- with men they loved? Because of the growing, public criticism that marriage was a form of prostitution, which had rapidly become the conventional wisdom among the conventionally wise. It didn't matter that the criticism was false. Because the criticism was now out in the open, marriage had to find a way to prove it wrong. How do you prove you're not a prostitute, even if you married your only client? How do you prove your wife is not a prostitute, especially if no one else would touch you for less? How do you prove your deal isn't a quid pro quo? Can't hide the quid, it's there on your finger, so you hide the quo. "Good heavens, what an impertinent suggestion, barter my sex for security? Have I awoken in Utah? I'll have you know, we don't even *have* sex." NB the actual Latin translation of quid pro quo is substitution not transaction, this *instead* of that, e.g. marriage instead of sex, which is literally more accurate, and would have been a good clue we were interpreting it wrong, on purpose.

The novels of Jane Austen are dripping with the precum of rich bachelor quid, yet nowhere in the books do any of the women inspire any overt lust nor do the men feel it; the quo is repressed, and returns as cunnilingus in conversation, and if you want an easy example of regression to the oral stage I present you with the following:

> Emma listened, and then cooly responded, "I shall not be satisfied,
> until he comes."

And cut.

"The act of sex was a sin." I'm not sure you know what acting is, let alone sin. "Sex was a sin for women." Why would women be more guilty than the men, especially if the men paid to get it? Why would masturbation be a sin? The reason Freud was able to detect guilt for repressed thoughts was that it was only the thoughts that generated guilt; one cannot be guilty for actions alone, not when they are impulsive, compelled, or for some other reason. The sin wasn't in the sex act, but in the lust, which is why there are countless varieties of manifestations of sexual guilt but I have never met nor heard of a man who felt guilty about the act of rape.

The sin was always the idea of the act, something only an omniscient God would be able to detect; so we had to abandon an omniscient God. Lust was bad enough, but way worse was causing lust in another person, being too comely would be her undoing-- and his. Men felt lust, but it's laughable that a man could cause lust-- except in another man, and therein you see the problem. But a woman could generate lust merely by being *described*, turns out men aren't particularly visual after all, which is why in Jane Austen when a woman plays matchmaker, she describes the woman to entice the man; but she has to detail his situation of 300 pounds a year to get the woman on board. Any of you progressives want to try setting your friend up on a blind date based on compatible interests alone? "He's interested in investment banking." Then we're compatible. It was even a sin for a wife to be a temptation to her husband, not into having sex-- sexual congress between a wife and husband was perfectly ok-- but into lust, on those occasions whereby ankle slip or Freudian slip or nothing she did at all, she tempted him into desiring her. In fiction, wives were never beautiful-- unless they were scheduled to fall in Act II, but prostitutes were always beautiful. Today it's the

imagination. Here is the consequence of not being able to fantasize: you can only know what you are told, you can only want what someone else wants; and so your happiness becomes logically relative to someone else's. Why the shift from fighting absolute poverty to fighting relative inequality? In your heart you'd rather the poor were poorer if it meant the rich were less rich; so the powerful slogans will target the 1% but the urban activists will physically target the 40%, then the 80%, then 101%. The grass is always greener on the other side of the fence, yet you both have grass, we could try making your grass greener or his grass browner but the human eye has been trained to detect the subtlest differences in hue, so that neither will ever be fair enough. The current impasse of today is historical: first we blamed ourselves, later we blamed the other guy, but now your omniscient mind blames the fence; but hell no are you going to risk doing anything about it because if you fail the other guy will laugh at

---

opposite, being able to generate lust in another person is celebrated as an evolutionary progress, so every wife's a MILF while prostitutes are... not constrained by societal beauty norms. You don't want to be caught going to one but a blowjob hardly counts against the ledger. True also in prison. I mention these historical changes so you're not surprised when your kids bring them back, it's the generational punishment for your selfishness. The logical extension of this would be modern fiction in which the "other woman" is beautiful, but the wife is also beautiful but less sexual, and consequently since neither of them can be logically immoral or weak-- they both have the power of attractiveness-- the story has to make them become friends or at least not enemies: the wife takes credit for the other's sexuality by being proximate to it. The weak or morally flawed character would thus be the husband. "It's women sticking together." Maybe they shouldn't. If your chromosomes trump your marriage you need to detox from your preferred sedative and apologize to your kids. "I suffer from anxiety." It's because you identify as a symptom.

You wouldn't speak of it in polite company, but as long as there was implicit transactional logic to all female sex-- prostitutes and mistresses got paid with money; wives with home and security-- everything made sense. The problem was how to understand, for example, wives cheating on their husbands? Taking such a huge risk for seemingly no reason? What kind of a woman would risk her husband, savings and her capital for a guy with mutton chops and an Inverness cape? "He's such a sensitive, delicate soul." It's porphyria.

A lawyer friend of Freud's tried to disprove Freud's "dreams are wish fulfillments" theory by recounting a not very fulfilling nightmare Freud secretly wished he had had: in the dream, a cop pulls up in a horse carriage and the man is "arrested for infanticide"; he asks for time to get his affairs in order. Freud's analysis is textbook a-ha: men can't be charged with infanticide because it is a female crime, so the wish fulfillment is that the mistress he was ejaculating on didn't get pregnant.

If it's a wish fulfillment, why did it manifest as a nightmare? Freud says the anxiety wasn't caused by the dream, but that pre-existing anxiety is what caused the wish fulfillment dream to manifest into a nightmare. Ok, would you like to know what Freud thinks is the source of the "neurotic anxiety" that distorted the dream? It was the lawyer's practice of "coitus interruptus". Pulling out is what did him in. This was before cumshots were eroticized practice, because this was before photography set the eroticized practice. Freud says that pulling out is not just less sexually satisfying, but more dangerous, it increases the pressure in a man's steampunk libido and kaboom.

To get to this conclusion, Freud obtains, then bafflingly ignores, some key facts in the lawyer's history: that the guy was cheating on his wife; with a woman who was herself married; and that he had already cheated on his wife with another woman whom he had once gotten pregnant-- and this woman then went and got an abortion, though the man was quick to point out that he "had nothing to do with her carrying out her intention." Nope, none of that caused anxiety. To Freud, the whole trouble was "coitus interruptus", which unlike "abortion" is an act so unspeakable that without Latin obfuscation it is even unwritable.

you. The political question is, how long can you stand the other guy's not browner grass? Ok, you will always want to murder him, but what will be the precipitant for actually trying? It's history, not math, so the answers aren't in the back of the book but in the front: it will be when you give some other omnipotent entity all your power to act for you, and then it tells you you're obligated to act for it.[80] [81]

It seems like every girl with a complicated backstory likes to be choked during sex, so if choking means male power and dominance, then women wanting it must mean they miss male power and dominance, and you can see where all this is going. She doesn't just miss this male power in her own sexual life; as a reliably voracious omnivore of on camera reality, this

---

But hear him out: Freud says neurotic anxiety is only fastened on to the idea which accompanies it, as with a phobia; that neurotic anxiety corresponds to a libido which has been deflected from its object. "Like masturbating to porn?" Back then yes, now no. By the theory, masturbation to porn would lessen anxiety. The "object" isn't necessarily a penis or vagina; it is whatever your delirious libido is aimed at; and in your case the normal object is the porn. On the other hand, this logic would imply that in the age of porn, a full ejaculation into a real life person not just fails to satisfy but increases inner tension. Madness? Gentlemen: have you ever ejaculated during sex but still had to masturbate afterwards because it didn't-- take? Yeah. Remember how that used to be the kind of thing a girl would do? Still is.

Freud may have loved cocaine but so did Sherlock Holmes, and both of them were good at detecting a liar; though admittedly Freud was really bad at this with women. So take him at his word: what if all those other facts weren't relevant-- to the lawyer? What if Freud sensed in this man a total absence of guilt about cheating, aborting, anything? What if this guy's soul was so made of battery acid and urinal cake that the only thing he felt after two duplicitous near misses was "Phew!" and a wish to upstage Freud?

Then Freud would be a genius, and I'm not saying he's not, but here again Freud doesn't apply his own method, and you should observe that every time Freud interprets a dream presented to him as a counterexample of his dream theory, he misinterprets it.

In this case, not getting her pregnant is not an unconscious wish, it's a straight up, down on your knees, prayer to the Almighty. Freud's interpretation that the lawyer is worried she'll get pregnant is so obvious *to the lawyer* that Freud's *interpretation* can only be the dream's defense against interpretation. In fact, according to the rules, the repressed wish would return in its inverted form; but in a person who knows the method like this lawyer does, the inverted form is the *interpretation* that she doesn't get pregnant, while the repressed wish is *literally* that she does get pregnant and then kills it. That is why the dream is associated with anxiety, even as it is a wish. Infanticide is a female crime, so him being arrested for it = she being arrested for it= it is all her fault, none of it is his fault. Hold on: not her pregnancy-- she's not actually pregnant-- but the *sex*. The wish fulfillment is that even the law (=some other omnipotent entity) recognizes that it's all the slut's fault that he cheated on his wife, because she's a horny temptress as proven by-- how easily he was tempted? How much she wanted it? No: how easily she got pregnant. Because those other things can't be seen by an omnipotent (=not omniscient) God. He needs concrete proof she wanted it. Pregnancy, like spreading her legs, is a choice, sometimes consciously and always unconsciously, until a highly controversial=publicized discovery made by men a hundred years later made pregnancy almost obsolete as a modern marker of her desire. "The Pill?" No, the vaginal orgasm.

A prostitute doesn't get pregnant by any one man, there's too many of them, her pregnancy is a manifestation of the amount of guilt in her ledger, it is cumulative, just like syphilis, proportional to the number of partners. Don't roll your intellectually superior 10th grade biology eyes at me and say no one's believed that for millennia, in my lifetime Freddy Krueger was backstoried as the evil spawn of a nun who got gang raped by 100 maniacs, even a kid who got a 6/10 on the meiosis quiz

is what she finds lacking everywhere. In other words, if she wants you to choke her, it means you look like you would but she knows you can't.

Never mind why some women might "secretly" crave male power, take them at their word. If it's male power they want, why are they content with only the appearance of it? Doesn't the reality of "he's not actually going to choke me out since I can stop him any time I want to" detract from the eroticism of the "male power?" "It's just fantasy." Yes. "The fantasy is the loss of control." Why are you only interpreting half of it? How is a loss of control a *fantasy*? "What I want is a guy who wants me so much he'll do anything to seize me." Except actually seize you. "It makes me feel desirable to be taken, wanted so much." But who are you fooling? You know he's faking it, and he hopes to God you know he's faking

---

knows it doesn't work that way, but how and precisely when the soul enters the body is still an open scientific question, and God knows there's no reason it can't be epigenetic, or at least probabilistic. But a mostly oligamous mistress and a Don Juan lawyer is tricky business. Who is guilty for that sex, if she's not slutty enough for it to be only her? If no one confirms it is her fault, then it might be his. I'm not even suggesting he should he feel guilty, this is beyond him and anyway there's always brandy; but according to the ledger someone has to pay and it's damn well not going to be him. How can he trick her into assuming all of the debt? Don't speculate, the answer is literally right there in Freud's description: when the lawyer had a previous affair with a different married woman and got her pregnant, she went and had an abortion; of course, he had "nothing to do with her carrying out her intention... but for a long time I naturally felt very nervous in case the business came out." Why, if infanticide is a female crime? Because in 1895, the business he would have been blamed for is the sex.

It is basic market psychology: the moment people understood Freud's explanation for how guilt was handled by the unconscious, everyone's unconscious stopped handling it that way-- it became the defense. In this dream and its wish you have a description of the modern approach to guilt, where instead of a Sophoclean, "even though I didn't know, still I am guilty"-- which sounds worse but allows for redemption-- we instead find someone with the power to assign guilt to people: we lose any hope of redemption but we know exactly who we have to fool. Look carefully, and feminists grab a pen: the woman didn't ask him for his permission to get the abortion not because he would have said no but because he would have had to say yes, *and then he would have exploded.* He caused her not to ask him for permission, so that he could truly believe=say that he would have forbidden it-- yet simultaneously benefit from it, and cause her to assume all the guilt. "That bitch did exactly what I wanted twice against my demands!" That's the social contract: you have the privilege of guilt free sex, but it's a woman's right to choose.

It is not hard to see in this lawyer's words and his mistress's actions the future of abortion. The way it did not go is that pregnancy triggered an ethical obligation. Neither a civil obligation, such that however it goes the man is liable for damages. The public debate became about *rights*: rights of the fetus vs rights of the woman, and this was very loud; but the form of the debate quietly divided sexual *power* precisely at the moment of conception. For one group of lunatics, all *sex* was inherently coercive, women were at best unknowing victims on a spectrum of rape or institutionalized prostitution, even affirmative consent still exists under invisible but oppressive structural pressures, so these ever-victims need some power after the fact to mitigate the damage; while for the opposing group of maniacs, all sexual power was front-loaded to women, her looks alone can kill, if you had the ability to act on her then she must have caused you to want it; so it was only fair she subordinate herself after the fact.

This, not the rights question, was the insoluble binary even in the 19th century. The vociferous public debate about changing the status of abortion was an end in itself, as evidenced by the fact that the status of abortion did not change at all, see also now; it did not enter the public consciousness in what way each of the *three* groups-- individual men, individual women, and the audience-- benefited

381

it. The fantasy isn't the loss of control-- the fantasy is having a loss of control AND full control, simultaneously-- that's a fantasy because it is impossible to have these things at the same time, they are logically exclusive. The only way for it to be possible is if you are *acting* for someone-- or something-- who is watching, if it is pornographized: you know you have full control, but to a hypothetical observer, it looks like a loss of control. It *looks* hot-- so it is hot. The problem with being the main character in your own movie is that in order for it to be satisfying, you need an audience. "Because ultimately we really just want to be looked at?" Ha. No. Because someone has to be seen being deprived.

There's a joke, and the joke is a rape joke, which I'm told is never funny, unless it's told

---

not from abortion but from the abortion debate, regardless of whether abortion remained legal or illegal: in both cases, if the debate was framed as about women's rights, men had no choice but to disavow any responsibility even as they retained the power. Responsibility not just for the decision to abort, or the cost, or the consequences; never mind if the man was secretly relieved she chose to abort; her act of abortion absorbed all of his responsibility in the sex act: obviously, she, not he, *always* had more power to act. Of course she probably still thinks of herself as not having much power since, after all, she felt compelled to get the abortion, but-- and I'm only quoting the feminist primary sources-- no one cares what she thinks. A peek into the secret ledger of the dreaming lawyer, i.e. being publicly charged with a crime he *literally* could not have committed, confirms the spectacular logical consequence. He may have cheated on his wife with her, but her getting an abortion against his will meant she was worse, she was the guilty one. *He was redeemed through her.*

So Freud was wrong. Yes, of course he consciously prayed she wouldn't get pregnant, but the unconscious wish is not that she wouldn't get pregnant, the unconscious wish-- the wish he is not allowed to have-- is that she *would* get pregnant, and then commit infanticide, so that he could not have been guilty. Coitus interruptus prevented a pregnancy, phew! But Latinizing-- medicalizing-- normalizing-- a camera ready sex act left him with all of the guilt, all of the responsibility for atonement. The cops won't be looking for him but the Devil surely will. You with me so far? Well, it's much worse than that.

Here's Freud's description of the dream:

> [For this example dream] I am indebted, not to a patient, but to an intelligent jurist of my acquaintance.

> "I dream," my informant tells me, "that I am walking in front of my house with a lady on my arm. Here a closed carriage is waiting; a man steps up to me, shows me his authorization as a police officer, and requests me to follow him. I ask only for time in which to arrange my affairs..."

> -Do you happen to know upon what charge you were arrested?

> "Yes; I believe for infanticide."

> -Infanticide? But you know that only a mother can commit this crime upon her new-born child?

Well, I'm no jurist, so I'll admit when I first heard this I didn't know that, but obviously an intelligent 19th century German jurist would. So it's a really good thing he's an intelligent 19th century German jurist, because for an intelligent 19th century German anything other than jurist, "infanticide" has a very different association. In other words, he's not a jurist, Freud made that up. Just stay with me.

382

by an attractive woman, in which case it's smart, or an unattractive woman, in which case its subversive. The rules keep changing, and NB it makes no difference what the actual joke is. Anyway, here is a definitionally smart joke which turns out indeed not to be funny:

"Have you ever noticed that your ugliest friend is most afraid of being raped?"

The rest of the joke is, "get in line," but it's not relevant here.

If you find yourself caught in an insoluble argument, with both sides not simply disagreeing but utterly unable to understand the other's perspective-- the same phrases being repeated louder, "wait, wait, wait: yes or no-- just answer! Yes or no?!" and, "what part of this don't you understand??!?"-- then look around, a third party is involved, he is forcing you

---

> ...By the dream you are assured that you have not begotten a child, or, what amounts to the same thing, that you have killed the child.

Do you really think Freud thinks this? Preventing it is the same as, say, drowning it? Those aren't even medically equivalent, and Freud was a neurologist. But more importantly, begetting is a male crime, it says it right there in the law, a child is begotten of the father, through whom all things are made. Freud wants to force an Oedipal parallel, so a child needs to be killed by its father, he wants to lead the lawyer into thinking that pulling out is equivalent to him Oedipally murdering a delivered child, conveniently supporting his theory of the Oedipus Complex. But they're not equivalent, it's insane, there's no way Freud could demonstrate the connecting links.

> I can easily demonstrate the connecting links. Do you remember, a few days ago we were talking about the troubles of matrimony, and about the inconsistency of permitting coitus so long as no impregnation takes place, while at the same time any preventive act committed after the ovum and the semen meet and a foetus is formed is punished as a crime? In this connection we recalled the medieval controversy about the moment of time at which the soul actually enters into the foetus, since the concept of murder becomes admissible only from that point onwards.

I can't imagine how high two people have to be for the conversation to go from something like "my prudish wife won't blow me" to pontificating on the exact moment of ensoulment; but you may be surprised to learn that the medieval debate was settled in favor of way later than you think. Aquinas was an Aristotelian, an empiricist not a dogmatist, so the immortal soul entered the body not theoretically at conception but when it caused reliably observable effects on the body, about one to two months later, at the quickening. See? Now the *Highlander* makes sense. Off topic and fun, the modern Catholic Church's position on "life begins at conception" draws support not from theological sophistry but on "the valuable confirmation of modern genetic science", though under its breath the Church still mutters eppur si muove. Even more interestingly, the Orthodox Church went Pythagorean not Aristotelian, and have always maintained the inseparability and immediacy of body and soul, now and unto the ages of ages, and all this may seem like a debate with little relevance today but does usefully explain why there are no Greeks in the *Highlander*.

The biggest clue that this is Freud pulling a fast one is that the subsequent associations don't come from the jurist's unconscious: they come from Freud's mouth. Instead of asking the jurist to free associate, he plants the idea into his mind, tricking the jurist into thinking the idea was his all along. If that's not suspiciously Unfreudian enough for you, Freud then interprets the dream with something that happens *after* it had been dreamt:

> "Of course, too, you know the gruesome poem by Lenau, which puts infanticide and birth-control on the same plane."

to accept the form of the argument so that he can profit from the discussion and prevent the true question from being articulated. Let's see if this is true for rape.

First, note that we are not allowed to consider as pathological the amount someone fears rape, ever.   This does not apply to a straight male's fear of rape, where it is the only consideration. The second indisputable fact-- which is the consequence of the first-- is that the stats on rapes show they are as plentiful as they were when TV was first invented, according to the media that invented the stats. Sure, the official rape statistics say there's been a decline of 50%, but those women don't count, the official rape numbers don't really target the only demographic that media-matters: college girls. Best to focus on frat party rapes because the assailant can reliably code as a lacrosse player and the victim can reliably code as

---

> "Strangely enough, I happened, as though by chance, to think of Lenau this morning."

Never mind psychoanalysis, he invented Inception. It's possible the dream did trigger the waking thought about Lenau's poem, but if that thought came to this jurist after the dream, then Lenau isn't part of the meaning, it's part of the distortion, it's part of the dream's defense. However…. there is in fact a poet that is referenced in the dream, but it isn't to Lenau, which is why Freud tries to fool him with Lenau instead of asking him to free associate from "infanticide". Because if you say "arrested for infanticide" to any intelligent 19th century anybody with the possible exception of a jurist, the immediate association would be to *Faust*. Especially for Freud, who was obsessed with *Faust*. We all remember Sophocles but he's persona non grata, it's Goethe who is everywhere in Freud's writings, needlessly or out of context, there's even a Goethe quote a few paragraphs up from this very dream, if you read Freud and *Faust* a few times or once at the same time you will never be able to unsee it-- unsee it, as he wants us to. Faust is the solution to Oedipus, reversed; so goes the psychology of the 19th century, and 21st.

Freud suggests to the fake jurist that infanticide is "legally a female crime" to moor it to real world boring legal procedure and block it from *Faust*. He tells us this man is a jurist so that this sounds believable to us. Then he suggests it's a poem by Lenau so that it's definitely not *Faust*. Well, what happens in *Faust* that he doesn't want said? Faust seduces Gretchen and then abandons her; she goes bananas and kills the baby, and is sent to prison and then executed for infanticide. In the very end not only does Faust not get punished, but when in her death she accepts all the guilt, he is also spiritually redeemed, through her.

This isn't simply a literary reference, the "jurist's" dream doesn't merely associate to *Faust*; in fact, the dream is an acting out of Chapters 23 and 25, in which Mephistopheles offers to help Faust save Gretchen from prison. Faust will bring Gretchen out, where Mephistopheles will have horses waiting. But Gretchen refuses to be saved, so Mephistopheles tells Faust to come with him-- and leave Gretchen behind-- but Faust delays, he has to get his affair in order, finally going with Mephistopheles only after Gretchen is judged-- *and he is redeemed*.

The inciting event of *Faust* is the bet of his soul, which he wasn't using anyway, that Mephistopheles can't show Faust some experience that satisfies him. It's not in the primary or secondary sources, but Mephistopheles technically won the bet; Mephistopheles does give Faust an experience which satisfies him, Faust may not say "stay, thou art so fair" but he does say stay, and he says it to Mephistopheles. He's the experience. Mephistopheles's presence means Faust is special. In the Marlowe version Faust sells his soul, here it's a bet, the difference is that in the original Faust knows the devil is real and in Goethe's story Faust is surprised that he's really there. In Marlowe the devil is real and always right around the corner, willing to bargain for anyone's soul, and in Goethe the devil's only interested in Faust, obviously because Faust is worth it. In Marlowe, the soul has value that can be exchanged. Here the soul only has value because of the bet. In fact, if you take this to the end, the only person who values the prize is Mephistopheles.

hot, and even if they're not their hot friends are always happy to be outraged on camera.

Decades of awareness programming haven't budged the prevalence of campus rape: One in five women is sexually assaulted in college, though according to a reliable secondary source only about 12 percent report it to authorities, but apparently 100% report it to secondary sources. I wonder if that's 12% of the 20% = 2% of the 100%, or 12% of the 100% which is 50% of the 20%? I suppose it's too hard to figure all this out, for a reason. "No one wants to send their daughter to a rape school," some person who didn't think it through said about why campus rapes might be deliberately underreported, as if the daughter might run the numbers and think it was well worth the risk. "I like the school's active social life." It's safer than you think, in 4 years there's only about 330 higher risk days, if you count

---

Note this "jurist's" sexual history: a cheater who's been with at least two married women; Freud knows his sexual technique well enough to "assume that you took this precaution several times during the night". The man thinks of himself as a seducer, a manly sophisticate of manly will and decision who manily pursues beauty and pleasure, though if you described this lothario to anyone who knew him they'd cock an eyebrow and say, "are you talking about Henry from accounting? His hobby is sandwiches." So much for being a Don Juan, the next best thing is to sublimate it all-- to make it sublime-- so he can become a Faust. I know I can be deplatformed for saying this, but Faust is a jerk. Faust, the great hero of the Enlightenment, is man who has no fear talking to the devil but is too afraid to approach a woman. He couldn't talk to let alone seduce Gretchen on his own-- he literally needed black magic. Faust is a story for a key male demographic that longs for an emperor; 20 years earlier that demographic was committing suicide because they identified with fictional Werther, who suicided because a married woman wouldn't sleep with him. Is that Oedipal? He can't kill her, or the husband, or move on, so he kills himself, which causes her to be miserable, which I'm pretty sure was the goal and I'm going to posit is anyway how she would have felt if she had slept with him. I recognize that's not the standard interpretation. "This world is not built for people like me." Well, that's true, anyway. The impossible desire to be a Don Juan becomes the unfulfilled wish to be a Faust, but no one's going to believe it unless you are chosen by a Mephistopheles, and since the devil doesn't exist and anyway couldn't be less interested in you you're going to need a Gretchen, simply find a woman who's been underestimated all her life and temporarily overestimate her. The envy of the effortlessly mutual carnality that seems the privilege of others but barred to him is transformed into an overvaluation of his own self-worth-- "I know too much"-- such that he is worthy of being redeemed.

Except there's a pathological level to this, it's not simply that the wayward pixie dream girl mediates the redemption of the manic sinner and then has the good sense to eternally vanish. Unlike Christianity which is redemption for your sins, in *Faust* committing the sin is the way to redemption. If he doesn't trick her, she won't love him, and if she doesn't love him, he's screwed. But since sex is always a trick-- either he manipulated her or she did it for some other reason-- how can he be sure she will redeem him, how can he be sure she wants him? Wisdom won't help, he needs a sign that by him she is well pleased. It's the 19th century, female orgasms haven't been discovered. So he has to get her pregnant. He doesn't want to get her pregnant, of course... but only that will count.

If you do the stats on Freud's writing-- or even take this case history as an example: the man committed adultery with two married women-- then in the era of sexual repression there are 2x more sexually adventurous women than men. I don't know if that was actually true, I only know that it appeared true, if not on a walk home from the opera house than at least from the contemporary media. Women were not actually pure and sexless, they were supposed to be pure and sexless, but not because of an evolutionary fear about paternity but so that by being upright they could pull a man up and *if they fell they could push a man up*. Faust was an alchemist so we should take his chemistry to the end: if he could take a pure woman, transform her into a slut, and then into a mother, and then into a murderer, it would mean he had been purified. This is the strategy we use

385

Thursdays, which you'd be a nerd not to.

There is no way for me to verify the statistics, but fortunately the caring folks at RAIIN had also found that 25% of college women had been raped, and they at least referenced the study that let them find this. I'm not bad at math, so I tried to hazmat my way through the referenced 433 page study from the American Association of Universities. Turns out the stat is from a 5 minute internet survey sent to college students, only about 20% of whom responded. The AAU designed a study to maximize selection bias and still could only engineer a 25% positive? Couldn't you get the governor to invalidate some of the other votes? Let me be mathematically precise: I'm not saying those numbers are wrong, I'm saying they're not even wrong. The actual rate could be *higher*, or lower, or equal-- those figures

---

today, the modern innovation is to transform the mother back into a slut that you won't touch. "Alchemy's not real." Fair enough, but you don't know any chemistry, either, so what's the difference?

The patient told the dream to Freud as a counterexample to the theory of wish fulfillment, knowing in advance that whatever the dream meant Freud would necessarily use it to find an Oedipal interpretation. But the real wish was indeed that the woman would be arrested-- and executed-- for infanticide, that someone would die for his sins, out of love for him. That sounds like what Christ was supposed to have done, but once someone invented steam engines it was hard to imagine love coming from anyone who identified as a man. What Goethe had done was suggested that a woman could redeem us, here on earth, and that was a savior everyone could get from behind. "Go," says the woman offering her head so that others may have it, "your sins are forgiven." Finally, a religion that speaks to modern issues.

This is the purpose of the infanticide, but Freud wants the dream to be Oedipal guilt and coitus interruptus, with the wish that she doesn't get pregnant. So instead of Goethe's *Faust*, Freud throws him off the trail and suggests/plants that the appropriate reference is the infanticide poem by Lenau. Notice the name of the poem is missing. That's weird, you should here suspect something is amiss. Omission is a signal of repression, but it's too late for Freud to go back and untypeset the reference to Lenau, so Freud now has to get Lenau to point to something else. So later editions of *The Interpretation Of Dreams* are helpfully revised to include the name of the= a poem:

> "Of course, too, you know the gruesome poem by Lenau (*Das Tote Glück*), which puts infanticide and birth-control on the same plane."

> "Strangely enough, I happened, as though by chance, to think of Lenau this morning."

Which assures the reader that *Das Tote Glück* is the relevant poem and thus guarantees no one will ever go look it up. Well, I did, it's irrelevant, which makes the editor an accomplice. You know what poem Lenau did write that might have been relevant? *Faust*. In which the phrase "das tote glück" happens to appear in the very last stanza. Inception will work if you go deep enough but the repressed always returns.

The poetry and science fiction of the 19th century may seem irrelevant in a world intoxicated with the advances of modern genetic science and late stage capitalism, but you can learn a lot from history, not because history repeats or rhymes, but because when people regress, they choose a place and time in which whatever knowledge they think they have today might have been powerful then; so it's useful to study their fiction and see how far back we have to go to get them to believe they could act. Nowadays for women it's the Jazz and Gilded Ages and for their male counterparts it's a kind of Middle Ages; and by no coincidence whatsoever that's exactly where Mark Twain regressed his counterpart. It's regression elevated to progression as a cover for aggression. It would be as if the world's post-grads took a break from fantasizing the annihilation of their parents and said, "look,

386

aren't even estimates, they are rhetoric, seriously, why not just make them up? What's the difference? Never mind why the asparageniuses would publish this study, or even conduct it; why would anyone with even a high tolerance for embarrassment use it as a primary source?

Unless you're suggesting that the statistics are hyped by the media, this generation's satanic murders or serial killings? Or are the stats consciously inflated by the activists because they want to have a reason to activate? No? Rape is still ubiquitous? Ok, we'll go with that.

"I am committed to activism and awareness because rape is a real problem." It is a problem, but why is it a problem for you? Just because it's real doesn't mean the fear isn't pathological. If my teenage daughter was so obsessed with rape that she submitted angry

---

I don't know if anyone has ever thought of this before, but instead of disavowing our common material humanity, why don't we just wear diapers? And we should make sure they're biodegradable and available to everyone." That's the kind of forward thinking that gets you a MacArthur Genius Award, or tenure.

There's no chance you've ever heard of Lenau, he was the product of his time, the same time that produced so much opium that capitalism demanded cocaine, so you will likely not be aware that Lenau had the 19th century's Most Punchable Face, just picture a guy with bulging self-righteousness and low muscle tone and add a wispy mustache to it. Yes, you knew him in college.

Lenau was of the literary school in which the universal could be found in the particular, particularly himself, so Lenau's Faust is less *Faust* than Lenau's ideal self. His actual self was an aimless, drifting 29 year old Hungarian law and medical school graduate, wistful for the now extinguished German romantic splendor of his youth. "Go West, young man," commanded Manifest Destiny a decade early, but lacking the spleen and spunk for physical exertion he got as far as Indiana. Yes, that Indiana. Alas, there was nothing for him there either. Disillusioned with all the productivity requirements he returned after a year. When an aspiring young man expects, and then fails, to make it in America, and now living off the inheritance from his appropriately deceased grandmother finds himself surrounded by phonies, brutes, and hypocrites, it's a good bet he's either going to try and write a *Faust* or end up in a mental institution. Lenau did both. "The problem is the system." If you can't make it in either two continents or three languages, you might want to consider the problem is you.

Lenau's Faust charts a similar course minus the charts and the course. Melancholic, passionate, directionless, he turns first to biological science-- nothing is to be learned from psychology, metaphysics, and definitely not religion-- he's a scientician, truth is in the material bodies, the physical organs. He dissects a cadaver, but the organs are of no help. Maybe dissect the organs? Smaller scales as the path to omniscience? And it beats seeing the whole. But nothing satisfies, so he goes with melancholia. If Goethe's Werther hadn't committed suicide, he would have become Lenau's Faust, and not coincidentally Lenau's Faust eventually commits suicide. "What is Truth?" It doesn't look like you really want an answer.

Lenau's Faust thinks his one problem is that he doesn't have enough knowledge. This is incorrect. Lenau's Faust has a second problem he doesn't understand is his only problem: he cannot act. The implication is that by learning more, he will gain more power, but that's not what his own story shows. He's trying to learn in order to not act. There's a gap: while questions within serve only to enrage him, outside rules the Will that doesn't much engage him. Early on this angry young man of science climbs a mountain expecting natural science to be the best teacher; but nature is indifferent to his education. So what does he do? Down in the valley the dummies are celebrating Easter, and since he's on higher ground and also they can't hear him he tells them that there is no God and He's not coming, let alone back. Preoccupied with fantasizing he is depriving others of their satisfaction, he almost trips-- jumps?-- off the edge, but Mephisto happens to be nearby hunting for idiots and, well, catches one in his arms. They talk, and Mephisto offers to give Faust knowledge. This next

387

articles to feminist media where she'd preach to highly converted free-rage thinkers how terrible rape culture was thus effecting absolutely no changes whatsoever, i.e wasting her time, I would have to conclude that either a) this was a coping mechanism for having already been raped; b) she has created an unnecessarily complicated but highly effective maneuver for avoiding math homework. I guess math is worse than rape. "Maybe activists just care about helping other people." HA! No. No one who brands themselves by their rage cares about other people, it's not a logical possibility. You should write that down, it is always true and there isn't much in life that is always true.

The weapon of choice is speech, it is your right to have it but it's use is tightly regulated and requires a background check. No one's figured out how to put a safety on a text, so for

---

point is usually shrugged off as obvious but is worth your meditation: Faust accepts-- because Faust thinks Mephisto *has* it. There may be no God, but there are demons, and, as you may have heard: demons know.

Goethe's Faust looks for Truth outside himself, while Lenau's Faust would rather not work so hard and so concludes Truth is to be found inside himself. See above, it's a half-assed pursuit. But if you read the poem, you'll observe that what Lenau's Faust does pursue-- it's the only thing he does at all-- is women. So we should probably look at his pick up strategy.

Faust and Mephisto go to a peasant wedding, and he meets Hannachen, the comely daughter of a peasant. Faust wants to engage in intercourse, but gets too nervous to go up to her. Mephisto laughs at him: you had no problem talking to the Devil, but you're afraid to approach a woman? Mephisto takes the fiddler's violin and plays a magic waltz which intoxicates the horny Faust into becoming an extrovert, in a wild dance Faust whirls the full... bodied... beauty right out of the room and her clothes, and finally off camera they have sex. NB the devil's magic music is used to intoxicate Faust, not Hannachen. She doesn't need it, she has no problem acting on her desire. To be rigorously psychoanalytic about this, think of the Mephisto's magic as Jager.

Off topic, here's an example of art repressing the truth so it can return as art. Liszt took this scene and wrote piano waltz for it, it is quite lively and upbeat, and hearing the melodic notes played over the subtext (?) of the dance music I guess it's a fair representation of 19th century authentic peasant lust as imagined by people who listen to piano waltzes and know little of peasants, or lust. But if Mephisto is actually playing violin, why is this a piano waltz and not a violin waltz? Well, try it. Aside from the fact it's next to impossible unless you're Paganini, on the violin it sounds eerie, uncanny, sinister: it reveals that the Devil is playing it.

Next Faust meets the comely wife of a blacksmith. What does he do in an attempt to woo said strumpet? He could try to be funny or friendly; or suavely touch her elbow in that way that immediately makes me spit rum out of my mouth and light it; but as a recently experienced seducer he now knows exactly what the ladies want from a man, and that thing is close up magic. "Ta da! Nothing up my sleeve!" Or down your pants, you're as useless as that was. "Want to see me escape from a restraining order?"

Suddenly, Hannachen shows up, yelling about how Faust abandoned her. I realize this is not the point of the story, but this is a key moment in a guy's life: the new girl is watching. You got busted, ok, anyone can slink away in shame and anyone can try to deny it, but a true player James Bonds the situation and starts juggling both balls, in full view of everyone. Anyway, Faust is not James Bond, he drops both balls and runs away screaming. There's some symbolism in Hannachen's changed appearance to ugly and destitute, and she's holding a baby, and really I'm not even sure it actually is Hannachen, but the point for us here is 2/2 encounters, this is a man who wants women but this is not the behavior of a man who wants to get women.

Mephisto tries to cheer him up by bragging how he once scored a young nun right there by the lake,

now we're left with a warning near the trigger. These warnings are easily decried as idiotic, and because they are usually directed at the young and/or female, they must mean that cowards and babies can't handle the big bad world that that has excluded them entirely from it. Did you think this? Then they worked. But what do they do, exactly? They don't perform any action, they don't even censor or redact anything, they merely announce what it knows is coming. It's a spoiler alert for reality.

As you've been encouraged to criticize what trigger warnings mean you won't have paid enough attention to where they are used-- in secondary sources describing a primary source-- and how they are used: by walling off the primary source, you get the knowledge from the secondary source, the one that announces the trigger warning. You'll say many people blow

---

got her pregnant, and she committed suicide. And infanticide. Wicked cool. Why Mephisto would want a nun— or any woman-- is not explained, more importantly, it is not even questioned; the idea that evil would desire to spoil good is taken as axiomatic, in order to suggest that Faust must be good, look how much time Mephisto's spending on corrupting him. Mephisto has a memento of the nun-sex, would you like to see it? Into the lake he goes, and out he comes holding the bones of a baby. Faust looks upon it in horror. It's a major scene. Note that Goethe merely describes Gretchen's infanticide, while Lenau shows the dead baby. Why the visual? That's easy: the only way to elicit feeling in a person whose only authentically felt emotion is rage is to pornographize it. But there's a logical argument being made: the scene of Mephisto corrupting a woman who got pregnant and committed infanticide follows the scene of Faust corrupting a woman who got pregnant and did not commit infanticide. Redemption through the woman is not possible, because women-- desirable women-- they fall for devils, not for nice guys like Faust. The only type of woman who would fall for Faust is whatever Hannachen turned out to be when the Jager wore off.

Next he meets Maria, the sexy fiancée of the Duke; and I hope you have noticed that 3/3 cases Faust's model for a desirable woman is another man's woman. This third encounter is the most telling, because it is Faust finally manning up and attempting to win her over with his charm and personality. It's a disaster. What does he do? He asks to paint her. He uses her as… a model. And to make sure he's in the painting, too, he paints stormy seas, get it? After idealizing her into an impossible image he then professes his love to her, he tells her how important she is to him, how much he needs her, and not surprisingly, she thinks he's a nut. The Duke has suspected Faust was up to no good (and Mephisto rats him out), they get into a fight and Faust stabs and kills him. Is that an act? In an opera maybe. You might think it would be easier to get up the courage to seduce a woman than to murder a man, but then you're probably a woman, or a man. He's neither. True to the personality type, Faust can't act, but he can react. So when he then feels guilty for the murder, you should understand that he doesn't feel any guilt for the murder at all, the guilt is a way of taking credit for acting like a brute and instead of what he actually did, which was reacting like a brat. Then he finds solace in Jager and crying at his mother's grave. Even she sighs.

I suppose Lenau meant his story as a reimagining of Goethe's *Faust*, but it's not, it's basically a first draft of Lenau's *Don Juan*, in which Don Juan isn't after multiple women but the perfect woman. NB that would be an impossible love, and predicts suffering for everyone else. In that story his third conquest is the fiancée of the Duke, but instead of the dark arts he uses darkness and sneaks into her room, bed, and vagina, and all the while she thinks he's the Duke and doesn't notice how easy it suddenly is to fellate him. Agreed: it's off campus and no one heard her scream so it couldn't be rape but even then it was an underhanded way to get sex, but getting sex wasn't the point. In other writers' versions of the Don Juan story he beds the Duke's fiancée, the difference is that in those versions she's either in on it or finds out later, but in Lenau's version he *tells* her that he fooled her, while they're in bed. He has to make her feel bad about it. He's proud he cuckolded the Duke, he's proud he tricked the fiancée, but it isn't enough that he had her, or tricked her, or tricked him, or took her from him or took her from herself; with his penis now safely back inside his vagina he then tries to completely deprive her, showing off his sophisticated knowledge of human nature by telling

389

past the trigger warnings and read the primary sources anyway, but the purpose isn't to block knowledge but establish authority. That trigger warnings on knowledge occur almost exclusively in universities and popular media isn't ironic but entirely the point: secondary sources have to be the authority. The ones applying the warnings become authorities. They exert power not over people or their behaviors (this they cannot control) but over knowledge. So you can follow the order: first, there is no desire for power. In order to cope with this-- not the loss of power but the lack of desire for power-- one conveys the impression of having knowledge. The warnings aren't for the victims to protect them from their impotence, but for the impotent warners to signify omniscience. They aren't fighting oligarchs and oppressors, they have no power to fight them, they are medieval clerics, their purpose is to distinguish

---

her that since she could be fooled, she doesn't really love the Duke, but only some ideal mental image of love; and that she's never actually "with" this ideal love, she's cheating on this ideal love even when she is with the real Duke. He tries to deprive her even of her love for the Duke-- but not by making her fall in love with himself, which would still allow her the satisfaction of loving-- but by completely obliterating any possibility of love for anyone. He's trying to trick her into confirming his nihilism. He wants a powerful woman to declare that love doesn't exist.

Don Juan doesn't end well for Don Juan. How does Lenau's *Faust* end? In contrast to Goethe, Lenau has his Faust sell, not bet, his soul. For how much? Nothing. So what does he ask for? Nothing. Seriously, it's nothing. When the end comes and he realizes he received nothing, why is he surprised? He'd been to America, he should have known better, capitalism won't give you what you need or even what you want, it will give you exactly what you pay for, nothing more-- and nothing less, that's the part everyone wants to forget. Having done literally nothing on his own throughout the whole story, in the final lines he performs the ultimate act and stabs himself-- in the heart, get it? Well, no, that would be an act, and he cannot act: he *imagines* he stabs himself. "I am a dream with lust and guilt and pain, I dream this dagger into my heart." And Mephisto shrugs, this lunatic's lust, guilt and pain aren't any more real than the dagger, or his heart. As above, so below, when you save a man's life it becomes your responsibility, and no woman wants that job so I guess it's up to me. You once jumped into my arms, now I have you again, for I have become a catcher of men.

80 Video games or imagination play? It's universally acknowledged that the latter is "better". But is it normal? Go to any middle school: the kids who played video games are more... normal than the ones who did not; the imagination kids are more likely to lie at the extremes of the curve of socialization, grades, mental disorders, happiness-- and, since you care, income. One might say that odd kids are naturally drawn to imagination play over video games, but this implies the kids made the choice from equally available options, as if the parents offered them both but they played with the stuff that doesn't play itself. Yes, double entendre. Then you could say the type of parent who doesn't let a kid play video games is outside +/-2 SD themselves, but that only pushes the question back a generation. Whatever the "cause", what becomes normalized is a way of thinking, a way of wanting; so that the person who reads someone else's derivative work of BDSM feels no shame but rather empowered-- *because* it is someone else's derivative work, normalized, approved by society. They are more a part of society, it is encouraged by the system; whereas a moment lost in fantasy is either disciplined as a waste of time or... abnormal. Like most of my examples, I chose "BDSM" not because I care about it but because it's easy for you to agree with, here's the word I actually wanted to use: "'journalism".

81 Though Thucydides never makes a separation, the secondary sources typically divide the Peloponnesian war into two time periods with a huge gap in between, for no intelligible reason skipping over almost a decade of fairly significant events that can only be understood as part of the War. I'll give you an example: according to this division, the invasion of Melos did not happen

themselves from the rest of the impotent, whom they consider irredeemable anyway. "We know how things really work." And we can only learn it from you? They are traitors.

"A lot of these conflicts are really class war in disguise." What article did you quote that from? Just so I know which disguise to wear, is the rallying factor the class of the victims or the class of the oppressors? It's easy to be united in hatred, I know, I know. 99% of the people who have detected a class war in disguise dramatically underestimate which class they're in, and if the revolution comes you may find you don't get to decide which side you're on. "Look-- no socks! I count myself as a radical!" Meh, you'll serve the cause better if we knit your name as Royalist and decapitate. The important thing is to keep score. It was the

---

during the War. Ok.

If you feel you must skip over some part of the war, and you're willing to let that part be the end of it, then a better division for the war would be the three Acts that follow the previous tyranny: Pericles, Cleon, and Alcibiades. Now you're going to reply that you can't just skip over the end of the most significant event in ancient history up to that point, but Thucydides did just that, on purpose. Following his lead, Pericles was the superego trying to manage the id; Cleon was ego free from superego; Alcibiades was id that everyone wanted to be superego. "You mean was driven by desire and passion?" I mean he was the jerk who drove around his parents' sports car like he built it, and convinced people to follow him and hang on his every lisp. R's, not S's.

If you ask any secondary source about Alcibiades, you'll learn he was the most beautiful man in Athens, a great general, a hedonist, and the favorite student of Socrates. Remarkably, Thucydides doesn't say any of these things. In fact, he doesn't describe Alcibiades at all. Thucydides gives an explicit personal judgment about everyone from Hipparchus to Brasidas, and even minor characters like Hyperbolus get a few choice adjectives, but the man who is almost personally responsible for the end of the Athenian Empire gets almost nothing more descriptive than the single observation that he was personally responsible for the end of the Athenian Empire. There is a speech Thucydides has Alcibiades give in which Alcibiades describes himself, but the only valid information you should take from it is that Alcibiades liked to describe himself. An 8th grader once had to perform his Sicilian invasion speech, so to get her into character I recommended playing him like a cross between any guy not wearing socks and Zaphod Beeblebrox. She nailed it. If Alcibiades is key to the demise of Athens, then Thucydides's understanding of Alcibiades is key to his understanding of that demise. Who he was didn't matter. What mattered is what he did and for what purpose.

Here's an example. Not only was he almost unilaterally responsible for the death of 40000 Athenians; not only does he defect to the Sparta and betray Athens; but while hiding out in Sparta, he then decides it's a good idea to seduce the Queen of Sparta and cuckold the King. It wasn't. "Was she hot?" I'm sure that didn't matter. "I want my sons to be the heirs of Sparta," he explained for the anecdote, "or the victims of Athens, either way counts." I made that last part up. Still true, though. "Good looking, unempathic, goes for what he wants-- that's alpha male behavior." You keep using that word. I'm not sure it means what you think it means. If you want to get an idea of how much the variance in sexual attractiveness and dominance signaling is related to culture vs. biology, go find a statue of Alcibiades, look upon the most beautiful alpha male in Athens, and despair. Hard to believe, but that's the actual face that launched a hundred ships. The other thing is, he had a lisp, r's became l's and it appealed to the masses, it made him seem more interesting. This is a complicated sentence, but 100% true: he appealed to the kind of men who thought Alcibiades was appealing to women because he was better than them. "Wait-- what does the 'them' refer to?"

In some ancient biography young Alcibiades is back home from Yale, and now that he knows everything goes full sophist and tries to trap his uncle Pericles into admitting that since coercion is unjust, a legitimate democratic vote is also unjust because it coerces the minority. Overworked Pericles has no time for sophistry, he has a democracy to run and a majority to coerce, so he shuts

best of times, the worst of times; superlatives without metric, rage without accountability. Why should you be surprised at the savage and pitiless excesses of people who began the struggle not in a class but in a party spirit? In that confusion, human nature, which always wants to rebel against something greater than it, gladly displays itself as passionate, the enemy of all superiority, placing revenge above morality and gain above justice-- all from the fatal power of envy. In fact, people too often make it a requisite of their revenge to publicly make an example of doing away with the laws, instead of keeping them just in case they need them themselves.

But it's not for me to criticize what you want, only describe how you want it, and see

---

down the discussion with the kind of thing your Dad would say as he left the house for work: "ah, we used to be so smart at your age, playing these philosophical games." And Alcibiades responds with the kind of thing you would say living off your Dad's work: "Then I wish I could have known you when you were smarter." Zing. Supposedly completely unrelated, in some other ancient=contemporary dialogue Callicles muses about the importance of education and philosophy in the young; but when you get older, he says, you're supposed to put away childish things and start doing something useful with your life. "Philosophy is like a lisp: cute in a child, hatable in an adult." Put these together and what appears to be a dismissiveness of philosophy or youth is actually disdain for Alcibiades.

If coercion of some kind is at the heart of any democracy, what did Athens use their coercion for? Athens was a direct democracy in which everyone participated, excluding women, slaves, and idiots. And by direct I mean inescapable and by idiots I mean idiots. All things were up for a vote, all things were decided immediately. It took them one night to vote for three decades of war with Sparta. Anything was a majority vote away. Given this, why didn't the overwhelming majority of citizens who were poor do what to anyone today would have seemed the most obvious thing ever: redistribute all the wealth? Not only did they not do this, no one even proposed it. A generation before the war, the majority poor Athenians discovered a massive silver mine and suddenly everyone was paper rich, but when they gathered to decide how to distribute the dividends, the poor people decided instead to invest the money in-- and boy oh boy are you not going to believe this-- a stronger military. Can you even imagine it? If you accept the logic of Thucydides, it was decisions like that that made the Spartans to attack.

If America could add a binding proposition to the national ballot to confiscate all the wealth of the top 0.001%, or 30% of the wealth of the top 0.01%, or whatever arithmetic is easy, not even in order to "redo the national energy grid" or some public works project, but simply on the general principle of Even Steven, you'd think the American citizens would vote for it almost unanimously. The American Founding Fathers set up the "democracy" as a republic so that that couldn't happen, so it was structurally impossible. But if the Athenians had the power to do so, if it was so easy to do so, why didn't they do it?

A possible answer is that the rich manufactured the appearance of democracy to delude the poor, let them think they had more power than they previously had (which they did), more money than they previously did (which they had)-- to appease them while the rich continued to exploit the labor of the poor on the backs of the slaves. Of course, personally fighting a 27 year long war against a slave exploiting oligarchy for no material gain doesn't sound like what an oligarchy would do; neither does telling them to abandon their wealth to come inside and die with their slaves, yet both of those happened; but going 800 miles into the sunset to invade a peaceful democratic state expressly for material gain does exactly sound like what an oligarchy would do, which is why Alcibiades convinced the democracy to do it.

One way to handle a people is to conquer them, 40% success rate but can last for centuries; another way is to absorb them, 100% effective but only good for a generation. Elsewhere is a story about what happens next. I do believe these activists, whatever their motivations, are earnest and want dramatic changes. Fair enough-- can we all agree they have mostly failed? E.g. taking you at your word-- you're the expert after all-- sexual assaults are as frequent as ever; but now they get recorded for others to enjoy, which is literally quite a dramatic change. So the question is, in the face of all this very public and vocal activism, why does e.g. sexual assault still occur as much, "even more", than before? Why did so much activism fail?

Let's assume as per the postulates that the system is truly patriarchal, even misogynist; not merely considerably so but *inherently* so, structurally so; as if to truly eradicate the misogyny you'd have to entirely rebuild the system. If you believe this is the case, how does the system prevent that change? How did the system deal with this core existential threat

young Cyrus, prince of Persia, on vacation at his grandfather's palace in Media, and you may not know this from watching *300* but Persia was a liberal, open democracy, everyone was entitled to be educated in public schools and subsequently free to hold any position or government office; or, said a different way, Persia was a clever democracy, everyone was free to hold any position or government office subsequent to being educated in a public school, which was so cost prohibitive so that only the entitled children of the positioned or government officials would go.

In this story Cyrus is about 12 and tries to convince his mom to let him stay and live with his cool grandfather, and she asks how will he be educated since his teachers are back home. No sweat, he responds, I already know everything. "Ok, smarty pants, what about things like justice?" Total mastery, he says smugly, he knows so much about justice that he got only one question wrong on the oral exam, and he learned even more from the mistake: his teacher asked him to judge the case of a small man with a big coat who meets a big man with a small coat, and the big man forces the small man to switch their coats. Cyrus decides it is just, since it was to both their benefit, ultimately each man got what he deserved and deserved what he got. His teacher slaps the gums off his teeth. Hey, stupid, the law doesn't allow anyone to redistribute property by force; and violating the law destroys trust in the law.

Well, what lesson are we to learn from this story? Maximal utility? Trust in the laws is more important than social justice? Today we know that the risk is chaos, both good and bad laws are what stand between civilization and anarchy, because if any two men desire the same thing which they can't both enjoy, they become enemies; where there's no law, there can be no injustice, and force and fraud become cardinal virtues. Political philosophy becomes political science. It's a good theory, but it's not supported by experiments. There have certainly been chaotic civil wars, but except in science fiction anarchy is not, and has never been, the risk. Neither was bigger men making policy decisions for smaller men. The risk was Cyrus. That's why the teacher slapped him. When Cyrus decided that redistribution was just, the one who decided that was Cyrus. Once Cyrus okayed the redistributed coats, both of the men got a fitting coat and both of them lost their power. It all went to Cyrus. He became the tyrant. No one can ever be responsible again. No one can act again. They can't even desire again. The most they can do in the future is try to fool the master.

So the lesson we should learn from this story is that in a republican democracy laws are necessary to prevent a tyranny, because every single person thinks they know what's best, and one of them might have the power to decide on his own, which is the last thing a republican democracy should want.

You may disagree and say the story has nothing to do with tyranny per se, but is in fact about preventing anarchy and the importance of trust in laws. Well, a few things about this story. First, it is probably made up, by an Athenian for Athenians. Anarchy was not much on their minds, the only time anarchy in its "chaotic" sense was used in Athens was by Critias, who apocryphally was trying to convince people that they should have a tyrant. Which he later became, deciding that what was best was purges. Then they killed him. Those last two aren't apocryphal.

Second, the way the republican democratic tutor taught Cyrus this lesson is by beating it into him.

from activists? If it *needs* rape, how does it allow itself to continue to rape?

More generally: how does a system that requires exploitation in its business model continue to do it? This is not the same question as, "how does one get away with a crime?" Here we are accepting the premise that the crime is necessary to the business model, it is founded on it, it needs it to continue. What are the mechanisms and maneuvers that permit exploitation to occur, while under heavy and public assault to change?

One way is to give individual activists precisely what would satisfy them. Careful; this is not change, which is what they want. What satisfies them is "to be heard", an audience. The media gives it to them, it lets them win battles in media.

That would be a joke if it wasn't the whole point. According to the book, the only way to prevent a budding or possible tyranny is with the very violence the laws are supposed to stop, because tyranny is gravitational; it requires work not to fall into it, not just the temptation to become a tyrant, but to accept tyranny. You have to beat that impulse out of them when they are children, before someone beats it into them as adults, or they just drift into it as democrats.

Third, and importantly, the story doesn't say that redistributing the coats is wrong. You should think about this carefully. It says only that it wasn't Cyrus's job. It's the law's job. You'll say that the majority would never pass such a law, it requires, well, "strong leadership", but the reason the story was made up for Athenians in the first place is because the Athenians had the power to do it.

Fourth, and very importantly, Cyrus says he learned the lesson, but the story doesn't explain what lesson Cyrus learned.

Most people who know the story from secondary sources don't know the really important part, which is what happens next: after telling the coat story to his mom to prove how much he's learned about justice vs. tyranny, for the purpose of not to having to go back to live with his republican democratic father, he then reassures his mom that if he has any further questions about justice, he can always ask ... his grandfather. Who is literally a tyrant. His mom grimaces. "Be careful that you don't learn the lesson that you should have more than anyone else." Cyrus tells her not to worry. "My grandfather would never teach me to have more than anyone else. He teaches everyone to have less than he does." In other words, the lesson Cyrus learned is that it is not his job to judge justice. So he should find a way to make it his job.

If you doubt this is the lesson he learned note that adult Cyrus chooses a middle path between tyranny and democracy, and finds a way to make all his subjects as happy as possible and to endear himself to them. With a fixed currency this is usually hard to do, so he does what anyone leader with a fixed currency does, which is to conquer everyone else. Those conquests take up the other 87.5% of the book. Lesson learned.

But our lesson is the other one, reinforced by the end of the book: Cyrus dies. And the whole thing collapses. Tyrants usually get killed by their people, or conquered; Cyrus had a longer run because he legitimately tried to be a just tyrant. But it doesn't take, because he's still a tyrant. So you swap the coats, now both men have the coat they deserve. But the small man is now resentful, because the big man got a new coat. Yes, he is aware he got a new coat, too. Doesn't count. He isn't jealous of the big man, he envies the big man, not for what he got but because it was he who got it. He hates the big man. He probably hates the tyrant, too.

That actually happens to Cyrus. Cyrus is such a benevolent tyrant that everyone loved him. So his uncle hates him. "If a man came and treated your wife well, so that she fell for him, would you thank him for his kindness?" A hundred bucks says you completely missed the point, because you only read the quote. Read the paragraph again. Do you get the point now?

Americans pretend to want to redistribute the coats, this is a lie, they want the coats to be

But the moment they entered media, they became a brand, another choice among rival choices. Brands can be attacked, destroyed, without ever touching the substance of the product. For example, it's easy to cast activists as ugly, not because they are ugly, but because it is easy to cast them as ugly. Find a few ugly activists and give them an interview on TV; they know TV is superficial, yet they never ask if their face is super enough to best represent their brand. "But it's not about me, it's about the issues." It was, until you went on TV. "No one even watches TV anymore, stupid." I don't know if you know what TV means, let alone what it's for.

There are some attractive activists, but these people are usually celebrities and mostly idiots. Again, not because they *are* idiots, who knows, but because it's easy to cast them as

---

redistributed. There's a difference, and the difference is Cyrus. The Athenians did not have a Cyrus; if they wanted to redistribute, it would be they themselves who did the redistribution. And so it couldn't be done. The only people who might be able to do it were proto-tyrants like Alcibiades, but frustratingly they wanted to do other things, like take other countries' coats, which is great and all, sigh, but it's just not the same.

You can see this if you look at the speeches. How did the politicians speak to the people? I am aware of the mechanics of rhetoric, this is not what I mean. Yes, as propaganda they were trying to persuade people to do something; but as rhetoric, what did they want people to believe?

Diodotus's and Cleon's speeches are so pragmatic that they sound like they could have been given in Congress today. Yet there's a difference. In Athens, the rhetoric spoke to those with power, while the American rhetoric speaks to victims. I don't mean it speaks only to the victims: I mean that when it speaks, it speaks to the audience as if they are victims. This is true for both parties equally. The message of American rhetoric is that "they" have deprived you, I will set things right. If Pericles had wanted to redistribute the wealth of the Athenians, he would try to persuade the rich to do it, not the poor that it should be done. He might appeal to idealism, or scare them with threats of civil unrest, or offer them tax incentives-- or just flatter them. These could all be lies. The rich could know they are lies. Whatever lie he says to them, he wants them to act; but the message he wants them to believe is: you have the power.

You will want to argue that nowadays this approach will not work, e.g. the rich won't willingly part with their money. And even some poor people, blinded by ideology, will support them. What's needed is a strong leader to do what's right and redistribute the coats over anyone's protests.

Never mind if this is true; as an argument it is flawed, because it pretends to want a result. It doesn't. The result is of secondary importance to the rhetoric. The Athenian rhetoric promises a gain to you. American rhetoric promises the rival will be deprived. If Pericles came to the US and convinced the rich to willingly part with 50% of their wealth-- then for Americans it wouldn't be enough, it wouldn't count. But say you'll take away 10% over their protests-- that counts. You doubt this? Why do you think they are broadcasting their protests? It's not convincing anyone to their side who isn't already sympathetic-- what purpose does it serve?

If wealth inequality is a structural problem, you would think people would want a structural solution. But it will not be satisfying. They'll only be satisfied with an imaginary solution, and by imaginary I mean it looks good in images. The Athenians did not have a structural solution to use as a cover for depriving a rival. Their direct democracy was the only structure. As long as they knew they had the power, then every action was evidence of their desire. To redistribute wealth would be too clearly using the structure to settle personal rivalries and envies (e.g. the 4th Century); and the whole thing would collapse and a tyrant would inevitably take over. Their schizophrenic relationship to Alcibiades, love-hate-repeat, was a symptom of that ambivalence. They wanted him to act for them, they wanted to follow the leader, they offered him the power, but at the end of the day the power was still theirs, so bright and early the morning after they had to imagine he was

idiots, juxtapose their activism with a story about their clothes or their mating habits. "You're so right, I hate it when they do that, it deliberately trivializes their intelligence." To whom? If you're reading it, it's for you.

Remember, the premise is that the problems are structural, the battles are supposed to be against the system; but the system tai chi's the attack towards individuals by giving them structural sounding names, "X the Nazi!", "Y the neoliberal!" "Z the totalizing incrementalist!" Go get 'em. Nothing feels as good as publicly bringing down a structuralist, including bringing down the structure. Pic or it didn't matter.

Activists enjoy shaming people in media, they'll even skip porn to watch that. Force the offenders to give a public apology. "Yes, we are aware it's fake, but it's a start." Well hold on, why would the system go along with the demand for such an apology, especially when everyone agrees it is fake? Because the apology serves the status quo by its division into opposites: through the forcing of the apology, we all get the explicit message that the offense is *in fact* offensive to the *media* (=for their use as content) and the more powerful implicit message that the activists are bullies and should be marginalized. And it's in media, so: "What does the person who was offended look like?" we'll all want to know, no surprise, she's offensive, because of all the people who were offended, the system found the one that fit the character sketch.[82]

Negative branding of individual activists can work on a case by case basis, but the true efficiency of the system is revealed in how it deals with a truly powerful, organized, counter-systemic threat. Progressive activists are vocal, well connected, educated, and there's a lot of them. How does the system thwart what should otherwise be a juggernaut political block and social movement? What does it do to castrate them? Ask your kids, it's institutionalized: *it*

---

planning to take it from them. No, it doesn't make sense, and it didn't make sense to Alcibiades either. And even if those statues weren't defaced by this tyrant, it proves a larger point: it must have been by some other tyrant. If Alcibiades wasn't willing to take the role of tyrant, he could at least become the scapegoat.

There is a little known story about Peter three times in the night denying that he was a follower of Christ; after the rooster crowed he realized what he had done, and wept. Well, what did he feel guilty about? It doesn't take a psychologist to see that he once lied to a woman and another woman twice because he was scared they would know who he was, but that would be grossly underestimating what was at stake, something so important the story isn't so much recounted as framed as a biblical prophecy. The risk was not that he was a follower, for which he might get killed; the risk was that he was the future leader, for which he was definitely going to be killed. Because somebody has to be. You can run from danger or your responsibilities but what you can't run from is your power, that you have to give up willingly, to someone else, whether they want it or not. It doesn't take a Freudian to see that every boy will one day overcome his father, for which the boy can be forgiven, but once the father is overcome the thing you can't do is go back to being the boy. Your god is dead, now you are the father, and either you start using your power for good or you move back with your mother and rot.

82 And they will work *very* hard to cast appropriately. There was once a comic who made a rape joke, and a woman in the audience yelled, out loud, that rape jokes aren't funny. The comic then said to the audience how funny it would be if everyone suddenly raped her. When the story hit the pornotron there was the usual outrage and demands for an apology; however, the "face" of the woman demanding an apology wasn't the actual woman at the comedy show, but a friend who was not even at the show, which, incidentally, would make her a secondary source. I'll leave you to work out the casting details.

offers them unlimited knowledge while taking away their power.

The jargon of rape discussions is easy to spot: patriarchy; hegemony, intersectionality, and some chemistry terms safely detached from chemistry. They're very descriptive, evocative, apocalyptive words, words that help make sense of the hidden forces at work around us. Where did you learn them? Never mind what they mean: *where can you use them?*

Your thesis is that the system is e.g. male and oppressive right to the girders-- that patriarchy is part of the structure of the system, and that's what you're fighting against. Then why was your interest in destroying it legitimized-- *encouraged?* Why was there a major in *college* that allowed you to deconstroy patriarchy, organize movements against it? Or did you think the university was a "safe space" outside of the "patriarchal system" from which to "critique" it-- for $50k/year? Every college course is for the system, every master's or PhD seminar is 100% in the service of the system, sometimes the link is straightforward like engineering or Business Mandarin but all of the courses conspire to 4% annual GDP growth. Lots of professors are socialists, but are there any Maoists, "political power comes from the barrel of a gun?" And yet there is ROTC, I learned to assemble and fire an M60 in under 4 minutes, eight of us were women, *and they taught me that for free.* Ok, it was at 5 am, *but it was free.*

You're a radical? You're going to break down the existing system, change the basic foundations of a "white, male, privileged structure?" Do you think your university would allow this? That your parents would pay for it? That the U.S. Government would loan you $$$$$ for it? Do you think you there's a degree in Subversion? In Toppling The Male Majority? If there is it's a BS. "I love how you don't seem to be aware you can major in Gender and Ethnic Studies." I love how you think that contradicts my argument.

"But there is a rape culture in America!" But by your assertion it *is* the system, so it certainly poses no threat to the system. *You* do. That's why it noticed you were trouble and it encouraged you to major in-- anything but math. Why did the system promote that opportunity? Why did the system offer you a dead-end life path? Because it wanted you to wield power, or it wanted you out of the way? The reason you're able to fight the system is because the system told you you were allowed to. And it fooled you by letting you think you were getting away with something. "I learned how things really work." Did you learn that they can work without you?

You'll counter that "the system" does not exist, it's just an analogy, a symbol, but then who are you fighting against? It either exists, in which case it is way more clever than you, or it doesn't, in which case you should probably see a psychiatrist.

The only thing your unemployable major allows you to do is work for the university that made you unemployable, and now you are neutralized. After the near miss of progressive rage of the 1960s and the stupendous moronity of the Y2Ks, the system needed a way to contain the lunatics, and boy oh boy did it luck out, because the only thing they needed as compensation for not effecting the changes they thought were so important was credit for trying. They failed, therefore they wanted to be recognized for their attempts, and an assistant professorship was all it took. Today they barely even try, they'll take any nominally academic sounding appointment as credit for imagining they could. "I've been an adjunct professor for 5 years, but I can't even afford rent." I don't even have a joke for that. I know the standard conservative complaint is about pervasive liberal bias in academia, but you bow ties are silly, you're looking at it the wrong way: better there than at General Dynamics. Or do you really want the person who teaches "Imperialism, Colonialism, Genocide" working at the

Department of Defense? Give them the unattainable goal of tenure to work for and an unreadable journal to write for and they become invisible; and the only people who will suffocate through their rhetoric are precisely the people whom it is for. Don't worry about the grades, everyone gets an A for effort.

And this isn't to imply that what they teach isn't true, but like psychoanalysis, the point of it now isn't change, it is to defend against change. In this way the university's discourse serves the master's discourse. "What?" DoD technical jargon; just know that the master's discourse consists ultimately of just one question: what should I allow these sophomores to think they're getting away with so they'll let me go back to the not enjoyable job of running things?

That's the system. It serves one group's greed and the other's envy, and as you like to tell everyone, you detest greed. Any dangerous ideas, any threats to status quo become absorbed by the university or its much better looking co-conspirator the media. Politics is Hollywood for ugly people, so the news follows a beat sheet. "Controlling idea! Audience revelation!" It doesn't try to hide anything-- it floods you with the information, even gives you the proper lexicon, just like porn. "I'm sex positive." I'm positive it requires porn. And you develop insights, "figure things out"-- and stay walled off, envy turned up to eleven, except for the occasional pointless marches or to get chased through the frat by misogynists. "What can I do? He's more powerful than me." Why not break that little glass panel on the wall that's labeled In Case Of Emergency? At least that's thinking outside the box. "I shouldn't *have* to do that." Yes, that's why it labeled In Case. I'll explain that one for free: it's a metaphor for utilizing all of the available resources of society as your power ante bellum, instead of hoping you have any power post bellum; and they made that power so easily accessible it is not only merely behind glass, it is in the enemy's own territory. But what you want is something that should not be-- a specific form of power for every specific situation-- because that would be someone granting you power, which then makes not so much a power as a privilege. Power doesn't care if it's by a hammer or an anvil, so long as the work gets done. "The glass that needs to break is the ceiling." Are you insane, what the hell for? It's glass-- can't you see they're not up there, they're not even in the same building? Your knowledge is the trade off for your impotence, and impotence is what you want, so that no one can depend on you. If it's being taught in a university and it doesn't have numbers in it, it is 100% a defense against change.

It encourages people to think of universities as having gnosis for the select, "here's our framework, here's some jargon." It encourages people to believe that public media is a neutral place to discuss ideas, and does not tell them that except for these discussions they will be utterly useless to the world. "Knowledge is power. Having a voice is power. Being able to affect what's in media is power." Yes, I agree you were told that.

The sweater vests have long debated whether had the Athenians followed Pericles's advice and stayed within the walls, could they have won a defensive war. But it's an invalid question; the reason Pericles thought this "defensive" plan would work is that it wasn't defensive at all: unlike the other walled cities of the time, Athens *wasn't* walled. The Athenians still had open access to the outside world through their port; and as they had the strongest navy in the world, they could project massive power, they could still go on the offensive, and the whole world knew it. What enraged the Spartans camped outside isn't that the Athenians wouldn't come out and fight like men, but wouldn't come out and fight like Spartans. "Why the hell would we? *We have boats.*" And NB the Spartans finally won by fighting like Athenians, and you better write that down, it's a near biblical prophecy. In the first year of a "defensive war" and "hiding" inside the walls, Pericles himself lead an attack out and back again with a huge army almost as big as the one that didn't came back from Sicily. But even with such access to the outside, the act of *partially* walling themselves in killed them-- including and especially the people who wanted to go outside and act. The problem wasn't the strategy, the problem was literally the walls. You are worse off, today you've allowed yourself to be *entirely* walled off inside universities and media, a media that encourages the jargon of universities, you can't project any power outside of those walls, which is why conversations with your dad are so frustrating. "You need to educate yourself!" Nah, I'm good. Pass the turkey. I realize that media appears like a kind of power, an access, but it's only access to other medias, tunnels connecting to tunnels that never open to fresh water; conduits for the transmission of a plague that contaminates not just you but everyone else who would have acted. You know that argument that finance careers are siphoning the best minds away from more noble pursuits? Not only is that wrong, it's irrelevant, by your own calculations it's only 1% of us. But the lure of "making a difference" and "having a voice" is flushing everyone else from everything else. We're now up to two generations of obviously bright and passionate people who are strategically planning to waste their entire lives one day at a time, in front of a teleprompter, complaining that they're not being heard. You say you want to change the future but your entire focus is the present progressive, current events that are happening, sentences people are saying. It's infected even the schools, if your college essay isn't at least peripherally related to social justice, MIT and RPI might assume autism but all the other admissions committees will simply press reject. Besides, humaneeds majors never ask for tuition reduction, they're just happy they got accepted.

You aren't fighting the good fight, you are poisoning all your fighters.

The system is often criticized as chaotic, but you need to stand way back and marvel at its efficiency, because once you've been bankrupted by a worthless degree that cost the same as the Harvard brand one thanks to the laws of supply and dumand, and obtained knowledge and techniques that can't project power, the system has castrated you; the productive world will never take you seriously again and your power dials down to negative. I'm sure those grads are smart and "know what needs to be done"-- see any of them in power? Slow down phenomenologists, not in office-- in power. Plenty of them end up as spouses/employees of power, though, that's interesting and shhhhhhhhh. The ferocity of your commitment to your cause is equalled only by the intensity with which you refused to learn math. True story and opposite to the conventional wisdom: in college I met more physics majors who considered themselves monotheists than considered themselves activists, doubly true for medical school, I'm sure they must have suspected that one of those was incompatible with science but the consensus was that the other was a total waste of their minds. Another separate observation, which is the same one: they were mostly uninterested in consumer electronics and media. The further you get from math the more sure you are of the power of technology-- technique-ology-- and revel in its jargon. Four to eight years after your cynicism + idealism you're in debt to the system and completely impotent, all you can do is buy your chosen Contrabrand and "contribute to the debate," this couldn't have worked out better if they planned it. They planned it.

Oh, but the sweater vest counter-argument-- which is the same argument: "The university system is broken, it's been appropriated by business interests and serves their needs, that's why it prefers science and engineering to philosophy and literature. College has become a tool of corporate capitalism. We're forgetting how to be human beings." That's your critique? It's hardly a critique, it's the standard conventional wisdom, it is... *obvious,* it's why your Dad mindlessly intones you should major in something that will get you a job. Both declare that college is necessary. That's propaganda, not rhetoric-- do you think it cares why you think you should pay for it? Ok, flip it around: if science is so objective and lucrative, why do you need to go to college to study it? At the undergraduate level it matters not a bit who teaches your class in physics but at least it's arguable you need a Thucydides scholar to help you with Thucydides. If your argument is you need to go to college and study something that will "get you a job" then you are a blatant propagandist for the student loan industry, it's the one thing you don't need college for. Same goes for the pro-mo pop sociologian who just finished a Mad Lib on "how the system works" and who thus believes girls should "be encouraged" to "pursue STEM" in college: you might want to start saving for her wedding, or rent. You don't need to go to college to learn STEM, you can do it from the woods, all of the relevant lessons can be pulled out of thin air for free. But no capital F Feminist will ever say this to a girl, you will not train them to self-study, you will believe the solution is to major in STEM, and when I tell you why you will catch your breath and demand that I hate women: *because then you don't actually have to learn it.* The university *declares* that you did. Try to learn math on your own and it is hard, very hard, because you are accountable only to the math; the math is easier in a university because less is expected of you, when the math seems really odd you can just skip the evens, you can figure out what might be on the test, there's a curve, you will be given the appearance of the blessing of knowledge and if all else fails you can always convert to a BA. As a secondary sources= primary outcome, you never imagine you'll ever be "smarter than the professor"-- do you even know that is something you should want? "I have the credentials, so why do I feel like I have imposter syndrome?" I'm sorry, who are you? So the university remains your master. "But don't you actually need to know how to do math to get the job?" Yes, but learning math is way harder than getting a degree and then loudly blaming structural oppression, and you can't use exclamation marks in math. Well, you can, but you won't.

While you're skipping physics to march for climate change, Elon Musk actually made it cool to have an electric car. Yes, I know, we're supposed to hate him for some reason. Off topic, here's an alleged Elon Musk interview question:

> From a certain location on Earth, you can go one mile south, one mile west, and one mile north, and you're exactly back where you started from. Yes, the bear is white, good job with elementary school. Is there any other point where you can go one mile south, one mile west, and one mile north, and end up exactly where you started?

Good news is there is more than one answer. The bad news is you won't learn this in college. I mean that there can be. The criticism used to be that colleges had "preferences" or even "quotas" that pushed out "the more qualified candidates" as defined by their utterly meaningless GPA. Remember how angry you got-- both of you? Those days are gone. What they have now is a recipe for a cake people will only lick the frosting of. This will seem obvious after I say it but just ponder the egalitarian implications: if you're a high schooler of given demographic and last year the College's class had 15% of your demographic, then you are not competing against other demographics *at all*, only against that one demographic, for those 15% of seats. Ok, I can see you're confused, I'll walk you through it: "I just got accepted into Harvard's Asian/Male/Non-legacy freshman class." Wow, you must be *really* smart.

The problem isn't even college, the problem is the debate about college. The debate about college protects college, protects universities from your frantic energy, so you can pay to attend them to display your frantic energy. It encourages the belief that colleges are vital to the productive/capitalist aspect of society by (pretending to) minimize the liberal arts; while also reminding the other everyones that college is the only place liberal arts (types) are valued. Are the outcomes the same? Universities protect the status quo by letting you protest the status quo. Go ahead and organize a march there, the police will helpfully block off the roads so you can get a video of you screaming at them for blocking off the roads. Frantic energy as a defense against impotence, what could be more American?

"None of this changes a basic fact: women work the same as men but get paid less." It doesn't even give you pause that every male corporate board in America has publicly and enthusiastically agreed with you? They adore you as the kind of forward thinking progressive they want because the outcome of this complaint will be that men will get paid less; the irony being that if you're satisfied with that outcome they won't actually need to hire you. It is interesting that no woman ever thinks to complain that they work harder but only get paid the same, I guess that's more of a guy thing.

You're not going to like hearing this, but these debates about sexism in the workplace always occur in the media because this is the place where the mediocre debate. Sexism occurs most viciously at the level of mediocrity because the mediocre can afford to be sexist. The real sabotaging of women is ignored because the culprit doesn't cast correctly. There is a legitimate argument to be made that girls are not encouraged to believe they are good in math, but it is only legitimate if we specify that it is the mediocre students who are not encouraged, and then honestly specify by whom. It could be rapey old white male colonialists, but it could also be that her peer group of Adderall and teleprompter addicts discourages anything other than photography, social justice, and cybergossip. And then maybe we can discuss whose fault that is. No? Walk into any high school's-- not AP calculus class, but multivariable calculus class-- a class which like page 101 of *Inside UFO 54-40* both exists yet cannot be accessed by any sanctioned pathway-- and ask the girls there if they were not encouraged to do math; or, if you have the nerve for it, who was prevented from discouraging them. You can ask the boys, too, but there's going to be about 70% fewer of them and they usually won't much like talking.

You think you figured that we have a "rape culture" all on your own? Systems of domination? Totalizing discourses? You detected the truth? The Oracle told you exactly what you needed to hear, and not a syllable more, the modern update was simply *to make you think you came up with it yourself*. Are you seeing the pattern?

You will engage in boisterous ineffectual activism by day, but when you go home at night you will return to your obedient status as consumers. First step: settle in and watch other people act. By day you will argue that slutty clothes are irrelevant in rape, but at night you'll tell your daughter to go upstairs and change into something more appropriate. Before you silence me as if I'm the one who doesn't understand the difference, please go back and meditate on what your monorail brain blew right past: she owns a lot of clothes. *She even bought clothes she can't wear*.

Why do you all use the same terminology, the same jargon? Is it because it explains reality, or because it is so internally consistent you don't have to look at things from anyone else's perspective? Is it a sign of inclusion, or a signal to everyone else that you can be

401

ignored? Let's ask everyone else.

"Capitalism is exploitative--" Yes, I've read the books you read about. As part of a battery of psychological testing I make people read *The Communist Manifesto.* Relax, it's only 30 pages, and it even comes with a Q&A. There are those who find it devastatingly accurate, and immediately want to join the movement; and there are those who find it devastatingly accurate, and immediately think, "holy crap, I better start accumulating capital, *fast.*" It's only capital if you use it, otherwise it's hoarding. "You missed the point of it, the bourgeoisie's existence is no longer compatible with a post-industrial society--" Wait, you're demanding change because you think that change is *inevitable?* Even your eschatology requires nothing of you, it is on autopilot, yet you want the credit. Turns out you're an Evangelical, Bible study is Wednesdays, swingers night's on Saturday, and don't forget to set your clock back an hour. See you in church.

You assert that capitalism is this giant, oppressive force that controls even the way we think-- and you're going to destroy it by explaining it? By making the unconscious conscious? From a merely strategic perspective, shouldn't the fact that you're still standing be evidence that capitalism let you live? Even Coca Cola observed that young people are less brand loyal than ever, they are turned off to consumerism and prefer broadcasting experiences, so the winning corporate strategy would be to encourage them to self-declare multiple identities each with their own jargon, codes, and products, fracturing their power and making it easier for marketing to parse the demographic and help them bury themselves alive in cryptoconsumerism, snapshots and self-righteousness. They know you won't be caught dead drinking their highly advertised carbonation and sugar water, and that you'll pay 3 times as much for their ad, sugar and carbonation free water to prove it. "We're pushing for revolutionary social change, against the 1%." I know math isn't your thing but your 1% is more like 40%, and did no one notice that your key ideological supporters are the actual 1%? Of course, they self-identified as socially responsible and anti-suit, so you thought they were one of you, never mind that unlike the suits their "services" have absolutely no social let alone productive value, they weren't even enjoyable as much as compulsive, 100% online gambling with 0% payoff. "We give everyone a voice and help people connect." You are a war criminal. You want the abandonment of traditional hierarchies in order to open up a space for radical new freedoms, well, check your balance to see exactly how much money they made off the identity they let you believe you came up with yourself. "I'm my own man." No trigger warnings on these Glocks. "I'm a victim." These oversize sweaters stretch all the way to the fingertips. "I refuse to be labeled." Have we got the TV show for you.

The capitalist critique of the critique of capitalism is that after WWII, the Marxists had to contend with a reality that didn't jibe with theory: why didn't the proletariat rise up? It had to be the seductive, oppressive "western capitalist traditions", Hellenism-monotheism-rationalism= colonialism-fascism-math that kept the proles out of power and blinded them with ideology. Only by bringing down these traditions, revealing their inherent binaries and inconsistencies, would the proles finally see they were slaves and rise up.

Well, never mind that's not entirely accurate, what you should be asking is why the Marxists needed the proles at all, why didn't the Marxists just do it all themselves, or at least lead the charge? And that's easy, they know everything, and therefore can't act; proles are ignorant but have the strength of ten Marxists. Once in a while you see a Marxist who does rise up, but usually he and the other avatars will only storm a dean's office or circle a square, which is pointless. Don't bother disputing this, you posted the pictures yourselves. Another good thing to ask is why, theoretically, opening the proles' eyes to future historical necessity necessitated that the proles not think about past historical necessity? But if this is the version of events you want to tell, if "cultural Marxism" was supposed to be the back door to class socialism, if the post WWII plan was to lift the fog of capitalist ideology so then people could see clearly for themselves the socialist/feminist/anti-imperialist truths that should have been obvious except for the fog, then boy oh boy were they way off because what happened next was Margaret Thatcher. I guess 1970s historical necessity, let alone 1870s, didn't see that coming. Sigh, if only she had watched Foucault on TV instead of bothering her pretty little head with math. As an aside, if you require an example of the desperate performance of omniscience as a defense against impotence, I offer you the French post-everythingists. Feminists, if you really think it's so symbolically important to just to have a female President, have you considered running a Republican? Because they seem all in. That wouldn't count? For reasons that wouldn't make sense? Got it.

It's not hard to understand what really went wrong if you simply... strip away all the ideology. Because while they thought they had "de-privileged the western canon", what they had inadvertently done was topple the primacy of *primary sources*-- including Marx. Careful: not pomo relativism, where one primary source can not be better than another; primary sources as a class was demoted, but since it is impossible under this logic not to bow to some authority, primacy went to secondary sources about primary sources, so they could tyrannize all of us. And that's how we got deconstruction. Lifting the fog of ideology did not deploy the proles; so the new strategy was to deploy experts to teach the proles a new ideology. Now we get dialectical materialism from the pages of *The New Yorker*, a publication so encephalotoxic that the best thing that ever happened to curb its 100% mortality rate was the capitalist paywall. That's either ironic, natural selection, or the system is sound. "People still need to be educated about what's going on." Umm, really? If they just knew more, they'd do more? Wasn't that Protestantism's gimmick? "Religion is the opium of the masses." I'm pretty sure opium was the opium of the masses, which is why Freud had to invent cocaine. Now opioids are the opium of the masses, how long can you be wrong before you sing a different song? As much as SPECTRE owed its techniques to psychoanalysis it utterly missed its basic clinical prediction: once the Western superego was destroyed, capitalism became the superego. We've known since the Romans that man cannot serve two masters at a time, but we've known since the Greeks you'll be damned if you don't serve one.

Let me see if I've got this right: the Horesemen of the end of capitalism are today's looming catastrophes of global warming, income inequality and migration-- too much energy, too much money, and too many people; throw in obesity and you also have too much food. I know, it's not distributed correctly, the problem here is the internal inconsistency of the catastrophes: too many of 3 don't think 1, 2 or 4 are a problem, they'd even be willing to move to California just to try out for the capitalists. Do you have a country or an NFL team? I don't know if I'm the first to say this, but I won't be the last: the catastrophic events of our time are nowhere near as catastrophic as was the Great Depression, the World Wars and the Cold War, and at least two of those were explicitly trying to destroy capitalism. Those catastrophes you are shown on your teleprompter aren't the demise of capitalism. They are the last gasps of socialism. [4.40] Go into any MLA format critical theory classroom and listen to the thirtyish adjunct longingly reminisce about how terrible things were for the old Marxy revolutionaries back during the Cold War, "oh god, the blacklisting, and the persecutions, and the pogroms, where could a Derrida go to be safe from a Reagan?" They are nostalgic for a time when it sounds like dreaming was considered a radical act; nowadays even 14 year olds have that same dream so distinguishing themselves as Professor/Radical requires the kind of action no one can even imagine. Time for a nap. I'm supposed to say that your dream is dead, try to dream a little bigger, but I don't really believe it was your dream, it was always someone else's. I think your true wish has always been for a tyranny, you can caption it Beneviolent but the key is it uses guillotines. You may take some comfort in knowing that I think you have never been closer to the fulfillment of your wish.

You can't change the system from the outside because you are the most inside, for you there is no outside, not anymore, because as much as you say you want to do things what you really want is not to do things and therefore to know things. Well, you got it. Meanwhile the system isn't political or cultural, it is technological, like the Matrix, you can't unplug. If you really wanted power, if you really wanted to a/effect the course of history or at least be at the top of the list for the evacuation pods, you would have to escape the walled city of Public and go all in on privacy. Any advertising exec has 10x the power of a college professor though of course the system doesn't let either know this, it is the former that decides how we view women or war, not the latter; quietly control the capital and you'll have the power to change the official language to Klingon if you want, or at the very least invade it should it be discovered to have dilithium crystals. "I would never invade another country." Well, it's not up to you, which is kind of the point. They say the future is decided by those who create the technologies, that is wrong, because they won't believe they have power either, they will think it resides with and be taken from investment bankers, beautiful women, alpha males, sports stars-- always the Other, always what they envy. You think it's because they don't *know* better? It's because the premise is envy. Since you don't feel you have the power to decide, no one else should have it. And no one will. The question of abortion will be solved not by ethics but by perfect contraception; the problem of rape will be solved not by "words mean words" but by ubiquitous 3D surveillance and nanotasers. And eventually we'll leave the planet and try feudalism again. Sorry Marx, turns out it's pretty easy to derive an entire system of critical logic if you start from axioms that are false. Human beings have abdicated moral, social, and political power to the technologies, much as you've done with your sexuality, which means any moral/social/sexual progress it seems to have made is entirely illusory. Doesn't it make you nervous that the crime rate will be inversely correlated to battery life? I know, I know, there are fewer killings than ever before in history; even the trauma surgeons have been convinced it's because of a higher social consciousness. Whatever humans say they believe, they await a technology to lead them into the future, but without the concomitant spiritual maturity they are slaves to the power generators=generators of power. Better hope they stay running, capitalist or not. Protest all you want, there will be no further social progress until someone invents the next big tech, or, said a different way, you can send an entire society's value system back in time just by throwing the appropriate kill switch. Maybe you'll think all this speculation hysterically unnecessary, so here's some historical necessity: when the Overlords approached, filling the horizon with their big ships, the awesome reality of their material arrival made people turn away from ideology and theology and go all in on technology. There were some holdouts, but when the Overlords showed them evidence that their prophets were just regular guys surrounded by science fiction writers, humanity embraced the Overlords and discarded their beliefs; and the next thing that happened was that the Overlords discarded them. "Yeah, we're going to leave you here to die, but we're taking the children." First of all, am I the only person who reads that as creepy, and second of all-- all of them? "I don't think it happened like that." If you had a child, then it happened exactly like that. One of the unintended lessons of the book is that while you shouldn't judge people by their appearance, you probably should judge them by their appearance if they have the ability

404

to choose their appearance and the appearance they choose is bananas. "Maybe if I cradle these two nine year olds in my arms, you won't notice I'm not returning them." Or that you're not wearing pants. You might counter-argue that humanity's pointless arguments over such silliness as "logos" and "I AM" in the face of malevolent alien invasion wouldn't have saved them anyway, but it's an odd argument to make since it's precisely such a faith that gave the Overlords their power. "But--" I know, I know, any sufficiently advanced technology is indistinguishable from magic, the trick is no one believes in magic, so everything we don't understand gets labeled as technology. "It works like magic!" Neato. The psychological benefit of the latter isn't that it is "real" but that it has an appeal to authority, to some other omnipotent entity. NB: as did magic. You are not living in an age of science, you are living in an age of science journalism. I'm sure pushing it all up one level and calling it materialism makes you and the other Sans-kulaks feel superior to the opiate addicts, and I'm sure thinking the book shows false religions will eventually be replaced by true science is a good way to punch your dad in the face, but such an interpretation is a cover for the colonialist tyranny we secretly wish for but aren't supposed to want. "We've come to plan the next stage of your evolution." Thank God! I get so much more out of watching you work and now I have both hands free to work on myself.

He approached the two fishermen who were leaning over their nets...
"Come, I shall make you fishers of men."

The above is from a novel by Nikos Kazantzakis, this part a retelling of Mark 1:17; the translation isn't literally accurate or even doctrinally pure, though at least Kazantzakis could read the original Greek. But he originally wrote the novel in English and later translated it into Greek, which makes this English the original and Greek the translation, all of which was too much for the Orthodox originalists, who banned him in every translation. In English there's the saying, "beware of Greeks bearing gifts," but the Greeks have a different one, it's etched in the Pnyx: nobody likes a wise guy.

The context creates the meaning: "fishermen" leads to "fishers of men", the meaning comes directly from wordplay which is why everyone remembers it, and to prove this there's a different passage in Luke where he simply tells the fishermen "from now on you will catch men" and no one remembers it.

But then we have a structural problem: the context is only literary, not cinematic, i.e. the wordplay depends on you reading it, not watching it, because the word "fishermen" is in the book but it's not in the movie. Jesus's lines aren't, "hey Simon and Andrew, you fishermen, come and I'll make you fishers of men." The word "fishermen" exists only for the reader, in the narration.

Of course an audience watching the movie might hear the words "fishers of men" and see two "fishermen" and make the association themselves. That would be fine for the audience to do if it were possible to do this, but it isn't possible to do this, not before 1600, because in Greek there's no such word as "fishermen". No one could have *thought* this word.

"Fisherman" in English is a compound word, formed by taking the agent noun "fisher" and adding "man." The Greek doesn't have such a compound word, the word erroneously translated "fishermen" is simply the agent noun "fisher," and the word "man" isn't there. The text literally says Jesus saw two fishers, and told them he would make them "fishers of men". There's still wordplay, but now there's a new ambiguity: what does the "of" mean? "Fishers fishing for men" or "men's fishers"?

Greek, not to mention Jesus, is unbearably ambiguous but Latin is supposed to be infuriatingly precise--

venite post me et faciam vos fieri *piscatores hominum*

come after me and I will make you become fishers of/for men.

--except here. I'm sure Jerome or whoever meant "fisher(men) fishing for men", and not "men's fishers", but it doesn't prove that Mark meant that, and for sure I know he didn't hear that.

I have been repeatedly told that the Bible is the embodiment of the word of God, all 5000 versions of it, but on this point God's word is fortunately unanimous that "men" is in the genitive. I say fortunately because if it was in the ablative you'd want to kill yourself, it's the sledgehammer of grammar and can mean almost anything though is primarily used today to lower the curve on the Latin final. The genitive is slightly less ambiguous in that it is only often ambiguous. A textbook Latin example, see if you can guess who requires consent:

amor *patris* (gen)= "father's love"

amor *patris* (gen)= "love for the father"

Sometimes there is no ambiguity because both meanings overlap:

nolite fieri servi *hominum* (gen)= "don't become slaves of men"

nolite fieri servi *hominum* (gen)= "don't become slaves for men"

But let's pretend that the Bible is in *fact* the "word" of God. What would that mean? At best, only the Greek-- or Aramaic, if the Overlords recorded it-- can have any possible claim to literal accuracy. And even if we knew what it literally said, who knows what it means? Even divine stenography would require interpretation in a whole other language. I certainly don't mean symbolically or analogously, where stuff stands for stuff. The language would have to be something that could speak more immediately, more necessarily, yet without needing supporting evidence, analogous to the language of the unconscious. It would be like the interpretation of someone else's dream, and what matters in an interpretation is the telling of the dream.

And the interpretation couldn't be more obvious: Jesus makes a simple analogy, he sees two fishermen fishing for fish, ok they haven't actually caught any fish at all that day, but he figures he can teach them to fish for a lifetime.

The problem with this wordplay analogy is that it's not an analogy. It is *only* wordplay. As an analogy it would necessarily fail. The purpose of an analogy is to deliver more clearly, not less clearly, a complicated meaning. But this analogy doesn't simplify or clarify, in fact it requires you to make necessary adjustments all along. Ok, fishermen, now they're fishers of men, except they're not actually going to capture any men, or gut them, or sell them, or lie about how big they were; these fishers of men are going to save their catches, protect them-- from other fish? Other fishers of men? "Fishing for men" doesn't get you there, unless you think the analogy is that the fish/men are supposed to be killed, and if you think no one would ever think this note that Julian The Convert thought exactly this when he observed that "the apostles were just like the fishermen who draw the fish out from the water where they were free and happy, into a place where they can't breathe and will soon die." Guess what happens next.

Imagine that Simon and Andrew were veterinarians. "I will make you become veterinarians of men." Now it's an analogy, it takes you all the way to the end, it allows for reasoning by analogy but keeps it channeled within a specific use. Healing animals, now you heal people; treating life, now treat souls; what you were doing is noble, but this is more noble; etc. Some of those interpretations could be wrong, but the analogy works.

Shepherding sheep is also an analogy which works, because even though the animals eventually might get slaughtered, that's not in the analogy: the specific task of a shepherd is to feed the flock and keep them safe from wolves or thieves. Fishermen don't do this, their allegiance isn't to the fish, unless they were shepherds of fish or veterinarians of fish, which they are not. They are fishers of fish. For men.

You'll say that anyone who has read even an excerpt of Mark can see the context directly supports the usual interpretation. I'm not sure which Mark they haven't read the rest of. Because while this Mark is full of nouns and action verbs, none of them are fishing or even catching men. The next thing that happens is Jesus casts out a demon, then he casts out another demon, then he casts out a lot of demons, then he takes a break, then he cures a leper, then he hangs out with a bunch of sinners-- whom he called, not caught, because he says the healthy have no need of a doctor, only the sick do, NB therefore the sinners are ill, not evil, instead of quarantine their illness can be cured. Then some more philosophy, some dogmatics, he heals another patient, then a whole bunch of people-- and then the words get really interesting, by which I mean repetitive.

In Mark 3:13 he appoints twelve apostles to go do two very specific verbs: "preach" and "cast out" demons. NB: those two things only, and "cast [out]" is the same word as "casting [nets]", which is what Simon and Andrew were doing when Jesus recruited them to be "apostles", which is the same word as "preach." I can't say the Bible is to be taken literally, but I can see God's biographer has a very tight vocabulary. Then he goes home where he is mobbed by more people, and his family sees the chaos and conclude he's a nut. The scribes helpfully explain that the only reason he can cast out demons is because he's possessed by one. NB: they don't say he didn't do it. They only explain how.

So Jesus gives a response with an obvious meaning that Lincoln remixed that actually makes no sense if you look at the words: "How is it done that Satan Satan casts out? A kingdom divided against itself cannot stand. A strong man's house can't be plundered unless you bind the strong man first."

Let's just leave for later that those three sentences could not possibly ever mean, "if I was possessed by a demon, I w/sh/couldn't do this"; for now observe that none of these verbs have anything to do with fishing or catching, but extracting. Does anyone ever actually "fish" or "catch" anything in Mark? Yes: the one time and thing they do actually fish is actual fish, which they use to feed actual men; and they do it twice. To be fair, if you simply assume the whole thing is magic, was the magic that they magically caught fishes for the crowd or that they "caught" the crowd with magic fishes? I'll give you a minute. You'll say that "fishing for" men comes later, the apostles catch fish into the church, and the gospel is the net. Thank you Lex Luthor, but the Bible doesn't say that. In fact, to be literally accurate, the only person in the New Testament who is described as catching any men is Satan.

Here's the Luke version that no one remembers:

> ...let down the nets for a catch....

> "We have toiled all night and have taken up nothing... but I will let down the nets..."

> ...they enclosed a huge amount of fishes... they called to the other boat to help them [take them up]... And they filled the boats, so that they began to sink.

> Having seen this, Simon Peter fell down at Jesus' knees, saying, "Depart from me, for I am a sinful man, O Lord."

> [for everyone there marveled] at the catch of fish they had taken up...

> And Jesus said to Simon Peter, "Fear not. From now on you will _____ men."

Note how varied the verbs are. "Let down [nets]" twice; derivatives of "taken up" three times, "enclosed" once; the noun "catch" twice. What kind of odds do you want for what goes in that blank? It's an all or nothing bet but in an unexpected direction, if you get it wrong you lose nothing but if you get it right it will have cost you your life.

The word Luke used was none of those, and NB "fishing" doesn't occur at all. In KJV it's "catching", but the actual word is ζωγρῶν, and that word *is* a compound word: "catching" and "alive," but it doesn't refer to animals, it refers to people, either to take prisoners instead of killing them, or to rescue them from being killed.

The KJV translation emphasizes a parallel between the objects, between the catching of fish and the catching of men, but in the Greek it's the verb that's different, the distinction is between catching dead and catching alive. Note the weird inclusion of the part where Peter falls to his knees-- in *fear*. What's he afraid of? Why would Peter tell Jesus to go away? Because if fish are men Jesus is catching them dead, which explains Jesus's very precise response to Peter's fear of being caught dead: "Fear not. From now on, men you will capture alive."

But these meanings reveal Luke to be unhelpfully uninterested in fishing, and syncretism, or making an exciting movie, so some work had go into creating a link to Mark when there was none. One sophist noted that Luke 5:10 is almost a direct quotation from Socrates, who said: "Try to be good and to catch the good. I will help you, for I know the art of catching men." That's a great save except that it requires you to hope Xenophon wrote in English and then translated it into Greek, because not only is his meaning totally different, but in Greek none of the words he uses are the same as Luke's, not "catching" nor "catch", not even "men"; and it further requires you to disavow that what Socrates was talking about catching was "friends". *Greek* friends. Everybody get it or do you need a video?

But even as early as the 400s the major studios execs weren't happy with Luke's script, his version was too different from Mark and Matthew's which were often word for word identical, hmm, and proving they too were aware of the ambiguity of the genitive they rewrote Luke and also used it to *fix* Mark and Matthew-- use the bird in the hand to kill the two in the bush, and what's the harm? Luke wasn't even there-- so the Latin remake Codex Bezae replaces the Greek Luke 5:10's very simple

Fear not, from now on men will you capture/catch alive

with the Latin jambalaya:

venite et nolite fieri piscatores piscum faciam enim vos piscatores homini

come and don't be fishers of fishes, as I will make you fishers of man

That's how you rework a film for a mostly illiterate audience, replace Luke with Mark and then add an explanation for Mark in Luke, and if you want an example of on the nose dialogue, there you go. The *enim*, which is roughly translated as "duh", is just plain pandering. Except... and I'm sure it's just a typo but boy oh boy would it be hilarious if it was an unconscious slip of the pen, or accurate, but *homini* with no *s* isn't genitive but dative singular, which would make that last part actually read, "fishers to man." As they say in psychoanalysis, oops.

But there's more serious problem with the obvious fishermen/of men analogy, which is that Jesus made it. According to the book, and Jesus, Jesus used parabolic analogies not to deliver the meaning more clearly, but to deliberately obfuscate the meaning. In other words, if "fishers of men" is indeed an analogy that Jesus used, then it probably *doesn't* mean what it obviously means.

Along with "fishermen", the English adds another word that is missing from the Greek:

KJV:

> [They were] casting a net into the sea, for they were fishermen.

> And Jesus said to them, "Follow me, and I will make you fishers of men."

Greek:

> [They were] casting around in the sea, for they were fishers.

> And Jesus said to them, "come behind me and I will make you to become fishers of men.

Never mind they're not very good or at all *fishermen*, these fools are playing without a net. The KJV actually invents the direct object "net" where before there was none, and thus obliterates the other meaning of the verb "cast." The word "cast" and its Greek prefix "amphi-" means "around" or "both sides"; change the prefix to "ek-", as in Mark 3:13, and it means to cast out, and now there is a semantic parallel between what the two brothers are doing before, and what they are explicitly sent to do after, using the same word. First they are unproductively casting about, then deliberately casting out.

The other thing about Greek and Latin is that in the absence of punctuation or boldface, emphasis must be signaled by rhetorical devices such as alliteration, repetition, rhythm, rhyme, etc. A famous example: "Verily, verily I say unto you" and then he goes on to say something verily important, and you know it's important because he repeated verily. But in Greek the rhetorical emphasis is even more pronounced as it comes with both repetition and alliteration:

ἀμὴν ἀμὴν λέγω ὑμῖν

"aMEEN, aMEEN, LEgo eeMEEN." The repetition says it's important, but the lyrical lightness ensures you remember it.

Here's Martin Luther on fishing:

> 65. Igitur thesauri euangelici rheti sunt, quibus olim piscabantur viros divitiarum.

> Therefore treasures of the gospels are nets, by which once were fished men of wealth.

> 66. Thesauri indulgentiarum rhetia sunt, quibus nunc piscantur divitias virorum.

> The treasures of indulgences are nets with which one now fishes for the wealth of men.

Note the contrast between 65 and 66 is highlighted by mirroring the pattern of the words; and while they don't exactly rhyme, there's a gayness to the endings that is might seem suited for poetry or entertainment, but nevertheless captures the listener's attention.

So if you listen to Greek Mark 1:17 ("come behind me and I will make you to become fishers of men.") -- or just look at the words--

δεῦτε ὀπίσω μου

καὶ ποιήσω ὑμᾶς

γενέσθαι ἁλιεῖς

ἀνθρώπων

words 2 and 5 not only rhyme, but taking the first six words, their rhythms are mirror reflections of one another:

X - - X - -   (come you in back of me)

  - - X - - X (and I'll make of you now)

- X - - (-) X   (a fisher of fish)

- X -   (for humans)

(The translation's not the point, I was trying to mimic the rhythm.)

If there is wordplay to hear here, the wordplay is between "behind" ὀπίσω (o-PEE-so) and "make" ποιήσω (pee-EE-so) "[you get] behind [me]" and "I will make [you]"-- the emphasis is on the logical connection between doing and becoming, not on fishermen and fishing. And even though there are several other applicants, it's said specifically *to* Peter as a metaphor *for* everyone else. It's not a job offer. It's an ultimatum: Come you in back of me, or get thee behind me.

Well, all good in theory, but it's all Greek to me, so I asked a few diner owners what what they thought the Greek actually meant. "Fishermen fishing for men." Hmm. I asked two native Greek classicists and a Greek priest what they thought it meant. "Fishermen fishing for men." So I was wrong.

But I wasn't trying to be right. I was just playing the odds, the payoff odds, given that everyone is betting the other way. If I'm right I win big, but if I lose I've lost nothing. Said the other way: if you're right you've won little, but if you're wrong--

To be a fisher of men is a magnificent calling that requires nearly no effort whatsoever, and for damn sure you aren't metriced on your catch. You eat either way. So what is this passage supposed to mean for the reader? Ok, fine, Peter, Simon and Andrew were unambiguously called to be fishers who catch men. So what does he need you for? To do what Peter was called to do, except for quo vadis and literally everything else-- as if God might want freelancers so he wouldn't have to cover retirement? "I've been a private fisherman for about 5 years, I charge an hourly rate and I'll need a retainer, though I'm willing to offer a sliding scale." How generous, but we got guys in house. "Yes, but I have a master's." You are illiterate in over 20 languages and can't do high school algebra, the only thing you've ever read are quotes from things you haven't, meanwhile you watch 12 hours of

411

TV a week and I know how much porn, you should pray someone is fishing for you. "I'm not saying I'm perfect, but I deserve credit for trying." Of course. The ledger must be balanced, even if the rest of the world must be deprived.

In even the most socialist parts of America the basic practical strategy is merely to give those with a disadvantage a leg up, which for some reason drives those with the advantage bananas. But even if this reversed the winners and losers, it cannot change that there are winners and losers, so in the future the dream will be to handicap the advantaged, make them do math with half a slide rule or swim the 200m butterfly wearing all previous medals. This may seem like an idiotic strategy for promoting productivity or excellence, and it is, except that this strategy is not for promoting either. It is for making people equivalent, by which I mean cattle, by which I mean chattel. If you want you can get on the internet and argue about what this means for humanity, but if this strategy is a structural response to a structural problem, then there must be some structural benefit separate from how this might benefit individual people. Based on the form of this analogy, a good guess would be this keeps everyone else betting, so the house can profit from the bets.

"The Rocking Horse Winner" is a short story about a pedigreed English family in the 1920s that seems never to have enough money, making the mom twitchy in the paddock and the boy hypersensitive to the lack. "There must be more money," he thinks he hears whispered, so being 7 he decides the obvious solution would be to give her some. Well, a boy can give a mom a fish and she'll eat for a day, but teaching a boy to fish is mostly his Dad's job, and he's absent, so for financial advice he goes back to his mom, who is not aware that fishing or any other gerund is relevant in economics, which is why she tells him that the secret to getting money is luck.

Look, it's not a great answer, but it is an answer, and if you're clever you can take any ideology and make it work for you, or use it to deprive someone else, which is the criticism Marx had about ideology before he was reworked as an ideology to deprive everyone else.

So the kid tells his mom he'll go get luck, or get lucky, but she patronizingly dismisses this as childish thinking. That angered him somewhere, and made him want to compel her attention, which is a childish ideology. But let's see if he can make it work for him.

The mom is very badly named Hester, and her economic world is by definition limited to the home, but she does have a gardener who knows husbandry and a brother who knows horsemanship. So next the boy goes to his surrogate fathers for advice, and because they are idiots instead of teaching him husbandry or horsemanship they encourage him to play the horses; again, not a great answer but the kid's got a System, and sure enough he wins a lot, but the story's reveal is that his System is to manically ride his toy rocking horse until he somehow divines the winner, an OCD ritual which also drains him of his life. With his final pick he wins 70 grand, and loses everything else. The last line of the story is a favorite prompt for discussion in 7th grade classrooms, of course there are no wrong answers except deviation from ideological purity, please raise your hands if you can tell me what society demands you to think this means:

> "Poor devil, he's best gone out of a life where he rides his rocking-horse to find a winner."

Anybody? Why do your parents bother to get you prescribed stimulants if they're not going to make you study? "She said it's because her doctor is an arrogant jerk." Well that clears that up. Ok class, put your hands down and turn your palms up: in one hand put "gone out of life" and in the other put "rides his rocking horse to find winners." Which is best?

If you picked the latter, or the former, you have been tricked into accepting the form of the debate and missed something important: the third choice, which is staying alive and not chasing winners, by which I mean losers. 7th graders do not think to suggest this third possibility, nor are they encouraged to do so, mostly because their teachers aren't betting on the outcome, they are benefitting from the debate. Importantly, however, in everyday life teachers themselves choose this third choice, e.g they won't play Russian Roulette no matter how much the prize. You don't need to be the math teacher to know that the probability is in your favor but the odds are not.

If you did play, and you won, you'd be a nut to play again if the cylinder's not respun. But the story's last line doesn't consider not playing as a possibility, as long as he lives the child will always keep chasing winners. That's what the kid does on his rocking horse, short odds get longer fast, and the only people who chase the long odds are losers, winners, and aspirational gamblers. So the analogy here is to a compulsive=competitive gambler, who, win or lose, can't=won't stop; i.e the compulsion isn't to gamble but to gamble enough times to be able to call yourself a gambler, even better if you win a few to prove it, and boy oh boy doesn't it count double if you win right after you point at a potential mate and say, "never tell me the odds." Except this kid's not a compulsive gambler, he's a kid, and he was perfectly willing to stop. Does anyone else have some ideas? This is D.H. Lawrence, and the mother is blonde, so there's a possible analogy between "rocking horse" and rocking your horse, but that's mostly the wish fulfillment of masturbators who wish it could pay off. This kid is doing the opposite of masturbating. He's riding to satisfy his mom; and the kid's got heart, I'll give him that, but he's a kid, he's a bit excitable and anyway his hamstrings are too weak for a twitchy mare. It never seems to be enough for her.

You could go psychoanalytic and say he wants to figure out what it is his mother desires, so he can give it to her. That thing is quite obviously money. He gives it to her. He observes it does not satisfy her. So he gives her more. Still not satisfied, it even seems to create a greater desire in her.

That would be a good guess, except there are two other key facts in the story. The first is that she does not know where all the new money comes from; the boy launders it, makes it look like it was an inheritance from a distant relative. The second is that she spends the all money-- not frivolously, e.g. she does get the boy a Greek and Latin tutor-- but fastly.

I guess there's an analogy to capitalism, always growing, always seeking more, but please observe that this bright young thing doesn't want *money*, she doesn't want to keep the money, she doesn't use it to acquire more capital, she's not even aware what the means of production are, let alone wanting control them; and she can hardly be accused of exploiting labor if she doesn't even know about the factory, which is what Marx would say the ideology was for.

If you're trying to understand what it is that satisfies her, you are chopping up the wrong tree. That void in her heart can't be satisfied by money, money's only a fetish for something else, here irrelevant. Neither is her satisfaction obtained by depriving anyone else, that's not what she's accounting for in her ledger.

What's hard to see is that though she's rich, she's singularly poor, and rather than detest her you should feel a downright compassion for her. Don't laugh. She has a reputation she has to live up to, responsibilities, and is no doubt called upon to make many costly sacrifices, failing any of which no one would tolerate her. She's obligated to entertain important guests, lubricate social relations, host dinner parties, and if that actually sounds wonderful I will here assume you are not, nor even know, an introvert, or what introvert means. Hosting a dinner party as an introvert is like having to eat with seven people. Yes, that's the whole analogy, you get it or you don't. Four hours later while you're autoclaving the silverware the methane machines are calling each other from their cars to crowdsource that your husband is definitely abusive, cheating, or gay. No thanks, and I'm not going to be coming to your key party either. This is the wife's plight, introvert or extrovert she better be in a pencil skirt, she lives in a democracy but in many ways it's still an oligarchy: let her fail in her obligations to raise the next class of officers/statesmen/board members, or fail to patronize the school-- never mind wealth taxes so onerous there's no way she can pay them. Remissness in respect to any of these will be visited upon her by the egalitarian citizens of the democracy no less strictly than if she was caught stealing from them. She may be gentry but she's no longer landed, the problem isn't wealth but cash flow, if she wants income she's going to have to work, and even that's become harder since she has small children and that dizzy slut Jenny took all the steady work from home jobs. And she'll get no assistance from her friends, at that level of bourgeoisity her friends are her friends in order to receive assistance from her.

You might suppose that her ever increasing spending is a function of the psychological expansion of desire from demand: the more she gets the more she'll ask for, but this isn't the case here because even though she wants money, she never demanded any money. From anyone. It just appeared. She spends more and more because she keeps getting more and more; give her less and less and she'll spend less and less, but always all of it. She's not spending it; she's getting rid of it. Now she got money she didn't pay for, which means that money counts as a debt.

You'll say that money carries no debt precisely because no one gave it to her, it came by luck. It cost her nothing. It was free. But counterintuitively except mathematically, money that came at no cost and from no source puts her infinitely indebted to the world, just look at the graph. You did your Algebra homework with the TV on? Ok. Let's start from x=1.

Imagine one day a guy you know gives you a fat stack of Pinocchio money, wow, you're elated. But let a few weeks pass and you'll hate the sight of him, especially if he's affluent or affable or never mentions it again. At least have the decency to insinuate I have sex with you so I have an explanation for why I detest you. Well, what if he's a stand up guy and doesn't want anything from you? If he's not toxic then the money is, you have to get rid of him, or it. You can't spend it on a house or a car, which becomes the physical manifestation of your debt to him, but on something that will itself disappear; the track, whores and heroin are common write offs for those who've declared moral bankruptcy, which is why they're all called horses, but for the average debtor the best way to publicly dispose of a finite debt is to use the money to pay off your other debts to everyone else. Use the bird in the hand to kill two in the bush. Sorry man, I'm not trying to be a problem, but your charity's not in my assets column, yes old liabilities were made to become less but into the liabilities column nevertheless.

Owing two creditors is even better, because now you owe only half to two people; a hundred creditors and the math shows you only owe each a tiny fraction, and by the only rules of significant figures you can still remember you thus don't owe anyone anything, which is how your accountant got you out the social contract.

But to the mother that money appeared as if by luck, i.e. no creditor to whom she can avoid being indebted to through a thousand psychological defenses ranging from fetishistic disavowal to grabbing a servant by the throat. No one to be indebted to means division by zero, and what she owes is infinite. God forbid her luck someday changes she will be required to pay it all in full, or else be sent to torturers who will extract whatever is left worth extracting. She is no miser, the money can't be saved, let alone hoarded. And she's not a capitalist, that capital can't be put to work to produce more money, remember: money comes from luck. Money only has value if it moves, so move it she will. She's not going to be frivolous with the money, but she has to get rid of it, fastly, because if she's one day caught by Fate with even a penny it will be taken from her.

The kid just wanted to be nice to his mom, I get it, but having had early instruction in Greek and Latin but not enough in two column accounting he made things worse, not better. If he had given her the money straight, and also explained clearly what it had cost him, she would never have let him do it again AND she would have used that money cautiously, slowly, reverently, because of what he had to pay for it. If he had given her the money straight but still hid from her what it cost him, she very likely would have demanded more-- and why not, if it's free? You'll wonder why this free money doesn't incur a debt, but it absolutely does-- but it is to her *child*. She is willing to incur any debt to him, even an infinite one, *because she loves him*. Wait, that's the part you doubt?

In paragraph 1, in great detail and for no reason, it is explained that the mother married for love but the love turned to dust; she's not gay and no one is dying, so her only option is her children, but alas, she could not love them either. The center of her heart was a hard little place that could not feel love, not for anybody; and she knew it, and her children knew it. Small aside and NB her brother comes around a lot.

The obvious and illogical reading is that she isn't capable of love and she loves money, which according to 7th grade teachers means she's a bad person. Because of the second thing, not the first thing. Yet she never does anything bad, and she doesn't actually love money. How can money make her good or bad? Look at how everyone admires the horses. Do the horses have any money? And yet without money, a horse is good or bad. You would think that it's thus possible for a woman to be good or bad based on what she does. Well? What does she do?

There's a reversal throughout the story that you don't notice because you want to hate her: it's not that she doesn't love anyone, it's that no one loves her. I checked. There's not a moment of affection for this woman in the whole story, no one gives her a tender word; even when her son is dying two of the idiots go off to play the horses, and when the boy dies after the big win the uncle actually tells her that at least her ledger is balanced. That's nearly a quote. And when I said Dad's absent I don't mean he's dead, which he should be, no, he's downstairs, making a whisky and soda. Apparently it's excellent. Why isn't he trying to control the capital or fish for his wife, or at least doing deadlifts to strengthen his husbandry? Nah, he prefers the life of apathetic leisure that deliberately low testosterone affords him. I have no idea what his job is, his main skill is waiting for prospects that don't "materialize"-- you know, like a fetish-- and at that he's excellent; meanwhile like any other low income household the woman is the one who has to go out looking for work. He's vain, passive; she's hard, active. She worries about the boy's future, she's anxious about his health. The father doesn't worry about anything, except running out of soda, that's not excellent, he likes the bubbles and otherwise the whisky makes his mouth ouchy. We're told the husband is well bred, handsome and has expensive tastes, but we're not told what his name is, like with any other trophy husband it's irrelevant and he gets on without all right. Other than blocking her orgasms he makes only one contribution to her story, in the form of a single statement, and it is so jaw-droppingly imbecilic that I'm going to quote it verbatim: "I don't know." Thinking gives him wrinkles. And you think the mother is to blame? This might be the most sexist thing that can be said, or the most gendered thing that can be said, but this poor woman is surrounded by women.

Sure, the mother also spends the money on "womanly" things, like throw pillows, colors, and entertaining; and it doesn't require a philosopher or mercenary to inquire whether she shouldn't aspire to a simpler house. But what she doesn't spend money on is herself. That would be her husband, who is more of a dandy man then a handyman, let alone a gentleman.

Using more technically accurate psychiatric terminology: the center of her heart isn't a *void*, it's a charcoal briquet, her heart doesn't need to be filled, it needs to be ignited; but never mind flint rock and magnifying glasses, no one in her blast radius bothers to push the red button that says ignite. So she remains cold and hard. She is neither Mme Bovary nor Cde Defarge, she can be forgiven if she spanks herself with interior design catalogs or gets all oxytociny when she can finally prepay Eton, at least she's not gang banging herself between a cocktail and 2 teleprompters, I might say she is too much in the world but at least she is not trying to obliterate the world, or herself, or everyone else. Nor does she sneakily untie herself and present to some Don Juan to mount her up and ride her bareback until she felt exquisitely guilty, but even if her husband heard no protests or caught her in the act it's not like he'd would be hurt or even angry so much as annoyed. "Must you, on the good sheets?"

The correct interpretation of her strategy is that she does not take the easy way out; though no one loves her she does not retreat to love for a child, even when he is dying. This isn't to say she doesn't love him; it's that she doesn't wear that love like a mask to avoid loving anyone else, to pretend to herself that she's a person whose heart is overflowing with love so she can get away with-- with what? The selfishness of spending money she doesn't have on a gardener to do what her husband has plenty of free time for and at least would teach him a skill? She just stays hard. Look, it's not a great solution, but if you're a clever person you can make it work for you, or use it to deprive someone else, and credit to her that she does not choose the latter.

And let's assume that while the husband is brainless he isn't blind, we can all see she probably doesn't much love her husband, nor her husband her; she probably thinks he's a bit of a burden, and he probably sees that she thinks him a burden. The danger here is that their dislike will grow, their former love will turn to dust-- but if she just exerted her authority and made him work, the result over time will be that she'll love him and he'll love her, and he'll feel like he's *useful* to her and makes her happy. They will be better friends, feel more at home together: they will be indebted *to each other*.

This isn't really the kind of analysis you give 7th graders, well, not most 7th graders, but if you went to college to major in English and spent any time analyzing the symbolic meaning of the race horses' names then it was very likely a defense against learning the math necessary for the actually useful analysis: the Rocking Horse System is garbage. Look, I made a chart:

HORSE/RACE	ODDS	BET	% of Bank	Profit/Loss	NET
Blush of Dawn	?	5s		-	-5s
Singhalese	?	10s		+	5s or 10s?
(one year passes since Blush of Dawn; various races, including Sansovino/Ascot)				"steady, all things considering" +	300 (+20 in reserve at Turf Commission)
Daffodil/Lincoln	4-1	300+5	93%	1200+20 (-5 payback to Uncle)	1520
Lively Spark/Leger	10-1	1000	66%	10000	11520
(Gives 5000 to mom)	EVS				6520
Grand National	?	100	2%	-100	6420
Lincoln	?	50	1%	-50	6370
Malabar/Derby	14-1	5300?	85%	74200?	80570?

I'll summarize: loses, wins, wins, wins, wins, loses, loses; wins. And dies. The Sharpe ratio is nearly zero, if it's not actually negative. Why not just flip a coin, at least you keep the coin? "There must be more money!" whispers the house, because the house always wins.

You'll say that even if the system is unreliable, when it flashes green you're sure to hit, so run a backing strategy and keep bets small when the odds get long. Well, don't quit your day job.

The boy says God is the one who gives him the luck, but you can probably guess what kind of a god D.H. Lawrence believes in. Hint: the Dad is absent. What the Rocking Horse system appears to give him is omniscience, but what the kid needs is power. This puts the kid at a disadvantage, for two reasons.

First, most people have enough high school to know that "probabilities" aren't the same as "odds", Russian Roulette is 5 in 6 and 5 to 1; but in this case "10-1 odds" aren't the odds of the horse winning. Those are the payoff odds, 10-1 means bet 1 to win 10, and they're determined not by the probability that the horse will win but by how much of the total bet across all horses was on that horse. They do indirectly represent the crowd's belief about the probability of the horse winning, I guess, but the crowd is comprised of idiots and they're right about 30% of the time. And most of the gentry who go the Grand National are English majors, or married to them, and extroverts, they didn't go to win money but to mingle with the best people, so they simply bet on the horse with the name that has symbolic meaning for them. Statistically speaking, therefore, 14-1 means not that the horse is mathematically unlikely to win because he is twitchy in the paddock but that the extroverts dismissed him as a loser because his name sounded stupid. Which is 7th grade all over again.

Second, the System tells him which horse will likely win, but it can't cause a horse to win. Neither can the System create the odds. If Lively Spark paid 4-1 instead of 10-1, then all the rest of the story equal the mom would have ended up only six thousand to the good. And a poor devil of a son to the bad. Even in your ledger I doubt you would say that it would have been worth it, and it's not a story you're going to read in 7th grade.

You therefore can't use those payoff odds to determine the probability that a horse will win the race. But you don't need to, because the probabilities are already known: they're all the same. The thing about the Olympics unlike the Grand National is that the fastest biped is not asked to sprint the 100m carrying two bandoliers full of depleted uranium to give the guy from whatever country will soon be in Russia a sporting chance. But at the Grand National, all the quadrupeds have been systematically= physically handicapped so that in theory they would all tie. In other words, the handicap the horse is *carrying* reflects the probability of the horse winning *before* the handicap. The whole point is for the bookmaker to make it interesting, to bring in more bets, get the over-round percentage >100 and pocket the difference. You could collect a hundred different variables from mud viscosity to orgone pressure, but the handicapper has already accounted for these, so unless your ideology, Oracle, or algorithm can better interpret the data, the probability of you picking the winner in a 15 horse race is 1:20. My math is correct. You're bad at money.

Next you'll tell me that the boy would adjust his bets, only go all in when he's certain. That's a very interesting hedge for you to make, and brings us to the second disadvantage of the Rocking Horse System, because he didn't do this in the story. The only reason you imagine he=you would do this is because I just pointed out the unreliability of the Rocking Horse system *and this weirdly convinces you that the system must therefore be valid*. In reverse: you would bet 100% of your bankroll when you think it's 100% certain, but this would imply the reason he doesn't bet 100% is that he is not actually 100% certain. He doesn't make the odds, so the best proxy for his confidence is the percent he bets. That's *his* system, and in his system, the worst thing he can do is go all in because one bad bet and he's out. But betting less means he has to play more times, which drains him of his life, because, surprise, instead of playing the horses he's been playing Russian Roulette. Which is 7th grade all over again.

You'll now shake your head at all the sophistry and maturely announce that since the System couldn't actually magically kill you, if you had such a system, you'd soberly adjust your bets and over the long run keep winning. I don't know how you can believe that 50% of a valid system can be dismissed as impossible magic while keeping the other 50% that is equally magical just so you can tell me how sophisticated a gambler you could be. That's magical thinking. That is the thinking of a child, and even the child in the story doesn't think like this. And I can say with 100% confidence you have many such childish systems for every aspect of your life, and none of them have worked. "The whole game is rigged!" And yet knowing it hasn't stopped you from playing it.

Which is the third disadvantage of the Rocking Horse System: any system which can reliably generate positive returns over the long term   will always, over a shorter term and in the hands of an idiot, result in disaster.   Always=100%. Here's an example. A generally reliable system is to simply bet on both the first and second favorite horses, since one of them wins 57% of the time, and to finesse it you can bet in a ratio, say the favorite pays 3-1 and the second 5-1 and you're willing to bet $10, you'd bet 4 on the first and 6 on the second. Ok? Well, I don't know anybody who does this. Nobody has the patience and everybody knows better. Say the Rocking Horse System tells a guy to bet 90% when his certainty is >90% and 75% when his certainty is 75-89, etc. What will happen is when his confidence is around 80, or the horse pays more than 10-1 or it's raining or his wife is a nagging bitch, he'll nudge his confidence up 1 or 2 or 30 and bet 90%. "The game is rigged!" Why would they bother? You could play Russian Roulette with an unloaded squirt gun and kill yourself with a panic attack. Yeah. Trigger warning.

You can even suggest he'll always bank his profits, give them to his mom-wife, and only ever bet from a fixed pool. That's even worse: it leads to divorce, and maybe homicide. The day after he gets wiped out he's going to start hating her, all he's asking for is a short term loan from the money he hard earned for a sure thing at long odds but this small minded interior decorator turned seamstress wants to spend it on tutors and tuition and deprive him of his satisfaction. "That slut never believed in me."

The father's to blame, but the tragic flaw is in the boy, he's misread the situation, no surprise, he was never taught to read situations, no one taught him it was not his job to satisfy his mom. Both of those are actually his Dad's job, but he failed the boy, also no surprise, because he failed the mother. No one taught the boy how to be a man. Or a gentleman. Or how to run an economy. You could show off your wonderfulness and say there's no reason a mother couldn't teach a boy to be a man, thank you stupid, but it is hard to argue it's entirely her responsibility when there's an actual man downstairs drinking responsibly. And so the kid really does have only two choices, ride that iffy system all the way to the winners and incessantly, or die trying and inevitably; he doesn't know there's a third possibility, and please observe carefully that both of those offered choices guarantee he never grows past the 7th grade, let alone up.

Imagine a story in which a wife goes to a Halloween party and mistakenly has sex with a different man who is wearing less of the same costume as her husband. As some of you are so brittle as to be unable to fantasize without safeguards within the fantasy, I'll say explicitly that the masked stranger wasn't trying to trick her, he just thought some MILF in a slutty nurse costume was into him.

So in Act I the story shows us an adult wife, no nonsense and perfectly loyal, who agrees to her husband's adolescent request to wear a slutty nurse costume. She thinks it's weird that he wants other people to ogle her, because what she wants is for him not to want this AND not to mind if she does. NB it's a "male" sexual fantasy, so her face doesn't get masked, her body does, opposite for male horror, and double opposite for female fantasies of each. In Act II she's drunk, flirts with people who are not who they appear to be, then aroused by all the new desire from new people, she ends up with a masked but naked man she thinks is her husband. Then the mask comes off, oops, turns out he's not. In the climax she climaxes. In Act III she convinces herself it's too late to stop now, may as well enjoy it, and she'll just have to explain to her husband she was drunk, didn't know what she was doing, and this wasn't at all what she wanted, all of which are facts.

Yes, she enjoyed it. And Captain Marvel could beat up Thor. I'll again say explicitly that if this fictional comic book scenario of confirmatory assent isn't sufficiently preposterous that you can still pretend it cuts you to the quick and want to warn others about the pain, I can't stop you, just know that no one can feel safer when they discover the one looking out for them is you. What they feel is embarrassed.

But the husband had actually stumbled into the room back in Act II, and in a drunken haze immediately deduced that she was drunk, didn't know what she's doing, and this is exactly what she wanted. Of course he is incapable of doing anything to stop it so convinces himself it's too late to stop it now, and so ends up hiding in the shadows holding his dick. Let's go with metaphorically. Maybe later on she tries to make it up to him in the language of porn, i.e. erotic frustration: "I'm sorry baby, if it's any consolation he probably wasn't interested in me, he just saw some blonde in a nurse hat and wanted to make her come so he could brag about it. You're not mad, are you?"

The husband and you can make the required interpretation. Not knowing until "it was too late" that there was something unusual about how hard it was to fellate her husband sounds either preposterous or like a woman who very much doesn't want to know-- *in order* to be able to act on her secret desire. The naughty wife unconsciously gets what she wants, with no responsibility for acting on it. And when the mask comes off she tries to ride the momentum of "too late to stop now" through a few more orgasms, which only proves she secretly wanted this to happen.

But what you need to prepare yourself for is that you did not interpret this; your obvious interpretation of the story is the story, it's the manifest content, but you're tricked into thinking you've found the secret so you stop looking. All those eyes wide shut and legs wide open moans and squeals look like she secretly wants to have sex with another man, but that's not what she wants.

It starts with the mask, the husband's mask, the basic assumption is it allows her a certain amount of fantasy, e.g. she'd be able to have sex with her husband while imagining it's someone else. But the very literal description of what is happening here is that she is having sex with someone else while imagining it's her husband.

Obviously the mask is supposed to facilitate projection of your secret desires. It's erotic because you feel that your ultimate desire is under that mask, and it can be fantasized to be anything you want. Of course, in reality your secret desire isn't really under the mask; but not because what's under the mask is realistically different than your secret fantasy, but because you don't have any secret fantasies at all. The whole reason it works is that the mask lets you think you merely don't know what they are, but that they exist. It makes them as potentially real as they can ever be. Horror works the same way: under that mask is your ultimate fear, but you don't actually have such an ultimate fear, so the mask is terrifying because it says you do, and ta da. The first horror movie I saw as a kid that scared me was the original *Halloween*, and more than scare me it *shook my soul*, for the first time I was seeing a true psychopath, pure will with no other needs or desires, its force directed towards only one goal rendering all other events meaningless, including gunshots, his will made him supernaturally invincible; but the moment his mask came off for two paused frames on the VCR my only thought was how easy it would be to cram his head into a microwave and set it to clean. I didn't know a lot of physics back then, but I just got a crash course in psychology. For this reason the mask is often labeled the "cause of desire". Take that mask off and it is never as scary or erotic as it is supposed to be (which is why in horror movies they cheat and use a second mask (uncanny face; no face; the victim's own face)). The cause of desire (or terror) is the mask-- not what lies underneath.

If you follow this logic of lust and anxiety, then it's a simple translation to tragedy: whatever is actually under that mask logically *cannot* be what causes your desire. The mask negates the desire for what is actually underneath.

It's not like this is a recent innovation. They wore masks in Venice in 1268, but not just during Carnival or the Purge or to get away with chucking eggs at the chicks. In fact, everyone had already been wearing masks intermittently for the past 6 months, not to hide their identity but to negate their class, giving everyone the otherwise sociopathic freedom to intermingle freely. Taking away knowledge meant everyone could act.

And ancient Greek actors wore masks, for the same reason they never showed graphic violence on stage. Did you think it was because they were uptight? A culture as sexual and violent as theirs didn't make the show PG because they-- the men-- couldn't handle PG-13. They may have wondered if Jocasta was really hot, but no one looked at the masked actor who played Jocasta and wondered if she was really hot, or a she. The mask negated the actor, converting the stage biped into a blank screen for the projections of each audience member's unconscious. Which means the masks also negated any *underlying* universality of the character. All that was left is the story. You weren't supposed to learn about Oedipus and his motivations, you're supposed to fantasize your Oedipus and motivations into the concrete story. There's nothing universal in the character of Oedipus, what's universal is the story of Oedipus. In order for your Oedipus to feel guilty, it had to be for something that could make *you* feel guilty. Not the shameful act of incest, but the repressed guilts each individual would have that could *safely* manifest in the play as incest. The masked Oedipus becomes each viewer's Oedipus; then the story "adjusts" you, to improve you. You came at it individually, you come out of it together.

The same play performed today doesn't "resonate with modern audiences" because when an unmasked actor portrays Oedipus, the actor becomes *an* Oedipus, *that* Oedipus, so it's your fantasies that are negated. Performing a modern play with *known* actors-- worse, being clever and changing the age/race/gender of the individual actors-- may improve the box office but undermines its purpose. At that point, why bother to hide the sex? It's already pornography and it's not about you, so what's the difference?

For this reason, when Aristotle wrote about tragedy, he focused on story. He didn't care about the acting or even the theme, it made no more sense to offer a critical analysis of the symbols of *Oedipus* than to say a unicorn in a dream symbolizes a virgin. To whom? Unicorn-- as in rhinoceros? Virgin-- as in boy? The story's meaning wasn't the point, the point was the catharsis. An example from within a movie: the *Eyes Wide Shut* party is meaninglessly cathartic, what matters isn't whether that's the same girl or whether that's really Ziegler. Your experience of the party, your projections, how it changes the protagonist-- and you-- is the purpose of those scenes. The movie hid the characters's faces yet showed the sex, not because it was titillating but so that you couldn't fantasize it, so that the fantasy could only be your projections on the characters, not the sex. And it's telling that some people experienced the masked attendees as omnipotent and just submitted to it like, well, a sub: for them, high end BDSM and luxury esotericism became the ultimate safe space; while the reversal of what was hidden made others experience the party as so uncanny, so castrating, that they ran screaming into a frame by frame analysis of each image, sound, and movement, and detected a real life Illuminati expose. They couldn't let the scene exist ambiguously *especially in a movie* – someone *else's* fantasy-- because the feelings elicited were too terrifyingly real to them. In short, they fled into omniscience, as a defense against impotence.

Meanwhile, the omniscient Illuminati hunters missed the really useful component of the fantasy: Tom Cruise's character is a frustrated not-even cuckold, not because his wife desired a man in a costume, not because another man so easily could have taken his wife-- and not because he is powerless around real men at the big scary party. What sent him on an odyssey to Troy was envy of his wife's power to be desired. The fantasy isn't that she can seduce whomever she wants, but that she can be seduced by whomever she wants-- through no action of her own. This is why the object of desire of every desirable woman in the movie is him. They all *want* him. That's the fantasy. But he keeps turning them down. You think it's because they're not desirable? It's because it doesn't count.

The masked attendees may still be Illuminati, but not symbolically Illuminati but literally Illuminati characters. But then what's to interpret? And so what? And of course everyone knows this movie is based on the novel *Traumnovelle*, but this has failed to provide any useful insights into the movie. Do you know why? Because it isn't based on the novel *Traumnovelle*, it's based on-- and I can't believe no one has noticed this before-- the *movie Traumnovelle*. There are entire sections which are shot for shot identical, and others... which are not. Kubrick's film is in dialogue with that film, what he changed vs what he left the same-- e.g. "*Naval* officer", "*elevator*"-- i.e. the particular vs the universal. But the kind of hyper-scrutiny of the film that favored "uncovering power structures" = rationalizing their own self-serving impotence, and the assurance that it was based on an old book they were never going to read made it impossible e.g. to see what was shot slowly, in close up, in broad daylight, with no other audio-visual distractions: the person who gives Tom Cruise the warning letter through the mansion gates is Senator John Waltzer.

In the Halloween story he's masked; but to her, his mask isn't hiding his identity. To her, that mask means that's her husband, that's how she knows it's him, it is evidently a more reliable signal than his penis. She's not imagining he's someone else. But the thing under the mask cannot be what causes her desire. That thing (she thinks) is her husband. The mask negates her husband as the cause of her desire. She thinks it's him, she's turned on, but what turns her on is not-him.

In other words, what makes the story erotic is that it looks like she got what she didn't know she wanted; but what makes it tragic is that she didn't know she got what for sure she didn't want-- so she needs to enjoy it. I'll explain and you won't like it.

In Act I you have a basic setup of the disavowal necessary to have sex with someone you love. The "love" side of him is negated by the mask, and what's left is the real part, which in Act II seems bigger, but then again she's in a slutty nurse costume (results may vary). Both masks validly negate the "mystical essence" of the other person, take them out of fantasy, and ground them in real material reality. You've been regularly assured by non-sluts and real nurses that a slutty nurse costume is fantastically unrealistic, but the sure bet is you've seen more slutty nurse costumes in your life than mystical essences.

The tension builds with her not realizing until too late that sometime after the Pledge the husband has been switched out for another man. Ta da. Now she's past the point of no return, so she adjusts her hat and coos, "Too late to stop now!"

But it's not enough to just make the husband disappear. You have to bring him back. So in Act III she has to get caught. She must get caught by an omniscient but impotent husband, audience, narrator or reader; no matter how jealous or horny you are you can see she didn't know what she was doing, she wasn't acting on any desire of hers to sleep with a stranger;

even if she had had such a desire, in this case she was only acting on his desire. Who could fault her? The only thing she could be blamed for is continuing the sex after the mask comes off; therefore it continues after the mask comes off. If it makes the husband feel better I guess he can yell at her about that, but I suspect the only thing enraged will be his penis.

But that's the trick. The reason she doesn't stop isn't that she secretly wants it, even if she now does. Take her literally: it is too late to stop. She cannot stop. Or start. The desire she is compelled to act on is not hers, it's the other's. Imagine the stranger pulls out and grabs his pants, and says, "Oh God, you thought I was your husband?? I'm so sorry!!" Would she *then* tell him it's too late for him to stop now, so get back in there?

No. She didn't find a way to cheat, because she doesn't want to cheat. But what other obvious conclusion could anyone reach except that all along she secretly wanted it? Isn't the husband's reaction-- rage, paralysis, arousal, whatever-- not a response to the act (she is blameless up to then) but to the "discovery" that she must have wanted something like this to happen? His intense frustration-- here sexualized-- is that he knows this is her secret desire.

But if it is her secret wish, it's hardly worth all this. What woman needs to repress-- not suppress-- a desire to have sex with someone else? Nor is it the more specific, wicked wish "to cheat"-- that cruelty can easily be reframed with some self-aggrandizing rationalization ("I have a wild side"; "truth is, I admit I'm getting back at him") and that kind of guilt is also safe to pretend to have. The fantasy further manifests a false interpretation by making the husband get impotently erect by the whole thing, as if the "meaning"-- that he is shamefully willing to admit to himself-- is that he's a good man but "deep down inside suspects" he's a loser, so he's eroticized his humiliation into voyeurism to at least enjoy that.

Well, none of this happens. In fact, nothing happens. She didn't get caught in Act III, she got caught in Act II. She *learned* she was caught in Act III. We still don't know anything about her motivations. Or his. Yes, she has sex with the guy. But we don't know what happens next.

If this were the true repressed fantasy of the husband, then whatever desire is *obvious* within it cannot be the true desire. What's eroticized is not her secret wish to be with another man-- it's safe to eroticize because that *isn't* her secret desire-- but that she got her secret wish *whatever it is*, and that she got her wish *through no actions of her own*, that in the fantasy *manifests* as being with another man. What is eroticized isn't jealousy, but envy. *There can't be any jealousy, because none of the characters want anything.*

The story is insoluble because it isn't a story, it's only part of a story. That's how it defends against the meaning. Yes, she has a climax but the story does not, it's absurd but not a comedy, if it was a horror movie it would have to end with the possibility/futility of hope or the eternal recurrence of despair, and if it was a love story there needs to be a double reversal, here, I'll make one up now: shaking off his envy and humiliation, he finally mans up. Slowly, dramatically, careful not to shatter the fantasy he is stepping in to, he peels off his clothes and discards his mask and walks over to his wife riding the man, and starts kissing her deeply while she takes his manhood out of his hand. It's the ultimate climax for her, being desired totally, as woman, wife, conquest, conqueror, real and fantasy; the incompatibility of love and lust overcome, come over, it took one and a half men and 5-14 inches but all in one magical moment. No longer accounting for who gained and who lost, she forgives his pride and accepts him as her husband, and he accepts the legitimacy of her desire for him because it comes authentically from her as herself, and thus succeeds in having her as both wife and

423

sexual fantasy. "You're a cheating slut," he says tenderly, ejaculating on her breasts. "I knew you wouldn't be mad at me," she smiles, blowing him a kiss. Fade out. You don't like that ending? Here's another of the exact same form: he pulls out a Glock, pistol whips the rival and puts the gun into her vagina until she signs the divorce papers granting him 100% of the marital assets. Yes, he carries a copy with him. And a Glock. He takes a few pics to send to her job, slips his camera into his tumble drys and goes back to being assistant manager of management disgusted by all the liberal entitlement. The End. The tissues are over there. "At least he's not a bitch ass beta cuck like the first guy." Hmm. It may be hard for you to see them past your polarized snipers and tucked in muffin top, but every time you wear khakis women can see the pee drops on the front. Time to get a chiton.

In the *Hauge-Truby Handbook of Clinical Psychoanalysis*, the authors describe the stages of character development, and make the assertion-- more accurately it's an observation, based on years of working with poorly developed character structures-- that what shapes the person's character isn't his internal state, nor the sum total of his past experiences-- though something like a trauma may be relevant if it is used as something to overcome-- character is formed by action *only*, and only in response to conflict. Literally nothing else matters.

So imagine this sexual fantasy as a movie, and since I have no patience for any of this nonsense I'm only writing the cold open. If you can't get them hooked in under a minute and get to climax in less than ten then your head's not in the game:

A woman has come out of the shower and put on a clean tank top and underwear.

HIM (holding her discarded hospital scrubs in one hand and thong in the other.) My hot ass wife is a sexy ass nurse.

HER (posing): I'm not a nurse, I'm a sorority girl.

HIM: I've never had sex with a sorority girl.

HER: Overrated, most of us just liked the attention. Nurses are way more fun.

HIM: Did you have more sex as a nurse or a sorority girl?

HER (giving him a sly look): Way more as a nurse.

HIM: But you had sex with more people as a sorority girl.

HER (sorority girl voice): Well, duh. We have a fucking reputation to uphold.

HIM: Ok, let's not use that word.

HER: (She reverts to her own voice.) Aww... you know I love you. And I'm afraid I'll ruin the fantasy, but the best sex was as a wife. (Blows him a kiss.)

HIM (slapping her ass): A naughty wife.

HER (sultry voice, posing like a centerfold): I'm not naughty, I'm just shot that way.

HIM: That's nurse again.

HER: Oops... then I guess it's the wife that's imaginary...

It's not an Ice King opening but 100% you'll stay to see what happens next. There are four women in that scene, woman, naughty wife, slutty nurse, and sorority girl, but he can only have sex with one of them, and NB he doesn't. There's no point. Obviously, a quadrilateral woman can be highly desirable, but one into four cannot go, and the tragedy is that he really wants something he shouldn't want: to be desired as much as he believes his wife is desired, and in the same way: passively, variously, without actually doing anything. If this were a fantasy to be interpreted the question would be why does he want this? But we're writing a movie to be watched so ok, if this is what the character wants, *what does he do about it?*

He's split the woman into pieces, but unlike an apple and exactly like an atom the split pieces are separate and distinct objects, they don't exist as referents to a previous whole. This allows him a tranquil enjoyment of the sexual object with minimal competition or aggression towards others. But now that these pieces exist, the woman has no value, because she no longer exists. He can't pull a proton out of his craft beer and say, "This is identical to a gold proton, I'd like it converted to $1.02E-26$ bitcoin, please." And whereas before he had some idea of what the woman wanted, now he no longer can know what she wants, because she no longer exists. What exists are subatomic particles. Meanwhile, to everyone else who is not a particle physicist or a lunatic, only the woman matters, not the particles. So he tells someone, "that slut just wants someone with a big dick," and they say, well, why'd Helen fall for you in the first place? "Because that gold digger just wanted security." Security? Didn't she cheat on you with a condom?

It's hard enough to get people to sufficiently accept the difference between the manifest dream and the latent dream such that they don't make arguments derived from the manifest content, ignoring the need to interpret the dream. But often when people do reliably substitute the latent meaning for the manifest, they then completely ignore the dream work, the process by which the latent thoughts become a manifest dream. Movies get dreams wrong: they're full of symbols which are used as devices to *convey* information about or to the dreamer, instead of as the *consequences* of the attempt to hide information. Now the cultural shift from psychology to sociology makes it harder to get people interested in dreams at all, "they don't mean anything" really stands for "they won't mean anything to anyone else," no one else wants to hear them and telling them is a very inefficient way of signaling how complex you are when you're not really. You need a story.

This is why journalism today is both the most popular form of continuing education while simultaneously being utterly useless as actionable knowledge: even though the story might be factually accurate, it Gay Taleses the facticons using the structure of narrative fiction, the purpose of which is to create a central conflict in order to produce an emotional reaction. Throw in some eye candy, comic relief and state of the art CGI, cut the dialogue down to soundbites and zingers, and have all the big set pieces dazzle the audiences with infotainment. I doubt any of the writers at *The New Yorker* know what a beat sheet is, but all of their articles follow one.

What I should do is explain why wanting to be the main character in your story is bad for everyone else in your blast radius, but this is pointless because: 1) you have no interest in anyone who is in your blast radius, only those who aren't; 2)-- and I can't believe I live in a world where I would ever write this-- you don't want to be the main character in your story. You want to be the main character in a story written by someone else.

Wanting to be the main character in an other's story requires a series of sacrifices. The first one is a consequence of a social=technological change: story=video. Even podcasts hav to be videos, how else is anyone going to see how much you spent on a mic and pop filter? There's no way you could ever imagine yourself as the main character in a novel. Everything with you is seeing, your primary sensory intake that makes your dream live is seeing: reflections, mirrors, images. So you pursue life moments that script like shots, the modern innovention is to actually shoot those shots. "Here's me hitting squats back in Act I." Foreshadowing the deadlifts, nice. No, a nap? Oh well. The trade off of using video for story is that you can shoot cool moments, but you can't shoot your inner journey. It doesn't work. Of course a movie character can have an inner journey, but it has to take place as a result of action that can be seen by the audience, the pursuit of a clear external goal, against conflict. The consequence of a video life is that any inner life that cannot be videoed cannot be lived. It cannot even be *imagined*. What are you going to do show quiet desperation, or even math homework? Cut yourself? Actually do math? In movies they would shoot math like they're hackers pinpointing a location: books and papers everywhere, manic, escalating tension as they try to solve the Lagrangian, building to the eureka moment in rapid cuts, dramatic camera sweeps, and techno frenzied dialogue with the other supermodels pulling pencils out of their now cascading anime hair. "Hey doll, nice specs, you look like a sexy scientist." They help me see where to stab you.

The second sacrifice is that the more detailed and intricate your character is-- surprise-- the worse the story is. What you have so far for plot, setting and theme could fit on the back of a 3x5, but for your character sketch you could write a novel, which is curious because you didn't, see above. "I really wanted there to be a strong symbology there." Symbology? It seems like we have a new heir to the King Bonehead crown, I'm sure the word you were looking for is *symbolism*. "A person's character is mostly genetic." I think you mean genitive. Since story requires the character to change, your intricately delicate character must *avoid* story, or you will break. You have put yourself-- a highly characterized character-- into a series of hyperbolic situations which you react *to*-- which are absolutely 100% unable to affect you. There can be no growth there, no desires can be fulfilled, as evidenced by the relationships you have with other people just like you, whose favorite force is centripetal and it points towards a television. Weeee. "But why do I feel like I'm being pushed outwards?" I know it feels like there's a force vector pushing away from the television, but in reality no such force exists.

You will push back on this, and say the situations often put your character at great risk. Rather than explain how it only appears that way, I'll just say it differently: whether or not there is a risk, these situations do not require you to be responsible for the consequences.

The third sacrifice-- and these are 100% amateur mistakes any UCLA Annex student would pick up just from the pitch-- is that "despite" wanting to be the main character, *you don't know what the main character wants*. So nothing can be pursued, and the 3D character in full symbology just wanders through cool scenes and situations like he's on vacation in Prague. A car chase needs a destination; a Glock needs a target; a kiss needs a purpose unless the purpose is the kiss; otherwise such adventures are boring to an audience, which is why you perceive your life to be boring and blame the adventures, or audience. You want nothing, so you are nothing. Even the deplorable "to do the right thing" or "to be desired" could still be legitimate story desires, as long as the character pursues those desires. That is not you. You'll tell me you're out there grinding every day to attain your goal, but anyone in the audience could see there's no connection between what you're doing and what you vaguely think you might want to be doing later, you are yet another guy who thinks upping their powerlifting PRs is going to lead to-- to what? $$$$$? How? It barely worked for Lou Ferrigno and now the Hulk is CGI. I can squat 315x5 like anybody else, the difference is what I wanted was a physical hour to listen to math lectures, so I could write a book about pornography, so I wouldn't destroy the lives of the people around me. See that? Clear desire, clear goal, clear actions, even if they are insane.

So the lack of a desire line makes the script irredeemable, no amount of gun shots or cum shots will make it interesting to anyone, including you, because however cool those scenes are individually, they are episodic, they all hit the same beats-- they do not move the story forward, they do not satisfy. *The Honeymooners* was a 1955 TV show so comedically primitive that a later reboot was set in the stone age, but in its time it was wildly successful; yet after one season Jackie Gleason refused to do a second even for all that moolah because he felt-- you should sit down for this-- they had run out of ideas. And away he went. But what makes this all a paradox is that while the most fundamental drive for story is absent, you still want the story that has no motive drive to drive you to your desire.

The character's fundamental flaw is actually that he can't act on his desire, made harder because he doesn't even know what it is-- he needs the audience to tell him-- and by fate, determinism, or an omnipotent director, this desire is supposed to be detected from 120 pages of mostly stylized character sketch and drifting aimlessly to the single page you've carefully scripted that has the big reversal in which you react and emote spectacularly. "It's a very powerful scene." That's one thing you can be certain it isn't. No one should invest time, money or genitals in your poorly fantasized clip show just because what you do have planned to the voxel is what you'll say in interviews. "I'm not great at writing plot, my forte is dialogue." You're actually terrible at that too, and it's the same reason for both. "Don't get it right, get it written" is standard advice for modern journalism but not a script, because once you bang out the first draft you will resist editing most of it but *especially* your precious lines of dialogue, which are also simultaneously the worst part of your horrible script. Here's the reason: the only action you can imagine your character actually doing is talking to other people, yet all you know how to actually do is use other people's lines to talk about yourself.

Let's look closely at what you have so far: highly detailed character, careful attention to wardrobe-- authenticity is soooo important-- but no clear desire line. A series of intense but disconnected needs, no visible overarching goal. A series of visually exciting scenes; but no rising tension. Plenty of overdramatic dialogues and punchy one liners, but which don't move the story along. Conflict everywhere; no central conflict. The character reacts dramatically, emotionally-- reactively-- to events which carry them along, but never deliberately acts on the desires they don't have. Maybe I've got the genre wrong: are you the victim in someone else's horror movie? Or a chick in a porno? *The Final Girl Finally Cums?*

In structural terms, the problem with your script is that you haven't written a story, you've written The Neverending Act I. Let me tell you a little secret: in movies the big battles are in Act III, but in real life the body count is in Act I. Most people never make it out of there alive.

You'll nod introspectively here and own up to your failing: "I'm waiting," you'll admit, "waiting for the Call To Adventure." But stupid, it isn't an actual call to you, it's simply an event, in *Star Wars* he got someone else's call and his first impulse was to erase it.

427

Now the liar in you will admit your shame: "truth be told, I'm afraid, afraid to Cross The Threshold into Act II." So you got the Call, but you're Refusing it? "No, if I got the Call, I wouldn't refuse it." The Call is Refused not because it's dangerous, but because it requires the character to give up some part of himself in advance of the pursuit, which in movies they shortcut by taking away some part of himself. No chance, you'll go as far as Anchorhead but you need to be home by midday to jerk off yourself or your boyfriend for another 6 mos too long or until one of you finds a new identical replacement. "It's complicated." And now it isn't.

"You're wrong about *Star Wars*, Leia's recording wasn't actually The Call, technically The Call was when Luke is asked by Obi Wan to go to Alderaan." Yes, that is the kind of mistake you would hope I made. I didn't. That's actually Meeting the Mentor. But you want it to be the Call. Having no clear desire and not wanting to act, you're waiting for a Mentor to *be* the Call, to tell you who you are supposed to be and what you're supposed to do. Unlike movies the Mentor should have been your parents way back in backstory, but now with college educated genitalia and a pre-K attention span you need a guru or that great unpaid internship to plug you into your own individual monomyth. Worse, now that psychology is no longer satisfying, that Mentor becomes less individualized and more socialized, it can't be a personal relationship since the point isn't to teach you anything but to invite you to the adventure, so it has to be an idealized entity, a corporation, a hierarchy, an authority. "I just want a seat at the table." You can have mine, I am done with these stupid meetings, I have work to do.

Even though you're the main character, your new hope is that the movie will be produced and directed by some other omnipotent entity, who will put you with a great cast, set safe boundaries for experimentation, shoot a lot of great footage and then fix it all in post. This is terrible movie making, and madness, and will fail because you're not actually an actor, you're an idiot. *You want to be lead.*

"No I don't." Yes you do. Here's a practical analogy: anyone could film a studio-quality movie today, for no money, all on your own. But that would be entering Act II with no money, all on your own. "How am I going to afford an Act II apartment?" You want to be hired by a studio, because that will cause you to make a full movie. The meta-irony is that no studio would hire you to make a movie about being hired by a studio to make a movie. But a studio would hire you to make a movie about making a movie without a studio, which is exactly the story you want, and would mean in real life your character arc was from passive-regressive dreamer to cowardly liar. Your life is now a tragedy, the studio will make a profit, and you'll tell everyone you were exploited and the marijuana is for anxiety. You'd be 50% right, just like in math.

Look, you don't even need to read your script to see the problems, just look at the scene sequence. Do the scenes advance the pursuit of the goal? You haven't written out the scene sequence, you just started filming? What is the story about? Who is it for? "It's not for anyone, it's just my life." Then why live it, let alone film it? "It's for me." What kind of a lunatic spends their life making B-roll of themselves? Here's an accidental metaphor too good to resist: in Final Cut Pro, B roll automatically takes precedence over the main movie timeline. At least, I'm hoping that's just a metaphor.

So we're back to *Trickx or Treats*, the torrid and titillating tale of the Halloween hotwife and her hapless husband. Hilarious! The Treats are hard R, but the Trick is rated X. Here's the trailer script, I even put in some music cues which I hope I got right, it's hard to consciously work this out in your head, just imagine it with a full orchestra and a competent editor.

OPEN ON:

INT. BEDROOM

SILENCE

Close up of the interior of an open safe. On the left half of the middle shelf: bundles of dollars hidden behind a dozen tubes of bullion coins. The right half of the middle shelf is empty except for a camera lens cleaning cloth and an SLR camera flash with its translucent white cap. On the upper shelf: two copies of the same issue of Playboy Magazine, each in plastic sleeves. A third empty sleeve lays askew on top of them.

In the otherwise silent background, the sound of a magazine page being turned.

CUT TO:

BLACK

                    WHISPER (V.O.)
          Open your eyes.

OPEN ON:

429

INT. BATHROOM

Close up POV looking down on MAN's two upturned hands, the left
holding pair of red nurse's scrubs, the right dangling red lace
underwear from the index finger.

                                                        CUT TO:

BLACK

                        MAN (V.O.)
            My hot ass wife is a sexy ass nurse.

                                                        CUT TO:

INT. HALLWAY/BATHROOM

As seen through the display of a camera's view screen ("REC"): FS of
WOMAN, just out of the shower in front of the mirror, damp light
brown hair, wearing white underwear and white tank top (the mirror
shows her shirt has a Pig Pen-- the Peanuts character-- on it.)
Without turning her head, she smirks at him through the mirror, and
responds to his stare with a single hand wave "Hi".

                                                        CUT TO:

BLACK

OPEN ON:

INT. KITCHEN

CLOSE UP of the invitation in WOMAN's hand in a darkish/bluish room,
but the invitation glows a faint white light; it is hand written in
unintelligible calligraphy, except for parts of a few words which are
in print: "BE COMIN"; "IN APPROPRI"; "A VID". It has lipstick marks
pressed into it at the bottom.

                    WOMAN (O.S.)
         "...a kind of charade…"

                                                          CUT TO:

MAN in khakis and blue button down shirt sitting at an empty kitchen
table, wiggling it to figure out why it's unsteady.

                    WOMAN (O.S.)
         Please say yes, you won't regret it!

                    MAN (not even looking up)
         Well if everyone's in masks, maybe you could go as--- would
         you wear the dress?

                    WOMAN (O.S.)
         Oh God, that's where your head goes? It's fine if I'm
         recognized in the dress, but I'd be mortified if someone
         recognized me from the dress.

                    MAN
         The only way they'd recognize you from the dress is if you
         weren't wearing it.

431

INT. BATHROOM

MFS of WOMAN's reflection in the mirror, exaggeratedly posing and twirling her hair, feigning a "dumb blonde" facial expression.

                          WOMAN
                (obviously fake sorority girl voice)

    I'm not a nurse, I'm a sorority girl.

                                                    CUT TO:

EXT. FRAT PARTY POOL

CLOSE UP/POV of PLAYER's hands pressing a rolled up magazine into WOMAN'S right hand, and three condoms into her left hand.

                          WOMAN (O.S.)
                What shall I do with these?

                                                    CUT TO:

OTS of PLAYER wearing a red and gold football jersey with no name, standing before WOMAN, here with platinum blonde hair, in a red bikini, who has just stepped out of the pool; she is smirking, holding the magazine and condoms in her upturned hands high near her shoulders. (The bikini is actually underwear; a small white pleated skirt is on the ground behind her.) On a small pool table next to a chaise is a (faux) wood push button telephone, and a point and shoot camera with a wrist strap. Off screen, some machine is projecting a light foam, dispersing over the pool area. He reaches for the front clasp of her bra.

                    PLAYER
          Just throw them anywhere, I won't be needing them till
          morning.

                    WOMAN (giggle)
          Don't you think we should be introduced first?   .

                    PLAYER
                 (nods towards the magazine hand)

          Mu Theta Y.

                    WOMAN
          That's good enough for me.

He unclasps the bra.

                                                          CUT TO:

INT. KITCHEN

OTS of MAN standing next to the kitchen table, looking down at WOMAN
seated in a chair, adjusting the table in front of her which is
upside down.

                         WOMAN (looking up at him excitedly)
          Will you let me go? Please?

                    MAN
          You will tell the truth?

                         WOMAN (mock affront)
          I promise! (tilts head upwards and puckers her lips)

                                                          CUT TO:

INT. STRIP POKER GAME

BLACK. SILENCE.

                    MAN (V.O.)
          Deal.

Sound of dice in a cup being shaken, then

OPEN ON:

INT. GAME ROOM

SLAM. Extreme close up of a black dice cup upside down on a red felt tabletop. It sounds as though there are several people playing, background sounds of rustling, laughing.

                    WOMAN (O.S. shivering/laughing)
          Brrr! I'm ready...

Camera PANS with dice cup as it is slid across the table to the left, dragging its dice with it, coming to rest next to some other player's cup.

                    MALE VOICE (O.S. sing-songy, gloating)
          Are you sure? Very well, but I warn you...

Both cups are tilted slowly upwards. The dice are revealed to cheering. A white garter is tossed onto the tilted cups.

                                                        CUT TO:

INT. STAGE

Tracking into FULL SHOT of the backside of WOMAN, platinum blonde hair pulled forward over her right shoulder, wearing a sexy white nurse dress, white pumps, nurse hat, and pearl necklace; facing slightly parted red curtains, about 6 feet high and 6 feet wide, as might surround a hospital bed. To her left is a footstool on which is seated a small stuffed animal. To the left of it is a bed table with a pitcher, and a bowl and sponge. On the floor to her right is a bedpan and slippers. A few feet behind these red curtains, visible over the top and past them on the right, stretching floor to ceiling is a heavy black drape lining the walls; at the far right of frame, someone's head is peeking in through a parting of this black drape; behind him is visible another fan, both in baseball caps turned backwards. She drops her dress completely off her now nude body but catches it in the crook of her left arm, and places her left foot/shoe on the stool. There is the sound of a camera shutter and motor taking rapid fire pictures. Turning back to look over her left shoulder, smirking coyly, she taps her butt playfully with the back of her right hand.

The sound of a vintage camera and flash is heard (O.S.)

                                                    BACK TO:

INT. BATHROOM

MCU one shot, profile of MAN, holding up his camera as he speaks, but peeking over it to see her directly.

                         MAN
          I've never been with a sorority girl.

                                                    CUT TO:

INT. PARTY

A tall, handsome, totally naked man with chiseled muscles-- the
epitome of a greek god-- is standing serenely by himself in a dark
area of the party against a wall, a bronze helmet on his head but
pushed up off his face on a mop of curly hair, leaning casually on
the spear propped in his right hand. His genitals can't be seen
(because they are stuffed into a flesh colored pouch). A
drunk/giggling WOMAN, wrapped in a blue sheet-- a mini-toga?-- is
walking hand in hand with someone ahead of her and already just out
of frame; they walk past GREEK GOD; his eyes widen and his head
tracks the spectacular blonde as she passes directly in front of him.
She makes eye contact and sensually drags her free hand across GREEK
GOD's bare chest as she is pulled away, then arches her head and
chest back teasingly as if to stay with him a while longer.

                      WOMAN (V.O.)
           Overrated. Most of them just want attention.

                                                  BACK TO:

INT. BATHROOM

WOMAN sending him a knowing glance through the mirror.

                      WOMAN (deeper, sultry voice)
           Nurses are way more fun.

                                                  CUT TO:

INT. HALLWAY

OTS of HELEN and WOMAN standing at the far end of a dark hallway in
an illuminated spot in the doorway of a partially open door, darkness
within. They are giggling conspiratorially, HELEN in a sexy Greek
costume, pressing up against WOMAN in nurse costume, nose to nose.
HELEN is rubbing the open front of WOMAN's dress through her fingers
admiringly. They look up to realize someone is there, and stifle
their giggles, but neither show surprise.

                    HELEN (vampishly looking at their observer,
                    hooking her finger up through the silver
                    dollar sized ring on the zipper of WOMAN's
                    dress and pulling it gently like a leash to
                    lead her through the door)
There is something very important we need to do...

                    WOMAN (smiling, obviously feigning bubbly
                    ignorance)
What's that?

                                      CUT TO:

INT. BATHROOM

MAN in profile looking directly into his camera viewer.

                    MAN
      But you had sex with more people as a sorority girl.

                                      CUT TO:

INT. HOUSE

All else in darkness, the back side of a privacy screen illuminated
from the inside: through it is visible the blurry shadows of some
distant shapes, and closer the sharp silhouette of a standing woman
slowly pulling off her clothes, and right below her, a man laying in
a bed.

                    HELEN (V.O.)
          Sweet, thoughtful, Mandy.

                                                    MATCH CUT:

INT.   HOUSE

Large room saturated in bluish light from an off screen TV. The back
of nude WOMAN standing with one knee on the side of a futon where a
nude man reclines. The futon is set into an L shaped partition, about
6 feet high, along the futon's far side and foot; silent darkness
around and behind it. She has just removed what she was wearing
(apparently a large striped flag) and is holding it daintily high up
in the air with her left hand, while her right is about to release
her hair from its bun. At that instant, a bare chested man with a
towel wrapped around his waist rounds the corner of the partition at
the foot of the futon on her right; he freezes, holding his breath,
his face still in the shadows but the rest of him in the light. They
see each other, and she pulls her bun loose.

                    WOMAN (V.O. sorority girl voice)
        Soooo many, I don't know how many I was with.

                                                    CUT TO:

INT. BATHROOM

TWO SHOT of MAN looking into camera as WOMAN reaches out and softly
pushes his hands and camera down, forcing him to look up.

                        WOMAN (intimately)
            But I'm afraid the best sex was as a wife.

                                                    CUT TO:

INT. PARTY

Loud party. MAN stands immobile; his face tense and expressionless.
WOMAN is sensuously pulling a stocking down over his head and eyes,
her own face tenderly amused by his plight, like a mother consoling a
child with a boo boo. Off screen, some unseen people are watching
this and snickering. She pauses at his nose when, in a hushed voice
trying not to move his lips, he mutters:

                              MAN
          You owe me.

WOMAN lovingly/patronizingly puckers her lips...

                                                      BACK TO:

INT. BATHROOM

                         WOMAN (L CUT/V.O.)
          ...Awwwwww...

WOMAN affectionately blows MAN a kiss as she slides past him.

                                                      CUT TO:

EXT. - NIGHT

Looking into the open back door of limo, a woman has extended her
bare right leg out of the limo, while inside she slips a small white
fold of paper in the white garter on her exposed left thigh.

                    FRENCH ACCENT MALE VOICE (V.O.)
          A necessity for both parties.

                                                      BACK TO:

INT. BATHROOM

MAN, now facing the other direction since she has just passed him,
while trying to look into the camera and keep the framing, reaches in
to spank her ass.

                        MAN
            A naughty wife.

                                                    CUT TO:

INT. BEDROOM

An extreme close up a screen, a yellowish tinted network of pixels
evident, on which there is a paused image of a video. A rapid PAN
from the bottom left of the screen up and to the right stops on the
bottom left quadrant of the fuzzy frozen image showing a man
reclining in a bed, bare torso. The bed and he are well lit, though
the shot's frame cuts off just above his chin-- his fingers there
seem to be adjusting a mask or helmet. Next to him on the left: a
nightstand, bowl and decanter, lying on the floor. Standing at the
side of the bed, barely in the frame on bottom right, is a woman's
bare left foot; and at top right a portion of her left arm holding up
a sliver of white garment.

                        WOMAN (V.O.)
            If you only knew...

                                                    CUT TO BLACK

SILENCE.

OPEN ON:

SILENCE. Close up of the torso of a butler in a tuxedo, white gloved
hands holding up a dinner bell (a small, metal xylophone), but
instead of a mallet the butler wears a thimble over his finger. He
moves his finger to strike the first chime--

CUT TO:

BLACK.

Heard as V.O., the bell plays along the same 6 notes of the
background music.

At the beginning of the third note--

OPEN ON:

INT. LIMO - NIGHT

442

From the back seat: a hatch in a limo's privacy screen sliding open, through it and out the front windshield can be seen the illuminated mansion they are approaching along the semicircular driveway. Another distant limo's headlights appear in the rear view mirror.

> DRIVER (turning his head just enough that the silhouette of the side of his nose is visible)
> This might be a good time to put on your mask, sir.

CUT TO:

INT. PARTY MAIN ROOM

Doors swing open to:

Fleeting establishing shot of huge circular ballroom full of men and women, party in full swing. The party room is three stories high; in the center of the room is a fake tree coming out of the floor, its base must be another story beneath the floor level; the trunk extending up into the second story, and above that to the domed ceiling is the tree's crown. Into the body of the trunk are hundreds of elaborate carvings of people's faces, each one different. The room's second story has a balcony circling the perimeter over the main room, on which various revelers congregate or look down over the party. GREEK GOD is up there on the left, talking to another Greek costumed man with a mask and laurel crown. Half of the crowd is in ancient Greek costumes; the other half in modern Halloween costumes, the women particularly noticeable in cliché sexy costumes: a FAIRY, a BRIDE, FRENCH MAID, KITTEN, BUNNY, CHEERLEADER, etc. None of the women are wearing masks on their face. Only the Greek costumed men are wearing masks or helmets.

The party hosts, MENELAUS in a blue Greek robes eating an apple and HELEN in a sexy Greek costume, long blonde hair tied in loose bun held together by a white beaded diadem, stand in front of MAN and WOMAN who have just entered the mansion. WOMAN in tightly belted

443

camel hair jacket and white nurse hat is visibly nervous as MAN, in buttoned buckskin coat and mask hastily and awkwardly pushed off his face onto his head) is frantically searching his coat's pockets.

                         MAN
          I seem to have forgotten it.

                         MENELAUS (disinterested; lecherously eyeing
                         WOMAN's long, tanned legs.)
               That's unfortunate.

HELEN rolls her eyes at MENELAUS'S performance and slaps him playfully on the arm, causing him to laugh and his entire demeanor to change. Now friendly and affable, MENELAUS tosses the apple to WOMAN, which she catches in surprise, and welcomingly steps forward and spins MAN around to assist him.

                                        CUT TO:

Medium shot from the back of MENELAUS, who is facing the back of MAN as MAN is unbuttoning his coat. WOMAN, now in between and to the right of them, facing MENELAUS, begins to untie her coat as MENELAUS says:

                         MENELAUS (to MAN, kindly)
               Remove your mask.

As MENELAUS helps take MAN's coat, he turns his head back to WOMAN.

                         MENELAUS (to WOMAN in stern command)
               Remove your clothes.

WOMAN opens her eyes wide in amused surprise.

                                        CUT TO:

INT. DOORWAY

444

PUSH IN behind MAN (waist up) to over his shoulder. MAN is
shirtless, maskless, standing in a dark room, but his backside is lit
by the open doorway (not visible) behind him. A few steps in front
of him is a dividing wall about 6 feet wide, unconnected to any other
walls as some light passes diffusely behind it from the room's bright
left to the right while he remains in darkness; and there are sounds
of sex right behind the wall. His right arm hangs slightly behind
him, while his left hand appears to be grasping something below frame
in the front, just at crotch level. Over his shoulder, diagonally
into the room past the wall on the left side is a chair, on which
lays the nurse dress. Near the chair on the floor are white pumps.

MAN (whispering to himself)
...oh God, if he takes off the mask, I'm dead...

CUT TO:

INT. PARTY GREAT ROOM

445

A grinning man with the demeanor and expression of an amused pothead
is dressed as a cartoonish parody of JESUS, with overly bronzed skin
and painted on musculature, fake wig of long hair, fake beard, and
fake crown of thorns; he is getting into position on an elevated
platform which is bathed in a dim yellow light, in front of a fake
wooden cross set on the wall. Getting into character, he drops his
smile, rolls his eyes upwards and stretches out his hands to complete
the pose in front of the crowd.

The onlookers (off screen) make increasing oohs and ahhs as they see
the special effect manifest.

                                                        BACK TO:

INT. BATHROOM

From MAN's camera viewfinder: WOMAN has walked past him down the
short hallway away from the bathroom. She has paused briefly to
assume a model's pose, her weight on the right leg, left leg bent and
raised on its toes, looking behind her over her left shoulder at the
camera, the back of her right hand on her butt, as she seductively
bites a finger on her left hand.

                        WOMAN (sultry voice)
            I'm not naughty, I'm just photographed that way.

                                                        CUT TO:

INT. PARTY GREAT ROOM

JESUS posing before the crowd. More lights of various colors from different angles shine on him. ZOOM IN as he freezes the pose, and the staged effect that manifests is an uncanny still image-- a flat, two dimensional Byzantine icon of Jesus on the cross: the musculature realistic, the face tragic, the blood on his hands now realistically black. Attached to the cross above him is a small sign that reads "SAVE YOURSELF" followed by other words obstructed by his head. Off screen is the sound of someone repeatedly dinging his glass to silence the crowd. Several camera shutters can be heard. Amidst the oohs and ahhs, an unseen REVELER calls out drunkenly, affecting pretentious religious speech:

REVELER (O.S.)
I will be a testament to the truth!

CUT TO:

INT. BATHROOM

MAN
(peeking over the camera as he holds it steady)

That's nurse again.

CUT TO:

INT. ROOM

447

Close up looking down on WOMAN's face while she is laying flat, in the beginning of orgasm, as she reaches up (off screen). Her eyes widen, then shut as the orgasm overtakes her.

BACK TO:

INT. BATHROOM

WOMAN

    Oops…

CUT TO:

MONTAGE

Fleeting images:

--From behind: a totally naked, muscular man, posing with arms outstretched as if bragging. He is standing almost knee deep in an outdoor pool; past him along the pool are (out of focus) admiring onlookers. Two pairs of hands, one female, the other indistinct, have snaked upwards between his legs and around his waist to caress his butt and thighs.

448

--An extreme close up of a screen with many "l"s scrolling across (as if someone was holding the l key down).

--In front of a bed or couch is a small stool, on which is seated jovial MENELAUS, apparently naked except for a red knit cap with a pom pom tassle, and a blue robe flipped behind his back like a cape. He is seated angled with his legs off to his left, while his torso is turned to his right to look up at WOMAN, platinum blonde hair and nurse costume, standing next to him with her legs crossed, leaning slightly sideways against MENELAUS, her left arm draped down over his left shoulder to his chest; his right hand is holding her left forearm. He is looking up at her and smiling; she is also smiling but looking at the floor, as if ashamed to be enjoying this. MENELAUS's left hand is propping up a large professional camera on his left thigh.

                    HELEN (V.O. during montage)
          You had disadvantages.

                    MAN (V.O.)
          What disadvantages?

                                    CUT TO:

INT. BAR ROOM

The modernist BAR ROOM is completely white: white walls, white doors, white chairs. MAN is seated at the bar, though in this brief shot he is not visible. HELEN, now wearing WOMAN's nurse dress, is standing behind the bar. Smiling, but with the embarrassed stare of one forced to say what the other is obviously only pretending isn't relevant, she is holding up two cocktail spears, one in each hand: one short, held just near her lips; the other almost twice as long, its tip resting against her slightly puckered lips.

                                    BACK TO:

INT. BATHROOM

Empty hallway as seen through MAN's camera.

                  WOMAN (V.O.)
          Then I guess it's the wife that's imaginary…

                                    CUT TO:

TITLE CARD (white letters on black background):

TRICKX OR TREATS

                                                          CUT TO:

BLACK.

SILENCE.

Fade in the background noise of a party outside a room, and then--

                    MAN (O.S.)
          But that's not the end, is it? Why don't you tell me the
          rest of it.

                                                         OPEN ON:

ClOSE UP of WOMAN as seen through a camera, lounging-- posing--
sexily on a kitchen table, shoulders bare, twirling her pearl
necklace in a finger and nibbling it, smiling guiltily.

                    WOMAN
          It was your fault... we were making love and... I wanted
          to... make fun of you... (giggle)...

                                                          CUT TO:

EXTREME CLOSE UP of an SLR camera lens. MAN takes a picture, and a
flash whites out the frame.

                                                         FADE IN:

450

TITLE CARD (black letters emerge on white background):

COMING THIS HALLOWEEN

THE END.

"To the very end," I said, shakily. "I heard his very last words…" I stopped in a fright.

"Repeat them," she said in a heart-broken tone. "I want-- I want-- something-- something-- to-- to live with."

I was on the point of crying at her, "Don't you hear them?"

Some men just want to watch the world burn.

"If only I knew more about myself." Yes, you are being lied to, by yourself. "If only I knew what to do with my life." As if the reason you can't act is that you don't know enough. I've seen that movie before, too, when you finally get the knowledge you think you need in order to act, you gouge out your eyes to ensure that you can't, and everyone else's to ensure that they won't. Blindness as a defense against impotence. Or did you think you were punishing yourself?

"Did Oedipus feel shame, or guilt?" You don't care which he felt, you just want it to be shame, which is why you want his crime to be incest. "But back then shame was much worse than guilt." Back when? 2500 years ago? 3000 years ago? 30 minutes ago? How come no one today self-mutilates out of guilt? "Cutting is my secret shame." How can it be a shame or a secret if you keep telling everyone about it? "Maybe it's a cry for attention." You may want attention, for which you pretend to be ashamed, but we both know you'll secretly only be satisfied if someone else is deprived. I doubt you feel any guilt about that.

What Oedipus felt was guilt. If it was shame he would have done what you would have done, which isn't take out his eyes but stab out everyone else's. If it was shame he would have felt rage at the world, not himself; but as someone with power his rage would have compelled him to act, he would have retreated from Thebes and reorganized in Corinth, recruited an army and returned in force, you think I'm going to let you judge me by the sex I had and not the sex I deserve? As if that counted? Retaliation would have been inevitable. That didn't happen. It wasn't shame. It was guilt.

Guilt, not for incest but for being a coward: he was born with power, or he could have taken power; but he preferred to be appointed king so he wouldn't have to act, like the idiots he ruled he wanted to be ruled like an idiot. He didn't want power, he wanted knowledge; he wanted to be desired, and in him power found an easy puppet. Then years later on an otherwise random day, power decided he could now best serve them as a symbolic sacrifice, not as a scapegoat but as escapist tragedy, for what greater purpose the gods only know; but for multiple generations of Theban kings the gods evidently took advantage of facts on the ground. He went quietly because he was allowed to go famously, or infamously, all the same to them and anyway all the same to him. A real man, let alone a man with power, let alone a tyrannosaurus, would have listened to the accusations, looked around incredulously at all the hysterical herbivores and wondered if he wasn't trapped in someone else's dream. "The prophecy foretold this would happen? The gods said I have no choice? Maybe I souvlaki everything from here to Delphi over the smoky charcoals of the Oracle and see if the gods can prophecy what I eat next." And he would have acted. "But no one is more powerful than the gods." I don't know why you of all people keep saying that. The gods do not exist.

Whatever your personal religious and political beliefs, it is a fact that our Western morality is a straight line from Judeo-Christian traditions, and our political beliefs a straight line from Greco-Roman traditions, and regardless of how much you believe times have changed or how bad you are at math you should still be able to observe that those are two separate lines. Your personal conscience, however improvised, followed a different line than your political ideology, however plagiarized. You may think that they are 100% congruent or at least parallel but ask anyone else, they are not. The best you can do is change the angle between them and affect the rate of their con/divergence, under your guiding principle of maximally depriving the other.

457

This was not the case for the Greeks, not at the beginning, anyway. Personal morality was inseparable from the state's morality, they were not overlapping, they were the same single thing; but in the opposite way you're imagining it, not because the State was all powerful but because the state was themselves. Personal morality vs. social standards; public behavior vs. private thoughts-- for at least 50 years it would have been inconceivable to an Athenian that those were different things. I don't mean they thought whatever the state wanted them to think, that's as meaningless as saying people think what their brains want them to think. And I do not mean there weren't bad people; I mean there was no recourse to the psychological position of "I'm not a bad person, I just did a bad thing." When we say the Athenian democracy required full participation, it should be taken literally. The citizens didn't just make up their own laws or fight their own wars, they thought the same thought: the state was the highest-- not power, not might-- but good. The highest good. Think about this. Think about whether you can think about this. Think about whether you have no other way to think about this except to think "O'Brien"-- assuming you could even think "O'Brien" and not default to "Hitler". Yet early Athens was not a surveillance state, it did not need to know-- though admittedly every government will patronizingly embrace its sycophants-- it left the accumulation of knowledge and power to the citizens so they could act, as it. This is why that period of history is so unique and so unrepeatable. For the first time and the only time and never since time, knowledge was used for action; the purpose of knowledge was to act; the purpose of earthly knowledge was to be able to act like gods with restraint. Not only for a handful of "great men"; they all thought this, it was the cultural standard. And then the war came, and the plague came, and the plague came again, and the sophists came, and the idea of man's greatness through obligation   became more fantastical than 12 hairless gods on a cold mountaintop wrapped in bedsheets, or on them. What good are gods in heaven if they won't send my neighbor to hell?   For all but a few, math became arithmetic and philosophy became accounting, and getting some power was far less satisfying than depriving the other of theirs. And here we are.

When I say Oedipus felt guilty, I mean Oedipus's superego was the state. This is what Freud got backwards-- no, let me amend that-- this is what Freud flipped upside down so that the people of the new century could turn guilt into shame and invent TV. Freud was wrong, Oedipus's latent wish wasn't to kill his father and sleep with his mother, that is the manifest content of the dream. The latent guilt-- the reason Sophocles picked the Oedipus story to train the audience-- is that he had failed in his duty to be the state by wanting his duty to be to the State, failed to serve the people by wanting to serve the State. And this is even surer if you're one of those who think Sophocles was here criticizing Pericles as the pollution, whose monomania had "caused" the plague: of course those things weren't true; those things had to become true. Because otherwise it was all on you. Oedipus stood for every single Athenian in the audience, who used to be the state and who now wanted to serve a State; who in theory had all the power, and now did not want it. They wanted to know-- only. "What do you think of what the State did?" Discuss. Sophocles, as tragedian of Athens, told an audience who no longer shared a collective superego-- they were discovering their individualism under paternalism, aka dysentery, and the consequent benefits of shame instead of guilt-- and tried to remind them that they could be guilty; not for incest-- who cares anymore, especially if she's hot enough or the union is useful-- "You know I would never do or think anything except as you would have it" -- but for failing in their duty to act. Even if it required them to blind themselves-- they wanted to be lead.

"Incest was the worst of all shames, a pollution, it was unthinkable!" They thought of it

458

as a pollution because they didn't actually think it was a pollution, do you think they thought about it so much because it was unthinkable? Sure, it was shameful, I guess, but not shameful enough-- to explain a plague. They had to set their stories in their *past*-- when incest may have been the most shameful act, the way today a story about the terrible consequences of female infidelity can only be set in our past, when we could hope there may have been terrible consequences. "Well, in the past there were terrible consequences." But why tell the story today? Or why not set it today and show-- no consequences? Because your rage needs a reason, because your rage matters, and it needs to have a basis in the physical world, in the ledger, so unless society is damaged or you can damage society no one will care about your rage. Modern infidelity's only consequence of individual psychic pain is reinterpreted on the previously real background of damage to the society-- which you then apply to today. To show how much she damaged you, you show how much infidelity damaged society. I know you'll retort those stories are for women but then men are the collateral, you are both in the same demographic, the form of the story is the same: to show a woman how explosively powerful her personal sexuality can be, you set the sexuality in the past and then press explode. Now your hero's journey can be elevated from I'm kind of being a jerk to an act of social rebellion by recalling a time when it could look like it was and pretending that it counts today. What's the result? "I guess it makes me feel better?" No, idiot, this is the whole point, what you feel doesn't matter. The result is that in order to prove it is bad or empowering, it has to be seen by an audience that can be taught to see it that way. And the consequence of that is you will fight for the status quo, you need it to exist so you can be shown exploding it, even as you say you desperately want to change it. I was going to write, "it couldn't have worked out better if they planned it," but that would be a lie. They didn't plan anything, because they don't exist. You only wish they exist.

"Free." This was the selling point of the rise of the Athenian democracy, 490-431, my dates are correct and so is my math, its synonym is guilt. Guilt is freedom: you bond yourself to yourself and free yourself from everyone else. "What if I think everything I do is perfect?" Then I'd say you're a person without guilt. Let's see how good you are at math... what follows? Oh, you're not good at math. Arguments about whether people were inherently unequal-- which would mean they couldn't be educated-- came later. Regardless of differences in wealth and penis size, all were equal under the law if they shared the gift of justice. Whether that gift had come from Athena or Marathon, justice was equally understood by all men which meant all men were equal, and the reason justice was the only factor in determining equality is that it was justice that allowed men to form a state. Justice came before the state. They didn't know why, they just knew that. But in Act III they flipped it and introduced a logical fallacy: since what gives the State its existence is a shared sense of justice and nothing else, then it should be the State that decides things like equality and justice. Everyone's a cook and there's too many of us in the kitchen, preparing the food is far too stressful and even less satisfying, let's all dress up nice like waiters, and serve it.

Which is why when Oedipus goes to Colonus in 401 and asserts he can't be guilty because it was all the gods' fault, he isn't really trying to get out of his guilt, he is trying to reassert the omnipotence of the gods, because the alternative is he didn't do anything for 30 years. Because he didn't. And the gods that he has caused to manifest are happy to accept the power, the Oracle announces he is required to die there, not as punishment or redemption, but for the benefit of the State. "But first, confess!" This is the solution the Athenians had waited on for an entire generation, this is what they wanted. And everyone just accepts the verdict. Not just Oedipus, not just the characters in the play; everyone accepts the gods' verdict. "Yes, but you can't go against the gods...." Are you not listening? The gods do not exist. And yet two years later the Athenians execute Socrates for impiety, hoping to cause them to exist. "But first, confess!" What could he do in the face of such madness but roll his eyes and reach for a drink, "pass me that cup because oh my God these people idiots." Then another generation of stagnation, of banality, where frivolous courts were clogged with ridiculous civil suits about unbalanced ledgers. And then-- can you guess what happens next? You want to ask the gods?

"Superstition is giving way to science, and fetishist ideology is giving way to collectively agreed upon social principles." You could not be more wrong, you, the next generation of 4th century Athenians, you think just because you follow one or two Platos on your teleprompter you must be an Aristotle. You think you know, you think you're getting wiser. You think information is a weapon and knowledge is power. "Education needs to be inclusive." As long as it doesn't include math. You should also take a quick glance at Raphael's famous fresco and not just the answer key, skip over the symbolic meaning of the karate chop as a response to being given the finger and ponder that while the title is School of Athens, the actual school was in Colonus; and while both men and women were inclusively welcome in his school of philosophy, no one ignorant of geometry could even apply. I guess I could make the joke that in America that would be a Title IX violation, but it wouldn't be a joke.

"We are all secular humanists now." I don't know what those words mean, and you don't know how right you are. It's a commonplace to divide the millennia long history of philosophy as a transition between "God is the measure of all things" to "Man is the measure of all things", and of course everyone's learned that the Athenians were able to shift their whole psychology from one to the other in only a few decades. But what gets obfuscated in the secondary sources and what should stop your blood dead cold is that the first maxim came last-- they started with man and moved towards god, man was observed to be an invalid and wholly unreliable measure of anything, god came at the end of the experiment. That could only happen because people did not consider themselves free anymore-- so the state was no longer considered just, let alone ideal. Let's be precise: it came when their state was no longer considered just. Wait, still not right: it came when they did not want to be free and prayed the State was unjust so they could justify stealing from it. Let me tell you exactly what kind of a person you are so you can plan your obsolescence or at least your contraception: so desperate were they to get away from the responsibility of their freedom that whenever they won major battles they then turned around and exiled their generals, even Thucydides was ostracized and Paches was so annoyed he killed himself in open court; but when 404 came and they lost the long war, when the Spartan general Lysander beat them at their own game and conquered them once and for all, not only was there no weeping or gnashing of teeth, but the people were so relieved that *they worshipped him like a god*. Read it-- and despair.

"That's not what happened." Yes, you will say that in 399, hoping no one remembers how the walls came down to the sound of you playing the flute so well. "But many of the Athenian colonies were happy to be freed from the rule of the Athenian crypto-oligarchy." Sure. They must have figured things were going to get a lot better under an actual oligarchy. Huh, just like today. "It was because they expected to be massacred, but Lysander spared them." And yet no Mytilenian erected a shrine to Diodotus, I guess Lysander was shrewd enough not to send two boats. Lysander was a god not because he spared them but because he was powerful, took away their power and also flattered them, he let them believe they had fooled him into thinking they were worth sparing-- all of those words are correct, that's what they wanted from their omnipotent god. He let the people who wanted no part of the responsibility for their state take credit for its past while having little they could do in the future but obey. He took their hubris and massaged it into pride, he let them take pride in their hubris and-- and they started masturbating ferociously. "Take from us, O Lysander, our beautiful Athens and rape her, rape her here before us, slay her with your phallus, remind us of our desire, and failure to satisfy her."

This is the democracy that was so moved by *Medea*. Medea isn't about Greek ideals like fate or honor, or even interest, it isn't about anything higher than 4'11", but about divorce. It's tempting to see Medea as "loving too much", too deeply, too pathologically, or if that seems unacceptably emotional you can say she overestimated the value of one man, if only she had been more Stoic about it all. But the only thing she overestimated is her own self-importance: my pain matters so much. It is a play where banal personal feelings are worth writing about simply because they feel important. But to justify the intensity of our feelings we today want to make it about something more, something universal. Medea isn't only about divorce, it's about social violence, she's heralded today as a proto-feminist tragic hero fighting the structural op/re/suppression of women. "We suffer," she says, "we are victims!" We? Who's we? Never mind you have magic powers, you're the queen. Her monologue against misogyny is ambitiously quoted, but I should point out that her revolutionary takedown of patriarchy ultimately concludes that women are better than men because fighting in three wars is nothing compared to the pain of giving birth. This is what she came up with. It's ridiculous on its face, but how can you argue with how true it feels? You can't, which is the point. These are the musings of an idiot and wouldn't be worth discussing unless-- unless they were the only things people were discussing. In Aeschylus the consequence matched the crime; in Sophocles the consequence needed a crime to match; in Euripides there wasn't even a crime, the consequence needed to match the feelings. "The plays of Euripides, more than Aeschylus, speak to the modern reader." Then you should align your calendars and see what happens next.

Medea's rage seems so modern not because the institution of marriage still carries the same structural imbalances but because she uses the trick everyone today thinks we invented as a social critique: she takes a personal rivalry and casts it as a structural problem. It has to be patriarchy, because otherwise she got screwed by a nut. While it is coincidentally correct that her plight mirrors the plight of many women, she has no interest in women, and I know this because she kills not Jason but his new wife; and not even because of a rivalry with the new wife but only as a tool to hurt her real rival: Jason.

Reframe your understanding of power before it gets us all killed: applauding a person's non-choices because a type of person made them and they deprive another type of person isn't justice, it is envy. Worse, it is envy that longs for tyranny even as it pretends to hate it. The first thing she did on the path to defeating the patriarchy is subordinate herself to an even bigger patriarch, that lucky accident was step 1, it's what allowed her to do everything else. You think she's able to imagine an alternative modernity? You can't find the true feminist play *Prometheus* staged anywhere, but a thousand college campuses, every one of them does *Medea*, this is the play that resonates with our future thought blockers. "I understand why she acted that way-- she just went too far." Are you sure? Because it looks to me like every verb in that sentence is a lie. Poor Medea, it's not Jason's cheating per se, what he did that was so terrible is taking her and all the glorious things her nobility and master's in sorcery promised, moving

461

her to the middle of nowhere and then abandoning her. No one thinks she was going to do anything anyway, and it's certainly not clear she loves him, but now he's disrupted her status quo and the prospect of decades in front of the television. What can she do? He knew about her nobility and her master's, of course, but still didn't agree to see her as a noble master's kind of woman. So she'll show him. Everyone parrots the one sentence disclaimer about the excessiveness of revenge scheme, "I don't condone it, but I understand", but you need to pay much more attention to the scheme's form. She originally wanted to gut him with a sword but decided against that plan, do you know why? "It's wrong? It doesn't represent justice? The kids would be sad?" No. *Because if she fails, people will laugh at her.* I wish I was making this up. But there will be some/all of you who so closely mirror her psychology that you will read this backwards, you will defend shame as socially useful, you will say it was that very shame of failure that kept her from stabbing him, but this is wrong. If she wasn't driven by shame, she would not have wanted to kill him at all. "But then what was she supposed to do? How could she make him suffer?" Yeah. A thousand college campuses.

And rather than causing him to suffer directly, she causes him to suffer indirectly using a scheme so bafflingly complicated... never mind. Instead of laughter being how we bear tragedy, creating tragedy becomes the defense against being laughed at, and then we all wonder how it came to this.

I know, it's easy to side with her because Jason is so hatable, he dumps Medea not even because he loves the new woman, he doesn't love her, but because it's a good marriage for him, which, if you follow the internal politics of Greek mythology, it actually isn't. His brain is made of earwax and it melted in the sun. You can see why she'd be baffled all this. To make sense of it all Medea even tries to suggest *to him* that maybe it's a love triangle, a rivalry between herself and the younger blonde bimbo, but Jason tells her flat out his desire has nothing to do with it, nope, he would never have acted simply out of desire, which is 100% true on every level. Does this dolt think that's supposed to make her feel better? So even their prior love was a lie? What did he expect her to feel when he forced her to know how he wants? He says he wants power but evidently what satisfies him is to be desired by others more powerful than himself. "Creon likes me! He wants me to marry into his family!" What are you, a girl? It's almost as if he expected Medea to be happy for him. "Look, I don't expect you to condone it," says an imbecile to an idiot, "but ----- but you understand, right?"

And she could have. It's not like Euripides left this middle aged single mom without any options, she had plenty of money and a new boyfriend who's a definite upgrade that she managed to land that same day-- how lucky is that?-- she can go nobly to Athens and be the matriarch of the future Athenian empire-- that would have been a kind of feminist move, and hell, maybe that would show him, too?-- but no, she had a ledger to balance, how much she gains counts less than how much he loses. He must be deprived. The parents do what they will, and the kids suffer what they must. A thousand college campuses.

On the way from the "man is the measure" to "God is the measure" was Sophocles, he was Hans Brinker, he was going to reinforce the dike, idealism and justice holding back the waters of imperial inevitability. It is a credit to Sophocles's-- persuasiveness is almost an insult-- his ability to modulate the audience's brain waves that he was able to take the plague that had almost turned the Athenians into Lefty Bank existentialists, relegate it to a disavowed subplot in a very flawed whodunit and thus remind their unconscious that it could be anything-- ANYTHING-- but random: Fate, Ares, the Oracle, global warming, whatever-- things could still be affected by their actions, they should still act. That kept democracy going for another generation, that's something, I guess.

I know it seems ridiculous to be critical of thousands of people thousands of years ago, especially when thousands of secondary sources are unanimous that those people produced Western Civilization. I don't know if you understand how time works, but the 5th century Greeks didn't produce Western civilization. They started with that. What they produced was the 4th century. And about 20 years from now, it will be correct to say that other than being ruled by conquerors, what the Greeks have spent more of their history on than anything else is socialism.

Of course that ancient democracy informs our society even today, to the point where it has become a standard criticism that it shouldn't. But how does it? Consider that while we've built an entire liberal education out of selected excerpts from that time, the average Athenian citizen would have had a real time immersion to all of it. A modern student will spend years studying the secondary sources to understand their meaning, but a semi-literate Athenian would have been expected to get the point from hearing the primary source once, and then use it. And yet they collapsed. So the question is, what happened? And what chance could we possibly have?

What happened to them is what's happening to us: we want to know more-- in order to do less. Every generation prides themselves at discovering anew what no one in history had ever thought of before: that democracy is a majority of idiots preventing the noble judgment of a wise minority from forcing the majority do what needs to be done. "Is democracy really the best form of government? Discuss." How about we start with something a little more basic, like what's the worst form? The single reason the Athenians chose democracy is so trite that it's easy to overlook, but it is the reason that makes everything else that happened intelligible, including the paradox of a democracy that excluded women and slaves but in which therefore the wealthy were expected to fight all the wars. It wasn't class struggle, it wasn't a belief in the wisdom of crowds, it wasn't racial pride and it wasn't a shared sense of community. They did not think a democracy would make the best decisions or the fewest mistakes. No. They chose democracy simply because the alternative was tyranny, and they for sure didn't want a tyranny. That's it. The successes and failures in every other metric do not weigh in its grade, the only question on every exam was circle Yes or No: was a tyranny prevented? They ostracized their most powerful and celebrated men, men they actually needed-- because they were too high risk, not just that they might be tempted to want to become tyrants but that the people might be tempted to want them to become tyrants. Thank you Cimon, we owe you our lives, but that mess in Ithome has opened our eyes. Power to the people, 500 will do; we got your number, we'll call if we need you.

Criticize their democracy any way you want and all you want-- misogyny, exploitation, idiocy-- but was it a success by the only metric that ultimately mattered to them? Yes. It was so successful that in 200 years, a tyranny was only conceived once. It was aborted after a trimester. Yes.

Monarchy, oligarchy, and democracy aren't opposites, they can co-exist and share power. The logical negation of these is a tyranny. Tyrannies arise when oligarchies disagree internally. And oligarchies arise when democracies disagree externally. I realize you learned that in the opposite direction. Nowadays American sophisticates nod their head in agreement when Thucydides has Cleon explain that a democracy is incapable of sustaining an empire, but Thucydides wasn't trying to critique the limitations of a democracy but rather that

463

democracy's desire for a tyrant. He put those words in the mouth of Cleon because he hated Cleon, Cleon was a liar, Cleon was the enemy. Thucydides might have been cool on democracy, he certainly preferred a mixed regime, but what he didn't want was a Cleon. So you can imagine how he felt when Cleon died and the Athenians wanted an Alcibiades.

"All of this is ancient history. Democracy doesn't work anymore, we need _____." Fill in the blank, I dare you. Because your personal psychology's premise is that you know what needs to be done but can't do what needs to be done, you know better but can't do better, so what's going in that blank that you're not even aware you want? A tyranny. There are no other choices. "No, not a tyranny, I just want a government above populist pressures, one that has all the power, whatever it does is just, it acts in the best interest of its people." That used to be called a Dad. Sometimes it takes 2500 years, but the repressed always returns.

Thirty years later Socrates annoyed the democrats, "why is it so important for you to believe you have knowledge, especially since it's fake?" and for this they sentenced him to death, a sentence he readily accepted because, well, he didn't care for the Statesmen but he believed in the state. I disagree, escaping and then returning in force to overthrow the wanna-be slaves posing as democrats would have been what I believe his ideal of the state would want from me, but it's easy for me to say that from the safety of the woods that are still in America. I guess it doesn't matter now. "Socrates wasn't killed just for that, it was for his relationship to Alcibiades and Critias, for Sicily, for the Thirty!" That's what you came up with? 27 years of grinding war, multiple plagues and a giant volcano, countless atrocities and worshipping your conqueror, your democracy had to be wrenched back for you by a man whose name you don't even remember and his crew that you'd rather forget-- and after all this, the first thing you do with your second chance is blame it all on-- Socrates? "We lost the war because we had poor leadership!" Poor leadership, what the hell are you talking about, you were supposed to be a democracy! But you want no responsibility for the democracy, you want to be lead. Look around you at the results. Thucydides was so disgusted that he just gave up writing, stopped mid-sentence, no ending was necessary, the whole thing is the ending. Here is the summary of your world, you can put it on a poster and hang it in your high school or give it to your enemies as a reason to invade: of all the achievements of ancient Athens, its greatest and most enduring product is the prophetic written history of its suicide; and nobody reads it, we only read about it. Madness. The final fall of Athens was even more absurd than the first, because rather than an unnecessary war becoming inevitable an inevitable war was dismissed as unnecessary. "It didn't seem to be a real threat." A real threat?! You're going into the finals against a team that's undefeated-- and they've absorbed all the other teams! What are you waiting for? The League to intervene? They're the enemy! There is no one else, there is never anyone else, if not you, who? But you couldn't act-- so you disavowed it, you blind yourself and pretend you know better. Marbles Mouth told you what was coming, he had read the actual Thucydides's Trap and warned you again and again and again and maybe even again, until at last he took charge and the army and heroically blocked the road, a last stand against the regression to the mean of history past and future, but by then it was far too little way too late. If you want to see hypocrisy etched into history the inscription on Demosthenes's statue reads, "If only your power had been equal to your knowledge, never would Greece have been conquered by a warlord", and I have to push my eyes into into my skull to hold back a fission reaction, pot/kettle/black-- you're blaming Demosthenes? But it's easier to blame a leader and worship your conqueror, crown the new tyrant a king and pretend he represents you, now and forever you can take credit for his actions and steal a little bit of satisfaction for yourself. That's the past you want, so it will be the future that satisfies you. Do you hear that, Mr. Anderson? The great experiment of freedom vs. tyranny deteriorated into knowledge vs. power, then the illusion of omniscience as a defense against impotence, and finally while you're rubbing your genitals to images of other people's actions that you didn't think of and don't even want omnipotence came at you with 16 foot spears after first taking out the Oracle of Delphi. They say it was close, we can pretend it was close, but we both know you never had a chance. In the land of the blind, the one eyed man will have become king. It was over. It is accomplished. *It is inevitable.*

Printed in Great Britain
by Amazon